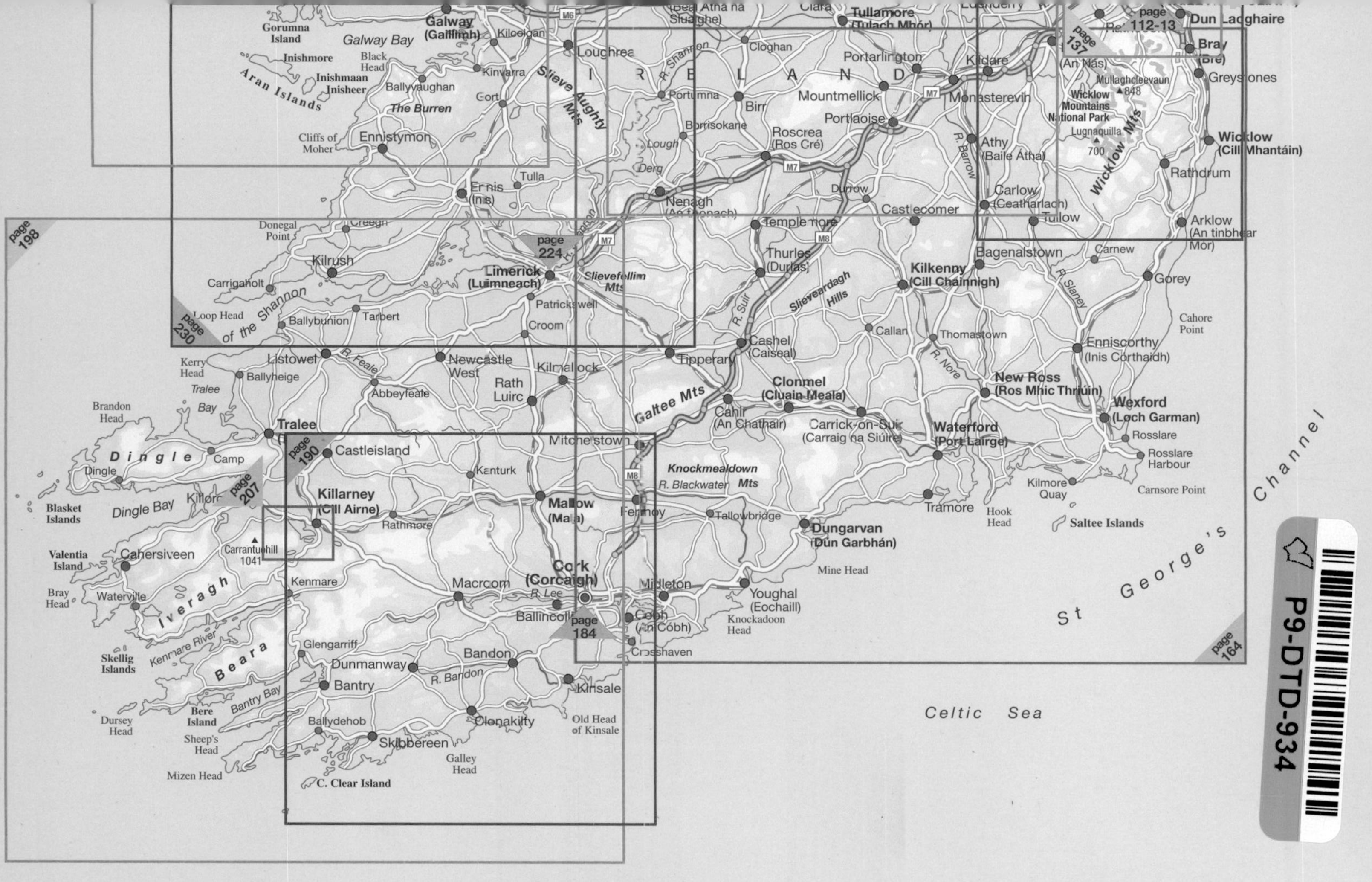
I R E L A N D
Galway (Gaillimh)
Galway Bay
Gorumna Island
Inishmore
Inishmaan
Inisheer
Aran Islands
Black Head
Ballyvaughan
The Burren
Kinvarra
Kilcolgan
Gort
Cliffs of Moher
Ennistymon
Loughrea
Slieve Aughty Mts
Ennis (Inis)
Tulla
Tullamore (Tulach Mhór)
Clara
Cloghan
Portumna
Birr
Borrisokane
Lough Derg
Nenagh
R. Shannon
Portarlington
Mountmellick
Portlaoise
Roscrea (Ros Cré)
Kildare
Monasterevin
Athy (Baile Átha)
R. Barrow
Carlow (Ceatharlach)
Tullow
Durrow
Castlecomer
Templemore
Thurles (Durlas)
Slieveardagh Hills
Kilkenny (Cill Chainnigh)
Bagenalstown
Carnew
Gorey
Arklow (An tinbhear Mór)
Rathdrum
Wicklow (Cill Mhantáin)
Wicklow Mts
Wicklow Mountains National Park
Mullaghcleevaun ▲848
Lugnaquilla ▲ 700
(An Nás)
Greystones
Bray (Bré)
Dun Laoghaire
page 112-13
page 137
page 198
page 224
page 230
page 190
page 207
page 184
page 164
Donegal Point
Creegh
Kilrush
Carrigaholt
Loop Head
of the Shannon
Ballybunion
Tarbert
Limerick (Luimneach)
Slievefelim Mts
Patrickswell
Croom
M7
M8
M6
Kerry Head
Ballyheige
Listowel
R. Feale
Newcastle West
Abbeyfeale
Rath Luirc
Kilmallock
Tipperary
Cashel (Caiseal)
R. Suir
Callan
Thomastown
R. Nore
R. Slaney
Enniscorthy (Inis Córthaidh)
Cahore Point
New Ross (Ros Mhic Thriúin)
Wexford (Loch Garman)
Rosslare
Rosslare Harbour
Carnsore Point
Kilmore Quay
Saltee Islands
Hook Head
Waterford (Port Láirge)
Tramore
Clonmel (Cluain Meala)
Carrick-on-Suir (Carraig na Siúire)
Cahir (An Chathair)
Galtee Mts
Mitchelstown
Knockmealdown Mts
R. Blackwater
Fermoy
Tallowbridge
Dungarvan (Dún Garbhán)
Mine Head
Youghal (Eochaill)
Knockadoon Head
Brandon Head
Tralee
Tralee Bay
Dingle
Camp
Castleisland
Kanturk
Mallow (Mala)
Killarney (Cill Airne)
Rathmore
Killorglin
Dingle Bay
Blasket Islands
Valentia Island
Cahersiveen
Carrantuohill 1041
Bray Head
Waterville
Iveragh
Kenmare
Kenmare River
Macroom
Cork (Corcaigh)
R. Lee
Ballincollig
Midleton
Cobh (An Cóbh)
Crosshaven
Skellig Islands
Beara
Glengarriff
Dunmanway
Bandon
R. Bandon
Kinsale
Old Head of Kinsale
Bantry
Bantry Bay
Bere Island
Dursey Head
Sheep's Head
Ballydehob
Skibbereen
Clonakilty
Galley Head
Mizen Head
C. Clear Island
Celtic Sea
St George's Channel

INSIGHT GUIDES

IRELAND

APA PUBLICATIONS

Part of the Langenscheidt Publishing Group

INSIGHT GUIDE
IRELAND

Editorial

Project Editor
Alexia Georgiou
Picture Manager
Steven Lawrence
Series Manager
Rachel Fox

Distribution

UK & Ireland
GeoCenter International Ltd
Meridian House, Churchill Way West
Basingstoke, Hampshire RG21 6YR
sales@geocenter.co.uk

United States
Ingram Publisher Services
One Ingram Blvd
PO Box 3006
La Vergne, TN 37086-1986
customer.service@ingrampublisherservices.com

Australia
Universal Publishers
1 Waterloo Road
Macquarie Park, NSW 2113
sales@universalpublishers.com.au

New Zealand
Hema Maps New Zealand Ltd (HNZ)
Unit 2, 10 Cryers Road
East Tamaki, Auckland 2013
sales.hema@clear.net.nz

Worldwide
Apa Publications GmbH & Co. Verlag KG (Singapore branch)
7030 Ang Mo Kio Ave 5,
08-65 Northstar@AMK, Singapore 569880
apasin@singnet.com.sg

Printing

CTPS-China

First Edition 1986
Eighth Edition 2011

CONTACTING THE EDITORS
We would appreciate it if readers would alert us to errors or outdated information by writing to:
Insight Guides, PO Box 7910, London SE1 1WE, England.
insight@apaguide.co.uk

www.insightguides.com

ABOUT THIS BOOK

The first Insight Guide pioneered the use of creative full-colour photography in travel guides in 1970. Since then, we have expanded our range to cater for our readers' need not only for reliable information about their chosen destination but also for a real understanding of the culture and workings of that destination. Now, when the internet can supply inexhaustible (but not always reliable) facts, our books marry text and pictures to provide those much more elusive qualities: knowledge and discernment. To achieve this, they rely heavily on the authority of locally based writers and photographers.

How to use this book

This book is carefully structured to convey an understanding of Ireland's people and culture and to guide readers through its many attractions:

◆ The **Best of Ireland** section at the front of the guide helps you to prioritise what you want to do.

◆ To understand Ireland today, you need to know something of its past. The **Features** section, indicated by a pink bar at the top of each page, is a series of illuminating essays that cover the natural and cultural history of the country, as well as daily life, architecture and the arts.

◆ The main **Places** section, indicated by a blue bar, is a complete guide to all the sights and areas worth visiting. Places of special interest are coordinated by number with the maps.

◆ The **Travel Tips** listings section, with a yellow bar, is a point of reference for information on transport, hotels, activities and shopping, and includes an A–Z section of essential practical information. An easy-to-

LEFT: Bloomsday, when many Dubliners re-enact events from James Joyce's *Ulysses*.

find contents list for Travel Tips is printed on the back flap, which also serves as a bookmark.

◆ **Photographs** are chosen not only to illustrate geography and buildings but also to convey the many moods of the country and its people.

The contributors

This new edition of *Insight Guide: Ireland* was managed by Insight Guides editor **Alexia Georgiou**, edited by **Mick Meikleham** and updated by **Alannah Hopkin**, **Jackie Staddon** and **Hilary Weston**.

It builds on the edition produced by ex-Insight Guides' editorial director, **Brian Bell**, an Irishman who began his publishing career as a journalist in Belfast. Working with **Alannah Hopkin**, a West Cork-based writer with an encyclopedic knowledge of Ireland's attractions, he assembled a team of specialist local writers. Bell also wrote the introduction and history chapters, while Hopkin penned the chapters on The Southwest and Contemporary Art as well as compiling the Best Of and Travel Tips sections and several information panels and photo features.

The Food chapter and the restaurant listings throughout the book were the work of **Biddy White Lennon**, a former actress who is now a noted cook and author of cookery books.

The chapters on Sport, Golf and Angling were produced by a writing team from **Maxmedia Communications** in Dublin.

John Daly, a Cork-based journalist and travel guide writer, revised the chapters on the Southeast, Cork & Surroundings, and Inland Ireland. **Paul Clements**, a former staffer with the BBC in Belfast, performed the same service for the chapters on Limerick & the Shannon Region, Galway & the West, and The Northwest, as well as writing on Pubs and Walking.

Jane Powers, a writer on sustainable development for the Irish Times, wrote the Day Trips from Dublin chapter as well as panels on Green Ireland and the Bungalow Blight. **Tina Neylon**, who has written for the Cork Examiner and produced several travel guides, wrote the pieces on Music, Literature, the Irish Language, and Horse-drawn Caravans.

The chapters on Northern Ireland and Belfast were reworked by **Seth Linder**, editor of a listings magazine in Belfast.

Much of the stunning photography is the output of photographers **Kevin Cummins** and **Corrie Wingate**. Out-of-house designer **Andy Hunter** worked on the layout. Thanks also go to **Sue Pearson** who proofread the guide.

Map Legend

- International Boundary
- County Boundary
- National Park/Reserve
- Ferry Route
- Airport: International/Regional
- Bus Station
- Tourist Information
- Church/Ruins
- Monastery/Abbey
- Castle/Ruins
- Mansion/Stately Home
- Archaeological Site
- Cave
- Statue/Monument
- Place of Interest
- Beach
- Post Office
- View Point
- Golf Course

The main places of interest in the Places section are coordinated by number with a full-colour map (eg ❶), and a symbol at the top of every right-hand page tells you where to find the map.

Contents

Introduction

History

Features

Insights

Places

LEFT: the Ring of Kerry.

Travel Tips

Maps

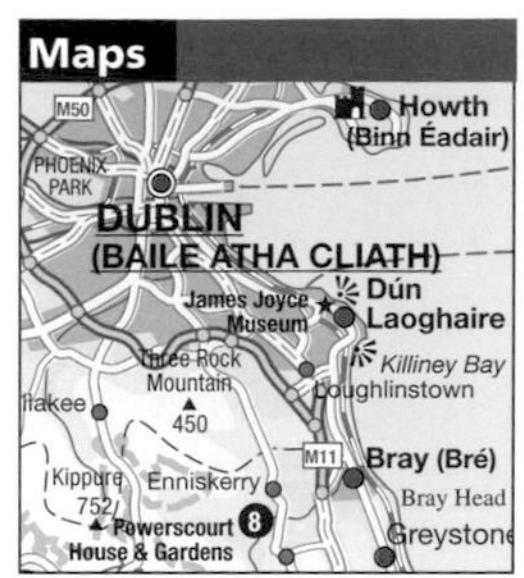

The Best of Ireland: Top Attractions

There's a lot of variety packed into a small island, from the slightly faded elegance of Dublin to the wild remoteness of windswept Connemara

△ **Dublin** retains some of its Georgian heritage – for example, the characteristic doors. But the real appeal is the Dubliners' vibrancy and sense of fun. *See pages 115–45.*

▽ **The Giant's Causeway**, an astonishing assembly of more than 40,000 hexagonal basalt columns on the north coast, is one of the world's wonders. *See pages 327–8.*

▷ **Ancient relics** such as this round tower at Glendalough *(see page 149)* are a striking reminder of Ireland's Golden Age when, after the fall of the Roman Empire plunged Europe into the Dark Ages, monks in Ireland ("the Land of Saints and Scholars") kept alight a lone beacon of learning and civilization.

▷ **The Rock of Cashel**. Towering above Tipperary's green plain is a dramatic cluster of romantically ruined stone buildings dating to the 12th and 13th centuries and the former stronghold of the Kings of Munster. *See page 177.*

△ **The Ring of Kerry**. This scenic drive takes in a panorama of coastal and mountain scenery as it passes by small villages, lush vegetation and sandy beaches. *See page 209.*

▷ **The Glens of Antrim**. A goat sculpture at Cusdendun represents the magic of the nine steep valleys which reminded the novelist William Makepeace Thackeray of "Switzerland in miniature". *See page 325.*

▽ **Connemara**, in the far west, is iconic Ireland – a landscape of wild, rocky bogland, its deeply indented coastline covered in autumnal shades of seaweed, its stunted pine trees struggling for a foothold and mirrored in the surprisingly blue water of its many loughs. *See page 255.*

▽ **Traditional Irish music**, which has influenced so many styles of music around the world, can be heard at its authentic best everywhere from street buskers to sessions in city and country pubs. *See pages 65–9.*

△ **The Burren**, a moon-like plateau in Co. Clare, contains ancient tombs and a remarkable variety of rich flora. *See pages 242–3.*

◁ **The Aran Islands**, beaten by the Atlantic, are an unspoiled Irish-speaking community that echoes a much older Ireland. *See pages 256–7.*

The Best of Ireland: Editor's Choice

Setting priorities, discovering secrets, the best festivals, the top sporting events, unique attractions... here, at a glance, are our recommendations plus some tips and tricks that even the locals won't always know...

Only in Ireland...

- **Newgrange, Co. Meath** This ancient passage tomb predates the Egyptian pyramids by centuries. *See page 153.*
- **Kissing the Blarney Stone** Even if it doesn't bestow the "gift of the gab," it's a dizzying experience. *See page 189.*
- **Trinity College, Dublin** With its cobbled courtyards, elegant Georgian buildings and bustling student population, it has a unique ambience. *See pages 117–9.*
- **Cruinniú na mBád** Traditional wooden boats with brown sails, laden with turf, race across Galway Bay in August. *See page 239.*
- **Croagh Patrick** Thousands of pilgrims, many of them barefoot, walk up Mayo's "holy mountain" on the last Sunday in July, as did their grandparents before them. *See page 258.*
- **Sunset on Bloody Foreland** Spectacular red sunsets over the Atlantic in Donegal. *See page 294.*
- **Derry's walls** The last walled city to be built in Europe is the centre of a vibrant culture. *See page 302.*
- **Budweiser Irish Derby** Held in June at the Curragh Racecourse in Co. Kildare, the most popular event on the colourful horseracing calendar. *See page 369.*

Best Fairs and Festivals

- **Bloomsday** Fans of James Joyce's *Ulysses* celebrate 16 June (the day it is set, in 1904) by proceeding around Dublin in period costume. Alcohol is consumed. *See pages 146–7.*
- **Fleadh Nua** Fleadh means festival, and in May Ennis's *Fleadh Nua* (*Nua* means new or modern), attracts thousands of traditional musicians, amateur and professional, with the music continuing at night in bars. *See page 232.*
- **The Auld Lammas Fair** The oldest fair in Ireland, dating from 1606, held in Ballycastle, Co. Antrim, still sees traditional horse trading alongside a busy trade in dulse (edible seaweed) and yellowman (hard toffee). *See page 326.*

Above: Bloomsday performer in a James Joyce mask.
Left: kiss the Blarney Stone to gain the gift of the gab.

BEST TRADITIONAL PUBS

- **The Crown Liquor Saloon**
46 Great Victoria Street, Belfast. Its ornate Victorian interior is cared for by the National Trust.
- **Gaughan's**
O'Rahilly St, Ballina, Co. Mayo. Town-centre bar with gleaming brass fittings. Good food.

ABOVE: Guinness, worth raising a glass to.

- **Hargadon's**
4 O'Connell Street, Sligo. A great "brown" pub (furniture, floors, walls, ceilings: brown). Good food, music.
- **MacCarthy's**
Main Square, Castletownbere, Beara, Co. Cork. The front is a grocery shop, used by local trawlermen; behind it is MacCarthy's Bar.
- **M.J. O'Neill**
Suffolk Street, Dublin 2. An old-style pub, with a warren of "snugs".
- **Morrissey's**
Main Street, Abbeyleix, Co. Laois (on the N8 Dublin–Cork road). Opened as a grocer's in 1775.
- **Tigh Neachtain**
Cross Street, Galway, has stubbornly retained its old-fashioned painted wooden interior. Music.

ABOVE: traditional pubs showcase traditional music.

BEST BIG HOUSES

- **Dublin Castle**
The State Apartments showcase traditional Irish craftsmanship. *See pages 125–6.*
- **Castletown House**
Co. Kildare. One of the largest private houses, dating from 1722. *See pages 154–5.*
- **Fota House**
Co. Cork. Shooting lodge in the classical style. Arboretum. *See pages 190–1.*
- **Strokestown Park House**
Co. Roscommon. Grandiose Georgian residence. *See pages 271–2.*
- **Castle Ward House**
Magnificent site overlooking Strangford Lough. Two facades: one classical, one Gothic. *See page 321.*

RIGHT: Dublin Castle.

TOP MUSEUMS AND GALLERIES

- **National Museum**
A wealth of priceless Irish treasures, including Celtic antiquities, Bronze Age gold jewellery and early Christian crosses. *See page 121.*
- **National Gallery**
Paintings by Vermeer, Rembrandt, Poussin and Goya: plus a major collection of Irish art. *See page 122.*
- **Chester Beatty Library**
Exquisite collection of Islamic and Far Eastern art housed in a wing of Dublin Castle. *See page 126.*
- **Irish Famine Museum**
Strokestown, Co. Roscommon. Visit for a compelling account of 1845's tragic scourge. *See page 272.*
- **Hunt Museum**
Limerick. Celtic and medieval treasures in historic Customs House on the River Shannon. *See page 225.*
- **Model Arts & Niland Gallery**
Sligo. Converted "model school" houses superb collection of paintings by Jack Yeats. *See page 285.*
- **Ulster Folk Park and Transport Museum**
Reconstructed houses and cottages bring Ulster circa 1910 to life. Transport ranges from huge locomotives to the De Lorean sports car (one of which featured in the film, *Back to the Future*). *See page 323.*
- **Dublin City Art Gallery, The Hugh Lane**
Imposing 18th-century town house in the Palladian style; collection of Impressionists plus 19th and 20th-century Irish art. *See page 132.*

Recommended for Families

- **Viking Splash Tours**
Use amphibious vehicles for a hilarious orientation tour of Dublin by land and water. (Departs St Patrick's Cathedral and St Stephen's Green). *See page 378.*
- **The Ark**
Eustace Street, Temple Bar, Dublin. This cultural centre for children has a gallery and workshop space. *See page 123.*

- **Carrick-a-Rede Rope Bridge**
Ballycastle, Co. Antrim. Spans a 60ft (18-meter) gap between mainland and Carrick-a-Rede Island. Strictly for thrill-seekers. *See page 327.*
- **Dublinia and the Viking World**
St Michael's Hill, Dublin. A reconstruction of life in medieval Dublin with high-tech displays. *See page 127.*
- **Bord na Móna Bog Rail Tour**
Shannonbridge, Co. Offaly. Discover the secrets of an Irish bog by taking a narrow-gauge train ride across the bog. *See page 266.*
- **Cobh Heritage Centre**
Cobh, Co. Cork. Compelling recreation of the emigrant experience. *See page 191.*
- **The Chimney**
Smithfield, Dublin. One of the original chimneys of the Old Jameson Distillery now has a thrilling glass elevator that whisks you to the 185ft (55-metre) tall observation tower. *See page 134.*
- **Bunratty Castle and Folk Park**
Bunratty, Co. Clare. The huge 15th-century castle is authentically furnished, while the village is inhabited by real people and animals. *See page 230.*
- **Sheep & Wool Centre**
Leenane, Co. Galway. Twenty breeds of sheep graze around the house, where craftspeople show how sheep's fleece is turned into wool. *See page 258.*
- **Whowhatwherewhen why**
(W5). Belfast. Interactive discovery centre, with 140 hands-on exhibits. *See page 341.*
- **Ulster Folk and Transport Museum**
See Museums, page 9.

Above: medieval feast for tourists at Bunratty Castle.

Best Beaches

Irish beaches are generally undeveloped, with free car parking. Beaches are popular wth walkers outside July and August.

- **Banna Strand**
Co. Kerry. West-facing beach backed by dunes big enough to get lost on. Fine views over Tralee Bay.
- **Benone Beach**
Part of Magilligan Strand on the north coast near Derry, is uncrowded but has good facilities.
- **Brittas Bay**
Co. Wicklow. White sand backed by dunes interspersed with small coves. Popular holiday spot for Dubliners.
- **Curracloe Beach**
Co. Wicklow. Stood in for Normandy for the D-Day landing scenes in the 1998 film *Saving Private Ryan*. Stretches for 5½ miles (9km). Nature trails and birdwatching hides to observe winter migrants.
- **Horn Head**
Co. Donegal. Dunfanaghy is a handy base for visiting the extensive, often deserted sandy beaches south of Horn Head.
- **Inch Strand**
Dingle, Co. Kerry. Stretch of golden sand running for 5 miles (8km) on a spit of land protruding into Dingle Bay.

Left: single horsepower on a County Antrim beach.

BEST CRAFTS SHOPS

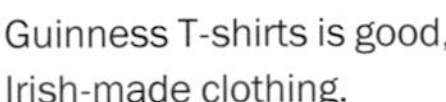

• **Avoca Handweavers** Killmacanogue, Bray, Co. Wicklow (also Dublin, Killarney and Letterfrack). Flagship store of a family-run chain known for their jewel-coloured, hand-woven rugs and throws. Also famed for fresh wholesome food.

• **Blarney Woollen Mills** Blarney, Co. Cork (also Killarney and Tipperary). Amid the leprechaun key rings and Guinness T-shirts is good, Irish-made clothing.

• **Waterford Experience, The Mall Waterford** A 50-minute tour takes visitors through the various stages of production. Wide range of crystal on sale in the retail centre.

• **The Kilkenny Design Centre** Kilkenny Castle. Well-designed Irish-made ceramics, jewellery, clothing and textiles.

• **Design Concourse Ireland** Kirwan's Lane, Galway. The best of hand-crafted design: ceramic, wood, textiles, glass and basket-ware.

• **Belleek Pottery** Co. Fermanagh. Fine bone china.

• **Smyth's Irish Linens** 65 Royal Avenue, Belfast. Wide range of goods in Irish linen.

ABOVE: a grandfather clock made from Waterford Glass.

ABOVE: a scenic walk in the Gap of Dunloe, Co. Kerry.

BEST WALKS ON THE WILD SIDE

Ireland's scenery can be enjoyed on way-marked paths suitable for all levels of fitness.

• **The Grand Canal Way** Flat canal bank walk from the Dublin outskirts to the little-visited Midlands (highest point, Lowtown, 280ft/85 metres).

• **The Kerry Way** Passes through some of Ireland's most beautiful scenery between Glenbeigh and Killarney.

• **The Slieve Bloom Mountains** Inland route close to exact centre of Ireland. Quietly spectacular.

• **The Ballyhoura Way** Easy walking on an inland pastoral route though low hills with views of the Golden Vale.

• **Beara Way** A variety of coastal and mountain scenery on one of the southwest's less frequented peninsulas.

• **The Sperrin Mountains** Sparsely populated area in the northeast of County Tyrone; bog, heather and moorland.

MONEY-SAVING TIPS

• **Heritage Cards** An OPW Heritage Card gives you unlimited admission to all 780 sites in the Office of Public Works scheme for one year. At €21 adult (€16 seniors, €55 family) it will quickly pay for itself.

• **Golden Trekker** is a scheme offering free rail travel for visitors aged 66 and over, introduced in 2010, and will continue, subject to demand. Details at www.discoverireland.com Tickets can be purchased in blocks of four days for unlimited free travel on mainline and commuter trains.

• **Hostels** To save on hotel costs, consider the 100 options listed by Independent Holiday Hostels of Ireland (9 in Northern Ireland), with no curfew or membership needed. Some are in historic buildings, all are friendly and well-run. Outside Dublin expect to pay under €20 per night in a double room (in Dublin around €30). www.hostels-ireland.com.

• **Bed and Breakfast** If you are staying for more than one night, ask for a reduction on advertised price. Check online for the amazing special offers available since the downturn.

• **Early Bird or Special Value/ market menus** Many restaurants offer cheaper two or three-course menus before 6.30 or 7.30pm.

• **Bar Food** is a thrifty alternative to restaurant food. Drink tap water (free) rather than expensive drinks.

Shop
here
FISHING TACKLE
B179
H1120

THE NEW IRELAND

Both parts of the island have been transformed in recent years. The Republic has reinvented itself as a secular, Europe-oriented state, and Northern Ireland has progressed from terrorism to power-sharing

Guinness, the heavy, dark stout that has become an Irish icon, was once marketed in the Caribbean as possessing aphrodisiac qualities. Similar whimsy has long infused the advertising campaigns of Ireland's tourism authority, which once boasted about how irresistible the Vikings, Normans and Saxons had found Ireland, and promised potential visitors: "So think what a grand time we'd show you. Especially since you'd be the only ones of the lot we actually invited."

Such blarney – talk that aims to charm, flatter or persuade – is a potent sales tool. An alluring "brand image" has been created for Ireland over the years, portraying an unspoilt green land with hospitable people, a leisurely pace of life and an uncanny ability to generate enjoyment. But then it's always been known for its fairy tales...

Not that any of the above is untrue. But the truth, as ever, is more complicated.

A changed society

Today's visitors who enjoy having their preconceptions demolished will indeed have a grand time in Ireland, on both sides of the border.

A dramatic transformation has taken place in the Republic. Branded 40 years ago by Northern Protestants as an economically deprived, priest-ridden country whose most prolific product was emigrants, the Republic has gone full circle economically since joining the European Union (then the EEC) in 1972. The Irish took full advantage of the subsidies that the EEC provided for its poorer members. Adopting the euro in 2003 distanced the country decisively from its old imperial master, Britain, which clung to sterling. Irish culture, it

PRECEDING PAGES: mural in Killarney town; Dublin's Liffey, spanned by the Ha'penny Bridge; Ardglass Marina and castles, County Down.
LEFT: whisky-laced Irish coffee or espresso, the choice is yours. **ABOVE FROM TOP:** an ancient dagger hilt; leprechaun souvenirs conjure up fairytale Ireland.

found, travelled well, whether in the form of the decidedly bogus "Irish pub" which took root in 42 countries or as cunningly modernised traditional music and dance epitomised by Riverdance. The global success of stadium rockers U2, and of Bob Geldof's Live Aid gave Dublin a new hip identity, consolidated by the highly successful early days of its buzzing Temple Bar district.

A job market flooded with well-educated, personable graduates, and generous tax breaks encouraged multinationals – from Pfizer and other pharmaceutical companies in the early days, to Google and other hi-tech operations, including Microsoft – to establish Irish operations, often basing their European headquarters in this hospitable and welcoming eurozone country. Many of those who had emigrated returned to a new Ireland with a booming economy, and were joined by emigrants from eastern European countries and elsewhere who flocked to Ireland to take up the lower-paid jobs that no one else wanted, diluting the former homogeneous population of white, Irish-born Catholics. Embracing globalisation, the Republic took as its model not its fellow European countries, with their emphasis on social welfare, but the US, with its stress on individual achievement. It was, the saying went, "more Boston than Berlin". Tipping its hat to US values, the low-fare airline Ryanair shamelessly modelled itself on America's Southwest Airlines, and became the biggest airline in Europe.

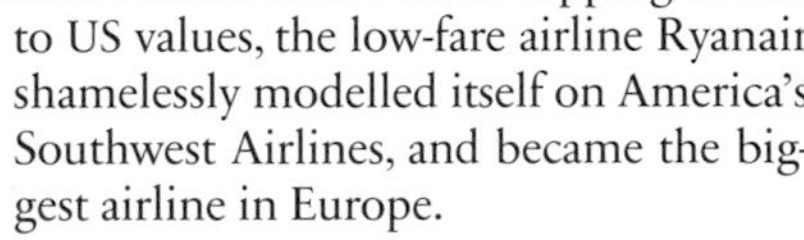

Boom and bust

In more recent years however, the 26-county Republic, traditionally seen as a pastoral and pious, though somewhat poverty-stricken land, has endured a dramatic cycle of boom-and-bust. From being the economic wonder of the European Union, Ireland, like many other countries, has fallen into recession, the legacy being an excess of 15,000 hotel rooms (good news for holiday-makers looking for competitive rates), untenanted office blocks and unsold apartments and houses. By 2010 activity in the construction industry was down to 5 per cent of its 2005 peak and over half of Ireland's architects were unemployed. Ireland now has the second highest rate of emigration in Europe, as people once more travel abroad in search of work.

The country is still in a state of shock at this new scenario, as people face pay cuts, pension cuts and years of negative equity while the huge debts run up by a coterie of irresponsible bankers and developers are paid off. What makes the Irish recession different is the level of "cronyism" emerging, with a handful of bankers, property developers

and politicians flaunting the normal regulatory process and the basic rules of banking in search of ever bigger profits. Criminal prosecution of key figures may well follow.

A social upheaval

A social revolution has accompanied Ireland's economic metamorphosis. Change took time: divorce, even for non-Catholics, was not decriminalised in the Republic until 1995 and homosexuality until 1993. Abortion is still unobtainable, with Irish women forced to travel to the UK for terminations. Continuing revelations about paedophilia in the priesthood led to the unprecedented resignation of several Irish bishops in 2010, and widespread anger. The Church had long been aware of the problem of child abuse but had knowingly covered it up and misled the public, failing to report offenders. Such is the level of disillusion that a website enabling Catholics officially to leave the Roman Catholic Church (www.countmeout.ie) has attracted over 10,000 people in its first year.

The Northern transformation

Northern Ireland meanwhile, once known chiefly for urban terrorism, broadcast daily on television, is selling itself as a great place to play golf. What caused this transformation? The answer is comparatively straightforward. After three decades of bloodshed, both the IRA and the British forces decided that it was time for a compromise. First, the Republic amended its constitution to abandon all claims of sovereignty towards Northern Ireland. Then the IRA agreed to lay down its arms. This enabled the North's fiery Protestant leader, the Rev. Ian Paisley, to agree to enter a power-sharing Assembly with his former enemy, Sinn Fein, a political party closely linked to the IRA. The British government, believing that one cause of "the Troubles" had been economic neglect, poured money into the province. Given that Northern Ireland has more than its fair share of the island's physical attractions – the Giant's Causeway, the Mountains of Mourne, the Antrim Coast Road, Fermanagh's lakeland, the Glens of Antrim – tourism has begun to revive.

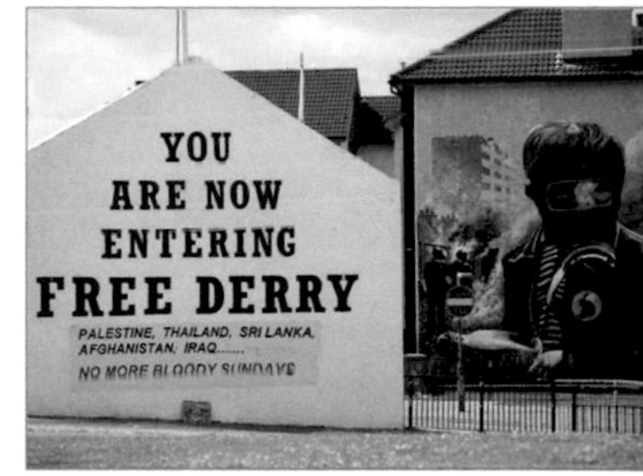

Ireland's continuing allure

Although the country has long outlived its Hollywood image, it manages to combine a modernised lifestyle with traditional hospitality and unspoilt scenery. The weather may not always be great and the prices may not always be cheap, but the people still have an outstanding capacity for enjoyment that they are more than willing to share with their visitors. ❑

LEFT: refurbishing Dublin Castle as the imperial past becomes a tourist attraction.
TOP: the iconic Ha'penny Bridge glowing through the Dublin night.
ABOVE RIGHT: thought-provoking murals in Northern Ireland.

THE IRISH CHARACTER

Take generous portions of charm, wit, congeniality and loquacity. Then mix in melancholy, daydreaming, opportunism and a history of violence. Stir gently...

With a cheerful disregard for political correctness, the Irish take a perverse delight in the universal jokes made against them. Indeed, they even print selections on linen tea-towels, which they sell at fancy prices in souvenir shops. That explains the perverse delight, of course: there's money to be made in conforming to a stereotyped image and, by appearing to be dim, the Irish can lull potential opponents into an ill-advised sense of superiority.

The trick works on tourists. In Co. Cork, guileful guides, deploying words like grapeshot, can charm the most sceptical travellers into paying good money to kiss the Blarney Stone, at the same time reassuring them fulsomely that its promised ability to confer eloquence on all who kiss it is, in itself, just a bit of blarney.

Love at first sight

Millions of visitors respond to this captivating charm by falling in love with Ireland at first sight. Yet many in Ireland question the extent to which the colossal social and economic changes that have taken place in recent decades *(see pages 19–21)* have eroded the traditional Irish values of courtesy, hospitality, spontaneity, sportsmanship and sense of fun.

These critics argue that Ireland is selling its soul in return for a rootless cosmopolitanism, ruining the attraction of its unspoilt countryside by ill-thought-out and badly-designed developments, while ignoring the widening gap between the rich and the poor. Countering these arguments, others – in an echo of Oscar Wilde's dictum –"Those who live within their means suffer from a lack of imagination" – insist that the Irish are bringing to bear on the wrecked economy the creativity they have always deployed in literature and the arts.

> “*How do you recognise an Irishman in a car wash?* He's the one sitting on the motorbike.”

As usual, the truth lies somewhere in the middle. Certainly, the Republic, with its car-dependent, increasingly suburban commuter lifestyle, and its preference for British and American TV channels, has become more like everywhere else. But enough people have realised the danger of diluting Ireland's unique cultural identity, and are working hard to promote a pride in, and affection for, all things Irish, including the language, the music, even the soccer team, and the (sometimes elusive) idea of a less stressful way of life. Visitors, therefore, once they have recovered from the shock of discovering how expensive everything is, are likely to find that the time-honoured sense of hospitality has survived, sustained by an innate gregariousness.

The two Irelands

After achieving independence from Britain in 1921, an event accompanied by bloody internal strife, the new Republic signalled its priorities in its currency, with coins displaying images not of rulers or tyrants but of pigs, hens, hares and salmon. But only the coins of *the Republic*, of course, for there are two Irelands. One consists of the 26 counties of the Republic, which evoke images of black beer and green shamrock. Then there are the six counties of Northern Ireland, part of the United Kingdom, a harder place whose unhappy political history inspired the celebrated slogan daubed on the side of a derelict house in Belfast: "Is there life *before* death?"

Britain's colonial involvement with Ireland over many centuries ensured that there are many facets to the Irish character. In terms of personality, the Northern Protestant is generally regarded as being more earnest, more unimaginative than the Northern Catholic, who is in turn seen as less outgoing, less impulsive than the Southern Catholic. And it doesn't take long for the enquiring visitor to begin pondering such puzzles as why a Dublin Roman Catholic will in all probability distrust the British but respect the English, while a Belfast Protestant may badmouth the English yet swear eternal loyalty to the British.

Such stereotypes, naturally, soon turn into absurd over-simplifications. An English journalist, for instance, despatched to Northern Ireland in the 1970s to discover why its Protestant and Roman Catholic communities were at each other's throats, reported: "They are incomparably more pleasant to the outsider than any other people in the British Isles. Even the terrorists have excellent manners."

It was the German writer Heinrich Böll who identified the two turns of speech most characteristic of the Irish as "It could be worse" and "I shouldn't worry." In a world where worries proliferate daily, Ireland retains an insane optimism.

Naturally the Irish have written down this philosophy on linen tea-towels, which they will sell to passers-through at a decent profit. It reads: "There are only two things to worry about: either you are well or you are sick. If you

LEFT: hamming it up for St Patrick's Day.
ABOVE LEFT: striking a pose by James Joyce's statue during Bloomsday. **ABOVE RIGHT:** a fan of Guinness.

are well, then there is nothing to worry about. But if you are sick, there are two things to worry about: either you will get well or you will die. If you get well, then there is nothing to worry about. If you die, there are only two things to worry about: either you will go to heaven or to hell. If you go to heaven, there is nothing to worry about. But if you go to hell, you'll be so damn busy shaking hands with friends, you won't have time to worry. Why worry!"

A strong theatricality

Not that the Irish won't give you cause enough for perplexity. Their character can be as elusive as the fairy gold to be sought at the end of Irish rainbows and the conversation as elliptical as an incomplete jigsaw puzzle.

Unarguably, there is a strong theatricality about their character. There's a recklessness, a tendency towards exaggeration. There's a love of "codology", the Irish equivalent of "leg-pulling." But there's an introversion, too, the proneness to melancholy captured by George Bernard Shaw in *John Bull's Other Island*, a play set in the land of his birth: "Your wits can't thicken in that soft moist air, on those white springy roads, in those misty rushes and brown bogs, on those hillsides of granite rocks and magenta heather. You've no such colours in the sky, no such lure in the distance, no such sadness in the evenings. Oh the dreaming! the dreaming! the torturing, heartscalding, never satisfying dreaming, dreaming, dreaming."

You can sometimes sense this aspect of the Irish character in a pub when, after the talk – once called "a game with no rules" – has achieved an erratic brilliance, the convivial mood abruptly changes to one of wistfulness and self-absorption, and you know it's time to go. This contradictory character led the 19th-century philosopher Søren Kierkegaard to muse that, if he hadn't been a Dane, he could well have been an Irishman: "For the Irish have not the heart to baptise their children completely, they want to preserve just a little paganism,

WHY DUBLIN IS DIFFERENT

Just as London is not representative of England, nor New York of the US, so the gap has widened between a fast-paced Dublin and the rest of the country. If the whole of Ireland had the same population density as Dublin, there would be more than 300 million people living there. As it is, the Republic's 4.3 million population produces a density of only 57 people per sq km (148 per sq mile). Once, just about everyone you met in the capital's streets or pubs would be a Dubliner. Recent immigration has eroded that homogeneity as Ireland edges its way warily towards becoming a multiracial society. To get a feel for the "real" Ireland, it's more necessary than ever to travel beyond Dublin.

and whereas a child is normally completely immersed, they keep his right arm out of the water so that in after-life he can grasp a sword and hold a girl in his arm."

Violence and vendettas

The Irish themselves look less whimsically at their native land. The poet Louis MacNeice, for example, described it as a nation "built upon violence and morose vendettas", and a wit defined Irish Alzheimer's as a disease that makes you forget everything except the grudges.

Perhaps the island's location is to blame. "With the exception it may be of Malta and of Iceland," wrote the Irish actor and theatre director Micheál MacLiammóir, "no European island lies in so lamentable and hostile a solitude as Ireland, who has no neighbour on her right hand but her conqueror, and nothing at all on her left hand but the desolate ocean, not one dry step until you get to America."

The history of this "wretched little clod, broken off a bigger clod, broken off the west end of Europe," as Shaw called it, encouraged it to develop a sense of victimhood, which in turn underpinned the moral authority that singers such as Bono and Bob Geldof assumed when they lectured world leaders face-to-face on the need to get to grips with the causes of world poverty. Enya's easy-listening take on traditional Celtic rhythms was judged poignant enough to be used as the soundtrack to TV replays of the collapse of the World Trade Center.

An attitude to life

In an age that esteems brand awareness, Ireland's international image is a potent one. It contains an echo of an 18th-century pace of life that has not completely faded away, a psychological climate in which a racehorse attracts more glances than a Rolls-Royce. It reflects the values of the rural railway guard answering a traveller who complained that the train was already half an hour late: "You must have a very narrow heart that you wouldn't go down to the town and stand your friends a few drinks instead of bothering me to get away."

It's this attitude to life, never far beneath the surface despite the upheavals, that makes Ireland such a rewarding place to visit. As the US-born novelist J. P. Donleavy, an exemplar of the less folksy style of Irish writing, expressed it winsomely in *The Ginger Man*: "When I die I want to decompose in a barrel of porter [*dark beer*] and have it served in all the pubs of Dublin. I wonder would they know it was me?" ❑

LEFT: street performers in Galway. **ABOVE:** when U2's Bono and The Edge were given the Freedom of the City of Dublin, the honour carried with it the right to graze sheep on St Stephen's Green.

Ireland in the Movies

Bejasus, it's them leprechauns again! The cinema has usually reinforced the stereotyped image of the Irish. Do they care? Not if it spells profit

Ireland's first dedicated cinema, the Volta in Dublin's Mary Street, was opened in 1909 by none other than James Joyce – an indication that the Irish have always valued the word more than the visual. But the country had no film studio until 1958, when Ardmore Studios opened in Bray, Co. Wicklow. It was thus left to Hollywood to portray Ireland to the world, and it did so by peddling whimsicality to the huge audience of Irish-Americans who had a sentimental attachment to the pastoral ideal most potently portrayed in John Ford's *The Quiet Man*. The Irish, who were in reality facing hardship and chronic emigration, didn't object to such a portrayal: indeed, they built a tourist industry on it.

The leprechauns massed in 1959 for *Darby O'Gill and the Little People*, in which a pre-007 Sean Connery sang and danced with Janet Munro and gangs of diminutive actors. No cliché was left unturned and Walt Disney ended up with a pot of gold.

Three decades of terrorism produced a muted response from international film-makers – Neil Jordan's *The Crying Game* was a rare success. The best recent film about the Irish civil war was made by Englishman Ken Loach: *The Wind That Shakes the Barley* (2006) is set in 1920 and was filmed on location in rural Cork, starring Cillian Murphy.

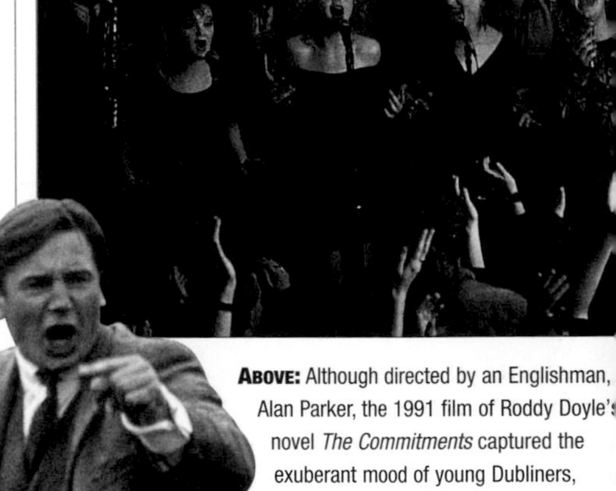

Above: Although directed by an Englishman, Alan Parker, the 1991 film of Roddy Doyle's novel *The Commitments* captured the exuberant mood of young Dubliners, expletives and all. This was no feel-good tale of a pop group – it chronicled their disaffection with life in Dublin and referred to Ireland, whose tiger economy was still in the future, as a Third World country.

Left: Neil Jordan's 1996 biopic *Michael Collins*, was dubbed Ireland's first national epic film, though it was US funded. Jordan sacrificed historical detail for dramatic impact, but Liam Neeson conveyed the romanticism and ruthlessness that characterised Ireland's struggle.

Above: Alan Parker's faithful 1999 version of *Angela's Ashes*, Frank McCourt's boyhood memoir of growing up in Limerick, was felt locally to have overstated the level of poverty. Others complained that pain was driven out by glossy photography and sentimentality.

ABOVE: The movie that did most to cement the image of the Irish as fighting boyos with a pre-feminist outlook was John Ford's 1952 production *The Quiet Man*, in which John Wayne slugged it out with Victor McLaglan and Maureen O'Hara in a virulently green landscape. Americans loved it – and so did the Irish.

ABOVE: Veteran Hollywood director John Huston, who came of Irish stock and had a home in Ireland, captured the country's streak of Chekovian melancholy in his last film, *The Dead* (1987), adapted from a classic short story by James Joyce.

BELOW: Neil Jordan's *Ondine* (2010) is a far cry from his 1992 hit, *The Crying Game*. Filmed in Cork, it's a modest fable with Colin Farrell as a moody fisherman and Stephen Rea stealing the show as parish priest.

RARE SPOTLIGHTS ON SOCIAL REALISM

Peter Mullan's critically acclaimed 2002 film *The Magdalen Sisters* (pictured above) told the story of the young girls – perhaps 30,000 of them over the years – who had been sent to live-in convent laundries as a punishment for having premarital sex or becoming pregnant out of wedlock. These sadistic labour camps, finally closed in the 1990s, had been a well-kept secret for most of their existence.

Such movies could not have been shown in Ireland during the long period when the Catholic church exercised a tight grip on moral values: in the first 40 years of the Republic's independence, an average of 75 films a year were banned and another 200 censored, most often for sexual content.

With the Irish box office representing less than 0.5 per cent of the global market there was limited scope for purely Irish films. So the government tempted foreign producers with tasty tax breaks. This persuaded Mel Gibson, for instance, that, although his 1995 *Braveheart* portrayed a legendary Scottish hero, the stirring battle scenes would look no less patriotic if they were filmed in Ireland.

RIGHT: the debut feature film of playwright Martin McDonagh (pictured), *In Bruges* (2008), a black comedy starring Colin Farrell and Brendan Gleeson as a pair of Irish hitmen hiding out in Belgium's medieval city, proved an international triumph and raised the profile of the Irish film industry overseas.

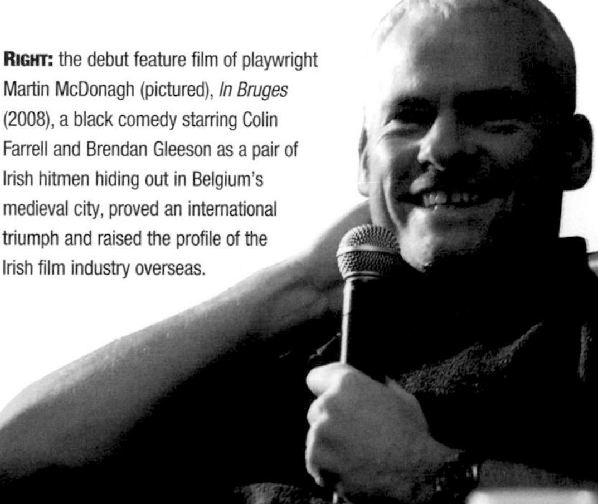

DECISIVE DATES

c.7000BC
Archaeological evidence of Mesolithic hunter-fisher people (flints, etc) along the coast dates from this period.

From c.3000BC
The Neolithic period sees megalithic tombs appear. Signs of prolonged settlement, agriculture and cultural sophistication (portal tombs) grow more frequent. From around 500BC, the migration of Celts from Britain marks the start of Ireland's Iron Age.

c.AD300
Stone-carved inscriptions appear in the "Ogham alphabet", a rune-like script.

431
The Pope sends Palladius as a bishop to Ireland. This implies that Christian communities existed before St Patrick arrived.

c.432
St Patrick (later Ireland's patron saint) comes back to Ireland as a missionary. At 16, he had been abducted from Britain and taken to Ireland, but later fled to France.

From c.800
Viking attacks begin. After a series of raids (many monasteries are plundered) the Norsemen found settlements which grow into harbour towns (eg Dublin).

976–1014
Brian Ború, crowned King of Munster in 976, proclaims himself High King of Ireland in 1002 and defeats the Vikings near Clontarf in 1014. After his murder later that same year, the kingdom falls apart again.

From 1169
Anglo-Normans – sent to Ireland by the English king Henry II after a request from Dermot MacMurrough, who is losing the fight for the Irish throne – conquer large areas of the island and settle there. A system of Feudalism is introduced and castles built.

1366
The Statutes of Kilkenny represent an attempt by the English crown to stop its barons from assimilating, marrying Irishwomen or speaking the Irish language.

From 1541
England's Henry VIII declares himself King of Ireland and begins asserting British supremacy over the Irish clan princes.

1607
The most powerful of the Irish clan princes flee to Spain (called the "Flight of the Earls"), marking the end of Gaelic supremacy.

1608
James I starts the systematic settlement of Protestant Scots and English (dubbed "the Plantation of Ulster").

1641–53
A rebellion by Irish Catholics

against the English settlement policy is initially successful. In 1649, after his victory in the English Civil War, Oliver Cromwell (pictured) conquers Ireland in a merciless campaign.

1690
England's Catholic King James II loses his throne to William of Orange at the Battle of the Boyne, and the period of "Protestant Ascendancy" begins.

1691
The Irish-Protestant parliament in Dublin passes the "Penal Laws" which exclude Catholics from public office, deprive them of their property and their right to vote.

1791
Influenced by the revolutions in France and America, the United Irishmen movement is formed in Belfast. Its leading light, Wolfe Tone, is a Protestant coachbuilder's son.

1800
The Act of Union makes Ireland part of the United Kingdom. The parliament in Dublin is dissolved and Ireland is represented by 100 MPs in the House of Commons in London.

1829
A Catholic politician, Daniel O'Connell (known as "the Liberator"), forces the London parliament to pass a law emancipating Catholics.

From 1840
Nationalist movements gain strength (Irish Republican Brotherhood founded in 1858, Irish National Land League founded in 1879). There is a renewed interest in Gaelic culture (the Gaelic League is formed in 1893).

1845–51
The Great Potato Famine deprives more than one-third of the Irish population of their main source of nutrition. An estimated 1 million people die between 1846 and 1851 of malnutrition, typhus and other diseases; approximately 1 million others emigrate.

From 1880
The Land League and the Irish Home Rule Party led by Charles Stuart Parnell employ parliamentary means in their struggle for Irish autonomy and land reform. In 1886, the

FAR LEFT TOP: the Battle of Clontarf in 1014, won by Brian Ború, the High King. FAR LEFT: St John, from the late 9th-century *MacDurnan Gospels*. LEFT: the English besieged Enniskillen Castle in 1593. ABOVE TOP: Cork in the late 18th century, painted by Nathaniel Grogan. RIGHT: a penniless family evicted during the Great Famine of 1845–51.

first of several draft resolutions for Irish independence is rejected.

1905–08
The group known as Sinn Féin ("We Ourselves") is formed "to make England take one hand from Ireland's throat and the other out of Ireland's pocket".

1912
Almost three-quarters of all Ulster Protestants sign a solemn pledge to stop all attempts at autonomy "by all necessary means". The Ulster Volunteer Force is formed in 1913 to enforce the pledge.

1916
On 24 April around 1,800 volunteers, led by Pádraig Pearse and James Connolly, occupy public buildings in Dublin and declare the formation of an Irish Republic. This "Easter Rising" is put down six days later. Britain's harsh response strengthens the nationalist cause.

1918–23
In elections to the UK Parliament, Sinn Féin wins 73 of 105 Irish seats. Their MPs announce the formation of an Irish parliament in Dublin, with Éamon de Valera as president; the British government sends in troops. During the Anglo-Irish War of 1919–21 the Irish Republican Army gradually gains the upper hand against the British. In 1922 the Irish Parliament narrowly accepts the Anglo-Irish treaty for the foundation of an Irish Free State excluding the six counties of Ulster with Protestant majorities. Civil war ensues between forces in favour of a Pan-Irish Republic and the pro-treaty Free State government, which wins.

1937
The Free State (now called Éire) adopts its own political constitution.

1939
Éire declares its neutrality during World War II. Germany tries to damage Britain's interests by supporting the IRA.

1949
Éire leaves the British Commonwealth to become the Republic of Ireland.

1969–70
A demonstration by the Northern Irish Civil Rights Movement is attacked by loyalists in 1969. The IRA, which has been fighting for a united Ireland since the 1930s, splits into two factions in 1970. The Provisional IRA intensifies its "armed struggle" in Northern Ireland.

1972
Thirteen demonstrators are shot dead by British soldiers on "Bloody Sunday". The parliament in Belfast is dissolved and Northern Ireland is ruled directly from London.

1973
The Republic joins the European Economic Community along with Great Britain.

1990
Mary Robinson becomes the first woman president of the Republic.

1997
In the Republic, divorce becomes legal, and Mary McAleese, a Northerner by birth, becomes president.

1998
A Northern Ireland peace treaty is signed by all parties, including Sinn Féin. David Trimble and John Hume receive the Nobel prize. A car bomb in Omagh kills 29.

1999
An all-party Assembly with limited powers set up in Northern Ireland. The Republic drops its claim to sovereignty over the North.

2002
The Republic adopts the euro. In the North, rule from London is reimposed.

FAR LEFT TOP: Eamon de Valera, opposing the 1922 treaty that divided Ireland. LEFT: unionist mural in the Newtownards Road area of east Belfast. TOP RIGHT: Sinn Féin chief Gerry Adams clutches the Good Friday Agreement. ABOVE: Mary Robinson. RIGHT: To universal surprise, former sworn enemies Ian Paisley (left) and Martin McGuinness agree to work together as the Northern Ireland Assembly's first minister and deputy first minister – smiling so much that they are dubbed the Chuckle Brothers.

2005
The IRA declares that its war is over and its weapons destroyed. The legendary Irish footballer George Best dies.

2007
Ian Paisley's Democratic Unionists and Gerry Adams's Sinn Féin dominate elections in Northern Ireland and agree to work together. An influx of migrant labour, chiefly from countries in Eastern Europe, boosts Ireland's population by approximately 10 per cent to 4.3 million.

2008
After almost 11 years as Taoiseach (Irish Prime Minister), Bertie Ahern resigns in May, following intensive questioning by the Mahon Tribunal public inquiry regarding his financial affairs during the 1990s, and hands over to his Minister for Finance, Brian Cowen. By September of the same year the international financial crisis starts to have a major impact on the Irish banking sector and the recession begins.

2010
The full scale of the financial losses that Irish banks face from irresponsible loans to property developers leave tax payers facing a €60 billion bail out, and many home-owners in negative equity or living on reduced pensions. Revelations of the Catholic Church's institutional failure to protect children from sexually abusive priests leads to the resignation of several Irish bishops, and widespread disillusionment with the once all-powerful Church.

IRLANDIÆ REGNUM.
Miliaria Ibernica Commimia
5 10 15 20 25 30 35 40
VERGINIUS
OCEANUS
Galway
Lymerik
ORMOUND
WEST BREANNY
EAST BREANNY
ANNAVE
Erne
Tyrew
Nalmoyan
Glan
The Grange
OWEN ENIS
Cork
Waterford
Wexford
Clare
Offa
Dungal

IRELAND'S INVADERS

First the Celts came, then the Vikings and Normans. The English decided to stake a strategic claim, and that's when the trouble really began

The key to much of Ireland's blood-stained history lies in the extraordinary love-hate relationship that it has had with its more powerful neighbouring island to the east. Ireland's history, in a nutshell, is its resistance to England. In this geographically forced marriage, the dominant partner sometimes deliberately abused the weaker, more often unthinkingly ignored her; yet the Irish, while hating the English for their arrogance and neglect, also admired them for their character and achievements and, until a surprisingly late stage, had no great wish for the marriage to be totally dissolved.

The first conquest

Evidence of Ireland's earliest inhabitants survives in the form of thousands of megalithic burial chambers. The Newgrange passage-grave in the Boyne valley, near Dublin, for example, is thought to be 5,000 years old. From the Bronze Age, when Ireland was one of the world's largest metal producers, beautifully crafted leaf-shaped swords and gold ornaments are preserved.

Several centuries before the birth of Christ, the island's first conquerors arrived. The Celts (or Gaels), masters of horsemanship, came not from England but from mainland Europe, mostly France and Spain, to this wild, wet island at the continent's fringes. Europe's next conquerors did not get as far as Ireland. The Roman legions, hard pressed to hold southern Britain against incursions by Picts and Scots, were disinclined to take on more trouble. Their inaction had far-reaching consequences: if Julius Caesar had successfully ventured west, it is unlikely that Ireland's character today would be so distinct from Britain's.

The Celts brought with them from mainland Europe a loose tribal structure, the blueprint for building a civilization, and had little trouble in overcoming the natives, a primitive people known as the Firbolg ("Big Men").

LEFT: Ireland in 1606 as portrayed by an Amsterdam atlas, the Mercador-Hondius.
RIGHT: The Arrest of Christ, from the *Book of Kells*.

The Golden Age

The divergences between the two cultures widened still further when the fall of the Roman Empire plunged Europe into the Dark Ages.

Ireland, in contrast, entered its Golden Age, becoming a lone beacon of learning and civilization – "the Land of Saints and Scholars".

Christianity had been brought to the island by an English-born rustic missionary, St Patrick, who had been kidnapped as a youth and taken to Ireland to tend sheep. Later, he travelled widely in France and Italy, returning to Ireland in 432 to spread the word of Christ. He found a largely peaceable people, though there was intermittent feuding between provincial kings.

Viking raids plagued the island in the 9th and 10th centuries *(see box below)*, but the Norse tyranny was destroyed at the Battle of Clontarf in 1014 by the High King, Brian Ború, who saw himself as Ireland's Charlemagne. Less destructive but no less ambitious visitors were Norman such as Strongbow, an English earl who came looking for land. Having gained a toehold, the Normans built a power base with fortified stone castles. This alarmed England's Henry II, who promptly paid a visit, inaugurating an involvement between the two countries that was to last, with immeasurable bloodshed, for 800 years.

The Normans go native

Over the next three centuries, the Normans, intermarrying with the natives, expanded their influence. Many of the country's elaborate castles, such as Blarney in Co. Cork and Bunratty in Co. Clare, date from this time.

Saved by the Monasteries

In the absence of a Roman substructure of towns and cities, monasteries became centres of population. The kings kept treasures there, which made the monasteries a target for plundering bands of Vikings, who sailed to Ireland from northern Scandinavia in the 9th century. Tall round towers, many still standing, were built by the monasteries to serve as lookouts and refuges as well as belfries. Also surviving are some of the monks' exquisite manuscripts, such as the *Book of Kells*, which the Vikings, being unable to read, ignored. Ireland's tradition of storytelling dates from this period. It can be seen on sand-stone high crosses, designed to teach Bible stories by means of elaborate carvings.

But, as the barons thrived, the English Crown's authority gradually shrank to an area around Dublin known as "the Pale". It was Henry VIII, determined finally to break the local nobles' power, who proclaimed himself "King of this land of Ireland as united, annexed and knit for ever to the Imperial Crown of the Realm of England". When the nobles resisted, Henry seized their lands, resettling them with loyal "planters" from England and Scotland.

His daughter, Elizabeth I, fought four wars in Ireland. As well as trying to impose the Reformation on the country, she wanted to protect

England's right flank against an invasion from her principal opponent, Spain.

Later, James I defeated a particularly powerful baron, Hugh O'Neill, Earl of Tyrone, at the Battle of Kinsale and planted new settlers on O'Neill's lands in six of the nine counties of the ancient province of Ulster. The new settlers were Protestants, firm believers in the Calvinist work ethic, and the racial mix they created led to strife in Ulster in the 19th and 20th centuries.

An early sign of the troubles ahead came in 1641, when Ulster Roman Catholics, hoping to recover their confiscated lands, rebelled at Portadown. The facts of the rebellion were rapidly overwhelmed by the legend as lurid tales spread of a drunken Catholic pogrom against the God-fearing settlers, with 12,000 Protestants knifed, shot and drowned, pregnant women raped, and infants roasted on spits.

The Gaelic Irish had further cause to worry when, after Charles I was beheaded, the new Puritan Parliament in England began suppressing the Roman Catholic religion. Fanned by the flames of this resentment, a new Catholic revolt began to spread. This "Great Rebellion" was ruthlessly suppressed by the English Protector, Oliver Cromwell, whose 20,000 Ironside troops devastated the countryside. By 1652, about a third of the Catholic Irish had been killed. Much of their land was handed over to Protestants.

When the monarchy was restored, Charles II disappointed Catholics by throwing his support behind the Protestants, on whom he depended for power. His successor, James II, himself a Roman Catholic, raised hopes by introducing an Act of Parliament that would have ousted the Protestant settlers; but, before it could be put into practice, James was defeated in 1690 at the Battle of the Boyne, near Dublin, by William of Orange. William had been called in by the English establishment to end James's "Popish ways" and his success in doing so is still commemorated annually on 12 July with mammoth parades by Protestant Orangemen throughout Northern Ireland. From that day in 1690, Roman Catholics became a persecuted majority in Ireland. New anti-Catholic legislation, the "Penal Laws", barred them from all public life and much social activity.

LEFT: England's Richard II made two expeditions to Ireland, in 1394–95 and in 1399.

ABOVE: William of Orange, who defeated James II at the Battle of the Boyne in 1690.

The land problem

Pressure for change was applied by Protestant patriots such as Henry Grattan. The threat of force was added in the shape of the Irish Volunteers, 80,000 strong by 1782. London caved in and agreed to a separate parliament in Dublin. But a fatal flaw in all this was that the Catholic majority (three-quarters of the population) were still denied a political role and the extensive patronage at the disposal of the English parliament allowed it to manipulate policy in Dublin.

The government in London thought it had done rather well to pass two Catholic Relief Acts giving Catholics limited voting rights and allowing them once more to own or lease land. As so often in Ireland, however, a well-meaning policy gave birth to anarchy. Catholics began buying land in Ulster, forcing up prices and alarming the Protestants, who formed a vigilante outfit, the Peep o' Day Boys, to burn out Catholics in dawn raids.The Catholics set up their own vigilante force, the Defenders. The lines of a long conflict were drawn.

Yet Ulster was the cradle in 1791 for a brave attempt by Protestants and Catholics to fight together for reform. Wolfe Tone, the son of a Protestant coach builder, set up the first Society of United Irishmen club in Belfast and a second soon opened in Dublin. It began well, largely as a debating society, but was suppressed within three years when British Prime Minister William Pitt feared an alliance between Ireland and France, with whom Britain was then at war. Tone, condemning England as "the never-failing source of all our political evils", fled to America.

Government anxiety increased when the United Irishmen, largely a middle-class Protestant group, began forging links with the Defenders, mostly working-class Catholics. And soon an even more threatening alliance was being forged: the United Irishmen persuaded Tone, who had been thinking of becoming a farmer near Philadelphia, to sail to France and rally support against Britain. Tone assured the French that their arrival in Ireland would trigger a national uprising, supported by the Irish militia, and on 16 December 1796 a French battle fleet of 43 ships set sail.

It was the weather that came to England's rescue. Severe storms dispersed the fleet, and the few troops who landed at Bantry Bay, on the southwest coast, were greeted rather unenthusiastically by the Irish peasants, who believed that the French really had been sent by the northern Protestants to suppress them further.

In the end, it was the United Irishmen who were suppressed. Pitt, fearing a second French expedition, imposed harsh martial law in Ulster. The army, four-fifths of whom were themselves Catholic Irish peasants, began arresting the organisation's outlawed leaders, identifying

ABOVE: Thomas Robinson's *Battle of Ballinahinch*, portraying a County Down clash in 1798.
RIGHT: The English built many grand mansions in Ireland such as Powerscourt in County Wicklow.

them as a result of information partly provided by informers, partly extracted through brutal beatings. Soon Ulster was in the grip of terror and the stage was set for a new group to enter

By the middle of the 18th century, only 7 per cent of Irish land was in Catholic hands, and peasants had the status of slaves.

the Irish drama. These were the Orangemen, whose role in Ulster remains central today.

The movement began in 1795 after a clash between Protestant Peep o' Day Boys and Catholic Defenders at the Battle of the Diamond, near Armagh, in which 30 men died. The Protestants, fearing worse was to come, reorganised as the Orange Society, named after their hero, William of Orange, and preyed as lawless bandits on Catholics. In defeating the United Irishmen, the government was glad of their vicious support.

Ireland joins the British Empire

The Great Rebellion of 1798 *(see box below)* exhausted what little patience the English had. William Pitt's exasperated response was to propose a full union between Britain and Ireland. The 300-seat Irish parliament in Dublin would be abolished and 100 seats for Irish representatives would be created within the Imperial Parliament in London. Englishman, Irishman, Welshman and Scot would be treated equally.

Opinion in Ireland was split, less on any patriotic principles than on cool appraisals of individual self-interest and economic prospects. But London's mind was made up and, after a period of political wheeler-dealing, a majority of five voting *against* the union was turned into a majority of 46 voting *for* it. Ireland's parliament had, in effect, abolished itself.

On 1 January 1801, Britain and Ireland entered, in Pitt's phrase, their "voluntary association" within the Empire with "equal laws, reciprocal affection, and inseparable interests". As with most marriages, the intentions were good. Perhaps the two partners might even live happily ever after.

It was not to be. No one present on that day early in a promising new century could have imagined the terrible suffering that lay ahead. ❑

THE GREAT REBELLION OF 1798

Disaffection with English rule climaxed in May 1798 in a major rebellion. But by then so many of the United Irishmen's leaders had been arrested that most of the risings throughout the country were too ill-organised to succeed. Also, the native yeomanry, revealing the ruthlessness that is a disturbing aspect of the Irish character, reacted by torturing and shooting indiscriminately, often butchering the rebels after they had surrendered.

Within six weeks, it was all over. Perhaps 30,000 had died, giving birth in the process to countless ballads commemorating a small nation's struggle for freedom. The notion of an Irish patriotism independent of England's fortunes was taking root with a vengeance.

Napoleon Bonaparte, pressed by Wolfe Tone not to abandon French support for Ireland, belatedly agreed to another expedition, which set sail that August. But again the French had been misinformed. When one party landed at Killala, Co. Mayo, having been led to expect enthusiastic, disciplined battalions, they found instead supporters whom they disdainfully regarded as rapacious simpletons.

In October Tone himself tried to land in Co. Donegal with a party of 3,000 French, but they were beaten back by a Royal Navy force. Tone was captured and died in prison after an attempted suicide. His martyrdom was assured: several Gaelic football clubs are named in his honour and a 1960s rebel music band called itself the Wolfe Tones.

The Joy of Ruins

Visiting ruins not only unveils the drama of Irish history, it often takes you off the beaten path to unusually beautiful corners of the countryside

To understand why Ireland has so many churches in ruins, consider its history. Located at the western edge of the known world, Ireland escaped conquest by the Romans, and continued to follow a Celtic religion until the mid-5th century, and the arrival of St Patrick and other missionaries. It was a peaceful conversion, and Celtic customs were absorbed into Christian ritual. The earliest monasteries became important centres of learning. Stone carving was used on High Crosses to tell the Gospel story to an illiterate population, and in architectural decoration.

In contrast, Christianity's subsequent history in Ireland has been turbulent. The monastery at Clonmacnoise, established on its vulnerable Shannon-side location in AD545, had a typical fate, surviving numerous attacks from warring Irish clans, then Viking raiders, and then Normans, only to be destroyed by the English in 1552.

The Penal Laws

In the 12th century the Anglo-Normans arrived, and inter-married with the Irish chieftains. The Normans endowed Continental monastic orders, including the Cistercians, and built abbeys on an ambitious scale But these institutions were short-lived. From 1536 onwards, the Reformation led to the suppression of the monasteries, and by 1653 Oliver Cromwell had finished off the job. The infamous Penal Laws that followed prohibited Catholic participation in public life, and most of the ruined churches and abbeys were never rebuilt.

But because of the beauty of the stone carving, their scale – which ranges from ambitious to extremely modest – and their often tranquil locations, the ruins of these buildings are most rewarding to visit.

Left: these decorative Celtic crosses, some dating from the 7th century, are found all over the country. They combine the traditional cross symbolising the Crucifixion with a circle that is usually held to represent eternity.

Above: a cliff-top site on a narrow promontory makes a stunning location for the ruined 12th-century Ardmore Cathedral, Co. Waterford. Its sturdy Hiberno-Romanesque arches contrast with the slender, conical-roofed Round Tower. St Declan's Oratory and Well nearby date from the 9th century, and are still visited by pilgrims annually on 24 July.

SKELLIG MICHAEL

The monastery of Skellig Michael, 8 miles (13km) off the southwestern coast, is dramatically situated on a barren rocky island. It is the most remarkable Early Christian site in Ireland, and can be visited by boat between May and September. Dating from around AD800, the monastic remains are on a saddle of rock reached by climbing 600 stone steps. Six beehive huts, in which the monks lived, and two rectangular oratories, where they prayed, were built of dry stone on a cliff edge around a small garden area. They are surprisingly well-preserved, given their exposed Atlantic location. Below the huts are the remains of a 12th-century church, and there are also early Christian cross slabs and hermitages. Shortly after AD1200, the monks transferred to the mainland at Ballinskelligs, partly, it is thought, due to persistent Viking raids. The monks, seeking to emulate the desert fathers in their isolation, survived on a diet of fish, seabirds and their eggs (which they traded with passing seafarers), and vegetables from their garden. The island was a place of pilgrimage for penitents until the 20th century.

ABOVE AND BELOW: when the monastery at Clomacnoise, Co. Offaly, was founded by St Ciarán around AD 540, its Shannonside location marked the boundary between the provinces of Leinster and Connacht. Today it is a remote spot, frequented only by visitors to the monastic remains, which include six churches, a cathedral, two round towers and three High Crosses.

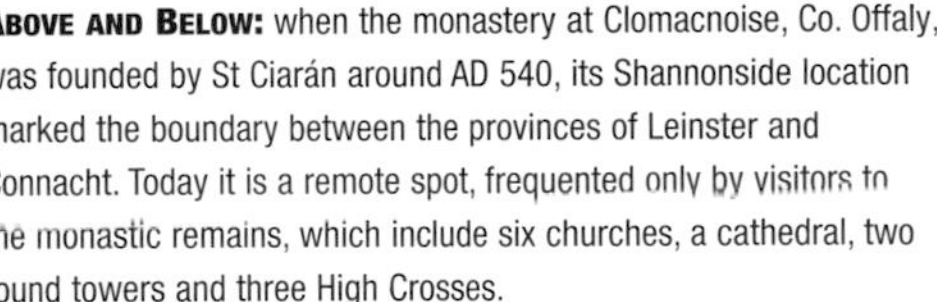

BELOW: influences from both Burgundy and the west of England have been detected in the richly carved Cistercian abbey that is Boyle Abbey, Co. Roscommon. Rounded arches of the Romanesque style were in favour in the late 12th century, but in a later phase of building, pointed Gothic arches were introduced.

LEFT: once the ecclesiastical capital of Kerry, today Ardfert is a small village known for its impressive church ruins and monastic site. The roofless Ardfert Cathedral dates from the 12th to 17th centuries and has a fine Romanesque doorway and a beautiful row of lancet windows. There are three smaller churches associated with St Brendan the Navigator, interesting carvings and an ogham stone on site.

RIGHT: the beautiful and remote valley of Glencolumbkille, Co. Donegal, associated with St Columba (Latin) or Colmcille (Irish), runs down to the sea at Glen Bay and contains 15 Early Christian pillars and cross-slabs decorated with cross-motifs and geometric designs. At midnight on 9 June a barefoot pilgrimage around the sites begins, as it has done for time immemorial.

THE MAKING OF A NATION

The union with Britain brought little happiness to either partner. And the divorce would involve more than a century of bitter bloodshed

Like many of his contemporaries, Daniel O'Connell, a Catholic lawyer from a well-off Kerry family, had been educated in France, and the ideals of the French Revolution had entered his thinking. Although he recognised that none of Ireland's basic problems had been solved by the union with Britain, he wanted no revolution in Ireland, not even a separation from the British Crown. What he campaigned for, with powerful oratory, was the right of Catholics to become Members of Parliament. Sir Robert Peel, Britain's prime minister, was forced to introduce a Catholic Emancipation Bill, which was passed.

Once in the House of Commons, O'Connell, by now "the uncrowned king of Ireland", began to rally support for his next cause: a repeal of the union. When his appeals struck few chords in parliament, he took his arguments to his countrymen, holding monster rallies throughout Ireland. One meeting was attended by 300,000.

Ireland's greatest disaster

At that point, fate intervened in the form of the Great Famine that began in 1845. In reality, it wasn't a true famine at all; rather a failure of the potato crop. At its height, wheat and barley were being freely shipped to England, together with tens of thousands of cattle, sheep and pigs. But such produce was beyond the pockets of the peasants, whose every penny went towards paying rent to the series of middlemen – often as many as seven – who stood between them and their land's ultimate owner. All they could afford was the humble potato. When it was blighted, they starved.

Out of a population of 8 million, 1 million people died in the Great Hunger and well over a million set off in squalid emigrant ships for a new life in America, where they would pass down to future generations a deep anti-British resentment. Around a third of the land in Ireland changed hands as estates went bankrupt, but the new landlords, who were mostly Irish (of both religions, now that Catholics were allowed to buy land), were even harsher than their predecessors in increasing rents. O'Connell's talk of non-violent nationalism seemed quite irrelevant. He died in 1847, aged 71, his dreams shattered.

In 1848, a year which saw nationalist uprisings in several countries of Europe, an attempted rising in Kilkenny was easily put down; it was a bungled fiasco, with little support from a weakened populace. A few wild plans, like one to kidnap Queen Victoria during her visit to Dublin in 1849, didn't materialise.

The birth of the Fenians

On St Patrick's Day, 17 March 1858, James Stephens, a Kilkenny railway engineer, founded a society which came to be known as the Irish Republican Brotherhood, dedicated to the idea of an independent democratic republic. An American branch was set up, called the Fenians after ancient Gaelic warriors. The American Civil War, Stephens noted, had given his supporters there valuable experience of battle. After a skirmish in Canada, Fenian participants were referred to as "The Irish Republican Army." It was the IRA's first appearance on the world stage.

Stephens was deposed as leader after his failure to organise an army of liberation from the US, but by 1867 armed and well-drilled bands had been set up throughout Ireland to revolt. Some trains were derailed, marking the arrival in the country of a strategy that would shape Ireland's struggles: guerrilla warfare. An explosion meant to spring other Irishmen from Clerkenwell prison killed 12 Londoners and maimed 30.

The fight for Home Rule

But it was not terrorism that was to further Ireland's cause most at this time. The two principal engines of change were driven by William Ewart Gladstone, who came to power as Britain's prime minister in 1868, and Charles Stewart Parnell, an English-educated Protestant landowner from County Wicklow.

"My mission," said Gladstone, "is to pacify Ireland." He began in 1869 by removing one chronic grievance. Since the Reformation, the Protestant church had been the established church in Ireland, although it represented only a sixth of the population. Gladstone abolished this privileged

LEFT: the formidable Daniel O'Connell, "the Liberator". **ABOVE:** a destitute family about to be evicted from their dwelling during the Great Famine of 1845.

ENGLAND'S ROLE IN THE FAMINE

The British government was not unaware of the Great Famine's effects. One MP described a large-scale eviction as "the chasing away of 700 human beings like crows out of a cornfield". England's refusal to provide relief is regarded by many today as a horrifying failure of imagination, one of the worst in its colonial history. Even compassionate and otherwise enlightened men lacked the vision to question the wisdom of the prevailing economic orthodoxy, the rigid belief that it would make matters even worse to interfere with natural economic forces. The same principle was applied to the industrial working classes in England's factories, but their lot was less desperate.

position. Next, he introduced a land Bill designed to make it less easy for landlords to evict tenants. Sensing new hope, nationalists began to demand once more that Ireland should have its own parliament for Irish affairs, leaving international matters to the Imperial parliament in London. This aspiration was known as Home Rule.

On reaching the House of Commons in 1875, Parnell, son of an Irish father and an American mother, scorned its cozy, club-like conventions and perfected filibustering techniques for blocking parliamentary business: proposing endless amendments, and making long. speeches. In one case, he forced an infuriated House into a continuous 41-hour session.

With Michael Davitt, Parnell set up the National Land League of Ireland. Funds from America flowed in to help the victims of oppression and threats of violence, frequently carried out, gave teeth to the Land League and left it in control of some areas of the country.

Ulster goes on the alert

A million Protestants still lived in Ireland, almost half of them in the northeast area of Ulster, and Home Rule would have severely limited the power of this influential minority. These Ulstermen saw themselves as different, as indeed they were. Their Presbyterian tradition had always been more radical than the loose Protestantism of their southern co-religionists and had given them a formidable self-reliance – some would say stubbornness. Although security of tenure had always been greater in the northeast, the Protestant descendants of the 17th-century Scots settlers felt far from settled; they had retained an ineradicable tribal fear of being dispossessed of their lands by the Catholics, and it was largely their opposition to change that led to the first Home Rule Bill being voted down in 1886.

> *The one part of Ireland to benefit from the Industrial Revolution was Ulster, where linen and shipbuilding took off. Therefore, Ulster Protestants saw their prosperity being threatened by anyone who wanted to weaken the link with England.*

In southern Ireland, a literary revival was growing, creating a new appreciation of Celtic culture and myths and a new respect for the Irish language, hitherto regarded as a fast-dying vulgar tongue. W.B. Yeats, the son of a Protestant Irish artist, published collections of folk tales such

ABOVE: an 1874 St Patrick's Day parade in New York features a bust of Daniel O'Connell.
RIGHT: Ulster Unionists bring out the guns in 1912 to demonstrate their resistance to Home Rule.

as *The Celtic Twilight*, conferring a new dignity on the often ridiculed Irish peasantry. A Gaelic League was set up, declaring itself the archer that would slay the plundering crow of the English mind, its arrow being the Irish language.

In the political arena, however, there were setbacks. Parnell lost political support when the scandal of his long-time affair with Kitty O'Shea, who had borne him three children, erupted in 1889. Parnell died two years later, after being soaked with rain at a political rally in Galway. Gladstone himself retired from the scene in 1893, aged 84, having failed to get his second Home Rule Bill, which had been approved narrowly by the House of Commons, through the Upper Chamber, the House of Lords. It was time for the baton of the Irish cause to pass to a new generation.

The 20th century

As a new century dawned, a Conservative government in England held out no hope of Home Rule. Queen Victoria's visit to Dublin in 1900 and Edward VII's in 1903 were well received, but new forces of nationalism were being assembled by Arthur Griffith, a Dublin printer and journalist, and John McBride, a Mayo-born republican who had fought against the British in the

THE PROS AND CONS OF HOME RULE

Gladstone's 1881 Land Act was regarded as revolutionary. It granted fixity of tenure to tenants who paid their rent; laid down that a tenant should be paid when he vacated a holding for improvements he had made; and decreed that fair rents should be defined not by the landlord but by a Land Court. Progress seemed possible. But then Lord Frederick Cavendish, the new Chief Secretary for Ireland and Gladstone's nephew by marriage, was knifed to death in Dublin. Reform slid down the agenda.

Parnell's next move was to found the Irish National League to campaign uncompromisingly for Home Rule. A general election in 1885 gave him control of 85 of the 103 Irish seats in the House of Commons – and the balance of power between the Liberals and Conservatives. Home Rule became the main issue in English politics.

The Conservatives argued that Home Rule would still leave the Imperial parliament controlling international affairs, war and peace, even customs and excise. How could any Irishman be satisfied with that? And yet many educated Irishmen, including nationalists, were happy to remain within the British Empire – as long as they could control their domestic affairs. Had Home Rule been granted in 1886, therefore, Ireland might well still be part of the United Kingdom, having "a distinct but not separate identity" rather like Wales and Scotland. It is one of the big "ifs" of Irish history.

Boer War. Griffith and McBride demanded "an Irish Republic One and Indivisible".

Two general elections in Britain in 1910 left the Liberals and Conservatives almost equally split in parliament. Once again the Irish Party, now led by the moderate John Redmond, used its balance of power to press for a new Home Rule Bill. Such a Bill was introduced in 1912 by prime minister Herbert Asquith and looked likely to become law in the foreseeable future.

The Protestants in Ulster began arming themselves. They found as leader a Dublin MP and lawyer, Sir Edward Carson, who had been Solicitor General in a Tory government and who had acted as prosecuting counsel against Oscar Wilde in 1895. What, asked Carson, was the point of Home Rule now that most Irishmen owned their farms, all major grievances had been removed, and even a Catholic university had been set up?

In 1913 recruiting started for a 100,000-strong Ulster Volunteer Force and large consignments of rifles were imported. "This place is an armed camp," said Carson. The southerners responded by setting up a counter-force, the Irish National Volunteers, whose badge carried the Letters "FF", for Fianna Fáil, a legendary band of warriors. The problem could be simply stated. The Protestant majority in the northeast wished to remain full British subjects and were prepared to fight Britain to retain that status. The Catholic minority in the area, like the Catholic majority in the rest of the island, sought a more Irish identity. The two attitudes seemed irreconcilable.

Sir Winston Churchill, then a Liberal Minister, was first to voice publicly one possible solution. Of the ancient province of Ulster's nine counties, six – those most heavily settled by Protestants in the early 1600s – might be excluded from Home Rule. Redmond, under pressure to get results, conceded that these six counties could *temporarily* be excluded for six years, after which time he hoped the Unionists would see the wisdom of rejoining their fellow Irishmen. From the nationalists' point of view, it was a fatal concession.

The Easter Rising

As England became preoccupied with fighting the Great War *(see box below)*, a handful of Irishmen were not prepared to shelve their nationalist demands for the duration of hostilities.

The Impact of the Great War

Larger problems than Ireland loomed for Britain in 1914 with the outbreak of World War I. A deal was rapidly done under which politicians in London passed a Home Rule Act, together with an order suspending its implementation for the duration of the war or until such time as some kind of amendment could be added to take account of the concerns of Ulster Unionists.

Ireland was thus bought off, to the extent that a greater proportion of Irishmen – from both the north and the south – volunteered for the British army than any other part of the United Kingdom's population. Irishmen won 17 Victoria Crosses in the first 13 months of the war. Surely, the Irish nationalists reasoned, such courage would eradicate even Ulster Unionist worries about the reliability of their Catholic countrymen.

The reality was different. Sir Edward Carson, now a member of Britain's War Cabinet, saw the Ulster regiments' heavy losses in the war, particularly during the Battle of the Somme in 1916, as a subscription towards permanent membership of a grateful UK.

In Dublin, not everyone was prepared to wait until the war with Germany ended. Many still remembered the old adage that England's misfortune is Ireland's opportunity, and nationalists led by Arthur Griffith began grouping under the broad banner of Sinn Féin (pronounced *shin fayne* and meaning, self-reliantly, "We Ourselves").

James Connolly, a labour organiser born into a poor Irish family in Scotland in 1868 and a soldier in the British army at 14, had embraced socialist thinking, setting up an Irish Citizens' Army to defend striking workers against brutal police suppression. Pádraic Pearse, a shy, austere school-master, had developed a mystical belief that bloodshed was needed to cleanse Ireland, in the same way as Jesus Christ, by shedding his blood, had redeemed mankind. Philosophy and physical force came together on the sunny spring holiday morning of Monday, 24 April 1916.

As Pearse, commander of the patriots determined to liberate Ireland, set out to march down Dublin's Sackville Street, his sister pleaded with him to "Come home, Pat, and leave all this foolishness". Most Irish people would probably have echoed her sentiments if they'd had an inkling of the ambitions of the small band of unrepresentative middle-class intellectuals behind the Easter Rising. But Pearse proceeded and, with 150 others, armed with a variety of venerable rifles and agricultural implements, took over the city's General Post Office and solemnly read out, to the reported apathy of bystanders, the proclamation of the new Irish Republic.

Another 800 or so civilian soldiers took over a brewery, a biscuit factory, a lunatic asylum and other key points. Eamon de Valera, a young maths teacher born in America of an Irish mother and a Spanish father, liberated a bakery against the wishes of its workers, who had felt that even in a republic people had to eat.

Soon Dublin ground to a halt. Alarm and rumours spread. The poor looted stores and children ransacked sweet shops. A British gunboat on the River Liffey began to shell the rebel strongholds. The inevitable end, when it came, was swift. The British set fire to the area around the GPO. By the time Pearse surrendered on the Saturday, 64 rebels, 134 police and soldiers and at least 220 civilians had died. The centre of Dublin lay in ruins. Martial law was imposed and 4,000 jailed. "So far the feeling of the population in Dublin is against the Sinn Féiners," one Irish MP wrote to his party leader, Redmond. "But a reaction might very easily be created." He then added the prophetic words: "Do not fail to urge the government not to execute any of the prisoners."

LEFT: Sir Edward Carson, although born in Dublin, rallies Protestant Ulster against Home Rule.
ABOVE: Dublin's O'Connell Street in ruins after being shelled by British gunboats during the Easter Rising.

A terrible beauty

Fatally, Redmond's urgings went unheeded and on 3 May the first three leaders, including Pearse, were shot at dawn. The next day, four more were shot. On 5 May, one more. On 8 May, four more. On 12 May, two more – including Connolly, who, because a bullet during the fighting had fractured his ankle, sat in a chair before the firing squad. Nobody knew how long the executions would go on. It was, someone said later, "like watching a stream of blood coming from beneath a closed door".

That Christmas, as a goodwill gesture, David Lloyd George, the "Welsh wizard" who was now Britain's charismatic prime minister, released 560 Irish internees from prison in England. Among them were Arthur Griffith, Sinn Féin's founder, and a 27-year-old west Cork man, Michael Collins, formerly a clerk in London with the British civil service. Another batch of prisoners given an amnesty at Easter 1917 included Eamon de Valera, the sole surviving Easter Rising commandant. The cast was in place for the climactic act of Ireland's drama.

The rise of Sinn Féin

In April 1918, panicked by a setback in the war in France, Britain finally extended conscription to Ireland, throwing in as a sop new Home Rule legislation based on partitioning the island. It was a foolish move. The Catholic Church's hierarchy condemned conscription – which turned out to be unnecessary anyway, as the war was soon to end – and the Irish Party walked out of the Commons. Sinn Féin, having found a rallying cry, won sweeping victories in the post-war general election of December 1918. The new MPs boycotted the Commons, forming their own parliament, Dáil Eireann, in Dublin's Mansion House. As president of their new "republic", they elected de Valera, still languishing in jail at the time.

Standing behind Sinn Féin were the Volunteers, known in the countryside as the Irish Republican Army, who increasingly saw violence as an effective weapon. They began killing anyone in uniform who stood in their way, then progressed to selective assassinations. Like so many Irish conflicts, this one rapidly took on some of the characteristics of a civil war. The

THE WEAPON OF HUNGER STRIKES

Sinn Féin candidates stood for parliament at by-elections, and began winning. Jailed supporters, on having their demand to be recognised as political prisoners turned down, staged hunger strikes. When one striker died after being force-fed, Collins organised a show funeral, massively attended. Arms were stockpiled. Lawlessness reminiscent of the 18th century started spreading in rural areas. By the time the Irish Party's leader John Redmond died (of natural causes) in March 1918, his hopes of bringing about Ireland's independence peaceably had turned to dust. And the tactics deployed at that time by Irish nationalists were revived with uncanny fidelity in the 1970s and 1980s.

corpses found labelled "Spy – Killed by IRA" were usually those of Irishmen.

After an attempt was made in broad daylight on the life of Viceroy, the king's representative in Ireland, England, perplexed as ever, suppressed Sinn Féin. Undeterred, Sinn Féin did well in the municipal elections held in January 1920.

When some of the boycotted police force resigned, they were replaced by recruits from England, many of them demobilised soldiers hardened to killing on the battlefields of France. Forming motorised squads, they hit back quickly at any trouble. But there were areas into which even they dared not go. In these, policing was taken over by the Volunteers, who arrested petty criminals and enforced licensing laws. The government, with 10,000 police and 50,000 troops, was humiliated. Before long, the police began fighting back, carrying out undisciplined reprisals after every IRA atrocity. On 21 November 1920, "Bloody Sunday", Michael Collins had 12 British officers shot dead, mostly in their beds. That afternoon, at a Gaelic football match in Dublin's Croke Park, police shot dead 12 civilians. In the countryside, fearful families took to sleeping in hedgerows to escape the revenge killings. Guerrilla warfare spread, out of control.

LEFT: on 6 December 1921, in London, Michael Collins signs the controversial treaty setting up the Free State. Arthur Griffith is seated on the left.
ABOVE: children in Dublin wave American flags to celebrate the ending of the Anglo-Irish war in 1921.

A deal is done

In May 1921 Britain tried out a new idea, holding elections for two Irish parliaments, one in the North, one in the South. Sinn Féin swept the board in the South and the Unionists dominated the North. In October, a conference was called in London at which Britain and Ireland, faced with the prospect of declaring war on each other, sat down to thrash out a settlement.

The compromises were agonising. But on 5 December 1921, at 2.20am, a deal was done. The island was to be divided. The consequences would be huge, for this was the first fissure, signalling the eventual break-up of the British Empire. To those present, the significance was narrower. Eight centuries of attempts by England's monarchs and ministers to rule their neighbouring island had, with surprising abruptness, come to an end. ❑

> *Slowly, in Ireland, derision for the upstarts turned to sympathy, then support. As Yeats wrote in a famous poem, the rebels had been "changed, changed utterly. A terrible beauty is born."*

First a Revolution, Then a Civil War

Bullets and shellfire ripped the heart out of the city centre between the Easter Rising of 1916 and the end of the Free State's bitter and bloody civil war in August 1923

Few ordinary Dubliners supported the small band of middle-class intellectuals and their 150 supporters who, armed with a variety of rifles and agricultural implements, took over the city's General Post Office on the spring holiday morning of 24 April 1916 and solemnly read out, to the apathy of bystanders, the proclamation of the new Irish Republic. Many, indeed, saw the action as treacherous: World War I was at a critical point and many Irishmen were serving – and dying – in British regiments in France.

It was only when Britain, having crushed the revolt, began to execute the rebels, a few at a time, that derision for the upstarts turned to sympathy. The way to post-war independence was clear, but the compromise that led to Britain retaining six northeastern counties divided the nation and led to a civil war in the new Free State in 1922. O'Connell Street was in flames again, with 60 dying in the first eight days of fighting. Between 1916 and 1922, three-quarters of the street was demolished, never to regain its former elegance.

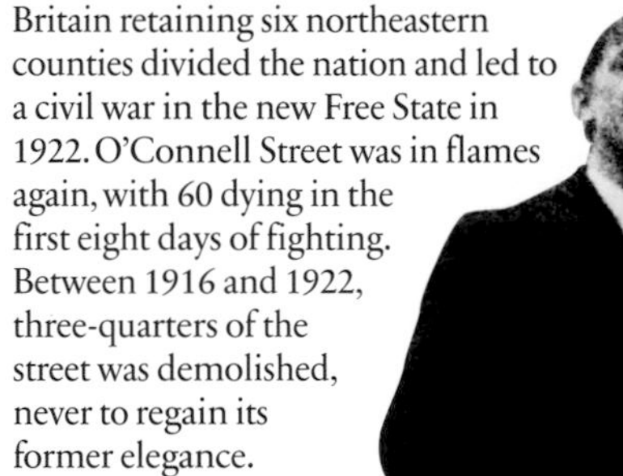

Below: This 1922 battle caused a fire at the Four Courts which destroyed historic deeds and documents dating back to the 12th century.

Left: Eamon de Valera defended Boland's Mill during the 1916 Rising. His rejection of the treaty with Britain led to civil war.

BOVE: The 1916 Rising ended when a British gunboat on the Liffey ıelled rebel strongholds, burning out the revolutionaries.

ELOW: Church Street after the 1916 Rising. The death toll was 64 bels, 134 police and soldiers and 220 civilians. Martial law was ıposed and 4,000 were arrested.

IGHT: Constance Markievicz, an Irish otestant who had married a Polish ›unt, was a 1916 rebel. Later she was e first woman elected to the London ırliament.

DE VALERA: THE GREAT SURVIVOR

In 1916, Eamon de Valera, a 33-year-old maths teacher liberated a bakery against the wishes of its workers, who felt that even in a republic people had to eat. Because he had been born in New York, of an Irish mother and a Spanish father, he was the only Easter Rising commandant not to be executed by the British.

Although president of Dáil Eireann in 1921, de Valera sent others to London to negotiate an independence treaty. That left him free to oppose their compromise, setting him against them in the civil war that followed.

The war ended in 1923 with de Valera's effective surrender and he did not achieve power until he headed the Fianna Fáil government in 1932. The economy stagnated, but he built Fianna Fáil into a formidable populist party and kept Ireland neutral during World War II. He served two terms as Irish president (1959–73) and died in 1975, aged 92.

ABOVE: suspects are frisked by troops in 1920. Many troops, recently returned from World War I, were not best suited to civilian duties.

RIGHT: Michael Collins, head of the provisional government, leaves Dublin Castle in January 1922. He would be shot dead 19 months later.

Living with Partition

Instead of coming together, the Catholic South and the Protestant-dominated North ignored each other for 50 years. Then civil strife and terrorism erupted in the North

To David Lloyd George's dexterous political mind, the fact that the Anglo-Irish Treaty gave everyone *something* they wanted but nobody *everything* they wanted meant it must stand some chance of success. This was the old mistake: the belief that the Irish were really Englishmen with brogues. In reality, the two peoples' expectations were quite different and, after eight centuries during which Irishman had fought Irishman over conflicting national allegiances, the first fruit of independence was true civil war.

The treaty gave the nationalists more than many had expected: an Irish Free State with a dominion status within the British Empire similar to Canada's. This was far greater freedom than Home Rule had ever promised.

The border question

But one dark cloud cast a shadow over the deal. Six counties of Ulster – Antrim, Down, Tyrone, Fermanagh, Armagh and Derry – were retained within the UK, the British having recognised that even a world war had not softened the resolution of the Protestants. Sir Winston Churchill expressed the dilemma graphically: "As the deluge subsides and the waters fall short, we see the dreary steeples of Fermanagh and Tyrone emerging once again. The integrity of their quarrel is one of the few institutions that's been unaltered in the cataclysm which has swept the world."

To sell the long-resisted division of Ireland to nationalists, the government added a proviso: a Boundary Commission would decide which Roman Catholic-dominated areas of Northern Ireland would later be incorporated within the 26 counties of the Free State. This promise permitted patriots such as Michael Collins to swallow the bitter pill of partition: after the Catholic areas of Tyrone, Fermanagh and south Armagh had been removed, they reckoned, what would remain would not leave the new north-eastern state a viable entity.

But Collins's hopes, faint though they were, were not universally held. Ferocious arguments split the infant Free State, laying bare long suppressed personal animosities. On the one side stood the pro-Treaty provisional government led by Arthur Griffith; on the other, the anti-Treaty forces massing behind Eamon de Valera. After a bitter 12-day parliamentary debate, the Treaty was carried by 64 votes to 57.

It was too narrow a margin to ensure peace, especially since the Irish Republican Army, mirroring the split in the country, was marching in opposite directions; about half with Collins, transforming itself into the regular army of the Free State, and the other half refusing to recognise the new government, relying instead on force to win them a free and united Ireland.

By 1922 Dublin's O'Connell Street was in flames again, with 60 dying in eight days. Northern Protestants, looking on, vowed to have nothing to do with any redrawing of borders, declaring: "What we have, we hold." Fighting broke out in Northern Ireland, too, with the death toll rising to 264 within six months.

The new Ireland's first prime minister did not live to see the end of the struggle: in August 1922, heavily overworked, Griffith collapsed and died. Collins had a more violent end, being shot dead in an ambush on the Macroom to Bandon road in his native County Cork. He had been expecting just such an outcome: after putting his name to the Anglo-Irish Treaty, he had written to a friend: "Will anyone be satisfied with the bargain? Will anyone? I tell you this – early this morning I signed my death warrant."

The Boundary Commission recommended only minor adjustments, and even these were never implemented. De Valera's view of the border as "an old fortress of crumbled masonry, held together with the plaster of fiction" had proved false. Permanent partition had arrived.

Fine Gael and Fianna Fáil

The civil war ended in 1923 with De Valera's effective surrender. But it was to dominate every aspect of political life in the Free State for the next half-century. The country's two main political parties today, Fine Gael (*Tribe of Ireland*) and Fianna Fáil (*Warriors of Ireland*) are direct descendants of the pro- and anti-Treaty forces.

In 1927, De Valera entered parliament (the Dáil) at the head of Fianna Fáil. He came to

LEFT: a farewell to Empire as Queen Victoria's statue is removed from outside Ireland's parliament building. **ABOVE:** Eamon de Valera addresses a rally.

EAMON DE VALERA'S VISION

As the new leader of Fianna Fáil, de Valera declared: "No longer shall our children, like our cattle, be brought up for export." He spelt out his vision for the Free State's future in a famous St Patrick's Day address, in which he described his ideal Ireland as "a land whose countryside would be bright with cozy homesteads, whose fields and villages would be joyous with the sounds of industry, with the rompings of sturdy children, the contests of athletic youths and the laughter of comely maidens, whose firesides would be forums for the wisdom of serene old age."

It was a noble enough aim. It just didn't particularly belong to the 20th century.

power in the 1932 election, vowing to reinstate the ancient Gaelic language and culture, ushering in a new era of pious respectability, based firmly on Catholic values. The poet W. B. Yeats, a member of the Irish Senate, warned Eamon de Valera of the dangers of alienating northern Protestants by allowing the Catholic Church too much influence in the South. "If you show that this country, Southern Ireland, is going to be governed by Catholic ideas and by Catholic ideas alone, you will never get the North," said Yeats. "You will put a wedge into the midst of this nation."

In the following three decades, De Valera built Fianna Fáil into a formidable populist political

movement, drawing support from small farmers, the urban working class and the newly moneyed. Fine Gael's heartland was among larger farmers and the professional classes. The Labour Party, which pre-dated partition, found it hard to build support: the trade unions, while nominally pro-Labour, often did deals with Fianna Fáil, and the Church's anti-communist propaganda encouraged a fear of the Left.

Endless emigration

"Dev", as he became affectionately known, pursued a policy of economic nationalism, raising tariff barriers against England, which retaliated. A tax was even imposed on English newspapers. Yet not everyone was thrilled when, for example, Dev announced that Ireland was self-sufficient in shoelaces. Emigration, mainly to England and America, claimed yet another generation of younger sons unable to inherit the family farm and younger daughters unable to find husbands. In the early 1920s, an astonishing 43 per cent of Irish-born men and women were living abroad. At the opposite end of the social scale from the farmhands, the once affluent Anglo-Irish – sometimes called the Protestant "Ascendancy" – fell into decline and their "Big Houses" at the end of long, tree-lined avenues began to look dilapidated.

Many southerners began to question the wisdom of following their leader's "Small is Beautiful" signposts. "It was indeed hard," said one observer, "to muster up enthusiasm for the carrageen moss industry, in the possible utilisation of the various parts of the herring's anatomy, down to the tail and the fin, in portable, prefabricated factories themselves made of herringbone cement along the west coast."

But what was the alternative? Certainly not to imitate the UK, Dev insisted, and, to emphasise the point, he produced a constitution in 1937 which abolished the oath of allegiance to England's king, claimed sovereignty over all 32 counties of Ireland and underlined the pervasive influence of the Roman Catholic Church.

The new constitution created a curious equilibrium. The bishops in the South and the Orangemen in the North each exercised a sectarian and politically conservative pressure on their respective parliaments.

Although the Unionists would have been happy to remain an integral part of Britain, Lloyd George, emphasising Ulster's "otherness", had given them their own parliament, Stormont – built on the outskirts of Belfast in the style of Buckingham Palace, only grander. And they had lost no time in making their makeshift state impregnable. London, relieved to be rid of the perennial Irish problem, did nothing to stop them. Nor, fatally, did the Roman Catholics' elected representatives, who boycotted Stormont. The assembly, the Unionists boasted, was "a Protestant parliament for a Protestant people." The historic hatreds between the two communities were left unhealed.

LEFT: Eamon de Valera's vision for a new Ireland had a strong emphasis on rural values.

RIGHT: a traditional family of travelling people.

If anything, they were deepened. Taking advantage of the nationalists' boycott, the Unionists made sure that the plum jobs and the best housing went to their own supporters. Two distinct communities developed: Protestant dentists pulled Protestant teeth, Catholic plumbers mended Catholic pipes.

An all-Protestant part-time special constabulary (the "B" Specials) maintained close links with the Orange Order and helped the police keep dissension under control. The IRA, making little headway in Ulster, began a campaign in English cities in 1938, setting off suitcase bombs, but the English declined to over-react.

World War II

While Irish history was repeating itself, European history concocted another world war. The Unionists felt their self-interest had been justified when, as soon as Britain declared war on Germany in 1939, De Valera announced that Southern Ireland would remain neutral. Behind the scenes, Winston Churchill, Britain's new wartime leader, offered De Valera a united Ireland at some point in the future if Ireland were to enter the war and allow the British navy to use its ports.

De Valera said no. After all, to enter the war would leave Ireland – with no navy or air force – wholly dependent on the protection of its old

THE TRAVELLING PEOPLE

There are probably more than 3,000 families of travellers in Ireland, adding up to an estimated 25,000 people. Although they bear some resemblances to the Gypsies of France, Spain and Romania, they are entirely Irish in their ethnic origins – the true Romanies, like the Romans, never reached Ireland.

Many live in illegal campsites by road sides, on waste ground, or on land cleared for development, and are frequently forced to move on. Local councils have tried to persuade them to move into rented housing, but most cling to the travellers' way of life. Once, they fulfilled a useful economic role in a society that was still mainly rural: mending utensils, making baskets and sieves, peddling knick-knacks, dealing in horses and selling scrap. Today's consumer society has little need of such services.

Until the early 1960s, almost all travellers lived in brightly-painted horse-drawn caravans or in tents. They dressed differently from other people – especially the women, with plaid shawls wrapped round their head and shoulders. Then, as demand for their trade diminished, they began drifting into urban areas such as Dublin and the caravans were often superseded by motorvans.

Travellers traditionally had large families, and children had the security of an extended family if not a reliable education. It appears, though, that many of the current generation may adopt a more settled urban life.

enemy, England, and its long-term prospects if Germany won the war, which seemed entirely possible, would hardly be enhanced.

Churchill's fears had not been unfounded. The Germans had been planning an invasion of Ireland, "Operation Green", as a springboard to an assault on Britain. In a handbook designed to brief their battalions, they noted that "the Irishman supports a community founded upon equality for all, but associates with this an extraordinary personal need for independence which easily leads to indiscipline and pugnacity."

Northern Ireland became a target. A ferocious night raid on Belfast in April 1941 killed more

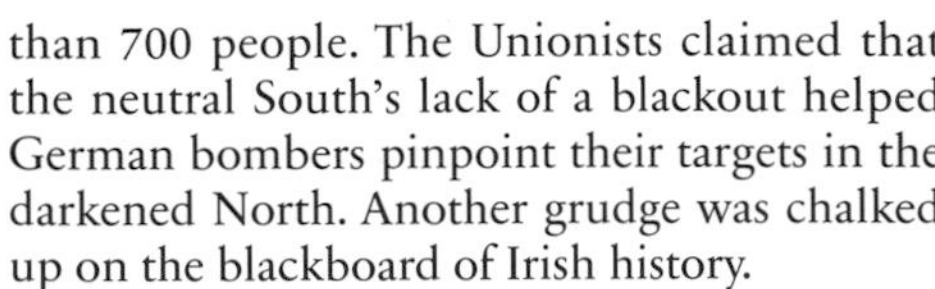

than 700 people. The Unionists claimed that the neutral South's lack of a blackout helped German bombers pinpoint their targets in the darkened North. Another grudge was chalked up on the blackboard of Irish history.

Over the years even the name of the Free State had been fiercely argued about. Both the English and the Irish seemed to find "Eire" (Gaelic for "Ireland") acceptable. But in 1948 a coalition government fixed the name of the country as the Republic of Ireland. Britain declared that, as a result, Ireland was no longer part of the Commonwealth. At last, Ireland – or at least 26 counties of it – was politically free.

The green consumers

In 1958, under the premiership of Sean Lemass, Ireland decided to rejoin the 20th century. He set out vigorously to create new jobs by opening up the economy to foreign investment, attracting light engineering, pharmaceutical and electronics companies.

The dream of de Valera – now the president, a largely symbolic office – faded fast. Interest in Gaelic language and culture waned and the voice of management consultants was heard in the land. The Irish, embracing consumerism with relish, were becoming more like the English. Even the IRA failed to command much support in its fight for a united Ireland. A campaign of border raids between 1956 and 1962 netted a few arms hauls but then petered out. By 1965, it seemed the most natural thing in the world for Lemass to have a neighbourly meeting with Northern Ireland's premier, Captain Terence O'Neill. But it seemed shockingly unnatural to hardline Union-

WHY THE NORTH DISTRUSTED THE SOUTH

Although politically free, the 26 counties of the Free State remained economically and culturally chained. Emigration reached epidemic proportions, triggered not only by the loneliness, dullness and generally unattractive nature of life in rural Ireland but also by the restrictions placed on entertainment. In 1954 a record 1,034 books were banned, and cinemagoers, if they wished to follow the plots of many films, had to cross the border to see the unscissored versions. London's more lurid Sunday newspapers published tamer Irish editions.

In *Mother Ireland*, the novelist Edna O'Brien described the constricting parochialism and the awful predictability that led her to flee to London: "Hour after hour I can think of Ireland, I can imagine without going too far wrong what is happening in any one of the little towns by day or by night... I can almost tell you what any one of my friends might be doing, so steadfast is the rhythm of life there."

Northern Protestants noted not only the southern state's poorer standard of living but also its intrusion into personal freedoms – its outlawing of divorce, for example, and its ban on the importation of contraceptives. Northern Ireland, Britain had pledged when the Republic left the Commonwealth, could remain part of the United Kingdom as long as a majority of its people wished. Since Protestants outnumbered Catholics by two to one in the Six Counties, that might mean forever.

ists. Several Cabinet colleagues and a popular fundamentalist preacher, the Reverend Ian Paisley, reminded him that Lemass's Republic still claimed jurisdiction over the Six Counties.

The upper-class O'Neill was ill-equipped to cope with the Pandora's Box that was opened

As Britain rebuilt its economic strength in the 1950s, Northern Ireland began to feel the benefit of its welfare state and industrial incentives, while the Republic remained essentially a humdrum peasant economy.

just three years later. It began routinely enough, when a Unionist-controlled council in Caledon, County Tyrone, where many Catholic families were badly in need of housing, allocated one of its dwellings to a young, single Protestant girl. Local nationalists, following the example of blacks in the US, first staged a sit-in, then a civil rights march. A second march was planned for October 1968, inside the walled city of Londonderry. This is a symbolic place for Unionists, who still commemorate the breaking of the city's siege in 1689 when Protestant supporters of William of Orange defeated Catholic supporters of James II, thus cementing Protestant supremacy (Nationalists, equally tutored in the city's history, reject its "English" name in favour of the original Derry).

O'Neill's government, viewing the march not as a civil rights protest but as a nationalist conspiracy, banned it. Two thousand people marched anyway, and were met by the massed forces of the RUC, complete with two mobile water cannons. TV viewers around the world were treated to the ensuing battle, as the RUC took their truncheons to the demonstrators with what looked suspiciously like enthusiasm. Further marches ended in violence and O'Neill, having seen his dreams for a civilised relationship between the two Irelands consumed by the fires of sectarian hatred, was forced out of office by militant Unionists.

Almost inevitably, the Protestants' annual march through Londonderry in August 1969 sparked off violence. Petrol bombs were hurled, along with broken-up paving stones. The police replied with CS gas. Fighting spread to the Catholic Falls Road and the Protestant Shankill Road. The RUC, hopelessly out of its depth, appealed for reinforcements and, on 16 August, a reluctant British government sent troops on to the streets of Derry and Belfast "in support of the civil power". What was the choice? Northern Ireland was, after all, part of the United Kingdom. It was meant to be a temporary arrangement. ❑

LEFT: the Rev. Ian Paisley, rallying Protestants in the late 1960s to oppose links with the Republic.
ABOVE: British troops sent to keep the peace in 1968.

Ireland Transformed

As violence dragged on from the 1970s into the '80s, the South left the North to fight its ancient battles and looked instead to Europe, overhauling its economic and social values. Finally the North reached a military impasse and adopted power-sharing. Meanwhile the Republic's economic boom quickly turned to bust

At first the British soldiers arriving in what was technically British territory were welcomed as saviours. Catholic housewives, many of whom had been preparing to take refuge in the Republic, plied them with endless cups of tea. Girls smiled sweetly at them. Perhaps, it seemed for a moment, all would be well. But it was already too late for such hopes, for this latest chapter of Ireland's Troubles had caused a fearful resurrection: that of the IRA.

As a fighting force, the Irish Republican Army had virtually ceased to exist in 1962. By the late 1960s the declared aim of the small group of Marxists who constituted the rump of the IRA was to overthrow the conservative establishments in both parts of Ireland, then set up an ill-defined workers' republic. Lacking modern weaponry, they were acutely conscious of their failure to protect Catholic communities against Protestant mobs, a failure brought painfully home by graffiti which interpreted IRA as "I Ran Away". The movement split into two groups: the traditionalists ("the Officials") and a new Provisional wing (the "Provos"). Recruitment to the Provos soared when the British army embarked on late-night arms searches in Catholic areas of Belfast and soon the army, having arrived as mediator, found itself in many areas the enemy.

Violence spreads

The IRA's armed offensive gathered pace, spreading terror by means of snipers' bullets, booby-trapped vehicles and bombs in crowded bars. Protestant vigilante and terrorist groups such as the Ulster Defence Association and the Ulster Volunteer Force began to match violence with violence. The situation worsened dramatically when, on 30 January 1972, shooting broke out

at an anti-internment rally in Londonderry. At the end of it, 13 civilians lay dead, shot by paratroopers. The date, Bloody Sunday, became yet another Irish anniversary to be commemorated violently. The following month, as a reprisal, a bomb exploded at Aldershot Barracks in England, killing seven.

Ireland joins Europe

As bombs and bullets ripped Northern Ireland's economy to shreds, the Republic was enjoying unprecedented affluence. After the country's entry into the European Economic Community at the beginning of 1973, financial subsidies descended, as seemingly inexhaustible as Ireland's rain. Former farm labourers, much to their delight, found themselves earning good money assembling electronics components, and one euphoric trade minister dared to describe Ireland as "the sunbelt of Europe".

Culturally, too, the climate was brightening. Writers and artists, once forced to emigrate in search of intellectual freedom, were exempted from paying income tax on their royalties. Some well-known names, such as thriller writer Frederick Forsyth, moved to Ireland to take advantage of the concession. One or two more provocative authors found it peculiar that, while one arm of the government was allowing them to live free of income tax, another was banning their books.

by Britain's prime minister, Margaret Thatcher, and 10 men starved to death.

Economic recession, and the reluctance of industrialists to site factories in Northern Ireland, made unemployment seem as great an evil as terrorism. And in this respect the South was faring little better. As the effects of the 1970s oil crisis became felt, industrial unemployment rose and inflation neared 25 per cent. Both governments were chasing the same investors. The North had the bad luck to win the tussle over who should build John de Lorean's gull-wing sports car: the Belfast factory closed after the UK had invested £17 million.

London takes control

In the North, the sky was darkening further. Britain abolished the 50-year-old Stormont parliament, imposing direct rule from London, and tried unsuccessfully to persuade Protestant and Catholic leaders to set up a power-sharing executive. As atrocities multiplied, the death toll passed 2,500 and an entire generation reached adulthood without ever having known peace. Even well-tried nationalist tactics were failing to work any more: a hunger strike in an Ulster prison was ignored

LEFT: a mural proclaims loyalties in Derry City.
ABOVE: the worst car bombing was in Omagh in 1998 when 29 people were killed.

THE TWO TRIBES

Trust between nationalists and Unionists in Northern Ireland had always been elusive because the two cultural traditions had so few points of contact. Protestant children attended Protestant schools supported by the state, while Catholic children went to schools managed by their church. Catholic children were taught Gaelic games, Protestants played cricket. Catholics learned Irish, Protestants didn't. Integrating the schools would have meant bussing thousands of children from one area to another and was a difficult policy to implement because the Catholic Church in particular argued strongly that Catholic children must have the spiritual nourishment of a specifically Catholic education.

The Haughey era

At one stage in 1981–82, there were three elections in the Republic within 18 months. A complex system of proportional representation meant that Fianna Fáil minority administrations, now led by the charismatic Charles Haughey *(see panel below)*, alternated with Fine Gael-Labour coalitions. The last of these coalitions, from late 1982 to 1987, had one major achievement: it succeeded in negotiating, with the British Prime Minister Margaret Thatcher, the Anglo-Irish Agreement. This gave the Irish Government a consultative role in the administration of Northern Ireland, while committing British and Irish law and security forces to work together against terrorism and reaffirming that the Six Counties would remain part of the United Kingdom as long as a majority of their people favoured that option.

THE HAUGHEY PHENOMENON

Once compared to a Renaissance potentate, Charles Haughey dominated politics in the Republic for two decades. In 1970, when Minister for Finance, he had been acquitted of conspiring illegally to import arms for use in Northern Ireland. As prime minister, he lived flamboyantly beyond his means.

Suspicions grew about his financial probity and in 1992 he was forced from office. Five years later he was charged for having received while in office millions of pounds of undeclared funds from Ben Dunne, a supermarket tycoon. Condemned by the *Irish Times* as a "symbol of the degeneracy of political culture," he died in 2006 at the age of 80.

It was a Haughey administration that eventually introduced fiscal measures brutal enough to halt the Republic's economic deterioration. Public services were cut and unemployment soared, but the ground was laid for better times in the 1990s. That decade was ushered in by the election as Ireland's president of the left-wing Mary Robinson, a leading lawyer and feminist who stood for liberal and pluralist values. In her seven-year term, she was to transform the presidency from being a dumping ground for retired politicians to a force for social change.

Bounty from Brussels

The European Union was largely responsible for the economy's upturn. Jobs were created and roads built as billions of pounds poured into the country from the European social fund. A sharp fall in interest rates gave rise to a boom in property development and construction. Cheques from Brussels made up almost half the income of Irish farmers. Psychologically, any lingering inferiority complex towards Britain was eroded as the new wealth reduced the country's economic dependence on trade with its larger neighbour.

Ireland began promoting itself as the Silicon Valley of Europe. Its combination of a youthful, well-educated workforce and generous grants and tax incentives lured more than 300 electronics companies to the Republic. Computer giants such as Dell and Gateway began assembling computers there, and Microsoft established its European operations centre in Dublin.

The buoyant job market eroded the emigration figures, which had reached 30,000 a year in the 1980s – mainly to Britain and the United States. Suddenly many of those who had gone in the 1980s came home, flaunting the experience they'd gained abroad and grabbing many of the new jobs. Refugees from destinations as diverse as Romania and Zaire, learning of Ireland's comparatively liberal immigration laws, arrived in Dublin. Applications for asylum, which had been only 30 to 40 a year at the beginning of

LEFT: Charles J. Haughey addresses a party meeting.
RIGHT: Dublin women attack anti-abortion laws.

The inward investment policy brought real, not fool's, gold to the end of the Irish rainbow. Large Mercedes and Toyotas sped German and Japanese execs through rural lanes, adding more unpredictability to Ireland's devil-may-care driving conditions.

the decade, soared to several thousand a year. As unemployment figures among the Irish dropped, people overcame their resentment of economic migrants from the EU, prepared to do the menial jobs spurned by the newly affluent Irish. The newcomers were accepted, many intermarried, the Irish even started learning a few phrases in languages such as Polish from their new workmates.

Happily, Europe loved Ireland just as much as Ireland loved Europe – if nothing else because its support acted as a useful counterweight to Britain's often antagonistic attitude. Being small and remote lent enchantment, too: Ireland could never have got away with offering corporate tax incentives that made a mockery of EU harmonisation if it had been a serious economic competitor to France or Germany. The effects weren't wholly beneficial. For example, because agricultural subsidies favoured sheep farming, the republic's

THE GREAT DEBATES OVER ABORTION AND DIVORCE

In 1992 voters in the Republic were asked to adjudicate by referendum on a bizarre debate about abortion. The government's chief legal advisor had sought an injunction to prevent a 14-year-old rape victim going to England to have an abortion. To many, the proposal seemed both hypocritical and irrelevant since an estimated 4,000 Irish women travelled to Britain each year for abortions. But after a vitriolic public debate, the Constitution was amended to defend the right to life of the unborn.

The issue would not die down and, after continuing acrimony, it was agreed that women could continue to go abroad for abortions and would be permitted freedom of information "relating to services lawfully available in another state." While abortion is legal in theory, the medical licensing body considers it malpractice for doctors to perform the operation, so women seeking a termination still have to travel abroad.

But the ground was shifting significantly on major social issues and a 1995 referendum on divorce gave the pro-divorce faction the slimmest of majorities: less than 1 percent. Such a result would have been inconceivable a decade earlier.

Despite the closeness of the vote, enough politicians of all parties were sufficiently emboldened to ensure that divorce finally became legal in the Irish Republic two years later.

sheep population more than trebled to more than 5 million and overgrazing threatened to turn lush parts of the west into rocky hillsides.

The Alice in Wonderland nature of Irish politics was highlighted in 1997 by the election of Mary McAleese, a Belfast academic with strong nationalist sympathies, to the presidency. Being a citizen of Northern Ireland, Mrs McAleese could not cast a vote in the Republic's presidential contest, yet she could legally stand as a candidate – and win.

Tourism benefited as Ireland suddenly became a chic tourist destination. Part of this popularity could be traced to the success of bands such as U2 and the impact of Riverdance, the show that sexualised traditional Irish dancing. The Irish talent for making merry was also highlighted by the creation of more than 1,000 Irish theme pubs overseas, from Durty Nelly's in Amsterdam to O'Kims in Seoul. For the first time, a £30 million ad campaign promoted both the Republic and Northern Ireland as a joint destination.

Criminal racketeering

But the Emerald Isle hadn't become a Garden of Eden. Dublin in particular was bedevilled by racketeering, much of it centred on the drugs trade. The scale of the problem became apparent in 1996 when gangs gunned down Veronica Guerin, a leading investigative journalist.

The Irish, now led by a pragmatic prime minister, Bertie Ahern, had few qualms about embracing the euro in 2002 (although Northern Ireland, as part of the UK, retained the pound). Suddenly the Irish discovered the joys of cheap credit, made possible by Europe's low interest rates, and embarked on a spending spree. At home, they bought foreign holidays, new kitchens and sport utility vehicles, and built themselves ever-bigger houses and holiday homes on former greenfield sites. Property prices spiralled, especially in and around Dublin, and in a bid to create affordable homes, the commuter belt expanded to estates built on the outskirts of towns an hour's drive and more from the city. Abroad, people invested in more property, taking particular advantage of a weak dollar to buy apartments to rent in Manhattan. But not everyone found gold at the end of the rainbow. As in the UK and the US, the poor got poorer while the rich got richer. And many

The Environment: Is Ireland Really Green?

Ireland's green credentials are somewhat mixed. On the one hand, its per capita emissions of greenhouse gases are surpassed in the EU only by Luxembourg and emissions from transport have been growing as more cars take to the roads. The widespread use of peat to generate electricity also adds considerably to greenhouse gas production.

On the other hand, renewable energy sources are increasing steadily, with one-tenth of electricity generated from wind, hydro, biomass, landfill gas and biogas. Wind power is the fastest growing sector, with 88 wind farms in 19 counties, including 12 facilities in Northern Ireland, and one offshore scheme at the Arklow Banks, off the east coast.

Although fertiliser use is decreasing, only 0.9 percent of farmland (39,000 hectares) is under organic cultivation. The Department of Agriculture has a target of 3 percent. Irish consumers have opened their wallets to embrace the organic idea, dramatically increasing their spending on ecologically-raised products.

In 2005 the government introduced refuse charges for all domestic waste, transforming the Irish into a nation of recyclers. A tax on polythene carrier bags was introduced in 2002, the first such levy in Europe. The 22-cent tariff, collected by all retail outlets, goes into an environmental fund. Ireland was also one of the first countries to ban smoking in public places, including bars. The prohibition has created the new sport of "smirting" outside pubs – smoking and flirting.

> *Dublin companies spent heavily on commercial properties in England and America, prompting the view that skyscrapers built with Irish labour were now owned by the labourers' descendants.*

worried that rampant cosmopolitanism would destroy irreplaceable values. Church attendance, which had slumped, began to recover. The number of Irish-language schools increased from just 25 in 1990 to more than 200, and a new Irish-language TV channel was launched in 1996.

In Northern Ireland, a peace agreement has been signed in the early hours of Good Friday 1998 by all the main political parties, including Sinn Féin, and the Republic changed its constitution to renounce its territorial claim to the North. In 2005 the IRA formally declared that the armed conflict was over and that they had scrapped their weaponry.

Peace breaks out

Although a low level of violence continued in both of Northern Ireland's communities, everyday life in Belfast seemed relatively normal. Clubbers from Britain and further afield discovered the city's vibrant nightlife, and the growth of low-cost airlines such as Ryanair enabled them to sample it. The city even hosted the British Council of Shopping Centres' annual conference.

But insecurities lived on, and subsequent elections saw middle-of-the road politicians mowed down by firm Unionist support for the Democratic Unionists, and equally decisive nationalist support for Sinn Féin.

Paradoxically, the success of the so-called "extremists" on both sides made a breakthrough possible. Having been stubborn enough to resist all compromises, the Unionists' leader, the Rev. Ian Paisley told his supporters that his essential demands had been met and that he was now satisfied enough to join a power-sharing Assembly with his former sworn enemies. Because responsibilities were allocated among the various parties in proportion to their performance at the polls, no parliamentary "opposition" was built into the system and co-operation was essential. So, as first minister, Protestant firebrand Ian Paisley had to get on with his deputy, former IRA man Martin McGuinness, or the Assembly would collapse.

LEFT: Bertie Ahern heads for another election win.
ABOVE: Ryanair boss Michael O'Leary.

Property bubble bursts

The first rumblings of trouble in the financial sector surfaced soon after the resignation of Bertie Ahern in May 2008, after nearly 11 years as leader following intensive investigation of his personal finances while in office by a government tribunal. In September of that same year, it appeared that the international financial crisis was affecting the Irish economy. However, it eventually emerged that the Irish economy was suffering a home-grown crisis, and was massively under-capitalised.

Irish banking had been operating in an effectively unregulated environment, encouraging

speculation by property developers, leading builders into dire trouble, precipitating mass unemployment as workers were laid off, leaving few if any buyers for thousands of houses and offices built during the boom.

In a desperate measure to save the Irish banking industry, pay cuts and pension cuts were imposed on public sector workers, one of a series of stringent measures designed to put the country back on course economically.

By the middle of 2010, despite the economic crash, Ireland still had a higher income per head of the population than the European average, and economic growth was once more on the horizon. ❑

ABC
Belfast's
Wonder
Theatre
RITZ
January 1946
Ritz
Phone
22494
all Proceeds
donated to a
Ritz bed in
the
Royal Victoria
hospital
MEMORIES
of
BELFAST CINEMAS

MUSIC

Many kinds of music, from classical to rock, are popular in Ireland. Whatever your taste, there are performances to enjoy all over the country

Irish traditional music is organic, constantly evolving. It has always drawn on many influences and sources, absorbing, retaining and changing them. Over the centuries hornpipes, polkas, barn dances, waltzes and other styles were imported from all over Europe and acquired a distinctly Irish flavour.

There are two basic types of Irish tune – the jig and the reel. The reel is the older and faster form, played in 4/4 time, while jigs have a 6/8 rhythm. Many thousands of different tunes make up the repertoire, which each musician performs in his or her unique style. Some airs and songs or how they are performed are associated with a particular area of the country.

Wherever you travel in Ireland you will encounter traditional music – from buskers performing on the streets to the hundreds of regular sessions, (*seisiún* in Irish), running year round all over the island – many with free admission.

Traditional variations

Traditional music falls into two categories – instrumental and song. Instrumental music was originally dance music but gradually evolved and nowadays is also performed for a listening audience, as well as to accompany dancing. Musicians usually perform sets of, for example, two different jigs followed by a reel, which builds up excitement as the music speeds up.

There is also a very strong song tradition – including unaccompanied solo singing known as *séan nós*, usually performed in Irish, as well as accompanied songs in English.

PRECEDING PAGES AND LEFT: traditional music is played in many pubs.
RIGHT: an Irish poet and a heraldic bard.

The harp, a national emblem, is the instrument most associated with Ireland but, while still widely played, you should not be surprised if you attend a music session where it does not feature. Other instruments include uilleann pipes, fiddle, flute, tin whistle, banjo, button accordion, bodhrán, harmonica and the spoons.

Uilleann pipes (pronounced *ill-un* or *ill-yun* and meaning "elbow") are bellows-blown bagpipes which evolved between the 18th and 19th century to their present form. The player performs seated, with the bag under one arm and the bellows under the other. The bodhrán (pronounced *bow-raun*) is a hand-held drum made from goatskin, which has become particularly popular since the 1960s. Ordinary spoons, in the hands of a master, produce a great sound, often setting the pace of a piece of music.

Comhaltas Ceoltóiri Éireann, founded in 1951, is the largest body involved in the promotion of Irish traditional music; its activities include concerts, festivals, competitions and summer schools, with workshops and classes in a range of instruments. It is well worth looking at its website: www.comhaltas.ie.

Revival of interest

While traditional music was always popular, it was a predominantly rural phenomenon until the 1960s, when there was a massive revival in interest, at least partly influenced by composer Sean Ó Riada, and the founding of companies including Claddagh Records. Nowadays it is played and enjoyed everywhere.

Music composed in earlier times has been revived and given new arrangements. Works by, for example, Carolan, the 18th-century itinerant blind harper and composer, are enjoyed again.

Some of the groups formed in the 1960s continue to tour today – among them The Chieftains, one of the most influential in building the international appeal of Irish music. Never afraid to push the boundaries, the group has

Irish Dancing: Alive and Kicking

Irish dancing is enjoying a popularity like never before. Ever since Riverdance burst onto TV screens in 1994 as an interval act during the Eurovision Song Contest, people find its toe-tapping rhythms irresistible. That magical performance by a troupe of dancers, led by Irish-Americans Jean Butler and Michael Flatley, to music composed by Bill Whelan, transformed perceptions of traditional Irish dance forever. The eponymous stage show continues to tour world-wide.

Until then, Irish dance was seen by many as stiff and uninspiring, and associated only with competitions or féis (pronounced *fesh*) which still take place – not only here, but also wherever the Irish emigrated. At them you see young girls in heavily embroidered dresses, their hair in ringlets, and young men in white shirts and black trousers, their arms stiff by their sides, compete for coveted awards.

What its critics had forgotten was that Irish dancing was also great fun. Similar to the barn dance or square dance, the ceílí is the best introduction, particularly when instructions are called out. There are four basic dance steps – the reel, light jig, slip jig and hornpipe – with many variations. There are more than 100 different dances with titles including *The Siege of Ennis* and *The Walls of Limerick*.

The Irish word *ceílí* means a gathering of neighbours in a house to enjoy music, dance and storytelling and, while today they are held in halls or pubs, that welcoming atmosphere survives. Avoid those organised purely for tourists.

collaborated with some of the biggest names in rock and pop, including musical legends Sting and Van Morrison, as well as with symphony orchestras and traditional groups worldwide. The vocal group The Dubliners also continues to entertain audiences in Ireland and overseas.

Music in Great Irish Houses hosts summer chamber music concerts in impressive historic homes, including Castletown House, Co. Kildare, Kilruddery House, County Wicklow and Emo Court, Co. Laois, www.musicgreatirishhouses.com.

Enya was a member of successful Donegal group Clannad with her siblings, but today is the best-selling Irish solo artist. She rarely performs in public and has not toured since 1988. She became known worldwide when one of her songs, *Only Time*, was used by TV stations to accompany archive footage of the World Trade Centre collapse.

The huge popularity of the Irish band, Kila, fusing music played on traditional Irish instruments with the strong and varied percussive beats of world music, is seen by many as evidence of the growing multicultural nature of Irish society.

Celtic fusion

Irish music has fused with rock and roll, punk and other genres since the 1970s, when Horslips merged the traditional and rock. Some fusion artists have been very successful both at home and internationally – among them the uncompromising Van Morrison and the wistful Enya.

Van Morrison's songs are often described as Celtic Soul. He was exposed to many musical influences, growing up in Belfast, as his father collected US jazz recordings and his mother was a singer. His work is thoughtful, and combines elements of jazz and R&B with Irish traditions.

LEFT: Irish dancing the way it used to be...
ABOVE: ...and at a pub's Irish music and dancing night.

Pop

Showbands were an Irish phenomenon in the 1960s and early 1970s. The largest of them were modelled on American big bands. They toured dance halls all over the country, performing covers of American and UK chart hits. They died out with the arrival of television and the closure of most halls, particularly those in rural areas.

That tradition lives on in a different form – with boy bands. The most successful of them internationally is Westlife. It should not surprise anyone to learn that both Westlife and its precursor Boyzone were manufactured and managed by Louis Walsh, who learned his trade on the showband circuit. Like the showbands, the groups' songs are covers of hits by other artists.

The most famous and successful of all Irish musicians on the contemporary scene is rock band U2. Their soaring stadium sound is not obviously influenced by Irish traditions.

Singing

The Irish love singing – and do so at any opportunity – just listen to them at a sporting event or on social occasions. Traditional songs fall into four categories: historic lays, fictional ballads, documentary come-all-ye's (so named as they start with "Come all ye...") and lyric song in Irish or *sean-nós*. The majority of songs in the Irish language collected in the 19th and 20th centuries are love songs, most composed between 1600 and 1850. After that period, and the disastrous famine, there was a growing dependence on English and that is reflected in the songs – some are bi-lingual, but most are in English.

Political songs support the Irish against the foreigner or glorify the feats of heroes including Fionn and Brian Ború. Others commemorate a disaster, such as a ship sinking, or are about the heartbreak of emigration. "Rebel songs," as they came to be known, with titles including *Kevin Barry* or *Boolavogue*, hark back to times of British oppression. The band The Wolfe Tones, formed in the early '60s, continues the tradition of singing rebel songs, and still tours to the UK and the US.

Most young Irish nowadays are unlikely to know the words of traditional songs, although they will be familiar with *The Fields of Athenry* (about deportation), and similar songs, written in recent decades and popular at sports events

Singers

Christy Moore is one of the country's most popular solo artists, who performs troubadour style. His songs reflect contemporary concerns – for instance, unemployment when it was an issue in Ireland. He rarely performs now and when he does tickets are at a premium. In the past he was also a member of bands, including Planxty and Moving Hearts, whose recordings are still available. That versatility is typical of many Irish traditional musicians – they may even belong to more than one group at a time.

Another popular singer is Daniel O'Donnell, who performs "middle of the road" love songs and ballads. There is nothing distinctly Irish about his choice of material.

Classical music

The main classical performing groups are the National Symphony Orchestra of Ireland and the Ulster Orchestra, based respectively in Dublin

LEFT: Van Morrison. **ABOVE:** Ronan O'Snodaigh of Kila. **RIGHT:** bodhrans are manufactured from goatskins.

and Belfast. Visitors to Ireland are surprised at the low ticket prices for their concerts, excellent value for world-class orchestras. Also look out for performances by students and graduates of colleges of music, particularly when visiting Belfast, Dublin, Cork or Limerick.

This being Ireland, politics naturally gets a look-in. In the hope that music might be the fruit of love, the Cross Border Orchestra of Ireland brings together 130 Protestants and Catholics aged from 12 to 24 from both sides of the border in the hope of breaking down prejudices.

The only Irish classical composer to be known internationally is John Field (1782–1837) who invented the nocturne. His music was brought to new audiences in the 20th century by Irish pianist John O'Conor.

Opera has always been popular, and in the 19th and early 20th centuries attracted huge audiences. Today, Opera Theatre Company tours all 32 counties and Opera Ireland presents two seasons in Dublin annually, while Castleward Opera and Loughcrew Opera mount productions in historic settings. Classically trained singers still lack career opportunities, and often have to go overseas. Some have formed trios such as The Celtic Tenors and The Irish Tenors, performing a mixture of classical and traditional songs. ❑

Where to Find the Best Music Festivals

The **West Cork Chamber Music Festival** (June–early July), epitomizes the specialist music festival: a beautiful location – Bantry House, overlooking Bantry Bay – and an intensive programme of international stars performing highlights from the chamber repertoire, public master classes and a Young Musicians platform. The day starts at noon with a Coffee Concert and ends with a Late Night Concert at 10.30pm, with two major concerts in between, and various events featuring young musicians. Tel: 027-52788, www.westcorkmusic.ie.

Opera lovers in evening dress enjoy full-scale performances in the Coach House at **Castle Ward** during three weeks in June, while many others take part in the **Opera Fringe Festival** in Downpatrick, Co. Down, with nightly concerts at the Down Arts Centre and Downpatrick Cathedral. www.operafringe.com.

The **Shannon International Music Festival** (mid-July) showcases the Irish Chamber Orchestra and guests – some from the world of jazz – with 11 concerts in five days in the riverside city of Limerick. www.irishchamberorchestra.info.

East Cork Early Music Festival (mid-September) uses historic buildings as venues for small ensembles, including Cloyne Cathedral, Ballymaloe House and the Palladian masterpiece, Fota House. www.eastcorkearlymusic.ie.

The **Sligo Baroque Music Festival** (in the Model Arts and Niland Centre, October holiday weekend) has four days of concerts, workshops and talks. www.modelart.ie.

THE IRISH WAY WITH WORDS

Whether in the theatre or the street, in parliament or the pub, the Irish are renowned for having the gift of the gab. Where did they get it from?

The Irish love telling stories, and many of them are very good at it – that's one of the reasons Irish writers are so popular all over the world and why an evening in a Dublin pub can be vastly entertaining.

Before the population of the country could express itself on paper, travelling storytellers – *seannachie* (pronounced shan-ah-key) – entertained and informed; their stock-in-trade included discursiveness, allusiveness, hyperbole and lots of high spirits. That tradition lives on today in the popularity of Irish stand-up comedians and broadcasters in the UK and abroad.

Writing in Irish

For centuries the Irish language survived despite invasions by the Vikings and Normans, and the arrival of English and Scottish planters. It was not until the mid-19th century that its use began to decline, to be replaced by English. This was due to the introduction of the National School system in 1831 and the effects of the 1845–49 Great Famine and the mass emigration which followed. The erosion was dramatic: in 1835 there were an estimated 4 million Irish speakers, but by 1891 the number had tumbled to 680,200.

It's not only the Irish ability at storytelling which attracts admiration: the Irish are also admired for their imaginative, even magical, ability with words.

As Ireland established its independence in the 20th century, interest in the native language increased, though its everyday use was confined mainly to the Gaeltacht areas along the western seaboard. Some writers produce work in both languages, slipping easily from one to the other.

Yet how English is spoken and written in Ireland differs greatly from how it is used elsewhere. Here it is less precise and concrete, much more lyrical, often using phrases directly translated from Irish. The almost physical delight in words seems to spring from a sharpened sensitivity to a language that has never been entirely adopted.

ABOVE: Mary Donnegan, a traditional Irish storyteller from Donegal, photographed in 1947.
RIGHT: James Joyce's *Ulysses* is acted out each year in locations from the book, such as Sandycove.

The Irish love of language

If you travel on public transport in Ireland, you will see how much its people enjoy reading. If you get to know Irish people, you will be surprised to learn just how many of them write poetry or try their hand at prose. These literary inclinations probably explain why, although successful writers are admired, their fellow countrymen are not over-awed by them.

Public readings of poetry and prose are relaxed, enjoyable occasions where all are welcome. Writing competitions and festivals are hugely popular, many of them offering workshops with experienced writers, which are often over-subscribed. The Arts Councils on both sides of the border encourage writing by giving financial assistance.

Learning about writers

There are lots of places to visit where you can learn more about writers. They include the Irish Writers' Centre and the Writers' Museum next door to each other in Dublin *(see page 132)*. In the Munster Literature Centre in Cork, visitors can discover short story writers Frank O'Connor and Seán Ó Faoláin, among others. Seanchaí, the Kerry Literary & Cultural Centre in Listowel, focuses on writers from that area, including the late John B. Keane, whose plays are hugely

IRELAND'S BEST LITERARY FESTIVALS

• **Dublin Writers Festival** is a four-day event featuring 30 of the world's most celebrated poets and fiction writers, coinciding with June 16, Bloomsday, which commemorates James Joyce's *Ulysses*. www.visitdublin.com.

• Galway's **Cuirt International Festival of Literature** is a big event in a small, festival-friendly town, held over six days in late April. It prides itself on showcasing local, national and international talent. Past visitors include Nobel Prize winners J.M. Coetzee, Nadine Gordimer, Derek Walcott and Seamus Heaney. It's a convivial event, with morning masterclasses, book launches and theatre performances, readings and debates. www.galwayartscentre.ie.

• **Listowel Writers Week** is held in late May in a north Kerry town (pop. 3000) that prides itself on its literary connections, including the late John B. Keane *(The Field)*. It includes writing competitions. www.writersweek.ie.

• **West Cork Literary Festival** in Bantry has free lunchtime readings from writers, many of whom also offer afternoon masterclasses. The pleasant seaside location attracts some big names, and an enthusiastic audience who enjoy the informal contact. Many people stay for all six days. www.westcorkliteraryfestival.ie.

• **Immrama**, a mid-June weekend of literary events organized around a travel writing theme, is held in Lismore, an attractive village in west Waterford and the home of travel writer Dervla Murphy. www.lismoreimmrama.com.

popular. The Verbal Arts Centre in Derry and the Creative Writers' Network, based in Belfast, both organise readings and workshops. Events featuring writers also take place in libraries, bookshops and arts centres all over the country – look out for posters or call in and ask.

It is often difficult to categorise Irish writers, as many work across various genres – poetry, novels, short stories, stage plays and screenplays.

Notable writers of the past

Jonathan Swift, satirist and author of *Gulliver's Travels*, playwright Richard Brinsley Sheridan and poet and dramatist Oscar Wilde are among Ireland's writers whose works continue to be enjoyed all over the world.

John Millington Synge (pronounced *sing*) used his knowledge of Irish to transform theatrical language in works including *The Playboy of the Western World* (1907), which caused a riot when first performed at the Abbey for its depiction of peasants.

James Joyce rewrote the rules of prose. His novel *Ulysses* follows one day in the lives of a Dublin Jew, his wife and Stephen Dedalus, based on himself. It is celebrated annually on June 16 as Bloomsday *(see pages 146–7)*.

Contemporary writers

A ruthlessly selective list would include:

Michael Davitt (1950–2005) attended university in Cork, where his lecturers included two Irish language poets – Seán Ó Tuama and Seán Ó Ríordáin. He founded the poetry magazine *Innti* in 1970 and is credited, along with Nuala Ní Dhomhnaill, Liam Ó Muirthile and Gabriel Rosenstock, with much of the continuing interest today in poetry written in Irish.

John McGahern (1934–2006) wrote about a society moving from insular repression in his early work towards self-confidence and freedom in his final novels, *Amongst Women* (1990) and *That They May Face the Rising Sun* (2001). He was a teacher when his second novel, *The Dark* (1965), was banned by Ireland's censors. He lost his job, and the resulting isolation touched his writing.

One of Ireland's most prominent playwrights is **Brian Friel**. Born in Omagh, Co. Tyrone, in 1929, some of his writing is influenced by his experience of the political situation in North-

IRISH WINNERS OF THE NOBEL PRIZE FOR LITERATURE

- **George Bernard Shaw** (1856–1950) spent most of his life in England. He wrote more than 50 plays and revolutionised the theatre with his dramas about ideas and issues. Works include *Man and Superman*, *Saint Joan* and *Pygmalion* which inspired *My Fair Lady*.
- **W.B. Yeats** (1865–1939), a hugely influential poet and dramatist, was a founder of the Abbey Theatre, the Republic's national theatre. His plays are rarely performed today, but he is considered one of the most influential poets of the 20th century. Although patriotic, he hated the bigotry of the nationalist movement, reflected in some of his best known poems.
- **Samuel Beckett** (1906–89) spent most of his life in Paris where, during World War II, he worked with the French Resistance. He wrote most of his work in French and then translated it into English. His best-known play, *Waiting for Godot*, was first produced in 1953.
- **Seamus Heaney** was born in 1939 into a Catholic farming family in Co. Derry, his early works combine personal memories with images of Irish heritage and landscape. His collections *North* (1975) and *Field Work* (1979) explore the political situation, while later works, including *Station Island* (1984) and *Seeing Things* (1991) convey an individualistic and meditative mood. As a translator, his work includes *Sweeney Astray* (1983) from a medieval poem in Irish, and the Anglo-Saxon poem *Beowulf* (1999).

ern Ireland. His most successful play is *Dancing at Lughnasa* (1990) which, after runs at the Abbey Theatre and in London's West End, won three Tony Awards on Broadway. Among his other works are *Philadelphia, Here I Come!*, *Lovers*, *Making History* and *Translations*.

Much of **Paul Durcan**'s poetry is satirical and idiosyncratic. He is compared to Patrick Kavanagh (1904–67) who also attacked Irish society.

Roddy Doyle's first novel *The Commitments*, made into a successful film, is part of his Barrytown trilogy, an accurate and funny portrayals of contemporary working-class life in Dublin written in the language used on its streets. His most

recent novel, *The Dead Republic* (2010) completes a picaresque trilogy following protagonist Henry Smart through 20th-century Irish history.

Joseph O'Connor (b. 1963, brother of singer Sinéad) has written seven novels, and is popular on the middlebrow Irish literary scene. He was first known for his witty newspaper articles, and gained international recognition with *Star of the Sea* (2002), which focused on the Great Famine and emigration. *Redemption Falls* draws on some of the same characters in that bestselling novel, and *Ghost Light* (2010) will complete the trilogy.

LEFT: Jonathan Swift's *Gulliver's Travels*, a parody of travel literature, was also a biting satire.
ABOVE: Roddy Doyle and Maeve Binchy.

Martin McDonagh (b. 1970) was born in London to parents from the West of Ireland, where he spent many holidays. His plays are black comedies, written in a language much influenced by the way English is spoken in Ireland. *The Beauty Queen of Leenane*, which won four Tony Awards on Broadway, and his debut feature film, *In Bruges*, were highly praised.

The tradition of short-story writing has been carried on by Neil Jordan (better known as a film director), John McGahern and William Trevor. A younger generation led by Claire Keegan (b. 1968) and Kevin Barry (b. 1969) is making its distinctive voice heard.

Popular fiction

Maeve Binchy, a former journalist with the *Irish Times*, is one of the country's most successful writers of short stories and novels, both at home and overseas. Among her best-selling books are *Evening Class*, *The Lilac Bus*, *Circle of Friends* and *Light a Penny Candle*.

Patricia Scanlan's novels, about family loyalties, acceptance and intolerance, pain and jealousy, are enjoyable and written with warmth. Among her novels are *Two for Joy*, *Francesca's Party* and *Divided Loyalties*.

Other notable contemporary writers of popular fiction include the often amusing Marian Keyes, Cathy Kelly, Sheila O'Flanagan and romance writer Cecilia Ahern. ❑

Arts Festivals

The economic boom has not only given Ireland traffic jams and housing estates. The new wealth has also led to a boom in the arts

The Irish have an international reputation as entertainers. But the visual artists, musicians, dancers and actors who once had to emigrate to find work now have jobs at home in these better economic times. Most Irish towns have a busy multi-purpose arts centre with exhibition spaces and auditorium.

Participating in cultural activities is one of the most popular pastimes for visitors to Ireland, and this has led to an explosion in the number of arts festivals taking place around the country, livening things up for residents as well. The concept of "the arts" involved is the broadest possible one, with comedy, cabaret, street performers and rock gigs sharing the programme with more conventional theatre, dance, classical music and readings.

Film and theatre

Autumn and winter are the time for film festivals – in Cork, Dublin and Belfast – and theatre festivals. In a country that loves to party, arts festivals are easy-going, unstuffy affairs, with many events held in pubs. The big summertime arts festivals – the Cork Midsummer Festival (June), the Galway Arts Week (July) and the Kilkenny Arts Festival (August) – co-exist with lively festivals in smaller towns that present ambitious multi-disciplinary programmes of theatre, music, cabaret, comedy, street entertainment, childrens' workshops and visual art. The talent might be mainly local, or you might be surprised by a big international name. While the main events will usually have modest ticket prices, all arts festivals generate free entertainment, and an unforgettable party atmosphere – which also makes them great places to meet people.

LEFT: the popular resort of Kinsale, south of Cork city, makes the most of its magnificent harbour during Arts Week in early July. Concerts of rock and traditional music in the stunningly-located historic site, Charles Fort, are a highlight.

ABOVE: the long summer nights with light until after 10pm are use to the full by the Cork Midsummer Festival, a lively multi-disciplinar festival. It has a high reputation for theatre, favouring open air promenade productions. Local company, Corcadorca, who gave Cillian Ryan his first break, are working their way through Shakespeare's comedies.

RIGHT: the medieval city of Kilkenny has a strong craft-making tradition and is at its best during the 10-day Kilkenny Arts Festival i August, the most highbrow of Ireland's arts festivals and particularl strong on visual arts and classical music. Pictured is the Ulster Orchestra.

OVE: overseas visitors (especially Americans) throng the steets of blin on 17 March, many of them taking part in the city's massive Patrick's Day parade. The St Patrick's Festival provides a full ek of carnival, music and street theatre, but its highlight is still traditional parade through the city centre.

GALWAY: FESTIVAL CITY

Galway is the closest Ireland gets to a city that never sleeps: its compact centre and lively pub scene make it an ideal festival venue. Its festival calendar is a challenging test of stamina: late April heralds the Cúirt Literature Festival, five days of readings from Irish and international authors. If you think literary festivals are quiet, polite occasions, Galway will change your mind. July is the year's highlight, with the five-day-long Galway Film Fleadh (over 70 Irish and international features, with master classes, seminars etc) leading up to a 10-day extravaganza, Galway Arts Festival, the biggest such event in Ireland with hundreds of events taking place day and night. Does Galway then take a quiet break and catch its collective breath? Not on your life: It's straight off to the Galway Races Festival, which brings the city and its ring road to a standstill, so that the preferred way to travel to the race course is by helicopter. Some 48,000 revellers attend Ladies' Day. The merry-makers assemble again in late September for the Galway International Oyster Festival. Then, in order to get the younger generation into training, mid-October sees the week-long Báboro (above), Ireland's first arts festival purely for children.

ABOVE: Cathedral Quarter Arts Festival, in Belfast's oldest area, reaches a peak during 11 days in early May with a feast of music (featuring US art-rockers Devo, above, in 2007), theatre, comedy, literature, circus and visual arts.

RIGHT: an "urban Glastonbury", the high-spirited Festival of World Cultures transforms sedate Dun Laoghaire on Dublin Bay for the last weekend in August. It has over 160 events, with artists from 50 countries.

CONTEMPORARY ART

Ireland's ancient tradition of visual art was neglected in the 20th century, but a new generation of painters and sculptors has recently been making an impact

Ireland's artistic reputation rests largely on the genius of its writers, but since the late 20th century, the visual arts have been flourishing. Irish artists are now fetching unusually high prices at auction, and sales are held regularly in London and New York as well as Dublin. Sotheby's has been conducting an annual Irish sale for more than 10 years, and proceeds can exceed £5 million. Early 20th-century artists John Lavery, Roderic O'Conor, Jack B. Yeats, William Orpen and Paul Henry all command high prices. Orpen's *Portrait of Gardenia St George,* at £1,985,500, is the most expensive Irish painting ever to sell at auction (bar the works of Francis Bacon, whose 1976 Triptych fetched \$86.3m at Sotheby's New York in 2008). The recession has put an end to such mad prices, but Irish painting, especially landscapes, continues to be sought after by collectors worldwide.

These artists are being joined by the next generation, born pre-1930, including Belfast's Gerard Dillon, Dublin's Patrick Collins, Louis Le Broquy (a living artist, born 1917), and Cork-born Patrick Scott. Galleries showing contemporary art are thriving in Dublin and Belfast, and younger artists are encouraged by both the Arts Council in Dublin, and the Arts Council of Northern Ireland. Irish art colleges are over-subscribed, with the University of Ulster at Coleraine having a particularly high reputation for post-graduate work in contemporary art. Irish artists Sean Scully and Felim Egan have gained international reputations as abstract artists.

Ancient inspiration

There has of course always been visual art in Ireland, from the spirals, loops and geometric forms of the Stone Age passage and burial graves at Newgrange and Knowth, to the La Tène period of Celtic art which arrived from continental Europe around 500BC. After the arrival of Christianity, artists and craft workers continued to enjoy the Celtic artists' privileged position in society, producing elaborately bejeweled chalices and shrines, as well as manuscript illumination.

The latter led to some of the greatest achievements of Celtic art in works such as the *Book of Durrow* and the *Book of Kells*, whose intricate

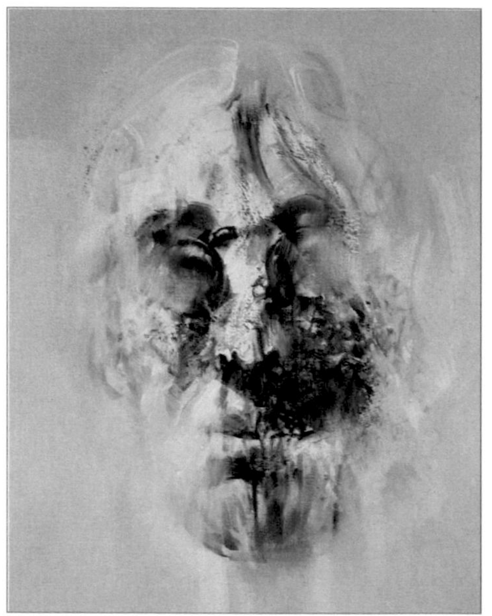

ABOVE: Louis Le Broquy's *James Joyce, Study 64* (1977), from the Irish Museum of Modern Art.
RIGHT: Barrie Cooke's *Megaceros Hibernicus* (1983), from the Irish Museum of Modern Art.

ornamentation and seemingly endless inventiveness can still take your breath away.

Stone crosses and ornamental metalwork are the only artifacts to survive successive waves of invasions, civil wars and general upheaval which began with the Vikings in the 9th century and lasted well into the 17th century. While the prosperity of the 18th century produced some of Ireland's greatest architecture, it was influenced more by English and continental traditions than indigenous ones. The Royal Hibernian Academy was established in Dublin in 1823, in the tradition of its London counterpart. Many Irish artists emigrated to London, and had a significant impact on English art – for example, James Barry (1741–1806), Daniel Maclise (1806–70), Francis Danby (1793–1861) and sculptors such as John Henry Foley (1818–74) and John Lawlor (1820–1901), who worked on London's Albert Memorial.

Many artists choose to live in scenic areas where property prices are still reasonable, and have consequently revitalised hitherto underpopulated areas: Counties Leitrim and Roscommon, Mayo, Sligo, Clare, Kerry and west Cork in particular.

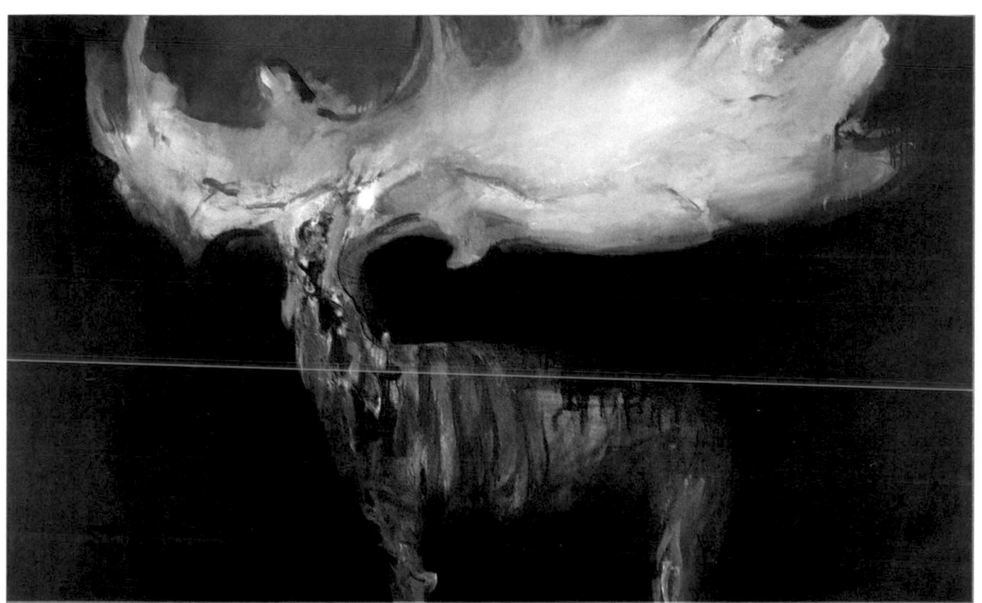

TEN CONTEMPORARY ARTISTS TO LOOK OUT FOR

Basil Blackshaw: Northern Ireland artist known for his depiction of horses and dogs, and latterly barns, in rough sketch-like paintings that capture the essence.

Barrie Cooke: American-born and educated in England, Cooke has lived in rural Ireland since the 1950s. Recent work depicts water pollution in lakes near his Sligo home.

Dorothy Cross: works mainly in three dimensions, sometimes in video and performance, and famously created a real "ghost ship" in Dublin Bay.

Martin Gale: paints eerie super-realist landscapes that mirror the changes taking place in the Irish countryside.

Brian O'Doherty: New York-based Irish-born conceptual artist and critic, formerly known also as Patrick Ireland.

Clare Langan: artist and cinematographer whose spectacular video work offers visions of a future in which civilization has apparently been overwhelmed by nature.

Sean MacSweeney: has repeatedly painted the bog pools near his Sligo home, on small and large scale.

Anne Madden: paints on a massive scale, usually abstract paintings inspired by landscape or mythology.

Vivienne Roche: sculptor working on a large scale, often in welded steel, whose austerely beautiful work often uses motifs from Viking and early Christian Ireland.

Sean Scully: New York-based, Dublin-born painter whose cool, almost monotone abstracts have their origins in his study of the stone walls of the west of Ireland.

The Celtic Revival

The Celtic Revival (c.1880–1930), with its use of the Celtic motifs from illuminated manuscripts, metalwork and monastic architecture, was an Irish version of the Arts and Crafts Movement, closely allied to the movement for Irish independence. The Honan Chapel at University College, Cork is a prime example of this style.

Impressionism began to influence Irish art around the turn of the century, with the work of Nathaniel Hone, John Butler Yeats, John Lavery, Sarah Purser, Walter Osborne, William Orpen and, most importantly, Roderic O'Conor. Jack B. Yeats (1871–1957), brother of the poet W.B. Yeats, stood head and shoulders above his contemporaries, and led the way in his adoption of Irish subject matter, favouring outdoor scenes of his native Sligo, circuses and horse races.

The best-known artist of the time was Paul Henry who had studied at Whistler's studio in Paris before settling in Connemara to paint archetypal images of the west of Ireland landscape, cottages set against blue mountains and tumbling grey skies, that were used as posters to advertise travel to Ireland. Events of the Civil War and the establishment of the Irish Free State were captured in a series of historical paintings by Sean Keating (1889–1997), and social realism became the dominant style, espoused by the academic tradition.

Art ignored

Economic conditions, Ireland's cultural isolation during World War II and the dominant ethos of Catholic conservatism did not add up to a favourable climate for artistic activity in the mid-20th century. Stained-glass artists were among the few to flourish, including the Harry Clarke Studios, whose work can be seen in Dublin's Hugh Lane Municipal Gallery. It was hard to make a living in a country where art was not taught in most schools, and art colleges did not award degrees. This is the era that has given rise to the belief that Ireland has no visual art tradition.

However, the first public gallery in the British Isles devoted to contemporary art was Dublin City Gallery – The Hugh Lane (as it is now known), established in 1908. Its collection of Irish and European late 19th- and early 20th-century art was an inspiration to many Dublin

How Ireland Rewards Creativity

Aosdána, an association of writers and artists, was set up in 1981 by the Taoiseach, Charles J. Haughey (1926–2006), who as Finance Minister in 1969 had introduced tax exemption for writers and artists. Both initiatives were intended to lure home Irish artists living abroad. Haughey's cultural advisor, the poet Anthony Cronin, inspired by the Celtic respect for the *aes dána* – the men of talent – drew up the plan.

Membership, limited to 250 people, includes most but not all of Ireland's artistic elite: Seamus Heaney is in, but John Banville opted out. It was intended as a recognition of artistic achievement. But to ensure that a new generation did not suffer the poverty of their predecessors, many of whom, like James Joyce and Samuel Beckett chose to emigrate, membership also gives optional access to an annuity of €12,000, created to enable members to work full time on creative projects.

The assembly meets once a year to elect new members, and debate resolutions, many concerning its own workings. It was originally limited to writers, composers or visual artists, but architects and choreographers are now eligible, but not performing artists. In 2006, 124 of the 213 members made a claim, costing the government about €1.5m – a fraction of the €72.31m overall arts budget. But in a nation famous for "begrudgery", many consider the subsidy excessive, and it has become Aosdána's most controversial aspect. Website: www.artscouncil.ie/aosdana.

artists. Inspired by what they had seen, Louis Le Brocquy, Norah McGuinness, Evie Hone, Mainie Jellett and others traveled abroad and experimented with Cubism, Futurism and Dada, returning home to lead the modern movement in Irish painting. In 1943 they founded the Irish Exhibition of Living Art as a *salon de refusés* for those whose work was consistently refused by the annual exhibition of the Royal Hibernian Academy. This evolved into an annual show called The Living Art exhibition, which became a forum for artists whose influences were derived from the international language of visual art: Patrick Scott, Patrick Collins, Gerard Dillon, Nano Reid, Barrie Cooke, Cecil King and Tony O'Malley. Living Art also embraced video and performance art, and persisted into the 1980s.

The Irish Museum of Modern Art opened in 1991, but meanwhile the creation of an improved infrastructure for the arts, the establishment of tax exemption for artists in 1969 and the introduction in 1981 of the island-wide Aosdána scheme did much to improve working conditions for artists. There has been an unprecedented growth in venues, subsidized exhibition spaces and also commercial galleries, both in Dublin and Belfast, and all around the country, and a corresponding upsurge in artistic activity. Many artists, such as the Manchester-born Hughie O'Donoghue, have returned from long or short stays abroad and set up studios in Ireland, some combining their artistic practice with teaching and lecturing.

International taste

Many of the younger generation of artists – Clare Langan, Linda Quinlan and Amanda Coogan, for example, working respectively in video, installation art and performance – produce work that is indistinguishable from their contemporaries in London, Paris or New York. Others continue to be inspired by landscape, even though their work may use forms belonging to the international contemporary art scene. Examples include Sarah Walker's coolly modernist wild flower grids, Charles Tyrrell's rigorous abstracts and Gary Coyle's dramatic photographs of Dublin Bay from a swimmer's perspective.

There are many less ambitious contemporary artists who continue to work in the old tradition, producing attractive landscapes and easy-to-live-with genre scenes of Irish life, whose work can also be found in contemporary galleries. With prices starting from around €200 for a landscape by an up-and-coming artist, it could well be worth making an investment. ❑

LEFT: Alice Maher's *Berry Dress* (1994), made from rosehips, cotton, paint and sewing pins, part of the collection of the Irish Museum of Modern Art (**ABOVE**).

FOOD

Despite an abundance of fresh ingredients, the Irish have never shown much interest in haute cuisine. Until recently...

Ireland has long been promoted as "Ireland, The Food Island", an ingenious marketing slogan invented by Bord Bia (The Irish Food Board). Despite the recent cycle of economic boom and bust, Ireland remains an agricultural country that produces far more food than it can eat. Its grass-fed beef and lamb produce superb meat and dairy produce and speciality foods including a completely unique range of farmhouse cheeses that are exported throughout the world. Stand in any fishing port and see how foreign fish merchants covet the fresh seafood caught in the country's clean Atlantic waters.

Ireland is clean, green and fertile – a moist, temperate climate and the benign influence of the Gulf Stream deflect the cold temperatures of Northern Europe. Tourism is equally important, so there is a sophisticated hospitality industry.

Eating out

Ireland is not a low-cost destination. However, if good food is what you seek there is value for money to be had at all levels – if you know where to find it. The best value (as opposed to the cheapest) is offered on "Early Bird" or "today's market" dinner menus, fixed price 2- or 3-course menus, and (the Irish way to experience a meal in leading fine-dining restaurants without blowing your budget) at lunchtime.

The pursuit of individualism is strong in Ireland. This can make it difficult for visitors to tell whether an establishment offers formal/fine dining with set 4–5 course menus (with a price tag to match), or casual/informal food where you can order as much or as little as you like. You'll come across restaurants, bistros, brasseries, café/bars, wine/café bars, or just plain cafés, pub/restaurants, pubs with bar food, pub carveries and seafood bars. The only sure way to distinguish between the first three is to inspect the prices on the menu, which must, by law, be displayed outside (or check the entry in this guide).

Café/bars and wine bars usually offer informal meals where you can order as much or little as you wish; you rarely need to make a reservation. Some cafés are quite expensive, restaurants in all but name; most offer an all-day menu and (sometimes) a lunch menu.

Dining in pubs

Pubs vary even more widely – some have restaurants with full lunch and dinner menus. Others offer "bar food" – a proper lunch and dinner menu eaten perched uncomfortably at low tables with minimal service. Many pubs advertise a "carvery" lunch, a self-service, canteen-style meal featuring at least one joint of meat, carved to order, and other pre-cooked options, filling and inexpensive, but unlikely to be a culinary highlight. The best option is seafood (oysters, prawns, crab or mussels) at one of the coastal pubs offering freshly-landed catch.

Hotels and restaurants

If eating in a hotel restaurant seems a last resort, think again. As a result of intense competition, most 4- and 5-star Irish hotels place a great emphasis on dining and employ top chefs. Many have two restaurants, one fine-dining and another informal. Most are open daily – useful to know as many Irish restaurants close after Sunday lunch and do not open for dinner on Sunday or Monday nights. In tourist areas some restaurants concentrate on weekends and close for a couple of months in mid-winter.

Contemporary Irish cooking

A distinctive style of Irish cooking has emerged over the past 20 years. A new generation of serious chefs take pride in using indigenous foods and, supported by a growing number of artisan food producers making authentic foods using traditional methods, re-explore traditional Irish recipes and dishes. What has emerged is a lighter, modern style, an innovative spin on traditional dishes but firmly based on Irish foods

Many country house restaurants use produce from their own farms and gardens, rivers and game shoots. It's part of the fun to inspect the estate or the kitchen garden before dinner and guess what will be on the menu.

Left: the improved quality of Irish food, here in Dublin's Gruel restaurant, has become a major selling point. **Above:** fresh seafood is one of Ireland's specialities.

What is Euro-Toques?

A sign to look out for is Euro-Toques (the European Communion of Chefs), a pan-European organisation with 3,500 members. Euro-Toques is strong in Ireland with more than 200 members and has been influential in the creation of unique contemporary Irish cooking. All Euro-Toques support sourcing top-quality, non-genetically modified, local and seasonal food and deliver dishes of flavour and authenticity. They aim to protect the quality, diversity and flavour of regional food and promote indigenous, traditional production methods. Their support in buying (and naming on menus) artisan food products has re-awakened consumer appreciation and has helped young artisan food producers.

and themes. Leading chefs take enormous care to source Irish ingredients, wild or farmed using traditional methods, and support the ever growing number of artisan food producers.

Irish chefs continue to be trained in the classic tradition. Most go abroad for a few years for experience and bring back culinary influences from their travels and give them an Irish twist; the most ambitious compete to work under influential Irish chefs so the modern approach is not just confined to fine-dining establishments but can be found in many places. Talented young chefs have the confidence to open their own restaurants not just in Dublin and other cities but in provincial towns, villages and sometimes deep in rural Ireland.

In many fine-dining restaurants modern Irish cooking allows a natural mingling of traditional Irish produce with an innovative approach to the cooking and presentation of long-established Irish dishes. The result is a contemporary Irish cuisine that is "entirely itself", an idiomatic expression. The good thing is that this approach to cooking is not confined to formal fine-dining restaurants but can be on offer in establishments all over the country *(see the box on Euro-Toques on the previous page)*.

Ethnic restaurants

The Irish have multi-cultural tastes. Thriving ethnic restaurants are plentiful. Immigration during the boom years has increased their numbers and diversity. Once you might have been lucky to find French, Italian, Chinese or Indian restaurants; now you can choose from a far wider range of ethnic restaurants: Nepalese, Japanese, Vietnamese, Indonesian, Belgian, Breton, Polish and Thai, as well as Indian and Chinese offering authentic regional cuisine. The most recent trend has been a huge growth in informal restaurant/café/wine bars offering Spanish tapas, or using the tapas principle to showcase Irish artisan foods including farmhouse cheeses, black pudding, smoked chicken and locally-produced charcuterie, which has flourished following immigration from Eastern Europe.

Irish Country House Cooking

Some of the best dining can be experienced in Irish country houses, almost all located in rural

THE BEST PLACES TO SAMPLE MODERN IRISH CUISINE

Thornton's, Dublin. Base for superstar chef Kevin Thornton. Creative haute cuisine in elegant surroundings.

O'Connell's Restaurant, Bewley's Hotel, Ballsbridge, Dublin. Chef Tom O'Connell uses only top quality Irish ingredients, and showcases the cheese and charcuterie of artisan food producers.

The Tannery, Dungarvan, Co. Waterford. Flamoyant owner-chef Paul Flynn applies foodie trends to meticulously sourced Irish produce in an attractive warehouse conversion.

Ballymaloe House, Shanagarry, Co. Cork. Ireland's most famous country house hotel pioneered the use of fresh local produce. Book for Sunday buffet lunch.

Mulcahy's, Kenmare, Co. Kerry. The owner-chef, Bruce Mulcahy, uses Irish seafood and local meat in his fusion menu that has strong Thai and Japanese influences.

Cherry Tree Restaurant, Killaloe, Co. Clare. Chefs work in an open-kitchen, preparing truffles, foie gras, local lobster and crab at this elegant, waterside country restaurant.

McNean House & Bistro, Blacklion, Co. Cavan. A successful TV series and cookbook have not distracted young Neven Maguire from his main job as chef in his family's business. Worth the considerable detour.

Roscoff Brasserie, Belfast. Authors and TV chefs Jean and Paul Rankin have created a relaxed, atmospheric brasserie.

• *For contact details and opening hours, see restaurant listings at the end of chapters in the Places section.*

areas. At the top end the facilities are on a par with a four or even five star hotels, with restaurants and dining experiences to match. Most (although not all) at this level offer modern Irish cooking and menus, tend to be open to non-residents and often attract a loyal local following as well as tourists staying in self-catering accommodation. Other smaller country houses do not employ a large team of chefs. In these the cooking style and presentation is simpler, menus shorter, and feature traditional (even regional) dishes that place an emphasis on allowing natural flavours of carefully sourced local and seasonal foods to shine through.

Féile Bia

"Bia" is the Irish word for food and the word "Féile" means a festival or celebration. The thrust of this voluntary programme run by Bord Bia (The Irish Food Board) is for restaurants to source fresh, authentic Irish food. Members are required to provide information to customers about how the food they serve is produced and where it comes from; they must source meat, poultry and eggs from approved quality assurance schemes. There are 1,450 Féile Bia members in Ireland. Some top chefs and restaurants are not members as they source their foods from unique, organic producers and don't need it as a selling point. ❑

Farm to Fork

The Irish place high value on knowing where food comes from – the entire route from farm to fork – and, by and large, they want it to be from an Irish farm. To satisfy consumer demand, the name of a product, its producer or the locality in which it was produced, is often incorporated into a dish's menu description. There is a growing number of artisan producers offering traditional and speciality foods. The demand for organic food has grown too and is used as a selling point in many restaurants.

Left: tempting baked goods testify to the increased demand for artisan foods.
Above: farmers' market at Midletown, County Cork.

Farmers' Markets

A visit to a farmers' market is a food experience, a must for those on a self-catering holiday. Look out for farmhouse cheeses (each unique to the farm and the cheesemaker), cured, smoked, spiced and air-dried meats, dry-cured bacon, black and white puddings, speciality sausages and pâtés, fish and shellfish, mountain lamb, wild game, home grown fruit and berries, traditional breads and baking, jams, chutneys and sauces. For information on local markets, go to www.bordbia.ie/aboutfood/farmersmarkets.

Country markets – smaller affairs held weekly in nearly 60 locations by a long-established cooperative – specialise in home baking and local produce.

PUBS

The counterfeit Irish pub has conquered the world. But the authentic pubs in Ireland, whose most intoxicating product used to be talk, are struggling to come to terms with a changed society

Dublin's hostelries – there are more than 800 of them – are a mix of the very old and the very new. Some are vast drinking emporiums offering live sport on huge screens and palatable food to more than 1,000 people; others are spit-and-sawdust drinking dens. It's the characterful old-school watering-holes that are worth visiting: McDaid's, Neary's, Kehoe's, Doheny and Nesbitt's, O'Donoghue's, The Palace Bar, Mulligan's, the Stag's Head, the International and M. J. O'Neill's – to name but 10.

These classic Dublin bars are peopled with wisecracking philosophers sharing their observations with anyone who'll listen – or buy them a drink. Old wooden bars, with creamy pints of stout, remain untouched by the hand of the modernisers. They have a well-lived in and well-drunk in look and feel, decked out in brass and mahogany, with antique mirrors proclaiming the merits of whiskies long since defunct. Some such pubs look much as they did in 1850.

One hundred miles (160km) to the north, Belfast is also richly endowed with pubs. A rash of new bars such as the Apartment, Café Vaudeville, Bar Bacca, the Potthouse and the Cloth Ear are the new, cool venues. But the most visited remains the iconic Crown Liquor Saloon, owned by the National Trust, with its wood-panelled snugs, gas lights, ornate tiles, woodcarvings and brasswork. Other venerable venues include White's Tavern, the Duke of York, Kelly's Cellars, the Garrick, the Morning Star, Bittles Bar, Madden's or the John Hewitt, named after a local poet.

The drinking culture

A recent European Union survey showed that Ireland has the highest proportion of binge drinkers in any European country. Just over a third of people living in Ireland were reported to consume on average five or more units of alcohol in a single sitting – more than three times the EU average. And four out of five drinks are consumed in bars rather than at home, compared to only one in three in Germany, confirming the image of the Irish as an incorrigibly gregarious people.

Despite this, economists have long been predicting the downfall of the Irish pub, and many smaller rural pubs have indeed been forced out of business. But the country still supports 10,000 pubs (8,500 in the Republic; 1,500 in Northern

ABOVE: after the smoking ban, many pubs advertised facilites such as cigarette-friendly beer gardens. **RIGHT:** at the Gin Palace, Dublin.

Ireland), and the rural pubs that *have* survived remain the epicentre of small towns where the community still comes together for its social and neighbourhood business. The paint may be peeling in some, but traditionally, they have been places where people meet, not just to drink and hold parties or wakes, but to gossip, talk football, solve the world's political problems, try to pick a winner in the 2.30 Leopardstown race meeting, tell tall tales or simply céilí the night away.

These traditions survive. From the regular sessions of the *seanchaí* (storyteller) in the Red House in Lismore, west Waterford, to Osbourne's pub in Clongeall, south Carlow; from O Loclainn's in Ballyvaughan, Co. Clare, to Kate Lavin's in Boyle, Co. Roscommon; and from Blakes of the Hollow in Enniskillen, Co. Fermanagh, to Frawley's pub in Lahinch, the customs and atmosphere – like the best whiskey – remain undiluted.

Many bars – especially the part-grocery/part-pub ones – are family-owned and can trace their longevity back several generations, although only about 200 pubs have been in one family for at least 100 years. Some commentators have pointed out that if such a lack of stability of ownership was to be found in farming, it would be declared a national scandal. Fortunately the

How the Smoking Ban and the Breathalyser Made an Impact

The sight of small groups of drinkers standing huddled up outside the doorways of pubs blowing smoke into the air in a distracted fashion has become common all over the Republic of Ireland since 2004. (Northern Ireland bars went smoke-free in 2007). Ireland was the world's first nation to introduce a smoking ban in pubs and many felt it would spell ruin for one of the most convivial of meeting places.

Most bars adapted by cordoning off smoking shelters either at the front or in the yard at the back of the premises. There were a few short-lived acts of defiance against the ban, but the law, like a decent pint of Guinness, eventually settled down. Pubs in rural Ireland continued to close at the rate of one a day, but the smoking ban did not play a significant part in their demise – the trigger was the same social upheaval that was forcing the closure of village shops and many small post offices in remote areas.

The drink-driving laws have also hit hard. The traditional tolerance for the jovial drunk eroded as the number of young people killed or injured in early morning road accidents at the weekends spiralled to alarming numbers. The police took a strong stand by introducing random breath-testing of motorists, and some publicans, conscious of the lack of public transport in outlying areas, turned themselves into taxi drivers, transporting customers home in a courtesy minibus. If any single thing symbolises Ireland's embrace of modern European values, this behavioural change may be it.

days of the characterful country pubs with a thatched roof and turf fire have still not disappeared, although many don't open until early evening as there are fewer daytime customers.

Traditional music

Informal traditional music sessions or set dancing have great appeal, though performance times can be erratic and the entertainment may not start before 10pm. Most sessions are held indoors but during a *fleadh cheoil* (music festival) when thousands flock into towns, the performers spill out on to the pavement and music flows down the streets.

Generally, music sessions fall into two categories. Some bars hold set-piece evenings that are turned on like a tap for the tourists; these occur regularly and are premeditated with a practised set list. Others are spontaneous where the players drop in for an unplanned evening and the result is a happy meeting of musical minds. The quality of the playing in both is equally good, but the impromptu session often has the edge because the unexpected may happen.

The informal nature of it means that it's open to all-comers to strut their musical stuff whether playing, singing or dancing. Often these sessions are the ones that will be imprinted in visitors' minds. The memory of the haunting *Nancy Spain*, the well-worn words of *The Wild Rover* or *Whiskey in the Jar* and the intoxicating talk will all remain long after the recollection of a visit to a spanking new interpretative centre has faded to oblivion.

In some parts of the country, old customs live on; search hard and you will find in Cork city a few "early houses" – pubs that open their doors at 7am to cater for nightshift workers including dockers and bakers, or those in search of "the cure" (a remedy for the morning-after hangover). On a Monday morning around 9am

EXPORTING THE IRISH PUB

If America can persuade the world to eat hamburgers, can Ireland persuade it to drink Guinness? More than 1,000 "traditional" Irish pubs, from Durty Nellie's in Amsterdam to Finnegan's in Abu Dhabi, from Shifty O'Shea's in Leicester, England, to O'Kims in Seoul, Korea, are trying to do just that.

Never slow to spot an opportunity, brewers such as Guinness set up companies to export the Irish pub concept. They'll help entrepreneurs anywhere in the world to design their hostelry – you can pick a standard model such as Country Cottage, the Victorian Dublin or the Brewery – and also aid them in locating authentic fittings and recruiting staff.

ABOVE: the Crown in Belfast, a traditional pub.
RIGHT: Guinness tops the list of liquid favourites.

TEN BARS WORTH TOASTING

These are chosen with a geographical spread in mind, but also for their atmosphere and the passion of the musicians who (sometimes) haunt their dark corners.

O Loclainn's, Ballyvaughan, Co. Clare. This cosy pub (known locally as MacNeill's) has more than 40 brands of whiskey. The bar, in the heart of the Burren, doesn't open until 9pm as the owner farms during the day. It is full of intimate charm and quiet conversation, and occasionally echoes to the beat of the bodhrán. Its simplicity is the key to its success.

Tigh Neachtain, Cross Street, Galway, (known in English as Naughton's). A popular city centre bar with old-fashioned painted wooden interior and features. The building dates back to medieval times and the tiny snugs are more than 100 years old. There's an open fire in the back room and regular music.

Morrissey's, Main Street, Abbeyleix, Co. Laois. Opened as a grocery in 1775 and now solely a pub, it has the air of a venerable institution. Its dark shelf-lined walls, pot-belly stove and rules forbidding cards, TV and singing are all part of the attraction.

Tynan's Bridge House, St John's Bridge, Kilkenny. This antiquarian's delight beside the River Nore is one of Ireland's best preserved pubs, complete with gas lamps. In a former incarnation it was a pharmacy.

Shoot the Crows, Market Cross, Grattan Street, Sligo. Opened in 1876, this long narrow pub has retained its original features including the timber wainscoting. Each month a local artist produces a painting for the front window reflecting the mythology, legend or folklore of the area. Good music on Wednesday nights.

P.J. O'Hare's Anchor Bar, Carlingford, Co. Louth. P.J.s has been in the family for 150 years and is decorated with pub mirrors and curios. On sunny Sunday afternoons the yard becomes a dance area.

Anderson's Thatch Pub, Elphin Road, Carrick-on-Shannon, Co. Leitrim. This inviting roadside pub dates back to 1760. The owner, who plays 11 instruments, holds music sessions on Wednesdays and Saturdays.

The Corner House, Coburg Street, Cork. Art work, portraits and postcards decorate the walls of this 1853 bar. Music ranges from Irish traditional to cajun.

Nancy's, Front Street, Ardara, Co. Donegal. This tiny hospitable bar is now in the seventh generation of family ownership. Seafood, especially the chowder, is a speciality. Traditional music is played.

The White House, 52 O'Connell Street, Limerick. A place of dark wood and immediate friendliness. Poetry readings on Wednesdays and traditional music on Sundays and Thursdays.

as office workers throughout the city scurry to work, you may be startled to stumble across several bars in the docks area almost as busy as on a Saturday night.

The mystique of Guinness

The respect paid to this national beverage, a strongish black beer with a creamy white head, is genuine and not something conjured up by a marketing department. Brewed in Dublin since 1759, it is a temperamental drink, needing great care in pouring from the tap to the glass. Constant temperature in the cellars, the distance from cask to tap and the frequency of the flow

are all considered important factors in the art known as "the pulling of a good pint".

If the pint isn't good, it is sent straight back. Experts (which is to say anyone who drinks the stuff) embark on long discussions on the pint's quality in different bars throughout the country. The visitor's best criterion is this: if the place is crowded with locals, then the pint is probably good. And you'll know a good pint when you get one. It won't taste like what passes for Guinness in Britain, where the beer is sloshed into the glass by insensitive barmen, or like the Guinness in America, where the long sea journey from Dublin does nothing for the quality. It will taste, in a good pub in Ireland, as smooth as velvet. ❑

A SPORTING NATION

Hurling and Gaelic football make soccer seem tame by comparison. And then there are oddities like road bowls

Sport enthusiasts will have a field day in Ireland as all the major international sports are played to some extent and only a few, like soccer, athletics and hockey, are affected by the political division of the island. But the most popular sports are the native ones of hurling and Gaelic football. These are fast-paced, thrilling, high-voltage games, amateur in nature and organised around the parish and controlled by a body called the Gaelic Athletic Association.

The GAA was founded in 1884, in Thurles, County Tipperary by Michael Cusack, a fiery nationalist from the Burren in County Clare, who was immortalised by James Joyce as "The Citizen" in *Ulysses*. Organised for a purpose that was political as much as sporting, the association's *raison d'être* was to revive the native games, under native control, as a means of strengthening national self-respect at a time when national morale was at a low ebb.

At the end of the 19th century, most of those involved with the GAA were farmers, labourers and shopkeepers but by the 20th century the new Roman Catholic middle class fired up by a Celtic Revival joined the movement. In 1918, the GAA was included on a list of organisations banned by the British Government, but despite this Gaelic Games were still played and in the 21st Century they still hold a hallowed position in Irish culture and are intrinsically linked to a sense of independence and identity.

Hurling – what's it all about

Hurling has been played in Ireland since prehistoric times and some of the country's oldest sagas tell of hurling matches that went on for days. It's the fastest of all field team games and its rules are relatively simple, although watching it for the first time can be a dizzying, bewildering experience as the ball hurtles around at breakneck speed and players bat their hurleys about, narrowly missing teeth and foreheads.

The hurley itself is made from ash and is around 3½ft (1 metre) long with a paddle at the bottom that measures about 3 inches (7.6cm) across at its broadest. The ball consists of yarn, tightly wound round a ball of cork and covered with hard leather, stitched

ABOVE: Limerick and Clare clash in an All-Ireland Hurling Championship match at Dublin's Croke Park. **RIGHT:** Gaelic football is spectacular, but its rules are subject to constant revision.

> *The first mention of football in Ireland can be traced to 1308, when John McCrocan, a spectator at a football game at Newcastle, Co. Dublin, was charged with accidentally stabbing a player named William Bernard.*

along the outside in a ridge to facilitate handling. The object of the game is to get the ball between the posts and under the bar – to score a goal, in other words (a goal amounts to three points). A single point is scored when the ball goes between the posts and over the bar.

What makes the game so crazy to watch is that the ball can be propelled along the ground *or* hit in the air, but it can only be taken into the hand if it's been caught in full flight – something that requires considerable skill. The best players can take the ball onto the hurley, from the ground, while running at full speed and carry it, balanced or bouncing, on the broad end before passing or scoring. Tricky? Yes. Exciting to watch? Absolutely. The main traditional hurling areas remain south of a line from Dublin to Galway, with a small pocket in the Glens of Antrim. Cork and Kilkenny are the top hurling counties.

GREAT SPORTING MOMENTS

Croke Park in Dublin has been home to the GAA for over 100 years and is the largest stadium in the country with capacity for over 82,300. Steeped in history, the venue lies at the heart of Ireland's troubled history and in 1920 the British Crown fired into the crowd at a Dublin vs Tipperary match and shot dead 11 spectators – and the Tipperary captain – in a raid that became known as "Bloody Sunday".

Since those early days, the stadium has remained central to Irish sporting and cultural life and the last decade has seen an enormous transformation with over €260 million being invested to transform Croke Park into one of Europe's finest venues.

Having been exclusively used for Gaelic Games, 2005 saw a defining moment as the GAA agreed to allow "Croker" to host "foreign games" of soccer and international rugby, while their usual stadium of Lansdowne Road prepared for redevelopment.

The most controversial match of all was the 2007 Ireland vs England rugby international: because of Bloody Sunday, many Irish fans greatly objected to the British national anthem being sung in the stadium. On 24 February, with phenomenal media hype, the historic Ireland vs England match kicked off with emotions running high. As the Irish anthem was sung, there was barely a dry eye in the house with Irish fans and players feeling the weight of history thick in the air. Ireland won by 43–13.

Football, Gaelic-style

Like hurling, Gaelic football is played by teams of 15-a-side. The layout of the pitch and methods of scoring are also the same as for hurling. Played with a ball similar to that used in soccer, Gaelic football is something of an invented game so the rules are ultimately imperfect and subject to constant revision. Players can handle the ball, lift it off the ground with the foot, run with it while passing it between hand and foot, kick it, or fist it, or play it with the feet on the ground as in soccer. Its main flaw is that there is no clear method of dispossessing a player in possession. But it's a spectacular game, and attracts the biggest crowds of any sporting event in Ireland.

Australian Rules, although played with an oval ball on an oval pitch, has features similar to those of Gaelic football. It's thought that Irish emigrants had a hand in influencing long kicking and the great leaps in the air to catch the ball. In an attempt to gain an international dimension for a game played only in Ireland (with the exception of Irish emigrants in the USA and Britain) the GAA has run tours to and from Australia, with games played under compromise rules. The fact that the Australian players are all professionals have so far given the contests more bite than was anticipated. Pros don't relish being beaten by amateurs...

The high point of the GAA year is in September with the All-Ireland hurling and football Finals in Dublin's Croke Park, which now incorporates a museum devoted to Irish sports. Tickets for the Finals do not go on sale to the general public and are distributed for purchase only through clubs and county boards.

Hares and horses

Greyhound racing (on tracks) and coursing in enclosed fields with live hares are popular sports in Ireland. The fact that races are over in a matter of seconds is no deterrent to the small army of punters who attend. Coursing is a winter sport, which has come under fire from animal-rights campaigners because of cruelty to hares. Two dogs are released to chase a hare. Points are scored by deflecting the hare from its course, or by killing it before it gets to the escape exit. Protests have resulted in greyhounds being muzzled by law.

ROAD BOWLING

Road bowling is a strange game, played only in South Armagh, Cork and parts of Waterford and Limerick. The game is very simple: two players throw or bowl an iron ball along an ordinary public road, and the winner is the one who covers a set distance with fewer throws. The bowl, or "bullet," can be 28, 21 or 16 ounces (between 800 and 450 grammes). One of the skills of the game is the negotiation of a bend in the road, either by lofting the bowl over the corner or by curving the throw. If the bowl leaves the road, the player is penalised.

While it might not be the most organised of sports, road bowling attracts major betting and large sums of money change hands when noted players meet. Not only are bets laid on the result of the contest; side-bets are also laid on individual shots. Road bowling is illegal as sections of public roads are barred to traffic during the contest, but prosecutions are rare.

Sports in all its glory

Casual perusal of the sports pages of any Irish daily newspaper will show that an extraordinary range of sports is covered, and a surprising number of people excel in a variety of sports at the highest level. To mention just a few: Sean Kelly dominated the world of cycling throughout the 1980s, and in 1987 Stephen Roche won the sport's ultimate prize, the gruelling Tour de France. In professional boxing, world titles were held by Barry McGuigan, Steve Collins, Michael Carruth and Dave McAuley. Alex Higgins, Ken O'Doherty and Dennis Taylor all claimed the world championship at snooker. To that list can be added two players with the most international appearances: Mike Gibson, in rugby football, and Pat Jennings, as a soccer goalkeeper. In 1998 Sonia O'Sullivan crowned an already illustrious career in athletics by winning both the 5,000-metre and 10,000-metre European championship titles, and Catherina McKiernan won four silver medals in the World Cross Country Championships. Top golfers on the international circuit include Darren Clarke, Dubliner Padraig Harrington, who won the Open in 2007 and 2008, also winning the PGA in 2008, and Northern Ireland's Rory McIlroy, who turned pro in 2007 on reaching the age of 16. In 2010 McIlroy had his first PGA tour triumph, winning the Quail Hollow Championship days before his 21st birthday.

In international rugby Ireland fields a team drawn from Northern Ireland and the Republic. Rugby is the one international sport (except for professional boxing) that unites all political elements on the island, at least temporarily. In July 2010 the newly-built Aviva Stadium in Dublin's Lansdowne Road, home of both rugby and soccer internationals, with a seated capacity of 50,000, hosted its first rugby match. ❑

LEFT: breeding greyhounds is a minor industry.
ABOVE: a rainbow signals the end of a downpour at Dublin's Croke Park during a Six Nations rugby match.

THE SPLIT IN SOCCER

Soccer is split by the internal political border. The island fields two international sides: Ireland, as the Northern Ireland team is officially designated, and the Republic of Ireland. Despite limited resources, both have impressed: Northern Ireland qualified for the final stages of the World Cup in both 1982 and 1986, while the Republic stood out in the finals of the 1988 European Championships and in the 1990 and 1994 World Cup. The team failed to qualify for the 2010 World Cup, following a controversial ball-handling incident in a crucial match with France. Because Ireland's domestic football leagues are small, many top Irish footballers make names for themselves in the UK leagues.

Golf

Ireland may lack the sun-soaked allure of Bermuda or the cachet of the Caribbean, but it is one of the most exciting golfing destinations in the world right now. It's crammed with jaw-droppingly beautiful, impressively designed and technically challenging courses

Always a popular golfing spot for players in-the-know, Ireland hit the world stage in a big way in 2006 with the hosting of the Ryder Cup at the sleek and luxurious K Club golf resort in County Kildare. Major international Irish names, such as Padraig Harrington, Darren Clarke and Rory McIlroy have highlighted the finesse and skill of Irish golfers at international competitions, while the Irish Open and the Smurfit European Open, both part of the European Tour, attracted some of the world's greatest players to the island during the summer months.

The green, green isle

Golfers are spoilt for choice. There's the drama of Doonbeg in County Clare, the elegance of Druid's Glen in County Wicklow, and the untamed magnificence of links courses, such as the Old Head of Kinsale in County Cork or the magnificent lake and mountain scenery of the Killarney Golf and Fishing Club, host of the 2010 Irish Open. Dotted throughout the land and outside all the major cities are internationally recognised courses, as well as smaller lesser-known spots that can be equally delightful to play on, depending on what you're looking for.

Major thrills and hidden gems

Among the big hitters are Lahinch in County Clare; Ballybunion and Waterville in County Kerry; and the Royal County Down. If you're looking for a quieter course, then try a hidden gem like Enniscrone in County Sligo; Ballyliffin in County Donegal; Kenmare in County Kerry and Killerig in County Carlow.

There are also an impressive number of luxurious golf resorts where you can complement a round of golf with some fine dining, spa and leisure facilities, along with deluxe accommodation. Mount Juliet in County Kilkenny boasts the only Jack Nicklaus-designed course in Ireland and is famed for its 1,500 acres of lush, rolling landscape and exquisite Georgian house. Adare Manor in County Limerick, host of the Irish Open from 2007 to 2009, is an opulent castle hotel in a beautiful location, or if you fancy living it up like one of the landed gentry, Dromoland Castle has sumptuous rooms and fine food and wine.

The older the better

Unsurprisingly for a country with over 440 courses, the Irish take golf seriously. The country's golf pedigree dates back to the late 19th century and clubs, courses and even clubhouses battle it out for the title of "oldest". The Curragh Golf Club in County Kildare is reputed to have the oldest course in Ireland dating back to 1852; the oldest club, The Royal Belfast Golf Club was founded in 1881 and the Ardglass Golf Club in County Down has the oldest clubhouse – parts of which date back to the 14th century.

Traditional roots

While golf has attracted a new generation of hip, young swingers in the UK and the US, in Ireland the game is still rooted in tradition. There may not be as many Pringle jumpers on the courses as there used to be, but clubs like Portmarnock Golf Club in Dublin are stalwarts of the old-school and bastions of male privilege. This beautifully situated links, nestled into the curve of coastline formed by Howth Peninsula, refuses to relax its age-old rule that excludes women from becoming full members, although visitors of both sexes are warmly welcomed on the course as long as you have a certified handicap.

Ireland's small size means that it's easy to take in a few clubs in a short space of time. But give yourself plenty of time to meet your tee-off booking, too, as you can be seriously delayed behind wayward cattle along some rural backroads...

In terms of cost, green fees in Ireland are generally quite high – one of the most expensive is the Arnold Palmer-designed course at the K Club, which charges €300 for a non-resident from May to September – but if you're looking for a bargain there are lots of smaller clubs that will only set you back around €40 or so.

Remember to check with the specific club regarding rules as some can be somewhat picky about dress codes, and nearly all clubs require advance booking for play, particularly during the busy summer months. ❑

LEFT: signing autographs during a Ryder Cup game at the K Club in County Kildare.
ABOVE: the Royal Portrush Golf Club, Country Antrim.

IRELAND'S GREATEST GOLF COURSES

The K Club, Co. Kildare. Two parkland courses. The choice of plutocrats.
Portmarnock, Dublin. On a sandy peninsula north of Dublin; still holding out against women members.
Ballybunion, Co. Kerry. Tiger Woods warms up on the Old Course for a European tour.
Killarney Golf and Fishing Club. Choice of three courses amid stunning lake and mountain scenery.
Lahinch, Co. Clare. Challenging links course on the shores of the Atlantic, famed for its massive bunkers.
Royal County Down. Near Mourne Mountains. Tough.
Royal Portrush. Co. Antrim. The only Irish club to have hosted a British Open. Fine coastal location.

ANGLING

Unsurprisingly for a country that's surrounded by sea, that enjoys an abundance of lakes and has a whopping 14,000km of fish-rich rivers, Ireland is one of Europe's most popular angling destinations

Ireland's mix of year-round rain, reasonably mild winters and gentle summers results in a profusion of cold and warm water species, so there's a really broad range of experiences on offer including salmon fishing, coarse fishing, pike fishing, sea fishing and trout fly-fishing right across the island.

While it's undeniably possible that you might be lucky enough to reel in a Mediterranean bass for your supper, you're probably more likely to have success with one of Ireland's native fish. Coarse fishing in Ireland isn't enormously popular with locals so the country's lightly fished freshwaters are teaming with species like pike, bream, tench, roach, eel and rudd. Admittedly, you're unlikely to be rustling up a gourmet dinner with a freshly-taken rudd, but it's all about the experience, and coarse fishing in Ireland is contemplative and tranquil thanks to the haunting beauty of the magnificent landscapes.

From the big rivers like the vast River Shannon, which dominates the midlands, to the small crystal-clear waters of Ireland's loughs such as County Roscommon's Lough Gara, Ireland offers a diversity that few other countries can compete with, and coarse fishing is a sport that thrills regardless of your level or experience. Or you could always opt for a showdown with a pink-fleshed salmon, trout or sea trout, which hold an honoured place in Irish culture and folklore.

The reel regulations

You'll need a licence, though, which you can pick up from fishing tackle shops and fishery offices. And, as the majority of waters are either privately owned or owned by the state, you'll also need a fishing permit. There are strict by-laws and conservation measures governing coarse and salmon fishing, including bag limits, mandatory catch and release and gill tags. It's best to contact the relevant Regional Fisheries Board (for contact details for each region, check with the Central Fisheries Board (www.cfb.ie; tel: 00 353 1 8842 600) close to the time of travel as these regulations change.

On the seashore

Sea-fishing in Ireland is a real thrill, with more than 4,000 miles of coastline covering landscapes that range from towering sea-cliffs that plummet into the crashing Atlantic Ocean along the west and northwest coast, to the gentler waters of the sunny southeast. There are over 80 species in the waters and the warming influence of the North

Atlantic Drift means that you can take fish from spring to autumn, which would usually be found only in the summer months elsewhere. Whether you want to boat-fish languidly on a warm August afternoon, wreck fish for conger, ling, pollack or coalfish, or take the sociable approach with a big-

> *Pike fishing is a huge draw for competitive anglers – the largest line-caught pike in a lough is 39lbs 3oz and a whopping 42lbs in a river, but don't expect to hook a beauty that size; most pike average 20lbs.*

fun bout of deep-sea fishing on a chartered boat, you're guaranteed an exciting experience. Best of all, after a day bobbing around in sea-spray, a night in the pub dissecting the day's catch over a pint of Guinness is a particular treat.

For many anglers, Ireland is a dream location for shore fishing and nothing beats the pure adrenalin-rush of battling with big surf on the west coast during one of the area's legendary storms. This isn't for the faint-hearted, though.

There are few parts of Ireland that can beat the wild untamed beauty of the Beara, Iveragh and Dingle peninsulas in the southwest. It's a beguiling part of the country, with a raw magnificence and a physical vitality that never fails to impress, and these rocky coastal shores provide the angler with one of the most picturesque fishing locations in the world. In terms of fish, you'll find species of wrasse and pollack ready for the taking. But arguably the most Irish of angling experiences has to be a battle with the enormous native pike. The quality of the clear, clean waters is attributed to the large numbers of pike in Ireland, and the fisheries of the Shannon, Lough Allen, Lough Derg, River Suck and River Inny are prolific with these legendary creatures, which average around 20lbs. The chance of reeling in a vast fish fires up anglers from across the world who are drawn to Ireland because of the unspoiled habitat that enables the fish to breed and swell to such an impressive size.

LEFT: fishing for pike in Co. Monaghan.
ABOVE: fishing in the Shannon by Thomond Bridge, Limerick, Co. Kerry.

Conservation efforts

It's important to remember conservation issues, and this is evident in the ever-changing bye-laws. In sea-fishing, most cartilaginous fish are tagged and returned alive, and fresh-water anglers are encouraged to limit the number of wild fish taken. The aforementioned Central Fisheries Board can supply current details. The CFB also offers a free download of *Irish Sport Fishes – A guide to their identification* and more besides. ❑

WALKING IN IRELAND

"The men of Ireland are mortal and temporal, but her hills are eternal," wrote George Bernard Shaw. As well as nurturing a rich store of mythology and folklore, the Irish hills offer spectacular opportunities for walkers

From the top of Slieve-na-Calliagh (hill of the witch) in County Meath, it's possible, on a clear day, to look down across 18 Irish counties. No great effort is needed to reach the summit as it's only 911ft (275 metres), and you can drive to a small car park 10 minutes' walk from the top. If the spirit moves you, and you have the key, you can enter a cross-shaped chamber covered with a mound of stones. Inside, the stones are riotously decorated with ancient rock art carvings and radial line patterns including zigzags and spirals that, it is believed, mark the expected variations of the sunbeam with the drifting of the equinoctial rising sun.

Although not huge in European or world terms, the mountains of Ireland have a seductive and, in the case of Slieve-na-Calliagh, enigmatic quality. For walkers, the countryside offers a spectacular range of opportunities. From the high peaks of Cork and Kerry to the Glens of Antrim, and from the Donegal highlands to the small hills or drumlins of the midlands, the range of walking possibilities is enormous.

There are few mountains that need more than half a day to scale, but walking an entire range will take two days or more to complete. Most peaks have their own qualities of visual drama. Many, including the Twelve Bens in Connemara, the Mourne Mountains in County Down, or Ireland's most climbed holy mountain, Croagh Patrick, have a distinctive triangular symmetry. Brandon in Kilkenny and the quartzite cone of Errigal in Donegal have an implacable presence, yet are intimate and inviting, their significance to the people living around their foothills out of all proportion to their height. Others are more subtle and don't always emphasise their glories.

An average of two people a year have been killed recently on the MacGillycuddy's Reeks near Killarney. A mobile phone is useful in an emergency but network coverage is often poor in the mountains.

Well-run walks

Walking in Ireland has grown rapidly as an activity since the early 1990s; it is big business and well organised. There are more than

ABOVE: walking along the Beara Peninsula, Co. Kerry.
RIGHT: meandering in the Mourne Mountains near Slieve Bearnach.

30 national waymarked walking trails and 100 walking clubs. These include the delightfully-named Limerick Climbing and Crochet Club, the hooked needle element being added to attract more women members.

The clubs are all affiliated to the Mountaineering Council of Ireland which publishes a well-informed quarterly magazine, *Irish Mountain Log*. The waymarked ways offer 1,860 miles (3,000km) of marked walking routes and one of their most appealing aspects is that they are suitable for walkers of all ages and abilities. The network ranges from towpath strolls and walks along scenic coastal stretches, to circuits of the high mountainous peninsulas. You can take your pick from one of the shortest, the Cavan Way at 16 miles (26km), to the Kerry Way stretching to 133 miles (214km). These trails rarely rise above 3,000ft (900 metres). While there are a few rugged stretches over open mountain passes, the routes mainly follow disused roads, grassy trails or forest tracks. They are signposted with yellow arrows and a walking man to guide you through the countryside and over stiles and bridges.

Tougher hikes

For those wanting a greater challenge, there are much tougher day-long annual hikes across some

WHEN A WALK BECOMES A FESTIVAL

Practically every area that contains some high ground organises outings to the hills lasting a whole weekend (or longer) as part of structured walking festivals. Many of these take in features of the countryside led by local guides knowledgeable about heritage sites, the archaeology and geology of the area as well as the wild flowers and birdlife to be seen. There is also a social side to the festivals with evening entertainment in the pubs and they are a good opportunity to make new friends.

There are more than 30 walking festivals in Ireland. These include the Ballyhoura International Walking Festival cradled in the arms of the Ballyhoura and Galtee Mountains, the Castlebar International 4 Days' Walks, the Strolls in the Sperrins Festival (set in a sprawling range in Mid-Ulster) and *Sliabh an Iarainn* (Slieve Anierin) hillwalking in Leitrim. The Wee Binnians, which labels itself "the social group that walks", holds a popular annual festival in the Mournes.

The Slieve Blooms, in the centre of Ireland, offer Eco Walks as part of their bi-annual weekends. This range is in an almost forgotten area that people drive through at speed to reach the west of Ireland, yet it covers an astonishing 60,000 acres (24,000 hectares) spread across Laois and Offaly. The writer Hubert Butler once described the Slieve Blooms as "a low, demure-looking range of hills, very suitable for middle-aged, unadventurous mountaineers with children and picnic-baskets."

of the bigger ranges organised by mountaineering clubs. The Maumturks Walk in Connemara each spring covers 15 miles (24km), while the Glover Highlander in Donegal is held in early September. Most clubs have programmes of walks throughout the year and welcome visitors.

The mist can come down quickly in mountainous regions and it's easy for the walker to go astray, so check the weather forecast before setting out. The old red sandstone Kerry mountains are the most dangerous in Ireland and can be treacherous, as the mist can descend with no warning, severely limiting visibility. At 3,414ft (1,039 metres), Carrauntoohil is the country's highest mountain and attracts thousands of walkers annually.

It's essential to have proper gear: walking boots with ankle support, rainwear, warm clothes, gloves and hat, maps, compass and guidebook and sufficient snacks such as chocolate or fruit, as well as a warm or hydrating drink.

Planning an advance itinerary and working out a route using the Ordnance Survey (OS) maps is the safest way. You should also leave word with someone where you are going and your approximate return time. The OS maps in the Discovery Series, drawn up to 1:50,000 scale, will help you find ancient monuments, holy wells and castles

as well as landmarks in towns and villages. You will also find on them scores of names tucked away into the crevices and foothills such as Crotty's Rock, the Colleen Bawn Cottage, and, at the summit of Slieve Gullion in south Armagh, Calliagh Berra's Lake. According to legend, any man who swims in the lake comes out visibly aged.

Magnificent scenery opens up in many mountainous areas such as Mayo's Doo Lough Pass, the Spelga Pass in south Down and the bleak but beautiful Gap of Dunloe in Kerry. But be careful as you drive on these remote roads as a PhD in these parts refers to Pot-hole Dodging. ❑

ABOVE: it's essential to carry proper hiking gear to cope with rapidly changing weather conditions.

USEFUL WEBSITES

- For information on waymarked walking trails visit: www.walkireland.ie.
- For details of routes on loop walks, trails in forest parks, national parks and city or town walks (known as *Sli na Slainte*) as well as information on walking festivals go to www.walkingireland.ie.
- Seven pilgrim paths in Ireland follow medieval pilgrimage routes. Details: www.heritagecouncil.ie.
- The Mountaineering Council of Ireland has a helpful website: www.mountaineering.ie.
- To learn more about looped walks, forest and nature walks, festivals and events and accommodation for walkers visit: www.discoverireland.com/walking.

Ireland's Top 10 Walks

From The Brandy Pad and The Dingle Way to coastal walks and a climb up Diamond Hill, there are hikes to suit everyone in the Emerald Isle

A favourite walk is **Errigal Mountain** (Co. Donegal). The most direct route starts from Dunlewy at the car park on the main R521. After crossing heathery slopes, you will reach firmer footing and it's a relatively easy walk to pick your way to the top through rocks and over loose stones for a view that takes in a large area of the north-west of Ireland.

The Brandy Pad (Co. Down). This route follows an old smuggler's path across the northern section of the Mourne Mountains. The whole walk, which is waymarked throughout and marked on maps, is 7 miles (11km.). It is not overly strenuous and the reward is spectacular views across the highest mountain range in Ulster.

The Dingle Way (Co. Kerry). For a taste of dramatic scenery you could walk all, or part, of the 110-mile (180km) Dingle Way on the Dingle peninsula. The walk begins in Tralee, leads west to Camp on the northern side, then loops round the peninsula, taking in the imposing Brandon Mountain, and dropping down to Clogher Head before turning back along the southern stretch of the peninsula.

Croagh Patrick (Co. Mayo). Turn up on the last Sunday in July and you'll have trouble creating elbow room for yourself amongst 30,000 pilgrims on their annual hike to the summit. A well-trodden path takes you to the chapel at the summit of this conical, aloof peak, from which you can view the islands beneath you in Clew Bay.

Burren Coastal Walk (Co. Clare). Along the stunning coastline from Black Head down to Doolin, you will cross a variety of terrain that includes limestone pavement, beaches, grass and sand dunes all offering pleasant walking among grey walls, stones and rocks. You will come across seabirds and rare Arctic-Alpine plants that flower in the spring and early summer. The five-hour walk also takes you across Fanore beach, a European Special Area of Conservation.

Diamond Hill (Co. Galway). The path to the top of Diamond Hill starts from the visitor centre in Connemara National Park. The 5-mile (8km) route starts along the Sruffaunboy Nature Trail before branching off towards the cone of Diamond Hill. From the cairn on the summit ridge at 1,460ft (442 metres) the breathtaking view embraces islands, bays, beaches, loughs and mountains.

Sawel (Co. Derry). The large expanse of the Sperrin Mountains are in a sparsely populated region of north Tyrone. The walking covers bog, heather and moorland and will take you through quiet valleys and encounters with sheep and birds.

The Grand Canal Way (Co. Dublin & midlands). This flat canalside walk leads westwards from the outskirts of Dublin through the central plains to the village of Shannon Harbour, covering a distance of 80 miles (130km). The walk offers a variety of wildlife, canal features and pretty villages to stop in for refuelling. You can pause to explore Ireland's finest monastic settlement at Clonmacnoise.

RIGHT: hiking through Donegal.

The Slieve Bloom Way (Cos. Laois & Offaly). This 43-mile (70km) route covers a wide circuit of an isolated range of mountains in central Ireland and takes two days. It provides panoramic views from the paths and tracks through the bogland, and the ascents of the hills are not too strenuous.

Carrauntoohil (Co. Kerry). The most popular route to the top of Ireland's highest mountain is via the Devil's Ladder, although it can be dangerous in wet weather. Walkers have to scramble through a wide gully that has loose boulders that can easily dislodge. The return time is a minimum of five hours, so this one is for more experienced walkers. ❑

Ireland's Architecture

Ireland has history like dogs have fleas, and its buildings reflect not only a catalogue of conquest but also its roots as an agrarian economy

"Never accept a commission in Ireland," a 19th-century English architect warned his colleagues. His fear was that only the most rugged buildings could withstand the Atlantic winds and rain. In the 20th century, two greater threats emerged: bitter warfare which would see great Anglo-Irish manors burnt to the ground, and the rapacity of 1960s property developers which would devastate Dublin's Georgian heritage.

Ireland's buildings reflect a history of conquest. From the 12th century, Anglo-Norman fortresses were built to intimidate. But Ireland proved hard to subjugate and fortified tower houses continued to be built until the end of the 17th century. In the 18th century, the British imported Palladian and Georgian styles. Neo-classical influences spread to humble farm houses. But the crude thatched cottage didn't die: it evolved into the crude bungalows that disfigure the countryside today.

Above: the English tradition of fine carpentry did not extend to Ireland, and the limestone or clay thatched cottage was not built to last. Traditional long-houses combined a dwelling with a shelter for animals. Cottages were built where there was shelter from the wind and a spring could provide water. An open hearth fuelled by turf provided both cooking and heating facilities.

Below: Leamaneagh Castle is a striking ruin of an extended tower house, dating from 1480 and attached to a 17th-century four-storey mansion. It can be found in the Burren area of Co. Clare, on route R476 from Kilfenora through Killinaboy.

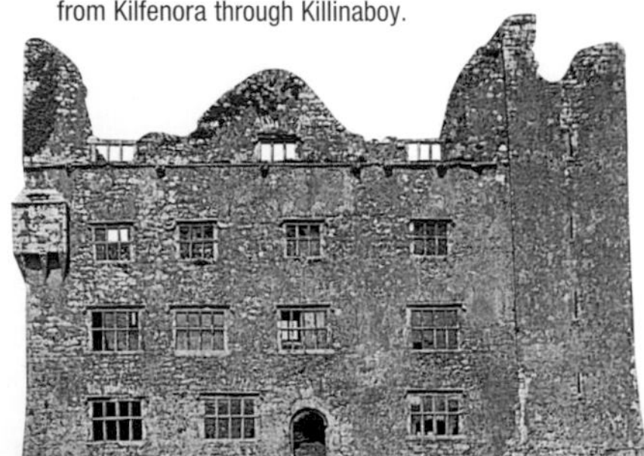

Below: Dublin became a showpiece city in the 18th century, with areas such as Fitzwilliam Square (pictured) conveying an elegant simplicity that implied social status. It was clearly a European capital. By contrast, Belfast was an industrial city, whose rapid growth in the 19th century produced a few grand civic edifices bu[t] mainly utilitarian Victorian buildings.

EFT: Kilruddery House in Bray, Co. Wicklow, is an example of a and country house within easy reach of Dublin. Built in the 17th ntury, it was later remodelled along neo-Elizabethan lines. A nservatory was added in 1852, its walls being masonry instead of ass because it was meant to house not only plants but also the atues collected by its owner, Lord Meath.

ELOW: the classic image of Dublin is of its elegant Georgian orways. But comparatively few have survived. unchecked velopers bulldozed many to create modern office blocks, and blic support for preserving Ireland's architectural heritage was metimes interpreted as nostalgia for the former colonial ruler.

THE FIGHT FOR OLD DUBLIN

Dublin in the 18th century was one of the ornaments of Europe, its Georgian buildings expressing a distinctive graciousness, the wide streetscapes framing distant mountain views, some of which can still be seen today.

Much of that heritage was destroyed in the unregulated property speculation of 1960s. Whole streets were razed and replaced by often unsympathetic office blocks. Classic Georgian terraces vanished. Protests peaked in the late 1970s after an important Viking site at Wood Quay was obliterated to build offices for city officials.

The recent record has been better. Plans for a huge bus depot in the Temple Bar area south of the River Liffey were shelved when the city authorities realised that the small shops, galleries and restaurants on the narrow cobbled streets of Temple Bar had turned the area into a prime tourist attraction. So instead of bulldozing the area, it was partly redeveloped, and is now home to the Irish Film Centre, The Ark (a children's cultural centre), Meeting House Square (an outdoor venue), galleries and artists' studios.

TOP CENTRE: Bantry House in Co. Cork is about as far as you can get from the cliché image of an Irish cottage, and hints at the lifestyle enjoyed by the Anglo-Irish aristocracy. When the 2nd Earl of Bantry inherited this Georgian house in 1845, he began turning it into a repository for the art and antiques he collected on his world travels. An amateur architect, he had a theatrical sense of design. Parallels with the Capitol Building in Washington DC reinforce the claims of Charles Frederick Anderson, who emigrated to the US and said he had a hand in both. Its collection of carpets, tapestries and furniture is open to the public, and it offers one of the best views over Bantry Bay.

BELOW: Avondale House, a Georgian building in Co. Wicklow, was the birthplace of the politician Charles Stewart Parnell (1846–91). Now a museum, it is surrounded by a forest park.

05 TAXI
36810 TAXI
19319

29769 TAXI
41138 TAXI
452
35279
TAXI

GLENDUN HOTEL
CUSH
B966

HOTEL
MARINER

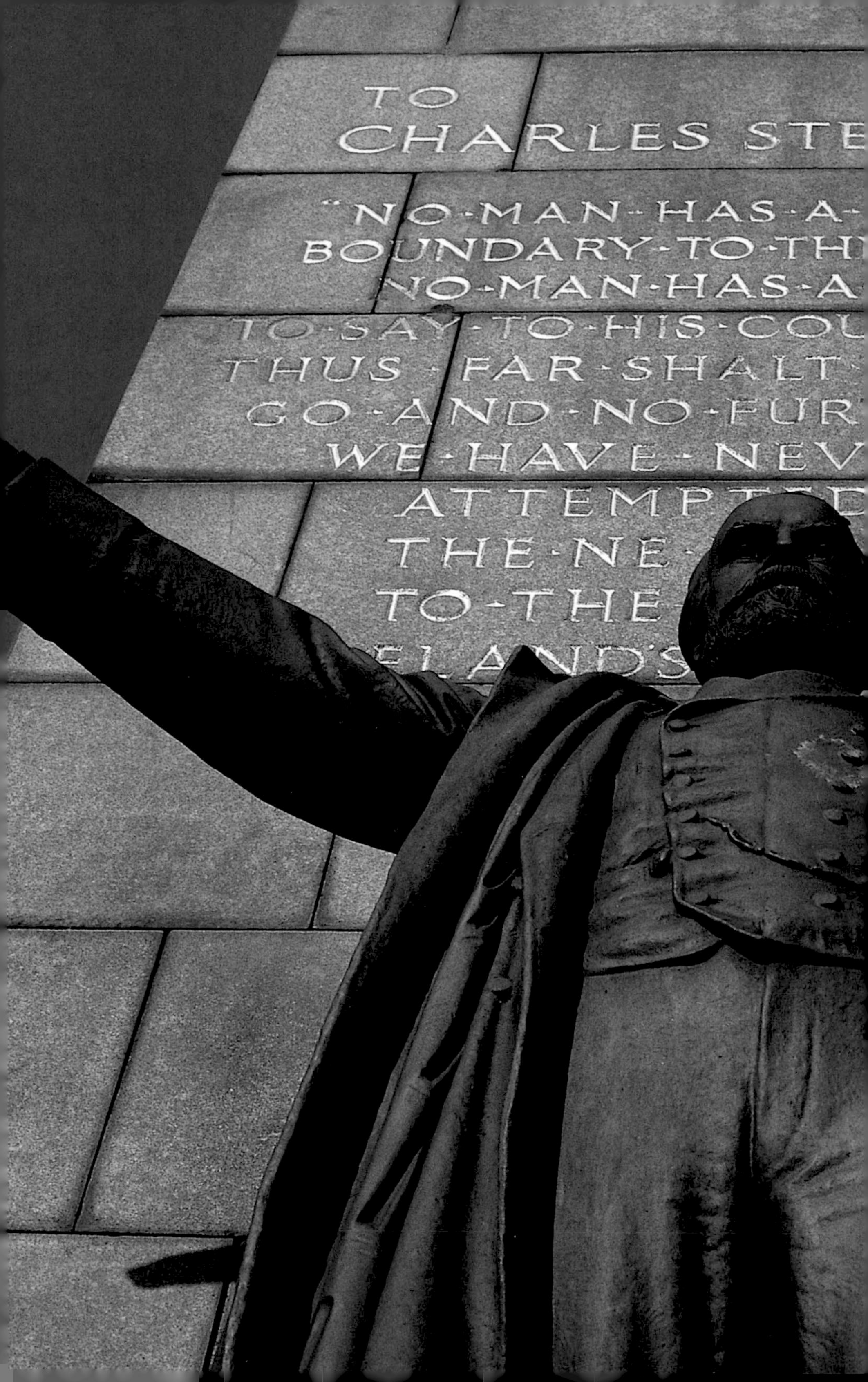
TO
CHARLES STE
"NO·MAN·HAS·A·
BOUNDARY·TO·TH
NO·MAN·HAS·A
TO·SAY·TO·HIS·COU
THUS·FAR·SHALT
GO·AND·NO·FUR
WE·HAVE·NEV
ATTEMPTED
THE·NE
TO·THE
LANDS

ART PARNELL·
HT·TO·FIX·THE·
ARCH·OF·A·NATION·
GHT·
RY·
OU·
ER
O·FIX·
ULTRA
ESS·OF
NHOOD
R·SHALL"
Go·soirbigid·Dia
éire·dá·clainn

VISA

PLACES

A detailed guide to the entire island and all its delights, with principal sites clearly cross-referenced by number to the accompanying maps

What other city but Dublin, capital of the Republic of Ireland, could boast a General Post Office as a national shrine? Where else but Belfast, capital of Northern Ireland, could have transformed itself in so short a time from car-bomb chaos to a clubbing destination for European partygoers? The stimulating thing about Ireland is that, having provoked so many preconceptions, it can constantly surprise.

Open-minded visitors, bringing raincoats and sturdy walking boots but leaving their preconceptions at home, will discover a beguiling Irish stew of hidden loughs and ancient towns, burial chambers and strange stone crosses, round towers and ruined castles, holy wells and high waterfalls. Racehorses are the local heroes and the villain is anyone too hurried to bid the time of day to a neighbour in a civilised manner.

Kerry beckons with opulent valleys, nurturing wild fuchsia and scented orchids; Killarney, with jaunting cars and leprechaun lore designed to charm the euros from tourists' pockets; Dublin, increasingly anglicised, americanised and hamburgerised, yet still the least lonely of cities; rivers like the Galway and the Shannon where you could knock a dozen salmon senseless with a single brick; and Fermanagh's resplendent lakeland, where boats are still gloriously few and far between. It is a small country but, like vintage wine, should be savoured slowly. Sometimes it has to be. A signpost may present you with three ways of getting to a destination or it may show none. Ask a passer-by and, if he decides you look a bit tired after a hard day's sightseeing and comparing pints of Guinness, he'll probably assure you it's "just a wee way ahead" because he doesn't wish to distress you by telling you it's really 40 miles by a narrow, twisting road.

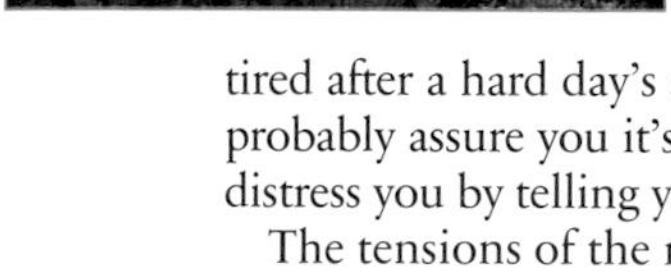

The tensions of the modern world have not bypassed Ireland, and the economic downturn has left a legacy of unfinished buildings and a shell-shocked national psyche. But a remarkable capacity for enjoyment has survived and most visitors find that enjoyment wildly infectious. ❑

PRECEDING PAGES: Dublin taxi rank; Cushendum, in Northern Ireland; the Parnell Monument in Dublin's O'Connell Street. **LEFT:** thatched cottage and garden, Adare, Co. Clare. **ABOVE FROM TOP:** Ring of Kerry; Blarney Castle.

Ireland
0 40 km
0 40 miles
N
ATLANTIC OCEAN
Malin Head
Tory Island
Tory Sound
Bloody Foreland
Gweedore
Derryveagh Mts
Aran Island
Dungloe
Gweebarra Bay
Portsalon
Millford
Letterkenny (Leitir Ceanainn)
Buncrana
Moville
Inishowen Head
L. Foyle
Derry
Limavady
Giant's Causeway
Rathlin Island
Ballycastle
Mull of Kintyre
North Channel
Portstewart
Coleraine
Antrim Mts
Cushendall
Ballymoney
R. Bann
NORTHERN IRELAND
Ballymena
Larne
Island Magee
Maghera
Randalstown
Antrim
M2
Carrickfergus
Bangor
Donaghadee
Newtownabbey
BELFAST
Newtownards
Strangford L.
Glenties
Blue Stack Mts
Ballybofey
R. Foyle
Strabane
Sperrin Mts
Magherafelt
Malin More
Killybegs
Donegal
Newtownstewart
Cookstown
Lough Neagh
Glenavy
Lisburn
R. Lagan
M1
Omagh
Coalisland
Dungannon
Lurgan
Craigavon
Portadown
Killyleagh
Ards Peninsula
Ballynahinch
Donegal Bay
Ballyshannon
Kesh
Belleek
Lower Lough Erne
Enniskillen
Armagh
Banbridge
Downpatrick
Lecale Peninsula
Erris Head
Downpatrick Head
Belmullet
Ballycastle
Killala Bay
Easky
Sligo Bay
Sligo (Sligeach)
Manorhamilton
Belcoo
Monaghan (Muineachán)
Keady
Rathfriland
Carrowmore L.
Mullet Peninsula
Bangor Erris
Ballina
Slieve Gamph or Ox Mts
Collooney
Dowra
Upper Lough Erne
Clones
Newry
Mourne Mts
Newcastle
Blacksod Bay
Nephin Beg Ra.
Lough Conn
Tobercurry
Lough Allen
Iron Mts
Drumshanbo
Ballybay
Castleblaney
Rostrevor
Kilkeel
Carlingford L.
Achill Island
Mulrany
Castlebar (Caisleán an Bharraigh)
Newport
Swinford
Boyle
Carrick-on-Shannon
Cavan (An Cabhán)
Carrickmacross
Dundalk (Dun Dealgan)
Dundalk Bay
Clare Island
Clew Bay
Westport
Bailieborough
Ardee
Dunany Point
Irish Sea
Dunleer
Inishturk
Louisburgh
Sheeffry Hills
Plains of Mayo
Ballyhaunis
Castlerea
Virginia
Granard
Ceanannus Mór (Kells)
Drogheda (Droichead Átha)
Claremorris
Longford (An Longfort)
Castlepollard
Duleek
Inishbofin
Partry Mts
Lough Mask
Ballinrobe
Roscommon
Navan (An Uaimh)
M3
Naul
Balbriggan
Skerries
Leenane
Clifden
Maam
Tuam
REPUBLIC
Dunshaughlin

I R E L A N D
Island
Galway Bay
Inishmore
Inishmaan
Inisheer
Aran Islands
Black
Head
Ballyvaughan
The Burren
Kinvarra
Gort
Loughrea
Slieve Aughty
Mts
R. Shannon
Portumna
Cloghan
Birr
Borrisokane
Lough
Derg
Portarlington
Mountmellick
Portlaoise
Roscrea
(Ros Cré)
Kildare
Monasterevin
M7
Naas
(An Nás)
Mullaghcleevaun
848
Wicklow
Mountains
National Park
Lugnaquilla
700
Wicklow Mts
Bray
(Bré)
Greystones
Wicklow
(Cill Mhantáin)
Rathdrum
Athy
(Baile Átha)
R. Barrow
Cliffs of
Moher
Ennistymon
Ennis
(Inis)
Tulla
Nenagh
(An tAonach)
Durrow
Carlow
(Ceatharlach)
Castlecomer
Tullow
Arklow
(An tInbhear
Mór)
Donegal
Point
Creegh
Templemore
M8
Carnew
Bagenalstown
Kilrush
Thurles
(Durlas)
Limerick
(Luimneach)
Slievefellim
Mts
Kilkenny
(Cill Chainnigh)
Gorey
R. Slaney
Carrigaholt
Slieveardagh
Hills
Patrickswell
R. Suir
Loop Head
Mouth of the Shannon
Ballybunion
Tarbert
Croom
Callan
Thomastown
Cahore
Point
Cashel
(Caiseal)
Enniscorthy
(Inis Corthaidh)
Kerry
Head
Listowel
R. Feale
Newcastle
West
Tipperary
R. Nore
Ballyheige
Kilmallock
Rath
Luirc
Abbeyfeale
Clonmel
(Cluain Meala)
New Ross
(Ros Mhic Thriúin)
Tralee
Bay
Galtee Mts
Wexford
(Loch Garman)
Brandon
Head
Cahir
(An Chathair)
Carrick-on-Suir
(Carraig na Siúire)
Tralee
(Trá Lí)
Mitchelstown
Waterford
(Port Láirge)
Rosslare
Dingle
Camp
Castleisland
Rosslare
Harbour
Dingle
Kanturk
Knockmealdown
Mts
R. Blackwater
Kilmore
Quay
Carnsore Point
Blasket
Islands
Dingle Bay
Killorglin
Killarney
(Cill Airne)
Mallow
(Mala)
Fermoy
Tallowbridge
Tramore
Hook
Head
Saltee Islands
Rathmore
Dungarvan
(Dún Garbhán)
Valentia
Island
Carrantuohill
1041
Cahersiveen
Cork
(Corcaigh)
Mine Head
Kenmare
Macroom
R. Lee
Midleton
Youghal
(Eochaill)
Bray
Head
Waterville
Iveragh
Ballincollig
Cobh
(An Cobh)
Knockadoon
Head
Kenmare River
Glengarriff
Skellig
Islands
Beara
Bandon
Crosshaven
Dunmanway
R. Bandon
Bantry
Kinsale
Bantry Bay
Bere
Island
Dursey
Head
Clonakilty
Ballydehob
Old Head
of Kinsale
Sheep's
Head
Skibbereen
Galley
Head
Mizen Head
C. Clear Island
Celtic Sea
St George's Channel

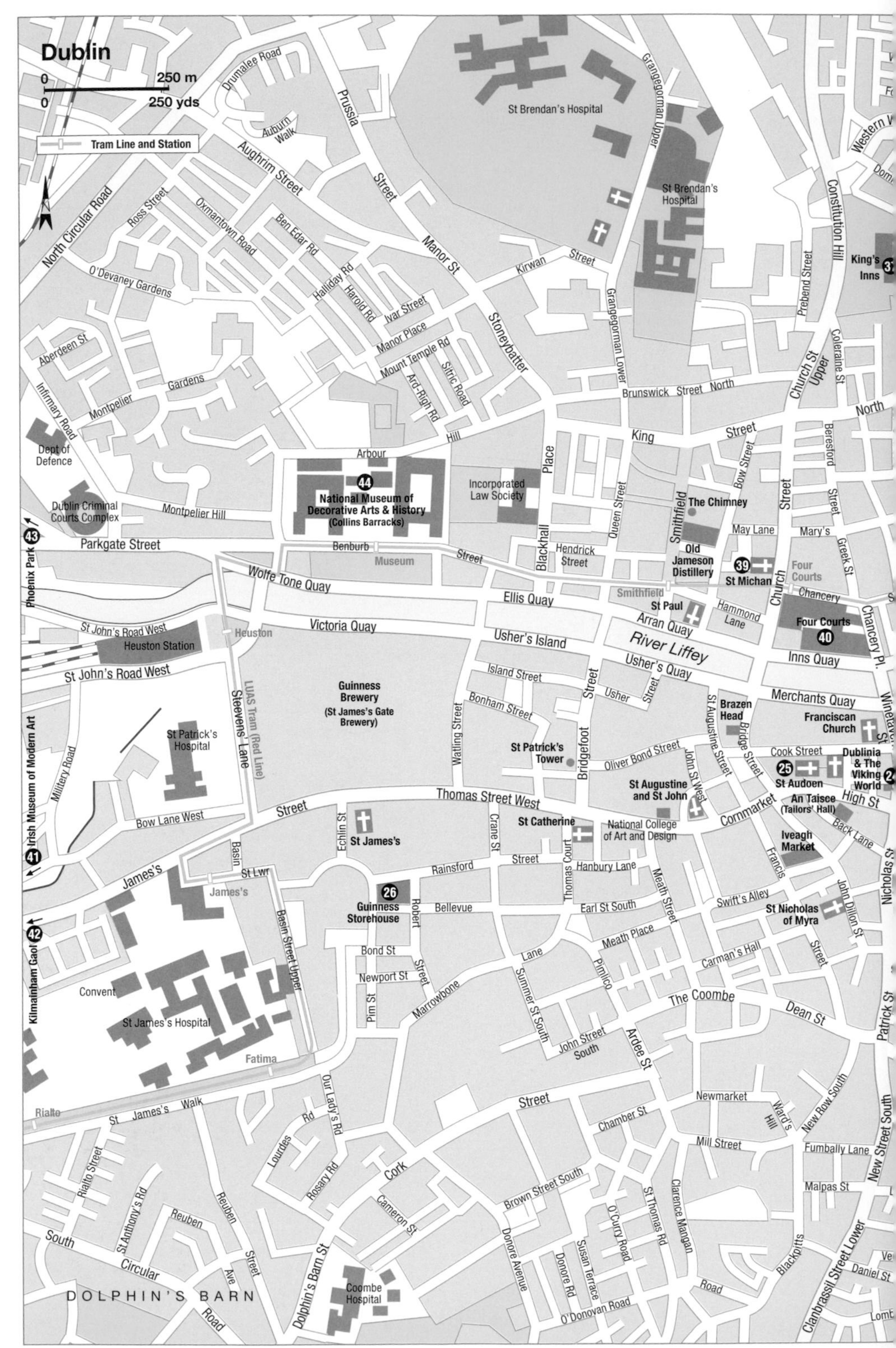
Dublin
0 250 m
0 250 yds
Tram Line and Station
St Brendan's Hospital
St Brendan's Hospital
King's Inns
National Museum of Decorative Arts & History (Collins Barracks)
Incorporated Law Society
Dept of Defence
Dublin Criminal Courts Complex
Phoenix Park
Heuston Station
Heuston
Museum
Smithfield
The Chimney
Old Jameson Distillery
St Michan
Four Courts
St Paul
River Liffey
Guinness Brewery (St James's Gate Brewery)
St Patrick's Hospital
LUAS Tram (Red Line)
Brazen Head
Franciscan Church
St Patrick's Tower
St Augustine and St John
St Audoen
Dublinia & The Viking World
An Taisce (Tailors' Hall)
St Catherine
National College of Art and Design
St James's
Iveagh Market
Irish Museum of Modern Art
Guinness Storehouse
St Nicholas of Myra
Kilmainham Gaol
James's
Convent
St James's Hospital
Fatima
Rialto
Coombe Hospital
DOLPHIN'S BARN
Parkgate Street
Wolfe Tone Quay
Victoria Quay
Ellis Quay
Arran Quay
Inns Quay
Usher's Island
Usher's Quay
Merchants Quay
Thomas Street West
James's Street
The Coombe
Dean St
South Circular Road
North Circular Road
Manor St
Stoneybatter
Prussia Street
Aughrim Street
Constitution Hill
Church Street
King Street North
Brunswick Street North
Benburb Street
Cork Street
St John's Road West
Steevens' Lane
Bridgefoot Street
Patrick St
New Street South
Clanbrassil Street Lower
Dolphin's Barn St

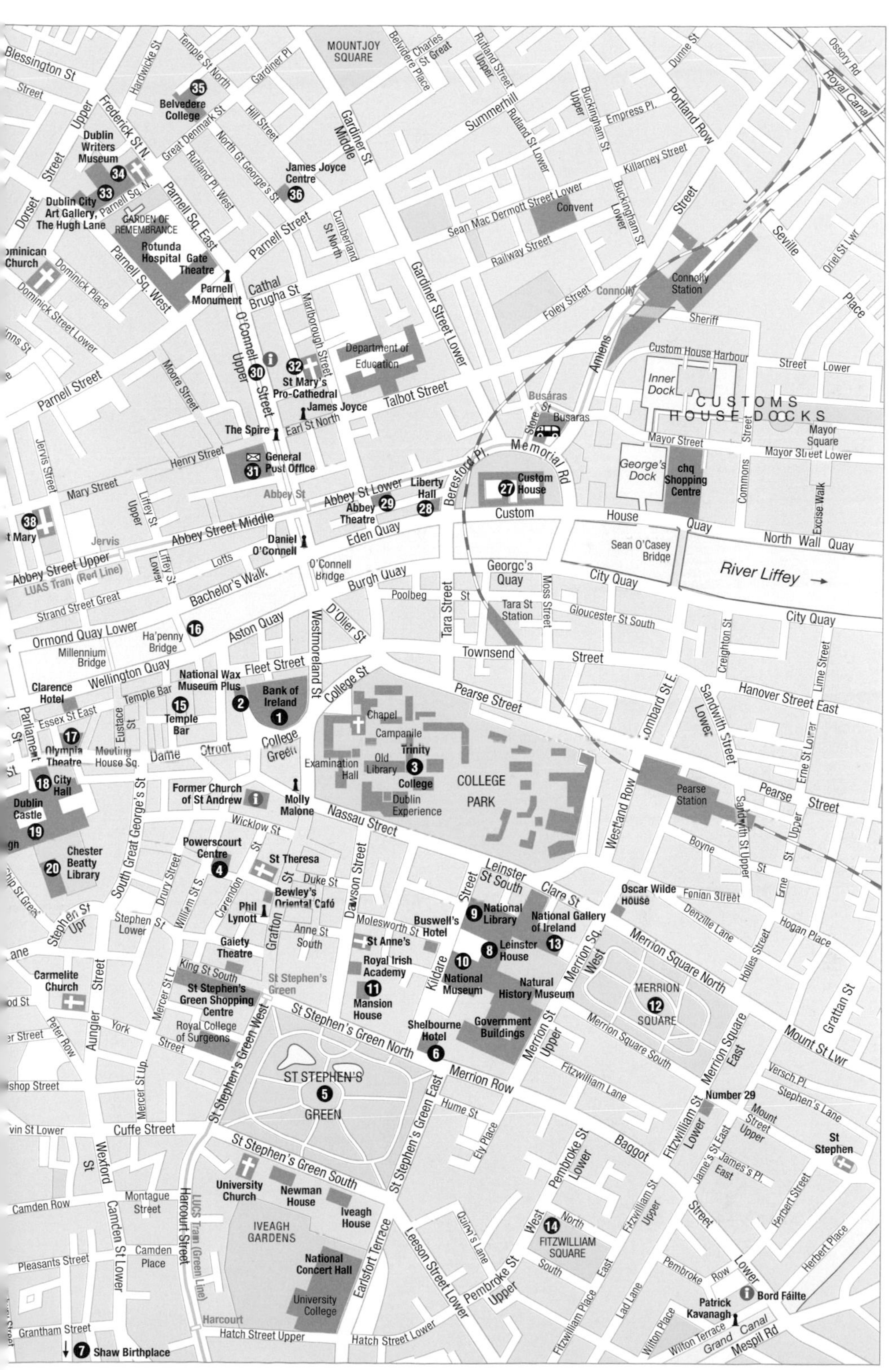

Blessington St
Temple St North
Hardwicke St
Gardiner Pl
MOUNTJOY SQUARE
Belvidere Place
Charles St Great
Rutland Street Upper
Dunne St
Ossory Rd
Royal Canal
Belvedere College
Great Denmark St
Hill Street
Gardiner St Middle
Summerhill
Rutland St Lower
Buckingham St Upper
Empress Pl.
Portland Row
Dublin Writers Museum
Frederick St N
Upper Dorset Street
North Gt George's St
Rutland Pl. West
James Joyce Centre
Killarney Street
Dublin City Art Gallery, The Hugh Lane
Parnell Sq. N.
GARDEN OF REMEMBRANCE
Parnell Sq. East
Sean Mac Dermott Street Lower
Convent
Buckingham St Lower
Rotunda Hospital
Gate Theatre
Parnell Street
Cumberland St North
Railway Street
Seville Place
Oriel St Lwr
Dominican Church
Dominick Place
Parnell Sq. West
Dominick Street Lower
Parnell Monument
Cathal Brugha St
Marlborough Street
Gardiner Street Lower
Foley Street
Connolly
Connolly Station
Sheriff Street Lower
Amiens Street
O'Connell Street Upper
Department of Education
Custom House Harbour
Inner Dock
CUSTOMS HOUSE DOCKS
Moore Street
Parnell Street
St Mary's Pro-Cathedral
Talbot Street
Busáras
Store St
James Joyce
Earl St North
Mayor Street
Mayor Square
Mayor Street Lower
The Spire
Memorial Rd
Henry Street
General Post Office
Beresford Pl.
Custom House
George's Dock
chq Shopping Centre
Commons Street
Excise Walk
Jervis Street
Mary Street
Liffey St Upper
Abbey St
Abbey St Lower
Abbey Theatre
Liberty Hall
Custom House Quay
North Wall Quay
St Mary
Abbey Street Middle
Jervis
Daniel O'Connell
Eden Quay
Sean O'Casey Bridge
River Liffey
Abbey Street Upper
LUAS Tram (Red Line)
Liffey St Lower
Lotts
O'Connell Bridge
George's Quay
Moss Street
City Quay
Bachelor's Walk
Burgh Quay
Poolbeg St
Tara Street
Tara St Station
Strand Street Great
D'Olier St
Westmoreland St
Gloucester St South
Ormond Quay Lower
Aston Quay
Ha'penny Bridge
Millennium Bridge
Townsend Street
Creighton St
Lime Street
Wellington Quay
Fleet Street
National Wax Museum Plus
Clarence Hotel
Bank of Ireland
College St
Pearse Street
Lombard St E.
Sandwith Street Lower
Hanover Street East
Temple Bar
Essex St East
Eustace St
Temple Bar
Parliament St
Chapel
Campanile
Olympia Theatre
Meeting House Sq.
Dame Street
College Green
Trinity College
Examination Hall
Old Library
COLLEGE PARK
Erne St Lower
City Hall
Dublin Castle
Former Church of St Andrew
Molly Malone
Dublin Experience
Westland Row
Pearse Station
Pearse Street
Wicklow St
Nassau Street
Boyne St
Sandwith St Upper
Erne St Upper
South Great George's St
Chester Beatty Library
Powerscourt Centre
St Theresa
Duke St
Dawson Street
Leinster St South
Drury Street
William St S.
Clarendon St
Grafton St
Bewley's Oriental Café
Clare St
Oscar Wilde House
Fenian Street
Denzille Lane
Hogan Place
Stephen St Upr
Stephen St Lower
Phil Lynott
Anne St South
Molesworth St
Buswell's Hotel
Kildare Street
National Library
National Gallery of Ireland
Merrion Sq. West
Merrion Square North
Holles Street
Gaiety Theatre
St Anne's
Leinster House
Royal Irish Academy
National Museum
Natural History Museum
Carmelite Church
King St South
St Stephen's Green
Mansion House
MERRION SQUARE
Grattan St
Aungier Street
Mercer St Lr
St Stephen's Green Shopping Centre
York Street
Peter Row
Royal College of Surgeons
St Stephen's Green North
Shelbourne Hotel
Government Buildings
Merrion St Upper
Merrion Square South
Merrion Square East
Mount St Lwr
Bishop Street
Mercer St Up.
St Stephen's Green West
ST STEPHEN'S GREEN
Merrion Row
Fitzwilliam Lane
Versch Pl.
St Stephen's Green East
Hume St
Number 29
Stephen's Lane
Cuffe Street
Wexford St
Ely Place
Pembroke St Lower
Baggot Street
Fitzwilliam St Lower
Mount Street Upper
James's St East
James's Pl. East
St Stephen
St Stephen's Green South
Fitzwilliam St Upper
Herbert Street
Camden Row
Montague Street
University Church
Newman House
Iveagh House
Camden St Lower
Harcourt Street
IVEAGH GARDENS
LUAS Tram (Green Line)
Earlsfort Terrace
Leeson Street Lower
Quinn's Lane
Fitzwilliam Square West
Fitzwilliam Square North
FITZWILLIAM SQUARE
Fitzwilliam Square South
Fitzwilliam Square East
Herbert Place
Pleasants Street
Camden Place
National Concert Hall
University College
Pembroke St Upper
Lad Lane
Pembroke Row
Lower
Bord Fáilte
Patrick Kavanagh
Grantham Street
Harcourt
Hatch Street Upper
Hatch Street Lower
Fitzwilliam Place
Wilton Place
Wilton Terrace
Grand Canal
Mespil Rd
Shaw Birthplace

DUBLIN

It's a small capital and not an especially pretty one – but the vivacity of its citizens and the hospitality they show to visitors have made it one of Europe's most popular destinations

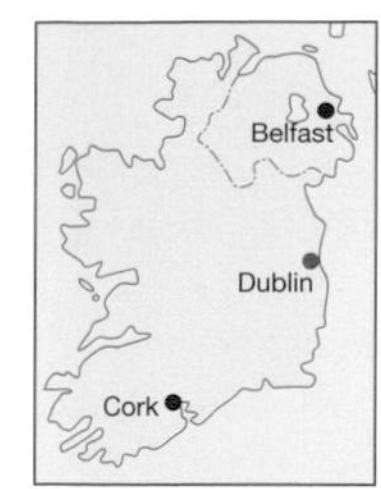

Main attractions
- Bank of Ireland
- Trinity College
- St Stephen's Green
- Leinster House
- National Library
- National Museum
- National Gallery of Ireland
- Fitzwilliam Square
- Temple Bar
- Ha'Penny Bridge
- Dublin Castle
- Marsh's Library
- St Patrick's Cathedral
- Guinness Storehouse
- Custom House
- O'Connell Street
- Kilmainham Gaol
- Phoenix Park

With its vibrant mix of traditional pubs, hip bars, elegant Georgian architecture, cool shops and a colourful cultural scene to rival any European capital, Dublin bubbles with an infectious energy. Despite the severe economic downturn Dublin continues to celebrate cosmopolitanism. The Irish capital is a lively place to be, from the café-packed side streets around Grafton Street to the African and Asian stores that rub shoulders with traditional street traders on Moore Street. Culturally, the city is famed throughout the world for its rich theatre, literature, art and music, which is no surprise considering that some of Europe's most prestigious artists, writers and musicians including Francis Bacon, James Joyce, W.B. Yeats, Brendan Behan, and, of course, U2 all hail from here.

Pubs and parks

As a city, Dublin means different things to different people. For some it's an inspirational centre of historical treasures from ancient Viking areas to the grand Georgian townhouses of the 18th century that give the city a grace and beauty. For others, it is a city of talkers, its pubs overflowing with Guinness and an inimitable atmosphere that makes locals believe Dublin pubs are the best in the world. Some fall in love with the quiet, sophisticated urban parks of Merrion Square and the Iveagh Gardens, while others gorge on the city's kaleidoscopic collection of chic boutiques, big-name chain stores and the super-luxurious Brown Thomas department store.

The first thing that strikes nearly all visitors is Dublin's superb natural setting. This vivacious spot sits on a wide plain bisected by the River Liffey, overlooked by hills and headlands and facing a broad sweeping bay. By contrast,

LEFT: the O'Connell Monument.
RIGHT: boardwalk along the Liffey, just the spot for a stroll.

A glass-topped boat, Spirit of Docklands (in foreground above) runs 45-minute river tours from 10.30am daily (not in winter; tel: 01-473 4082; www.liffeyvoyage.ie). In the background is the Jeanie Johnston, a replica famine ship with a museum (weekends only).

BELOW: Dublin's Capel Street in 1800, painted by James Malton (1761–1803).

the city itself has an untidy, abstracted elegance, as if its mind is on something more important than looking attractive, but Dublin can still sparkle when it tries.

A divided city

Dublin is divided by the River Liffey, which flows through its centre and also by the social differences, which the river delineates. In the early 18th century, the rich moved north across the river from the old medieval city with its teeming slums to fine new terraces and squares, such as Henrietta Street and Mountjoy Square. But within decades they doubled back again to establish fashionable residences on the south side in Merrion Square and Fitzwilliam Square, continuing in Victorian times through the suburbs of Ballsbridge and out along the coast to the attractive towns of Dun Laoghaire and Dalkey.

There are still middle-class enclaves on the northside, but by and large southsiders are better off, better dressed and (to their own ears) better spoken. Like any snobbery, of course, the north-south chauvinism works both ways, and just as many southsiders "wouldn't be seen dead on the northside", northsiders are inclined to judge the southside as a wasteland of snobbery and pretension. In the city centre, the divide is slowly being chipped away, though, as areas along Docklands' North Quays and around Capel Street teem with a new wave of hip bars and restaurants that tempt southsiders across the river in their droves. But the south is getting its own back with the developing Grand Canal Quay spawning trendy bars and a snazzy new theatre.

Bank of Ireland and around

A good place to begin a walking tour is O'Connell Bridge. Turn your back on the breadth and bustle of O'Connell Street and instead walk down Westmoreland Street into College Green, which contains two of Dublin's most impressive and historic buildings: the **Bank of Ireland** ❶

Paradoxes of Dublin's History

Dublin began by the banks of the Liffey, where Celtic settlements and churches existed at least from early Christian times, near a causeway crossing from which the city's Gaelic name, Baile Atha Cliath, "The Town of the Hurdle Ford", is derived. But towns as such did not figure in the old Celtic way of things, and it is generally accepted that Dublin was founded in the 9th century not by the Irish, but by the Vikings, who were plundering and colonising all the coasts of Northern Europe.

Dublin was soon a lucrative base for both raiding and trading and the Danes hung on to it – despite persistent attacks by local chieftains and a great defeat at the Battle of Clontarf in 1014 – gradually intermarrying with the Irish and adopting Christianity. The Anglo-Normans arrived in the 12th century. But, until Elizabethan times, direct English rule was restricted to a ribbon of land on the east coast known as "the Pale", running roughly from Dundalk to the north to a little way south of Dublin.

The colonisation by landlords from Britain in the 17th and 18th centuries created Dublin's "golden age", when many great buildings were erected and the city's social life was as fashionable as any in Europe.

Legislative independence was granted under the English Crown in 1782, but the Irish parliament in College Green was short-lived. After the rebellion of the United Irishmen in 1798, Britain brought Ireland under direct control again and began a long period of decline in Dublin life.

The city was at the heart of the ferment that led to the Rising of 1916, the subsequent War of Independence and the establishment of the Free State in 1921. The next 40 years were a time of economic struggle in a puritan atmosphere that was often culturally and socially stifling.

and Trinity College. The bank, with its curving, columnar, windowless facade, exudes loftier ideals than those of commerce and was begun in 1729 to house the Irish Parliament, whose builders could not have foreseen how brief its age of glory would be.

Just behind the bank in Foster Place is the **National Wax Museum Plus** ❷ (tel: 01-671 8373; www.waxmuseumplus.ie; daily 10am–7pm; charge), which relocated here in 2009. Displays include Irish history, literature, science and discovery, plus Irish music and sporting legends, the Enchanted World and a Chamber of Horrors.

The statue of Henry Grattan, the parliament's greatest orator, stands in the middle of College Green, in mid-gesture, apparently delivering one of his ringing speeches. "Nations," he once said, "are governed not by interest only, but by passion also, and the passion of Ireland is freedom."

The eastern front of the bank was added in 1785 by James Gandon. The building is open during banking hours; conducted tours are held on Tuesday at 10.30am, 11.30am and 1.45pm.

Trinity College

Trinity College ❸, whose sober facade is topped by a surprisingly bright blue clock, was founded in 1592 by Elizabeth I on the site of a confiscated monastery, but the frontage was built between 1755 and 1759. The porch inside the main gate leads to a spacious, cobbled quadrangle, on the right of which is the Theatre, or Examination Hall (1779–91), which contains a gilt oak chandelier from the old parliament and an organ said to have been taken from a Spanish ship at Vigo in 1702. On the left is the Chapel (1792) and beyond it the Dining Hall (1743). The 100ft (30-metre) campanile, which dominates the quadrangle was designed by Sir Charles Lanyon and erected in 1853 on a spot supposed to mark the centre of the medieval monastery church.

To the right of the second quadrangle is the **Old Library** (1712–32), containing in a glass case the *Book of Kells*. This magnificently ornate 9th-century manuscript copy of the gospels

Trinity College.

BELOW: the Long Room library at Trinity College.

Trinity's Traditions

Set up exclusively for the Protestant Ascendancy class, Trinity College nourished many of Ireland's greatest writers, scientists and politicians

Founded in 1591 by Elizabeth I on the site of a confiscated monastery, Trinity covers 16 hectares (40 acres) in the centre of the city on land reclaimed from the Liffey estuary. It doesn't quite have the grandeur of the nearby Bank of Ireland and was described by James Joyce in *A Portrait of the Artist as a Young Man* as being "set heavily in the city's ignorance like a dull stone set in a cumbrous ring."

Trinity remained an exclusively Protestant university for most of its history, having been set up by Queen Elizabeth to "civilise" the Irish and keep them from the influences of "Popery". The college has lost some, if not all, of its air of Ascendancy since the restriction on Catholic students was lifted in 1873. But until comparatively recently it was considered a dangerous place for church-going Catholics, and indeed it is only since 1970 that Catholics have attended in substantial numbers.

In academic circles, Oxford, Cambridge and Trinity were often mentioned in the same breath, and many English students who failed to make the first two ended up at "Trinners". Women students were admitted in 1903, earlier than in most British universities. Famous alumni include literary figures such as Oscar Wilde, Samuel Beckett, Thomas Moore, Sheridan Le Fanu, John Millington Synge, Oliver St John Gogarty and Bram Stoker. Politicians, rebels and statesmen, among them the likes of Edward Carson, Douglas Hyde (Ireland's first president), Henry Grattan, Wolfe Tone and Robert Emmet also made their mark.

Most of Trinity's buildings date from the 18th century. The entrance is flanked by statues of two of Trinity's many famous alumni, the historian and statesman Edmund Burke (1729–97) and the writer Oliver Goldsmith (1728–74). Goldsmith is missing a pen that he once held, and it is rumoured that the college declined an offer from a well-known pen manufacturer to replace it.

The Berkeley Library, built in 1967, is named after Bishop George Berkeley, the great 18th-century philosopher who came to study at Trinity in 1700 at the age of 15 and later served for a time as the college librarian. Regarded by some as the precursor of Einstein and the father of higher education in America, Berkeley, who was born in Kilkenny, was also a distinguished scientist, economist, psychologist and writer.

He tried unsuccessfully to found a college in Bermuda "for the education of the sons of English planters and of native Indians." He also advised his friend, the American philosopher Samuel Johnson, on the founding of what is now Columbia University of New York, donated his residence to Newhaven College, Connecticut, and helped to found the University of Pennsylvania. The University of Berkeley, California, is named after him. ❑

LEFT: a figure from the 9th-century *Book of Kells*.
ABOVE: statues of two famous alumni, Edmund Burke (top) and Oliver Goldsmith.

in Latin is the centrepiece of an exhibition "Turning Darkness into Light" (tel: 01-896 2320; www.tcd.ie; Mon–Sat 9.30am–5pm year round, Sun Oct–Apr noon–4.30pm, May–Sept 9.30am–4.30pm; charge) and should not be missed. It is the greatest artefact of the flowering of Irish culture between the 7th and 9th centuries, the era when Ireland was famed as "the land of saints and scholars" and Irish monks re-Christianised Europe after the Dark Ages. Also in the library are the *Book of Durrow* (7th-century), the *Book of Dimma* (8th-century) and the *Book of Armagh* (*c.*807). Upstairs is the breathtaking Long Room, nearly 210ft (64 metres) in length and containing 200,000 of the college's oldest books. Temporary exhibitions highlight the library's fine collection.

Grafton Street

Leaving Trinity by the main gate and turning left, you face the mouth of **Grafton Street**, the southside's principal shopping thoroughfare, a pedestrianised street teeming with people and home to a pavement café culture, which is beginning to rival the city's legendary pubs for custom – proof positive of Ireland's European atmosphere. A statue at the junction with Suffolk Street depicts Molly Malone who, in the famous song *In Dublin's Fair City*, "wheeled her wheelbarrow through streets broad and narrow." With typical Dublin wit, the statue was dubbed "the tart with the cart". Worth a visit for its gregarious atmosphere is **Bewley's Oriental Café**, a sprawling but beautifully presented historic spot that lies at the heart of Dublin's social life midway up Grafton Street. The café was recently given an overhaul and houses a popular eating and meeting place, serving breakfast, lunch and dinner. Upstairs the Bewley's Café Theatre is now a hotspot for lunchtime drama and a vibrant evening venue with comedy, jazz and cabaret.

Johnston's Court, a narrow alley off Grafton Street to the right, leads to the rear entrance of the **Powerscourt Centre** ❹, three storeys of stylish shops and cafés under the roof of the former Powerscourt Townhouse, built in 1771–74 for Viscount Powerscourt.

Molly Malone wheels her wheelbarrow in Grafton Street.

BELOW: St Stephen's Green.

TIP

To get about by bike, Cycleways Ltd (Parnell Street; tel: 01-873 4748; www.cycleways.com) offer Globe City bikes for rental, perfect for exploring the city. Irish Cycling Safaris run guided tours throughout Ireland. Contact Belfield Bike Shop, Belfield House, University College, Dublin 4; tel: 01-260 0749; www.cyclingsafaris.com.

St Stephen's Green

On returning to Grafton Street, a right turn and a short walk takes you to the corner of **St Stephen's Green ❺**, a delightful small park bordered by some fine houses, though there has also been some ruinous modern development – particularly on the westside, where the only surviving historic building is the neo-classical Royal College of Surgeons (1806). The green, formerly an open common, was enclosed in 1663, but it was not surrounded by buildings until the late 18th century, when it became very fashionable. The gardens, laid out as a public park in 1880, are a relaxing refuge from the traffic, contain several interesting sculptures and are crammed throughout the summer months with city-weary Dubliners who sprawl out on the lawns picnicking and sunbathing.

On the Green's south side are two elegant Georgian houses: **Newman House**, numbers 85 and 86 (tel: 01-716 7422; June–Aug Tue–Fri, public guided tours at 2pm, 3pm and 4pm; charge) once the seat of the Catholic University of Ireland at which James Joyce, Flann O'Brien and Gerard Manley Hopkins worked or studied; and **Iveagh House**, numbers 80 and 81, which was built for the Bishop of Cork, once housed the Guinness family, and is now part of the Department of Foreign Affairs.

The main attraction of Newman House is its fine interior plasterwork. In 1856 John Henry Newman, the English theologian who was rector at the forerunner of University College Dublin, directed the building next door of **University Church**, designed in a colourful neo-Byzantine style.

On the north side of the Green is the **Shelbourne Hotel ❻**. Built in 1824, the hotel has been an intrinsic part of Dublin's social and cultural life for over 180 years and re-opened in 2007 after an enormous refurbishment. It's now a grand, elegant and exceptionally sumptuous spot, which attracts well-heeled Dubliners to its bars and restaurants. In Earlsfort Terrace, which branches from the southeastern corner of the green, is the **National Concert Hall** *(see Travel Tips page 370)*. The building, beautifully renovated, has first-rate acoustics.

Fans of George Bernard Shaw (1856–1950) can divert about a mile southwest to the **Shaw Birthplace ❼** (tel: 01-475 0854; June–Sept, Tue–Fri 10am–5pm, Sat 2–5pm, closed 1–2pm; charge) at 33 Synge Street. Since Shaw moved to England at the age of 20, there's little here to indicate his writing activities, but the house nicely evokes the domestic world of Victorian Dublin.

Official Dublin

Back on the north side of St Stephen's Green, Kildare Street leads past the left-hand side of the Shelbourne Hotel and a block of modern state buildings to **Leinster House ❽**, built as a townhouse for the Duke of Leinster in 1746 and now home of the Dáil Eireann (Irish parliament). It is flanked by two, nearly symmetrical, edifices with columnar entrance rotundas. These are the National Library and National Museum, both built in 1890.

BELOW: Leinster House.

Apart from more than 500,000 books, the **National Library** ❾ has an extensive collection of old newspapers and periodicals and a gallery housing temporary exhibitions of its collection (tel: 01-603 0200; www.nli.ie; exhibition area Mon–Wed 9.30am–9pm, Thur–Fri 9.30am–5pm, Sat 9.30am–4.30pm). The large, musty reading-room is also well worth a look.

The **National Museum** ❿ (tel: 01-677 7828; www.museum.ie; Tue–Sat 10am–5pm, Sun 2–5pm) has exhibits ranging from prehistory through the early Christian period and the Vikings to the Independence struggle. Exhibits include such treasures as the Ardagh Chalice and the Tara Brooch, plus fine prehistoric gold artefacts.

Directly opposite Leinster House is Molesworth Street, and a few yards along it is **Buswell's Hotel**, a popular haunt among politicians and political journalists. At its far end the street meets Dawson Street, which boasts some stylish shops, as well as the decadent Café en Seine, and the more stylish Ron Black's, with its intimate Champagne Bar.

Turning left at the corner you find **St Anne's Church** (1720), a venue for concerts as well as religious services. A few metres up the street is the **Mansion House** ⓫, the residence since 1715 of the Lord Mayors of Dublin. A Queen Anne-style house, dating from 1705, it was decorated with stucco and cast iron in Victorian times.

Merrion Square

At the other end of Dawson Street (towards Trinity College), you can turn right along Nassau Street which quickly becomes Clare Street, past the Kilkenny shop and Greene's fine old bookshop, into **Merrion Square** ⓬, one of Dublin's finest parks. Laid out in 1762, it has had many distinguished inhabitants; Sir William and Lady "Speranza" Wilde, surgeon and poetess, and parents of Oscar, lived at number 1; Daniel O'Connell lived at number 58; W. B. Yeats, who was born in the seaside suburb of Sandymount

A memorial to Oscar Wilde in Merrion Square.

LEFT AND BELOW: classic Georgian door knocker and doorway in Merrion Square.

TIP

Good or bad art?
Curators at the National Gallery of Ireland hold a picture clinic in the Shaw Room on the first Thursday of the month (except Jan and Aug) from 10am to noon. They appraise paintings, prints and drawings brought in by members of the public. There's no charge.

but grew up mainly in London, lived at number 52 and later at number 83; Sheridan Le Fanu, author of the seminal vampire story Carmilla, lived at number 70. The Duke of Wellington, victor over Napoleon at the Battle of Waterloo, was born at number 24 Merrion Street Upper, which runs off the southwest corner of the square towards Merrion Row and St Stephen's Green. The lush gardens in the square are open to the public and are more recently used in summer for music and performance festivals.

You can access the **National Gallery of Ireland** ⓭ (tel: 01-661 5133; www.nationalgallery.ie; Mon–Sat 9.30am–5.30pm, Thur until 8.30pm, Sun noon–5.30pm, guided tours Sat at 2pm, Sun at 1pm and 2pm; free, charge for exhibitions) at both Merrion Square West, or Clare Street, which houses the beautiful, light-filled Millennium Wing. The statue on the lawn at Merrion Square is of William Dargan, who organised the 1853 Dublin Exhibition on this site and used the profits to found the collection. To the left of the entrance is a statue of George Bernard Shaw, who said he owed his education to the gallery and left it a third of his estate. Apart from a range of Irish work, the gallery has some Dutch masters and fine examples of the 17th-century French, Italian and Spanish schools. The "Amorino" is the work of the Italian sculptor Canova. The Yeats Museum is a tribute to the artistic achievements of the Yeats family, especially Jack B. Yeats. The Millennium Wing houses temporary exhibitions, the gallery shop and the With Taste Café and Restaurant.

Leaving the gallery and turning right up Merrion Street Upper past the lawns of Leinster House, there is a fine view to your left along the southside of Merrion Square towards the distant cupola of St Stephen's Church (1825), known locally as the Pepper Canister.

Passing the **Natural History Museum** on your right (closed for refurbishment, scheduled to reopen in 2012), you reach the imposing gates of **Government Buildings**, which house the office of the Taoiseach (prime minister) and the Cabinet room. Tours are available on Saturdays from 10.30am–1.30pm; tickets are free of charge and are available that morning from the National Gallery.

A left turn at the next intersection along Baggot Street, then a right up Pembroke Street leads to **Fitzwilliam Square** ⓮, the city's smallest, latest (1825) and best-preserved Georgian square. Jack B. Yeats lived at number 18, on the corner of Fitzwilliam Street, the longest Georgian street in Dublin. In an infamous piece of state vandalism, 26 houses on its eastern side were demolished in 1965 to make way for a new Electricity Supply Board HQ. Perhaps out of shame, the ESB helped restore **Number 29**, (tel: 01-702 6165; www.esb.ie/numbertwentynine; Tue–Sat 10am–5pm, Sun noon–5pm; charge) in Fitzwilliam Street Lower, as an elegant middle-class house of the late 1700s.

Wander back now to Trinity College, a good starting point to begin exploring the oldest part of the city.

BELOW: the Natural History Museum.

Temple Bar

With your back to the facade of Trinity and the Bank of Ireland on your right, walk along Dame Street, passing on your right the imposing, layered structure of the modern Central Bank. The network of small streets between the Central Bank and the river quays, known as **Temple Bar** ⓯, has undergone a remarkable renaissance in the past few years to become Dublin's "Left Bank", its cobbled streets full of studios, galleries, second-hand book, clothing and music stores, pubs, clubs, cultural centres, restaurants and craft shops. This is a buzzy area of Dublin, the streets are thronged with tourists in the summer and on Saturday nights the main street feels like a Disneyland of Irishness. The pubs are constantly packed, but most Dubliners now give Temple Bar a wide berth, preferring to socialise in the city's less overtly "touristy" areas.

There's no "best route" through Temple Bar; it's essentially a place for browsing. The area's renewal has been planned around two new public squares: Temple Bar Square, a meeting point for shoppers, and Meeting House Square, a cultural centre and performance space, which still draws the locals for its excellent Saturday farmers' market as well as its outdoor cinema events.

Just off Temple Bar Square, Merchant's Arch – a favourite spot for buskers – leads to the river quay and the **Ha'penny Bridge** ⓰ (1816) – so-called because of the toll once charged for crossing it. This cast-iron pedestrian walkway across the Liffey has become one of the best-known symbols of the city. It is a valuable link between Temple Bar and the bustling shopping streets of the Henry Street area across the river. Further west a companion footbridge spans the Liffey between the Ormond Quay and Wellington Quay.

The route from Temple Bar Square to Meeting House Square goes through **Curved Street**, which houses the **Temple Bar Music Centre**, a training centre/workshop and concert venue (www.tbmc.ie). You emerge in Eustace Street, which contains the **Ark**, a cultural centre for children (www.ark.ie).

Just up the street from the Ark, a covered passageway leads into **Meeting House Square**.

To one side of it are two of the area's main cultural attractions: the **Irish Film Institute** – an art-house cinema with a bookshop, café/restaurant, bar and film archive (www.ifi.ie) – and the **Gallery of Photography**, which shows both Irish and international work and has an interesting range of postcards

Pub entertainment in Temple Bar.

BELOW: the quirky Temple Bar area.

Temple Bar almost became a bus station. CIE, the state transport company, had bought up most of the buildings in the area and rented them out until it was ready to demolish them. Small shops and art galleries were among the renters, and an effective campaign was launched to build on their success and turn the area into a cultural quarter.

and books (www.galleryofphotography.ie). Just off the other side of the square is the Temple Bar Cultural Trust (tel: 01-677 2255; www.temple-bar.ie; useful for details of current events).

Continuing along Essex Street East, you pass the rear of the **Clarence Hotel** *(see Travel Tips page 357)*, which fronts onto the river quay. The hotel's current owners include members of the U2 rock band, and its stylish Octagon Bar is a fashionable meeting place.

At the riverside end of Parliament Street is **Sunlight Chambers**, a building with a beautiful Victorian frieze displaying the world according to the priorities of Lever Bros, soap manufacturers: men's toil makes clothes dirty, women's toil (and Sunlight Soap) makes them clean again!

Ancient Dublin

Venture across Parliament Street and down Essex Street into the quieter Old City section of Temple Bar and you'll find a more elegant and less-travelled path. Here there's a good collection of chi-chi interiors shops and small boutiques, as well as the hip Cow's Lane Designer Mart market, which takes place every Saturday.

Essex Street ends at its junction with **Fishamble Street**, the medieval "fish shambles", or market, whose existence can be traced back to 1467 and which winds upwards from the quay alongside the Civic Offices.

Back on Dame Street, opposite City Hall, you see on your right the ornate Victorian doorway of the **Olympia Theatre** 17. Despite its modest frontage, it is Dublin's largest theatre; its programme mixes plays, musicals and rock concerts.

City Hall

Dublin's medieval city once occupied the area between City Hall and Bridge Street, bordered by the riverbank to the north and defensive walls, which stretched as far as Bride Street in the south. **City Hall** 18 (tel: 01-222 2204; www.dublincity.ie; Mon–Sat 10am–5.15pm, Sun 2–5pm; charge) was designed in 1769 as the Royal Exchange by the London architect Thomas Cooley (who won a £100 prize for the plan) and served as a prison for

BELOW: one of Temple Bar's more extravagantly decorated pubs.

The *Messiah's* birth

The otherwise unprepossessing Fishamble Street is celebrated as the venue of the first performance of Handel's *Messiah*, conducted by the composer in 1742 in the Charitable Music Society's Hall, long since demolished. Because the hall was cramped and the attendance large, ladies were asked not to wear hooped petticoats and gentlemen not to wear their swords. *Messiah* was an instant success in Dublin, though London audiences remained cool towards it for several years. A hotel, named after the composer, stands beside the original site, and the *Messiah*'s birth is celebrated at this spot by a statue of the composer (in the nude) and at noon every 13 April by members of Our Lady's Choral Society (fully clothed), who sing a selection of choruses.

rebels in 1798, as a military depot and as a corn exchange, before being taken over by the Corporation of Dublin in 1852. The entrance rotunda has a splendid illuminated dome. On the mosaic floor is the city's coat of arms, with the rubric in Latin, "Happy the city where citizens obey" – not perhaps the most apposite motto for Dubliners. The exhibition The Story of the Capital is housed in the restored vaults of City Hall, and tells the story of Dublin through the ages.

Dublin Castle

Dublin Castle 19 (tel: 01-645 8813; www.dublincastle.ie; Mon–Sat 10am–4.45pm, Sun and public holidays 2–4.45pm; guided tours; charge), just behind City Hall, was built between 1208 and 1220 on the site of an earlier Danish fortress and was the symbol of English rule in Ireland for almost eight centuries. The building as it now stands is mainly 18th-century; the largest visible remain of the Norman structure is the Record Tower, in the lower Castle Yard, which contains the Garda (Police) Museum.

Dublin Castle.

The Bermingham Tower, tallest in the castle, was originally early 15th-century, but was rebuilt after an explosion in 1775. Many celebrated rebels were imprisoned here over the years, including Red Hugh O'Donnell and Henry and Art O'Neill, who escaped on Christmas Eve, 1591.

The most impressive parts of the castle are the **State Apartments** (viewed by guided tour only) – St Patrick's Hall, 82ft (25 metres) long and 40ft (12 metres) wide, with a high panelled and decorated ceiling, is probably the grandest room in Ireland. It was used by the British for various state functions and since 1938 has been the scene of the inauguration of Irish

BELOW: Dublin Castle's State Apartments.

Sir Alfred Chester Beatty was born in New York in 1875 and became a successful mining engineer in Colorado. Having collected minerals and Chinese snuff bottles as a child, he became interested in Japanese and Chinese paintings. His knighthood was a reward for his help in supplying raw materials to the Allies in World War II. He moved to Ireland in 1950 and built a library to house his art collection.

presidents. The Gothic-style Church of the Most Holy Trinity was built as the Chapel Royal between 1807 and 1814 to a design by Francis Johnston; it was taken over by the Catholic Church in 1943. The exterior is decorated with more than 90 carved heads of English monarchs and other historical figures.

To the castle's rear the Clocktower building has been extended to accommodate the award-winning **Chester Beatty Library** ⓴ (tel: 01-407 0750; www.cbl.ie; Oct–Apr Tue–Fri 10am–5pm, May–Sept Mon–Fri 10am–5pm, Sat 11am–5pm all year, Sun 1–5pm all year; free). The library has a fine collection of Chinese, Japanese, Persian, Indian and Middle Eastern manuscripts, paintings and ornaments. Audio-visual programmes provide background. It also houses the first-class Silk Road Café.

Leaving the castle, head a short way down Dame Street towards Trinity College and turn right up busy South Great George's Street; on the left side is a Victorian shopping arcade containing many interesting and colourful shops and stalls.

BELOW: the Chester Beatty Library.

Continuing into Aungier Street, you see on your right the **Church of the Carmelite Fathers**, the only church in Dublin to be re-established on its pre-Reformation site – the order had a church here in the 13th century. Thomas Moore, the 19th-century poet and songwriter, was born at number 12 Aungier Street. John Field, Ireland's greatest composer and pianist, was born nearby in Golden Lane in 1782. He created the nocturne and originated the style of romantic pianism, which culminated in Chopin's work.

Continue now into Wexford Street, turn right, and cross New Bride Street into Kevin Street Upper, where you find **Marsh's Library** ㉑ (tel: 01-454 3511; www.marshlibrary.ie; Mon and Wed–Fri 10am–1pm and 2–5pm, Sat 10.30am–1pm; charge), the oldest public library in Ireland and named after its founder, Archbishop Narcissus Marsh (1638–1713). Among its 25,000 interesting items is Jonathan Swift's copy of Clarendon's *History of the Great Rebellion*, with Swift's pencilled notes.

The Liberties

The next junction marks the beginning of the **Liberties**, an area so named because it lay outside the jurisdiction of medieval Dublin. One of the city's oldest and most characterful working-class areas, it was also filled with some of the worst 19th-century slum tenements. The Liberties is now on the list for a spot of urban regeneration so it's only a matter of time before the rich professionals move in. The Coombe road, which runs westward into the Liberties, was once the "coomb" (river valley) of the Poddle.

Make a note to sample the character of the Liberties another time and turn right along Patrick Street to **St Patrick's Cathedral** ㉒ (tel: 01-453 9472; www.stpatrickscathedral.ie; Mar–Oct daily 9am–5.30pm, Nov–Feb Mon–Sat 9am–5pm, Sun 9am–3pm; charge). Dedicated in 1192, St Patrick's has been restored many times and, like Dublin's other cathedral,

Christ Church, has belonged to the Church of Ireland since the Reformation. Jonathan Swift, Dean from 1713 to 1745, is buried in it, near his beloved "Stella", Esther Johnson. "Living Stones", a permanent exhibition, explores the history of the cathedral.

Continue now along Patrick Street and then Nicholas Street to **Christ Church Cathedral** ㉓ (tel: 01-677 8099; www.cccdub.ie; mid July–Aug Mon–Fri 9.45am–6.15pm, Sat 9.45am–4.15pm, Sun 12.30–2.30pm, 4.30–6.15pm, June–mid-July Mon–Tue, Fri 9.45am–6.15pm, Wed–Thur, Sat 9.45am–4.15pm, Sun 12.30–2.30pm, 4.30–6.15pm, Sept–May Mon–Sat 9.45am–4.15pm, Sun 12.30–4.30pm; charge). This prominent cathedral was founded by Sitric, the Danish King of Dublin, about 1040, and greatly expanded from 1172 onwards under the aegis of Strongbow and St Laurence O'Toole. The central tower was built about 1600 after storm and fire damage to the original steeples. Lambert Simnel, 10-year-old pretender to the English throne, was crowned here by his supporters in 1487. Christ Church became Protestant in 1551, though the Mass was restored for a short period under James II. The structure was greatly rebuilt in Gothic revival style in the 1870s. Two of the cathedral's many tombs are said to be those of Strongbow and his son, whom, according to legend, he executed for cowardice in battle.

Linked to the cathedral by a covered bridge is **Dublinia & The Viking World** ㉔ (tel: 01-679 4611; www.dublinia.ie; daily 10am–5pm, last admission 4.15pm Apr–Sept, 4pm Oct–Mar; charge), an exhibition, run by the non-profit Medieval Trust and given an overhaul, which was completed in 2009. State-of-the-art interactives and reconstructions give an insight into the medieval world of Dublin. There is also an archaeological lab and excavation site, and an exhibition of what life was like aboard a Viking warship. From the top of the 200ft (60-metre) St Michael's Tower, you can enjoy a

Stained-glass window, Christ Church Cathedral.

LEFT AND BELOW: Christ Church Cathedral.

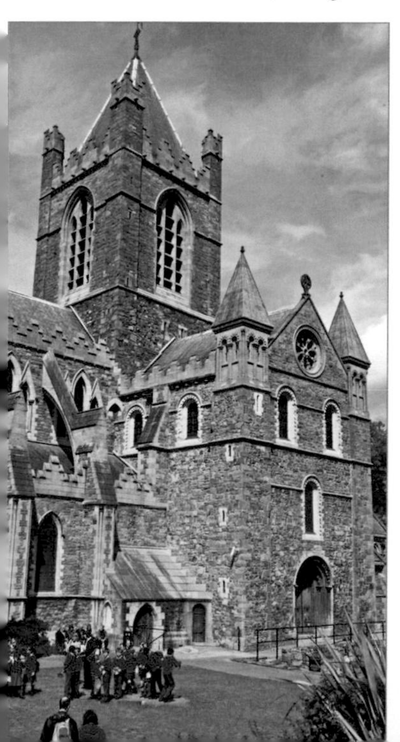

The toucan, Guinness's longtime symbol.

panoramic view over the city. Admission to Dublinia includes discounted admission to the cathedral via the bridge, but you can also enter Christ Church directly. Across the river to your left is the stately dome of the Four Courts (*see page 134*); save it for a later tour.

St Audoen's Church

High Street, which runs off the west side of Christchurch Place, was the backbone of medieval Dublin. Part of the old city wall and the only surviving city gate has been uncovered near the partially ruined **St Audoen's Church** 25 (tel: 01-677 0088; May–Oct daily 9.30am–5.30pm; free). It was named by the Normans after St Ouen of Rouen. Its aisle contains a font dating from 1194; the tower is 12th-century and three of its bells were cast in the early 15th century, making them the country's oldest.

On the other side of High Street, in Back Lane, is **Tailors' Hall**, the only surviving guild hall in Dublin, and now the offices of An Taisce, which works to preserve the country's natural and architectural heritage.

The Guinness tour

One part of the national heritage which seems well able to look after itself is enshrined half-a-mile (1km) to the west along Thomas Street: **Guinness's Brewery**, the biggest in Europe, churning out 2½ million pints of its celebrated black stout every day. The brewery doesn't admit visitors, but the **Guinness Storehouse** 26 (tel: 01-408 4800; www.guinness-storehouse.com; daily 9.30am–5pm, July–Aug 9.30am–7pm; charge, discounts on tickets available online) lets you explore – through sight, touch, taste and smell – the making and history of the world's most famous stout. The building also houses gallery and exhibition areas, events venues, an archives room and the **Gravity Bar**, the highest bar in Dublin with an incredible panoramic view of the city. The admission ticket entitles you to a complimentary pint in the rooftop bar – probably the best-

BELOW: break for a drink at the end of the Guinness Storehouse tour.

tasting Guinness to be had anywhere, since it hasn't had to travel.

If you don't feel like walking quite so far for a drink, you may enjoy a visit to the **Brazen Head**, nearer at hand in Bridge Street. There is said to have been a tavern on this site since Viking times, though the present premises date from only 1688. It was once a meeting place for the United Irishmen, and makes a nice place for a pint on balmy summer evenings, or on cold winter days when you can snuggle up inside. On your way back to O'Connell Street Bridge, you could cross over the narrow, arching footpath of the "Ha'penny Bridge", from which there are fine river views, especially at sunset. Alternatively, you can use its much newer neighbour, the Millennium Bridge.

North of the Liffey

O'Connell Bridge is once more your starting-point to explore Dublin's northern half, but before acquainting yourself with the main features of O'Connell Street, stay a little longer on the southside, walking east along Burgh Quay and under the railway bridge for a view across the river to the **Custom House** ㉗, one of the masterpieces of James Gandon, the greatest architect of 18th-century Dublin. Although English, Gandon looked to the Continent for architectural models and it is easier to imagine the Custom House transposed to the banks of the Seine than to the Thames.

Finished in 1791, the building was extensively damaged in a fire started by Republicans to mark the Sinn Féin election victory in 1921 and has been largely rebuilt. The central copper dome, 120ft (38 metres) high, is topped by a statue of commerce by Edward Smyth. The keystones over the arched doorways flanking the Doric portico represent the Atlantic Ocean and 13 principal rivers of Ireland.

Gandon later designed Carlisle Bridge (widened and rebuilt in 1880 and renamed O'Connell Bridge), the Four Courts, the eastern portico of Parliament House (Bank of Ireland) and the King's Inns.

The gleaming new building just downstream of the Custom House is the Irish Financial Services Centre (known as the IFSC), erected in the late 1980s, this area has been aggressively developed into Dublin's financial district but there's still room for the city's social and cultural life to flourish here with the restaurants, bars and shopping outlets that are spreading along both sides of the Liffey in the Docklands development.

The tall, nasty-looking 1960s building – one of Dublin's only skyscrapers – a little way upstream of the Custom House is **Liberty Hall** ㉘, headquarters of the country's largest trade union, the Services, Industrial, Professional and Technical Union. Its more modest predecessor was a nerve-centre of the labour struggle. At the far end of the place is the Busaras (central bus station), a daring work by Dublin stand-

One of a group of statues by the Custom House marking the Great Famine of the 1840s.

BELOW: the Custom House.

TIP

Cross the Liffey river over the Samuel Beckett bridge, opened in January 2010, to the south side to find newly developed Grand Canal Quay. Here, in the futuristic piazza, is the Grand Canal Theatre (capacity 2,000); the stunning design is by renowned architect Daniel Libeskind. The regenerated dockland district is continuing to attract trendy restaurants. From the square, head south along the canal to join the Grand Canal for a peaceful wander by the water's edge.

ards when built in 1953. More recently it has been described, rather unfairly, as a "hideous edifice".

The Abbey Theatre

Walk towards O'Connell Bridge along the north bank and turn into Marlborough Street, where you find the **Abbey Theatre** ㉙, Ireland's national playhouse (www.abbeytheatre.ie). The present building was erected in 1966 to replace a predecessor which was destroyed by fire.

The Abbey, founded in 1904 by W. B. Yeats, Lady Gregory and their collaborators, played a vital role in the cultural renaissance of the time and earned a world reputation through the great works of John Millington Synge and Sean O'Casey and for its players' naturalistic acting style. Performances were often turbulent: the most celebrated uproar was caused at a performance of Synge's *The Playboy of the Western World* by the use of the word "shift" (petticoat). Downstairs in the Abbey its sister theatre, the **Peacock**, is used to showcase more experimental work.

O'Connell Street

O'Connell Street ㉚ itself is not what it was. The latter-day rash of fast-food joints, amusement arcades, ugly modern buildings, billboards and neons signs may still darken its beauty, but there's been a concerted effort to upgrade this elegant street and generally give it a "face-lift". Broad and impressive, the street was planned (as Sackville Street) in the mid-1700s by the first Viscount Mountjoy, Luke Gardiner, who widened the existing narrow roadway, Drogheda Street, and planted trees on a central mall.

In 1794, the construction of Carlisle Bridge turned it from a fashionable residential promenade into the city's main north-south artery. A tall column surmounted by a statue of Horatio Nelson, like that in London's Trafalgar Square, was erected in 1815 to mark the famous sea victory over Napoleon; republicans blew it up, neatly, by an explosion one night in 1966 to mark the 50th anniversary of the Easter Rising.

Reaching to the sky is the **Spire of Dublin**, an aspirational and strangely

BELOW: the General Post Office, central to the 1916 Rising.

Key to the statues

The statues lining the centre of O'Connell Street are (from the bridge end): Daniel O'Connell (1775–1847), a great leader of constitutional nationalism; William Smith O'Brien (1803–64), leader of the Young Ireland Party; Sir John Gay (1816–75), proprietor of the *Freeman's Journal* (published 1763–1924) and organiser of the city's water supply; James Larkin (1876–1947), a famous trade union leader and co-founder of the Irish Labour Party; Father Theobald Mathew (1790–1856), the "Apostle of Temperance"; and Charles Stewart Parnell (1846–91), inspiration of the Home Rule movement and a tragic victim of intolerance whose career was ruined by the outcry over his union with Kitty O'Shea, who happened to be married to another Irish politician.

beautiful 390ft (120-metre) stainless steel pillar, which was given a variety of monikers including "the Stiffy by the Liffey" and "the Stiletto in the Ghetto".

Centrepiece of the street is the imposing Ionic portico of the **General Post Office** ㉛ (1815), headquarters of the 1916 Rising and the place where the rebels proclaimed the republic in ringing terms, to the initial bemusement of Dubliners – a reaction, in Yeats's words, "changed utterly" by the subsequent execution, one by one, of 15 captured leaders. The GPO's pillars are still pockmarked by bullets; although the building survived the fighting, much of the street was wrecked by British artillery and it suffered further in 1922 during the Civil War.

But those struggles are not the principal cause of O'Connell Street's fall from grace: it was rebuilt well enough in the 1920s but, as the journalist Frank McDonald wrote in *The Destruction of Dublin*, "the dignified and noble facades... got scant attention from the developers who descended on the street during the late 1960s and early 1970s." In McDonald's angry words: "This magnificent thoroughfare could have become Dublin's answer to the Champs Elysées, lined with fashionable shops and terrace cafés where people could sit and watch the world go by. Instead, the capital's main street was transformed into a honky-tonk freeway, cluttered with fast-food joints, slot-machine casinos, ugly modern office blocks, vacant buildings and even the odd derelict site." Things are now changing and O'Connell Street is generally scrubbing up well with increased pedestrianised areas and a defiantly less-shabby air to it, but there's still a way to go.

Moore Street market

Off O'Connell Street, just past the GPO, Henry Street is the northside's main shopping street. Its tributary to the north, **Moore Street**, is filled with fruit and vegetable stalls staffed by colourful and vociferous women. It is packed with a hive of ethnic food outlets and hair and beauty stores to cater for Dublin's burgeoning immigrant population. It's well worth visiting for a dose of down-to-earth Dublin, as well as Ireland's new multi-culturalism, and there are some great no-frills Chinese restaurants hidden beneath Mandarin-scripted signs.

On the opposite side of O'Connell Street, walk down Earl Street and turn left into Marlborough Street to visit **St Mary's Pro-Cathedral** ㉜ (1816–25), the city's main Catholic Church. John Henry Newman first publicly professed Catholicism here in 1851. The area was once a notorious red-light district, known as "Monto" (James Joyce's "Nighttown").

At the north end of O'Connell Street are the late 18th-century **Rotunda Rooms**, occupied in recent years by a cinema, and now a music venue. The **Rotunda Hospital** to the left (Europe's first maternity hospital) was financed by concerts in the Rooms. Built in conjunction with the hospital, the **Gate Theatre** at the bottom of Parnell Square East was founded in 1928

This life-size statue of James Joyce stands on North Earl Street, off O'Connell Street.

BELOW: the stainless-steel Spire on O'Connell Street.

ABOVE AND BELOW: Moore Street market.

by Micheál MacLiammóir and Hilton Edwards; the teenage Orson Welles made his first professional appearance here (www.gate-theatre.ie).

A few yards on past the Gate, the **Garden of Remembrance** (1966) commemorates Ireland's martyrs. The sculpture by Oisin Kelly, beyond the central lake, is based on the myth of the Children of Lir, who were turned into swans.

Modern art

On the northside of Parnell Square is the **Dublin City Art Gallery, The Hugh Lane** 33 (tel: 01-222 5550; www.hughlane.ie; Tue–Thur 10am–6pm, Fri–Sat 10am–5pm, Sun 11am–5pm; free). Its nucleus is formed by the mainly Impressionist collection of Sir Hugh Lane, who died when the liner *Lusitania* was torpedoed in 1915. As a result of a wrangle over his will, the collection was split, each half being alternated every five years between Dublin and London's Tate Gallery. In 1998 the gallery employed a team of archaeologists to painstakingly dismantle the London studio of Dublin-born artist Francis Bacon and faithfully reconstruct it here.

At 18–19 Parnell Square North, the **Dublin Writers Museum** 34 (tel: 01-872 2077; www.writersmuseum.com; Mon–Sat 10am–5pm, June–Aug until 6pm, Sun 11am–5pm; charge) displays photographs, paintings, busts, letters, manuscripts, first editions and other memorabilia relating to celebrated deceased writers such as Swift, Shaw, Yeats, O'Casey, Joyce, Beckett and Behan. The first-floor Gallery of Writers is splendidly decorated.

Parnell Street was always a bit of a rough-and-tumble type of spot with an atmosphere of urban degradation and some seriously dodgy pubs, but Dublin's growing community and Chinese business leaders are hoping to transform the street into Dublin's official Chinatown or China Village as it is known here, with a Chinese archway flanked by golden dragons. A Chinese New Year festival is held in the city annually.

At Parnell Square East, turn left and then right into Great Denmark Street. On the left is **Belvedere College** 35, a fine 18th-century mansion, which has been the Jesuit Belvedere College since 1841. James Joyce, who was a pupil here, described its atmosphere in *Portrait of the Artist as a Young Man*.

James Joyce Centre

Turn into North Great George's Street, where many grand Georgian houses have been saved from decades of decrepitude. At number 35 is the **James Joyce Centre** ㊱ (tel: 01-878 8547; www.jamesjoyce.ie; year round Tue–Sat 10am–5pm; charge, tours must be pre-booked). This addition to the literary tourist trail is located in a beautifully restored late 18th-century townhouse which features in *Ulysses* as the venue for dancing classes. The centre's most interesting exhibit is a set of biographies of real Dublin people fictionalised in Joyce's masterpiece. There are photographs and storyboards about Joyce's family and the many homes they inhabited. And, in a suitably Joycean collision of fact and fiction, you can view the front door of No. 7 Eccles Street, home of Leopold Bloom and his wife Molly, the central characters of *Ulysses* (the house itself was demolished). The centre's interior has splendid stucco ceilings.

Returning past the Hugh Lane Gallery to Parnell Square West, turn right, then left into Bolton Street, then right again at Henrietta Street, the oldest and once, it is said, the finest of the city's Georgian streets, the home of archbishops, peers and Members of Parliament. It is now mostly decrepit. At its far end are the **King's Inns** ㊲, the Dublin inns of court, where, in the English tradition, newly qualified barristers must eat a prescribed number of meals. The building was designed by Gandon at the turn of the 19th century (tours by appointment only; tel: 01-874 4840).

Continue down Bolton Street bearing left into Capel Street. To the left in Mary Street is **St Mary's Church** ㊳, built from 1697 by Thomas Burgh, architect of Trinity College library.

Where writers are remembered.

Here, in 1747, John Wesley preached his first sermon in Ireland. Theobald Wolfe Tone (1763–98), founder of the United Irishmen and father of Irish republicanism, was born nearby in a street now named after him.

St Michan's

To the other side of Capel Street, Mary Street leads via Mary's Lane to Church Street, where you find **St Michan's Church** ㊴, (Mon–Sat; charge for tour of vaults) founded in 1095 as a Viking parish church. The present structure dates from the late 1600s, but it was much restored in 1821 and again after the Civil War. Handel is said to have played on its organ.

In the vaults are 17th-century mummified bodies, preserved because the

BELOW: the hosts of a nightly literary pub crawl put a strong emphasis on Joyce's Dublin.

St Michan's Church contains 17th-century mummified bodies.

limestone walls absorb moisture from the air.

Leaving the church, turn down May Lane and left into Bow Street which will bring you to the **Old Jameson Distillery** (www.jamesonwhiskey.com; daily 9am–5.15pm, tours are continuous), a museum sited in the old warehouse of the 1791 whiskey factory.

A small lane will then take you to **Smithfield village**. Its distinctive architecture includes the distillery's 175ft (53-metre) chimney built in 1895 and now a viewing platform, accessible by glass lift, giving panoramic views (closed for maintenance at time of writing).

The Four Courts

Return to the quays and turn left to end this section of the tour as you began it: with a look at a Gandon masterpiece. The **Four Courts** ⓾ (visitors can witness most court proceedings, Mon–Fri 10am–1pm, 2–4pm) was built between 1786 and 1802. The dominant lantern-dome is fronted by a six-columned Corinthian portico surmounted by the statues of Moses, Justice and Mercy, and flanked by two wings enclosing courtyards.

In 1922, after the building was barricaded by anti-Treaty republicans, troops of Michael Collins's new government shelled it from across the river. In the ensuing fire, the Record Office was burnt, destroying priceless documents. Restoration was completed in 1932.

West Dublin

Board the westbound Red Line of LUAS at the rear of the Four Courts. After three quick stops, you'll be at Heuston Station.

From here it is only a five-minute walk west along St John's Road before turning north onto Military Road and the entrance to **Kilmainham Royal Hospital**, founded by Charles II (1680–84) "for the reception and entertainment of antient (sic) maimed, and infirm officers and soldiers." It's a beautiful French-style building with

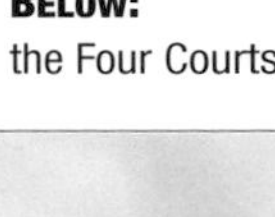

BELOW: the Four Courts.

exquisite grounds and now houses the **Irish Museum of Modern Art** ❹❶ (tel: 01-612 9900; www.imma.ie; Tue–Sat 10am–5.30pm, Wed 10.30am–5.30pm, Sun noon–5.30pm; free, charge for special exhibitions), which combines Irish and international 20th-century art with various educational and community programmes and performing arts. The permanent collection is patchy, but the temporary exhibitions can be interesting.

There's a nice café here and beautiful formal gardens that are a pleasure to lounge around in summer.

Kilmainham Gaol

Exit the museum the way you came in, a right turn onto Military Road and a right again onto Bow Bridge brings you to the South Circular Road and **Kilmainham Gaol** ❹❷ (tel: 01-453 5984; Apr–Sept daily 9.30am–6pm, Oct–Mar Mon–Sat 9.30am–5.30pm, Sun 10am–6pm; charge), which has been intimately connected with Ireland's struggle for independence from its construction in the 1790s until it ceased to be a prison in the 1920s. Visitors are invited to browse in the museum, which explores 19th-century notions of crime, punishment and reform through a series of well-captioned displays. The upstairs section is devoted to the nationalist figures, some famous, some more obscure, who were imprisoned here, many awaiting execution.

A guide then leads visitors into the vaulted east wing of the jail, with its tiers of cells and overhead catwalks, and upstairs to the prison chapel, where an excellent audio-visual summary of the nationalist struggle is shown. Visitors are then brought to the "1916 corridor", containing the cells that housed the captured leaders of the Rising, and finally led to the stone-breakers' yard where 14 of them were shot between 3 and 12 May of that year. Well worth a visit.

If you prefer a walk in the park to time in jail, turn left on Bow Lane from Military Road and left again on **Steeven's Lane.** Head past Heuston Station and cross the river to visit **Phoenix Park** ❹❸, whose southern boundary extends west on the Liffey's

After a bloody past, Kilmainham Gaol became a popular film location. Interior scenes for the prison in which Noël Coward planned his heist in The Italian Job *(1969) were shot here. So were scenes from* In the Name of the Father *(1993),* Michael Collins *(1996) and* Boondock Saints *(1999). Execution scenes for the TV mini series* The Tudors *(2007) were also filmed here.*

BELOW: Kilmainham Gaol.

The former Collins Barracks has been transformed into an outpost of the National Museum.

north bank for about 3 miles (5km). At 1,760 acres (712 hectares), it is over five times as large as London's Hyde Park. Its name is a corruption of the Gaelic fionn uisce ("clear water").

Among its features, all signposted, are: the Wellington Monument, an obelisk 197ft (60 metres) high, erected after Waterloo; Dublin Zoo (www.dublinzoo.ie), the third oldest public zoo in the world (1830), well known for the breeding of lions (it supplied the MGM announcer); the President's residence, Aras an Uachtaráin, formerly the Viceregal Lodge (1751–54); the US Ambassador's residence; and the "15 acres", an open space actually of 200 acres (81 hectares) containing playing fields – an 18th-century duelling ground.

On the way back to the city, on the north side of the quays, is the former Collins Barracks, now the **National Museum of Decorative Arts and History** 44 with displays of Irish silver, glassware, musical instruments and Japanese art (tel: 01-6777 7444; www.museum.ie; Tue–Sat 10am–5pm, Sun 2–5pm).

BELOW: showing the Irish at war at the National Museum of Decorative Arts and History.

Southside suburbs

Most places mentioned in this section of the book are served by various buses departing from Eden Quay, beside O'Connell Bridge, and by the DART suburban trains.

Travelling out through Merrion Square North, along Northumberland Road past the squat, circular block of the **American Embassy** (1964), you reach the prestigious suburb of **Ballsbridge** 45, named after the bridge over the River Dodder. The large greystone buildings to the right on Merrion Road, just past the bridge, are the headquarters of the Royal Dublin Society ("the RDS"; www.rds.ie), the sponsor of improvements in agriculture and stock breeding and the venue for the Dublin Horse Show (in August). The RDS's Simmonscourt Extension is used for exhibitions and concerts.

The main road south soon skirts the coast, affording fine views of the bay, and passes through **Blackrock** 46, where Eamon de Valera studied and later taught at the boys' college.

Dun Laoghaire

A couple of miles further on is the town and port of **Dun Laoghaire** 47 (pronounced *Dunleery*), departure point for ferries to Britain. The harbour, with its long, granite piers, was built between 1817 and 1859 and is exceptionally popular with locals right throughout the year. The pier is particularly beautiful on a summer's day when the sea twinkles and the views of craggy Howth are especially clear.

The next promontory, within easy walking distance, is that of **Sandycove**, with its Martello Tower where Joyce lived for a short time in 1904. He used it as the setting for the opening scene of *Ulysses* and it is now the **James Joyce Museum** ⓸⓼ (tel: 01-280 9265; Apr–Sept Tue–Sat 10am–5pm, Sun 2–6pm, closed between 1–2pm). The Forty Foot bathing place has been a popular spot for nude male bathers for years, but now the naked bits are covered up and swimmers of all ages come to plunge into the waters right throughout the year.

Dalkey

Just a 20-minute walk from Sandycove is the affluent and charming village of **Dalkey** ⓸⓽. **Dalkey Castle** (tel: 01-285 8366), a medieval tower house, has been restored and houses a heritage centre. Its battlements give excellent views of the surrounding land and seascape.

From nearby Coliemore Harbour there are summer boat trips to Dalkey Island, a stone's throw offshore; it contains another Martello tower and the ruins of a Benedictine church. The island is a bird sanctuary and the waters are rich with seals.

From Vico Road, which continues along the coast, you can enter Killiney Hill Park; motorists should drive instead up Dalkey Avenue, to the public car-park.

At the summit of the park is a Victorian obelisk commanding splendid views of the broad sweep of Killiney Bay (often likened to the Bay of Naples), Bray Head (the humpbacked promontory at its far side) and the two Sugar Loaf Mountains. DART travellers can easily continue on to **Bray** ⓹⓪; as a seaside resort it has seen better days, but the seascapes en route are impressive and Bray Head offers bracing walks and fine views to the south.

Northern suburbs

The attractions of the northside are more diffuse. But it's worth visiting the suburb of **Glasnevin** ⓹⓵ (buses 13 and 19 from O'Connell Street) to see the beautifully arranged **Botanic Gardens** (tel: 01-804 0300; www.botanicgardens.ie; daily, summer 9am–6pm, winter 9am–4.30pm; free, charge for guided tours). These are in the former demesne of Joseph Addison, the English essayist and founder of *The Spectator* magazine

The lighthouse at Dun Laoghaire.

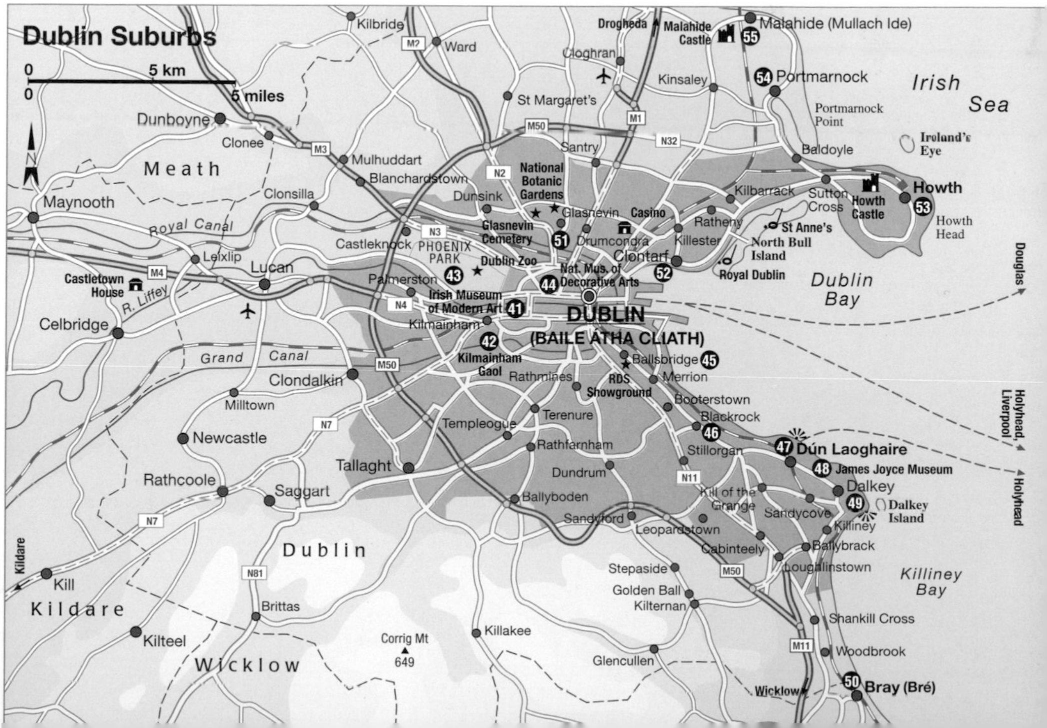

Dublin Suburbs

Glasnevin Cemetery.

BELOW: 90-minute tours of Glasnevin Cemetery are held on Wednesdays and Fridays at 2.30pm.

who lived in Dublin as secretary to the Earl of Sutherland.

Glasnevin Cemetery (tel: 01-830 1133; www.glasnevintrust.ie), the Republic's national burying ground, contains the remains of Daniel O'Connell, Eamon DeValera, Michael Collins, Brendan Behan and many others.

Clontarf

The coastal route northeast by the Custom House leads past Fairview Park to the middle-class enclave of **Clontarf** 52 site of the battle in 1014 in which Brian Ború defeated the Danes. Malahide Road branches off to the left and to the left again is the recently restored Casino, Marino, once part of the seaside estate of Lord Charlemont, whose town house is now the Hugh Lane Gallery. It is a small Palladian building, a gem of its kind, with several unusual features: the roof urns are actually chimneys and the columns are hollow, serving as drains.

Beyond Clontarf the coast road passes the **North Bull Island**, a huge sandbank growing from the North Wall of Dublin Port and containing two golf courses: St Anne's (www.stanneslinksgolf.com) and the

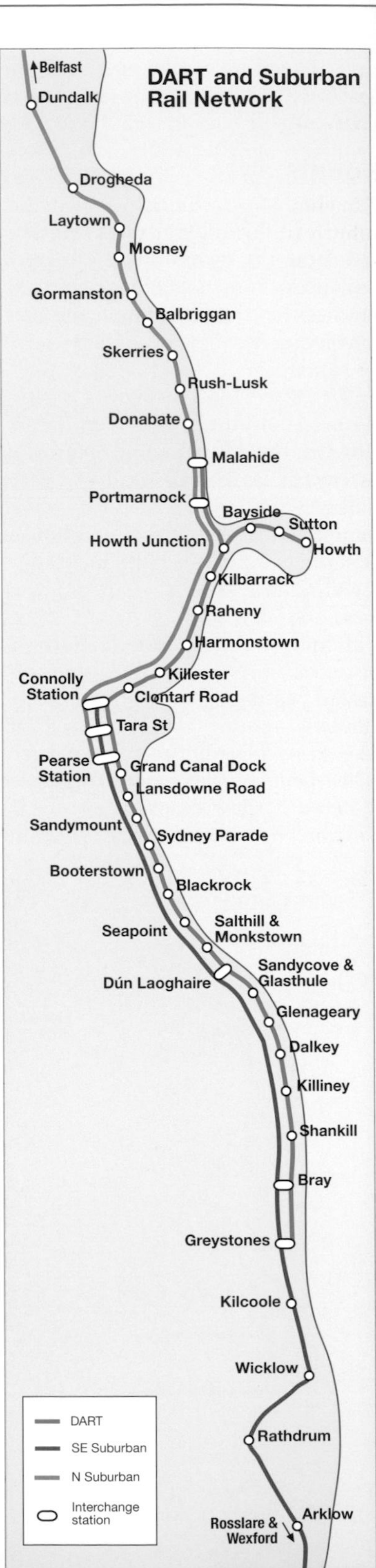

famous Royal Dublin (www.theroyaldublingolfclub.com). It is also an important sanctuary for winter migrant birds.

Howth

Carrying on via the isthmus at the suburb of Sutton you reach **Howth Head** (also accessible by DART and bus), whose rugged brow overlooks the northern entrance to Dublin Bay. You can go directly to the village of **Howth** 53 or start instead at The Summit and walk to the village around the nose of the promontory by a splendidly scenic cliff path, which descends steeply to the fishing harbour. The novelist H.G. Wells called the view from the head "one of the most beautiful in the world." The offshore island of **Ireland's Eye** was the site of a 6th-century monastery and is now a bird sanctuary. Howth, along with Malahide, is the most fashionable place to live on the northside, and it is easy to see why. The gardens at nearby Howth Castle are beautiful, especially if you like rhododendrons.

Five miles (8km) north of Howth lies the resort of **Portmarnock** 54, which has fine beaches and a championship golf course (www.portmarnockgolfclub.ie). West of here is St Doulagh's Church, claimed to be the oldest still in use in Ireland; its high-pitched stone roof is 12th-century. Doulagh Lodge, nearby, was the home of the landscape painter, Nathaniel Hone (1831–1917).

A crowded harbour at Howth village.

At **Malahide** 55, a pleasant resort and dormitory town 7 miles (11km) north of Howth, is **Malahide Castle** (daily; charge), inhabited by the Talbot family from 1185 until 1976, except for a short period in the mid-1600s when Oliver Cromwell was around. The castle, now publicly owned, houses many portraits from the collection of the National Gallery.

In its gardens is the **Fry Model Railway Museum** (tel: 01-846 2184; www.malahidecastle.com; Apr–Sept Tue–Sat 10am–5pm, Sun 1–5pm, closed for tours 1–2pm; charge). The models of trains and stations in this re-creation of Ireland's rail system are meticulous. ❑

BELOW: Malahide Castle.

RESTAURANTS AND PUBS

Restaurants

Prices for a three-course dinner per person without wine:
€ = under €25
€€ = €25–40
€€€ = €40–55
€€€€ = over €55

Dublin City

Bridge Bar & Grill
The Malting Tower, Grand Canal Quay, Dublin 2
Tel: 01-639 4941
Mon–Sat noon–10pm. All day menu **€€**
In an interesting location set beneath the DART railway bridge, this modern brasserie has lots of character. Quality ingredients are used and the emphasis is on flavour – game in season, crab cakes and fruit crumbles. Also has a cocktail bar.

Café en Seine
40 Dawson Street, Dublin 2
Tel: 01-677 4567
Mon–Wed, Sun 11am–midnight, Thur–Sat 11am–3am; food served: noon–9pm, Sun–Wed, until 10pm Thur–Sat. L **€**, D **€**
Stunning Art Deco interior with three-storey atrium featuring intimate bars within bars. It's the trendy place to be. The casual, contemporary food is on offer all day and well into the night.

The Cedar Tree
11a St Andrew Street, Dublin 2
Tel: 01-677 2121
Daily, D Mon–Wed 5.30–11.30pm, Thur–Fri 5.30–midnight, Sat–Sun 5.30–10.45pm. D **€€**
You could easily walk straight past this unusual Lebanese restaurant down in the basement. The food is authentic and gently spiced. Oriental dancing adds some interest on Friday and Saturday nights.

Chapter One
18–19 Parnell Square, Dublin 1
Tel: 01-873 2266
Tue–Sat, L 12.30–2pm, D 6–10.30pm. L and Early Bird **€€**, à la carte D **€€€€**
Michelin-starred. One of Dublin's leading restaurants, it has a well deserved reputation for suburb, friendly service, outstanding classic/modern Irish cooking that showcases specialist Irish produce. A highlight is the new Chef's Table, in particular the 6-course menu. A meal here is a special treat (reserve well in advance). Lunch, and their renowned pre-theatre menu (dessert served after the theatre show), are great value.

Chez Max
1 Palace Street, Dublin
Tel: 01-633 7215
Daily, L noon–3.30pm, Sat until 4pm, D 5.30–10pm, Sat–Sun until 11pm. L **€–€€**, Early Bird **€** (2 courses), D **€€**
This bistro, close to Dublin Castle, brings to mind Paris of the 1940s. Max Delaloubie brings his homeland to his dishes, including favourites such as French onion soup and *moules frites*. Frogs' legs are on offer, too, and some delectable pastries and desserts.

Clarendon Café Bar
Clarendon Street, Dublin 2
Tel: 01-679 2909
Mon–Thur 10.30am–11.30pm, Fri–Sat 10.30pm–12.30am, Sun 11am–11pm, food: Mon–Thur noon–9pm, Fri–Sun noon–7pm **€€**
A warm, friendly, place with bars covering three stories. The food is serious with a commitment to interesting menus, named suppliers and sound cooking.

Cornucopia
19 Wicklow Street, Dublin 2
Tel: 01-677 7583
Mon–Fri 8.30am–9pm, Sat 8.30am–8pm, Sun noon–7pm. L and D **€**
Informal, wholesome, home style vegetarian cooking, organic food and wine with yeast-free, dairy, gluten and wheat-free options.

Dax
23 Upper Pembroke Street, Dublin 2
Tel: 01-676 1494
L Tue–Fri 12.30–2.30pm, D Tue–Sat 6–11pm. L **€€**, Early Bird **€€**, D **€€€**
A rustic, yet elegant restaurant serving good seasonal food with French influences inspired by the chef/owner Olivier Meisonnave. It needs seeking out as it is tucked away in a basement at the quieter end of Pembroke Street.

Dunne and Crescenzi Café/Restaurant
14 South Frederick Street. Dublin
Tel: 01-677 3815
Mon–Sat 7.30am–11pm, Sun 10am–10pm. L and D **€–€€**
Close to Trinity College. Highly regarded for food

and wine. Light, stylish, authentic Italian food, wine and cooking.

Eden
Meeting House Square, Temple Bar, Dublin 2
Tel: 01-670 5372
L Mon–Fri 12.30–3pm, brunch Sat–Sun noon–3pm, until 4pm Sun, D Sun–Thur 5–10pm, Fri–Sat 6–10pm. L **€€**, Early Bird **€€**, D **€€–€€€**
Sit inside or out, this is the place to be seen. That it offers good food, imaginative, seasonal, contemporary Irish menus, atmosphere and value for money is a bonus.

ely hq Gastropub
Forbes Street, Hanover Quay, Dublin 2
Tel: 01-633 9986
Daily noon–10pm. All day menu **€€**
Located in the trendy newly developed Docklands overlooking Grand Canal Square, this pub serves wholesome organic food sourced from the family farm, and all washed down with a choice of good beer and wine.

Il Fornaio
IFSC, 1b Valentia House, Custom House Square, Dublin 1
Tel: 01-628 3774
Mon–Fri 9am–10pm, Sat 11am–11pm, Sun 11am–9pm. All day menu **€**
No frills but there is authentic home-made Italian food at reasonable prices. This is just one of several branches in Dublin and is located in the up-and-coming financial district. It's fairly small but has outdoor tables to enjoy al fresco dining in the better weather.

Gallery Restaurant at the Church
Mary Street, Dublin 1
Tel: 01-828 0102
Daily 5–10pm or later. Early Bird **€€**, D **€€–€€€**
Diners come here as much for the ambience as for the food as the setting is stunning. It includes a massive church organ and huge stained-glass windows. International cusine with an Irish twist.

Good World
18 South Great George's Street, Dublin 2
Tel: 01-677 5373
Daily 12.30pm–midnight. L **€**, D **€€**
Appreciated by the Chinese community and by Dubliners for extensive authentic Chinese food: dim sum a speciality.

Halo
at the Morrison Hotel, Lower Ormonde Quay, Dublin 1
Tel: 01-887 2400
Fri–Sat D 7–10pm. D **€€**
Halo has had a makeover and promotes a relaxed, informal atmosphere for the discerning diner. The menu features modern European with a twist of Ireland, with only quality Irish products used.

L'Ecrivain
109a Lower Baggot Street, Dublin 2
Tel: 01-661 1919
L Mon, Wed–Fri 12.30–2pm. D Mon, Wed–Sat, 6.30–10.30pm. L **€€€**, D **€€€€**
Michelin star. An exceptional place in every way. Chef/patron Derry Clarke and his gifted team have a unique cooking style based on classic French with contemporary flair and a strong leaning towards contemporary Irish cooking using carefully sourced ingredients from artisan producers.

L'Geuleton
1 Fade Street, (off Georges Street) Dublin 2
Tel: 01-675 3708
Daily, L noon–3pm, Sun 1–3pm, D 6–10pm, Sun until 9pm. L **€**, D **€€**
Dubliners love this no-frills French bistro. Interesting menu, food and cooking. No distinction between courses, good value casual dining. No reservations, so be ready for queues.

La Mère Zoë
22 St Stephen's Green North
Tel: 01-661 6669
Daily, L 12.30–3pm, Sun noon–3.30pm, D 6–11pm, Sun until 9pm. L **€€**, Early Bird (6–7pm) **€€**, D **€€**
Belgian/French based on classic country cooking. Reliable cooking, good food, served promptly and in comfort; reasonable prices. Live jazz on Friday and Saturday nights.

Les Frères Jacques
74 Dame Street, Dublin 2
Tel: 01-679 4555
L Mon–Fri 12.30–2.30pm, D Mon–Sat 7–10.30pm, until 11pm Fri–Sat. L **€€**, Early Bird **€€**, D **€€–€€€€**
Classic French cuisine at exceptionally reasonable prices for the high quality

LEFT: dining in ornate surroundings. **RIGHT:** go veggie at Cornucopia.

Prices for a three-course dinner per person without wine:
€ = under €25
€€ = €25–40
€€€ = €40–55
€€€€ = over €55

of food, cooking and table service.

Mermaid Café
69–70 Dame Street, Dublin 2
Tel: 01-670 8236
Daily, L 12.30–3pm, Sun brunch to 3.30pm, D 6–11pm, Sun to 9pm. L **€€**, D **€€€**
The food style combines classic French and American that come together in an individual way in this stylish, highly regarded and popular restaurant.

Monty's of Kathmandu
28 Eustace Street, Temple Bar, Dublin 2
Tel: 01-670 4911
L Mon–Sat noon–2pm, D daily 5.30–11pm, Sun until 10.30pm. L **€–€€**, D **€€**, Tasting menu (6 courses) **€€€**
Ireland's only Nepalese restaurant. Long menu offers authentic cooking of real character at reasonable prices in a comfortable setting. Good vegetarian choice plus their own specially brewed shive beer.

One Pico Restaurant
5–6 Molesworth Place, Schoolhouse Lane, Dublin 2
Tel: 01-676 0300
Mon–Sat. L noon–3pm. D 6–11pm. L **€€**, Early Bird (6–7.30pm) **€€€**, D **€€€–€€€€**
This fashionable fine-dining restaurant was refurbished in 2010. A varied menu from Early Bird to tasting menu and the food style is classic/modern French.

Panem
Ha'penny Bridge, 21 Lower Ormond Quay, Dublin 1
Tel: 01-872 8510
Mon–Sat 9am–5pm. L **€**
This café has the best baking in town. Everything is made on site: delicious croissants, biscuits, Italian and French bread and cakes. Light meals. Italian coffee and chocolate.

Pearle Brasserie
20 Upper Merrion Street, Dublin 2
Tel: 01-661 3572
L Mon–Fri noon–2.30pm, D daily 6–10.30pm. L **€€**, Early Bird **€€**, D **€€€–€€€€**
Chef/patron Sebastien Masi cooks unusual and beautifully presented meals in a contemporary style with a classic French base and an emphasis on flavours that highlight the quality ingredients. Children welcome.

The Pig's Ear
4 Nassau Street
Tel: 01-670 3865
Mon–Sat, L noon–3pm, D 5.30–10pm. L **€**, Early Bird (5.30–6.30pm) **€ €**, D **€ €**
Dine in either of the two lovely contemporary upstairs rooms overlooking Trinity College. Top TV chef Stephen McAllister gives Irish favourites a modern twist. Highly creative, right down to the little treats with coffee.

Port House
64a South William Street, Dublin 2
Tel: 01-677 0298
Daily 11am–1am, Sun until 11pm **€–€€**
Casual restaurant and wine bar. Wine by the glass; tapas. Authentic, good cooking.

Queen of Tarts
Cork Hill, Dame Street, Dublin 2
Tel: 01-670 7499
Mon–Fri 7.30am–7pm, Sat–Sun 9am–7pm. All day menu **€**
Sisters Yvonne and Regina Fallon trained as pastry chefs in New York but their gorgeous little teashop is Irish through and through. Treats include delectable savoury tarts, innovative salads and scrumptious cakes. There is another branch around the corner in Cow's Lane.

Restaurant Patrick Guibaud
21 Upper Merrion Street, Dublin 2
Tel: 01-676 4192
Tue–Sat, L 12.30–2.15pm, D 7.30–10.15pm. L **€€€**, D **€€€€**
Two Michelin stars. Long established; formal fine dining. Contemporary French cooking at its best and renowned for exceptional cuisine based on seasonal Irish foods. Highlights include the tasting menus.

Shanahan's on the Green
119 St Stephen's Green, Dublin 2
Tel: 01-407 0939
L Fri only 12.30–2pm, D Mon–Sat 6–10pm. L **€€€**, D **€€€€**
Luxurious, fashionable and very expensive American steakhouse. But the certified Irish Angus beef steaks are magnificent. Good wine list, strong on California.

Silk Road Café
Chester Beatty Library, Dublin Castle, Dublin 2
Tel: 01-407 0770
Mon–Fri 10am–4.30pm, Sat 11am–4.30pm, Sun 1–4.30pm, closed Mon Oct–May. Light meals **€**
Unusual café in the clock tower. The themes of the library are brought together in an unusual menu featuring Middle Eastern, Mediterranean, vegetarian and organic halal/kosher food.

Tea Rooms at the Clarence Hotel
6 Wellington Quay, Dublin 2

Tel: 01-407 0800
Daily, B 7am–11am, Sat–Sun 7.30am, L Sun only 12.30–7pm, D Thur–Sat 6–10.30pm, Sun until 9.30pm. B € €, L €€, D €€
Cool, elegant restaurant attached to celebrity hotel that has changed its menus to fight the economic downturn and offers some superb quality cooking at excellent prices.

Thornton's Restaurant
St Stephen's Green West, Dublin 2
Tel: 01-478 7008
L Thur–Sat noon–2pm, D Tue–Sat 6–10pm. L €€–€€€, D €€€€
One Michelin star for one of Dublin's special places. Kevin Thornton is a gifted chef, using fantastic ingredients beautifully presented, with emphasis on flavour, all in deep comfort with impeccable service.

Unicorn Restaurant
12b Merrion Court, off Merrion Row, Dublin 2
Tel: 01-676 2181
Mon–Sat, L 12.30–4.30pm, D 6–11pm, Fri–Sat 11.30pm. L €€, Early Bird €€, D €€–€€€
Regional/modern Italian food and superb Italian wine list. The antipasta table is legendary. Long established, packed with character. Piano bar and live music Wed–Sat 9pm–3am.

Ballsbridge

French Paradox
53 Shelbourne Road, Ballsbridge, Dublin 4
Tel: 01-660 4068
Mon–Sat, L noon–3pm, Sat continuous service noon–10.30pm, D 6–10.30pm. L €, D €€
Casual restaurant, wine bar and café with 70 wines by the glass and one-plate menu in addition to L and D. Food that gives a flavour of the south of France.

Lobster Pot
9 Ballsbridge Terrace, Dublin 4
Tel: 01-668 0025
L Mon–Fri noon–2pm, D Mon–Sat 6–10.30pm. L €€€, Early Bird (Mon–Fri 6–7pm) €€, D €€€
Charming relaxed old-world atmosphere in which to eat from the first-class fish menu. Choose something from the daily catch or the tempting seafood, but the meateaters will not be disappointed either.

O'Connells Restaurant
Ballsbridge Court Hotel, Lansdowne Road, Dublin 4
Tel: 01-665 5940
L Mon–Sat L noon–2.30pm, Sun 12.45–3pm, D daily 6–10pm, Sun until 9pm. L €, Early Bird €€, D €€–€€€
Tom O'Connell's kitchen produces first-class modern cooking, utilizing the very best of fresh Irish ingredients. Tasty roast dinners and succulent seafood are some of the highlights, accompanied by piano playing at the weekend.

Roly's Bistro
7 Ballsbridge Terrace, Ballsbridge, Dublin 4
Tel: 01-668 0623
Daily, L noon–3pm, D 5.45–10pm. L €, Early Bird (Mon–Fri 5.45–6.30pm) €€, D €€€
Renowned, very buzzy bistro. Quality and value is maintained. Classic French meets modern Irish with a few global wanderings.

Clontarf

Kinara
(Pakistani/north Indian restaurant), 318 Clontarf Road, Dublin 3
Tel: 01-833 6759
Daily noon–11pm. Set L €, Early Bird €–€€, D €€
Excellently cooked authentic north Indian/Pakistani cuisine. With emphasis on local and organic foods; wide menu includes vegetarian options. Gentle decor, comfort and attentive service.

Dalkey

Nosh
111 Colliemore Road, Dalkey, Co. Dublin
Tel: 01-284 0666
L Tue–Fri and brunch Sat–Sun, L 11am–4pm, D Tue–Sun 5–10pm. L €, D €€
Casual and contemporary. Seasonal menus, strong on fish and vegetarian choices. "Posh nosh" daily special and special prices Tuesday to Thursday and Sunday evening.

Dun Laoghaire

Cavistons Seafood Restaurant
59 Glasthule Road, Sandycove, near Dun Laoghaire, Co. Dublin
Tel: 01-280 9245
L Tue–Thur noon, 1.30pm, 3pm (3 sittings), D Fri–Sat 6, 8.15pm (2 sittings). L and D €€–€€€
Tiny, characterful and popular for the sparkling fresh quality and range of the seafood menu (they run a fishmongers and deli next door). Simple but skilled cooking presented with flair. Those in the know book the latest sitting and linger!

Hartleys
1 Harbour Road, Dun Laoghaire, Co. Dublin
Tel: 01-280 6767
L Mon–Fri noon–3pm, Sun noon–5pm, D Mon–Sat 6–late, Sun 5.30–9pm. L €€, D €€€
Located in old railway terminal building and overlooking the harbour. A lovely spacious dining

LEFT: cakes and pastries cater for the sweet tooth.
RIGHT: eating out, sort of, whatever the weather.

Prices for a three-course dinner per person without wine:
€ = under €25
€€ = €25–40
€€€ = €40–55
€€€€ = over €55

room where food is beautifully cooked. Particularly good are the fish choices including chowder and daily mussel dish.

Rasam
18–19 Glasthule Road, Dun Laoghaire, Co. Dublin
Tel: 01-230 0600
Daily 5.30–11pm, Sun until 10.30pm). Early Bird **€**, D **€€**, Set D **€€€**
An excellent and delighful Indian restaurant offering light, authentic, varied regional cuisine. Menu with clear descriptions. Drinks menu complements food. Top class cooking, service, fair prices.

Howth

Aqua Restaurant
1 West Pier, Howth, Co Dublin
Tel: 01-832 0690
L Tue–Sat 12.30–3.30pm, Sun noon–5pm, D Tue–Sun 5.30–10pm, Sun to 8.30pm. L **€€**, Early Bird **€€**, à la carte **€€€**
Modern restaurant with sea views. Contemporary Irish mingled with Cal-Italian style dishes with an emphasis on fresh seafood from the port. Simply presented.

King Sitric
East Pier, Howth, Co. Dublin
Tel: 01-832 5235
Mon, Wed–Sat, closed Mon in winter, L Sun only 1–7pm, D 6.30–10pm. L **€€**, D (Mon–Thur) **€€**, D **€€€€**
The setting for this long-established fine-dining restaurant is lovely. Chef/patron Aidan McManus is committed to fish fresh from the boats (or his own lobster pots) and has a fine wine list.

Leixlip

Becketts Country House Hotel
Cooldrinagh House
Tel: 01-624 7040
L Mon–Fri 12.30–2.15pm, Sun 12.30–6pm, Early Bird Mon–Fri 6–7.30pm, D 6–10pm. L **€**, Early Bird **€€**, D special **€€**, à la carte **€€€**
Located in West Co. Dublin, the restaurant is atmospheric, the welcome warm and the service good. Fairly traditional menu, but the cooking is sound. The set lunch, special dinner and Early Bird menus are good value.

Malahide

Cruzzo Bar and Restaurant
The Marina Village, Malahide, Co. Dublin
Tel: 01-845 0599
L Wed–Fri noon–3pm, until 3.30pm Sun, Early Bird Tue–Fri 6–7pm, Sat 5.30–6.30pm, D Tue–Sat 6–10pm, Sat 10.30pm. L **€€**, Early Bird **€€**, D **€€–€€€**
Built on a platform overhanging the water. Menus are fairly traditional but presented in contemporary style. There is a "real food" children's menu. Live music (mainly jazz – Sat and sometimes other nights).

Jaipur Restaurant
5 St James Terrace, Malahide
Tel: 01-845 5455
Daily 5.30–11pm, Early Bird 5–7pm. Early Bird **€€**, D **€€€**, Tasting menu **€€€**
Authentic yet contemporary Indian fine dining. Excellent food quality and cooking, colourful and beautiful presentation, served with flair, charm and style. Strong on vegetarian dishes. The (Indian) desserts are especially good.

Portobello

Nonna Valentina
1-2 Portobello Road, Dublin 8
Tel: 01-454 9866
Tue–Sat 6pm–late, Sun noon–late. L **€€**, à la carte **€€–€€€**
On the banks of the Grand Canal. Dunne and Crescenzi (who also have a group of renowned café/bars in Dublin) offer fine Italian dining with authentic ingredients and menus and a buzzy Italian atmosphere.

Seagrass
30 South Richmond Street, Portobello, Dublin 2
Tel: 01-478 9595
Wed–Sun, L noon–5pm, also brunch Sat–Sun noon–5pm, D 5.30pm–late, Sun until 9pm. L **€–€€**, D **€€**, Tapas tasting plates **€**
A fresh new approach to modern European food in pleasing surroundings. Dine in the main restaurant, intimate basement or on the outside terrace on warm days. Thursday night is bring your own bottle night.

Skerries

Red Bank House and Restaurant
5–7 Church Street, Skerries, Co. Dublin
Tel: 01-849 1005
L Sun only 12.30–4.30pm, Early Bird Mon–Fri 6–8pm, D daily 6.30–9.45pm. L **€€**, Early Bird **€€**, D **€€€**, Gourmet menu **€€€**
Atmospheric restaurant converted from a bank with vaults for the wine cellar. Renowned chef/patron Terry McCoy is a wizard with seafood fresh from Skerries harbour, and the menus are written in plain English. Vegetarian options and a good dessert trolley.

Terenure

Vermillion
94–96 Terenure Road, North Terenure, Dublin 6W
Tel: 01-499 1400
Daily 5.30pm–late. L **€**, Set value dinner Tue–Sat 5.30–

7pm **€**, D **€€**
Contemporary Indian decor with creative modern Indian menu and cooking style to match.

Pubs

Dublin City

The Long Hall in Great Georges Street Dublin 2 is a very fine Victorian pub in a perfect state of preservation; many would rate this Dublin's best pub – and you get to meet the locals. **O'Neills** is just opposite the Tourist Office and close to Trinity College whose students favour this wateringhole for the bar food and the traditional music on Monday nights. **McDaids** was once the haunt of Brendan Behan and other literary types. It's definitely a nice pub.

The Market Bar is beside the Georges Street Market Arcade; a new-style pub popular with the younger crowd, although everyone appreciates the excellence of the tapas.

Neary's, a stylish Edwardian pub close to the Gaiety Theatre, attracts theatregoers and actors and can get busy in the evenings. Near here, too, is the **Stag's Head** (Dame Court), one of the finest pubs in Dublin, with its mahogany bar and intimate snugs. **The Porterhouse** is a rather special modern pub close to Dublin Castle and Christ Church Cathedral; the attraction is the micro-brewery and a great selection of excellent beers brewed on the premises, an international selection of bottled beers and high-class bar food too. **The Brazen Head** near the River Liffey may well be (as it claims) Dublin's oldest pub; there was one on the site in the 12th century. It certainly feels ancient and dark but it's fun, offers traditional Irish dishes and live music nightly.

Doheny & Nesbitt (5 Lower Baggot Street), near the parliament buildings, is frequented by politicians, political writers and pundits. A good place to gossip, it's also a well-run pub.

Nearby and beside St Stephen's Green is **O'Donoghue's**, former haunt of the legendary Dubliners, (tel: 01-668 7194); the attraction here is live traditional music every night.

The Old Stand, handy to the Tourist Office, is a traditional rugby pub that gets packed to the rafters on International rugby weekends. It, too, lays a claim to be one of the oldest pubs in Dublin.

Co. Dublin

The fashionable watering hole in Dalkey is **The Queen's Bar**. Established in 1745, it retains many original features. It has good bar food and outdoor seating. **Johnny Fox's** in Glencullen is a carefully preserved rural pub where Dubliners wishing to entertain visitors bring them for a "Hooley Night" (touristy but fun). Although **The 12th Lock** (overlooking the 12th lock of the Royal Canal) has grown into a hotel and restaurant, at its heart are a lovely bar and outdoor area overlooking the Marina; this is a great place to while away the hours on a sunny day.

Abbey Tavern, Howth (tel: 01 839 0307) is a famous traditional music and dance pub; it's also an interesting place in its own right with parts dating back to the 15th century when it was, indeed, an abbey. Best visited in daytime unless you want to enjoy the dinner entertainment (for which you should book ahead in high season).

John Kavanagh is known as the "Gravediggers") because this pub is right beside Glasnevin Cemetery. An unspoilt Victorian haven. Go there and you'll often happen upon a Dublin "wake". It's said to serve one of the best pints in the city; basic food (soup and "sangers") is available as well.

Porterhouse North. Art Deco pub (originally a garage) which is now a trendy venue in Glasnevin. It's spacious and spread on four levels with a smoking area out the back. It's attractive to the young people on the town.

Ryans of Park Gate Street is one of the city's most appreciated Victorian pubs, with beautiful stained glass, a collection of antique mirrors and, that most beloved feature of visitors, lots of snugs where you can enjoy your drink in privacy. The elegant FXB Steak & Seafood Restaurant is located on the first floor.

Gibney's Pub, Malahide. A place of character with a large beer garden (where smoking is permitted). Good blackboard selection of wine by the glass. Also live music and sports TV.

Stoop Your Head, Skerries, Co Dublin, is a bar cum restaurant close to Skerries harbour. You don't have to eat but there is good seafood available – simple dishes but well done.

LEFT: soda bread, crumbly and nutty-tasting.
RIGHT: the venerable Doheny & Nesbitt pub.

Bloomsday

The action of James Joyce's *Ulysses* takes place on a single day in 1904. Each year on that day, 16 June, the novel's events are re-enacted

Polls of literary critics have deemed *Ulysses* the greatest novel of the 20th century, although even in Dublin it is probably more honoured than read. Thematically based on Homer's *Odyssey*, it documents a 24-hour period in the lives of an Irish Jew, Leopold Bloom, and a budding writer, Stephen Dedalus, as they move around Dublin; the story reaches its climax when they meet.

The novel was published in 1922 in Paris by Sylvia Beach's Shakespeare & Co bookshop. It was banned in Britain and America – though never, curiously, in Ireland, though it was difficult to obtain there. The first Bloomsday celebrations took place in Dublin on 16 June 1954, the 50th anniversary of the events depicted in the novel. Initially they were designed to appeal mainly to academics, but after Joyce's centenary in 1982, they became increasingly popular so that now they are rivalled only by St Patrick's Day. In 2004, the centenary celebrations of events in the novel included a five-month long ReJoyce festival.

Gorgonzola sandwich

Participants, wearing what approximates to 1904 garb, trace the paths of the book's characters. After a Bloomsday breakfast in Sandycove, they can listen to readings delivered by costumed actors, lunch on gorgonzola sandwiches and burgundy in Davy Byrne's pub, walk through the northside, taking in Hardwicke Street, Eccles Street, Gardiner Street and Mountjoy Square, enjoy more readings at the Joyce Centre, and then discuss the book's finer points over a few pints of Guinness.

LEFT: a street performer wears the letter "a" on his head. The 250,000 words of *Ulysses*, packed with puns, parodies and allusions, formed some of the 20th century's most experimental prose.

ABOVE: an actor in a James Joyce mask. Sinn Féin president Gerr Adams once said: "I have never completed his *Ulysses*. And I've n met anyone who has, although I've met people who say they have

JAMES JOYCE (1882–1941)

One of 10 children, James Augustine Aloysius Joyce was born at Rathgar, Dublin. He graduated from University College in 1902 with a degree in modern languages.

In 1904, while living briefly in the Martello Tower at Sandycove, he met Nora Barnacle, a simple country girl, and moved abroad, living mainly in Trieste and Paris; they had a son, Giorgio (who later became an alcoholic), and a daughter, Lucia (who became mentally ill), but did not marry until 1931. Joyce's eye troubles began in 1907, leaving him almost blind in later life.

Joyce remained an exile for the rest of his life. In Paris he mixed with writers such as Ezra Pound, Scott Fitzgerald, T.S. Eliot and Ernest Hemingway. As a young man, the playwright Samuel Beckett acted as his secretary. When war drove Joyce out in 1940, he moved to Zurich, where he died a year later. Nora remained in Zurich, where she died in 1951.

Joyce said of Ulysses: There are enough enigmas "to keep the professors busy for centuries arguing over what I meant, and that's the only way of securing your immortality."

The sculpture shown above is beside Joyce's grave at Fluntern Cemetery in Zurich.

AND ABOVE: *Ulysses* mentions so many bars that Bloomsday easily turn into a pub crawl. A prominent venue is Davy Byrne's oral pub" where Leopold Bloom enjoyed a lunchtime gorgonzola dwich and a glass of burgundy.

VE: Joyce was critical of the debilitating effects the priesthood on Irish life. At one point he has the hero of *Ulysses* – Leopold om, a Jew – praise psychological devices such as Confession.

LEFT: even the politicians join in – a government arts minister, John O'Donaghue, joins pupils from the Gaiety School of Acting during a Bloomsday reconstruction.

BELOW: Joyce once boasted that, if Dublin were to be destroyed, it would be possible to reconstruct it from the pages of *Ulysses*.

EXCURSIONS FROM DUBLIN

To the south lie the Wicklow Mountains, to the north the remarkable historical burial chambers of Newgrange and to the west some of the world's best racehorse country

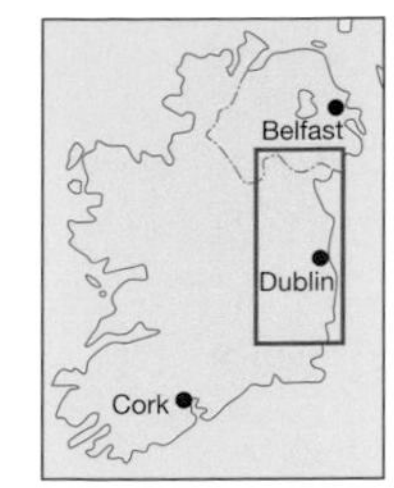

Wicklow (www.visitwicklow.ie) is known as "the garden of Ireland", and while there are scenic spots galore (including some glorious gardens), the county also possesses a savage beauty that equals that of the west of the island. The Wicklow Mountains (www.wicklowmountains nationalpark.ie), are a rugged mass of granite running from Dublin, through Wicklow and down into Wexford. Blanket bogs clothe the upper slopes, while peaty streams cascade swiftly downhill into deep lakes. The mountains run an impassable wedge through parts of the county, making it difficult to cover the whole area in one day – unless you drive at a non-stop clip.

West Wicklow

West Wicklow can be reached via the M50 and the N81. At **Blessington**, 19 miles (30km) from Dublin, the valley of the River Liffey was flooded in 1940, submerging 74 farmhouses and cottages to create a reservoir; a scenic drive skirts the perimeter. Less than 2 miles south is the grand, 18th-century, Palladian house, **Russborough** ❶. The house has an important collection of furnishings and paintings, including works by Goya, Gainsborough and Rubens (tel: 045-865 239; www.russborough.ie; May–Sept daily 10am–5pm, Apr and Oct Sun and bank holidays only; charge).

Follow the N81 to **Hollywood** ❷, no relation to its Californian namesake, but coincidentally, a location for the films *Dancing at Lughnasa* (1998) and *Michael Collins* (1996). From here, a 15-mile (25km) drive on the R756 brings you across the bleakly beautiful Wicklow Gap to **Laragh** where, in summer, teas are served in the grassy village triangle.

A mile before Laragh is the turn to one of the most visited sites in the east of Ireland, **Glendalough** ❸. Here, in the steep-sided valley between two lakes, St Kevin founded a monastic settlement

Main attractions
- BLESSINGTON
- GLENDALOUGH
- AVOCA
- POWERSCOURT HOUSE
- HILL OF TARA
- NAVAN
- SLANE
- NEWGRANGE
- MELLIFONT ABBEY
- DROGHEDA
- DUNDALK
- COOLEY PENINSULA
- CELBRIDGE
- KILDARE

LEFT: Powerscourt Gardens.
RIGHT: Powerscourt Waterfall.

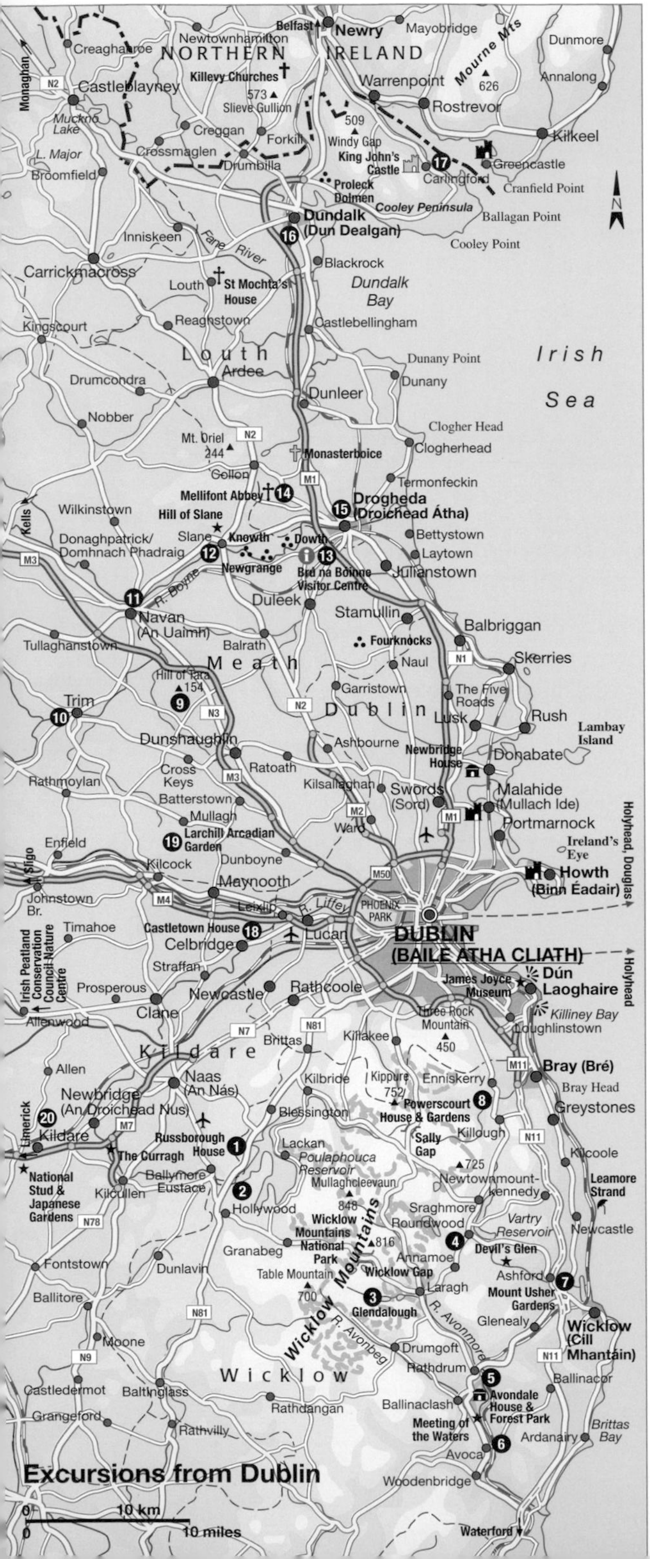

Excursions from Dublin

in the 6th century. The ruins – a 110ft (33-metre) round tower and sacred structures – date from the 11th and 12th centuries (tel: 0404-45325/45352; daily 9.30am–5pm Nov–Feb, Mar–Oct until 6pm; guided tours; charge).

Several roads meet in Laragh: take the R755 to the northeast, and after 6 miles (9km) you arrive in **Roundwood** ❹, purportedly the highest village in Ireland, 781ft (238 metres) above sea level. If you take the R155, to the northwest, you come to the gorgeous **Glenmacnass Waterfall**, 6 miles (9km) away.

Avondale

If you continue south from Laragh, the R755 leads through the gently-wooded Vale of Clara to **Rathdrum**, 7 miles (11km) away. **Avondale** ❺, the Georgian home of the great Irish politician, Charles Stewart Parnell (1846–91), is now a museum devoted to his memory and is surrounded by hundreds of acres of forest park (tel: 0404-46111; 17 Mar–31 Oct 11am–6pm, last admission to house at 5pm, house closed Mon in Apr, Sept and Oct, except bank holidays; charge).

 Map on page 150

The picturesque village of **Avoca** ❻ with its multicoloured houses and working weaving mill is another couple of miles south. Also at this end of the county is **Brittas Bay** (off the N11 at "Jack White's"), with its sandy dunes, beloved of Irish holidaymakers.

On the way back to Dublin, the beauteous **Mount Usher Gardens** ❼ (a must for tree lovers; www.mountushergardens.ie; Mar–Oct only) are off the N11 at **Ashford**. The Devil's Glen, a mile or two northwest on the R764 and R765, has a walk along the Vartry River and a sculpture trail. Birdwatchers should head for the coast (off the R761) between Newcastle and Kilcoole, where migrants often stop to feed.

Powerscourt

The village of **Enniskerry**, signposted off the N11 near Bray, has a lovely cut-stone clock tower at its centre. **Powerscourt House and Gardens** ❽ are about a mile to the south (tel: 01-204 6000; www.powerscourt.ie; daily 9.30am–5.30pm, dusk in winter; charge). The 18th-century stately home, gutted by fire in 1974, and restored in the mid-1990s, now houses upmarket shops, a garden centre and a restaurant. The grounds on one side are dominated by a golf course, but on the other, the heroic Italianate landscape designed by Daniel Robertson in the mid-19th century survives. Robertson, a martyr to gout and the sherry bottle, was said to have conducted operations from a wheelbarrow.

Powerscourt Waterfall, which has a separate entrance gate, is the tallest waterfall in Ireland (398ft/121metres).

One of many statues dotting Powerscourt's Italianate grounds.

EXCURSIONS NORTH

The countryside north of Co. Dublin is impressively larded with antiquities, and offers up well preserved pre-Christian monuments, monastic sites and heritage towns. Some of the attractions, such as the megalithic passage graves in the Boyne Valley, can easily consume the best part of the day.

Co. Meath, which wraps around the northwest shoulder of Dublin, was the

LEFT: Glendalough ruins.
BELOW: Powerscourt House.

Market day in Trim, County Meath.

terrain of the pagan High Kings of Ireland and is known as the Royal county (www.meathtourism.ie). The ancient seat of the rulers was the **Hill of Tara ❾**, 28 miles (44km) from Dublin, off the M3, 7 miles (11km) beyond the village of Dunshaughlin. The limestone ridge commands fittingly regal views over the central plain of Ireland, smokily framed by distant mountain ranges. Ring forts, ruins and a standing stone mark the place that was the island's spiritual and cultural capital for millennia (tel: 046-902 5903; access all year, guided tours end-May–mid-Sept; charge).

The town of **Trim ❿**, 13 miles (21km) to the west, has Ireland's largest Anglo-Norman castle, started by Hugh de Lacy in 1173 and used in the filming of Mel Gibson's *Braveheart* in 1994. The restored keep may be visited by guided tour, on a first-come, first-served basis (tel: 046-943 8619; groups must book in advance; charge). Trim is well furnished with other historic structures, which are strung along the heritage trail that winds through the town and along the River Boyne. In fine weather, the river banks are the perfect place to picnic.

Navan

The Boyne drive takes you to the market town of **Navan ⓫**, 9 miles (15km) away, with its fine Solstice Arts Centre (www.solsticeartscentre.com). Famous residents of the palindromic town include actor Pierce Brosnan, comedians Tommy Tiernan and Dylan Moran, and Francis Beaufort, who created the Beaufort wind force scale in 1805.

From Navan, a 7-mile (12km) drive on the N51 takes you to **Slane ⓬**, a beautiful 18th-century estate village above the River Boyne, and bedevilled by traffic travelling between Ireland's northwest and Dublin (it is 30 miles/50km from the capital on the N2).

The central crossroads contains a quartet of identical, three-storey, limestone Georgian houses, gazing implacably at each other across the square. The Gothic revival Slane Castle is the home of Lord Henry Conyngham, earl of Mount Charles, and is an annual venue for monster rock concerts. The castle and grounds are open from May to early August, Sunday to Thursday. Access to the castle is by tour only, with groups of 10 required to book in

BELOW: the Hill of Tara.

advance (tel: 041-988 4400; www.slane castle.ie; charge).

Less than a mile north of the village is the windswept **Hill of Slane** where in 433, St Patrick lit a Paschal fire to celebrate the arrival of Christianity in Ireland, much to the annoyance of the pagan high king, Laoghaire – who had decreed that no flames should be visible from Tara during the festival of Feis Temro. The hill, which is open all year, contains the ruins of a 16th-century Franciscan friary, and has good views of the surrounding countryside.

Newgrange

One of Europe's most important prehistoric clusters is just a few miles southeast of Slane: the neolithic burial mounds (a Unesco World Heritage site) at Newgrange, Knowth and Dowth.

Access to Newgrange and Knowth is solely by tour from the **Brú na Bóinne Visitor Centre** ⓭ near Donore (tel: 041-988 0300; Nov–Jan 9.30am–5pm, Feb–Apr 9.30am–5.30pm, May 9am–6.30pm, June–mid-Sept 9am–7pm, mid-Sept–end-Sept 9am–6.30pm, Oct 9.30am–5.30pm; charge; groups of 15 or more must book by fax: 041-982 3071).

Dowth may be visited separately (signposted off the N51) and viewed from the outside. Its shaggy, unrestored mound makes a contrast to the renovated structures of Newgrange and Knowth. Newgrange is the only one of the monuments where access is allowed to the interior passage and chamber – the latter is aligned so that the rising sun sends in a shaft of light at the winter solstice (entry to the chamber for that occasion is by lottery). Built around 3200 BC, Newgrange is several hundred years older than the Pyramids, and 1,000 years more ancient than Stonehenge. The sites are busy in summer, and entry cannot be guaranteed. Go early in the day, and allow at least three hours.

About 5 miles (8km) north, in Louth, Ireland's smallest county (www.louthholidays.com), stand the ruins of **Mellifont Abbey** ⓮ on the banks of the Mattock River. The first Cistercian house on the island, its earliest parts date from the 12th century. In 1690, the buildings were the headquarters of King William of Orange, who defeated James II at the Battle of the Boyne.

Mellifont Abbey.

Not far east of Mellifont is a modern monument that can be seen for miles, the **Boyne Suspension Bridge** at Drogheda. Completed in 2003, it has a main span of 555ft (170 metres) and a 310ft (95-metre) -high concrete pylon, from which 28 shimmering cables fan out like the work of a giant spider.

The busy town of **Drogheda** ⓯ is surrounded by rather utilitarian fac-

BELOW: an interior passage at Newgrange.

TIP

For a mini-trip to explore the lesser-known places around Dublin, drive to the Fingal area on the M1 north out of Dublin to the town of Swords, which has a fine castle. Just a little further north, on the R127, is the seaside town of Rush with the impressive Kenure House, a venue used for many film sets. North along the coast road are the attractive towns of Skerries and Balbriggan, and the famous Ardgillan Castle.

tories and retail outlets, but its core dates from Norman times, when it marked the northern boundary of the Pale. In 1649 the town was besieged and stormed by Cromwell and thousands of its citizens were killed, or transported to the Caribbean for slavery.

The **Millmount Museum** complex (tel: 041-983 3097; www.millmount.net; charge) includes a 19th-century Martello tower. The exhibits include a collection of trade and guild banners. At St Peter's Church, in the town centre, a shrine protects the embalmed head of St Oliver Plunkett (1629–81), the Archbishop of Armagh. He was the last Catholic martyr to die in England – hanged, drawn and quartered. The 13th-century Laurence Gate is an exquisite remnant of the city's medieval walls.

A mile and a half (2km) west of Drogheda (off the Baltray Road) is **Beaulieu House** (tel: 041-983 8557; www.beaulieuhouse.ie; charge), constructed in the 1660s in the Dutch style. The walled garden dates from the early 18th century. Half a dozen racing and rally cars from the 1960s and '70s are on display in the car museum.

BELOW: Drogheda.

Six miles (10km) east of Drogheda, via the R150, is the seaside resort of **Bettystown**, where the intricate Tara Brooch (now housed in the National Museum of Ireland), was found in 1850. A couple of miles further south is **Laytown**, where an annual horse racing event takes place on the strand in early September *(see page 158)*.

Drogheda is just 30 miles (50km) from Dublin on the M1 motorway that moves quickly up to Belfast. **Dundalk** ⓰, 23 miles (37km) beyond Drogheda, is the last town before the border.

To the east is the scenic **Cooley Peninsula** (www.carlingford.ie), the mythical stomping ground of the brown bull of Cooley (Donn Cúailnge), who was the object of legendary Queen Medb's cattle raid, The Táin. Dundalk Bay (on the south side of the peninsula) and Carlingford Lough (on the north) are both Special Protection Areas for wildlife, and are popular with birdwatchers.

The village of **Carlingford** ⓱ is an absolutely charming place where several stone-built medieval buildings nestle between the whitewashed houses on the narrow streets.

EXCURSIONS WEST

Kildare (www.visitkildare.ie), once known for its stud farms and lush green pastures, has gradually taken on the additional role of a dormitory county for Dublin. Quiet country towns and villages have sprouted apartment and housing developments, the homes of commuters who face a 60 to 90-mile daily round trip to the capital. Yet the county still holds many attractions, including some of the best horses in the world, grand houses and demesnes, and a peaceful network of canals and towpaths that are popular with walkers.

Castletown House ⓲ in **Celbridge** is 14 miles (22km) from Dublin, via the M4, taking the R449 Celbridge exit. Ireland's largest Palladian country house, it was built for the speaker of the Irish House of Commons, William Conolly in 1722 (tel: 01-628 8252; www.castletownhouse.ie; mid–Mar–Oct; charge).

Four miles (7km) to the southwest is **Straffan** with a steam museum and pretty 18th-century walled garden at Lodge Park (tel: 01-627 3155/628 8412; www.steam-museum.com; charge).

Head back north for 5 miles (8km) on the R403 and R406, and you come to the 18th-century university town of **Maynooth**, along the Royal Canal.

A few miles northwest (on the R148, R158 and R125) is **Larchill Arcadian Garden** ⓳, beyond **Kilcock** (tel: 01-628 7354; www.larchill.ie; May bank holiday weekends, June–Aug Thur–Sun and bank holidays, Sept Sat–Sun; charge). The restored ornamental landscape is a fine example of an 18th-century *ferme ornée*, with rare breeds and a large lake.

Head back to Kilcock, and take the R407 to the rapidly expanding village of **Clane**. From there the R403 passes through **Prosperous**, one of the first towns where the United Irishmen rose in the 1798 rebellion. The road continues to **Allenwood**, from where the R414 travels through the Bog of Allen to the Irish Peatland Conservation Council's Nature Centre at Lullymore, about 3 miles (5km) before **Rathangan** (tel: 045-860 133; www.ipcc.ie; Mon–Fri, 10am–4pm, except bank holidays, all year; charge). Here you may learn about bogs and peat, take guided walks and examine dozens of species of carnivorous plants from around the world.

Kildare

From Rathangan it is 7 miles (11km) southeast to the town of **Kildare** ⓴, on the edge of the Curragh, the central plain of Ireland, which lies like a flat green blanket on the landscape. A mile outside the town, at Tully, is the famous **Irish National Stud**, with its Japanese Gardens and St Fiachra's Garden. These attractions are fully covered on pages 172–3 of the Southeast chapter.

Just over 7 miles (12km) to the east on the M7 and the R445 is **Newbridge**, home of Newbridge Silverware (www.newbridgesilverware.com). From here, it is a 30-mile (50km) drive to Dublin via the R445, the N7, and – if you are feeling strong enough – the M50 *(see box)*. ❑

Tiger Woods walks past the waterfall on the 14th green at the K Club golf course at Straffan during a Ryder Cup game.

The M50

Dublin's ring road carries a massive volume of traffic, and often not very effectively. It was designed to cater for a maximum 45,000 vehicles per day, but now carries closer to 100,000. It has been under construction or in the throes of upgrading for 20 years. Its most famous junction, the Red Cow Roundabout (where it meets the N7), was quickly dubbed "the Mad Cow Roundabout" but this has now been upgraded, causing less of a tailback. Visitors may decide to give it a wide berth as the toll booths have been removed and you have to pay online or ring a dedicated phone line before 8pm on the following day after use. You cannot pre-pay. Morning rush hour is between 7.30–10am; the afternoon rush starting 4 or 4.30pm, the road remaining busy until 6.30pm or later. (www.m50.ie).

BELOW: Castletown House.

RESTAURANTS AND PUBS

Restaurants

Prices for a three-course dinner per person without wine:
€ = under €25
€€ = €25–40
€€€ = €40–55
€€€€ = over €55

Kilmacanogue

Avoca Fern House Café
Kilmacanogue, Co. Wicklow
Tel: 01-286 7466
All-day menu 9.30am–5pm (Sun until 6pm) **€–€€**
In a lovely orangerie-style conservatory, at this new restaurant you can choose between a light meal or three-course lunch. Also the Sugar Tree café, and the Foodhall for delicious home-made picnic treats. Note: Three further Avoca cafés can be found in Avoca village, Co. Wicklow, Mount Usher Gardens, Co. Wicklow, and at Powerscourt, Co. Wicklow.

Ballymore Eustace

Ballymore Inn
Ballymore Eustace, Co. Kildare
Tel: 045-864 585
Daily, L 12.30–3pm, D 6–9pm. L **€€**, all day bar food **€–€€**, D **€€–€€€**
Located on the Russborough House side of the Wicklow Gap with a terrific reputation for meticulously sourced local foods; enticing modern menu, fine cooking, hospitality and live music on some nights.

Aughrim

Brooklodge Hotel, Stawberry Tree Restaurant, Acton's Pub, Orchard Café
Macreddin Village, Nr. Aughrim, Co. Wicklow
Tel: 0402-36444
D June–Oct daily from 7pm, Apr–May Wed–Sun from 7pm, Nov–Mar from 7pm, **€€€**; excellent informal meals in Acton's Bar, Apr–Sept daily from noon, Oct–Mar Mon–Thur from 6pm, Sat–Sun from noon, **€**; Orchard Café Apr–Sept daily from noon, Oct–Mar Sat–Sun from noon, **€**
Worth a special trip to experience Ireland's first and so far only certified organic restaurant. Exceptionally innovative, fine Irish cuisine in the restaurant. Also features a microbrewery, bakery, smokery, deli and monthly organic market.

Blessington

Grangecon Café
Kilbride Road, Blessington Village
Tel: 045-857 892
Mon–Sat 9am–5pm (closes at 4pm Mon–Wed) **€**
The café is in a beautiful old building. Everything from bread, to pastries and ice cream. All food home cooked, organic or free range and local where possible; much is made on the premises.

Carlingford

Ghan House
Tel: 042-937 3682
L Sun only 5 courses, **€€€**; D (most days, call in advance) 7–9.30pm **€€–€€€**
Georgian country house in centre of medieval walled village/fishing port. Modern Irish cooking, based on homegrown vegetables and the best local produce including Carlingford oysters, seafood, Cooley lamb and beef.

Celbridge

La Serre Restaurant
The Village at Lyons Demesne, near Celbridge, Co. Kildare
Tel: 01-630 3500
Wed–Sun, L noon–3pm, D 6–9.30pm. L **€€**, D **€€**, set dinner Wed–Fri **€€**, D **€€€**
After TV chef Richard Corrigan's departure to Dublin, La Serre is fronted again by chef Paul Carroll, bringing back his modern European menu with carefully sourced food, beautifully cooked and presented. Lovely courtyard for alfresco meals.

Drogheda

D Hotel Viaduct Bar and Grill
Scotch Hall, Drogheda, Co. Louth
Tel: 041-987 7702
Fri–Sat, dinner only 6–10pm. D **€€**
Like its sister, the G Hotel, this stylish bar and restaurant is set in a contemporary development with lovely views overlooking the River Boyne. Chef Stephen Wolstenholme employs modern European cooking using locally sourced ingredients.

Dundalk

Rosso Restaurant
5 Roden Place, Dundalk, Co. Louth
Tel: 042-935 6502
L Tue–Fri 12.30–2.45pm, D Tue–Sat 6–9.45pm. Value L **€**, L **€€**, D **€€**
Under the direction of renowned head chef Raymond McArdle (of the Nuremore Hotel, Co. Monaghan), the stylish modern room matches the cutting edge, modern Irish cooking with a menu which is a combination of traditional, unexpected spins on classic dishes and high standard of cooking by head chef Conor Mee.

Greystones

Chakra by Jaipur
Greystones, Co. Wicklow
Tel: 01-201 7222
Daily 5–11pm. Early Bird (5.30–7pm) **€€**, D **€€–€€€**
Located in a seaside village (beside the DART rail station) this is a sister restaurant of Jaipur in Dublin, Malahide and Dalkey. It is a contemporary spin on traditional Indian food served in fine dining style. Great vegetarian options and dessert menu. Elegant double height room and fine service.

Kells

Vanilla Pod Restaurant
Headfort Arms Hotel, Kells, Co. Meath
Tel: 0818-222 800
D Mon–Sat 5.30–10pm, Sun all day menu 12.30–9.30pm. Early Bird (5.30–7.30pm, Sun all day) **€€**, D **€€**
Don't be fooled by the old-fashioned entrance to the hotel, this independent restaurant is modern and bright, and serves well-presented fare cooked using excellent locally-sourced ingredients. Expect the likes of crab and chilli risotto with parmesan crisp for starters, followed by herb-crusted rack of lamb on a bed of beetroot, rounded off with a home-made dessert or chocolate fondue.

Rathdrum

Bates Restaurant
3 Market Street, Market Square, Rathdrum,

Co. Wicklow
Tel: 040-429 988
L Tue–Sun 12.30–2pm, D 6.30–10pm, Sun until 9pm. L **€–€€**, Early Bird (Tue–Thur, Sun 6.30–7.30pm), **€€** set dinner and all day €21.95, D (à la carte) **€€**
Italian chef and Italian cooking but with some wonderful Irish and European influences, all offering great value. Bates is part of the complex that also features the Cartoon Inn *(see Pubs right)*.

Naas

Vie de Chateaux

The Harbour, Naas, Co. Kildare
Tel: 045-888 478
L Mon–Fri noon–2.30pm, D daily 6–10pm. L and D **€€**
A popular venue for locals, set beside the canal, this French restaurant brings both France and Ireland to the table. A good range of French wines are offered, including some by the glass. Try the delicious tartlets to start, then mains such as sea bass or guinea fowl, followed by scrumptious desserts.

Navan

Eden Restaurant

Bellinter House, Navan, Co. Meath (near Hill of Tara)
Tel: 046-903 0900
Food served daily 11am–11pm, L noon–4pm. Light meals **€**, L **€€**, Early Bird **€€**, Dinner **€€€**
Modelled on its sister Eden in Temple Bar, Dublin, County Meath has a great addition to its restaurant scene. An elegant dining room is the perfect place to enjoy seasonal fresh Irish food delivered with a distinctively modern flair in this historic country house hotel.

Roundwood

Roundwood Inn

Roundwood, Co. Wicklow
Tel: 01-281 8107
Bar menu daily noon–9.30pm, **€**; Restaurant L Sun only, **€€**; D Fri–Sat, **€€**
En route to Glendalough, you'll find this comfortable and hospitable 17th-century inn. The cuisine is a blend of German/Irish cooking based on local foods especially wild game in season, and Wicklow lamb and fish, suckling pig and goose.

Slane

Brabazon Restaurant

Tankardstown House, Rathkenny, Nr Slane, Co. Meath
Tel: 041-982 4621
Thur–Sun, L Sun noon–6pm, D Thur–Sat 5.30–10pm. Sun L **€€**, Early Bird (5–6.30pm) 3 courses €28, D **€€**
Serving a blend of international and Irish cuisine, Brabazon is in an old converted cowshed, part of a beautiful period conversion at Tankardstown. Opened in 2009, the menu at Brabazon is a sophisticated rustic style featuring Irish products such as Wicklow loin of venison. A more relaxed style of dining is to be found in the Bistro.

Trim

Franzini O'Briens

Frenche's Lane, Trim, Co. Meath (beside Trim Castle)
Tel: 046-943 1002
L Sun only 1–4pm, D Mon–Sat 6.30–10pm, children welcome before 8.30pm. L **€**, Early Bird **€**, D **€–€€**
Comfortable, modern and elegant. Informal, international style menu attractively presented.

Pubs

There are some traditional pubs close to visitor attractions worth a visit just to drink in the atmosphere and meet with the locals. **O'Connells** (traditional and unspoilt) rural pub Skryne, Co. Meath (tel: 046-902 5122). Just the place to recover from wandering around the nearby Hill of Tara.

At the **Spirit Store**, Georges Quay, Dundalk, Co. Louth (tel: 042-935 2697) you meet up with sailors from around the world for a pint or a cup of tea. At night the upstairs bar features music in a buzzy atmosphere favoured by the young.

Furey's Bar, Moyvalley, is a canal bank pub between Moyvalley and Enfield, Co. Kildare (tel: 046-955 1185). Conjured from a Victorian railway station, it features a cosy bar with snugs, a good varied pub food menu of home cooked food and a view of the boats coming and going on the canal. Meals are served all day, Mon–Sat noon–7.30pm.

Cartoon Inn, Rathdrum, Co. Wicklow, is a traditional pub featuring some great work by the prominent Irish cartoonist Martyn Turner, which will keep you amused while you sup your pint.

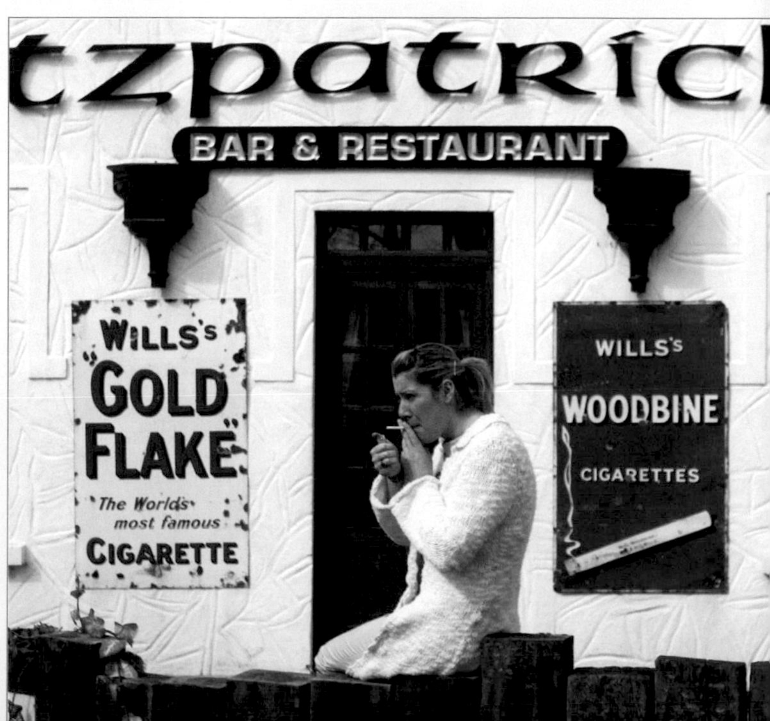

RIGHT: a bar near Dundalk after Ireland banned smoking in pubs and restaurants.

The Horse Culture

Whether they're breeding them, racing them, exporting them or betting on them, the Irish have an extraordinary affinity with horses

In 1809 *The History and Delineation of the Horse* recorded that "the Irish are the highest and the steadiest leapers in the world." They still are.

The pre-eminence of Irish-bred steeplechasers and hurdlers on the racecourses of Britain has been remarkable, and, given the legions of horses exported annually to trainers in England, it's even more remarkable that the greatest steeplechasers of modern era were trained in Ireland. Perhaps the greatest of all was Arkle, who won the Cheltenham Gold Cup three years in succession in the 1960s. Had Arkle entered a referendum for the Irish presidency, the world might well have had its first equine statesman since Caligula.

The Irish prefer the reckless and often threadbare thrills of steeplechasing to its rich relation, racing "on the flat". Whereas top-class flat-racing throughout the world is dominated by the commercial requirements of the multi-million dollar bloodstock industry, this aspect is absent from racing "over the sticks" because nearly all jumpers are geldings.

Left: Ireland's prosperous bloodstock industry owes much to a 1969 government ruling that fees for the services of thoroughbred stallions would be exempt from tax.

Above: Europe's only official race to be held on a beach takes pla in July/August (depending on tides) at Laytown, an east-coast resc

Above: many Irish people have a natural ability to understand an handle horses, which can still be seen in many small towns.

HORSES THROUGH HISTORY

Until the 1990s the Garda Síochána was one of the major police forces that didn't have a mounted police troop, but today a handful of Irish Draught Horses (a native breed, known for its versatility and good temperament) patrol the streets of Dublin.

Although horses have played a vital role in Ireland's economy over the centuries, it was the racing scene that inspired excitement. The Red Branch Knights of pre-Christian Ireland raced each other on horses, and horse-racing was an essential part of public fairs in the early centuries AD.

In Co. Cork in the year 1752, a Mr Edmund Blake and a Mr O'Callaghan raced each other on horseback across the countryside from Buttevant Church to the spire of St Leger Church 4½ miles away, jumping hedges, walls and ditches on the way. As a result, a new word, "steeplechasing", entered the English language, and a new sport was created.

Steeplechasing was soon all the rage. Races were run, like the original, across open country from one point to another with the precise course left largely to the discretion of the riders. A 19th-century Englishman returning from a holiday in Ireland wrote that steeplechasing was "a sort of racing for which the Paddies are particularly famous".

[ABO]VE: The Curragh is the fashionable setting for all the Irish classic [rac]es: the 2,000 and 1,000 Guineas, the Derby, the Oaks and the St [Leg]er. Prize money at the Derby now exceeds €1.5 million.

[ABO]VE: equine symbolism is frequently found in Ireland, as in this [stat]ue guarding the gates to the Powerscourt estate in Co. Wicklow.

LEFT: the occasional horse and carts still seen on Irish roads are a romantic echo of the old rag and bone collectors who made a living out of recycling before it became fashionable.

BELOW: bookmakers in Ireland have been slow to embrace online betting. Cynics claimed that's because the profit margins aren't so good.

THE SOUTHEAST

Between Dublin and Cork, you can find opera in Wexford, crystal glass in Waterford, horse-racing at the Curragh and ancient historical sites at Kilkenny and Cashel

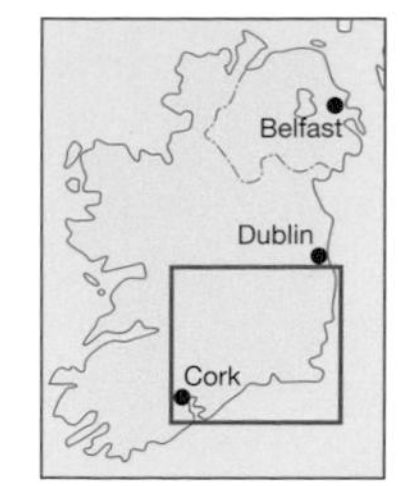

Main attractions
- ARKLOW
- WEXFORD
- SALTEE ISLANDS
- WATERFORD
- DUNGARVAN
- CAPPOQUIN
- LISMORE
- ARDMORE
- YOUGHAL
- MIDLETON
- KILDARE
- KILKENNY
- JERPOINT ABBEY
- CLONMEL
- ROCK OF CASHEL
- CAHIR

The "sunny Southeast", as it is popularly known, has one obvious advantage over the rest of Ireland: good weather. With almost double the annual sunshine quota for other regions, it has long been favoured as a holiday destination by the Irish themselves, and many Dubliners have holiday homes there. In high summer, therefore, traffic is heavy.

The region bears a distinct geographical contrast to the rest of the country with undulating flat plains intersected by meandering river valleys producing some of the most fertile agricultural land in Tipperary, Kilkenny and Carlow. Unlike the rugged South and West, the Southeast has a relatively gentle coastal aspect of long sandy beaches, rocky bays and low cliffs along the Wicklow, Wexford and Waterford shorelines.

This chapter suggests two different zroutes – one coastal and one inland – for exploring.

Option 1: Dublin to Cork via the coast

The first tour travels from Dublin to Cork, through Wexford, Waterford, Dungarvan and Youghal. This route takes 4½ hours –nearly two hours longer than the main N7/N8 route, but it is far more scenic, with frequent sea views, and far less congested. Take a full day for the drive, or plan one or two overnight stops.

Leave Dublin on the N11/M11 Bray road, and follow this through Rathnew to **Arklow** ❶. This is a small but lively fishing port and seaside resort on the estuary of the River Avoca known for boat building and for a pottery that produces everyday tableware.

Sir Francis Chichester's yacht *Gypsy Moth III*, in which he won the transatlantic single handed yacht race, was built at Tyrell's boatyard, as was the Irish Navy's late and much-lamented

PRECEDING PAGES: Lismore Castle.
LEFT: the Tipperary Plain.
RIGHT: Courtown Harbour, Gorey.

A life, and a living, connected to the sea.

sail training vessel, the brigantine *Asgard II*, which sank in the Bay of Biscay in 2008. The **Maritime Museum** (Bridgewater Centre, North Quay; tel: 0402-32868; Tue–Sat; charge) contains a comprehensive display of artefacts and memorabilia tracing the maritime history of Arklow through the centuries. Its eclectic collection includes World War II mines and salvaged items from the wreck of the *Lusitania*, sunk by a German submarine in 1915.

Gorey, the first town in County Wexford, has a more genteel ambience than Arklow. It is not actually on the sea, but nevertheless is chiefly a holiday resort. The seaside cottages will be found by turning left in Gorey on to the R742, a pleasant alternative route to Wexford.

The R742 passes **Curracloe Strand**, 7 miles (11km) northeast of Wexford Harbour. The totally unspoilt strand is backed by dunes, and stretches for 6 miles (10km). It "stood in" for the Normandy beaches when Steven Spielberg filmed *Saving Private Ryan* (1998). In winter it is home to numerous Canada geese. Information on the region's birds can be found at the **Wexford Wildfowl Reserve** (tel: 053-912 3129; free) which is signposted off the R741 just outside Wexford. The harbour is partly silted up, and its mud flats attract a variety of ducks, geese and swans.

The Southeast

0 — 20 km — 20 miles

Wexford

Wexford ❷ is a small, easy-to-explore town consisting of a series of quays parallel to the water, with a compact network of smaller streets parallel to the quays. Crescent Quay is decorated with a large statue on a plinth of locally-born Commodore John Barry (1745–1803) – *see panel, right*. Walking tours leave from the nearby Tourist Information Office (The Crescent; tel: 053-912 3111; daily 11am; charge) visiting the town's most interesting sites including the Westgate Tower, the only remaining of five fortified gateways in the Norman town walls.

Wexford, which has an interesting selection of small, old-fashioned shops and pubs, is at its best in October during the two-week run of the **Wexford Festival Opera** (tel: 053-912 2144; www.wexfordopera.com). Three full-length operas are performed at the **Wexford Opera House** (a €33million landmark building that opened in 2008), with an international cast of up-and-coming stars. The tradition is to choose little-known works, with consistently interesting results. A series of fringe events guarantee musical entertainment from 11am to midnight.

The **Irish National Heritage Park** (tel: 053-912 0733; www.inhp.com; daily, Mar–Oct 9.30am–6.30pm, Nov–Feb 9.30am–5.30pm; charge) at Ferrycarrig, 3 miles (5km) northwest of Wexford on the N11 Enniscorthy road, is an open-air theme park on the banks of the River Slaney. A couple of hours among its life-size replicas of typical dwelling places will make you an expert on Irish history and architecture, from Stone Age man in 6000BC, up to the 12th-century Norman settlements.

The 35-acre (14-hectare) open-air museum includes a prehistoric homestead, a *crannog* (lake dwelling), an early Christian fortified farm, a Christian monastry and a Norman castle. All the exhibits have guides dressed in the styles of the various periods.

Follow the N25 for 3 miles (5km) in the Rosslare direction to visit **Johnstown Castle Gardens** (tel: 053-914 2888; charge). The castle is a grandiose grey stone Gothic building dating from the mid-19th century. Only the entrance hall is open to the public but

At Crescent Quay in Wexford, a statue of Commodore John Barry remembers the local man who went on to become "the father of the American Navy". Born in Ballysampson in 1745, he emigrated to Philadelphia to make his name as a brilliant naval tactician during the American War of Independence.

BELOW: the harbour at Wexford.

Celtic cross at the Irish National Heritage Park.

BELOW: a child's view of history, exhibited at the Irish National Heritage Park.

the attractively landscaped gardens can be visited. Built for the Morgan family around 1810, the estate contains splendid plantings of Japanese cedars and Lawson cypresses, lakes, ornamental gardens, nature trails and the Devil's Gate walled garden set around the ruins of Rathlannon Castle.

The **Irish Agricultural Museum** (tel: 053-914 2888; charge) is in the stables. It has extensive displays of artefacts from Ireland's rural past, and a collection of Irish country furniture.

The scenic way to Waterford

The N25 travels to Waterford via New Ross, but we suggest this scenic alternative route to Waterford. Take the N25 in the Rosslare direction and turn off at Piercetown for **Kilmore Quay** ❸. This quaint little fishing village of thatched, whitewashed cottages and friendly pubs is built between the dunes and a stone harbour wall, and looks out to the uninhabited **Saltee Islands**, one of Ireland's most important bird sanctuaries. In late spring to early summer, 3 million birds from 47 species stop here, and can be observed from local boats.

In mid-summer, the sea bird colonies on Gannet headland make for a memorable, and noisy, sight with vast numbers of guillemots, fulmars and razorbills packing the cliff faces. Towards dusk, the sight of the puffins congregating in small groups near their nestling sites adds to the spectacle.

Heading west, the R736/R733 will take you to the **Hook Head Peninsula** and its lighthouse which forms the eastern side of Waterford harbour. Beyond Arthurstown is **Ballyhack**, a picture-book pretty waterside village on the estuary of the River Barrow, dominated by **Ballyhack Castle** (tel: 051-389 468; mid-June–mid-Sept daily; charge), a 16th-century tower house. The castle is thought to have been built around 1450 by the Knights Hospitallers of St John, one of the two military orders founded in the 12th century at the time of the Crusades.

Continue north on the R733 for 3 miles (5km) to **Dunbrody Abbey** (tel:

How the Southeast's history is littered with invasions

Given its close proximity to mainland Europe and Britain, the Southeast region carried the lion's share of invasions dating back to early monastic civilisation. The Vikings, who raided here regularly, were the scourge of early Christian settlements at Lismore, Kilkenny and Cashel. St Declan, who founded a monastery at Ardmore in 416, was preaching the Christian message long before the arrival of St Patrick, Ireland's patron saint.

The beautiful illuminated manuscripts and precious metal implements fashioned by monks during this golden age of learning were prized booty sought by the Vikings, who went on to found the cities of Waterford and Wexford sometime in the 9th century.

The Anglo-Normans led by the aptly named Strongbow arrived in 1169, ironically at the invitation of the then King of Leinster, Diarmuid, as part of a political alliance that would change the course of Irish history by allowing England a firm foothold for Henry II and his successors. At the behest of Henry VIII, Oliver Cromwell's bloody campaigns of 1650 destroyed many of the region's churches and monasteries. From the Middle Ages through to the 18th century, English influence in the Southeast was stronger than elsewhere in Ireland with many of the great estates of Russborough House, Kilkenny Castle and Johnstown Castle withstanding the political turbulence.

The most emotional touchstone of history in the region remains the 1798 Rebellion, when over 20,000 rebels wielding only pitchforks and clubs died in a hail of cannon and rifle fire at Vinegar Hill in Wexford. While the ill-fated attempt at forming a United Ireland inspired by the French Revolution of 1789 ultimately failed, it did ignite the fuse of liberty that would eventually succeed 100 years later.

Map on page 164

051-388 603; charge), an impressive ruined Cistercian abbey dating from 1175. A further 5 miles (8km) north is the **John F. Kennedy Memorial Forest Park and Arboretum** (tel: 051-388 171; charge). First planted in 1968, the 4,500 species of trees and shrubs are now reaching maturity.

The forest plots are divided into areas containing trees from each of the five continents. A particularly colourful feature is the ericaceous garden with rhododendrons, azaleas and heathers. The Visitor Centre, in Liscannor stone and Western red cedar, includes the Kennedy memorial and fountain, a lobby with explanatory display and an audio visual room.

The farmhouse near Dunganstown from which US President John F. Kennedy's grandfather emigrated to Boston is now the **Kennedy Homestead** (tel: 051-388 264; daily May, June and Sept 11.30am–4.30pm, July–Aug 10am–5pm, or by appointment; charge). From here, the shortest route to Waterford is back to Ballyhack for a five-minute car ferry ride to the Waterford side.

Waterford

Waterford ❹, a city of 49,000 people, has a proud past as an important European port, but nowadays its wide, stone quays are mainly used for car parking. Its heyday was in the 18th century, when the famous glass-manufacturing industry was established.

The Tourist Office is on Merchants Quay, in the same building as the **Waterford Museum of Treasures** (tel: 051-304 500; June–Aug Mon–Sat 9am–6pm, Sun 11am–6pm, Sept–May, Mon–Sat 10am–5pm, Sun 11am–5pm; charge). The museum has an audiovisual presentation, The Stones of Waterford, introducing the town's historic buildings. Its display of original artefacts includes 12th-century Viking jewellery and the sword of Thomas Francis Meagher, Irish patriot and hero of the American Civil War.

At the eastern extremity of the quays, you can see the distinctive landmark **Reginald's Tower** (tel: 051-304 220; charge), a massive, 12th-century cylindrical tower built by the Normans on a former Viking site. It is said that when the Norman Strongbow married the

The coat of arms of the Kennedys. This common Irish name whose Gaelic version, Ó Cinnéide, means "rough-headed", can be traced to a nephew of the 10th-century Irish king Brian Ború. John F. Kennedy received a rapturous reception during his 1963 visit.

BELOW: the Irish National Heritage Park.

Reginald's Tower, built by the Normans in the 12th century.

daughter of Dermot McMurrough, thus peacefully uniting the Norman invaders and the native Irish, the wedding took place here.

Georgian Waterford is only around the corner from Reginald's Tower, on **The Mall**. The **City Hall** (office hours; free) is a neoclassical building dating from 1788, which contains some good examples of early Waterford crystal, including a huge chandelier. The same building contains the Theatre Royal, which has been tastefully restored, and is one of Ireland's few remaining 19th-century theatre interiors with three tiers of horseshoe-shaped balconies. Just beyond it is **Bishop Foy Palace,** originally an imposing town house, which is also used by the Corporation as offices. Behind the palace is **Christ Church Cathedral** which replaced an older church in 1773.

Designed by local architect John Roberts (1712–96), it is the only neoclassical Georgian cathedral in Ireland with trademark white stucco trim designs of florets and laurels and huge Corinthian columns.

The ruins of French Church on Greyfriar's Street date back to an original 13th century Franciscan abbey. In 1695, it was given to a group of Huguenot refugees – hence the "French" prefix. A splendid east window is all that now remains intact.

Opposite the City Hall, **The Waterford Crystal Experience** (The Mall; tel: 051-351 936; www.waterfordvisitorcentre.com; charge) celebrates the city's long tradition of glass-making, which dates back to 1783. It is a substitute for the factory tour, which ceased when Waterford Wedgwood went into receivership in 2009. The dramatic 50-minute tour features glass blowing, before which the glass is heated to high temperatures in a blazing furnace, cutting and engraving carried out by skilled master craftsmen.

The main N25 takes a fast inland route to Dungarvan. If you have time, take the coastal route leaving Waterford on the R684 for **Dunmore East.**

BELOW: Waterford.

This pretty cliff-side fishing village and holiday resort of thatched cottages is on the open sea at the head of Waterford Harbour.

Tramore is a total contrast, with a long flat sandy beach, a fun fair, caravan parks and other facilities aimed at the budget holiday market. The coast road continues through a series of villages with good beaches – **Annestown**, **Bunmahon** and **Clonea**. Known as Waterford's Copper Coast, the region was designated European Geopark status by Unesco in 2004 in recognition of its volcanic geology and its 19th-century copper mining heritage. Find out more at the Geopark Information Point (Bunmahon; tel: 051-292 828; www.coppercoastgeopark.com). Elsewhere in the sandstone cliffs secluded coves can be reached by foot. **Dungarvan** ❺, situated on Dungarvan Harbour and backed by wooded hills, is the county town of Waterford. It has some lively waterside pubs, and is increasingly popular as a centre for activity holidays.

If you're headed for Cork, skip to Ardmore below. Those heading for Killarney, or with time for a scenic detour into the **Blackwater Valley**, should pick up the N72 Cappoquin road outside Dungarvan.

Vee Gap: the scenic route to Lismore Castle

Cappoquin ❻ is a quiet village nicely situated on a wooded hillside on the River Blackwater, a beautiful salmon and trout river. About 3 miles (5km) north of the village is **Mount Melleray** (tel: 058-54404; www.mountmellerayabbey.org), a Cistercian (Trappist) abbey dating from the mid-19th century that welcomes visitors in search of solitude. The Vee Gap route is signposted form here, going north on the R669 into the Knockmealdown Mountains. The Vee Gap is at the summit, from which you can see the Galtee Mountains in the northwest, and in good visibility the Rock of Cashel due north, rising out of the Tipperary Plain. Turn back here, and take the R668 to Lismore.

Lismore ❼, a pretty wooded village of 900 inhabitants approached over a stone bridge, was an important monastic centre from the 7th to the 12th centuries, which is why it has

Fishing boat at Bunmahon, along the coast from Dungarvan.

BELOW: celebrating Waterford's glass-making tradition.

The Clock Tower at Youghal.

BELOW: Lismore Castle.

two cathedrals. **St Carthage's** (1633) has some interesting effigies. More information on the village's past can be found at the Lismore Heritage Centre (tel: 058-54975; charge) opposite the castle car park. The village is dominated by the grey stone turrets of **Lismore Castle** (tel: 058-54424; www.lismorecastle.com; gardens and Art Gallery: 17 Mar–mid-Oct; charge). Built on a rock overhanging the river in the mid-18th century, the castle is a dramatic and imposing building. It is used as a summer residence by the Duke of Devonshire, and is not open to the public. The gardens include an 800-year-old yew walk. The Castle's west wing has been converted into a contemporary art gallery, and the gardens have a fine selection of contemporary sculpture by leading artists.

The structure, often described as the most spectacular castle in Ireland, dates back to 1753 and is situated in a panoramic position overlooking the Blackwater Valley with views over rolling, wooded hills to the Knockmealdown Mountains beyond. Private groups of up to 23 guests can rent the castle when the Duke is not in residence and are looked after by his personal staff.

Ardmore

If you are heading for Killarney, follow the Blackwater valley on the N72 from Lismore to Fermoy to Mallow, and on to Killarney, about a two-hour drive.

Beyond Dungarvan the main tour joins the N25, which climbs the **Drum Hills** giving good views back across Dungarvan harbour. **Ardmore** involves a 5-mile (8km) detour, but is worth the effort. St Declan established a monastery here in the 5th century. Today the remains of a medieval cathedral and round tower stand on the site of the original foundation, a cliff top with stunning views over Ardmore Bay. The 12th-century cathedral with its sturdy, rounded arches is a prime example of the Hiberno-Romanesque style, while the slender round tower with its conical roof is an elegant contrast. There are also interesting stone and carvings. The tiny village is at the bottom of the cliff, and is a pleasant place with good sandy beaches.

Youghal ❽ (pronounced *yawl*), famous for its long sandy beaches and historic town centre, found fame in 1956 when John Huston filmed the New Bedford scenes of *Moby Dick* here. Photos of Gregory Peck and other cast members on location can be seen in Paddy Linehan's Bar on the quay. Also on the waterfront, the Youghal Tourist Office (Market Square; tel: 024-92447) houses a heritage centre, and is the starting point for walking tours of the area that the town calls its "historic core" (May–Sept daily 11am, Oct–Apr phone to book). The Clock Tower is a distinctive landmark built in 1776 as a jail, that straddles the road in the town centre. The steps beside it lead to a street with excellent harbour views, and to the 13th-century St Mary's Collegiate Church. Sir Walter Raleigh (*c.*1552–1618) lived next door, where he smoked the first tobacco and planted the first the potato plant in Ireland – a claim disputed by several

other places. The famous sandy beaches which have made Youghal a favourite holiday destination for generations of Cork people (though nowadays beach lovers tend to live in Youghal and commute to work in the city) are outside the town on the Cork side, and extend for 3 miles (5km).

Quaker connections

Turn left off the N25 in Castlemartyr for **Shanagarry** ❾, a tidy village built of grey stone with many Quaker connections. To the east of the village is the famous hotel, **Ballymaloe House**. The **Ballymaloe Cookery School, Farm Shop and Gardens** (tel: 021-464 6909; www.cookingisfun.ie) in the village centre have a geometric potager, a formal fruit garden and a shell house. **The Emporium** (tel: 021-464-5838) beside the parish church, is a large craft shop with a good café, run by the Kilkenny Shop, stocking local ceramic artists including Stephen Pearce, with artists' studios in the basement.

For seconds and one-off pieces, visit the Jack O Patsy Pottery, a short walk from the Emporium. **Shanagarry House** where William Penn, the founder of Pennsylvania, grew up, is opposite the Emporium.

Ballycotton, 3 miles (5km) beyond Shanagarry is a fishing village built on a cliff top overlooking a small island and lighthouse. There are good cliff walks, and numerous nesting seabirds can be seen in early summer. The brightly-coloured fishing fleet supplies much of Cork city's fish.

Midleton ❿, a pleasant market town, is the home of Ireland's largest distillery. A new distilling complex was built in 1966, and the **Old Midleton Distillery** (tel: 021-461 3594; www.jamesonwhiskey.com; daily 10am–6pm; charge) now houses an audio-visual display and an optional guided tour which explains the distilling process of Irish whiskey. You can sample a drop of the famous product in a traditional Irish pub. Admirers of industrial architecture will enjoy the carefully restored 11-acre (4.5-hectare) 18th-century site. Most of the buildings are of cut stone, and the original waterwheel still functions. The N25 continues for 15 miles (24km) into Cork city.

Don't miss out on home-baked treats.

BELOW: Darina Allen teaches a class at the Ballymaloe Cookery School.

Jameson whiskey being distilled in Midleton.

Option 2: Kildare to Cashel via Kilkenny

This alternative, inland route from Dublin to Cork takes in some of the Southeast's most interesting historical sites. Kildare, with its Japanese Gardens and National Stud, has a Cathedral and a 12th-century Round Tower associated with St Brigid. The historic medieval town of black marble, Kilkenny, lies 23 miles (37km) south of Kildare, and the magnificently restored castle is a must-see.

You can linger in the Kilkenny area exploring the pretty riverside villages of the Nore and the Barrow, or continue to Clonmel, a compact market town on the River Suir, and head into the Nire Valley for a taste of unspoilt hill and bogland. Both options lead to Tipperary, and the spectacular ecclesiastical ruins on the Rock of Cashel.

At Cahir, there is a massive castle to visit, and quiet woodland walks through the relatively unfrequented Glen of Aherlow.

Leave Dublin on the main N7 Limerick motorway, taking the Kildare exit. The road cuts through **The Curragh** ⓫ a broad plain of 6,000 acres (2,400 hectares). The **Curragh Racecourse** is the heart of the Irish racing world, and the Irish Derby is held here every June. If you are lucky, you might see a string of race horses galloping by. Otherwise, the plain is used for exercises by the Irish Army which has a large camp here.

St Brigid founded a religious settlement in **Kildare** ⓬ in the 5th century. The present **Cathedral** dates partly from the late 17th century and partly from the 19th century. The 108ft (33-metre) **Round Tower** beside the cathedral belongs to a 12th-century monastery. If you're feeling lively, you can climb to the top for excellent views of the surrounding countryside.

The National Stud

Nowadays Kildare is a prosperous town, closely associated with the horse racing business, with dozens of small studs in the area. Admission to the most prestigious of them all, the **National Stud**,

BELOW: jockey Kieren Fallon after a race at The Curragh.

Selling the Auld Sod

When the Irish emigrated to America, it's said, they brought their churches, schools and music, but the only thing they couldn't bring was the soil. That omission was rectified in 2006 when the Auld Sod Export Company began selling 12oz (340gm) plastic bags of "Official Irish Dirt" from a field in the village of Cahir, County Tipperary, to a warehouse in Speonk, New York. At US$5 a bag (including a packet of shamrock seeds) it wasn't exactly dirt-cheap, but the company piled up $2 million of sales in its first four months.

Auld Sod advised the 40 million Americans who admit to Irish ancestry that they could use the soil to grow an Irish rose for their sweetheart or scatter it over the casket or grave of the dearly departed (www.officialirishdirt.com).

where top-class breeding stallions are stabled, and the **Irish Horse Museum** (tel: 045-521 617; www.irish-national-stud.ie; Mar–Oct; charge) also allows you to visit the rather strange **Japanese Gardens**, laid out between 1906 and 1910 by Japanese landscape artist Tassa Eida and his son Minoru, which have been carefully preserved as one of the country's horticultural gems. The significance of the gardens is not only artistic and horticultural but also religious, philosophical and historical.

Also in the National Stud grounds is **St Fiachra's Garden**, designed by Professor Martin Hallinan, a prominent landscape architect. St Fiachra, a 6th-century Irish monk, is the patron saint of gardeners. It was created to celebrate the Millennium with 4 acres (1.6 hectares) of woodland and lakeside walks. The centre of the garden is dominated by fissured limestone monastic cells within which are hand-crafted Waterford Crystal rocks and plants such as ferns and orchids. The gardens trace a symbolic journey through life, and are considered by experts to be among the finest in Europe.

Medieval Kilkenny

Kilkenny ⓭ was founded as a monastic settlement by St Canice in the 6th century. In 1641 a Catholic parliament, the Confederation of Kilkenny, tried to organise resistance to the persecution of Catholics. Cromwell's destructive 1650 campaign put a brutal end to such aspirations. While **Kilkenny** likes to promote itself as "Ireland's medieval capital", its rich heritage is not immediately obvious. Start at the Tourist Information Office in **Shee Alms House**, Rose Inn Street (tel: 056-775 1500; free) where you can equip yourself with free maps. This charming stone house with mullioned windows was built in the mid-17th century as a hospital for the poor. Frequent walking tours leave from here daily between March and October.

The sites of medieval Kilkenny start with St Canice's Cathedral at one extreme and end with the Castle at the other. Between them is a **Tholsel** (town hall) dating from 1761, the ruins of a 13th-century friary, the **Black Abbey**, and **Rothe House**, a 16th-century merchant's townhouse.

Horses have been bred in this area for seven centuries, but the first stud farm was not established until 1900. Its founder, a Scottish colonel, William Hall Walker, who later became Lord Wavertree, presented it to the British government in 1916 with the aim of founding a British National Stud. It was bought by the Irish government in 1943 and is run by the Irish National Stud Company.

BELOW: the Japanese Gardens at Kildare.

Ceramics at Kilkenny Design Centre.

Built by John Rothe around 1594, it is a fine example of a merchant's house of the Tudor period. Owned by the Kilkenny Archaeological Society, it contains a collection of Bronze Age artifacts, period costumes and Ogham stones. Rothe House also has a genealogical centre for tracing ancestors (www.rothehouse.com).

Kilkenny Castle (tel: 056-772 1450; guided tours only; charge, grounds and art gallery free) has been sumptuously restored. The grey stone, turreted landmark towers over the River Barrow, which serves as its moat. The original castle was built by the Butler family and dates from 1659. It has since been rebuilt several times.

The ornate Georgian stableyard of the castle across the main road is occupied by the **Kilkenny Design Centre** which has a big display of local and national crafts and several workshops.

While walking along Kilkenny's main street to reach St Canice's Cathedral note the narrow covered passageways on either side of the road that lead to cobbled alleyways lined by small houses, many with attractive floral displays. Known as "slips", these are a particular feature of Kilkenny, and a reminder of its medieval past.

St Canice's Cathedral, dating from the 13th century, is built in the Early English style. The Gothic interior is remarkable for its wealth of medieval monuments and life-size effigies, many carved from a locally quarried black marble. Amidst the many Norman memorials, be sure to view the female effigy in the south aisle wearing a Kinsale cloak, and St Ciaran's Chair, in the north transept, made of black marble with designs from the 13th century.

The 6th-century **Round Tower** in the Cathedral grounds is the only remnant of St Canice's monastery. You can climb its 167 steps, and enjoy an astounding view. In rainy weather it is closed to visitors for safety reasons.

Kytler's Inn on Kieran Street (tel: 056-772 1064) dates back to 1324 when Dame Alice Kytler, "the sorceress of Kilkenny", was accused of poisoning her four husbands, and of being a witch and brothel keeper. (She fled to England and stayed there.) The restaurant retains a medieval air with exposed

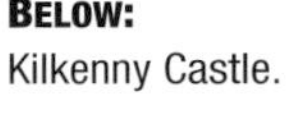

BELOW: Kilkenny Castle.

beams and 14th-century stonework. The area behind the inn and Kieran Street has a small park overlooking the River Nore and is a good place for a restful break.

Riverside villages

If you have time for a day-long drive around the Kilkenny area, explore one of the pretty villages on the rivers **Nore** and **Barrow**. The rivers meander through rich countryside with gently sloping wooded hills dotted with old villages of grey stone buildings, until they meet in New Ross and flow into the sea at Waterford.

Leave Kilkenny on the R700 south for **Bennettsbridge** ⓮. Some of Kilkenny's best craft makers live and work in this old-world village which straddles the River Nore, and have created their own craft trail. You can visit **Chesneau Leather Goods** (tel: 056-772 7456), makers of stylish handbags, wallets etc., the **Nicholas Mosse Pottery** (tel: 056-772 7505), which makes painted spongeware and also has a pottery museum, and candle makers Moth to a Flame (tel: 056-772 7826).

Thomastown is now a small market village (pop. 1,300) with a couple of delightful pubs, and a well respected college for craft makers, but in the 13th century it was walled and fortified. Its 18th-century stone-arched bridge over the Nore indicates its former importance.

Cross the bridge for a short (1½ miles/3km) detour to **Jerpoint Abbey** (tel: 056-772 4623; charge), one of the most attractive monastic sites in Ireland. The ruined Cistercian monastery is 12th-century. The church, with its Romanesque details, dates from this period. In the transept chapels the visitor can see 13th- to 16th-century tomb sculpture. The tower and cloister date from the 15th century. Another Kilkenny cottage industry craft maker, **Jerpoint Glass** (tel: 056-772 4350), where you can watch heavy, uncut glass being shaped by hand into modern designs, can be visited two miles beyond the abbey, just beyond the entrance to the **Mount Juliet estate**.

Return to Thomastown and cross the Nore again to reach **Inistioge**. The village is on a bend of the river and has a tree-lined square beside a 10-arched stone bridge. Its narrow, sloping streets of small stone houses make it a popular location for filming period movies such as the 1994 comedy-drama *Widow's Peak* with Mia Farrow and Joan Plowright, and in 1995, *Circle of Friends*, based on a novel by Maeve Binchy which starred Colin Firth and Minnie Driver. **Woodstock Estate Forest Park** which was laid out in the 19th century with interesting shrubs from the Far East, is open to the public, but the house itself was burnt down in 1922.

Seven miles (11km) south of Inistioge, turn left off the N700 to **The Rower**. This little village marks the start of an especially scenic stretch of road, with views over the River Barrow on the right hand side, and the Blackstairs Mountains beyond the river.

Graiguenamanagh ("the hamlet of the monks") ⓯ was an important

St Canice's Cathedral.

BELOW: a medieval lane in Kilkenny.

Leisure boating at Graiguenamanagh.

commercial centre in the 19th century, when the River Barrow was used to transport coal and grain. Nowadays herons fish along its weir, and one of its stone-built warehouses has been turned into a stylish waterside B&B and restaurant.

There is a genuinely nostalgic stretch of old-fashioned pubs on the hill to the west of the bridge, in whose dark interiors you can buy groceries as well as pints. At the top of this hill on the right is **Duiske Abbey**, a Cistercian Abbey founded in 1204. The exterior is pebble-dashed and does not look very promising. However, the main nave of the abbey was adapted in 1983 to serve as the parish church. Its combination of modern and ancient features is much praised by some, and lamented by others. Whatever your opinion, it is certainly worth a look at its light-filled interior. Look out for the **Knight of Duiske**, an effigy in chain mail, the hammer-beam roof in Irish oak and the magnificent Romanesque processional door in the south transept.

Both the R705 from Graiguenamanagh and the R700 Thomastown-Inistioge road lead to **New Ross** ⓰ where both the River Nore and the Barrow form a long estuary before reaching the sea. The town, which is in County Wexford, was built on a steep hill overlooking the River Barrow at a strategically important river crossing. On the river bank you will see the tall masts of the Dunbody Famine Ship (tel: 051-425 239; www.dunbrody.com; tours daily 9am–6pm, Oct–Mar until 5pm; charge), docked to the east of the river, a full-scale replica of a sailing ship built in 1845 to transport emigrants to North America. On board, actors tell the stories of the passengers, who

BELOW: Jerpoint Abbey.

travelled in this "coffin-ship" in order to escape the Great Famine. It is both entertaining, and a sobering reminder of the ordeal suffered by the 2 million and more people who emigrated from Ireland's ports in that era.

Clonmel

From Kilkenny, follow the N76 south to **Clonmel** ⓱, a busy Tipperary market town on the River Suir. The area to the north and east of the town is known for its apple orchards, and Clonmel is the centre of the Irish cider-making industry. However, travel to the south, and you will find another kind of scenery altogether.

The **Nire Valley Drive** is a sign-posted circular route of about 23 miles (37km) that travels along the edge of the **Comeragh Mountains** to **Ballymacarbry**, and the **Nire Valley**, returning to Clonmel through **Clogheen**. This is not for the faint-hearted; the roads are narrow, sometimes steep, and there are several hair-pin bends, but the forest and bogland scenery is magnificent. Ballymacarbry is a good base from which to follow the various way-marked trails in the area.

The Rock of Cashel

From Clonmel, head northwest on the R688 to **Cashel** ⓲. A cluster of romantic-looking, grey, turreted buildings stands on a limestone outcrop rising 60 metres (200ft) above the Tipperary plain, and absolutely every tour bus stops here. It will greatly enhance your visit if you can avoid the crowds by visiting the rock at lunch time or in the late afternoon.

The **Rock of Cashel** (tel: 062-61437; www.cashel.ie; charge) was probably once a centre of Druidic worship. By the 4th century AD Cashel was the ceremonial centre of the Kings of Munster. It was here, legend says, that St Patrick baptised King Aengus *(see margin note)*.

The largest building on the rock, the shell of **St Patrick's Cathedral**, built in the Gothic style, was in use from the 13th to the mid-16th centuries when it was desecrated in Oliver Cromwell's campaign. **Cormac's Chapel** is a simpler building dating from 1127, before the Norman invasion, with a high, corbelled roof similar to those found in early saints' cells in Glendalough and Dingle. Cormac's Chapel is generally considered one of the greatest achievements of native Irish church architecture. The entry archway is a fine example of the Hiberno-Romanesque style of architecture. The broken sarcophagus within the chapel is believed to be Cormac's final resting place. Don't miss the medieval paintings showing through the old plasterwork.

Spend some time lingering at Cashel, absorbing its unique atmosphere, and enjoying memorable views of the surrounding countryside. Rather than visiting the two heritage centres, concentrate on the Rock. Take a quick look at the town and maybe a light snack at the **Cashel Palace Hotel,** a red-brick, Queen Anne-style bishop's palace built in 1730. Note also the well-preserved wooden Victorian shop fronts across the road.

Cahir ⓳ (pronounced *Care*) situated on a hill above the River Suir, has a

The Rock of Cashel, according to legend, was created when St Patrick baptised King Aengus here in AD432, making him Ireland's first Christian ruler. The devil, displeased, flew over Ireland, took a bite out of the Slieve Bloom Mountains which got in his way and spat out his mouthful to form the Rock of Cashel.

BELOW: St Patrick's Cathedral on the Rock of Cashel.

The reason so many Irish place-names – perhaps as many as 5,000 of them – start with Bally is that the word Baile in Irish means "town". So Ballymacabry means Town of the Mac Cairbre Family.

certain faded charm, due chiefly to the well-proportioned Georgian houses in its Mall and main square. It is known chiefly for its antique shops and its castle. Cahir Castle (tel: 052-744 1011; charge) is a massive limestone fortress dating from the mid-12th century set on a rock in the River Suir. There is an informative guided tour, but avoid the audio-visual display. Walk up the hill beside the castle to the attractive main square. About a mile outside Cahir on the Clonmel road is the Swiss Cottage (tel: 052-744 1144; closed mid-Oct–mid-Mar; charge), a thatched *cottage orné* built in 1810 to amuse the Earls of Glengall. Bordered by verandahs fashioned from branched trees, it allowed its lordly aristocrats to play make-believe as "humble folk" for a day. To enhance the fantasy, hidden doorways were built to allow servants bring food and drink without being seen.

Walkers might like to detour northwest on the N24 for 14 miles (22km) to **Bansha**, and on to Tipperary town and the **Glen of Aherlow**, an excellent area for hiking with marked trails of various lengths. The Glen, which is partly wooded and runs alongside the Aherlow River, has great views of the Galtee mountains (sometimes spelt Galty), and is a good base for getting off the beaten track. The Glen of Aherlow leads to **Kilfinane** 20 at the heart of the Galtee and Ballyhoura Mountains. Its main feature, the Kilfinane Moat, is an ancient, flat-top mound encircled by three ramparts.

The Ballyhoura Way

The 56-mile (90km) **Ballyhoura Way** is a marked footpath through north Cork and County Limerick to Tipperary town. More than 930 miles (1,500km) of way-marked loop walks varying in length from 2 miles (3km) to 12 miles (20km) have been laid out, with a map board at the starting point of each walk. This is beautiful, unspoilt country, a mixture of pasture and woodland, with medieval and megalithic monuments.

From Kilfinane, continue driving west joining the N20 and turning south for Cork, or head south and join the N8 for Cork. Either way, Cork city is about one hour's drive. ❑

BELOW: Cahir Castle.

Horse-drawn Caravans

Slow travel doesn't get much slower, but these holidays appeal to anyone from students to retired executives who are looking for relaxation.

Holidays in horse-drawn caravans have been available for four decades. The caravans are of the type used by the nomadic ethnic minority, the Travellers, since the 19th century – barrel-topped and brightly painted.

Operators offering these holidays at first bought caravans from the Travellers, and made modifications to them. That supply dried up, however, as the real "travelling people" moved into modern caravans, towed by cars, or settled into houses. Today operators have the caravans made in the traditional style. Many of the horses, which are quiet and specially trained to pull the caravans, are descendants of those bred by the Travellers.

Today just a handful of operators in the Republic – in counties Mayo and Galway in the west, in Laois in the Midlands and Wicklow on the east coast – offer this kind of horse-drawn holiday *(see page 376)*. Clients come from all over the world, 85 percent via the internet. Most people take one-week holidays.

It can be a relaxing way of seeing a small area of the country. You clop along at about a mile an hour, so you only travel about 10–15 miles each day. You see and smell everything around you – the birds and animals, the hedges and fields. Maps with descriptions of interesting features to look out for en route are supplied. It's more about enjoying the experience than reaching a destination.

RIGHT: taking it slowly through the countryside.
ABOVE: horse maintenance at an overnight stop.

The caravans usually sleep four people – some can fit an extra berth – and are well equipped. Operators offer either fixed routes or will arrange alternatives in advance. Overnight stops are made at farms, pubs, guest-houses or hotels which are used to welcoming them.

Holidaymakers aren't sent on their way before receiving instructions and practice in leading and driving the horse. The instructor travels with them on the road until they feel relaxed and also meets up with them at their first overnight stop to help them unharness, and again next morning before they head off.

Some former clients of horse-drawn holiday companies in Ireland now run their own operations in Germany and the Czech Republic. One former client bought the caravans when an Irish proprietor retired and now runs a business in Normandy, France.

On a practical note

Expect to pay about €600–720 low season to €930 per caravan per week (4 people) depending on the region. A fifth person costs around 15 percent more.

There is a charge of about €20 per night per caravan per overnight stop which covers grazing, showers and so on. Oats for the horse are supplied by the operator, and the main problem is that some people tend to over-feed their horse. ❑

RESTAURANTS AND PUBS

Restaurants

Prices for a three-course dinner per person without wine:
€ = under €25
€€ = €25–40
€€€ = €40–55
€€€€ = over €55

Arklow

Kitty's of Arklow
56 Main Street, Arklow, Co. Wicklow
Tel: 0402-31669
Daily, L noon–5pm D 6–10.30pm **€–€€**
The most popular restaurant in town has a large, airy downstairs lounge bar and a more expensive restaurant upstairs with harbour views. Fresh fish specials – mussels, scallops, seafood chowder – sit beside traditional dishes such as Wicklow lamb and steak. There's a choice of set menus as well as à la carte.

Arthurstown, New Ross

The Harvest Room at Dunbrody Country House Restaurant
Arthurstown, Co. Wexford
Tel: 051-389 600
Mon–Sat 6.30–9.15pm, L Sun 1.30–2.30pm. L **€€**, D **€€€**, Tasting menu **€€€€**
Elegant, a place to treasure. A selection of menus built around local, artisan, speciality and home-grown organic food, offer classic and international influences on Irish themes including "a full on Irish" tasting menu.

Cappoquin

Richmond House Restaurant and Country House
Cappoquin, Co. Waterford
Tel: 058-54278
D daily 6.30–9.30pm
Early bird **€€**, D **€€€**
Popular with locals, a lively atmosphere. Careful sourcing of local food; a balanced mix of country house style and modern Irish cooked with care, imagination and confidence. Vegetarian menu available. Children are welcome.

Carlow

Lennon's Café/Bar
121 Tullow Street, Carlow, Co. Carlow
Tel: 059-913 1575
As a bar: daily 10am–11pm; B until 11am **€**; L Mon–Sat noon–3pm **€**; D Thur–Sat 5.30–9pm **€€**
Informal dining. Enticing menus are a mix of traditional and modern Irish with a sprinkling of international options. Great desserts.

Cashel

Chez Hans
Moor Lane, Cashel, Co. Tipperary
Tel: 062-61177
Tue–Sat 6–10pm
Early Bird D 6–7pm **€€**, D **€€€**, Informal daytime meals in Café Hans next door **€**
At the foot of the Rock of Cashel, a great setting in a converted church, family-run for over 40 years. Consistently excellent and great value.

Clonegal

Sha-Roe Bistro
Clonegal, Co. Carlow
Tel: 053-937 5636
Wed–Sat 6.30–9.30pm, Sun L 12.30–3.30pm. Sun L **€€**, D **€€€**
Off the beaten track but well worth a detour. A world-class chef, Henry White, a menu in tune with the seasons, meticulously sourced ingredients and faultless cooking in a beautifully restored 18th-century building.

Clonmel

Befani's
6 Sarsfield Street
Tel: 052-617 7893
B from 9am **€**; L 12.30–3pm; Tapas 3–9.30pm **€**; D 6–9.30pm **€€**
A spacious, simply and elegantly furnished Mediterranean and tapas restaurant. Outdoor patio dining. Open all day with menus for breakfast, lunch, tapas lunch and dinner. Good vegetarian options. Relaxed style.

Dungarvan

The Tannery
10 Quay Street (restaurant with rooms)
Tel: 058-45420
L Tue–Sun until 2.15pm **€€**; Early Bird D Tue–Fri **€€**; 6.30–7.15; D Tue–Sat 6.30–9.30pm **€€€**
One of Ireland's leading restaurants. Renowned chef Paul Flynn has a highly individual style and menus are based on local ingredients. Accomplished, often inspired, cooking influenced by global trends and regional cuisine, especially the Mediterranean.

Gorey

Marlfield Country House and Restaurant
Courtown Road, Gorey, Co. Wexford
Tel: 053-942 1124
Daily 7–9pm, L Sun 12.30–2pm, Light L daily in Library **€€€**
A romantic, elegant country house where guests are cosseted. Fine dining, classic and contemporary style; strongly seasonal menus with fruit and vegetables from the kitchen garden.

Graiguenamanagh

The Waterside
The Quay, Graiguenamanagh, Co. Kilkenny
Tel: 059-972 4246
Daily 6.30–9.30pm, L Sun only, 12.30–3pm, Light L in summer. L **€**, Early Bird **€**, D **€€**
Comfortable, not too formal; on the river bank with outdoor tables in summer. Enticing European style food plus local specialities: smoked eel from the river and local cheeses; good vegetarian choice.

Inistioge

Footlights
The Square, Inistioge, Co. Kilkenny
Tel: 056-775 8724
Daily noon–8pm, Fri–Sat until 10pm, Nov–Mar Sat–Sun only **€€**
The decor is stylishly contemporary at this child-friendly bistro in a period riverside house. Snacks include ciabattas, salads and pizzas, while mains are made with fresh local produce.

Kilkenny

Kilkenny Design Centre
Castle Yard, Kilkenny
Tel: 056-772 2118
Daily 10am–7pm, Jan–Mar closed Sun **€**

A lively first floor restaurant popular with both locals and visitors. Wholesome daily specials like chicken and broccoli crumble with Lavistown cheese, feature alongside imaginative soups, salads and home-baked cakes.

Lacken House
Dublin Road, Kilkenny
Tel: 056-776 1085
Tue–Sat 6.30–9pm, Sun in summer. Early Bird 6–7.30pm **€€€**, D **€€€€**
Mix of traditional and modern fine dining using the best local, mainly organic, produce. Great wine list.

Langton's
69 John Street, Kilkenny
Tel: 056-776 5133
Daily 9am–9.30pm **€–€€**
One of Ireland's premier bar restaurants, Langton's is a veritable warren of bars and restaurants, including child-friendly areas and a garden-patio. The kitchen is dedicated to using fresh local produce and regularly wins awards. The 67 Bar with full waiter service and a menu of local steaks and seafood is perennially popular.

Lismore

O'Brien Chophouse
Main Street, Lismore, Co. Waterford
Tel: 058-53810
Wed–Sat, L 12.30–2.30pm, D 6–10pm, Sun 12.30–8pm. L **€**, D **€€**
Charmingly converted Victorian pub with a pretty garden, serving robust versions of traditional Irish food, sourced locally and served simply.

Midleton

Ballymaloe House
Shanagarry, Midleton, Co. Cork
Tel: 021-465 2531
Daily, buffet meals only on Sun; children's high tea 5.30pm **€**; L 1pm **€€**; D 7–9.15pm **€€€€**
Forty years after Myrtle Allen opened Ireland's most famous country house hotel, Ballymaloe remains true to her vision. It presents an authentic experience with seasonally driven menus featuring their own farm and local artisan produce and seafood from Ballycotton, all cooked with flair and simply presented.

Farmgate Restaurant and Country Store
Broderick Street, Midleton, Co. Cork
Tel: 021-463 2771
Mon–Sat 9am–5pm, L noon–3.30pm, Thur–Sat, D 6.30–9.30pm **€€**
Informal and friendly, Farmgate features some of the region's best baking, as well as wholesome freshly prepared food using local ingredients, served in its rambling warehouse-like space, amid a funky collection of contemporary art.

Rosslare

La Marine and Beeches Restaurants
Kelly's Resort Hotel, Rosslare, Co. Wexford
Tel: 053-913 2114
Both daily, L and D. Beeches L 1–2pm **€€**, D 7.30–9pm **€€€€**; La Marine L 12.30–2.15pm **€€**, D 6.30–9pm **€€**
Family run for 100 years, Beeches is formal fine dining and provides classic cooking. Menus change daily. La Marine offers relaxed, contemporary European style menus with the odd Asian spin.

Waterford

La Bohème
2 Georges Street, Waterford, Co. Waterford
Tel: 051-875 645
Mon–Sat 5.30–10pm
Early Bird Tue–Fri 5.30–7pm **€€**, D **€€€€**
Run with style by owner/chef Eric Theze. A serious restaurant, French style all the way. Expensive, but worth it.

Wexford

La Dolce Vita
6–7 Trimmer's Lane, Wexford, Co. Wexford
Tel: 053-917 0806
Mon–Thur 9am–5.30pm, Fri–Sat noon–9.30pm, L noon–4pm. L **€**, D **€€**
One of Ireland's favourite Italian daytime restaurants, café and deli. Roberto's cooking and menus are enticingly authentic.

Youghal

Aherne's Seafood Restaurant
163 North Main Street, Youghal, Co. Cork
Tel: 024-92424
Restaurant: daily D 6.30–9.30pm, Set D **€€€**, à la carte **€€€€**; Seafood Bar: daily noon–10pm **€**
Renowned family-owned formal restaurant and all-day seafood bar, treasured for the simple but skilful cooking and presentation of fresh seafood straight from the boats.

Pubs

The 300-year-old **Suir Inn** at Cheekpoint, Co. Waterford serves keenly priced seafood. **Rockets of the Metal Man** in the seaside resort of Tramore is one of a few Waterford pubs to serve Crubeens (pigs' trotters).

Kilkenny's bars include the unspoilt **Bridge Bar** as you cross the river on the Dublin Road and the **Marble City Bar**, fashionable with good bar food. **Fury's Bar** at Moyvalley, Co. Kildare, down a slip road off a busy national route, offers a haven of snugs and a view of the canal.

RIGHT: simple style at Dunbrody Country House.

·MOSES·MADE·A·SERPENT·OF·BRASS·AND·PUT·IT·UPON

Cork and Surroundings

After experiencing Cork's gentle charms, you can explore the port of Cobh, visit an innovative wildlife park and aim to acquire eloquence (while abandoning dignity) by kissing the Blarney Stone

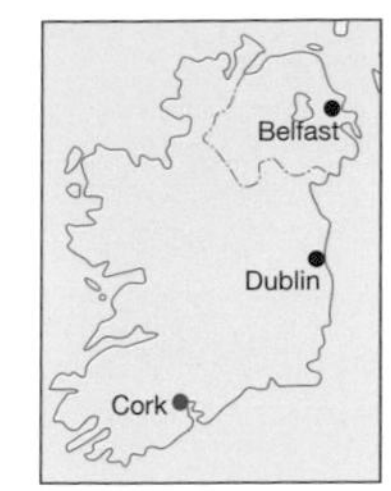

Main attractions
- St Fin Barre's Cathedral
- University College, Cork
- Princes Street Market
- Rory Gallagher Piazza
- Opera House
- St Anne's Church
- Cork City Gaol
- Blarney Castle
- Doneraile Wildlife Park
- Fota Wildlife Park
- Cobh

Pride of place runs deep amongst the natives of **Cork** ❶, an attitude ably underlined by its natives repeated reference to their city as "the real capital." Renowned as much for the sing-song lilt of their accent as for their traditional determination to usurp Dublin at commerce, culture and sport, the friendly population need little prompting to extol their proud birthright. "Up the Rebels!" will be heard frequently as both a hearty greeting and a sporting exhortation – a legend dating back to the 19th-century National Fenian Movement when Cork was the centre of political rebellion.

European immigration

With a population of more than 125,000, Cork has long divested itself of its sleepy second-city status with multinationals setting up "Silicon Valley"-style business operations combined with a growing influx of immigrants from the new European Union states such as Poland, Hungary and Lithuania. The result is a cosmopolitan city bristling with tapas bars, ethnic restaurants and festivals of which the Cork Jazz Festival (www.corkjazzfestival.com) in October and International Choral Festival (www.corkchoral.ie) in May reign supreme.

Lying at the mouth of the River Lee, the city's historic centre is formed on an island created by two channels of the river. Easily walked from end to end over a day, it allows the visitor easy access for sightseeing, shopping and idle strolling within convenient distance of any car park.

Founded by St Finbar in the 6th century, the name "Cork" derives from the Irish *Corcach Mór Mumhan*, translated as the "great marsh of Munster". The place was prone to flooding and allowed early civilisation to flourish only on marshy islands joined by bridges.

Over the centuries, Cork, like much of Ireland, was invaded by the Vikings,

LEFT: stained glass in St Fin Barre's.
RIGHT: bus mural beside the real deal.

A Polish food store caters for a new immigrant market.

the Normans, and the English – as well as an episode of the Black Plague in 1349 that almost wiped out the city. The McCarthy's of Desmond, a native tribe who grasped power in the 12th century, are credited with constructing the first city walls, built in the present-day Shandon area. Over the centuries, these defensive structures were extended to make Cork one of the great walled cities of Ireland's medieval period.

Cork was at its most affluent in the 18th century, when its butter market was a source of vast wealth. Much of the best architecture as seen in the wide streetscapes of the South Mall, Grand Parade and the North Mall dates from this period. This was the era of the "merchant princes" – local business families who still figure in much of the city's commerce and whose mansions in upmarket suburbs such as Montenotte and Blackrock remain in the same hands.

In the 18th and 19th centuries Cork's more affluent citizens lived in its waterside suburbs or on the high ground to the north of the city to avoid the diseases that proliferated in its marshy centre, where slaughter houses and tanneries proliferated. Nowadays people still prefer to live outside the city, commuting from its pleasant hinterlands, and the city centre itself on Lapp's Island has a very low population, measured in the hundreds. However, some 350,000 people live within a 45-minute journey of Cork city in attractive seaside locations such as Cobh and Kinsale, or satellite towns such as Midleton, Ballincollig and Carrigaline. The total student population of the city is in excess of 25,000 (University College and Cork Institute of Techonology combined), a figure which will not surprise anyone who has seen the young people pouring out of the city's bars and discos at closing time on the weekends. With traditional manufacturing industries like Ford and Dunlop long since closed, the city and its hinterland are now home to high-tech pharmaceutical, electronic, telecoms and computer multinationals such as

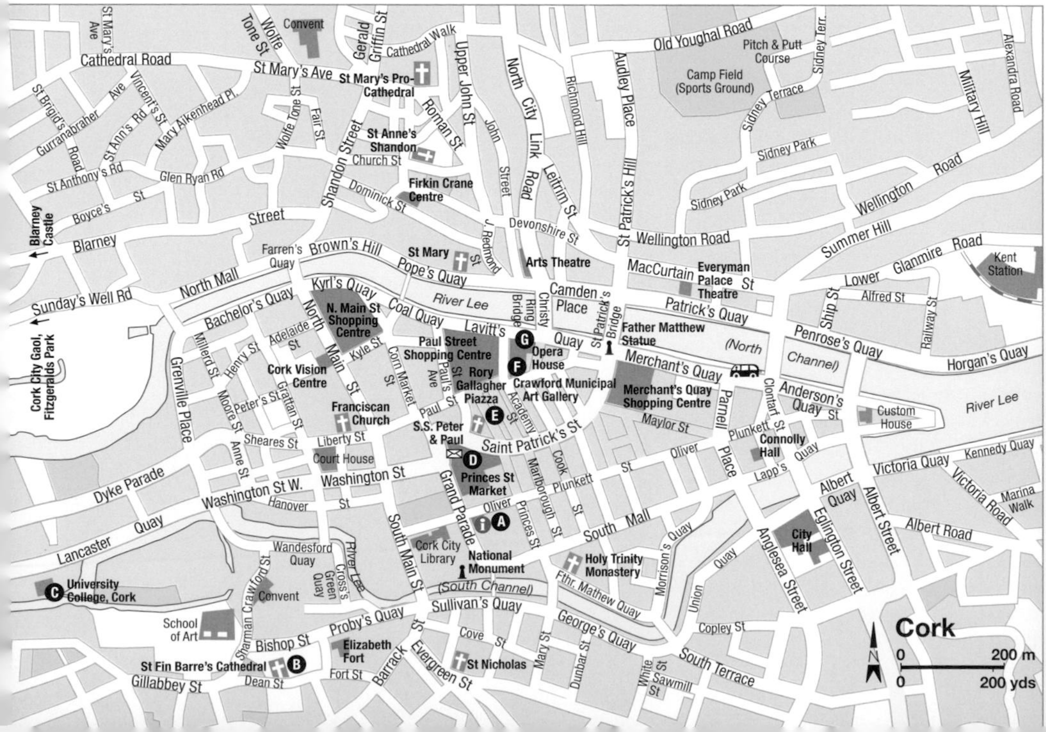

Pfizer and EMC as the city attracts the industries of a new age.

Cork's tenure of European Capital of Culture in 2005 prompted a redesign of the city's St Patrick's Street and Grand Parade by the Barcelona architect Beth Gallí, giving a pedestrianised focus with her pavements of polychromatic stone and futuristic street lights. A major programme of inner city development has led to a proliferation of lacklustre, sparsely tenanted shopping malls, and the disappearance of many of the quirky smaller shops, galleries and businesses. (Outside the traditional centre, several new office and apartment developments dating from the boom years remain largely unoccupied, including the city's much-vaunted tallest building, the Elysian Tower). The most successful regeneration project is the area between Patrick Street and the river, around Paul Street. The smoking ban has led to the installation of outdoor bar and café tables under awnings in these pedestrianised areas, where buskers are also encouraged, leading to an unusually lively street-life by (rainy) Irish standards.

The city centre

Cork's narrow lanes, half-hidden flights of steps and unexpected plazas lend themselves to lazy strolls or determined one-day sightseeing excursions. The city centre is often likened to Venice and Rome for its many bridges and steep hills, but, as in Venice or Rome, any geographical confusion that may occur will usually be solved by walking a straight line to a major landmark.

Start at the **Tourist Information Office** Ⓐ (tel: 021-425 5100; www.corkkerry.ie) on **Grand Parade**. Take a look across the street in front of the TIO at a terrace of three elegant Georgian houses with slate-hung, bow-fronted windows, typical of Cork's 18th-century prime. In the southwest, across the south channel of the River Lee, you can see the spires of **St Fin Barre's Cathedral** Ⓑ (www.cathedral.cork.anglican.org), where the city began as a monastic school in about AD650. Both the Gothic, late 19th-century cathedral, and the bridge across the Lee are built of characteristic white limestone. The cathedral, designed by William Burges, who also contributed the stained glass, sculptures, mosaics

Sculpture on St Fin Barre's Cathedral.

LEFT AND BELOW: St Fin Barre's Cathedral.

University College, Cork.

and metal work for the interior, had its foundation stone laid in 1865. The high columns of the nave are of Bath stone while the walls are lined with Cork red marble. Scenes from the Old Testament are depicted in the stained glass, and the organ dates from 1889.

Washington Street, which reaches Grand Parade in a T-junction, leads, after a 10-minute walk, to the campus of **University College, Cork** ⓒ The Visitor Centre (tel: 021-490 3000; www.ucc.ie; guided tours daily at 3pm, but telephone to confirm; free, charge for tours) is located in the north side of the 19th-century Tudor-Gothic style Quadrangle, adjacent to a display of ancient Ogham Stones – gravestone-like rock tablets with varying sequences of short lines etched along one side, recording events and occasions in an ancient language known as Ogham. Known locally as UCC, the college has 15,000 students. The new buildings on campus have been cleverly integrated to create a second focal area with a 21st century identity. The Honan Chapel, a Hiberno-Romanesque chapel dating from 1916, which showcases Celtic Revival arts and crafts, forms part of this vista. The campus has several other interesting buildings, notably the **Lewis Glucksman Gallery** (www.glucksman.org), a boldly designed art gallery with its top floor among the treetops, which was voted Best Public Building in 2005. The Crawford Observatory, dating from 1878 and designed by Howard Grubb, contains working models of his Equatorial and Siderostatic telescopes. The university was also where Professor George Boole, whose Boolean Logic has become the basis of modern day computer science, spent much of his working life.

Back at the Tourist Information Office on Grand Parade, walk a few steps to the left for a look at **South Mall**, Cork's business area in the city's 18th-century prime. It is now the legal and banking district. Prior to its 18th century development, "The Mall", as it is known locally, was a waterway where

BELOW: shopping at Princes Street Market.

The Cork Accent

The sing-song qualities of the local accent can often prove a tricky hurdle for the visitor to overcome, especially when combined with the speed of speech generally acknowledged the fastest in the country. With a rich vein of slang running through daily discourse, the need for a polite "pardon me?" will be frequent. Given the multitudes of invaders through the centuries, Viking, Norman, Elizabethan and Huguenot, to name but a few, Corkonians have assimilated a lexicon all of their own.

Cork Slang by Seán Beecher, on sale at local bookshops, provides a cultural tour of this essential quirk. Thus you will learn that a *flah-bag* is a promiscuous woman, a *masher* is an attractive man, a *ranker* is a coward, *scauld* is tea and *meejum* is a measure of stout.

merchant ships moored and the flights of stone steps still visible on its north side recall its maritime past.

The English market

Leaving the river to your back, walk along the Grand Parade to Cork's indoor food market, the **Princes Street Market** **D**, also known as the English Market, which extends across a whole city block. This huge market, with its ornate Victorian cast-iron frame, is one of the city's showpieces, where over 1,500 stalls of artisan food makers, continental delis and organic farmers sell their wares alongside traditional fishmongers, beef, lamb and pork butchers and poulterers. At the far (Princes Street) end of the market there is a top-lit piazza with a central fountain and the popular Farmgate Restaurant around the balcony above. Note the stall at the door with a display of tripe (cows' intestines) and drisheen (blood sausage), and the buttered eggs (the shells rubbed with butter to preserve their freshness) sold in the piazza.

Probably the best place in the city to hear the local accent in all of its wonderful cadences, the market has all the life of the city within its bounds – tourists, locals both young and old, Eastern European immigrants and musicians. Recently, some vintage clothing stalls have appeared, adding another flavour to this much loved institution.

Follow Grand Parade into the graceful curve of **St Patrick's Street**, Cork's main shopping street. The major department store, Brown Thomas, has a good stock of Irish crystal. Look up, because above the modern shop fronts many of the buildings on Patrick Street (as it is generally called in conversation) have retained 18th- and 19th-century features. After lunch you'll hear a unique Cork phenomenon – cries of "Eeeechooo!" from vendors of Cork's evening paper, the *Evening Echo*. A bronze statue of this quintessential Cork symbol, "the Echo boy", stands at the junction of Patrick Street and Cook Street.

About 20 metres along St Patrick's Street, on the left-hand side, a pedestrian alleyway next to the Body Shop leads to the **Rory Gallagher Piazza** **E**, a pedestrian square popular with buskers, named for the Cork-born rock and

EAT

As well as the meats and fish, Princes Street Market now has olive stalls, wine merchants, bakers and cheese makers – putting it on most foodies' must-do lists. While there, pause for a break at the first-floor Farmgate Café (inexpensive), one of the city's liveliest lunch spots and perfect for people watching.

BELOW: Woodford Bourne, once a famous tea and wine importer, now houses McDonald's.

The Firkin Crane Centre.

blues guitarist who died in 1995. This area is the closest Cork gets to a "left bank", with a cluster of design conscious home furnishing stores, fashion and vintage clothing boutiques and trendy cafés.

Turn right on to Paul Street for the **Crawford Municipal Art Gallery** Ⓕ (tel: 021-490 7855; www.crawfordartgallery.ie; Mon–Sat 9am–5pm; free). It has an interesting permanent collection, in which most major 20th-century Irish artists are represented, and a good collection of topographical paintings of Cork in its 18th- and 19th-century prime. It also mounts and hosts touring exhibitions in an extension, built in 2001, which wraps around the existing red-brick building, using the same material, in an adventurous design by Dutch architect Eric van Egeraat.

The **Opera House** Ⓖ (www.corkoperahouse.ie), just around the corner in the direction of the river, dates from 1965, and was recently given a stylish new façade and a pedestrianised forecourt, to the great delight of local skateboarders. The original structure, built in 1855, played host to Charles Dickens, who performed there twice – as did Irish patriot Charles Stewart Parnell, who made his famous statement upon its stage: "No man has a right to fix the boundary of the march of a nation."

To the right is St Patrick's Bridge, and straight ahead is the modern Christy Ring Bridge. Both lead from the central island of Cork to the northside.

Cross the Christy Ring Bridge, and climb the hill to the **Firkin Crane Centre**. Part of the centre, a classical rotunda attractively built in cut limestone, is used for dance performances, and part houses the **Shandon Craft Market**. The Firkin Crane Centre dates from the 18th century when much of Cork's wealth derived from the exporting of butter. Butter was packed in wooden barrels known as firkins, which were weighed here by a crane.

BELOW: Cork's Opera House.

The four-faced liar

Across the road is **St Anne's Church**, (www.shandonbells.org) the city's most enduring landmark whose Shandon Steeple is topped by a large salmon-shaped weather vane and its carillion of bells. Visible right across the city, the four-sided clock tower was known as "the four-faced liar" due to a peculiar quirk of its machinery that allowed four different times to be displayed. Strangely, all four faces synchronised perfectly on the hour. This malfunction was corrected some years ago, much to the chagrin of locals.

Built in 1722, the steeple has red sandstone faced with white limestone, a popular combination in local architecture, known as "streaky bacon", from which the colours of the Cork hurling and football teams are taken. A climb to the belfry rewards visitors with the chance to play a tune on the famous Shandon Bells – an exercise that will allow your inexpert rope pulls to echo discordantly across the city. Past the bell loft, a stairs leads to the tower's terrace and stunning views on all sides.

The old prison

A 20-minute walk starting at the North Mall beside the river at the foot of Shandon Street, uphill into Sunday's Well Road leads to **Cork City Gaol** (tel: 021-430 5022; www.corkcitygaol.com; charge), a 19th-century prison recreated in all its miserable conditions. With wax figures crouched in the tiny cells and the sounds of dragging chains, the atmosphere is sobering and perhaps not suitable for very young children. The building also houses a fascinating (but rather underpromoted) **Radio Museum** in the former studio of Cork's first radio station, with numerous genuine artefacts, providing a history of the early days of Irish and international radio broadcasting.

Walking back toward the city centre, cross the River Lee on Daly's Bridge, a pedestrian suspension structure known locally as "the shaky bridge", to **Fitzgerald Park.** Set beside the river with many benches and quiet corners ideal for picnics, the 18-acre (7-hectare) landscaped park is a favourite of all Corkonians with rose beds, spreading oaks and central pond. The **Public Museum** is housed in a two-storey Georgian house and contains many personal effects of Michael Collins, the Cork-born freedom fighter. The Riverview Café, in the museum's extension, fully exploits the commanding views of the River Lee and provides the visitor with a tranquil haven to enjoy a coffee and a snack.

Blarney Castle

A visit to **Blarney Castle** ❷ (tel: 021-438 5252; www.blarneycastle.ie; daily 9am–sundown, Sun until 5.30pm in summer; charge) makes a pleasant half-day outing. Don't be put off by Blarney's reputation as a tourist trap. The castle is surrounded by well-tended gardens, two rivers, a "Druid" grotto and parkland (don't miss the lake), and the experience is humorously presented tongue-in-cheek as a load of Blarney.

The castle is not furnished, but nor, like many castles of its age, is it a ruin.

Blarney Castle.

BELOW: there is no dignified way to kiss the Blarney Stone.

Giraffe roam freely in Fota Wildlife Park.

It is basically a 15th-century fortified home, and the staircase is narrow so that it can be defended by one man holding a sword. Kissing the **Blarney Stone** is supposed to bestow the gift of eloquence. The word Blarney has entered the English language to mean "smoothly flattering or cajoling talk", but the origins of the strange tradition are obscure.

Having ascended the castle's many steps to the stunning vistas offered by the rooftop viewing point, those who would romance the Stone are held by the waist while leaning over the battlements to offer puckered lips upon the legendary surface. There is no charge, but most people are so happy to survive the ordeal, they gladly pay €10 at the exit for a souvenir photo.

North Cork Excursion

Driving from Blarney on the N20, the fertile plains of north Cork start to beckon. A portion of the county often overlooked by visitors, its villages offer an interesting one-day excursion. A few miles beyond Mallow is **Doneraile Wildlife Park** (tel: 022-24244; free), an outstanding example of an 18th-century landscaped park in the Capability Brown style. Mature groves of oak trees, restored water features and a number of deer herds can be viewed along the many pathways within the Park. Doneraile Court, the former residence of the St Leger family, is situated within the park and will be opened to the public when it has been fully restored.

Heading west from Mallow on the N72 to Killarney, the ruins of **Kanturk Castle** are found on the town's outskirts. Dating back to the 16th century as a stronghold of the McCarthy clan, the castle and grounds were handed back to Ireland by the English National Trust, which had held the landmark since 1899.

Fota Wildlife Park

The east side of Cork Harbour is formed by three islands, **Little Island**, **Fota Island** and **Great Island**, all connected by causeways. The road from

BELOW: cheetah family at Fota Wildlife Park.

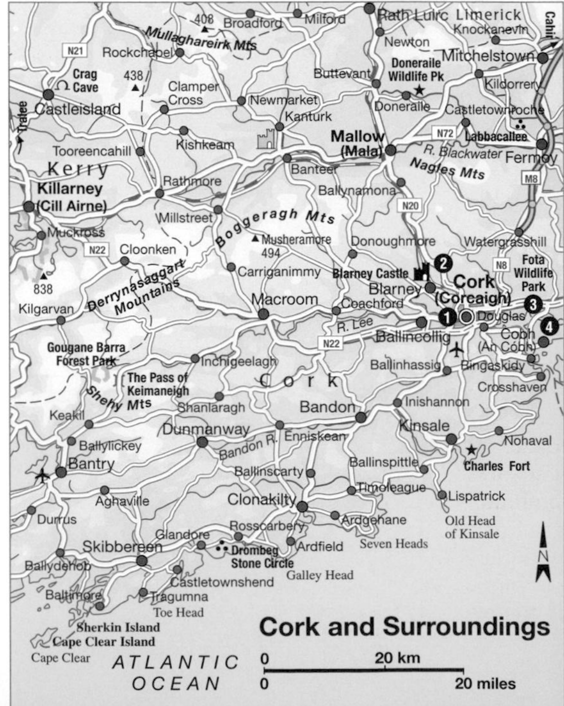

Cork to Cobh brings you past the walls of the 780-acre (315-hectare) **Fota Estate. Fota Wildlife Park ❸** (www.fotawildlife.ie; tel: 021-481 2678; charge) aims to breed certain species that are under threat in the wild. Giraffe, zebras, ostrich, oryx and antelope roam freely in grassland, monkeys swing through trees on lake islands, while kangaroos, wallabies, lemurs and peacocks have complete freedom of the park. Fota is the world's leading breeder of cheetahs, one of the few animals here that must be caged.

The freely accessible **Fota Arboretum** is beside the Wildlife Park, behind Fota House (tel: 021-481 5543; www.fotahouse.com; charge). The house, built as a shooting lodge, was enlarged in 1820 to a symmetrical neoclassical design. The arboretum has a beautiful collection of mature trees. The name derives from the Irish *Fód te*, meaning warm soil. Many of these specimens were introduced from Asia, Australia and the Americas during the 19th century.

The Cove of Cork

Cobh ❹ (pronounced *Cove*) was a small fishing village, referred to as the Cove of Cork. It grew in importance as a British naval base during the American War of Independence, thanks to its natural deep-water harbour. It grew again during the French Revolutionary and Napoleonic Wars (1792–1815). The fine cut-stone buildings on the two main islands in its harbour, built by the British Navy, date from this period. In Victorian times Cove became Queenstown, and after Independence reverted to its original name in Irish transliteration.

Cobh is attractively located on a steep slope with a Victorian-style promenade, and panoramic south-facing views of Cork harbour. It is a popular commuter town, linked by rail to the city. It is popular with visitors for its maritime history as the last – and first – European port of call for transatlantic shipping. Between 1848 and 1950 about 2½ million adults and children emigrated through the port. Their transport ranged from convict transports and the "coffin ships" of the famine years, overcrowded and unseaworthy, to the luxury of White Star and Cunard liners. Cobh was the last port of call of the *Titanic* in 1912, and it was to Cobh that most of the bodies recovered from the torpedoing of the *Lusitania* in 1915 were brought. The old railway station is now the Cobh Heritage Centre (tel: 021-481 3591; www.cobhheritage.com; daily 9.30am–5.30pm; free). The history of emigration from Cobh is covered in **The Queenstown Story** (charge), an imaginative audio-visual exhibition. Allow at least an hour.

A large, Gothic-revival church, **St Colman's Cathedral**, was built in granite between 1868 and 1915. From its parapet you can see Roches Point in the south, which marks the harbour entrance, and the open sea beyond. ❑

St Colman's Cathedral.

BELOW: memorial to emigration.

RESTAURANTS AND PUBS

Restaurants

Prices for a three-course dinner per person without wine:
€ = under €25
€€ = €25–40
€€€ = €40–55
€€€€ = over €55

Cork

Augustine's
7 Washington Street, Cork
Tel: 021-427 9375
Tue–Sat, D 6–9.30pm **€€**
Intimate city centre restaurant where the Irish owner-chef serves a six-course tasting menu based on fresh local produce from the English market across the street. For foodies.

Café Paradiso
16 Lancaster Quay, Western Road, Cork
Tel: 021-427 4973
Tue–Sat, L noon–3pm **€**; D 6.30–10.30pm **€€€**
Legendary vegetarian restaurant. Denis Cotter creates dishes that never fail to excite the palate so that even carnivores relish every mouthful. Good friendly service in spite of the rather cramped, ever busy space. Buy one of his books and you'll see the skill behind it all.

Cornstore Wine Bar and Grill
Cornmarket Street, Cork
Tel: 021-427 4777
Daily, L noon–4pm, D 5–10.30pm. L **€**, D **€€**
A granite warehouse conversion in Cork's open air market district, this is a buzzingly busy gastropub, said to make the best chips in town. Lobster is as speciality, as are their premium steaks, which include a 10oz T-bone. Pizzas are stone-baked to order, and the home-made desserts include mocha ice cream and a daily chocolate special.

Crawford Gallery Café
Emmet Place, Cork
Tel: 021-427 4415
Daily 9am–5pm, L from noon **€**
A team from Ballymaloe, Ireland's famous country house, offer light seasonal special and legendary home-made cakes and scones. The elegant room with tall windows is a restful haven in the city centre, and a favourite meeting point.

Farmgate Café
English Market, Cork
Tel: 021-427 8134
Mon–Sat 8.30am–5pm. B, L and light meals **€**
Located in the gallery of this famous food market. Good cooking and good value. The "full Irish" breakfast, traditional and regional dishes with produce from the speciality stalls in the market.

Flemings Restaurant
Silver Grange House, Tivoli, Cork (restaurant with rooms)
Tel: 021-482 1621
Daily, 6.30–10pm, D **€€€**
2½ miles (4km) from city centre in a large, elegant Georgian house and kitchen garden where much of the fruit, herbs and vegetables are grown. An excellent and stylish family run restaurant, with accomplished owner-chef providing classical and modern French cooking.

Greenes
48 MacCurtain Street, Cork
Tel: 021-450 0011
Daily D 6–9.30pm **€€€**
Located on a cobbled alley off the busy street, a natural waterfall is the view from a minimal modernist interior with bare stone walls. A continental menu with Asian Pacific influence delivers exciting fusion dishes featuring local seafood and meat.

Idaho Café
19 Caroline Street, Cork
Tel: 021-427 6376
Mon–Sat 8.30am–5pm, L 12.30–4.30pm. B **€**, L **€**
Great breakfast, with tempting home baking until noon. Good range of international lunch options. Great value.

Isaacs Restaurant
48 MacCurtin Street, Cork
Tel: 021-455 1348
Daily, L Mon–Sat 12.30–2.30pm, D daily 6–10pm. L **€**, D **€€**
Spacious converted warehouse. Relaxed, fun and buzzy. Good service, quality ingredients, consistently excellent cooking delivered at a fair price. Food style a mix of international and traditional. Good vegetarian options.

Jacobs on The Mall
30A South Mall, Cork
Tel: 021-425 1530

LEFT: lunching by the River Lee in Cork.
RIGHT: music enlivens a Cork bar.

Mon–Sat, L 12.30–2.30pm, D 6.30–10pm. L **€€**, D **€€€€**
Leading restaurant in the city. Once a Turkish Bath, the space is atmospheric. Innovative, contemporary European style cooking from fresh, seasonal, local and organic food – plus a spark of creativity that makes a meal here a special experience.

Jacques Restaurant
Phoenix Street, Cork
Tel: 021-427 7387
Mon–Sat 6–10.30pm, L **€**, Early Bird 6–7pm **€€**
Carefully sourced ingredients from network of producers (listed on the menu); a simple style of modern cooking consistent with a policy of letting the natural flavours of top-quality food shine through; good service and great value.

Les Gourmandises Restaurant
17 Cook Street, Cork
Tel: 021-425 1959
Mon–Sat 6.30–9.30pm, Early D **€€**, D **€€€**
The food is local; everything else is firmly like being in a rather stylish family-run restaurant in France. Menu is deceptively simple; this place delivers the goods at a fair price for the quality, including a special value "market menu". Michelin-trained chefs.

Liberty Grill
32 Washington Street, Cork
Tel: 021-427 1049
Mon–Sat, B and L 8am–5pm **€**; D last orders 9pm **€–€€**
Cheerful, family-friendly burger joint also serving traditional American salads and desserts. All food is freshly prepared and locally sourced, with crab burgers, lamb burgers and other variations for the discerning.

Blarney

Blairs Inn
Cloghroe, Blarney, Co. Cork
Tel: 021-438 1470
Daily bar food 12.30–9.30pm, L **€**
Riverside country pub offering sound cooking and fairly traditional Irish meat, seafood dishes, vegetarian and even game in season. Lunch and dinner is also available in the attached restaurant.

Cobh and East Cork

Ballymaloe House
Shanagarry, Co. Cork
Tel: 021-465 2531
Daily L 1pm, D 7.30–9.30pm, Sun 7.30–8.30pm. L **€€€**, D **€€€€**
Food lovers will want to make a pilgrimage to the pioneer of the Irish food revival, about 30 minutes' drive northeast of Cobh. The best of fresh local produce, much of it from their own farm, is simply prepared and served in gracious traditional surroundings. Be sure to book in advance.

Jacob's Ladder
Water's Edge Hotel, Cobh
Tel: 021-81 5566
Daily L noon–2.30pm, D 6–10pm. L **€**, D **€€**
The clean lined contemporary dining room really is on the water's edge, with panoramic harbour views from picture windows. There's an imaginative menu of superior pub grub with an Irish accent: baked ham with parsley sauce, for example.

Mallow

Longueville House
Mallow, Co. Cork
Tel: 022-47156
Daily, light meals 12.30–5pm **€€**; Early Bird 6–6.45pm **€€**; D and menu gourmand **€€€€**
Early 18th-century manor house; the restaurant includes a Turner Conservatory overlooking the River Blackwater. The river, family farm and kitchen gardens supply much of the food, and they make wine and apple brandy. Fine dining, classic and Irish country house cooking. Children welcome.

Pubs

Boqueria is a dark old-style pub and wine bar in downtown Bridge Street, Cork city (north of Saint Patrick's Bridge), which serves Spanish wines and Irish drinks. Good tapas.

Meet actors at **Dan Lowrey's Tavern**, 13 MacCurtain Street, Cork; beside the Everyman Palace Theatre, established in 1875 and named after the founder.

The Corner House, 7 Coburg Street (near MacCurtain Street) is a genuine "local" with live Cajun and Irish folk music at weekends.

Dennehy's, Cornmarket Street, still has its Victorian interior, and doesn't open until 5pm.

The Bosun on the pier at Monkstown, southeast of Cork city, is a well-run bar conveniently near the ferry that plies between Ringaskiddy and Cobh. Famous for its bar food, steaks and seafood.

In Blarney village, the **Muskerry Arms** is a lively place with traditional music in the bar most evenings.

Map on page 198

THE SOUTHWEST

This is where the Atlantic first touches Europe, and the mild climate enhances the spectacular scenery of Bantry Bay, Killarney, the Ring of Kerry and the Dingle Peninsula

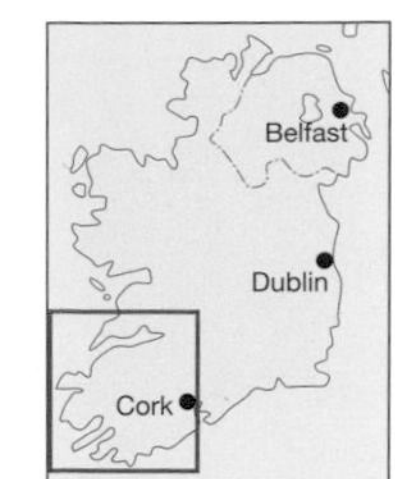

Main attractions
KINSALE
CLONAKILTY
ROSSCARBERY
GLANDORE
SKIBBEREEN
CAPE CLEAR ISLAND
MIZEN HEAD
BANTRY BAY
GLENGARRIFF
BEARA PENINSULA
KILLARNEY
RING OF KERRY
VALENTIA ISLAND
WATERVILLE
SNEEM
DINGLE
BLASKET ISLANDS
TRALEE

Cork and Kerry, Ireland's most southwesterly corner, offer an attractive combination of sea and mountain scenery, interspersed with lively small towns and villages – Kinsale, Clonakilty, Kenmare, Killarney and An Daingean/Dingle. Life is taken at a slower pace hereabouts, and old fashioned courtesies survive: for example, on the smaller, back roads it is still the tradition for the driver to salute the driver of the oncoming car, so do not be surprised if strangers wave at you. People find it quite natural to strike up conversations, just because you happen to be in the same place at the same time. A friendly informality prevails.

The rainbow effect

Bring strong walking shoes and waterproof jackets. The further west you go, the more likely you are to encounter rain, as the clouds scud in from the Atlantic, but it is seldom continuous heavy rain, and the showery weather typical of Killarney and Dingle often alternates with sunshine, creating some magical light effects, including numerous rainbows.

The rich farming country on the fertile plains of the Rivers Lee and Bandon give way to more rugged, hilly land, the closer you get to the coast. More than 600 miles (1,000km) of coastline include impressive slate and sandstone cliffs, long sandy beaches and rocky inlets, and easily accessible offshore islands, with abundant wild life. Because of the proximity of the Gulf Stream, parts of the coast of west Cork and Kerry, including Glengarriff, Killarney and Sneem, are frost-free year round, and have lush, sub-tropical vegetation, with massive rhododenrons and azaleas from mid-April to May.

An added bonus throughout the region is the high quality of its natural produce – farmhouse cheeses made from the milk of those sleek cows

PRECEDING PAGES AND LEFT: the Ring of Kerry. **RIGHT:** riding the Atlantic waves.

Kinsale's harbour.

grazing the fertile green meadows, locally-reared beef, pork and lamb, sea-fresh fish and shell-fish, local honey, home-grown potatoes, salads and vegetables (increasingly organic) will impress with their flavour and freshness. These are sold locally in specialist food shops and at farmers' markets, and used in restaurants and have given the area a high reputation among food lovers.

The pleasures of the southwest are chiefly rural. Most people who visit the area are here for the outdoors and the scenery. The lakes and mountains of Killarney can compete with the best Europe has to offer, while the Ring of Kerry presents a succession of spectacular seascapes. The less-frequented Beara Peninsula is preferred by walkers and cyclists who enjoy the relative lack of traffic and the simple B&B accommodation. The coast of West Cork also has its champions, people who like the relatively small scale of its cliffs and hills, the miles of fuchsia hedges, dripping with dark red, honey-scented flowers, clashing exuberantly with swathes of purple heather.

The most popular part of the west among visitors is the western tip of the Dingle Peninsula, a largely Irish-

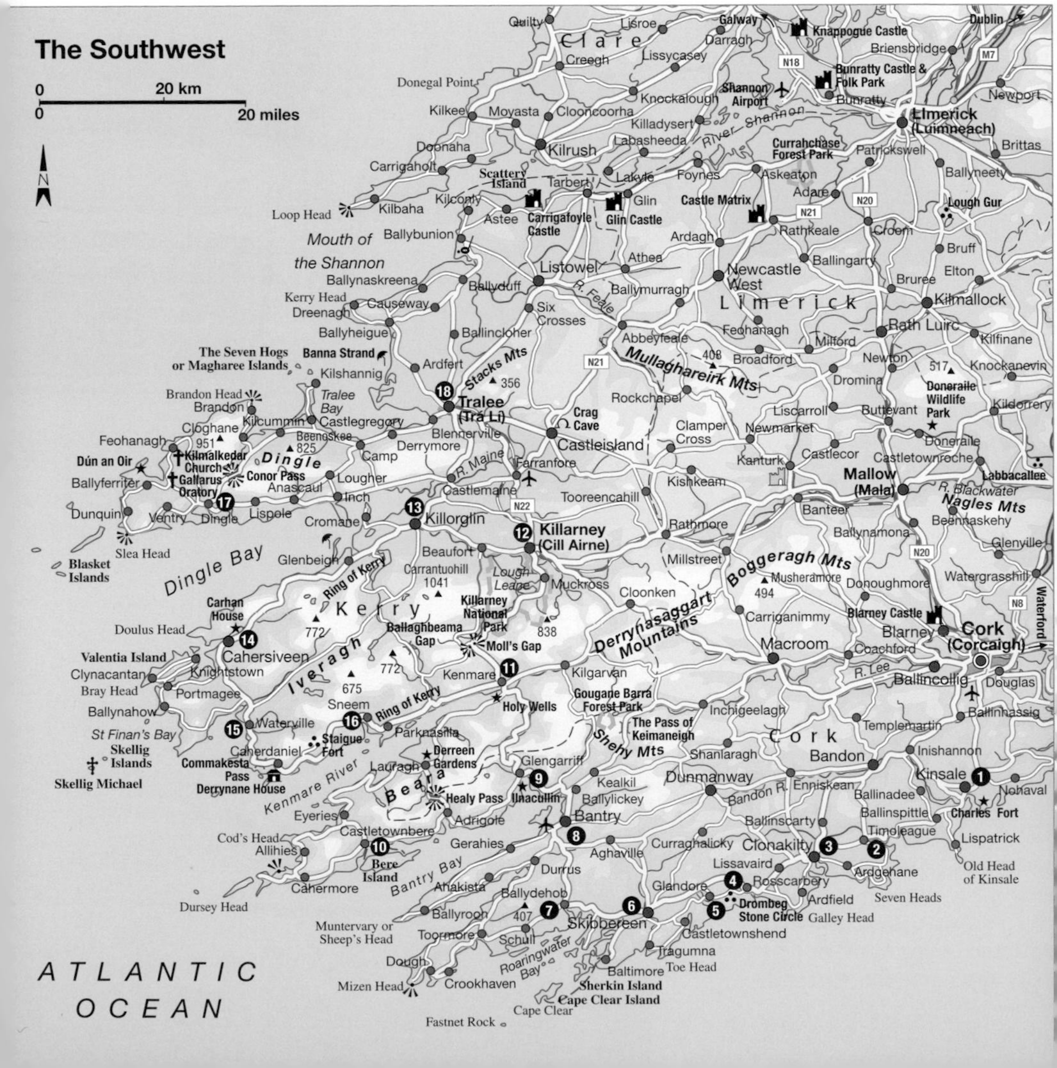

The Southwest

0 — 20 km
0 — 20 miles

ATLANTIC OCEAN

speaking area rich in prehistoric and early Christian remains, with some of the world's best coastal scenery and the country's best traditional music.

Kinsale

Kinsale ❶, 12 miles (19km) south of Cork Airport on the R600, is the big success story of Irish tourism. Once a run-down fishing port, it is now a wealthy resort with so many restaurants that it's known as "the gourmet capital of Ireland". It is situated at the top of a fjord-like harbour where the River Bandon runs into the sea. Craft shops, galleries, restaurants and antique shops abound. While the south-facing slopes of the inner harbour have been marred by up-market housing developments, including a series of large apartment blocks known locally as "Heineken Heights", the outer harbour is mercifully unspoilt.

The **Old Courthouse** in Market Square dates from 1600. In 1706 a Dutch-style gabled frontage and octagonal clock tower were added. The Courthouse contains the Kinsale Regional Museum (tel: 021-477 7930; charge), whose exhibits include mementoes of the *Lusitania*, sunk 14 miles (23km) off the coast by a German submarine in 1915.

Also of interest nearby are the 12th-century **St Multose Church** and the 16th-century restored **Desmond Castle** which houses a wine museum (tel: 021-477 4855; www.winegeese.ie; Apr–mid-Oct daily 10am–6pm; charge). (Many emigrant Irish families from the 17th century onwards got involved with the wine trade in Europe, Australia and the United States.) Originally built as a custom house, from the mid-18th century Desmond Castle was used as a prison, and it is known locally as the French Prison after a tragic fire in which 54 prisoners, mainly French sailors, died. **Charles Fort** (tel: 021-477 2263; daily, mid-Mar–Oct 10am–6pm, Nov–mid-Mar 10am–5pm; charge), a five-minute drive down Kinsale Harbour, is a star-shaped fort enclosing 9 acres (3.5 hectares) of ground, and was built in 1677. Because it is overlooked

Charles Fort.

BELOW: Kinsale.

TIP

Kinsale Arts Week
This takes place in the second week of July is one of Ireland's liveliest summer festivals, a spectacular nine-day event, featuring installations by major international artists, open-air concerts on the spectacular harbour, theatre, readings, street entertainment and workshops.

by high ground, it was never a great success militarily, and its working life as a recruit training centre ended in 1921 when the IRA burnt it down. There is good cut-stone work on many buildings, and wonderful sea views. On the outer harbour side of the fort an attractive footpath runs along beside the sea towards the harbour mouth for about 1 mile (2km; free).

Old Head of Kinsale

Leave Kinsale by crossing the River Bandon to the west. The R600 runs along the edge of the **Courtmacsherry Estuary** which in winter months is home to great flocks of plover, oyster catchers and curlew. In the summer cormorants, egrets and herons should be easy to spot.

The distant view of **Timoleague** ❷ is dominated by the grey stone ruins of a waterside 12th-century **Franciscan Friary**. Until the 16th century the monks were wine importers. The ruins are freely accessible. There are some garish modern graves inside, but the tall Gothic windows framing views of the estuary offer an irresistible photo-opportunity. The interior walls of Timoleague's tiny 19th-century **Church of Ireland** are entirely covered by a mosaic mural in the decorative style favoured by the Oxford Movement. The 20th-century Hiberno-Romanesque-style **Church of Our Lady's Nativity** contains some fine stained-glass windows by the acclaimed Dublin artist, Harry Clarke (1889–1931).

Clonakilty and Environs

Arriving at **Clonakilty** ❸, take the by-pass and park in one of the designated areas to explore the colourful and compact town centre on foot. **Emmet Square** is lined by tall Georgian houses. The **General Post Office** is in a small 19th-century church. Note the hand-painted shop signs above wooden shop fronts which have been revived in recent years. The **West Cork Model Railway Village** (tel: 023-883 3224; charge) in the old railway station at the east end of town is a 1:24 scale model of the towns of Bandon, Kinsale, Clonakilty and Dunmanway, as they were in the 1940s, and of the long closed West Cork Railway. Historians will like the

BELOW:
Michael Collins, two weeks before his assassination in 1922.

Fuchsia Branding

A logo featuring a fuchsia flower and the words "A place apart – West Cork" is part of a regional branding exercise designed to enhance the area's reputation for high-quality food, accommodation and craft products. Those sanctioned to use the fuchsia logo must adhere to strict quality criteria, and reflect local characteristics including environmental quality, and an awareness of the richness and diversity of local heritage. The fuchsia sign on a menu guarantees the best regional ingredients. Producers include Murphy's Irish Seafood, luxury cakes from Coolmore Foods, wild smoked salmon from Ummera Smoked Products, West Cork Bakery's hand-made bread, Skeaghanore Duck from Ballydehob (very flavoursome) and Follain Teo's high fruit preserves, relishes and marmalade.

eclectic **West Cork Regional Museum** (Old Methodist School, Western Road; tel: 023-883 3115; May–Oct; charge) which has memorabilia of the controversial patriot Michael Collins *(see pages 46–7)* among its extensive collection. Collins's birthplace, a dignified memorial featuring the walls of the family farmhouse and a bronze statue, is signposted 6 miles (9km) west of Timoleague, just beyond **Lissavaird.**

The **Michael Collins Centre** (2 miles/3km outside Clonakilty off the R600 Timoleague road; tel: 023-884 6107; July–Aug 11am–5pm, or by appointment; charge) offers an audio-visual display, photo and militaria exhibition featuring the local hero, and can organise guided tours (in your own car, or tour bus) of the somewhat scattered sites associated with Collins. Lectures and other events mark the anniversary of his death on 22 August, 1922, in an ambush at nearby **Béal na Blath.**

Continuing west on the N71, the road crosses a wide sea inlet at **Rosscarbery** ❹. This was an important monastic centre from the 6th to the 12th centuries. The small Protestant Cathedral (1612) has been attractively renovated and the pretty village square, on a hill above the main road, with craft shops and several bars and cafés, is worth exploring.

Turn left just beyond Rosscarbery on to the R597 Glandore road. From June to September this little road, and many others like it around west Cork, are lined by tall hedges of *fuchsia magellanica*, a shrub with bright red bell-shaped flowers imported from Chile in the 19th century. It has adapted so well to the climate that it grows wild in profusion.

About 2 miles (3.5km) along is the road to the **Drombeg Stone Circle** (free), one of the most complete and most impressively situated of the region's early Iron Age remains. The circle is oriented to the winter solstice. If it's cloudless on 21 December, it's an impressive sight as the last rays of the sun travel through a cut in the distant mountains and land on the flat stone at the far side of the circle.

In winter **Glandore** ❺, a tiny village built on the south-facing slope of a protected harbour, with a year-round

TIP

Boat trip

Skipper Colin Barnes runs a four-hour boat trip from Reen Pier, Union Hall, with regular sightings of dolphins, seals and fin, humpback and minke whales. Daily at 10am and 3pm, weather permitting, in summer, autumn and winter. Adults €50, group rates for 6+. Tel. 086-327 3226 or 028-36832.

BELOW: Drombeg Stone Circle.

EAT

Skibbereen is a great place to shop for food. Field's Supervalu is renowned for its range of local artisan foods (cheese, pâté, bread, charcuterie, organic vegetables) while you can stock up on wine and beer at Lidl.

population well below 100, will be virtually empty, while in summer it will be teeming with wealthy visitors and their yachts. This lovely spot is known locally as Millionaire's Row. **Union Hall**, on the opposite side of Glandore Harbour, is a small fishing village. The brightly-painted trawlers moor nearby at **Keelbeg Pier**. Note the characteristic multi-coloured houses: it's said this tradition began when fishermen used whatever was left over from the annual painting of their boats to brighten up their houses. The custom has been enthusiastically adopted by developers of new holiday homes, but you will quickly learn to distinguish the real thing.

Castletownshend

Castletownshend is signposted from Union Hall on an attractive back road which passes through **Rineen.** Castletownshend may be the prettiest village in west Cork, but it is also the least typical. Wander along its two streets, noting its large, well-designed three- and four-storey houses, often stone-built and neoclassical. These belonged to "planter" families – Protestant English ex-soldiers who were given lands in the area in the late 17th century.

A wall plaque in **St Barrahane's Church** enlarges on their history. Behind the church are the graves of Edith Somerville (1858–1949) and her writing partner, Violet Martin (1862–1915). As Somerville and Ross, they are best known for a series of comic sketches of Irish country life, *Some Experiences of an Irish RM* (Resident Magistrate). They also wrote a well-received novel, *The Real Charlotte*. There's a wonderful view of the sheltered anchorage from their graves.

Skibbereen

Skibbereen ❻ is a market town built in a solid bourgeois style in the 19th and early 20th centuries. Symptomatic of the changes that have taken place in rural Ireland since the economic boom, it now has a tiny (but very welcome) by-pass, in the form of a ring road studded with supermarkets and DIY warehouses.

The **Skibbereen Heritage Centre**, on Upper Bridge Street (mid-May–

RIGHT: the Baltimore Beacon warns ships of the treacherous coast.

Preserving a boating tradition in Baltimore

From May to September, Baltimore's fleet of gaff-rigged wooden sailing boats can be seen in the harbour. A group of enthusiasts rescued the bones of an old sailing ship rotting in the mud, and used it as a template to revive the area's traditional mackerel boats. These were built for speed, to get the catch back into port ahead of the pack, and provide exciting sailing. The boats, which were in use up to the 1950s, are built in a traditional yard at Oldcourt (just outside Baltimore) by Liam Hegarty and Fachtna O'Sullivan, whose families have been building boats here for generations.

There are now about 40 sailing vessels in the fleet of various designs, and several canoe-like currachs, traditionally built of tarred canvas on a wooden frame. The smaller "towelsail" yawls were used for crab fishing in inland waters, and are designed to navigate shallow rocky coves. The "towelsail" was a sail hung over the body of the boat to create a tent (teabhal in the local Irish dialect, pronounced towel) for the crab fishermen who spent many nights aboard.

The boats celebrate the start of the season every year on the last weekend in May with mussel eating and net mending competitions in the Baltimore Seafood and Wooden Boats Festivals (www.baltimore.ie). In summer the fleet, a much-loved spectacle and emblem of the region's maritime heritage, travels by invitation to regattas up and down the Cork coast.

mid-Sept daily 10am–6pm, rest of year Tue–Sat; charge) makes a good attempt to explain the causes of the Great Famine of 1845–7 which took the lives of over 10,000 people in the area.

Baltimore, 8 miles (13km) south of Skibbereen, is a popular sailing and holiday village on **Roaringwater Bay**. The bay covers an area between the Mizen Head in the west and Baltimore in the east which is known for its numerous rocks and islands. In good visibility, the **Fastnet Rock Lighthouse**, can be seen on the horizon some 14 miles (23km) to the south.

Baltimore is also the base for the mail boats and ferries servicing Roaringwater Bay's two largest inhabited islands, Cape Clear and Sherkin. **Sherkin Island** is only a quick hop (tel: 028-22001 or 087-911 7377 for ferry details). The ruins of a 15th-century Franciscan friary stand just beside the pier on Sherkin. The island is 3 miles long and 1½ miles wide (5 by 2.4km) with several pleasant sandy beaches, and good peaceful walking on its quiet, almost-traffic-free roads. It's popular for day trips.

Birdwatching centre

Cape Clear Island is reached by a thrilling 45-minute boat ride through the rocks of Roaringwater Bay (tel: 028-39153 for ferry details). There is usually a boat out at 11am, returning at 4pm). Cape Clear (pop. 170) is an Irish-speaking island about 3 miles long by 1 mile (5 by 2km). There are three pubs, a youth hostel, a bird observatory, a heritage centre and half a dozen B&Bs. Because of its southerly position, Cape Clear's Bird Observatory often reports landings of rare migratory birds, and the appearance of large flocks.

The N71 west leaves Skibbereen beside the banks of the **River Ilen**. About 6 miles (9km) out of town, keep an eye out to the left for your first panoramic view of Roaringwater Bay and its numerous islands.

Ballydehob ❼ is a lively, brightly-painted village built on a hillside, apparently in the middle of nowhere. Although it appears to be inland, Ballydehob has a harbour. Before the harbour silted up, the village was the marketing centre for the islanders of Roaringwater Bay. Now it's a popular

SHOP

Farmers' market

In summer, check out the Schull Farmers' Market which is held near the pier on Sundays from 10am to 3pm, May–Sept, and sells crafts as well as local artisan food products.

BELOW: Corpus Christi procession in Ballydehob.

Mizen Head, and the crashing waves of the Atlantic.

retreat for city folk – English, Dutch, German and even Irish – seeking a better quality of life.

Continue on the R592 towards Schull. In good weather you will see **Mount Gabriel** (1335ft/407 metres) on your right. The two white balls on its summit guide transatlantic air traffic. If you wake early in west Cork, you can often hear a stream of jumbo jets high above, heading for the airports of Europe. While Ballydehob has a reputation for being arty, **Schull**, 3 miles (5km) down the R592, is the heart of fashionable west Cork, a summer resort for wealthy Dubliners. Walk down to the pier for another look at Roaringwater Bay, then explore its one main street, checking out its restaurants, bookshops and craft boutiques.

Mizen Head

Leave Schull on the R592 to travel to the tip of the **Mizen Peninsula**. The road passes rocky, rugged bits of low-lying coast. About 4 miles (7km) west at **Altar**, there is a megalithic tomb on the left, known locally as the Altar Rock. The **Mizen Head** is a dramatic spot with wild Atlantic waves pounding the rocks even in the calmest weather. The lighthouse signal has been automatic, and the station unstaffed since 1993. The **Mizen Head Visitor Centre** (tel: 028-35115; www.mizenhead.net; mid-Mar–Oct daily 10.30am–5.30pm, Nov–mid-Mar Sat–Sun 11am–4pm; charge) is located in the lighthouse keeper's house on an island at the tip of the peninsula. To reach it you must cross a concrete suspension bridge while the waves swirl around 150ft (45 metres) below. It's worth bringing a camera.

The **Sheep's Head Peninsula** is a thin finger of land dividing Dunmanus Bay from Bantry Bay to the north. From Goleen or Schull, follow the R591 to Durrus, and follow signs for the Sheep's Head Drive (50 miles/80km) which leads to the N71, and Bantry town. The peninsula is small and sparsely populated, with most people living in scattered farmhouses. There is a timeless air about the gorse and heather of the heathland, and the rough green fields with grey stone walls. The marked Sheep's Head Way walking trail of over 60 miles (100km) has been designed with loop walks of 1 to 2 hours; maps are available locally. The views are superb, with the more sheltered south coast looking back across the narrow Dunmanus Bay to the Mizen Head, and the north coast overlooking the wide expanse of Bantry Bay, and the Beara peninsula. Stop at the Tin Pub in Ahakista to experience old-style hospitality, then explore the nearby megalithic stone circle, signposted as part of the waking trail. Near Kilcrohane is a plaque commemorating the novelist J.G. Farrell (*Troubles*, *The Siege of Krishnapur*) who was swept out to sea while fishing from the rocks in 1978, shortly after moving to live here.

The shores of Bantry Bay

The town of **Bantry** ❽ is distinguished only by its setting on the shores of **Bantry Bay**. **Bantry House and Gardens** (tel: 027-50047; Mar–

BELOW: Bantry House.

Oct daily 10am–6pm, café, craft shop; charge), a short walk from the town centre, is a large, mid-18th century mansion with a magnificent setting overlooking the famous bay (which is 4 miles/6.4km wide). The gardens have recently been replanted with some striking contemporary effects enhancing features such as an ancient wisteria trained on a circular trellis.

Inside, there is a fine collection of treasures, including Aubusson carpets, Gobelin tapestries, Russian icons, Chinese lacquer and a mixture of French and Irish 18th-century furniture.

Head inland from Bantry via **Kealkil** to visit **Gougane Barra**, a deep tarn which is the source of the River Lee. The lake is surrounded on three sides by steep precipices which run with cataracts after heavy rain. **St Finbar's Oratory**, a small stone-built chapel (a 20th-century replica) on an island in the lake, can be reached by a causeway. This is believed to be where St Finbar lived in the 6th century before founding his monastery in Cork city. A pilgrimage is still held on the first Sunday after St Finbar's Feast Day, 25 September. There's something special about the place, particularly if you arrive early, before the majority of day trippers.

Glengarriff

The N71 climbs above Bantry Bay into open, more rugged country, offering ever-changing views across the bay. **Glengarriff ❾**, a wooded glen with a sheltered harbour warmed by the Gulf Stream, has an especially mild climate, with an average annual temperature of 52°F (11°C). Azaleas, rhododendrons, magnolia and camellias grow in abundance. **Glengarriff Bamboo Park** is situated on 13 acres of a sheltered coastal headland, and has walks thgouh over 30 different species of bamboo and palm trees with superb sea views (tel: 027-63570; daily 9am–7pm; charge).

Glengarriff village is teeming with craft shops, serving coaches en route to Killarney, but **Ilnacullin Gardens** (tel: 027-63040; Mar–Oct; charge, boat extra) on **Garinish Island**, five minutes

St Finbar's Oratory.

BELOW: Glengarriff.

TIP

A nine-hole golf course, on the eastern side of Castletownbere, will accept visitors, charging reasonable green fees. Sea angling and coastal fishing trips can be arranged through local retailers, who will hire rods and tackle.

offshore, are well worth a visit. Allow about an hour and a half. Don't miss the Italian Garden, a formal garden with colonnades and a terrace heightening the contrast between the classical man-made beauty of the garden and the wild mountain scenery that surrounds it. Alternatively, for the same fare (€12) you can take a boat trip around the harbour without landing on the island. Except in very bad weather, you will see families of basking seals on the rocks between the mainland and the island.

The Ring of Beara

The **Ring of Beara** is less well known than its neighbour to the north, the Ring of Kerry, yet it also offers impressive scenery. It is a favourite haunt of walkers, cyclists, bird watchers and people who enjoy natural beauty. Although the drive covers only about 68 miles (110km), much of it is on narrow, winding roads, so allow a full day.

The **Beara Peninsula** stretches for about 30 miles (48km) southwest from Glengarriff, forming the north side of Bantry Bay. The **Caha** and **Slieve Miskish** mountains run down the centre of the peninsula, and the road around it is mainly on a narrow coastal plain.

A shorter route to Kenmare, avoiding the Ring of Beara, can be taken at Adrigole, about 12 miles (19km) beyond Glengarriff. The R574 climbs north across the peninsula in a series of small but sharp hairpin bends, leading to the **Healy Pass** (1,083ft/330 metres). Stop here to enjoy a panoramic view of Bantry Bay to the south, with the Kenmare river and the MacGilligcuddy Reeks in the north. Turn right at Lauragh on to the R571 Kenmare road.

Many would consider **Castletownbere ⓾**, with a population of about 850, little more than a village. However, it is a busy working port, home to Ireland's largest white fish trawling fleet. Get a feel for the place by walking along the quays and admiring the brightly coloured fishing fleet. In summer 2008 the writer and film director Neil Jordan, who has a holiday home nearby, filmed *Ondine* on location in the town and at Pulleen Harbour, two miles to the west. Its stars, Colin Farrell and Alicja Bachleda, fell in love in real life, as in the film, and now have a child together.

Leave town on the R575 for **Allihies**. After about 5 miles (8km) a sign on the left indicates the Dzogchen Beara Retreat Centre (tel: 027-73147), a Buddhist retreat with hostel, and in summer a café. Visitors are welcome to join daily meditation at their cliff top centre, or simply enjoy the gardens and sea view.

Allihies village is a straggling line of brightly coloured cottages set between sea and hills (now augmented by new replica cottages, mainly second homes), and was built for the copper miners working in the hills behind it. The sandy beach at **Ballydonegan** was formed of spoil from the mines. The **Allihies Copper Mine Museum** (tel: 027-73933; Mon–Fri 10am–5pm, Sat–Sun noon–5pm, café; charge) explains the history of mining in the area, from the Iron Age to the arrival of Cornish miners in the 19th century, and the subsequent departure of many miners

BELOW: the cliffs at Slieve League.

for Butte, Montana when the mines closed in the 1950s. The material is beautifully presented in a converted church, and there are also exhibitions by the many fine artists living locally. Walk up to the abandoned mines (marked by tall brick chimneys) and enjoy the views of sea and wild hillside. You can walk from here to the next village, **Eyeries** (7 miles/11km), on a grassy footpath that forms part of the Beara Way. Even if you only walk a few miles of it, the peace and isolation will be memorable.

The road between Allihies and Eyeries, another village of small, brightly coloured houses, is one of the highlights of the Ring of Beara. In good weather the **Iveragh Peninsula** is clearly visible to the north, across the **Kenmare River**, as are the conical shaped **Skellig Rocks** off its tip. You will get a closer look at these rocky islands from the Ring of Kerry.

Derreen Gardens (tel: 064-83588; charge) were planted 100 years ago beside Kilmakilloge Harbour, a sheltered inlet on the south shore of the Kenmare River. The woodland gardens run down to the water's edge and contain many azaleas and rhododendrons, massive stands of bamboo and groves of New Zealand tree ferns – all of which thrive in the mild air warmed by the Gulf Stream.

Kenmare ⓫, an attractive and cosmopolitan little town backed by hills, has a good selection of shops and restaurants. Guided eco-tours of the Bay and Islands are run from Kenmare Pier by Seafari (tel: 064-83171; mid-Apr–Sept). The **Kenmare Heritage Centre** (tel: 064-41233; Apr–Sept; charge) explores themes of local interest, including lace making. Sheep are still traded from makeshift pens at the traditional Friday market.

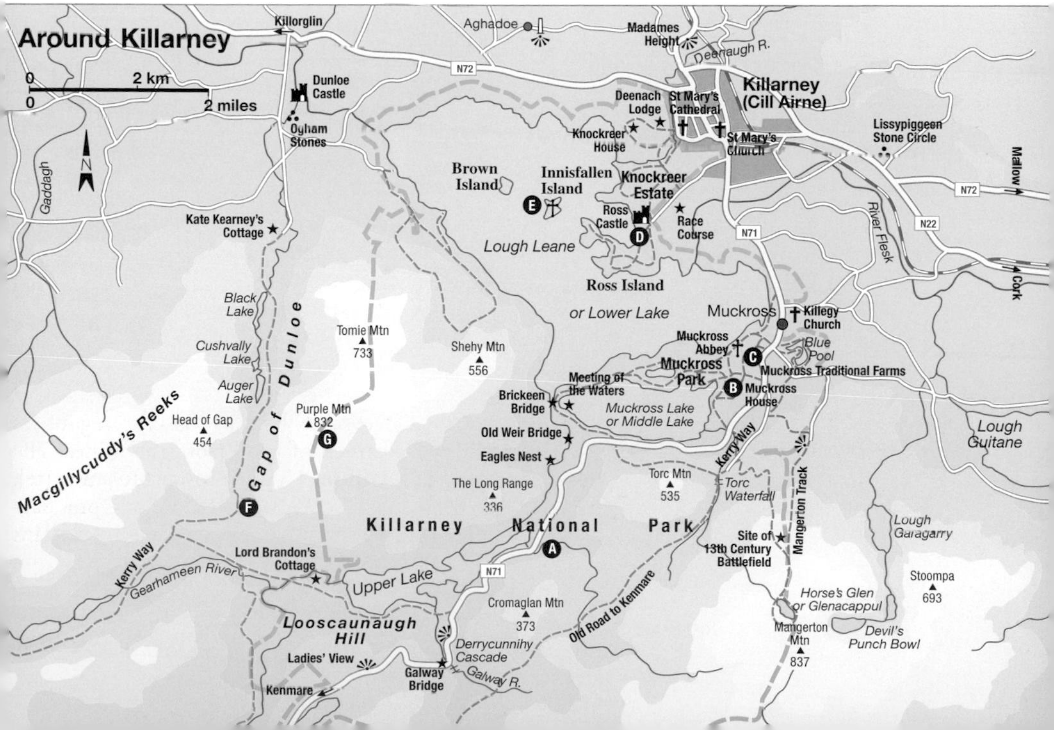

Killarney drinking hole.

Around Killarney

TIPS

Bird watching
Keep an eye on the sky: white-tailed sea eagles are being reintroduced to Killarney National Park. The first 75 chicks took flight in 2007 after an absence of over 100 years. When mature the wingspan is up to 8ft (2.5 metres).

Deer watching
A herd of over 500 red deer roam freely in Killarney National Park, mainly in the mountain areas of Torc and Mangerton, and also in Muckross and Knockreer Estates. Best time to spot them is early morning.

Killarney

Killarney ⓬ may be the most commercialised area in the Southwest, but it is still possible to avoid the crowds and enjoy the lakes and hills. The romantic scenery of boulder-strewn, heather-clad mountains, deep blue lakes dotted with wooded islands and wild woodland has been preserved within a large National Park. Avoid the town by day. Killarney isn't a great place to shop for crafts, as it caters chiefly for the first-time visitor, but it is always useful to visit the Tourist Information Office beside the central car park for details of special events, festivals, guided walks, and Gaelic Games (hurling and football). However, there are several good restaurants open in the evening, and the singing bars can be enjoyable if you don't mind organised fun.

Enjoying a visit to Killarney is largely a matter of attitude. You won't appreciate Killarney from the inside of a car. One great pleasure here is the damp woodland aroma that permeates the mild air. As in the rest of Kerry, it is important not to be put off by rain. Any weather, good or bad, tends not to last long around here. In fact, the lakes of Killarney look especially good when seen through a light drizzle.

Rather than regarding Killarney as a series of sights to be ticked off a list, it is more satisfying to do only one or two things in a leisurely way. Arriving from Kenmare, you may decide to stop on the N71 and climb the path beside the **Torc Waterfall** to enjoy the view.

BELOW: Killarney National Park.

Killarney National Park

A nice contrast to the wildness of Torc can be found across the road in **Muckross Park**, a neatly trimmed lakeside area with gravel paths that forms the nucleus of the **Killarney National Park** Ⓐ. This is a car-free zone, and it is a good place to take a ride on one of Killarney's famous jaunting cars (open horse-drawn carriages). The drivers ("jarveys") are traditionally great talkers. Don't be surprised if you hear a phone ring during your quaint ride; most drivers carry mobile phones to help locate their next fare.

Muckross House Ⓑ (tel: 064-31440; charge), built in the 19th century in the Elizabethan style, houses a folklore and farming museum. You can admire the rhododendrons and azaleas in the formal gardens free of charge.

Muckross Traditional Farms Ⓒ (tel: 064-31440; charge, optional joint ticket with house) is a largely outdoor attraction with a healthy walk between three different-sized farms, all inhabited by chatty, well-informed guides (disguised as farmers), illustrating farming methods before electricity and the internal combustion engine. This may be your only chance to get up close to a pair of Irish wolfhounds, huge but gentle creatures who live on the middle farm.

Ross Castle Ⓓ (tel: 064-35851; Apr–Oct) is a 14th-century castle keep that has been fully restored and furnished You can hire a rowing boat here, and take a picnic over to **Innisfallen Island** Ⓔ about 1 mile (1.6km) offshore. The wooded island has the remains of an abbey founded about AD 600, which is famous for the *Annals of Innisfallen* a chronicle of world and Irish history written in this remote and beautiful spot up to 1320 by a succession of monastic scribes.

Consider taking an organised half-day coach-horse-and-boat trip through the **Gap of Dunloe** F, a narrow mountain pass formed by glacial action. The organised trip has the advantage of allowing you to travel through the Gap on foot or horseback and then go back to town by boat without having to retrieve your car.

The Gap itself is an unpaved path that stretches for 4 miles (6.4km) between the **Macgillicuddy's Reeks** and the **Purple Mountain** G, which gets its name from the heather that covers it in the autumn. There is no motor traffic, but in summer there is a constant stream of ponies, jaunting cars and pedestrians. The scenery is first-rate, with a chain of five small lakes beside the road, and massive glacial boulders, but don't expect solitude.

The Ring of Kerry

You can drive non-stop around the 112 miles (180km) of the Ring of Kerry in under four hours, but allow a full day as you will want to make several stops. The Ring of Kerry is justifiably famous for its combination of lush, sub-tropical vegetation and rugged seascapes. In July and August the narrow two-lane road can be clogged by a slow procession of tour buses and RVs. If traffic and commercialism bother you, do the Ring of Beara instead, or go straight to Dingle.

Killorglin 13 is a busy village which makes the most of its strategic position on the road between Killarney and Dingle. Its focal point is now a modern square at the top of the town, a product of recent redevelopment. It is famous for Puck Fair – Ireland's oldest festival, dating back to pagan times – on 10–12 August. On the first day a mountain goat is crowned King Puck, garlanded with ribbon, and installed on a tall throne overlooking the town, where it stays until the evening of the third day. There are various explanations of its origin, but nowadays it is chiefly a drinking and horse-trading festival, and can get rowdy. A short drive inland from the road to Glenbeigh, **Caragh Lake** is a delightful, sheltered spot, popular with game anglers. The lake shore is discreetly dotted with luxury hotels and holiday homes, mostly 19th-century.

Glenbeigh is a good touring base, convenient for both sea and hills. Nearby **Rossbeigh** is a 3-mile (5km) long sandy beach facing west over Dingle Bay, backed by dunes. There are good walks here in **Glenbeigh Woods**.

Cahersiveen 14 (pronounced Cah-her-sigh-*veen*) is the chief market town for the Iveragh peninsula, but don't expect a buzzing metropolis. One of its newest features is a "ghost hotel", the remnant of a Celtic Tiger venture which proved definitively that the town was not the right location for a luxury "boutique" hotel. Don't miss the visitor centre, **The Barracks** (tel: 066-947 2777; charge), a community-led initiative occupying an exotic-looking, white-turreted building. The story goes that it

TIP

Fed up with driving? Several companies run day trips around the Ring of Kerry by minibus, including Kenmare-based Finnegan's Tours 064-41491, and O'Connor Autotours, Killarney tel: 064-31052.

BELOW: the Ring of Kerry.

Valentia's name
The name Valentia comes from the Irish name for the channel between the island and the mainland, Beale Inse, and has nothing to do with Spain.

should have been built in India, on the Northwest Frontier, but the plans were mistakenly sent to Ireland. In fact its architect, Enoch Trevor Owen, habitually built in what he called the Schloss style, and looked at from another angle, his design suits the hill-backed location very well. But why spoil a good story? Nowadays it houses an amusing and informative series of exhibitions.

Follow the sign outside The Barracks to the pier. The prettiest part of Cahersiveen is its backside which overlooks the wide estuary of the River Ferta and the green hills beyond.

Valentia Island

Look out for signs to the Valentia Island car ferry about 3 miles (5km) west of Cahersiveen. This lands you in **Knightstown** at the eastern tip of **Valentia**, a sleepy place, eerily quiet, with a couple of bars. The island is 6¾ miles (11km) long and 1¾ miles (3km) broad, a quiet place with a population of about 700. Its relative lack of traffic and wonderful sea views make Valentia a good destination for walkers; maps are available locally; don't miss the Tetrapod footprints near the Slate Quarry, made by a precursor of the dinosaur. The original transatlantic cable connecting Europe with Newfoundland was laid from here between 1857 and 1865. Valentia is connected to the mainland by a causeway at **Portmagee**. The **Skellig Experience** (tel: 066-947 6306; Apr–Nov; charge), beside the causeway, is an uninspiring visitor centre. Opt instead for a boat trip to the islands (tel: 066-947 6306; May–Oct). Bear in mind that all the boats are open, the water can be rough, and bad weather leads to cancellations, sometimes for days on end.

Skellig Michael, the largest of the three islands, was inhabited by monks from the 7th until the 12th centuries. It rises in a cone shape to a double peak 712ft (217 metres) high. A flight of over 500 steps lead to the monastery, built of dry stone with no mortar. It has had major restoration work to enable it to cope with the number of visitors. Enthusiastic guides, all trained archaeologists, live on the island from June to August, to supervise visitors and tell them the island's history.

BELOW: beehive stone huts and a gravestone shaped like a human figure are part of the ruins of St Finan's Abbey on Skellig Michael.

A scenic drive

If the weather is good, take the scenic road from Portmagee to Waterville through **Ballynahow**, along an impressive arc of coast and mountains with the best views so far of the Skelligs.

Rejoin the main Ring road just before Waterville. **Waterville** ⓯ is a popular base for golfers, who like the famous links, and anglers who have a choice of deep-sea fishing in Ballinskelligs Bay or angling on Lough Currane, half a mile inland.

The next stretch of road is one of the most scenic stretches, winding along the edge of **Ballinskelligs Bay** through rocky coastline backed by rugged green hills. **Derrynane House** (tel: 066-947 5113; May–Oct; charge) is a mile beyond **Caherdaniel**. The house belonged to Daniel O'Connell (1775–1847), remembered chiefly for his campaign for Catholic emancipa-

tion (granting civil rights to Catholics), in 1829. The 320 acres (130 hectares) of woods surrounding the house (year-round; free) have pleasant walks and access to an attractive sandy beach.

Castlecove is a small, friendly place with good sandy beaches. A narrow lane beyond the church climbs 1¾ miles (3km) to **Staigue Fort**. This is a well-preserved example of a prehistoric stone fortress, dating from 1500 BC. It consists of a circular dry-stone wall, 115ft (35 metres) in diameter, varying in thickness from 13ft to 5ft (4–1.5 metres). A series of steps in the walls lead to a platform with good sea views. A small donation is requested by the landowner.

Sneem ⓰ is another pretty but untypical village, laid out English-style around a village green beneath a semi-circle of low mountains. Some of the charm has been lost following over-intensive development of holiday homes. Turn your back on these and walk down the road beside the Blue Bull (signposted "Pier") past an attractive communal garden. Looking back through the reeds you can appreciate Sneem's sheltered location between the sea and the hills.

Sneem marks the start of the most sheltered part of the Ring of Kerry's coast. Here you will see lush, subtropical growth – wild rhododendrons, azaleas, camellias and bamboo – evidence of the benign effect of the Gulf Stream. The N70 continues past Parknasilla, a large hotel resort with pleasant walks in its wooded waterside grounds, on to Kenmare, where the N71 leads to either Killarney or Glengarriff.

The Dingle Peninsula

The weather can make or break a visit to **Dingle** ⓱ (now signposted as An Daingean by government decree: you will not see any signposts directing you to Dingle, *see p212)*. If the sea mist is down, consider postponing your trip. At Killorglin take the N70 to Castlemaine, and in Castlemaine take the R561, which gives good views across the bay of the coast of the Iveragh peninsula. **Inch** has 4 miles (6.5km) of sandy beach backed by dunes.

Dingle has a population of about 1,500, which can treble in summer.

TIP

Surf's up

Brandon Bay at the north side of the Dingle Peninsula, is a popular surf and windsurfing destination. It's fun to watch, or you can learn the sport at Jamie Knox Watersports; tel: 066-713 9411, www.jamieknox.com.

BELOW: Dingle's harbour.

The rose garden in Tralee's town park.

Its tourism was boosted by the filming of *Ryan's Daughter* in 1969. Since 1985, a wild dolphin, Fungie, has been entertaining visitors with his playful antics, and townsfolk recently erected a bronze statue of him on the pier. Skippers tout for business, offering "money-back if no dolphin sightings" deals.

Dingle, where you will hear the Irish language spoken in everyday dealings, is very popular with visitors, and offers seriously good restaurants and lively music pubs. A triangular 10-minute walk from the pier area, up Green Street (the best place for craft shops), down Main Street and back along the Mall to the pier takes you past most of the shops, pubs and restaurants.

An Diseart (Green Street; tel: 066-915 2476; grounds free) is a huge 19th-century convent, converted into an Institute of Education and Celtic Culture. Its walled gardens and graveyard create an oasis in the town centre, and the building has beautiful stained-glass windows in pre-Raphaelite style (charge).

Continue west on the R559. Between **Ventry** and Slea Head there are over 400 *clochāns* ("beehive" huts). The farmers charge you a nominal sum to visit them. These small conical huts of unmortared stone are not prehistoric, as the farmers claim; the oldest date from the early Christian period, the 5th to 8th centuries, and were used by hermit monks. Others were built within the past 100 years or less to house farm implements: there is little timber in these parts, so it is cheaper to build with stone. Dunbeg Fort (tel: 066-915 9755; Easter–Apr daily 9.30am–7pm; charge) just beyond Ventry, a properly excavated Iron Age promontory fort dating from about AD 800, built on a cliff edge, and the adjacent Visitor Centre (included in charge), are worth a visit, as are the clochāns half a mile further on, which look out to the Skellig Rocks. The road then climbs westward around Eagle Mountain to **Slea Head,** and has good panoramas.

The Blasket Islands

The group of seven rocky islands offshore are the **Blasket Islands**. The **Great Blasket,** the largest one, is about 4 miles (7km) long and ¾ mile (1.5km) wide. It was inhabited until 1953. The islanders were great story-tellers and

RIGHT: summer comes to Ventry Strand.

How Dingle fought to save its name

A new law in 2005 decreed that all Irish-speaking places must use the Irish-language version of their place name, and that only the Irish-language version can appear on legal documents, maps and signposts. The Dingle Peninsula is known as Corca Dhuibhne (pronounced *corka guiney*) in Irish, but Irish is spoken only at the far western tip of the peninsula, which is where the new legislation comes into effect. But the people of Dingle Town, officially within the Irish-speaking area, are reluctant to lose a name that they consider is effectively an international brand name, worth millions to its thriving tourist industry. Many refused to call their town An Daingean.

A local plebiscite was held in 2006. It favoured the bilingual name Dingle Daingean uí Chúis (the fortress of O'Cush – pronounced *dangan ee quish*), but the central government argued that complex legislation would be needed to create an exception to the rule protecting Irish-language place names – and anyway the Minister refused to make any exceptions. Meanwhile, the name "Dingle" was used by most local businesses, and the same government's tourist publications, while the legal arguments continued in Dublin. The Irish-language sign for An Daingean at the town's entrance was defaced by graffiti to read DINGLE. Another case of Only in Ireland…

Map on page 198

have made a lasting contribution to Irish literature. **The Great Blasket Centre** (tel: 066-915 6444; closed Oct–Easter; charge) tells their story using many old records and photographs. Below Mount Eagle is the village of **Dunquin**, a scattered settlement whose harbour was once the landing point for the islanders. Stop at Dunquin Pier, and walk down the steep, concrete path.

Boats go to the island regularly in the summer (tel: 066-915 4864; www.blasketislands.ie; Easter–Sept). The crossing takes 20 minutes, but until the long-promised new pier is built, landing is by transfer to dinghy, so you must be fit and agile. There are frequent crossings between 10am and 4pm, weather permitting, or you can opt for a two-and-a-half hour eco-tour of the islands.

On towards Tralee

Gallarus Oratory (well signposted) is an extraordinary little building of unmortared "dry" stone, which probably dates from the 8th century. It is in the shape of an inverted boat, with a door at the west and a window in the east wall. It remains as dry and solid as the day it was built, and is very dark inside.

Avoid the **Conor Pass** in bad weather – take the N78 through Anascaul instead. The drive is hair-raising in all weathers as you climb steeply to 1,496ft (456 metres) above sea level.

Both roads meet at Camp on the N86. Blennerville is a mainly Georgian village perched between Tralee Bay and the old ship canal. It still has a large working windmill, best viewed from a distance.

Tralee **18** (pop. 22,750) is the county town of Kerry, but don't expect a lot. While it may seem like a booming metropolis after a few days in Dingle, Tralee is a dull place with an impersonal newly-built, pedestrianised town centre. The exception is in August, when the whole town parties for a week during the **Rose of Tralee Festival**, a beauty and personality pageant, and then adjourns to the adjacent Ballybeggan racecourse for a six-day race meeting. The town's most attractive area is

Blennerville Windmill.

BELOW: Slea Head.

Woolly thinking.

near the museum: the **Town Park** and **Denny Street**, with its nicely proportioned Georgian houses.

The enjoyable **Kerry County Museum** (tel: 066-712 7777; charge) is in a neoclassical building at the top of Denny Street. Tralee is also the base for **Siamsa Tire** (tel: 066-712 3055), Ireland's national folk theatre, which stages nightly performances in summer of Irish folklore, music and dance.

The country to the north of Tralee is the flatter, more sheltered part of Kerry. Take the R551 north from Tralee to **Ardfert**, a small village with the impressive ruins of a large 12th-century Cathedral with Romanesque doorways and transepts restored (tel: 066-713 4711; May–Sept 9.30am–6.30pm; visitor centre: charge, ruins: free).

Access to **Banna Strand**, and a monument commemorating Roger Casement's landing from a German submarine in 1916 can be had about 2 miles (3km) north of Ardfert. The west-facing **Ballyheigue Strand** is popular for watersports and walking, with great views of the mountains of Dingle and the **Magharee Islands** across the bay.

BELOW: festival time in Tralee.

Ballybunion

The road continues to **Ballybunion**, a small, seaside resort famous for its championship golf course, dramatic cliff walk and sandy beaches. Beside **Lady's Strand** is the bath house (tel: 068-27469; June–Sept; charge), where farmers came to ease their aching bones after harvest time in hot seawater baths, containing a generous bucket of seaweed. It's still a great tonic, though the cheerful DIY atmosphere is far from the pampering treatments of the modern spa (as is the modest charge).

Listowel, a quite little place, mainly dating from the late 19th century, with a large main square, is the county town of North Kerry, known for the **Listowel Writer's Week** which takes place annually in late May, and **Listowel Races**, a lively seven-day race meeting in the last week of September, which originated as a post-harvest celebration.

From **Tarbert** on the banks of the Shannon Estuary a car ferry runs to Killimer in Co. Clare (tel: 065-905 3124), providing a scenic alternative to a long detour through Limerick. ❑

Irish makes itself heard

Even though the most famous Irish writers wrote in English, Irish is the Republic's official language. But how many people can speak it fluently?

From the foundation of the Irish Free State back in 1922, enormous efforts were made to encourage everyone to learn and use the language – including making it compulsory at school and awarding extra marks for answering in Irish in examinations.

The new Irish State also designated geographical areas, most along the western seaboard, as the Gaeltacht. Within them, people use Irish all the time, and residents receive grants from the government to promote the language and cultural heritage. There are sizeable Gaeltacht areas in counties Donegal, Mayo, Galway and Kerry as well as smaller parts of counties Cork, Waterford and, the only inland area, Meath. Generations of Irish teenagers have spent part of their summer on subsidised holidays in these areas – sent home if they speak English.

Visitors from overseas can also spend their holidays in Gaeltacht areas, learn some Irish, and enjoy pubs with traditional music sessions and *céilís* (literally translated as "dance gatherings"). Check out www.gaelsaoire.ie

Such is human nature, compulsory Irish at school had the opposite effect to its intent on the general population of the Republic. While everyone educated here has some knowledge of the language, until recent decades they usually denied they did, while using some words in conversation: *craic* (fun) probably the most commonly heard.

Attitudes to the language have changed over the last two decades, particularly in the Republic. A grassroots movement developed to increase the number of all-Irish schools – *gaelscoileanna* – where all subjects are taught through that language. Since the 1980s the number of schools has grown – by 2010 there were 207 of them, both at primary and secondary level, with over 30,000 students. In County Cork, for example, there are 21 primary all-Irish schools – there was only one until the 1980s.

There's been an Irish language radio station since 1972, Raidió na Gaeltachta, run by State broadcaster RTÉ, joined by the television service TG4 in 1996. There's also the Dublin community radio station Raidió na Life, and BBC Northern Ireland provides about 40 hours a week of radio in Irish. The weekly newspaper *Foinse* (meaning "source") is available nationally. *Lá Nua*, backed by both the British and Irish governments, is produced in West Belfast and the Donegal Gaeltacht, and appears five days a week.

The 2006 Census revealed that use of the language is dropping in Gaeltacht areas, particularly among the 20–44 age group. However, it also showed that among the general population 1½ million claim they can speak it, though a third of them admit they do not use it. The growth of all-Irish schools and the daily viewer figures for TG4 of more than 800,000, despite huge competition from overseas channels, show that an enthusiasm for the language survives. And on road signs in the Republic it shares equal billing with English. ❑

RIGHT: learning Gaelic at a rural school.

RESTAURANTS AND PUBS

Restaurants

Prices for a three-course dinner per person without wine:
€ = under €25
€€ = €25–40
€€€ = €40–55
€€€€ = over €55

Baltimore

Glebe House Gardens
Baltimore, Co. Cork
Tel: 028-20232
Easter–June Sat–Sun, June–Aug Wed–Sun, B and L, 10am–5pm, D June–Aug 7–10pm. L **€**
The prolific and ornamental kitchen gardens surround one of prettiest cafés in the country. Creative baking; short, enticing menu of light meals conjured from local produce and the organic garden. Eat inside or outside.

La Jolie Brise
Baltimore, Co. Cork
Tel: 028-20600
Daily, B 8.30am–12.30pm, L & D last orders 9.30pm **€**
This is the family-oriented, budget restaurant of three in the village, all run by Breton Youen Jacob and his Irish-born son, Youen junior. The best espresso for miles around is complemented by a menu of pizzas, fresh fish, simple grills and, of course, *moules frites*, with seating outdoors for sunny days. Seafood lovers should try Chez Youen (dinner only), a serious, Breton-style seafood place.

Bantry

O'Connor's Seafood Restaurant and Bar
Wolfe Tone Square, Bantry, Co. Cork
Tel: 027-50221
Daily, L 12.15–3pm, D 6–10pm, phone for hours in winter. L **€**, D **€€**
Town centre shop conversion with long established reputation for good seafood at very fair prices. Comfortable, buzzy. Modern Irish blackboard specials depending on catch.

Cahirsiveen

QC's Seafood Bar & Restaurant
3 Main Street, Cahirsiveen, Co. Kerry
Tel: 066-947 2244
L 12.30–2.30pm, Mon–Sat, June–Aug; D 6.30–9.30pm, daily July–Aug, Tue–Sun, May–June and Sept, Thur–Sun in winter, closed Jan–Feb. L **€**, D **€€€**
A Victorian bar converted to a restauarant and decorated with nautical bric a brac, appropriately as the menu highlights sea-fresh seafood from the owners' boats, cooked with a Spanish influence: prawns sizzling in garlic and olive oil, for example. Local meats are char-grilled to order, and can be served al fresco, Kerry weather permitting.

Castletownshend

Mary Ann's Bar and Restaurant
Castlestownshend, Co. Cork
Tel: 028-36146
Daily in summer, Nov–Mar Tue–Sun, L noon–2.30pm, D 6–9pm, also bar food 6–9pm. L **€**, D **€€€€**
Traditional and full of character with a courtyard garden for al fresco dining. Top quality food, fresh from the pier, seafood is the star.

Clonakilty

An Sugan Restaurant and Bar
41 Wolfe Tone Street, Clonakilty, Co. Cork
Tel: 023-883 3498
Daily, L noon–4pm. D 5–9.30pm. L **€**, D **€€**
Has a deserved good name for sound cooking – in terms of seafood especially, but it's a fine local eat for carnivores too. Menus change daily, depending on the catch.

Dingle

Ashe's Bar
Main Street, Dingle, Co. Kerry
Tel: 066-915 0989
Daily, L noon–2.30pm, D 5–10pm. L **€**, D **€€**
Ashe's pioneered bar food locally, feeding the cast of *Ryan's Daughter* in 1969. The pub is cosy, quirky and old fashioned, but the menu is bang up to date, with prawn tempura, oysters, rib-eyed steak and squid salad.

The Chart House
The Mall, Dingle, Co. Kerry
Tel: 066-915 2255
Daily in high season, restricted in low season 6.30–10pm. D **€€–€€€**
An outstanding restaurant where a talented team bring everything together into a harmonious whole; comfort, terrific service, creative cooking, stylish presentation, interesting menus and, with good value choice highlighted, great value for money – qualities that have helped it win numerous awards.

Doyles Seafood Restaurant
5 John Street, Dingle
Tel: 066-915 1174
Mon–Sat 6–10pm. Early Bird 6–7.15pm **€€**; D **€€€**
Casual, easygoing place full of traditional character. Seafood is the attraction but there are meat and vegetarian options.

Out of the Blue
Waterside, Dingle
Tel: 066-915 0811
Early Mar–mid Nov Thur–Tue, L noon–3.30pm, D 6–9.30pm. L **€**, D **€€**
Informal, great classic French cooking with odd modern twist. Seafood rules to the point that if the weather means no fresh fish they don't open. As their slogan says "meat eaters need not apply".

Durrus

Blairs Cove
Durrus, Co. Cork
Tel: 027-61127
17 Mar–Oct D Tue–Sat 7.30–9.30 **€€€€**
Restaurant (with rooms). Great atmosphere and stunning waterside location in courtyard of a Georgian mansion, and excellent cooking. Enormous and elaborate hors d'oeuvre buffet, meat and fish from wood fired grill; equally enormous dessert and cheese selection. Reservations required.

Good Things Café
Durrus, Co. Cork
Tel: 027-61426
Summer 11am–9pm, Wed–Mon L 12.30–3pm **€€**; D 7–9pm **€€€**
A foodie's haven; a simply furnished rather stark café/deli offering lunch and dinner composed of carefully sourced local and artisan ingredients and creative contemporary cooking.

Goleen

Heron's Cove
The Harbour, Goleen, Co. Cork
Tel: 028-35335
Daily in summer, phone to check days and times Nov–Mar, D 7am–9.30pm **€€€**
Overlooking the harbour, comfortable, lively and with a philosophy of the best of food cooked with loving care makes this a place where a good dinner is guaranteed. Balanced menu with a leaning towards abundant local seafood and an excellent wine list.

Kenmare

La Cascade
Sheen Falls Lodge, Kenmare, Co. Kerry
Tel: 064-41600
Daily 7–9pm. D **€€€€**.
Beautifully formal style overlooking the floodlit falls. Impeccable service. Excellent cooking, stunning presentation. Classic French cuisine (the menu includes only a very occasional concession to Irish food or food culture).

Lime Tree Restaurant
Shelbourne Street, Kenmare, Co. Kerry
Tel: 064-41225
Apr–Oct daily 6.30–10pm. D **€€€**
A place of character with consistent high quality food, good cooking and service. Style a mix of mainstream, modern Irish and world cuisine. Wide-ranging menu and interesting wine list.

Mulcahy's Restaurant
36 Henry Street, Kenmare, Co. Kerry
Tel: 064-42383
Daily 6–10pm. Early Bird and value menu **€€**, D **€€€**
Spacious, modern and eclectic in decor and food style. Exciting menu that ranges from Thai, to Japanese fusion and Irish. Produce is organic. Good vegetarian options.

Packies
Henry Street, Kenmare, Co. Kerry
Tel: 064-42135
Mon–Sat 6–10pm. Set D **€€€**, D **€€€€**
Relaxed atmosphere, friendly, efficient service, closely packed tables and a welcome for children. International menu and traditional Irish themes. Local organic/artisan ingredients.

Kilbrittain (near Kinsale and Clonakilty)

Casino House
Coolmain Bay, Kilbrittain, Co. Cork
Tel: 023-884 9944
Thur–Tue, D 7–9pm, L Sun only 1–3pm. L **€€**, D **€€€**
Old house, striking modern decor, warm hospitality and consistently good cooking that reflects its closeness to Union Hall fishing port. Good vegetarian options.

The Pink Elephant
Coolmain Bay, Kilbrittain, Co. Cork
Tel: 023-884 9608
June–Sept, daily L 1–3pm, D 6–9pm; off season Thur–Sat, D only, Sun L & D, but phone to confirm. L **€**, D **€€**
The elevated south-facing view across the Atlantic from this unpretentious bar/restaurant is unforgettable, and the food is good too, a short, simply-prepared menu using the best local ingredients, including steak, rack of lamb, lobster, shrimp, right down to locally grown potatoes and salad.

Killarney

Gaby's Seafood
27 High Street, Killarney
Tel: 064-663 2519
Mid-Mar–Jan Wed–Sat, D

LEFT: the day's specials at a Dublin bar.
RIGHT: traditional Irish stew features on many menus.

Prices for a three-course dinner per person without wine:
€ = under €25
€€ = €25–40
€€€ = €40–55
€€€€ = over €55

5.30–9.30pm. Reservations advised. **€€€€**
Belgian owner-chef runs one of Ireland's finest seafood establishments in the town centre of Killarney. Cooking is classic: the signature dish, lobster Gaby, is served with a cream and cognac sauce, or try the massive seafood platter. There is also a selection of steaks and local lamb.

Peppers Restaurant
The Malton Hotel (formerly Great Southern Hotel), East Avenue Road, Killarney, Co. Kerry
Tel: 064-31262
D Tue–Sat, 6.30–9.30pm. Reservations advised. D **€€**
A cheerful bistro-style venue, with imaginative Mediterranean menus, a wide range of steaks and consistently fine cooking make this one of Killarney's leading eating places.

Treyvaud's Restaurant
62 High Street, Killarney, Co. Kerry
Tel: 064-33062
Daily, L noon–5pm, D 5–10.30pm, closed Mon–Tue off season. Set L **€**, D **€€**
Attractive, comfortable and friendly place offering everything from a "tasty bite" through set lunch, dinner to à la carte dinner. Modern Irish with a few international offerings. Delicious food including breads and baking. Local game a speciality in winter.

Killorglin

Bianconi's
Lower Bridge Street, Killorglin, Co. Kerry
Tel: 066-976 1146
Food served: Mon–Sat, L 12.30–2.30pm **€**; D 6.30–9.30pm **€€**. Advance booking advisable for dinner in summer and at weekends.
An old coaching inn (it still has rooms) at the entrance to town, with a dark wood Victorian interior, Bianconi's is known for its reasonably priced food, served at tables of various shapes and sizes.

Nicks Seafood Restaurant and Piano Bar
Lr. Bridge Street, Killorglin, Co. Kerry
Tel: 066-976 1233
Daily in summer 6.30–9.30pm, Wed–Sun in winter. Set dinner **€€€**, D (à la carte) **€€€€**
This most famous old restaurant is ever young at heart. Classically cooked (seafood is the main event) with an Irish accent; but Kerry lamb and beef and vegetarian options. Music, outstanding and friendly service and Irish hospitality.

Kinsale

Fishy Fishy Café
Crowley's Quay, Kinsale, Co. Cork
Tel: 021-470 0415
Daily, Jan–mid-Apr, Nov–Dec, noon–4.30pm, May–Oct, noon–9pm **€€**
Huge stylish café/restaurant, with a great buzz, and loads of outdoor eating space. A relaxed casual place that takes seafood seriously and the range on offer is vast. Prices reasonable for the quality of food and the high standard of cooking.

Man Friday
Scilly, Kinsale, Co. Cork
Tel: 021-477 7177
Mon–Sat, D 6.45–10pm. **€€€**, Early Bird 6.45–7.30pm **€€**
Its rustic-cabin exterior leads to a busy, sophisticated restaurant, where friendly service and the owner-chef's generous portions of seafood and steaks ensure a satisfied clientele.

Max's Wine Bar
48 Main Street, Kinsale, Co. Cork
Tel: 021-477 2260
Mon–Fri L D, closed Tue Nov–Mar **€€**
Atmospheric restaurant in 800-year-old building complete with ceiling beams. Irish–French cuisine with emphasis on seafood. Good selection of wines by the glass.

Portmagee
The Bridge Bar, The Pier
Tel: 066-947 7108
Daily L noon–2.30pm, D 5.30–9pm, Oct–Apr no food Mon **€€**
Seafront pub with a rustic pine interior warmed by an open fire, it serves excellent bar food, while more formal simple meals are served in a separate restaurant space in the evening.

Toddie's @The Bulman
Summercove, Kinsale, Co. Cork
Tel: 021-477 2131
Daily L 12.30–2.30pm, D 5–10.30pm, but phone to confirm off season. L **€**, D **€€€**
At lunchtime a simple menu of *moules frites* and home-made burgers is served in the waterside bar, or on the quayside outside. Dinner in the upstairs restaurant is more ambitious contemporary Irish cuisine; the harbour view is stunning.

Rosscarbery

O'Callaghan-Walshe Restaurant
The Square, Rosscarbery, Co. Cork
Tel: 023-884 8125
Tue–Sun 6.30–9.15pm, Sat–Sun only in winter. D **€€**
A haven of relaxed warmth, good cheer and confident cooking. Great seafood bought daily at nearby fish auction at Union Hall. Menus change daily.

Schull

Grove House
Colla Road, Schull, Co. Cork
Tel: 028-28067
All year, Sat–Sun only off high season, D 6.30–10.30. D **€€€**
An old house full of character also offering bed and breakfast. Stylish dining rooms (al fresco eating as well when weather permits). Using the best artisan, organic foods and fresh seafood Katrinia Runske has long been delighting fine-diners with her excellent cooking and out of the ordinary menus (with distinctly Swedish leanings). Children welcome.

TJ Newmans Café
West Main Street, Schull, Co. Cork
Tel: 028-27776
All day 9–11pm, Sun from noon **€€**
Good stop at any hour for an informal meal. Café, pub and wine bar close to the marina. A delightful menu (such as platter of West Cork salamis, or cheese, and daily hot dishes), great cakes and desserts. Keenly priced wines by the glass.

Skibbereen

Island Cottage
Heir Island, Skibbereen, Co. Cork
Tel: 028-38102
www.islandcottage.com
Mid-June–mid-Sept, D Wed–Sat 8.15–11.45pm **€€€**
The simple cottage really is on an island, a 5-minute ferry ride from Cunnamore Pier. Your hosts have worked in prestigious European restaurants, and

the 5-course dinner menu based on local organic and wild ingredients will taste as good as anything you've ever eaten. Book well in advance, and be prepared to share a table. Off-season groups of 16-24 served by arrangement.

Over the Moon
46 Bridge Street, Skibbereen, Co. Cork
Tel: 028-22100
Mon–Sat, L noon–3pm, D 6–10pm. L **€**, D **€€**
A smart town-centre restaurant, casual by day, formal white linen by night, OTM offers a sophisticated menu, impeccably presented, thanks to the young owners' professional background in some of the world's top restaurants.

Tralee

An Pota Stóir
Meadowlands Hotel, Oakpark Road, Tralee, Co. Kerry
Tel: 056-718 0444
Daily, D Mon–Sat 7–9.30pm **€€**; L Sun noon–2pm **€**
This modern country house-style hotel in a quiet suburb of Tralee has a very popular restaurant with a rustic interior, serving seafood from the owner's own trawler, alongside locally sourced meat. The bar also serves above-average fare (**€**).

Waterville

Paddy Frogs Restaurant
The New Line, Waterville, Co. Kerry
Tel: 066-947 8766
Mid-Mar–Oct Fri–Sun 6.30–10pm, Tue–Sun July–Aug. D **€€€**
Shore-side location, eye-catching decor, modern cooking style that respects ingredients. Menus feature a balance between local seafood and meat. Separate vegetarian menu. Strong on desserts.

The Smugglers Inn
Cliff Road, Waterville, Co. Kerry
Tel: 066-947 4422
Daily, L noon–3pm, Sun until 4pm, D 6–9.30pm. Early D **€€**, D **€€€€**
Talented father-and-son team run the kitchen. Local ingredients. Seafood, meat and game are given classic treatment with a contemporary twist.

Pubs

The Spaniard is one of Kinsale's landmark pubs, serving good bar food, which can be eaten while basking in the sun on a wooden bench. The Wednesday night traditional session welcomes visiting musicians.

Grainne's in Timoleague serves home-prepared bar food in generous portions 'til 7pm.

An unusual spot is **Hayes Bar**, Glandore, Co. Cork. Overlooking the harbour, it's a "Little Spain" deep in rural Ireland; Spanish wines and sherry by the glass. Food all day. Tapas 6–9pm.

The Eldon Hotel in Skibbereen has a good reputation for bar food and has a large patio garden. Music sessions, too.

Bushe's Bar in Baltimore has impressive displays of local maritime memorabilia; good bar food as well.

Bunratty's in Schull in the town centre near the Allied Irish Bank, is a reliable year-round place for bar food, where the local business people lunch.

O'Sullivan's Bar, on the harbour in Crookhaven, is an attractive and comfortable traditional pub with simple fresh seafood on offer daily.

En route to Moll's Gap in Kerry is the delightful **Beaufort Bar and Restaurant**, a place of character that offers good dinners featuring high-quality cooking and a mainly traditional menu.

The Point Bar at Renard Point (Cahirsiveen side of Valentia Island) and beside boat departures to Valentia Island. A place to unwind and enjoy a bowl of chowder or seafood salad.

South Pole Inn, Annascaul. So named because of Antarctic exploration connections as Ernest Shackleton's second officer was Tom Crean, a native of this village, who returned to run this pub in 1920. Lots of memorabilia relating to these explorers, and a simple bar food menu.

Ashes in Camp on the Dingle peninsula; a well-preserved old pub in the same family for 200 years; a place to meet locals, have a chat and a freshly-prepared bar lunch.

Cassidy's on the Pier in Dingle town serves bar food all day long, starting with breakfast.

Seven minutes' walk from the Marina at Fenit is the **West End Bar** and Restaurant, a cosy bar with an open fire, good bar food and friendly staff.

Val O'Shea's Bar and Bistro in Bridge Street, Tralee, Co. Kerry, is ultra-modern, fashionable and very popular with the young. Good food both in the bar and the restaurant upstairs.

Bailey's Corner in Ashe Street, Tralee, will suit an older crowd with its church pews, sporting prints and good bar food.

Kate Brown's pub in Ardfert has an open fire and offers generous portions of wholesome, home-cooked food.

RIGHT: still the drink of choice in many pubs.

Sean
Kelly

LIMERICK AND THE SHANNON REGION

Within easy reach of Limerick is a region of ruined castles, a dramatic coastline, spectacular caves and the eerie moonlike landscape of the Burren

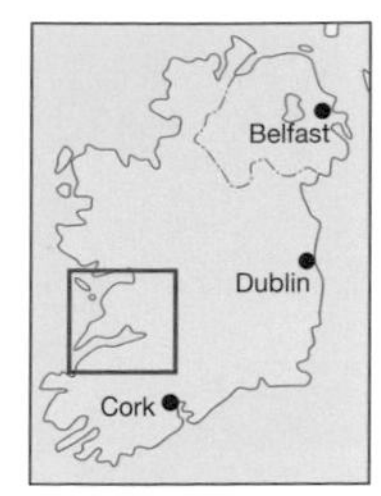

Main attractions
BISHOP'S PALACE
ST MARY'S CATHEDRAL
LIMERICK CITY GALLERY OF ART
UNIVERSITY OF LIMERICK
ADARE
BUNRATTY CASTLE
ENNIS
KILRUSH
LAHINCH
CLIFFS OF MOHER
DOOLIN
LISDOONVARNA
THE BURREN
BALLYVAUGHAN
COOLE PARK

The counties of Clare and Limerick constitute most of this prosperous region. Golfing, fishing, walking and surfing are amongst the main activities. The Cliffs of Moher rise almost vertically out of the sea and north of them lies the mysterious Burren, home to a remarkable variety of Alpine and Mediterranean wild flowers.

Limerick city

Limerick ❶ is a modern city (pop. 52,560, with another 38,200 living in the suburbs) with a medieval core on King's Island. It is more than 1,000 years since Viking traders established a sheltered seaport at the head of the Shannon estuary. But even today the city is full of historical reminders.

The bulk of the city lies to the east of the River Shannon, and until recently Limerick's city centre resolutely turned its back on the river, the wide, fast-flowing Shannon, its best asset. The city's high level of crime, reflected in feuds and drug wars, has given the tourist authorities a headache, but a regeneration programme is helping local communities tackle social problems.

An attractive riverside path, the Spokane Walk, skirts the Shannon and leads from the Tourist Information Office at Arthurs Quay Park, and over a steel footbridge to King John's Castle, so that the entire medieval quarter can comfortably be visited on foot while enjoying riverside views. Quayside pubs with outdoor picnic tables add to the friendly ambience.

The **Tourist Information Centre** Ⓐ at Arthurs Quay is a boldly designed modern building representing the outline of a ship. Ask here for details of historical guided city tours, or for *Angela's Ashes* walking tours of locations in Frank McCourt's memoir (tel: 061-317 522; www.shannonregionaltourism.ie; closed Sun except July–Aug).

PRECEDING PAGES: King John's Castle, Limerick. **LEFT:** grazing by the river. **RIGHT:** the Curragower Bar, Clancy's Strand.

Limerick's castle is one of Ireland's most impressive fortresses.

King John's Castle

To get a feel for the history of the place it's best to start in the medieval quarter. The top attraction here is the 13th-century **King John's Castle** Ⓑ on King's Island (tel: 061-411 201; www.shannonheritage.com; May–Sept 9.30am–5.30pm, shorter hours in winter; charge). The castle is one of Ireland's most impressively sited Norman fortresses, with curtain walls and drum towers surviving. Climb one of the round towers for an excellent view of both river and town. An audio-visual display recounts Limerick's history from its foundation by the Vikings in AD 992.

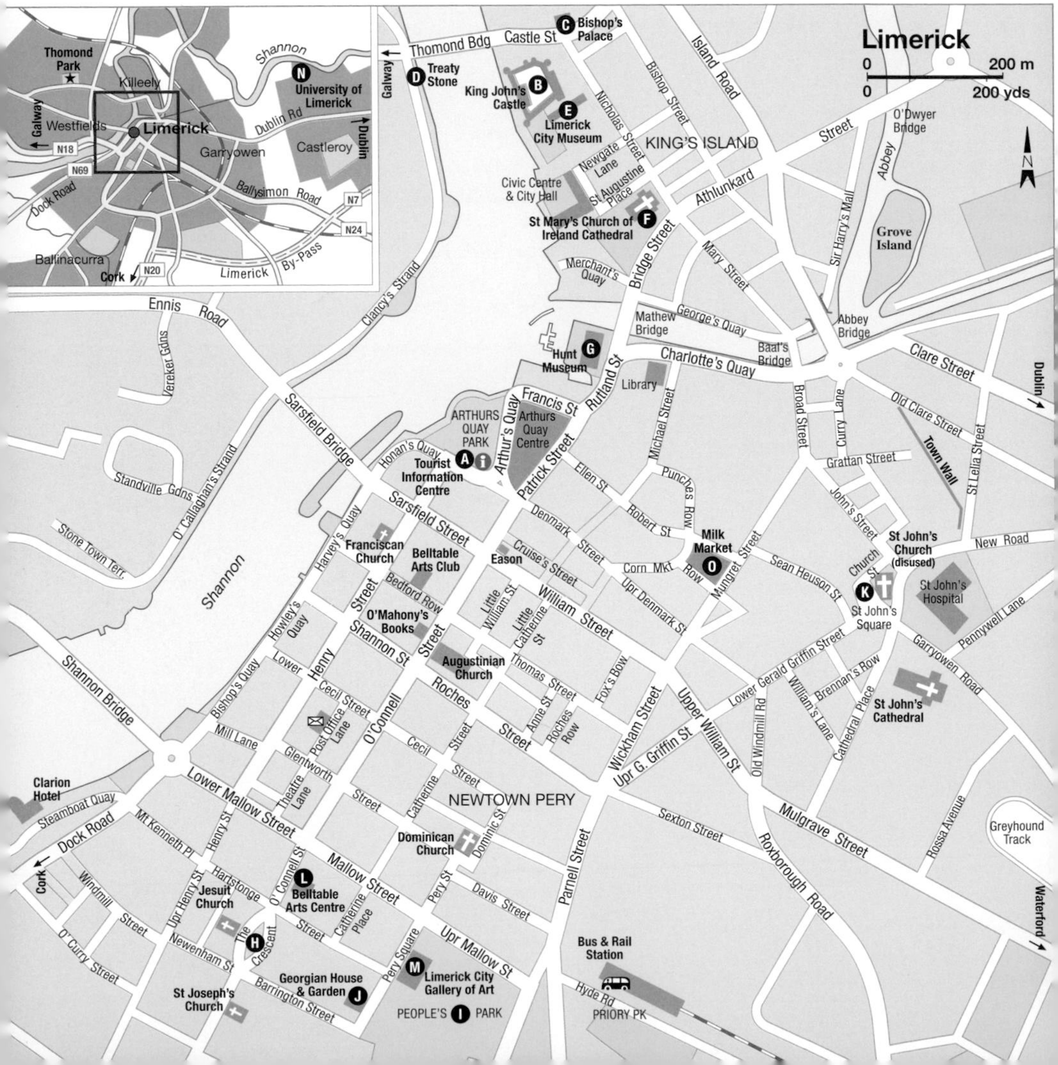

Look into the elegant **Bishop's Palace** Ⓒ, the former Palace occupied by the Church of Ireland Bishops from 1661 to 1784, which has been restored by the Limerick Civic Trust and is now its headquarters (Church Street, King's Island; tel: 061-313 399; www.limerickcivictrust.ie; Mon–Fri 10am–1pm, 2–4.30pm; free). The city's oldest example of Palladian domestic architecture, it houses a Hall of Fame Room comprising portrait drawings of 23 local people honoured for their outstanding achievements. One of these is Richard Harris, a rugby star turned actor, who made the London stage the launching pad of a cinema career spanning 50 years and was winning a new generation of fans in the Harry Potter films when he died in 2002. The recently-built curio wall in the courtyard is an extraordinary addition using salvaged, engraved and decorative stone.

A short walk across Thomond Bridge takes you to the **Treaty Stone** ❶, a rough-hewn limestone block raised on a pedestal. Tradition has it that on this rock the Treaty of Limerick was signed in 1691 marking the surrender of the city to William of Orange. The treaty demanded that the government promised to respect Catholicism, but it was rejected by the English and Irish Parliaments, allowing Limerick to be dubbed the "City of the Broken Treaty". The Latin inscription on the stone is taken from Virgil's description of Troy: "It was an ancient city, well versed in the arts of war."

Back across the river and in Castle Lane, the **Limerick City Museum** ❺ is based in a granary-style building housing more than 40,000 objects illustrating historical aspects of the city and surrounding areas (tel: 061-417 826; www.limerickcity.ie/museum; Mon–Sat 10am–5pm, Sun 2–5pm, Nov–Feb Tue–Sat 10am–5pm; free).

Limerick's cathedral

A short distance along Nicholas Street is what many regard as the *pièce de résistance* of the city's sights – **St Mary's Church of Ireland Cathedral** ❻ (tel: 061-310 293; www.cathedral.limerick.anglican.org; closed in afternoons Nov–Feb; free). Founded by King Donal Mor O'Brien on the site of his palace, it is the oldest building in daily use in Limerick and there is at least one daily service. Built in the form of a cross, it incorporates both Romanesque and Gothic styles.

The Romanesque West Door is magnificent, the black oak misericorde (mercy) choir stalls are carved with animal features, and there's a pre-Reformation altarstone, a leper squint window, and stained-glass windows. The Cathedral hosts many civic and musical events and has an unbroken tradition of choral music for more than 800 years.

Hunt Museum

From the Cathedral, cross over the Matthew Bridge and on Rutland Street you will come immediately to the former Custom House, now the **Hunt Museum** ❼ (tel: 061-312 833; www.huntmuseum.com; Mon–Sat 10am–5pm, Sun 2–5pm; charge). This superb private collection contains 2,000 original works of art and antiquity. They range from the 9th-century enamel Antrim Cross, to Egyptian, Roman and Etruscan pieces, Chinese porcelain, a drawing by

Verse and worse
Limerick claims the origin of the five-line verse known worldwide as the limerick and all too often beginning "There was a young lady from..." The genre, originally oral and frequently obscene, was most famously adopted by the English painter and humorist Edward Lear (1812–88)

BELOW: St Mary's Church of Ireland Cathedral.

TIP

For those wishing to start a visit to Ireland in this region, Shannon Airport, 15 miles (24km) north of Limerick, has good connections to North America (Delta, Continental, American Airlines, US Airways, Aer Lingus), Britain (Easyjet, Ryanair) and continental Europe (Ryanair). Bus services link the airport with Limerick's railway station.

Picasso, and masterworks by da Vinci, Renoir and the Irish artists Jack B. Yeats and Roderic O'Conor. The collection was assembled by John Hunt, a medievalist, and his wife Gertrude, and left to the nation on his death in 1976.

Limerick is full of delightful architectural surprises. From Rutland Street, a brisk 20-minute walk through the main shopping area (allow more time for window shopping) along O'Connell Street leads to the spacious streets of the Georgian area, a district known as **Newtown**. Turn a corner in this area with its well-ordered geometry and you'll be enchanted by a church, a square or a terrace of houses with brightly painted doors and semicircular fan-lights.

Elegant architecture

The Crescent H consists of elegant four-storey houses and has been well restored. Now mostly offices, they are occupied by accountants, solicitors and the like. From here Barrington Street leads to Pery Square and the **People's Park** I where workers bask on the grass at lunchtime with their sandwiches.

The **Georgian House and Garden** J (No. 2 Pery Square; tel: 061-314 130; www.georgianlimerick.com; Mon–Fri 10am–4pm; charge) is one of a terrace of six houses built around 1830. It has been furnished in 18th-century style with its original architectural features reinstated in precise detail. It also houses a display relating to the 1999 filming of *Angela's Ashes*.

Make a short detour down Parnell Street and along Upper and Lower Gerald Griffin Streets to take in the exquisite **St John's Square** K. This "square" is in fact a three-sided terrace of houses with a basement and three bays. The mid-18th-century houses are the earliest Georgian development in Limerick and were originally occupied by the gentry as townhouses during the winter.

The cultural scene

Music and the arts are flourishing in Limerick. The **Belltable Arts Centre** L (tel: 061-319 709; www.belltable.ie) at 69 O'Connell Street has contemporary exhibitions and a theatre. Established in 1981, it is a multi-purpose venue

BELOW: George's Quay and the Locke Bar.

with 257 seats offering world cinema, plays, music and cabaret, family events and visual art.

The **Limerick City Gallery of Art** Ⓜ in Pery Square (tel: 061-310 633; www.limerickcity.ie/lcga; Mon–Fri 10am–6pm, Thur until 7pm, Sat until 5pm, Sun 2–5pm; free) was once a Carnegie Library. Its permanent collection of Irish art ranges from the 18th century to the 21st. The gallery mounts a city-wide annual exhibition of visual-plus arts – ev+a (www.eva.ie) – that is regarded as Ireland's leading annual exhibition of contemporary art.

The university

The **University of Limerick** (www.ul.ie) Ⓝ, in the suburbs at Plassey, has established a reputation as Ireland's leading university in industry-led research. It is a successful showcase for contemporary Irish architecture and sculpture, and hosts concerts and musical events ranging from pop to classical.

Apart from its vibrant artistic side, the city is renowned for its passion for sport and one game in particular. For more than 100 years rugby has been part of the lifeblood of Limerick and has been played by all sections of the population. Some wags joke that the city has three cathedrals: St Mary's, St John's and Thomond Park, the "cathedral" of rugby fans, not just in Limerick, but throughout the entire Province of Munster.

Rugby is the game of the people, stirring passionate support and local loyalties. The oldest senior club, Garryowen, has even given its name to the game's international vocabulary – the Garryowen, called after the traditional attacking ploy: the "up and under."

Shopping centre

Many familiar chain stores have branches in Limerick. The liveliest part of the shopping district is the pedestrianised Cruise's Street area, off O'Connell Street. At numerous cafés, many with outdoor tables, you can choose from the usual range of espressos, mochas, cappuccinos or lattes, but for a change, try Captain Jack's coffee. You will also stumble across antique dealers, barbers, victuallers and saddlers, and Fox's Bow, an alleyway with

While walking around Limerick, you may be lucky enough to see "gigs", the specially trained trotting horses that are ridden around the streets in preparation for race meetings, and which cause additional headaches for motorists in the traffic-choked streets.

City of sieges

Limerick was besieged three times in the 17th century as Britain strove to subdue the Irish. The first blockade, in 1651, was led by Oliver Cromwell as part of a merciless campaign after the execution of Charles I. By the time the citizens surrendered five months later, 5,000 had died of disease or starvation.

The other two sieges, in 1690 and 1691, were linked to William of Orange's campaign to secure the English throne against the Catholic James II. After James fled to France, many of his supporters holed up in Limerick. William's first siege failed to dislodge them. The following year a more determined siege sapped the citizens' morale and they signed the Treaty of Limerick, which promised religious liberty and restoration of property but was not honoured.

BELOW: street performers.

Heritage on view at Adare.

quirky shops. Every Saturday (8am–2.30pm) the restored **Milk Market** ❿, at Corn Market Row, comes alive. At this food and flower market you can find cheeses, fish, seaweed, sausages, jams, chutney and breads as well as organic farm produce.

South of Limerick City

Attractions to the south include museums, visitor centres and charming villages. **Lough Gur** ❷ (tel: 061-361 511; www.shannonregiontourism.ie; 10am–6pm, closed Oct–Apr; charge), 12 miles (19km) south of Limerick on the N24-R514 near Bruff, is one of Europe's most complete Stone Age and Bronze Age sites. It has a horseshoe-shaped lake, rich in bird life. The **Grange Stone Circle** is 150ft (45 metres) across and contains about 100 boulders. More than 20 other stone circles, tombs, hut foundations, lakeside dwellings and ring forts have been excavated beside Lough Gur.

An interpretative centre built in the form of Neolithic huts houses a collection of artefacts and has an audio-visual presentation introducing the site.

Adare ❸, 10 miles (17km) southwest of Limerick, is one of Ireland's prettiest villages. Several of its stone-built cottages are thatched, and they all have colourful front gardens. Adare is noted for its antique dealers, but don't expect bargains. Opposite the Dunraven Arms Hotel is the entrance to Adare Manor, now an American-owned luxury hotel, **Adare Manor and Golf Resort.** It has twice hosted the Irish Open golf tournament, is regarded as one of Ireland's finest parkland courses. However, only golfers and hotel guests can pass the security barrier.

Adare Manor was the seat of the Earls of Dunraven, who built the picturesque thatched cottages that line the village for their workers. The original 18th-century manor was enlarged in the Gothic Revival style in the mid-19th century. In its grounds are the ruins of the 14th-century **Desmond Castle** and of a 1464 Franciscan Friary, accessible by a separate entrance.

The **Adare Heritage Centre** (tel: 061-396 666; www.adareheritagecentre.ie; all year 9am–5pm; free, charge for exhibition) has a helpful history display

BELOW: the stone circle at Lough Gur.

The Polish connection

Wander around the streets of Limerick and you will notice there is a multicultural feel to the city centre. You are likely to hear Polish, Russian or Estonian spoken as much as English. Poles make up nearly a tenth of the population and have opened their own shops selling Polish food, drink, newspapers and magazines. A Polish pub, the Bialo-Czerwoni (The Red and White) opened in Henry Street in 2005, and the local newspaper, the *Limerick Leader*, started a column in Polish.

Limerick has forged links with Europe and in 2006 formed a partnership with Brescia Tourism in Italy. As the gateway to the Shannon Region, the city is well positioned to benefit from the growth in air services and to cash in on the weekend visitor market.

and a model of medieval Adare. The 14-arch bridge dates from medieval times and leads to the Augustinian Friary built in 1315. The cloisters were converted into a mausoleum for the Earl of Dunraven in 1826 and the church was restored in 1852. The centre also houses a Tourist Information Centre (tel: 061-396 255).

The **Celtic Park & Gardens** ❹, near **Kilcornan**, is 5 miles (8km) from Adare. The park and formal gardens are on an original Celtic settlement and historically on one of the most important 17th-century plantations in Munster. Exhibits interpret the past through the physical structures associated with ancient Ireland (tel: 061-394 243; www.limerickgardentrail.com; mid-Mar–Oct, 9.30am–6pm; charge, under-12s free).

Flying Museum

On the south bank of the Shannon Estuary, **Foynes** ❺ played an important part in aviation history. In the late 1930s flying boats would land on the sheltered stretch of the Shannon between Foynes Island and the shore, having made the transatlantic crossing from Newfoundland. The award-winning **Foynes Flying Boat Museum** (tel: 069-65416; www.flyingboatmuseum.com; Mar–Oct 10am–6pm, Nov–Dec 10am–4pm; charge) commemorates those days with models and photographs, and includes the original terminal building, radio room and weather forecasting equipment.

Shannon Crossing

There is a pleasant drive along the wooded shores of the estuary. The turrets of **Glin Castle** are visible from the road, but the palatial home of head of the Fitzgerald clan, the Knight of Glin, is no longer open to the public.

From Glin it is only 4 miles (7km) to **Tarbert** ❻, where a car ferry will take you across the Shannon Estuary in 20 minutes to Co. Clare. The ferry is often accompanied by a pod of dolphins, whose presence will be announced over the loudspeakers.

North of Limerick City

This is castle country, with ruined stumps of crumbling tower houses dotted around the place. There were

TIP

Limerick has a good range of bookshops. O'Mahony's, established in 1902, and Eason's, both in O'Connell Street, sell new books. The Celtic Bookshop in Rutland Street appears to stock at least one copy of every book or pamphlet published about Ireland in the past 40 years. For secondhand and antiquarian books visit the Little Catherine Bookshop and Coffee House, in Little Catherine Street. The owner has extensive local knowledge and is a source of useful advice.

BELOW: Adare Manor.

Foynes Flying Boat Museum.

Irish coffee

It was at Foynes during the flying boat days that Irish Coffee – a mix of coffee and whiskey topped with whipped cream – was invented by barman Joe Sheridan, who wanted to cheer up a group of cold, travel-weary passengers who had been forced back by bad weather.

once more than 420 tower houses in the Shannon area. Few are as imposing nor as carefully restored as Bunratty whose rectangular 15th-century keep is surrounded by four corner turrets, each topped with battlements and a set of flags.

Bunratty Castle and Folk Park ❼ (tel: 061-361 511; www.shannonheritage.com; daily year-round; charge) is strategically placed on the road between Shannon Airport and Limerick city. It contains furniture and paintings from the 15th and 16th centuries. The Folk Park behind it consists of 25 acres (10 hectares) of reconstructed and fully furnished farmhouses, cottages and shops, as they would have appeared to a visitor to mid-western Ireland in the late 19th century. There is even a village street with blacksmith, pub, drapery, print works and post office. **Durty Nelly's**, an old-world Irish pub next door to the village, has been copied all over the world.

Another corny but enjoyable experience is the medieval Irish banquet, a purely tourist-oriented but good-natured event – essentially a meal with Irish cabaret during which the guests are serenaded by Irish colleens – which takes place twice nightly at Bunratty and at the nearby **Knappogue Castle** (tel: 061-360 788; charge) at Quin to the north of Bunratty. Knappogue is a 15th-century Macnamara stronghold, also restored and furnished in period.

The Craggaunowen Project

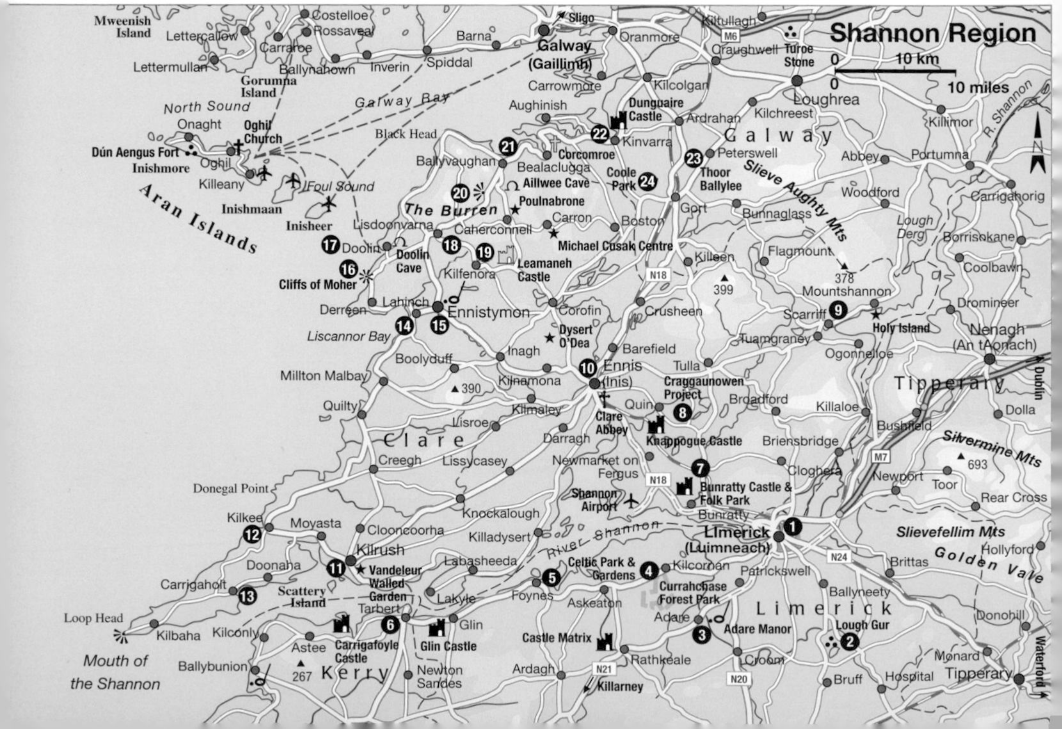

The **Craggaunowen Project** ❽ (tel: 061-367 178; mid-May–mid-Sept daily 10am–5pm; charge) is built in the grounds of another castle, a 16th-century tower house. The project has reconstructed authentic replicas of dwelling places in prehistoric and pre-Christian Ireland. On an island in the lake, reached by means of a footbridge, is a *crannog*, a fortified dwelling of clay and wattle. A small ring fort which shows how a farmer would have lived in the 5th or 6th centuries has been built. Also at Craggaunowen is the traditionally-built boat in which the writer and adventurer Tim Severin sailed to Nova Scotia in 1976, retracing the legendary 6th-century voyage of St Brendan, and making a plausible case for its historical reality.

To escape from the beaten path of the castle trail, consider an outing to **Scarriff** ❾, a quiet little town set on high ground overlooking Lough Derg. It is a rural backwater, popular with visitors in summer and sleepy in winter, which has a reputation for traditional music. **Drewsborough House** near **Tuamgraney**, to the south of Scarriff, is the birthplace of the novelist Edna O'Brien who has written scathing descriptions of the narrow-minded inhabitants of this area which was considered remote 50 years ago.

Both Scarriff and Tuamgraney are on the scenic drive that goes all the way around **Lough Derg**, a wide, almost sea-like part of the Shannon River which is popular with watersports enthusiasts. It is worth taking in at least the 5-mile (8km) stretch north-east to **Mountshannon**, a neat 18th-century village. Offshore you can visit **Holy Island**, an uninhabited 49-acre (20-hectare) island which had a 7th-century Christian settlement. There are the remains of five churches and a 79ft (24-metre) high round tower. The East Clare Heritage Centre, Tuamgraney (tel: 061-921 351; www.eastclareheritage.com; Mon–Fri 9.30am–5pm) is based in a 10th-century church and celebrates the rich heritage of this unsung area.

Ennis

Ennis ❿, a busy market town 23 miles (37km) west of Lough Derg, has an inviting cosiness, partly due to its size and human scale but also because a bypass has diverted much of the traffic. The town's proximity to Shannon Airport has meant that many people seeking asylum in Ireland were housed in Ennis while awaiting a verdict on their application, and opted to stay in the town when asylum was granted. Conseuqently Ennis now has a sizable West African population, which adds an exotic touch to its daily life. The Tourist Information Office (tel: 065-682 8366; www.shannonregiontourism.ie) is on Arthurs Row, off O'Connell Street.

The same building is shared with the **Clare Museum**, which tells the story of 6,000 years of history through the *Riches of Clare* exhibition (tel: 065-682 3382; www.clarelibrary.ie; June–Sept Mon–Sat 9.30am–5.30pm, Sun 9.30am–1pm, Oct–May Tue–Sat 9.30am–5.30pm; free).

Ennis Friary is a Franciscan Friary founded by the O'Brien Kings of Thomond in the 13th century. The ruins, well-preserved, consist of a nave, chancel, belfry and cloister (tel: 065-682 9100; Apr–Oct 10am–6pm; charge).

Ennis is known as a centre for traditional Irish music and dance. Performers and students (many of them youngsters) flock to the Fleadh Nua a competitive festival for musicians and dancers held annually at the end of May. At all times of the year, traditional musicians gather in the pubs of Ennis and hold impromptu music sessions, which can be enjoyed for the price of a drink. Ask locally where

EAT

For connoisseurs of the kitsch, Bunratty Castle's Medieval Banquets, held twice nightly at 5.30pm and 8.45pm for up to 141 people, take some beating. Goblets of mead precede the spare ribs with honey and whiskey sauce, and medieval madrigals aid the digestion. Prices start at around €60 for an adult. Details: www.shannonheritage.com.

BELOW: Bunratty Castle.

Fleadh Nua
Since 1974 Ennis has hosted what was the first traditional festival to bring together concerts, street entertainment, music, song and dancing workshops, exhibitions, lectures, film shows, pageants and parades. Around 50,000 people attend each May. www.fleadhnua.com.

to find music. More formal, ticketed events, and the finals of the Fleadh Nua are held at Glór Irish Music Centre (Friar's Walk; tel: 065-64 3103; www.glor.ie). The strikingly-designed modern building hosts well-known touring acts on the Irish music scene, locally produced drama, and there is also a craft gallery and coffee shop.

Moving down to the coast, **Kilrush** ⓫ is 5½ miles (9km) west of Killimer where the car ferry from north Kerry docks. Kilrush, with a population of 2,650, is the biggest town on the coast of west Clare. It was designed by a local landlord in the 18th century to complement his estate.

The style chosen for the town is pleasantly neoclassical, with wide streets and a main square big enough to accommodate horse fairs. Traditional livestock fairs (mainly horses, donkeys and sheep, with side stalls) are held in the square on the first Thursday of March, June and October.

The ruins of the Vandeleur family mansion, which was destroyed by fire in 1897, are at the centre of the 420-acre (170-hectare) Kilrush Forest Park. The **Vandeleur Walled Garden** (Vandeleur Demesne, Killimer Road; tel: 065-905 1760; www.vandeleurwalledgarden.ie; Apr–Oct Mon–Fri 10am–5pm, Sat–Sun noon–5pm, Oct–Mar Mon–Fri 10am–5pm; charge) is enclosed behind old stone walls at the centre of a woodland estate, and has a courtyard with a coffee shop and a Victorian-style glasshouse displaying unusual and tender plants.

A 15-minute boat ride from Kilrush Creek Marina (Griffin Boat Hire; tel: 065-905 1327; Apr–Oct daily) will take you to **Scattery Island** which has a 6th-century monastery founded by St Senan, the remains of five churches and a round tower The monastery was plundered by Vikings before being recaptured by Brian Ború. There is a Visitor Centre on the island, and guided tours are available free. Dolphin-watching cruises run by the Shannon Dolphin and Wildlife Foundation (Kilrush Creek Marina; tel: 065-905 2326; www.shannondolphins.ie; June–Sept) operate daily in summer, weather permitting, to watch families of bottle-nosed dolphins playing in the estuary. Another firm, the MV *Dolphin Discovery* (tel: 065-905 1327) also operates from Kilrush Marina in the summer.

Kilkee ⓬, 8½ miles (13km) to the west, is on the Atlantic coast of Clare, as opposed to the banks of the Shannon Estuary, and has a sandy beach. The village has been rather overwhelmed by bland developments of holiday homes (it is traditionally a favourite weekend spot for Limerick City people), but its centre retains an old world charm There is a scenic drive south to Loop Head lighthouse, a round trip of about 34 miles (55km). At **Carrigaholt** ⓭ a 16th-century tower house stands beside the pier with good views from its top floor across the Shannon Estuary to north Kerry.

Lahinch

The west-facing beaches, where long rolling waves break on the sand after their Atlantic crossing, are popular

BELOW: the Cliffs of Moher.

with water sport enthusiasts all the way up the coast to **Lahinch** ⓮, (sometimes spelt Lehinch) also famous for its golf links. This part of the west Clare coast has become the haunt of some of the world's leading surfers because of the immense size of its waves. A "new" wave *Aill na Searrach* (the leap of the foals), and with the nickname Aileens, was first successfully surfed in 2005 and has attracted many of the world's leading surfers. Aileens is hidden at the base of cliffs and rises to epic proportions of up to 25ft (8 metres). Those hoping to conquer it do so with the help of a jet-ski. The Clare waves suit surfers of all abilities when conditions are right and it is the country's fastest growing sport. For an updated daily surf report visit www.lahinchsurfshop.com; for general information on surfing in Ireland contact the Irish Surfing Association; tel: 096-49428; www.isasurf.ie.

From Lahinch, **Ennistymon** ⓯, 2½ miles (4km) inland is a charming, old-fashioned resort town on the Cullenagh River which has retained many original wooden shop fronts and some friendly pubs. The river has a series of waterfalls visible from its seven-arched bridge.

Local bakery, Kilkee.

The Cliffs of Moher

It was 17 years in the planning and cost more than €31 million, but one of Ireland's top attractions has finally been dressed up and garlanded with the inevitable "interpretative experience".

Towering to 650ft (214 metres) high and stretching for 5 miles (8km), the **Cliffs of Moher** ⓰ on the west coast of Clare have always been a popular destination. But with upwards of 1 million visitors a year tramping across them,

BELOW: beach in the Lahinch region.

Understanding the Cliffs

The Visitor Experience exhibition will teach you all about the ridged Cliffs of Moher, a protected haven for many species of seabirds

Formed by layers of siltstone, shale and sandstone, the Cliffs of Moher have long been recognised and protected. In 1988 the area around them was designated as a Refuge for Fauna and the following year became a Special Protection Area for birds. The layering of rock has led to the development of narrow horizontal ledges that provide nest sites for seabirds including fulmars, guillemots, razorbills and puffins. The area is Ireland's most accessible breeding site of puffins and hundreds of pairs of these comic-looking birds nest there. The designation includes the cliffs, cliff-top maritime grass and heath, and a 200-metre zone of open water.

For the real elemental experience and to properly feel the gustiness of the wind on your face and see the waves booming below, you should walk up to the edge. With binoculars you can look across to Liscannor Bay or pick out the Aran Islands. Friendly and knowledgeable "Moher Rangers" will guide you round and explain the significance of the site, taking you up to O'Brien's Tower built in 1835 by Cornelius O'Brien, a descendant of Brian Ború, the High King of Ireland. The best time to see the sea birds is at the height of the breeding season from early May to the end of July. You should have fine views of puffins wheeling in to land and be able to pick out rows of guillemots and kittiwakes crouched precariously on ledges.

The Visitor Experience's exhibition area features the Atlantic Edge (an optional multimedia exhibition; charge) incorporating the themed zones of ocean, rock, nature and man. It includes the Ledge, computer-generated images of life above and below water that lets you to see close-up the natural world from a bird's-eye perspective. You can also take a Clare journey with a high-definition cinematic aerial tour of varied landscapes tracked on a map of the county.

A touch-screen displays the changing earth over geological time; there are views of cave interiors and explanations of Clare's underground rivers. The human history of life has not been neglected and a rich fund of legends from the area are told through taped interviews and displays. It's a long way from the 1950s when a local guide, Dinney McMahon, realized he could make a living from trading to tourists at the cliffs. He sold postcards, tin whistles and shillelaghs, and charmed visitors with stories of local gods as well as the habits of the birds. He died of a heart attack at 80 while making his way to his stand on the cliffs; a memorial stone marks the spot.

Billed as one of Europe's busiest tourist attractions, the cliffs are worth a half-day visit. Add in lunch to the Atlantic Edge entrance charge and the somewhat excessive car parking charges and a visit can work out expensive. But this is one of Ireland's most popular locations and always manages to stir something within the imagination. In high season, get there early before the crowds arrive. ❑

ABOVE: O'Brien's Tower.
LEFT: it's a long way down.

they had started to erode and the old facilities were woefully inadequate. New features include an extension of old paths, elevated viewing platforms, more seating and the ecological reconstruction of the cliff wall and grass. For those who wish to keep dry and warm, the whole experience can now be enjoyed in the sparkling New Visitor Experience (tel: 065-708 6141; www.cliffsofmoher.ie; daily Nov–Feb 9am–5pm, Mar–Apr and Oct until 6.30pm, May and Sept until 7pm, June–Aug until 9pm; free, Atlantic Edge exhibition, charge, and charge per vehicle for parking; ATM facilities).

The centre is largely hidden from view as it has been subsumed into the contours of the landscape and covered by a hillside. As you approach, the building appears to be in darkness – the idea being to create a dimly lit cave-like effect *(see box, opposite page)*.

Doolin Cave

Just over 3 miles (5km) away you come to an experience that should feature on the itinerary of every tourist to County Clare: **Doolin Cave**, Pol an Ionáin "the ivy cave" (tel: 065-707 5761; www.doolincave.ie; daily 9am–5pm; charge). One of the world's biggest free-standing stalactites, "The Great Stalactite", opened in 2006 after a 15-year battle over planning permission. The stalactite – it's more than 600,000 years old – was discovered by two English cavers in 1952 and is an extremely popular draw.

A minibus driver brings you the short distance to the entrance where you are given a hard hat and torch before descending 125 steps to experience a stunning subterranean world and a memorable sight. The visitor is plunged into darkness and then in a flash the subtly-lit stalactite appears before you in the main chamber. The stalactite hangs more than 20ft (7 metres) from the ceiling and weighs in at 10 tons – and it is still developing. The cave tour takes one hour and numbers are limited to 20.

Doolin

Doolin ⓱ (also called Roadford on some maps) consists of a long straggle of B&Bs, hostels and hotels, several restaurants, craft shops and three pubs. The pubs are renowned for traditional

WHERE

The Cliffs of Moher lie 3 miles (5km) south of Doolin, and 6 miles (10km) from Lisdoonvarna.

LEFT: don't miss Doolin Cave.
BELOW: Doolin.

TIP

Aran Island hopping

Doolin Ferries (tel: 065-707 445; Easter–Oct; www.doolinferries.com) runs a service from Doolin Pier to the three Aran Islands. The Cliffs of Moher Cruises also operate daily services to one of the three Aran Islands, Inis Oirr, as well as a Cliffs of Moher cruise. The cruises leave from Doolin Pier and Liscannor, subject to tides and weather conditions (tel: 065-707 5949, daily Apr–Oct; www.mohercruises.com).

music. Some young musicians spend the whole summer camping here, learning from their elders.

Lisdoonvarna

Moving inland to **Lisdoonvarna** ⓲, if you visit the Burren Smokehouse (tel: 065-707 4432; www.burrensmokehouse.ie) you will be shown an exhibition kiln and smoke box with a short audio-visual presentation of the smoking process in action. The town developed as a spa centre for tourists due to the healing properties of its sulphurous spring water (the baths, alas, are no more). Today its main claim to fame is its **Matchmaking Festival** in September when shy farmers meet women under the direction of Willie Daly, matchmaker, horse whisperer and publican (his bar is at 1 Main Street, Ennistymon). The festival now offers a matchmaking website and speed dating (www.matchmakerireland.com).

Music is a permanent soundtrack to the lives of the people of Clare. The next village on the southern fringe of the Burren, **Kilfenora** ⓳ is famous for the Kilfenora Ceilí Band, a group of local traditional musicians which celebrated its 100th anniversary in 2009, and tours throughout Ireland and to the UK and USA. It is also the home of the **Burren Centre** (tel: 065-708 8030; www.theburrencentre.ie; June–Aug 9.30am–6pm, mid-Mar–May and Sept–Oct 10am–5pm; charge to exhibition). A multi-dimensional exhibition tells the story of the Burren and there is an informative video presentation. The centre also houses a tourist information point, exhibition area, craft shop and tea rooms.

Next door to the centre it is well worth a look at the 12th-century **St Fachtnan's Cathedral** with its fine collection of medieval high crosses. The recently-installed sloping glass roof on the north chapel has been added to protect the crosses from the elements. Information panels outline the details of the crosses, the most famous being the impressive Doorty Cross with its bishop holding his hand up in blessing.

BELOW: excitement mounts at Lisdoonvarna's Matchmaking Festival.

The Burren

Travelling east from Kilfenora you come to the beautifully proportioned ruin of **Leamaneh Castle** where you turn north entering the hauntingly magical kingdom that is the **Burren** ⓴.

This is botanical holy ground of a high order, a meeting place of plants from the Arctic, the Alps and the Mediterranean. Over 70 percent of Ireland's native flora is found here, including 24 species of orchid and 25 types of fern. The best-known flower in this wild rock garden is the spring gentian *(gentiana verna)* a dazzling small blue plant that can be seen in April and May. Search hard and you will find it growing alongside brightly coloured magenta geraniums, early purple-orchids and swathes of creamy mountain avens all sprouting from the grykes (vertical crevices that lie between the pavement). The clints are the glacially polished horizontal surfaces that you walk across and which occasionally wobble.

The Burren is renowned as a place of geological and archaeological wonder. Miles of gunmetal grey ancient stone walls thread in all directions. Everywhere there are giant boulders – glacial erratics – that were dropped by the glacier. These rock refugees are part of the topographical outdoor decor of the place and have stood for 15,000 years.

Spend just a short time here and you will be enthralled. You will quickly realise why the Burren means "rocky place." It is a Karst landscape (from an area in the former Yugoslavia with similar terrain) hewed from stone: stone monuments, stone cottages, stone fields, pavement, rocks and walls. With a patina all its own, it feels unlike anywhere else in Ireland – almost a different country.

• *For fuller coverage of the Burren landscape, see pages 242–3.*

Carron

Follow the road from Leamaneh Castle to **Carron** where you will see a *polje*, a geological term for a depression in the limestone and where a turlough, or seasonal lake (full of fresh water in winter and entirely dry in the summer) is to be found. Carron has the **Michael Cusack Centre** (tel: 065-708 9944; www.michaelcusack.ie; Apr–Oct, Mon–Sun 10am–5.30pm; charge). Cusack was the founder of the world's largest amateur sporting organisation, the Gaelic Athletic Association. The 19th century herdsman's cottage where Cusask grew up has been fully restored. The centre tells the story of his life from his humble origins in Carron through his travels and careers. Nearby, the Burren Perfumery & Floral Centre (tel: 065-708 9102; daily, May, June and Sept 10am–6pm, July–Aug 10am–7pm, Oct–Apr 10am–5pm; café) highlights the sensory side of the Burren and serves organic food.

Now retrace your route back to the main road and you will come to **Caherconnell Visitor Centre** (tel: 065-708 9999; www.burrenforts.ie; Mar–Oct Mon–Sun 10am–5pm, July–Aug 10am–6pm; charge).

This centre explains the circular and walled farmsteads found throughout the Burren that are known locally as "Cahers". There are more than 500

Finding fauna

The Burren lays claim to 30 of Ireland's species of butterfly and 100 species of breeding birds. On a walk across the limestone you are likely to come across parties of feral goats, herds of hardy cattle, perhaps a hare or fox and, if you are lucky, a pine marten – although they are mostly nocturnal creatures.

BELOW: exotic plants abound in the unpromising landscape of the Burren.

TIP

Exploring the area
The Burren and its surroundings are littered with the remnants of the past and a tremendous sense of antiquity. An essential *vade-mecum* for visitors is *The Burren* map produced by Folding Landscapes that plots every townland, dolmen, standing stone, ring fort, castle, abbey and ruined church.

of them, including the spectacular Cahercummaun. The best preserved is found at Caherconnell.

Poulnabrone

A short distance north you will see from the road what is unquestionably Ireland's best known, most-visited and most-photographed megalithic burial tomb, the **Poulnabrone** ("the pool of the sorrows") portal dolmen with its huge capstone. Ancient, baffling, yet strangely familiar as its image is reproduced all around you on postcards, T-shirts, book covers and holiday brochures; it was built about 4,500 years ago.

Each day numerous tour coaches stop at this dolmen which, although now roped off for protection, is in its natural state. A timeline on a signboard interprets its significance and puts it in context with information on the surrounding flora.

The dolmen was excavated in 1986 and the remains of 22 bodies – 16 adults and 6 children, male and female – were discovered. The bodies were reckoned to be at least 1,500 years old.

BELOW: the mysterious dolmen at Poulnabrone.

Aillwee Cave

Follow a twisting road with hairpin bends down Ballyallaban Hill for 3 miles (5km) and you come to another underworld adventure, **Aillwee Cave** (tel: 065-707 7036; www.aillweecave.ie; daily 9.30am–5.30pm, July–Aug 10am–6.30pm; charge), discovered around 1940 by a herdsman. Guides accompany you on a 35-minute tour through caverns, over bridged chasms, under weird formations, past pale threads of straw stalactites hanging down mysteriously and alongside waterfalls. The bones of a brown bear, a species extinct in Ireland for over 1,000 years, were found here.

Ballyvaughan

Picturesquely-sited **Ballyvaughan** ㉑ (pop 220) is the best base for exploring this unique landscape. The village has two hotels, pubs and cafés and a bicycle hire business – one of the best ways of appreciating the Burren is on two wheels.

Each May, Ballyvaughan hosts "Burren in Bloom", a month-long programme of talks and tours. Illustrated talks on the flora, birdlife, archaeology and geology as well as history and folklore tours, ghost tours of Aillwee Cave, workshops, concerts and traditional music nights are all on the packed itinerary (tel: 065-707 7077; www.ballyvaughanireland.com).

Before heading north out of the Burren it's worth a short detour off the main road to explore the well-preserved ruins of **Corcomroe Abbey**. Now roofless, this Cistercian abbey was built shortly after 1195 in a serene valley near Bell Harbour. According to legend, the stonemasons who built it were executed when they had finished their work to prevent them building a more beautiful church elsewhere.

Kinvarra

There is a pleasant scenic drive along the south shore of Galway Bay to **Kinvarra** ㉒, a charming fishing village at the head of Galway Bay with a grassy quayside and an alternative spelling of Kinvara. It is popular with visitors who enjoy its old-fashioned pubs and modern restaurants. The highlight of the year is the annual *Cruinniú na mBád* in mid-August, "the gathering of the boats". In this festive regatta, traditional Connemara sailing craft – the famous brown-sailed Galway Hookers, which were once used to carry turf across the bay – race against each other in a grand spectacle.

In spring, the *Fleadh na gCuach*, "the cuckoo festival", a traditional Irish music event, attracts large crowds.

The floodlit **Dunguaire Castle** (tel: 061-360 788; May–Oct; charge) is a four-storey tower house built by the shore in 1520. At night this lonely sentinel is used for medieval banqueting, hence the floodlighting. A recent addition to Kinvarra is **Murphystore**, a 200-year-old listed building on the quayside that has been restored from dereliction. Originally used as a grain store, it is now a coffee and craft shop specialising in seaweed-based products from Ireland's west coast. The work of local artists and potters is also on display (tel: 091-637 760; www.murphystore.com).

In the centre of Kinvarra, it's well worth visiting a small café and gallery run by Burrenbeo (www.burrenbeo.com), an information and education resource, with a good selection of books on the Burren.

Yeats associations

The final leg of a Shannon journey takes the visitor to **Gort**, a pleasant market town with a large main square, on the main road from Ennis to Galway. It is known locally as "Brazil", as it has a lively community of Brazilian residents, mostly from the same village in north-east Brazil, who came to Ireland originally to work in the meat-processing industry. Gort Forge is mentioned by the poet W.B. Yeats, who restored the nearby castle, **Thoor Ballylee** ㉓ (tel: 091-631 436; June–Sept) a 16th-century tower house which was the summer home of the Nobel prize-winning poet from 1917 to 1928. The restored tower, which the poet bought for £28, contains much of Yeats's original furniture. It is beautifully situated in a wooded area close to a stream.

The tower house was discovered for the poet by his benfactor, Lady Gregory (1852–1932), herself a playwright and collector of folklore. Her house at **Coole Park** ㉔, 2 miles (3km) northwest of Gort was demolished in 1947, but its grounds now form the Coole-Garryland National Park with a deer enclosure, forest walks and a lake whose petrified trees stick out of the water (Coole Park Visitor Centre; tel: 091-631 804; www.coolepark.ie; Apr–May and Sept Mon–Sun 10am–5pm, June–Aug 10am–6pm, park grounds: 8.30am–7.30pm, June–Aug 8.30am–9pm; charge, grounds free).

In the walled garden stands a great copper beech tree, the famous "Autograph Tree" on which Lady Gregory's guests – Yeats, the playwrights George Bernard Shaw, J. M. Synge and Sean O'Casey, the poet John Masefield and the painter Augustus John – carved their initials. ❑

Dunguaire Castle.

BELOW: there's no excuse for losing your way in Ballyvaughan.

RESTAURANTS AND PUBS

Restaurants

Prices for a three-course dinner per person without wine:
€ = under €25
€€ = €25–40
€€€ = €40–55
€€€€ = over €55

Adare

Adare Manor
Adare, Co. Limerick
Tel: 061-396 566
Daily, D 6.30–9.30pm, D **€€€€**
If you want to experience the high life you'll find it in this neo-Gothic mansion. The Oak Restaurant serves contemporary, classic cuisine. Much of the produce is sourced from the 900-acre (360-hectare) estate.

Maguire Restaurant
at the Dunraven Arms, Adare, Co. Limerick
Tel: 061-396 633
Daily 7.30–9.30pm, Sun L only 12.30–1.30pm. L **€€**, D **€€€**
Country house atmosphere and a menu that offers genuine traditional dishes. A big draw is real roast rib of beef carved at the table.

The Wild Geese Restaurant
Rose Cottage, Main Street, Adare, Co. Limerick
Tel: 061-396 451
Mon–Sat 6.30–10pm, Sun 6–9pm summer only. D **€€–€€€**
Fairy-tale pretty; a talented chef who sources ingredients with care; contemporary Irish menu and cooking style. The value menu with no time restrictions is great value.

Ballingarry

The Mustard Seed
Echo Lodge Country House, Ballingarry, Co. Limerick
Tel: 069-685 088
Daily D 7–9.30pm. Reservations required **€€€€**
Good food and exceptional country house hospitality. Wonderful cooking in individual, contemporary Irish style. Seasonal menus based on local/artisan and home grown produce from large organic garden.

Ballyvaughan
Gregan's Castle, Corkscrew Road, Ballyvaughan, Co. Clare
Tel: 065-707 7005
D Mon–Sat 6.30–8.30pm, Feb, Mar and Nov Fri–Sat only **€€€€**
Watch the sun set over Galway Bay at this elegant country house in the best restaurant around, serving a classic menu of local organic produce.

Bunratty

Gallagher's Restaurant
Bunratty, Co. Limerick
Tel: 061-363 363
D daily 5.30–9.45pm **€€€€**; L Sun 12.30–2.30pm **€€**
Contemporary seafood restaurant with a rustic interior in old-style thatched cottage sharing a kitchen with a popular gastropub. Warm welcome, relaxed style.

Doolin

Cullinan's Seafood Restaurant
Doolin, Co. Clare
Tel: 065-707 4183
D Thur–Tue 6–9pm **€€€**
Owner-chef and his wife offer a menu of local seafood and Burren lamb prepared in a contemporary style in a simple cottage-style restaurant overlooking the River Aille.

Doonbeg

Morrissey's Seafood Bar and Grill
Doonbeg, Co. Clare
Tel: 065-905 5304
Tue–Sat, L noon–2.30pm, D 6.30–9.30pm, closed Nov, Jan–Feb **€€**
A family pub in the village centre has been converted into a restaurant with a family-friendly menu offering local steaks and seafood from the grill.

Ennis

JM's Bistro
Temple Gate Hotel, The Square, Ennis, Co. Clare
Tel: 065-682 3300
Daily 7–10pm, Sun L 12.45–2.30pm **€€€**
Lofty old-world style room. Professional yet friendly service. High standard of cooking: modern Irish menus emphasise fresh seafood and local meat.

Town Hall Café
Old Ground Hotel, O'Connell Street, Ennis, Co. Clare
Tel: 065-682 8112
Daily 10am–9.30pm, L noon–4pm, D 6–9.30pm. L **€**, D **€€**
Well restored part of Ennis's venerable Old Ground Hotel, with airy high ceilings. Best stop in Ennis for informal, bistro-style lunches. At night, it moves up a gear.

Ennistymon

Byrne's
Main Street, Ennistymon, Co. Clare
Tel: 065-707 1080
Dinner only Mon–Sat 6.30–9.30pm, closed Nov and Feb. Set D **€€**, à la carte **€€€**
Airy space with high ceilings. Views of "the Falls". Imaginative modern Irish cooking with a leaning towards fresh seafood and good vegetarian options.

Fanore

Italian Trattoria
Fanore, Co. Clare
Tel: 065-707 6971
May–Sept 11am–11pm. L **€**, D **€€**
Authentic modern Italian cooking, simple, delicious food with a strong leaning towards enticing vegetarian dishes.

Killaloe

The Cherry Tree
Lakeside, Killaloe, Co. Clare
Tel: 061-375 688
Tue–Sat 6–10pm. D **€€€**
Charming location with floor to ceiling windows on to lake views. Consistently excellent contemporary Irish cooking. Impeccable service.

Kinvarra
The Pier Head, Kinvarra, Co. Galway
Tel: 091-638 188
Mon–Sat 5–9pm D, Sat L noon–2.30pm **€€**
Excellent seafood and steak served in a former pub on the pier overlooking the bay and its castle.

Lahinch

Bartra Seafood Restaurant
Lahinch, Co. Clare
Tel: 065-708 1280
Tue–Sun 5–10pm, closed Jan–Feb. Early Bird 5–6.30pm **€€**, D **€€€**
Cliff-top restaurant specialising in fresh, local

seafood and great fresh vegetarian options.

Vaughan Lodge
Lahinch, Co. Clare
Tel: 065-708 1111
Tue–Sun 6.30–9.30pm, closed Nov–Mar **€€€**
Stylish and spacious contemporary restaurant in small country house hotel specialising in seafood and local artisan foods.

Limerick

Aubars
49–50 Thomas Street, Limerick, Co. Limerick
Tel: 061-317 572
Tue–Sat 8am–9.30pm, bar meals daily, All day brunch, L noon–3pm, D 5.30–9-30pm. L **€**, D **€€**
Contemporary restaurant and bar. A celebration of traditional dishes presented in a modern style. Good vegetarian options.

Brasserie One
1 Pery Square, Limerick
Tel: 061-402 402
Mon–Sat 6–9.30pm, Sun 11am–7pm **€€**
Informal first floor restaurant of Georgian townhouse turned boutique hotel, with a classic Franco-Irish dinner menu and all-day brunch/roast dinner menu on Sundays.

Copper and Spice
2 Cornmarket Street, Limerick
Tel: 061-313 620
Daily, D 5–10.30pm. D **€€**
Stylish, authentic Indian, though menus also offer Thai cuisine. Children welcome.

Liscannor

Vaughan's Anchor Inn
Liscannor, Co. Clare (pub and restaurant)
Tel: 065-708 1548
Daily 12.30–9pm. L **€**, D **€€**
Alive with character, specialising in fresh seafood. Casual food all day. In the evening it moves up a gear. 20 varieties of fish, a menu that changes as the boats come in. Tradition with sophistication.

Lisdoonvarna

Sheedy's Country House Hotel and Restaurant
Lisdoonvarna, Co. Clare
Tel: 065-707 4026
Daily 7–8.30pm **€€**
One of the best in the West. A family enterprise offering understated elegance, stunning ingredients, accomplished contemporary Irish cooking, artistic presentation.

New-Market-on-Fergus/Shannon

Earl of Thomond Restaurant
At Dromoland Castle Hotel, New-Market-on-Fergus
Tel: 061-368 144
Daily 7–9pm, L Sun only 12.30–1.30pm. L **€€€**, D **€€€€**
Dine in elegance to the music of an Irish harp. Explore three classic menus: table d'hôte, vegetarian and à la carte. Cuisine is classic French using Irish ingredients. Service is impeccable.

Scariff

Mac Ruaidhri's
The Square, Scariff, Co. Clare
Tel: 061-921 999
D Wed–Sat, plus Tue in summer, 6–9.15pm, L Sun only noon–2.30pm. L **€€**, Early D **€€**, D **€€€**
Attractive space with friendly service. Balanced menu, modern Irish/traditional. Talented chef.

Tulla

Flappers
Main Street, Tulla, Co. Clare
Tel: 065-683 5711
Daily 9.30am–9.15pm. L **€**, D **€€**
Café-style restaurant with simple, well cooked food at lunchtime. The evening menus are more imaginative.

Pubs

In Limerick, **Nancy Blake's**, 19 Upper Denmark Street, has a good pint and good music.

The **Locke Bar and Bistro** is adjacent to Limerick city's riverside walk and has outdoor tables.

In Glin, Co. Limerick, just outside Glin Castle's walls, is the delightful **O'Shaughnessy's** pub, six generations in the same family. They keep "holy hours" by closing from 2.30 to 5.30pm.

Cruises, Abbey Street Ennis, Co. Clare is one of several pubs in the town known for traditional music sessions.

Gooser's pub, Killaloe, Co. Clare, is a popular Shannon-side pub with outdoor seating. Bar food.

Durty Nellies, Bunratty, Co. Clare. Beside Bunratty Castle, it's well run and the bar food is usually good. Evening live music.

J.C. Clarke's, Bunratty, Co. Clare is a large modern gastropub at opposite end of village to the castle, where the natives eat.

The Whiskey Still, Lough Derg, Dromineer, Co. Tipperary. Pleasant pub with outdoor seating within sight of the marina.

Larkins, Garrykennedy, Lough Derg. Whitewashed cottage on the lake harbour; a place to watch the boats and enjoy the bar food.

The Monk's Pub, Ballyvaughan, Co. Clare. Long cottage on the village pier, a seafood menu and traditional music on Sunday afternoons.

Hyland's Burren Hotel, Ballyvaughan, has all-day bar food, and in summer live music and storytelling.

RIGHT: Limerick signage.

The Burren

North Clare contains a strange landscape, a treeless limestone plateau that's a place of pilgrimage for botanists and geologists

A frustrated general serving Oliver Cromwell, one of the many ruthless invaders from across the Irish Sea, famously condemned this bleak place as having "not enough wood to hang a man, not enough water to drown him, not enough clay to cover his corpse." The view probably hasn't changed much in 350 years, but now the Burren (meaning great rock) is a national park. It covers 500 sq km (200 sq miles) of lunar-like limestone formation with delicate flora and fauna of Arctic, Alpine and Mediterranean origin, brought to the area by migrating birds. Here you will find, in seasonal abundance – but protected by the State – orchids, the purple bloody cranesbill and azaleas. The Burren is also an area of potholes, seasonal lakes, caves and streams.

The view from Corkscrew Hill

Properly appreciating the extraordinary nature of the place requires some study. The Burren Experience, on the northside of Ballyvaughan village, on the Kinvarra road, gives an introduction, but a finer overview can be had at the original Burren Centre, to the south in Kilfenora village. A good overall view of this "stony district" can be had from the so-called "Corkscrew" Hill on the road linking Ballyvaughan with Lisdoonvarna, but by far the best way to explore the fissured terrain is on foot.

Scattered throughout the region are tombs, chambers and dolmens of the Stone Age – notably, near Corkscrew Hill, the famous Poulnabrone Dolmen, dating from 2,500 BC.

Above: the Burren is home to many plants which flourish in its apparently inhospitable landscape. They are nurtured by a unique combination of soil, heat and mositure.

Below: Carron, east of the Burren, means the Cairn and has yielded up useful archaeological evidence of Bronze Age life. The stones that today form walls to keep the wind at bay were then used to construct a great cairn 8ft high and 50ft in diameter (2.4 by 15 metres) which protected the bodies in the burial mound. At Kilnaboy, in the upland part of the Burren, is the great stone fort of Cahercommaun (7th–10th centuries).

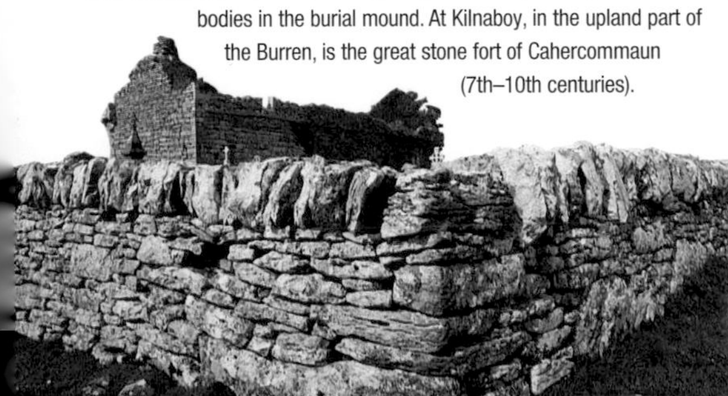

Right: It's surprising to find small green fields in such a stony landscape. But sheep farmers know how to survive the bleak winters in the west of Ireland. Animal farming flourishes due to the Burren's mineral wealth, which has especially helped horse breeding.

OVE: this bleak limestone terrain had its origins 70 million years when shells of marine animals were compacted on the seabed later pushed above the waves by geological shifts. A soft rock, limestone has been eroded by wind and rain, creating cracks crevices which both drain off rainwater and provide shelter for remarkable variety of fauna.

LOW: on the road through the Burren from Kinvarra lies the ruined comroe Abbey, founded by Cistercian monks around 1195. ough Henry VIII dissolved the monasteries in 1554, the abbey's oleness allowed the monks to remain for many years

THE TOMBS THAT HAVE DEFIED TIME

Poulnabrone Dolmen (above) dates from 25,00BC and is a striking example of the many ancient monuments which are particularly common in this part of Ireland because of the ready availability of limestone slabs. Its name means "pool of sorrows". Because its massive capstone is set at an angle, it has been fancifully been called a launching-pad for a Stone Age missile.

Such single-chambered portal graves were originally covered with a mound of earth and stones, and are a testament to the great reverence the Neolithic people had for their dead.

Passage-graves, in which the burial chamber was reached through a passage, reveal sophisticated building techniques and often intricate abstract carvings. Some of Europe's most spectacular examples can be seen at Newgrange, west of Drogheda in Co. Louth.

Stone circles, which served as prehistoric temples, are probably related to the megalithic tombs. Some of the most impressive can be found at Lough Gur in Co. Limerick and near Hollywood in Co. Wicklow.

The commonest monument is the ring fort – about 30,000 survive. These were circular stone defences surrounding dwellings or royal seats.

BELOW: Co. Clare is very much part of the western seaboard, from its natural boundary of the Shannon estuary to its northern border with Galway. The full force of the Atlantic can be felt here and lighthouses played a vital part in warning ships clear of the treacherous coastline. At Spanish Point, near the village of Milltown Malbay, some ships from the Spanish Armada sent to invade England were wrecked in1588.

GALWAY AND THE WEST

Beyond the liveliness of Galway city lies Connemara's wild, romantic landscape at the very edge of Europe where the Irish language is still spoken. But can the increasing number of visitors still find solitude?

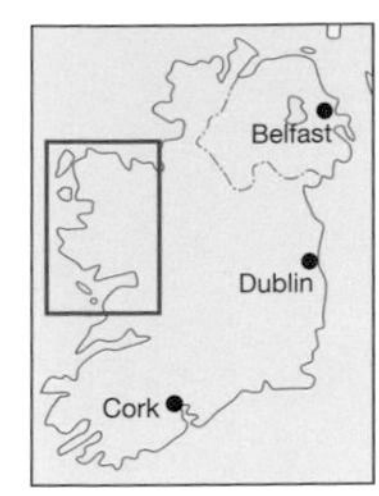

Main attractions
GALWAY CITY MUSEUM
LYNCH'S CASTLE
GALWAY RACES
GALWAY CATHEDRAL
SALTHILL
ROUNDSTONE
ARAN ISLANDS
LOUGH CORRIB
KYLEMORE ABBEY
WESTPORT
ACHILL ISLAND
KNOCK

The short-lived boom in the Irish economy led to rapid development in many parts of the west of Ireland, including Galway city which up until 2008 was frequently cited as one of the fastest growing cities in Europe. These days Galway city, with a population of 72,000 is surrounded by a dual-carriageway ring road which had, at last count 16 roundabouts, and the approach to the city is frequently grid-locked. However, most people live in suburbs which have grown up over the past 20 years, leaving the city's historic centre and docks relatively unscathed. It is hoped that the opening in 2010 of a rail link to Limerick will help to ease traffic congestion.

A compact city centre with numerous quaint shops, trendy boutiques as well as stylish cafés and pubs, **Galway** ❶ has developed a unique personality, combining a strongly Irish identity with exuberant cosmopolitan influences, epitomised by the broad cultural mix presented annually in the highly successful Galway Arts Festival.

The medieval city

The city lies on the northeastern shore of **Galway Bay**, the inlet that separates Co. Galway from Co. Clare. In the words of the poet Mary Devenport O'Neill (1879–1967), it is "a town tormented by the sea". Galway takes its name from the Irish *Gaillimh* (pronounced *Goll-yiv*). It has been shaped by a colourful past and by its status as a seaport of importance. Unlike some Irish cities, it wasn't conquered by the Vikings but was invaded by the Anglo-Normans in the 13th century.

The medieval city grew up on the eastern bank of the River Corrib, inside the stone walls between 1232 and 1243, developing as a thriving port for wine, spices and fish. It became known as the "Citie of the Tribes" because of

PRECEEDING PAGES: riding on Cleggan Beach. **LEFT:** Galway Cathedral. **RIGHT:** view of the Long Walk, Galway.

The Quincentennial Fountain is a representation of the sails of the Galway hooker, a traditional fishing boat unique to Galway.

the influence of 14 wealthy Anglo-Norman merchant families who ruled it as an independent city-state. These families held power in the town and county for many centuries. Each family had its own street and mansion with stone-faced designs. Remnants of the buildings and the stonework can be seen on a walk around the city.

The modern city

The logical starting point, and the place where most people arrive, is **Eyre Square**. The square, Galway's focal point and main public park, was officially presented to the city in 1710 by Mayor Edward Eyre. In 1963 it was where the US president John F. Kennedy made a speech when given the freedom of the city.

Long in need of a makeover, it had a dowdy appearance leading to its night-time nickname "eerie" square. The revamped square has recently been re-landscaped in a €10 million project, with a sweeping walkway, giving the city's iconic central point a much-needed facelift.

Fourteen flags, each one representing one of the Tribes, now fly along one side of the square. The adjacent **Quincentennial Fountain** Ⓐ, erected in 1984 to celebrate the 500th anniversary of Galway becoming a city, has been retained. The fountain is composed of sheets of iron depicting the area's distinctive sailing boats, the Galway hooker.

Browne's Gateway Ⓑ, the entrance to the town house of a merchant family originally built in 1617, is a cut-stone doorway and window, and stands somewhat incongruously beside the flags.

Moving statue

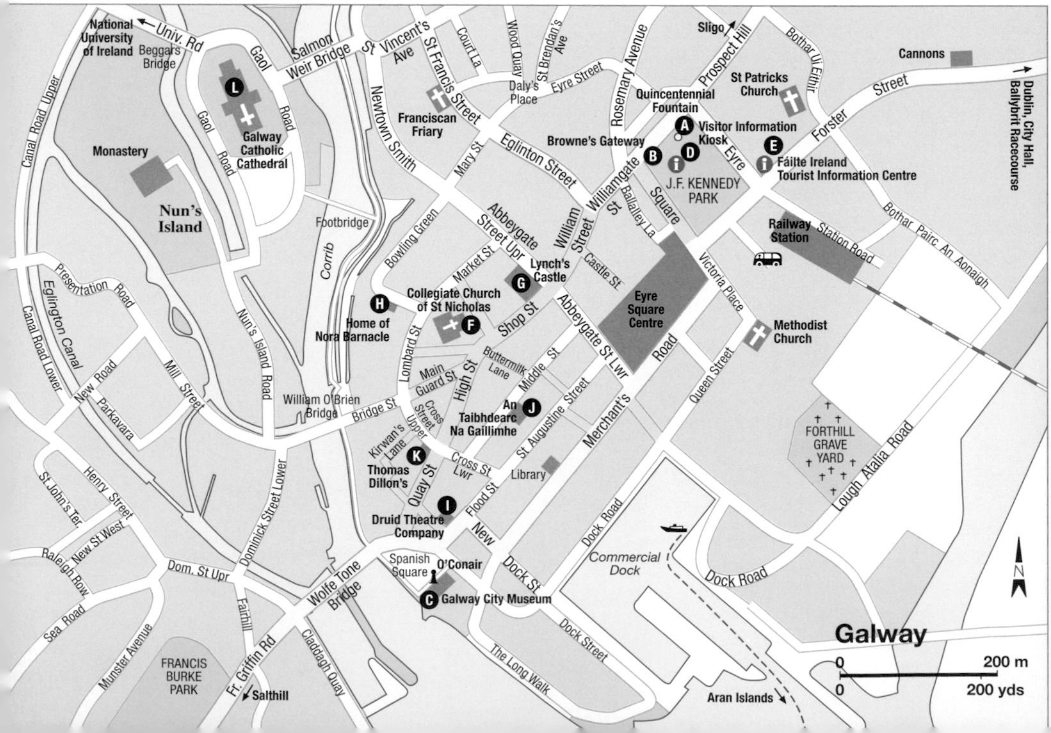

One controversial change was the removal of a limestone statue of Pádraic O'Conaire, one of Galway's most famous literary sons. A specialist in short stories, he is recognised as one of the first modernist writers of fiction in Irish. After returning from London in 1914, he spent the rest of his life roaming around Ireland, living off a meagre income from his stories and rural sketches. He died destitute in a hospital in Dublin in 1928, his only possessions his pipe and tobacco and an apple.

For years his seated figure, dressed in the worn clothes of a countryman, was a landmark in Eyre Square. Now his statute adorns the main entrance area of the **Galway City Museum** **C** (Spanish Parade; tel: 091-532 460; www.galwaycity.ie; June–Oct Mon–Sat 10am–5pm, Sun 2–5pm, Oct–May Tue–Sat 10am–5pm, closed Sun; free), a fine new building that was another product of the boom years. The ground floor covers the contemporary city, emphasising the arts scene, and two upper floors focus on medieval and post-Famine Galway.

The Square also contains a children's play area, and a **Visitor Information Kiosk** **D** (Mon–Sat 11am–5pm, Sun 9.15am–5.45pm, closes 1–2pm, limited opening off-season). The **Fáilte Ireland Tourist Information Centre,** **E** Ireland West Tourism, Forster Street (tel: 091-537 700; www.irelandwest.ie; Mon–Sat 9am–5.45pm) just off the eastern corner of Eyre Square, is awash with booklets, maps, postcards and gifts.

Galway, an ideal place for aimless wandering, is compact enough to not lose your bearings. The most notable ecclesiastical building is the Anglican Cathedral, the **Collegiate Church of St Nicholas** **F** (tel: 091-564 648). Built around 1320, it is the largest parish church of the medieval period in Ireland. It is dedicated to St Nicholas, a 4th-century Bishop of Myra in Lycia (southwestern Asia Minor). Although best known today as the patron saint of children, or "Santa Claus", he was during the Middle Ages more commonly found in medieval seaports such as Galway. Christopher Columbus is reputed to have prayed here in 1477 before setting off on his voyage of discovery.

Outstanding features of interest inside the Cathedral include the Crusader's Tomb dating from the 13th or early 14th century with an inscription in Norman French, a carved Baptismal Font of the late 16th or early 17th century and a Holy Water Stoup built into the church wall. An obelisk in front of the church made from Galway granite and limestone commemorates the tragic death of three young men drowned while sailing on Lough

Pádraic O'Conaire's limestone statue.

LEFT: pavement cafés contribute to Galway's cosmopolitan feel. **BELOW:** open-air chess.

Established in 1845 as Queen's College Galway, the National University of Ireland, Galway, on University Road (www.nuigalway.ie) has 15,000 students in its seven faculties. It has a strong commitment to teaching in the Irish language.

Corrib in 1887. The Saturday morning **farmers' market** beside the Collegiate Church of St Nicholas is not to be missed.

Lynch's Castle

Another historic building is **Lynch's Castle** Ⓖ in Shop Street. This was the town house of the premier Tribe and is now a bank displaying in its foyer a series of wall panels telling the story of the castle. The house – it was never a real castle, but an old custom in Ireland called anything more than a small house a castle – dates from the 15th century and is the city's only complete secular medieval building. The imposing smooth stone facade is decorated with carved panels and stonework, as well as gruesome gargoyles that include a lion devouring another animal, and a monkey and child. Inside, a reproduction of a 1651 map shows the symmetrical yet simple layout of the streets.

One of the most attractive parts of Galway is the area of its old lanes. **Buttermilk Lane** (off Middle Street) retains its quaint oriel-windowed houses still intact, and the pinnacles of the Augustinian Church loom in the background.

Hidden away in Bowling Green, a lane running off the north side of the Church of St Nicholas, is an unremarkable house that is now a museum. It was the tiny family home of **Nora Barnacle** Ⓗ James Joyce's wife and muse. It has been restored and gives a glimpse into how an ordinary family lived early in the 20th century (tel: 091-564 743; May–Sept; charge).

BELOW: gargoyle at Lynch's Castle.

Traditional shops

A stroll around the streets is an assault on the senses, particularly the smells and sounds. The streets that coalesce – **William, Shop, High** and **Quay Streets**, the latter leading down to the Spanish Arch and Wolfe Tone Bridge – are lined with dozens of restaurants and pubs. On spring and summer evenings many set up tables on the pavement, and the culinary choice is wide.

The survival of smaller independently owned businesses is part of the appeal. In many areas of Ireland, town centres have replicated high streets but in Galway the corporate giants sit cheek by jowl with shops that have deep-rooted connections with the past. Drapery stores, cheesemongers, bakers, barbers, bespoke tailors and shops selling shooting and fishing tackle continue to exist.

For more than 60 years, for example, the family-run **Ó'Máille's** (16 High Street; tel: 091-562 696; www.omaille.com) has specialised in handwoven tweed, including hand-knitted Aran sweaters. Its claim to fame is that it produced the costumes for John Ford's classic film *The Quiet Man,* filmed in the village of Cong, about an hour's drive north of Galway *(see page 26)*.

Charlie Byrne's (The Cornstore, Middle Street; tel: 091-561 766; www.charliebyrne.com; Mon–Sat 9am–6pm, Fri until 8pm, Sun noon–6pm) is a sprawling shop that stocks a huge selection of new and old books.

The centre of the city buzzes with

chic cafés, bakeries and bustling pubs. One shop worth visiting is **Griffins Bakery** on Shop Street, established in 1876. Using traditional recipes, the naturally fermented breads are baked fresh each day at the back of the shop. The mouthwatering variety of baps, pan loaves and breads includes rye, olive, ciabatta and spelt bread which is high in gliadin – a soluble protein – and low in gluten. A popular speciality is Guinness fruitcake.

Ubiquitous music

Catch the right morning and, amongst the cacophony of mobile phone ring tones, you will hear buskers opening up spontaneously with their guitars, banjos, tin whistles, bodhráns or uilleann (elbow) pipes, all adding to the bohemian mood music. French, Italian, British, Spanish and South American musicians often mingle with shoppers.

One of the curiosities of Galway buskers is that they seem to like entertaining passers-by while sitting down on the job. On speakers, rucksacks or beer barrels, perched on electrical distribution pillars (with the words "Danger, Keep Away") or leaning casually against shop window ledges, their stance appears to reflect the laid-back feel of this most westerly of all European cities.

More formal musical entertainment is available during festivals. Since its inception in 1996, the Galway Early Music Festival (www.galwayearlymusic.com) has held annual events celebrating the culture of Europe from the 12th to the 18th centuries in music, dance, costume and colour. The programme of baroque and renaissance music features atmospheric candlelit concerts in the Church of St Nicholas as well as workshops, masterclasses and street performances by internationally acclaimed ensembles.

Walking tours of the city are also held with the leader dressing in period clothing, whilst the walkers are serenaded around the streets by musicians. The tour is completed just in time for lunch at the **King's Head** (15 High Street), one of the city's oldest pubs, with a large open fireplace and flagstone flooring.

Apart from the melodic side, Gal-

TIP

Music for Galway
Between September and May, Music for Galway, a group formed in 1981, brings world-class musicians to local venues for concerts ranging from solo piano to full orchestras and jazz groups. Details: www.musicforgalway.ie.

BELOW: dressed for traditional dancing.

Festival Fever

If "festival-itis" is a disease, Galway suffers from it. As well as the **Galway Early Music Festival** *(see text above)*, there's the **Galway Arts Festival**, founded in 1978 and held during the last two weeks in July. This dynamic mixture of drama, music, poetry and dance showcasing local and national culture kicks off with a parade led by the flamboyant street theatre company, Macnas, whose name means "joyful abandonment". While **Cúirt International Festival of Literature** (www.galwayartscentre.ie), in late April, offers a cross-section of contemporary writing. It has in the past hosted an impressive array of literary talent including the Nobel Prize winners J. M. Coetzee, Nadine Gordimer, Derek Walcott and Seamus Heaney.

WHERE

The easiest way to get to Ballybrit Racecourse is by the shuttle bus that leaves regularly from Eyre Square in Galway throughout Race Week. Details from www.buseireann.ie; tel: 091-562 000.

way has a strong artistic and literary tradition, as evidenced by its rash of festivals *(see box on previous page)*. The city's most celebrated drama group, the **Druid Theatre Company** ❶ in Chapel Lane, presents work by Irish playwrights and has built up an international reputation. A theatre for plays in Irish, ***An Taibhdhearc Na Gaillimhe*** ❶ (pronounced *thive-arc*), is based in Middle Street, and holds summer shows and traditional singing and drama. For details of forthcoming events, visit www.antaibhdhearc.com.

The Galway Races

The Arts Festival is closely followed by the **Galway Races** (tel: 091-753 870; www.galwayraces.com), a week-long summer extravaganza running from late July to early August that brings in thousands of people to the city in search of the *craic*: after a day at the races the tradition is to party all night. Accommodation at this time is scarce, and prices shoot up: if you're not a racing fan, avoid Galway in race week. The races are held at **Ballybrit Racecourse** 3 miles (5km) to the east of the city near Galway Airport.

A sight not to be missed is the **Salmon Weir Bridge**, built in 1819. Lying north of the Church of St Nicholas, it is the last bridge upstream before the waters of the **Corrib River** open out into the lough. At the right time of year (generally early spring but sometimes later too) hundreds of fish wait under the shadow of the bridge before making their way upstream to spawn in **Lough Corrib**.

The Claddagh Ring

Across the Corrib River, on the other side from Galway, was the **Claddagh**, the original Irish settlement situated outside the city walls. There's little trace of the old thatched cabins in the area's current modest housing, but the fishing village gave its name to the **Claddagh Ring**. This was a traditional ring with two hands holding a heart that wears a crown. The heart represents love, the crown is loyalty and the hands symbolize friendship. According to tradition, the rings were handed down from mother to daughter.

One of Galway city's oldest shops, **Thomas Dillon's** ❿ (1 Quay Street;

BELOW: entertainment at the King's Head pub, Galway. **RIGHT:** Leisureland.

tel: 091-566 365; www.claddaghring.ie), established in 1750, sells fine gold and sterling silver examples of the ring. At the back of the shop, the small **Claddagh Museum** tells the story of this ring that is now a much sought-after fashion accessory and a symbol of romance.

The Spanish Arch

The only remaining gate of the walls that surrounded the ancient city, the sturdy **Spanish Arch**, still stands beside the **Fishmarket**. It took its name from the former trade with Spain and leads through to the **Long Walk** where small ships and boats are berthed and where you may sometimes see a flotilla of swans.

The Fishmarket is an outdoor area used 100 years ago to load kelp on to carts to be sold as fertiliser. Nowadays, groups of students, with bottles and cans of beer, gather here in circles on the grass holding drinking picnics. An eclectic mix of exhibitionists including jugglers, clowns, frisbee-throwers and skateboarders congregates in the area at weekends and in the evenings.

The Catholic Cathedral

From the Spanish Arch a pleasant riverside path will take you to **Galway's Catholic Cathedral** ❶ (www.galwaycathedral.org) – or, to give it its full magisterial title, the **Cathedral of Our Lady Assumed into Heaven and St Nicholas**. Built between 1959 and 1965, the Cathedral with its copper dome has an impressive variety of interior art. The last great building to be built of natural stone in Ireland, it is an established landmark. Its stained-glass windows depict John F. Kennedy, Christ rising from the dead and the Irish patriot Padraig Pearse.

If you wish to continue your riverside tour, some very attractive walks beside the Corrib have been developed by the Galway Civic Trust and lead from **O'Brien's Bridge** to the **Salmon Weir Bridge**.

When the pugnacious writer, raconteur and wit Brendan Behan visited Galway in the 1950s, he said he was sold 60 acres of land at a fair. The fairs have long gone, but Galway demonstrates how the old and the new can sit side by side. It is a mellow city that has aged well, reinvented itself many times and embraced the modern, presenting a vigorous and funky image.

The Spanish Arch.

Salthill

Almost conjoined, Galway's small neighbour **Salthill** ❷ is just 2 miles (3km) along the coast, and offers an escape from the city streets as well as tremendous views of the wide expanse of **Galway Bay**. This resort was built in the early years of the 19th century.

As befits such a place, it has its quota of amusement arcades, discos and a fairground. **Leisureland** (Salthill

BELOW: Galway Cathedral.

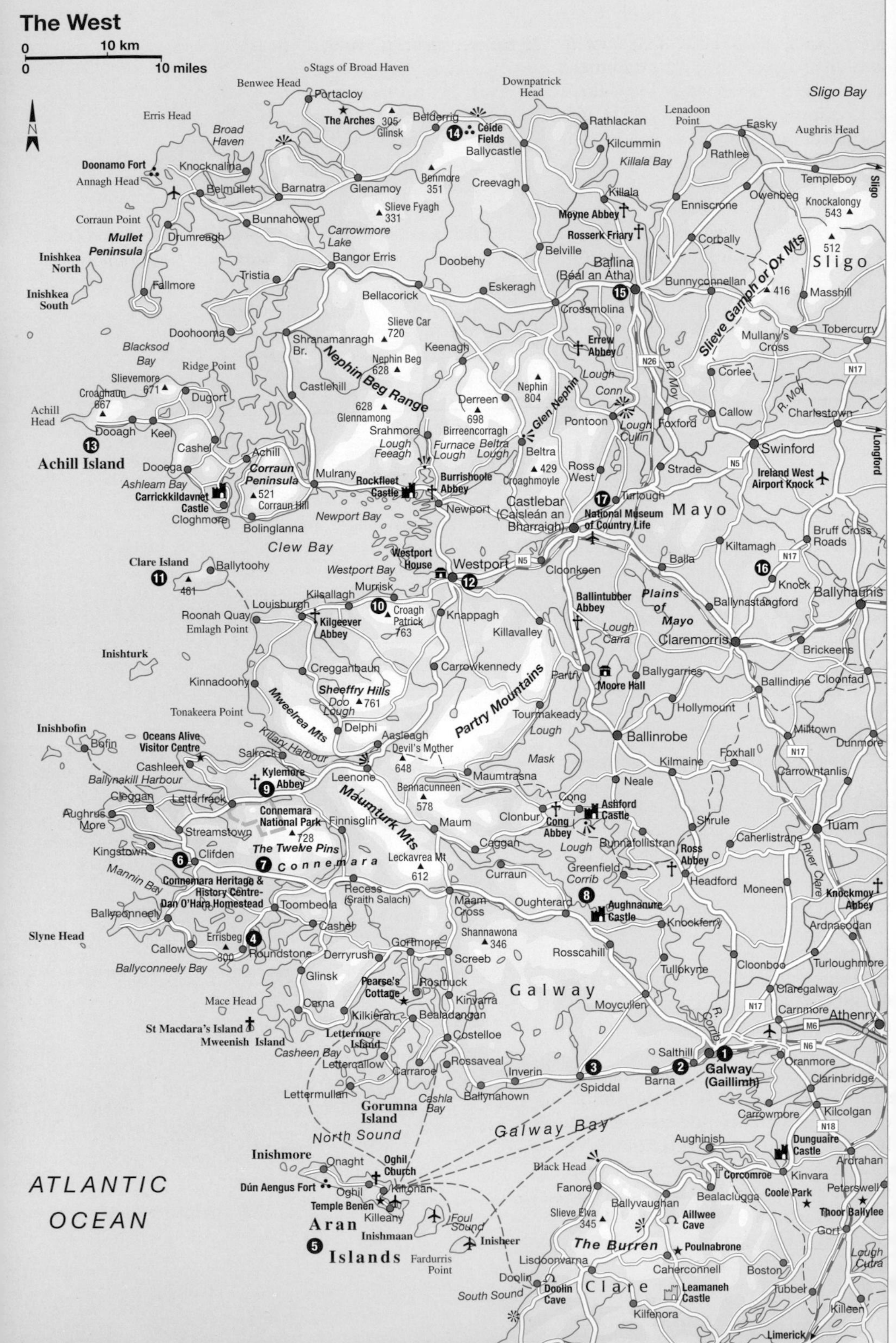

The West
0 10 km
0 10 miles
Stags of Broad Haven
Benwee Head
Portacloy
Downpatrick Head
Sligo Bay
Erris Head
Broad Haven
The Arches
305 Glinsk
Belderrig
Céide Fields
Lenadoon Point
Rathlackan
Easky
Aughris Head
Ballycastle
Kilcummin
Killala Bay
Rathlee
Doonamo Fort
Knocknalina
Benmore 351
Creevagh
Templeboy
Sligo
Annagh Head
Belmullet
Barnatra
Glenamoy
Killala
Enniscrone
Owenbeg
Knockalongy 543
Slieve Fyagh 331
Moyne Abbey
Corraun Point
Bunnahowen
Carrowmore Lake
Rosserk Friary
Corbally
Mullet Peninsula
Drumreagh
512
Belville
Inishkea North
Bangor Erris
Doobehy
Ballina (Béal an Átha)
Sligo
Tristia
Slieve Gamph or Ox Mts
Bunnyconnellan
Inishkea South
Fallmore
Bellacorick
Eskeragh
416
Masshill
Crossmolina
Slieve Car 720
Doohooma
Shranamanragh Br.
Tobercurry
Keenagh
Mullany's Cross
Blacksod Bay
Errew Abbey
Nephin Beg 628
N26
Ridge Point
Nephin Beg Range
Lough Conn
Corlee
N17
Slievemore 671
Castlehill
Nephin 804
R. Moy
Croaghaun 667
Dugort
Derreen 698
Glen Nephin
Callow
R. Moy
Charlestown
628 Glennamong
Achill Head
Pontoon
Foxford
Keel
Lough Cullin
Dooagh
Srahmore
Birreencorragh
Longford
Achill Island
Cashel
Lough Feeagh
Furnace Lough
Beltra Lough
Swinford
Achill
Beltra
Dooega
Corraun Peninsula
Mulrany
Rockfleet Castle
Burrishoole Abbey
429 Croaghmoyle
Ross West
Strade
N5
Ireland West Airport Knock
Ashleam Bay
521 Corraun Hill
Carrickkildavnet Castle
Turlough
Castlebar (Caisleán an Bharraigh)
National Museum of Country Life
Mayo
Newport
Cloghmore
Newport Bay
Bolinglanna
Bruff Cross Roads
Clew Bay
Kiltamagh
Westport House
Clare Island
N17
Ballytoohy
Westport
N5
Balla
Westport Bay
Cloonkeen
461
Knock
Ballyhaunis
Murrisk
Ballintubber Abbey
Plains of Mayo
Kilsallagh
Louisburgh
Croagh Patrick 763
Ballynastangford
Roonah Quay
Knappagh
Emlagh Point
Kilgeever Abbey
Lough Carra
Claremorris
Killavalley
Inishturk
Brickeens
Creggan baun
Carrowkennedy
Partry
Ballygarries
Kinnadoohy
Moore Hall
Ballindine
Cloonfad
Sheeffry Hills
Mweelrea Mts
Doo Lough
761
Partry Mountains
Hollymount
Tonakeera Point
Tourmakeady
Delphi
Lough
Inishbofin
Aasleagh
Ballinrobe
Milltown
Bofin
Oceans Alive Visitor Centre
Killary Harbour
Devil's Mother
Dunmore
Salrock
Mask
Kilmaine
Foxhall
648
N17
Cashleen
Leenone
Ballynakill Harbour
Maumtrasna
Carrowntanlis
Kylemore Abbey
Neale
Bennacunneen 578
Cleggan
Letterfrack
Maumturk Mts
Cong
Ashford Castle
Aughrus More
Connemara National Park
Finnisglin
Clonbur
Shrule
Maum
Cong Abbey
Tuam
Streamstown
728
Caggan
Bunnafollistran
Caherlistrane
The Twelve Pins
Lough
Ross Abbey
Kingstown
Clifden
Leckavrea Mt 612
Corrib
River Clare
Connemara
Curraun
Greenfield
Headford
Mannin Bay
Moneen
Knockmoy Abbey
Connemara Heritage & History Centre-Dan O'Hara Homestead
Recess (Sraith Salach)
Maam Cross
Oughterard
Aughnanure Castle
Toombeola
Ballyconneely
Knockferry
Ardnasodan
Cashel
Shannawona 346
Slyne Head
Errisbeg 300
Gortmore
Rosscahill
Callow
Roundstone
Derryrush
Screeb
Turloughmore
Cloonboo
Tullokyne
Ballyconneely Bay
Glinsk
Rosmuck
Galway
Claregalway
Pearse's Cottage
Mace Head
Kinvarra
Moycullen
R. Corrib
Carna
N17
Carnmore
Athenry
Kilkieran
Bealadangan
M6
St Macdara's Island
Mweenish Island
Lettermore Island
Costelloe
N6
Casheen Bay
Salthill
Lettercallow
Galway (Gaillimh)
Oranmore
Carraroe
Rossaveal
Barna
Inverin
Spiddal
Clarinbridge
Lettermullan
Gorumna Island
Cashla Bay
Ballynahown
Carrowmore
Kilcolgan
North Sound
Galway Bay
N18
Inishmore
Aughinish
Dunguaire Castle
Onaght
Oghil Church
Black Head
Ardrahan
ATLANTIC OCEAN
Dún Aengus Fort
Oghil
Kilronan
Fanore
Corcomroe
Kinvara
Temple Benen
Bealaclugga
Coole Park
Peterswell
Killeany
Ballyvaughan
Thoor Ballylee
Aran Islands
Foul Sound
Slieve Elva 345
Aillwee Cave
Inishmaan
Inisheer
Gort
The Burren
Poulnabrone
Fardurris Point
Lough Cutra
Lisdoonvarna
Caherconnell
Boston
Doolin
Clare
Leamaneh Castle
Doolin Cave
Tubber
South Sound
Kilfenora
Killeen
Limerick

promenade; tel: 091-521 455; www.leisureland.ie) is a family entertainment and amusement complex with three swimming pools and a waterslide. It is also used for concerts, exhibitions and conferences.

Atlantaquaria, the country's national aquarium (Toft Park, Salthill; tel: 091-585 100; www.nationalaquarium.ie; Mar–Sept Mon–Fri 9am–5pm, Sat–Sun 9am–6pm, Oct–Feb closed Mon–Tue; charge), is a good place to spend an hour on a rainy day and get acquainted with some of the 170 species of marine and freshwater life including seahorses, stingrays and the angel shark. The estuary exhibit shows the fish that make the mouth of the Corrib River their home.

Connemara

Connemara, Galway City's hinterland, is full of lakes, bogs and mountains, but almost empty of people. Traditionally its farming and fishing communities clustered around the coast, while its interior was inhabited chiefly by sheep farmers. Until Clifden was built in the mid-19th century, Connemara did not even have a town. It has always attracted visitors, especially painters who have found inspiration in the light and landscape. Two extensive ranges of mountains, the **Twelve Pins** (also known as **Twelve Bens**) and the **Maumturks**, dominate the views and suit all levels of walkers.

The visitor does not have to travel far from the city before entering the Irish-speaking area known as the **Gaeltacht.** The roadsigns are in Irish and one of the first places you will come to is **Bearna** (Barna), which has a golf club with an 18-hole championship course. Much new housing, most of it architecturally undistinguished, has been built along this stretch of coast, which is now a commuter belt; if such developments offend, take the inland N59 road via Oughterard, turning off for Roundstone west of Recess. The coast road wends its way around bays and inlets and through a series of former fishing villages which become more picturesque the further you go from the city, including **An Spidéal** (Spiddal), **Casla** (Costelloe), **Scrib** (Screeb), **Cill Chiarain** (Kilkieran), **Caiseal** (Cashel) and eventually **Roundstone.** This latter is a pretty holiday resort with a sheltered harbour for fishing and sailing boats, a little gem of a place which has attracted many artists and writers. Here you re-enter the non-Gaeltacht part of Connemara before completing the journey to Clifden, the "capital of Connemara".

Looking across Galway Bay towards the Aran Islands.

In both **Spiddal** ❸ and **Roundstone** ❹ local crafts thrive. **Spiddal Craft & Design Studios** (tel: 091-553 376; www.ceardlan.com) offers visitors the chance to see artisan craftworkers putting their skills on display and to buy directly from them. Workshops include candle-making, leather-work, pottery, screen printing, weaving and wood-turning.

In a former Franciscan Monastery in Roundstone, a bodhrán-making busi-

BELOW: Connemara is characterised by lakes, bogs and mountains.

Peaceful scenery near Roundstone.

ness, **Roundstone Music, Craft & Fashion** (tel: 095-35808; www.bodhrán.com; daily) is a popular attraction. Roundstone itself (www.roundstone.ie) is a pretty holiday resort with a sheltered harbour for fishing and sailing boats.

The Aran Islands

During a holiday in Connemara, a side trip to the **Aran Islands** ❺ (www.aranislands.ie) is regarded as *de rigueur*. Aran Island Ferries (tel: 091-658 903; www.aranislandferries.com), operates daily services from **Ros a' Mhil** (Rossaveal) on the Connemara coast, with a bus link to Galway City. An air taxi service (with a frequency of up to 25 flights a day during peak season) to the three islands is run by Aer Arann Islands (tel: 091-593 034; www.aerarannislands.ie) from Connemara Regional Airport, a 45-minute drive west of Galway city. The plane journey takes less than 10 minutes; the ferry journey to Inisheer (the furthest island) is one hour. The three Aran Islands – **Inishmore, Inishmaan** and **Inisheer** – contain many pre-Christian and early-Christian remains. Visitors should carry waterproof clothes and wear shoes suitable for uneven terrain.

Most noteworthy is **Dún Aengus** stone fort on Inishmore, one of Europe's finest prehistoric monuments. Perched on the edge of a vertical 200ft (60-metre) cliff, it consists of four semi-circular defensive walls. The experts have failed to date Dún Aengus with any accuracy: some say 4,000 BC and others 1,000 BC. But, apart from its historic interest, the view from its ramparts is one of the most striking imaginable. On a clear day the sweep of coastline from Kerry and Clare to the south, as well as the length of Galway to the western extremity of Connemara is visible.

One of the best ways of reaching the fort is to hire a bicycle in **Kilronan**, the main village. A visit to the Visitor Centre at **Kilmurvey** (tel: 099-61008; daily, Mar–Oct 10am–6pm, Nov–Feb 10am–4pm; charge) will provide useful information on the islands.

Fishing is still very important to the islanders, but tourism has been growing significantly. As many as 2,000 day-trippers a day in peak season can visit Inishmore, which has a permanent population of 900.

BELOW: castle ruins on Inishmore, Aran Islands.

St Macdara's Island

Another island that attracts visitors, a few miles off Connemara's coast near Roundstone, is **St Macdara's Island**. Although only 60 acres (24 hectares) in size, it has an exquisite 6th-century oratory, named after St Macdara, a protector of sailors and the first recorded Irish saint to have a surname. An annual pilgrimage is held on the saint's feast day, 15 July, when people make their way to the island to say Mass and for the celebration of the boats.

Clifden

Back on dry land, **Clifden ❻**, the region's principal town, is a lively spot with a good choice of hotels, Bed & Breakfast accommodation and restaurants, and is one of the best places to buy traditional tweed. In August the town hosts the Connemara Pony Show, an annual highlight based around these small sturdy local ponies.

Connemara National Park

Connemara National Park (Letterfrack; tel: 095-41054; daily, July–Aug 9.30am–6.30pm, June 10am–6.30pm, Apr–May and Sept–Oct, 10am–5.30pm; visitor centre charge, park freely accessible) is an unfenced nature reserve covering 5,000 acres (2,000 hectares) and is rich in wildlife. A series of summer programmes serves up an enticing choice of walks, talks and special events.

Nearby, hidden away in the hillside beneath the Twelve Pins, is the restored cottage of Dan O'Hara, a tenant farmer evicted because he was unable to pay his rent and who has been immortalised in song and story. The cottage is now part of **Connemara Heritage & History Centre ❼** (Lettershea; tel: 095-21246; www.connemaraheritage.com; Apr–Oct daily 10am–6pm) and gives visitors an insight into the life of the 19th-century farmer in the west of Ireland just before the 1845 potato famine. The centre provides an audiovisual tour of Connemara through the ages with reconstructions of a *crannog* (prehistoric artificial island home) ring fort and *clochan* (a dry stone hut).

It's worth an inland drive across to **Oughterard**, an angling centre on Lough Corrib, where you come to

Father Ted's blessing

Tourism to the Aran Islands was boosted in the 1990s by the popularity of the British TV comedy series "Father Ted". This featured the exploits of three priests on the fictional Craggy Island. This has inspired an annual festival, "Tedfest", held on Inishmore in February, inspired by the series' wacky sense of humour. See www.tedfest.org.

Inspired by Aran

The Aran islands have long attracted artists, novelists, poets, philologists, antiquarians and film makers. Robert Flaherty's 1934 film *Man of Aran* made the islands known to a worldwide audience. The playwright John Millington Synge wrote his book *The Aran Islands* while living on Inishmaan, where he also heard the plot of his most famous play, *The Playboy of the Western World*.

Inishmore has produced an internationally known writer, Liam O'Flaherty. Born in the shadow of Dún Aengus, he is famous for his nature stories and as author of the novel *The Informer* (filmed by director John Ford in 1935 and starring Victor McLaglen).

Irish is the daily language of the people of Aran, but most are equally fluent in the English language.

BELOW: Clifden.

WHERE

Several companies offer scheduled cruises on Lough Corrib from March to October: visit www.corribcruises.com (tel: 094-954 6209), or the Galway city-based www.corribprincess.ie (tel: 091-592 447).

Aughnanure Castle (tel: 091-552 214; www.heritageireland.ie; Mar–Oct daily 9.30am–6pm, guided 45-minute tours; charge), close to the shores of Lough Corrib. Standing on what is virtually a rocky island, the castle is a well-preserved example of an Irish tower house with the remains of a banqueting hall, a watch tower, an unusual double bawn and bastions, and a dry harbour.

Lough Corrib

Lough Corrib ❽ is the Republic of Ireland's largest lake. Renowned for its salmon and brown trout, it also has a number of islands – some with houses. You can take a day or evening cruise from Oughterard or **Cong** and sample the lake's tranquillity from the water.

Kylemore Abbey

The diversion to Lough Corrib aside, you will be confronted by one of Ireland's most photographed buildings – the dramatically sited **Kylemore Abbey** ❾. This late 19th-century limestone and granite building was erected by a Liverpool merchant as a gift to his son and is now run by the Benedictine nuns as a boarding-school for girls. The Abbey exhibition rooms, miniature Gothic chapel, craft shop and restaurant are all open to the public (tel: 095-41146; www.kylemoreabbey.com; Mar–Nov 9.30am–5.30pm, Nov–Mar 10.30am–4pm; Victorian walled flower and kitchen garden: Easter–Oct 10.30am–4.30pm).

The next village is **Leenane**, situated appealingly at the mouth of **Killary Harbour**, Ireland's only fjord, and marking the separation of counties Galway and Mayo. Its **Sheep & Wool Centre** (tel: 095-42323; www.sheepandwoolcentre.com) has live breeds, demonstrations of spinning and weaving, a multilingual historical video and, of course, a gift shop.

A choice of roads here will take you up to **Westport**, either via the spectacular **Doo Lough Pass** to **Louisburgh** or directly along the N59.

Croagh Patrick

Looming ahead you will see the unmistakable cone of **Croagh Patrick** ❿, Ireland's holy mountain. The Reek, as it is known, is climbed in honour of

BELOW: the much photographed Kylemore Abbey.

St Patrick by more than 30,000 pilgrims – many of them barefoot – on the last Sunday in July. Some set out before dawn and many are still descending as darkness falls. The Visitor Information Centre (Murrisk; tel: 098-64114; www.museumsofmayo.com; Mar–Oct 10am–5pm, closed end Oct–Mar) at the base of the mountain contains fascinating information about the archaeological discoveries on the summit. The remains of a dry stone oratory were carbon-dated to between AD 430 and 890. Across the road from Croagh Patrick, on the banks of Clew Bay, are the ruins of **Murrisk Abbey** (1456).

Clare Island

Clare Island ⓫ is well worth visiting to learn the seafaring exploits of Grace O'Malley, or Granuaile (1530–1603), a pirate queen who preyed on cargo vessels; late in her life she journeyed to London to do a deal with Queen Elizabeth I, negotiating in their only common language, Latin. Clare Island has a population of about 350 and holds much interest for the botanist. It measures 3½ by 1½ miles (5.5km by 2.5km) and has a small hotel and B&Bs. There is a ferry service of 15 minutes from Roonagh Harbour, Louisburgh to a new harbour on the island.

Westport

Picturesquely situated on the Carrowbeg River, **Westport** ⓬, a busy market town with colourful shop fronts, that attractively combines the old and the new, is designated as one of Ireland's heritage towns. A walk around the streets exploring its tree-lined riverside mall, fine Georgian buildings and octagon, is a pleasant experience. The town's quays, a ten-minute walks from its centre, are on Clew Bay, and the old warehouses have been nicely developed as tourist accommodation. This is the place for spectacular sunsets, to be watched, perhaps, from the terrace of one of the two waterside pubs. Don't miss **Clew Bay Heritage Centre** at The Quay for a look back at the way people lived (tel: 098-26852; www.museumsofmayo.com).

One of Ireland's most historic homes, **Westport House & Country Park** (The Demesne, Westport; tel:

Children enjoying the swan boats at Westport House & Country Park.

LEFT: an interior at Kylemore Abbey. **BELOW:** pilgrims climbing Croagh Patrick.

On the western side of Achill Island is Corrymore House, a former hotel built by Captain Charles Boycott, a land agent for Lord Erne in County Mayo who first came to Achill in 1857. His harsh tactics made him extremely unpopular and, as no one would work for him or even speak to him, his surname entered the English language as a word meaning to ostracise or shun.

098-27766; www.westporthouse.ie; Mar 11.30am–4pm, Apr–June 11.30am–5.30pm, July–Aug 11.30am–6pm, Sept–Nov 11.30am–5pm) is set in magnificent parkland on the outskirts of Westport and has attractions for children of all ages. It is owned by direct descendants of Grace O'Malley.

Achill Island

In 1910 the Belfast artist Paul Henry set out for **Achill Island** ⓭ for two weeks. He was immediately captivated by its beauty, tore up his return train ticket, and stayed nine years. Henry described it as "a windswept island at the back of beyond". But he felt it "talked" to him and that he had been carried there "on the currents of life".

Top to bottom, Achill Island measures just 15 miles (24km) by 12 miles (18km). It is joined to the mainland by a bridge built in 1888 but once you cross **Achill Sound** a feeling of isolation and other worldliness persists in the stark landscape. Acclimatising to Achill time and tuning in to its slow rhythm of life and its weather takes a few days. The island is largely shaped by the wet Atlantic climate. It rains with a grim persistence. Even the elegiac car bumper stickers acknowledge the harshness of the natural elements: "Achill: Beaten by the wind and rain – your beauty draws me ever more."

About 2,500 people live on the island. In the winter the caravan parks, B&Bs, craft and coffee shops are closed, the scattered villages deserted, the clusters of new holiday homes empty, and the long sandy beaches at **Keel, Dooagh, Trawmore**, as well as the silver and golden strands in the remote north side are deserted apart from wading birds. If you want to find peace and quiet, this is the best time to visit when you share the tranquil beaches with sanderlings, oystercatchers and golden plovers.

Birds are an important part of life here; in fact the name Achill comes from *Achaill*, meaning "eagle". In August, an influx of thousands of holidaymakers brings a needed boost to the economy.

To get a feel for the past, the visitor should take the narrow single-track road signposted to the **Deserted**

BELOW: Atlantic Drive, Achill Island.

Heinrich Böll's Achill

Achill Island has long had a magnetic pulling power for writers, poets and painters. The German writer Heinrich Böll, who won the Nobel Prize for Literature in 1972, spent 35 summers on Achill, visiting the island right up until his death, aged 67, in 1985.

Böll lived in a cottage in Dugort (*Dubh gort*, "black field" and pronounced with a heavy local emphasis on the second syllable sounding like *du-gort*). The cottage, where most of his novels were written, is now a residential retreat – a guesthouse for international and Irish artists and writers. When he first came to Achill, Böll said he felt like he was "playing truant from Europe". His *Irish Journal, A Traveller's Portrait of Ireland* (1957) shows a warm affection for the area as well as the country itself.

 Map on page 254

Village on the south-western side of **Slievemore Mountain**. More than 70 roofless stone houses are all that remain of this village that in 1837 was the largest human settlement on the island. A single grassed-over street runs between the houses and even today there is a feeling of desolation about it. If archaeology appeals, visit www.achill-fieldschool.com, which organises archaeological and environmental field schools lasting from one day up to seven days.

The most scenic route on Achill is the **Atlantic Drive** that loops round the south of the island and takes in **Carrickkildavnet Castle**, a 15th-century tower house.

The 21st-century face of Achill has changed radically. Clusters of holiday homes that remain empty for 11 months of the year have sprung up in many places and few parts of the island remain untouched by builders. There are also numerous single bungalows or detached houses pepper-potting every available patch of building land, to the point where many people prefer not to visit Achill at all.

Achill Island is a microcosm of Ireland: a self-contained world with its own smorgasbord of mountains, lakes, bogs, Blue Flag (EU-approved for cleanliness and safety for swimming) beaches, cliffs, rivers, cycle rides, enchanting birdlife and, at the last count, at least 10 pubs. For more information, contact Achill Tourism, Cashel, Achill Island; www.achilltourism.com; tel: 098-47353.

The Mayo coast

Crossing back to the mainland again, continue along the remote north Mayo coast road and you will be startled by the site of a pyramid-shaped building. This is the remarkable **Céide Fields** ⓮ (pronounced *kay-jeh*) Visitor Centre (Ballycastle; tel: 096-43325; June–Sept 10am–6pm, mid-Mar–May and Oct–Nov, 10am–5pm; charge). An extensive stone-age monument, the site includes field systems, dwelling area and megalithic tombs dating back 5,000 years. The bog's rare wild flowers and the spectacular cliffs opposite the centre attract botanists, geologists and birdwatchers.

Céide Fields Visitor Centre.

BELOW: the rugged cliffs at Benwee Head.

Irish performance dancing, characterised by quick, precise movements of the feet and a relatively still upper body and arms.

The neighbouring towns, **Killala** and **Ballina** ⓯, have their own particular charms for the visitor. Killala rises above a small harbour, its skyline dominated by a pencil-thin 10th-century round tower and the spire of the Church of Ireland. Ballina, with its streets sloping down to the River Moy (www.rivermoy.com), is the largest town in Mayo and is internationally renowned as an exceptional source of salmon. The area attracts large numbers of visiting fishermen and women for both game angling and coarse angling, and Ballina's bridges are busy during the season, with the Ridge Pool being a particular attraction.

Knock

An inland detour takes you to **Knock** ⓰ where in 1879 several people reportedly saw the Blessed Virgin silhouetted on the gable of the local church. The story is told by **Knock Folk Museum** (tel: 094-938 8100; www.knockshrine.ie; May–Oct 10am–7pm, Basilica: all year; main pilgrimage season from the last Sun in Apr to the second Sun in Oct).

The village is thronged year-round with shops selling souvenirs and religious artifacts. One of Ireland's most popular pilgrimage places, it is visited by over 1 million people each year. Many of those coming by air fly directly to the nearby **Ireland West Airport Knock**. From small beginnings in 1986, it has expanded considerably, bringing in visitors not only from Britain and Europe but, with the introduction of scheduled transatlantic services from New York and Boston in 2007, many tourists from the USA.

To end your cultural tour of the west with a reflective look at what life in Ireland used to be like, turn off the N5 to visit the award-winning **National Museum of Country Life** ⓱ at Turlough Park, 5 miles (8km) from **Castlebar,** Co. Mayo's capital. The museum, the first branch of the National Museum outside Dublin, houses the National Folklife Collection detailing the domestic lives of people who lived in rural Ireland from 1850 to 1950 (tel: 094-903 1755; www.museum.ie; Tue–Sat 10am–5pm, Sun 2–5pm; free). ❑

BELOW: the garden at the National Museum of Country Life.

RESTAURANTS AND PUBS

Restaurants

Prices for a three-course dinner per person without wine:
€ = under €25
€€ = €25–40
€€€ = €40–55
€€€€ = over €55

Ballina

Crockets on the Quay
Ballina, Co. Mayo
Tel: 096-22400
Bar/restaurant: daily, food all day, L 12.30–3pm; D 6–9.30pm; bar food from 4–9.30pm **€.** L **€**, D **€€.**
Bar food **€**
Interesting menus feature local food. Dark by day, lively by night. Informal atmosphere.

Barna

O'Grady's on the Pier
Seapoint, Barna, Co. Galway
Tel: 091-592 223
Daily, L Sun only, D 6–10pm. L **€€**, D **€€**
Seafood a speciality, fresh from the pier. Innovative and off-beat ideas.

Clifden, Connemara

Mitchell's Seafood Restaurant
Market Street, Clifden, Connemara, Co. Galway
Tel: 095-21867
Daily noon–10pm last orders **€€**
Former shop in town centre converted into an atmospheric restaurant with open fire. Seafood is local and simply prepared.

Recess, Connemara

Owenmore Restaurant
Ballinahinch Castle Hotel, Recess, Connemara, Co. Galway
Tel: 095-31006
Daily, L served in bar noon–3.30pm, D 6.30–9pm. L **€€**, D **€€€€**
Stunning setting overlooking the river. Cuisine is a blend of classic and modern and menus feature local produce like seafood, salmon from the river and mountain lamb.

Galway

Ard Bia/Nimmo's
2 Quay Street, Galway, Co. Galway
Tel: 091-539 897
Mon–Sat L noon–4pm D 6–10.30pm, Sun noon–6pm. L **€**, D **€€**
Located in a riverside warehouse, amid cheerful contemporary art. Casual, simple dining by daytime; fine dining by night upstairs in Nimmo's. Eclectic menu.

Goya's
2–3 Kirwan's Lane, Galway, Co. Galway
All day Mon–Sat, L noon–3pm. L **€**
Best coffee and cakes in town. Gorgeous bakery and café.

Sheridans on the Docks
Galway Docks, Galway, Co. Galway
Tel: 091-564 905
Pub: Mon–Thur 4.30–11.30pm, Fri–Sat noon–1pm; resturant: Tue–Sat 6.30–9pm. Bar food **€**, D **€€**
An old dockside pub is now run by cheesemongers, Sheridan's, but still serves the cheapest pint in the city and a wide selection of wines, as well as cheese platters and a daily blackboard menu of soups and stews. The chic upstairs restaurant (booking advisable) features seasonal wild food, foraged locally – sorrel, sea spinach, chanterelles – in many of its imaginative organically-based dishes.

Kilcolgan

Moran's Oyster Cottage
The Weir, Kilcolgan, Co. Galway
Daily 11.30am–11.30pm **€€**
Traditional thatch, on the waterside. Behind the tiny traditional bar overlooking the weir is a large restaurant extension, hugely popular. Great seafood menu, especially oysters from their own native oyster beds (Sept–Apr); otherwise local Gigas oysters. Details like that matter at Moran's.

Pontoon

Healy's Hotel, Pontoon, Co. Mayo
Tel: 094-925 6443
L noon–2.30pm **€**; D 6–9.30pm **€€**
Small and simple country inn favoured by fishermen with a stunning lake view, and generous portions of freshly prepared seafood and steaks.

Westport

The Tavern Bar and Restaurant
Murrisk, Co. Mayo
Tel: 098-64060
Bar food: daily noon–11pm **€**; restaurant: daily 6–10pm, closed some weekdays Nov–mid-Mar **€€**
Busy pub near Croagh-patrick, 3 miles (5km) from town with a child-friendly bar serving seafood and local artisan products, and a more sophisticated restaurant serving contemporary cuisine upstairs.

Pubs

One of Galway's most famous old bars is **Tigh Neachtain (Noctan's)** in Cross Street; unspoilt painted wooden interior, arty clientele and impromptu music sessions. The **Dáil Bar**, also on Cross Street, attracts a younger crowd and serves good food all day in a buzzing atmosphere. The **Front Door Bar** on High Street is a newish place, also for the younger crowd, with five bars spread over two floors and a good choice of food. For music, **The Quays** on Quay Street, further down Cross Street, is a tall narrow pub with three storeys known for its late-night music sessions.

All round the west coast you find traditional pubs like **O'Dowd's** in Roundstone, Co. Galway. It overlooks the harbour and you can watch the boats or sip a pint by the fire. **The Bard's Den** in Letterfrack is known for traditional music and also serves all-day bar food. **Hamilton's Bar** in Leenane is an old-style pub with a grocery shop in the front and pool in the back.

Matt Molloy's, Bridge Street, Westport is owned by a member of The Chieftains, so it's no surprise that traditional music is a major feature in the back room. **Gaughan's**, O'Rahilly Street, Ballina is a fine example of a Victorian town pub interior and also does great food. **Polke's**, Main Street, Ballycastle, Co. Mayo is a well maintained 19th-century pub behind a shop.

Inland Ireland
0
10 km
0
10 miles
NORTHERN IRELAND
REPUBLIC OF IRELAND
Enniskillen
Enniskillen
Omagh
Manorhamilton
Lough Macnean Upper
Belcoo
A4
Maguiresbridge
Castle Leslie Hotel
Middletown
Parke's Castle
N16
Blacklion
L. Macnean Lower
Florence Court
Scotstown
Glenfarne
Marble Arch Caves
Florence Court Forest Park
Drumcard
Lisnaskea
Monaghan (Muineachán)
L. Gill
Tiltinbane 592
Upper Lough Erne
Derrynawilt
Rossmore Forest Park
Dromahair
Glangevlin
Cuilcagh 665
Derrylin
Smithborough
Clones
Leitrim
Dowra
Swanlinbar
Newtownbutler
Scotch Corner
Creaghanroe
Ballintogher
N2
Drumkeeran
Ballinagleragh
Derrynacreeve
Teemore
Wattle Bridge
Newbliss
Swan's Cross Roads
Castleblayney
Lough Allen
496
Benbrack
Source of the Shannon
Slieve Rushen 405
Bellamont House
Ballybay
L. Major
Iron Mts
519
Bencroy or Gubnaveagh
Ballyconnell
Belturbet
Scotshouse
Monaghan
Heapstown Cairn
Geevagh
Slieve Anierin 586
Milltown
N3
Cootehill
Arigna
Garadice Lough
Drumlane Abbey
Butlersbridge
Shantonagh
Sligo
Lough Arrow
Drumshanbo
Ballinamore
Moyduff
Corrigeenroe
R. Shannon
Doogary
Killashandra
Bellanacargy
Shercock
Ballinafad
Lough Key
Leitrim
Garvagh
Killykeen Forest Park
Lough Oughter
Cavan (An Cabhán)
Canningstown
Carrickmacross
Boyle
Knockvicar
Carrigallen
Cornafean
Dún A Rí Forest Park
Lough Key Forest Park
Carrick-on-Shannon
Cloone Grange
Bellananagh
Cavan
Kingscourt
N4
Drumsna
Arvagh
R. Erne
Cross Keys
Bailieborough
Croghan
Mohill
Billis Bridge
Hill Street
Lough Boderg
Rinn Lough
Ballyjamesduff
Lough Bofin
Dromod
Virginia
Ballyroddy
Kilcogy
Lough Sheelin
Mullagh
Roscommon
Roosky
Drumlish
Lough Gowna
Lough Ramor
Moynalty
Rathcroghan
Lough Forbes
Granard
Finnea
Strokestown
Ballinalee
Oldcastle
Tulsk
Scramoge
N4
Longford
Ceanannus Mór (Kells)
Loughcrew Passage Grave
Crossakeel
Strokestown Park House & Famine Museum
Termonbarry
Carriglas Manor
Lisryan
Castleplunket
N5
Longford (An Longfort)
Mostrim (Edgeworthstown)
Coole
M3
Four Mile House
Cross Keys
Castlepollard
Meath
Tullynally Castle
Runnabackan
Coolshaghtena
Killashee
Lough Lene
Lanesborough
Lough Derravaragh
Collinstown
Clonmellon
Rathowen
Corlea Trackway Visitor Centre
Roscommon
Keenagh
Carrickboy
N4
Multyfarnham
Crookedwood
Delvin
Athboy
R. Suck
Newtown Cashel
Bally-nacarrigy
Lough Owel
Trim
Lough
Mullingar (An Muileann gCearr)
Athleague
Knockcroghery
Ballymahon
Ballivor
Skeagh
Ballygar
Rahara
The Downs
Raharney
Ree
The Pigeons
Westmeath
Four Roads
L. Ennell
Rathmoylan
Galway
Ballymore
Longhanavally
Belvedere House & Gardens
Curraghboy
Kiltoom
Glasson
Kinnegad
Dublin
M4
Ballykeeran
Milltownpass
Enfield
Brideswell
Moyvoughly
Ballynagore
Rochfortbridge
Athlone (Baile Átha Luain)
Kilglass
Moate
M6
Castlejordan
Carrowreagh
Corraree
Horseleap
Tyrrellspass
Johnstown Bridge
Edenderry
Kilbeggan
Cornafulla
Rhode
Ballynahown
Clara
Carbury
Ballydangan
Kiltober
Clonmacnoise
Grand Canal
Grogan
Bog of Allen
Galway
Ballinasloe (Béal Átha na Sluaighe)
Clonfinloughstone
Tullamore (Tulach Mhór)
Rathvilla
Kildare
M6
Aughrim
Daingean
Shannonbridge
Clonbullogue
Charleville Forest Castle
N6
Brackagh
Allen
Crossconnell
Ferbane
River Suck
Geashill
Rathangan
Laurencetown
Cloghan
Bracknagh
Hill of Allen
Killeigh
Blue Ball
Galway
Newbridge
Shannon Harbour
Offaly
Drumatober
Kildare
Banagher
Clonygowan
Portarlington
M7
Kilcormac
Clonaslee
Dublin
Killimor
Taylor's Cross
National Stud & Japanese Gardens
Cloghan Castle
Mountmellick
Monasterevin
R. Shannon
Fivealley
Rosenallis
Cadamstown
Emo Court
Pike
Slieve Bloom Mts
Birr
Coolbanagher Church
Nurney
Portumna
The Cut 411
New Inn
Fontstown
Abbey
Kinnitty
Laois
M7
Vicarstown
Portumna Castle
Carrigahorig
Drimmo
Rock of Dunamase
Woodford
Aderin 527
Portlaoise (Port Laoise)
Athy (Baile Átha)
Lough Derg
Terryglass
Sharavogue
Ballinderry
Boheraphuca
N7
Stradbally
Ballingarry
Mountrath
Gorteeny
Mount St Joseph's Abbey
R. Barrow
Camross
Borrisokane
Pike of Rush Hall
Cromoge
317
Ballylynan
Coolbawn
Tipperary
Shinrone
Timahoe
N8
Cloghjordan
Roscrea (Ros Cré)
Dromineer
Abbeyleix
Castledermot
Dunkerrin
Garrykennedy
Ballybrophy
M8
Nenagh (An tAonach)
N7
Moneygall
M7
Durrow
Limerick
Toomyvara
Cork
Rathdowney
1
2
3
4
5
6
7
8
9
10
11
12
13
14
15
16
17
18
19
20

INLAND IRELAND

Water, in the form of bogs, lakes and rivers, dominates the often overlooked counties in the middle of the country. Fishing and boating are the big attractions, and the landscapes are seductive

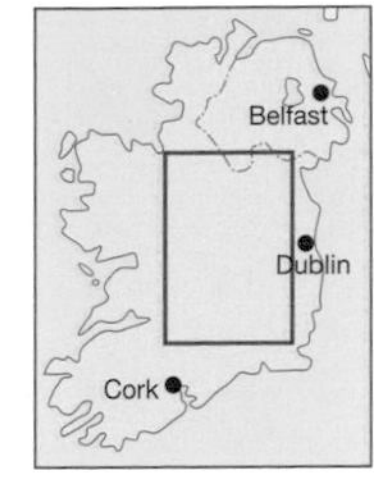

Main attractions
CLONMACNOISE
BANAGHER
BIRR CASTLE
LOUGH DERG
NENAGH
EMO COURT
KILBEGGAN
MULLINGAR
STROKESTOWN PARK HOUSE AND FAMINE MUSEUM
ROSCOMMON
ATHLONE
CAVAN
BELLAMONT HOUSE
CLONES
CASTLE LESLIE
PATRICK KAVANAGH CENTRE

Geography class for Irish primary schoolchildren traditionally reduced their country to a common item of domestic tableware – a saucer. With the outer rim representing the ragged, mountainous coastal regions, the Midlands were credited with the dubious honour of being Ireland's flat centre.

In a region marked by the relative absence of physical drama, where bogland and lake account for much of the terrain, the counties of Longford, Laois, Offaly, Westmeath, Roscommon, Cavan and Monaghan have long played second fiddle to the more popular tourist regions of the South and West.

However, bisected by the River Shannon, the region is rich in varied recreation options, from fishing on the many lakes, walking the Slieve Bloom hills, to exploring the slower pace of life in its sleepy towns and villages.

Echoes of the past

Perceived by many, including the Irish, as a rather dull part of the country, the Midlands are, in fact, one of the last remaining regions where the pace of life harks back to an Ireland of 30 years ago. The attendant bustle and ubiquitous traffic jams are happily still absent. Life here is still unhurried and friendly.

The inland counties offer much for the visitor – especially Clonmacnoise, Ireland's most important and atmospheric monastic site. Grand mansions and castles pepper the region, and emerging farmers' markets and espresso bars sit comfortably with centuries-old pubs and grocery shops, and new blood mixes happily with old, unchanged ways.

From bogs to monasteries

Ballinasloe ❶, the chief town of east Co. Galway, has long been an important crossing place of the **River Suck**, and marks a kind of border, more

RIGHT: the green fields of rural Tipperary.

The big houses
The great period of country house building in Ireland began in the early 1720s. English architects who had studied in Italy introduced Palladianism, and soon a diluted version of the style appeared everywhere, from village churches to farmhouses.

psychological than physical, between the west of Ireland and the Midlands. Every year during the first week of October Europe's oldest horse fair takes place here. Between Ballinasloe and Loughrea, off the M6, is the **Dartfield Horse Museum and Heritage Centre** (tel: 091-843 968; www.dartfield.com; daily 9am–6pm). The museum occupies a courtyard of the original Dartfield House. As well as an exhibition on the history of Irish horses and Connemara ponies, together with farm machinery and carriages, there are 350 acres to enjoy, and a walking tour to see a variety of animals including horses, deer and sheep. Horse riding is also available.

From Ballinasloe take the R357 to **Shannonbridge** ❷. This is the point where county Galway meets counties Offaly and Roscommon, and the River Suck flows into the River Shannon. There's a lot of bog in the Midlands, in various stages of development. The state-run Irish Peat Board, Bord Na Móna, who run the Blackwater Power Station, closed the passenger railway line in November 2008 but they are working closely with the Irish Tourist Board (Fáilte Ireland) to develop eco-tourism in the bogland.

BELOW: Clonmacnoise monastic site.

Clonmacnoise ❸ (tel: 090-967 4195; daily; charge) is one of Ireland's most important monastic sites, superbly located on a bend in the River Shannon. It was built on an esker, or natural gravel ridge, that overlooks a large marshy area. The monastery was founded in AD 545 by St Kieran and was the burial place of the Kings of Connaught and Tara. While it may appear remote today, in earlier centuries transport for pilgrims was easier by water than over land.

The earliest of the surviving ruins dates from the 9th century. The monastery was plundered from then onwards by the Irish, the Vikings and the Anglo-Normans until it was destroyed in the Elizabethan wars of the mid-16th century by the English garrison from Athlone. Yet there's still plenty to be seen. The Visitor Centre has a collection of carved grave slabs dating from the 9th to the 12th centuries, as well as a helpful audio-visual presentation.

Among the older surviving buildings of the complex are the shell of a small cathedral, two round towers, the remains of eight smaller churches and several high crosses. There are various doorways and chancel arches in the Irish Romanesque style. One of the churches, Temple Connor, was restored by the Church of Ireland in 1911 and is used for services.

Around Lough Derg

Head south for **Shannon Harbour**, the junction of the Grand Canal and the River Shannon which is a popular mooring place for river cruisers. About 5 miles (8km) further south is **Banagher** ❹, another popular boating centre with a new marina. This pretty, one-street village will be eerie and empty in winter, and bustling with river enthusiasts in summer.

The town has two notable literary connections, the first of which was Anthony Trollope, who worked in the area as a land surveyor in 1841 and

 Map on page 264

penned his first novel, *The Macdermots of Ballycloran*, here. Charlotte Brontë spent her honeymoon in the area. A common Irish exclamation: "That beats Banagher!" dates back to a period during the 19th century when the town was ruled by corrupt officials and gave rise to this definition of poor standards still in popular currency.

Signposted from the centre of the village and lying a mile or so outside it is the lovingly restored **Cloghan Castle** (used for private functions only).

Birr

Birr ❺ is an attractive Georgian town, more or less in the centre of Ireland, dominated by **Birr Castle and Demesne** (tel: 057-912 0336; www.birrcastle.com; daily; charge). As an estate town that grew in tandem with the castle, Birr is a good example of Georgian town planning, with many original entrance fan-lights, door panelling and iron railings still intact.

The gardens of Birr Castle cover 100 acres (40 hectares) and have more than 1,000 species of trees and shrubs with an especially strong Chinese and Himalayan collection. In spring, magnolias, crab apples and cherries will be in flower; in the autumn, maples, chestnut and weeping beech supply colour. The box hedges subdividing the formal gardens are the highest in the world.

The 17th-century castle is private, but its stable block now houses **Ireland's Historic Science Centre** (tel. as above). The owners of Birr Castle, the Parsons family, later ennobled as the Earls of Rosse, have manifested a scientific bent for several generations. In the 1840s the 3rd Earl of Rosse built the Great Telescope which enabled him to see further into space than any of his contemporaries. The telescope, which has a 56ft (17-metre) tube and a 6ft (1.8-metre) mirror, was in use until 1908 and has been restored to working order.

Walk into town along **Oxmanton Mall**, a tree-lined thoroughfare which leads from the castle gates past a row of elegant Georgian houses. **Emmet Square** in the town centre is the location of one-time coaching inn **Dooly's**

The Great Telescope at Ireland's Historic Science Centre.

BELOW: the gardens at Birr Castle and Demesne.

The neo-Gothic St Mary of the Rosary Church, Nenagh, built in 1895.

Hotel (dating from 1747; www.doolyshotel.com), which gave its name to the Galway Blazers when they set fire to it after a Hunt Ball in 1809, almost destroying the building.

Lough Derg

From Birr, head to **Borrisokane** and the eastern shores of **Lough Derg** ❻. At Lough Derg the Shannon widens into a 50 sq mile (130 sq km) lake that is about 10 miles (16km) across at its widest point. This side is in County Tipperary and the west of the lake is in County Clare. The circular **Lough Derg Drive** (about 50 miles/90km) passes through a succession of pretty villages, but the lake itself is not always visible. The villages on this side of Lough Derg are peaceful, out-of-the-way places to stay that have recently been gaining in popularity. Most visitors either have a boat of some kind or are interested in fishing – mainly coarse angling – on the lake. Others enjoy walking, both near the lake and on the other side of Birr in the way-marked trails of the **Slieve Bloom Mountains**.

Terryglass is one of the prettiest villages near Lough Derg, although you have to leave the main road to find the lake. **Dromineer** on the other hand is right on the water, and has a ruined castle on its pier. Many of the people you meet in the pubs will be temporarily living on river cruisers, which they own or have hired.

A very accessible range of low-lying hills perfect for either leisurely strolling or steep hiking, the Slieve Bloom Way is a 20-mile (32km) circular trail through mostly uninhabited landscape and hidden vistas. You can dip in and out of the trail at many points, but the villages of Cadamstown and Kinnity are ideal starting points.

Nenagh

Nenagh ❼ is a Tipperary market town now bypassed by the busy Dublin-Limerick main road. All that remains of the original Norman settlement is the **Nenagh Castle Keep**, or donjon, with walls 20ft (6 metres) thick. It reaches to a height of 100ft (30 metres). Across the road in the **Governor's House** of the old town gaol is the **Nenagh**

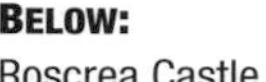

BELOW: Roscrea Castle.

Heritage Centre (tel: 067-33850; free), which includes the condemned cells and execution room of the gaol, and a museum of rural life.

Roscrea ❽, further up the M7 in the Dublin direction, has long been plagued by traffic and will certainly benefit from the new motorway. From the road, you can see the west façade of the 12th-century St Cronan's Abbey, which is all that remains, with a round-arched doorway containing a moulded figure of St Cronan.

Roscrea's Norman castle contains an 18th-century town house, **Damer House**, within its walls. The 13th-century castle is a polygonal structure with two D-shaped towers. The gate house is topped by 18th-century gables and chimneys. It now houses the **Roscrea Heritage Centre** (tel: 0505-21850; www.roscreaheritage.com; charge also includes Damer House), which has an interesting exhibit on Norman castles.

Damer House, which stands inside the castle walls, is an elegant, 18th-century, three-storied house with a plain, symmetrical façade and a handsome pine staircase. It was completed in the 1720s and became a Bishop's Palace before being converted to a military barracks in 1798. It was very nearly demolished in the 1970s to make room for a car park but was saved through the vigilance of the Irish Georgian Society.

Great Irish houses

Travel east again, by-passing **Portlaoise**, to visit **Emo Court** ❾ (tel: 057-862 6573; www.emocourt.net; house closed Nov–Mar; charge). This fine Georgian mansion was built in 1792 for the Earl of Portarlington in the Classical style by James Gandon, best known for Dublin's Four Courts and Custom House. It was restored and donated to the nation in 1996 by a private benefactor.

Approached via an avenue of splendid Wellingtonia trees, the house is certainly worth a visit. Built over a 70-year period as a result of the 1st Earl's fluctuating financial fortunes, the house is the only large-scale domestic example of Gandon's work apart from the Custom House. Pride of place goes to the domed rotunda, designed by Gandon's successor, William Caldbeck, a mix of marble pilasters with gilded Corinthian capitals supporting the enormous blue painted dome which was inspired by Rome's Pantheon.

Damer House.

The gardens were created in two parts. The Clucker, named because it was once the site of the nun's quarters of an ancient abbey, is planted with azaleas, rhododendrons and Japanese maples. The Grapery is planted with trees and shrubs and leads down to the peaceful lakeside walk.

Nearby is **Coolbanagher Church,** also designed by Gandon, within which are the original 1795 architectural plans. An intricate 15th-century font from an earlier church has been incorporated. Close by is Gandon's mausoleum for Lord Portarlington.

There is another interesting house in an entirely different style to the

BELOW: a Gaelic football game in Tipperary.

Locke's Distillery, fed by springs from Lough Ennel.

north near Tullamore, **Charleville Forest Castle** ⑩ (tel: 057-932 3040; all year but times vary so check first; charge). The castle is gradually being restored by volunteers.

Designed by Francis Johnson, the architect responsible for many of Dublin's Georgian houses, this fine example of Gothic Revival style was commissioned by Baron Tullamore in 1812. With its flag tower and castellated turrets rising high over an estate of pleasant woodland walks and gardens, the house is built of grey limestone with an internal gallery complete with some intricate plasterwork running the entire length of the garden front.

BELOW: shearing a sheep at Mullingar.

Five avenues lined by Irish yew trees radiate from the house. The grounds contain many impressive trees including an oak believed to be 700 years old. Tullamore is also where Irish Mist and Tullamore Dew liqueurs are made. The drinks' histories and traditional distilling methods are explained in the **Tullamore Dew Heritage Centre** (tel: 057-932 5016; www.tullamoredew.com; daily all year; charge).

Around Lough Ennel

Follow the N52 from Tullamore for 7½ miles (12km) north to **Kilbeggan** ⑪. **Locke's Distillery** (tel: 057-933 2134; www.lockesdistillerymusem.ie; daily all year; charge), advertised for miles around, is on the banks of the River Brosna which is fed by springs from nearby Lough Ennel. It claims to have been the world's oldest pot-still distillery. After closing in 1957, it was reopened as a museum in 1987.

It is said that all good whiskey depends on the water that goes into the distillation process. The distillery was in use from 1757 to 1953 and much of the original equipment is still in place. There are enticing smells of malt and oak as you view the equipment, and a tasting.

The low-lying **Lough Ennel** can be seen from the N52 between Kilbeggan and Mullingar. It is a popular place for swimming, boating and fishing. The restored **Belvedere House and Gardens** (tel: 044-934 9060; www.belvedere-house.ie; daily all year; charge) is remarkable for its beautiful setting, with terraced gardens descending in three stages to the shores of the lake.

Mullingar ⑫, the chief town of County Westmeath, is an important cattle-dealing centre which is also popular with anglers. If things military appeal, the **Military Museum** (tel: 044-934 8391, call in advance for appointment) should not be missed. It contains weaponry from both world wars, uniforms and flags from all over the world and a section dedicated to the old IRA (as distinct from the more recent incarnation). The museum is run by the army, curated by an army captain who will show you around and is actually located in the **Columb Barracks**.

Around Lough Derravaragh

Tullynally Castle ⓭ (tel: 044-966 1159; www.tullynallycastle.com; house closed Sept–Apr; charge), to the north of Mullingar, just beyond **Castlepollard**, used to be known as Pakenham Hall. This massive, grey stone, turreted house overlooking **Lough Derravaragh** is well worth a visit. It has been the seat of the Pakenham family, now the Earls of Longford, since 1655. The current family includes the children of the late British peer Lord Longford: his historian son Thomas, and his daughters, biographer Antonia Fraser and novelist Rachel Billington. The castle is the home of Thomas Pakenham.

The original fort was converted into a two-storey house in the 18th century. A Gothic facade was added in the early 19th century, and in the mid-19th century Sir Richard Morrison designed the central tower and two wings. There is an entertaining upstairs-downstairs guided tour, which includes the Great Hall, the library (which is one of Ireland's largest private collections with over 8,000 volumes), the drawing room and also the kitchen and laundry, fully equipped as in Victorian times. The landscaped gardens, which include a grotto, have spectacular views of Lough Derravaragh.

Multyfarnham, a 2-mile (3km) detour off the N4 Longford road, is a one-street town with some good old-fashioned pubs. Multyfarnham's **Cistercian monastery**, founded in 1306, has an attractive slender tower 88ft (27 metres) high. The abbey was restored by the Franciscans in 1973. Its new stained-glass windows show the legend of the Children of Lir who were turned into swans and lived nearby on Lough Derravaragh. The Franciscans have built a life-size Stations of the Cross in a grove of evergreens beside a fast-flowing stream.

Just to the north of Longford is **Carriglas Manor** (under renovation at the time of writing). Its stables are considered more interesting architecturally than the grand house itself – mainly because they were designed by James Gandon. The house itself was designed in the Gothic Revival style by Daniel Robertson in 1837 for Thomas Lefroy, the Lord Chief Justice of Ireland *(see margin note)*. The estate now boasts a top-class golf course, hotel and newly-built houses.

To the south of Longford off the R397, the **Corlea Trackway Visitor Centre** at Kenagh (tel: 043-332 2386; Apr–Sept daily; free) interprets an iron age Bog Road dating from 148 BC – the largest of its kind ever to be uncovered in Europe.

Famine Museum

If you can only visit one stately home in the Midlands, then follow the N5 for 25 miles (40km) west of Longford to **Strokestown Park House and Famine Museum** ⓮ (tel: 071-963

Austen associations
Thomas Lefroy, who built Carriglas Manor, was apparently the great love of novelist Jane Austen's life – as celebrated in the 2007 film Becoming Jane. *Austen supposedly based the character of Mr Darcy in* Pride and Prejudice *on him. The Lefroy descendants sold the manor to golf developers.*

BELOW: Lough Derravaragh.

Foxgloves in Co. Wicklow.

3013; www.strokestownpark.ie; closed Nov–mid-Mar except for pre-booked tours; charge). The village leads to an imposing Georgian-Gothic arch that leads to the house. The village, with its exceptionally broad main street, was laid out in the early 19th century to complement the new entrance. The house itself is a fine Palladian mansion designed by Sir Richard Cassels in the 1730s. The central block was the family's residence while the wings either side contained the stables and the kitchen areas. The kitchen is especially interesting. A gallery runs above it from which the lady of the house could oversee the staff without entering the kitchen itself. Each Monday morning she would drop a menu with instructions for the week's meals. Tunnels to hide the movements of tradesmen and servants link the main block of the house to the kitchens and stables. The walled garden has also been restored in line with horticultural practices of the 18th century.

The house, accessible by guided tour only (40 minutes), was at the centre of a large estate. It stayed in the Mahon family until 1979 when it was bought and restored by a local businessman. Allow another hour for the **Famine Museum**, housed in the stable yard *(see box below)*.

West of Strokestown where the N5 crosses the R367 lies **Tulsk** and the **Cruachan Aí Visitors Centre** (tel: 071-963 9268; Mon–Sat all year and Sun June–Oct; charge), which explores the archaeological, historical and mythological aspects of Cruachan, burial place of the Kings of Connacht.

Roscommon

Roscommon ⓯, to the south of Tulsk, is a pleasant market town built on a low hill in the midst of rich cattle and sheep country. **Roscommon Castle** (freely accessible), to the north of the town, is an impressive ruin on a green field site. It was originally a 13th-century Norman stronghold. It has massive walls defended by round bastions at each corner, and the mullioned windows can still be seen in some of the remaining walls.

Adjacent to the town are the remains of the 12th-century **Roscommon**

BELOW: fishing along the 17-mile (27-km) length of Lough Ree.

Recalling the Famine

The Famine Museum at Strokestown Park House presents a vivid display tracing the history of the family and the estate and links this to the national events in 1845–50 which led to Ireland's Great Famine and the resulting mass emigration or death of more than 2 million people – almost one-quarter of the population.

It balances the history of the big house with the experiences of the peasants who worked the land. Moving documents record the pleas made to the Mahon family by tenants starving as a result of a devastating potato blight, together with the response they received. The Museum also aims to create a greater awareness of contemporary famine by demonstrating the link between the causes of the Great Irish Famine and the contemporary spectacle of famine in the developing world.

 Map on page 264

Abbey founded by Felim O'Conor, king of Connacht, who was buried there himself in 1265. Eight sculpted figures represent the "gallowglass" – professional soldiers for hire used extensively during the period. Much of the remaining structure dates from the 13th century.

Around Lough Ree

Thanks to the ring road around Athlone, it is possible to drive from Roscommon to **Glasson** which is about 6 miles (10km) outside Athlone, without fighting Athlone's traffic. Glasson is one of a series of pretty villages on the eastern shore of **Lough Ree** ⑯, part of the River Shannon. There are good amenities for water sports, attractive country pubs and restaurants, and a series of lake shore and forest walks. The poet and dramatist Oliver Goldsmith (1730–74), best known for his 1773 comedy *She Stoops to Conquer*, is associated with this area.

The play's central device, by which a traveller mistakes a private home for a country inn, supposedly happened to Goldsmith at Ardagh House in Ardagh, which is now a school. The house where he grew up, Lissoy Parsonage, is now in ruins. The **Three Jolly Pigeons** pub (tel: 090-648 5162) on the Ballymahon road, is the headquarters of the annual Oliver Goldsmith Summer School. Though he rarely returned to his childhood county, his recollections of Longford are also thought to have influenced his epic poem *The Deserted Village*.

Athlone

Athlone ⑰, which straddles the River Shannon at an important strategic point to the south of Lough Ree, has the distinction of being half in Co. Westmeath and half in Co. Roscommon. It is an important commercial centre, and the busiest town in the Midlands (www.athlone.ie).

Athlone Castle (tel: 090-647 2107; closed Oct–Apr, open for Easter; charge) is a squat, 13th-century building, which

Athlone Castle from the River Shannon.

BELOW: Athlone.

Bungalow Blight

Ireland's legendary green countryside is defaced by a rash of houses built with unsuitable materials and painted with more exuberance than taste. Why?

Promotional photos of Ireland could lead visitors to believe that the majority of the rural population lives in small, two-room cottages nestling in the landscape. On the contrary, most country people have given up their dark, cramped accommodation in favour of something more commodious – and visible. From the 1960s, new homes began to appear, often next door to the old cottage. The preferred design was, at first, a modest bungalow, with larger windows, decent plumbing and perhaps an extra bedroom or two. Their owners, seized by fits of individuality, often painted the walls in colours that were unexpectedly cheerful (or garish, depending on your outlook), or added panels of stone cladding.

Over the years, rural homes have become larger and more embellished – although many retain the one-storey format. Some are garnished with Georgian porticoes and balustrades, others loop off into Spanish-arched verandas, while still others sprout eagle-topped gateposts and gold-tipped wrought-iron gates. Tyrolean barge boards, Victorian lamp stands and fairytale wishing wells have likewise found a place in the Irish countryside. The more exuberant homeowners have gone for a jolly *mixum gatherum* of the whole lot – causing architects and purists to despair.

Not only have many of the new houses turned their broad backs on the traditional designs, but they do not conform to the way that buildings have been placed in the Irish countryside since time immemorial. In the past cottages and farm structures were snuggled into the landscape unobtrusively – in the lee of a hill, in the fold between two fields, in the armhold of a hedgerow. But the new residences are often displayed monumentally on the brow of a hill or dropped importantly into the middle of a plot.

County council planning departments issue booklets on careful site selection and layout, and on appropriate design and materials, but this advice is blissfully ignored by many home builders. Indeed, the most famous catalyst for the new style residences was a pattern book called *Bungalow Bliss*, by Jack Fitzsimons, first published in 1971, and which ran to at least a dozen editions over 30 years. This and other pattern books include self-build designs that often pay no heed to traditional materials, form or scale.

Fitzsimons's book title has given rise to cries of "bungalow blight" and "bungalow blitz", in protest against the proliferation of single houses spreading ribbon-like along the rural roadsides of some counties. The National Trust for Ireland, An Taisce, is in constant battle with local authorities over the granting of planning permission for such "one-off" houses. But some county councillors are reluctant to veto the building projects of their constituents. There is a visceral desire among many Irish to have a house of their own, and this is hard to disregard. An Irishman's home is all-important. It is definitely his castle – and it may equally be his Spanish hacienda, Texan ranch or Tudor mansion. ❑

LEFT AND ABOVE: the ever popular rural bungalow.

was badly damaged in 1690 when the Irish made a stand here against the advance of Cromwell's forces. The castle keep now houses a **Folk Museum** that includes souvenirs of the tenor John McCormack, who was born in Athlone in 1884. The area behind the castle is being promoted as Athlone's "Left Bank". There are some nice town houses dating from the 18th and 19th centuries, several good restaurants and bars, but the project has a way to go yet.

You will notice that even relatively modest restaurants in Athlone tend to have trilingual menus. This is because the town is very popular with holidaymakers on Shannon cruisers, most of whom eat ashore as often as they can. The nicest thing to do in Athlone is to take a boat trip up the Shannon to Lough Ree. Boats leave regularly between June and August for a 90-minute cruise from the **Jolly Mariner Marina** (tel: 090-647 4386) on the Shannon's Right (west) Bank.

Cavan's cruising

Across the border to the south of Enniskillen, landlocked Co. Cavan, emptied by emigration, bridges the two Irelands by providing the source of two great rivers: the **Shannon,** which flows south to the Atlantic, and the **Erne**, which flows north into Fermanagh's magnificent lakes. Both rivers are ideal for cruising. Most of the county's scattered towns and villages have small hotels, which cater for visiting fishermen. The Ballinamore-Ballyconnell canal linking the two river systems has been reopened and pleasure trips along the canal are in demand (Inland Waterways Association of Ireland; tel: 01-890 924 991; www.iwai.ie).

Cavan town ⓲ is the site of a 14th-century Franciscan friary, of which only a belfry tower remains. The Roman Catholic Cathedral, in contrast, dates from 1942. **Cavan Crystal** (Dublin Road; tel: 049-433 1800; free) has an attractive showroom displaying the collection of delightful crystal, plus a range of silverware and homeware.

St Feithlimidh's Cathedral at Kilmore is just off the main Cavan-Crossdoney road, 3 miles (5km) from Cavan town. It has been a place of worship for up to 15 centuries. The cathedral is built in the Early Decorated or Middle Pointed style with a cruciform plan, consisting of nave, aisles, transepts, chancel and a central tower which is finished by a four-sided pyramidal roof.

Killykeen Forest Park (tel: 049-433 2541) 5 miles (8km) from Cavan town, covers 600 acres (240 hectares) of mixed woodland overlooking Lough Oughter on the Erne river system and offering a picturesque landscape of lakes, islands and woodland. It is especially popular with fishing enthusiasts, as well as walkers, thanks to its forest walks and trails.

A bit further north just off the R201 near Milltown is Drumlane Abbey (www.drumlane.ie), located in a peaceful setting on the Erne River. The Augustian St Mary's Priory was founded here in the 12th century, although the buildings possibly date back to the sixth century. There are remains of the round tower minus its roof, a church, graveyard and stone crosses.

Angling attraction
Fishermen like Irish trout because most are wild – a rarity in the rest of Europe. Some lakes are stocked with fully grown fish, but fingerlings reared from wild stock are more usual. There are also some lakes stocked with rainbow trout.

BELOW: where freedom is a cabin cruiser.

TIP

Co. Cavan's tourist office can be found in Farnham Street, Cavan town (tel: 049-433 1942; www.cavantourism.com). **Monaghan**'s tourist office is located at Mullacroghery, Clones Road, Monaghan town (tel: 047-81122; www.monaghantourism.com).

Village Ireland

A tour going west and north from Cavan would take in **Arvagh**, a peaceful village 14 miles (22km) south-west on the R198 by Lough Garty; 17th-century **Cloughoughter Castle** on an island in Lough Oughter and nearby **Killeshandra**, a popular spot for anglers; **Dowra**, to the north-west on the R200 near the Black Pig's Dyke, thought to be an ancient frontier earthwork; **Swanlinbar on the N87**, with its faded, once-a-spa charms, on the Border; **Blacklion**, on Lough Macnean 33 miles (52km) north-west on the N3/R200, a hamlet surrounded by many prehistoric ringforts and cairns including a beehive-shaped sweat house, a Celtic form of Turkish bath; and **Butlersbridge**, 4 miles (6km) north on the N3 near which Ballyhaise House, now an agricultural college, has a rare 1733 oval saloon and two storeys vaulted over in brick.

A tour going east and south would cover: **Cootehill**, 16 miles (26km) north-east on the R118 which has a splendid 1730 Palladian house, **Bellamont House**, built for the Coote family in Bellamont Forest. Often hailed as Ireland's loveliest 18th-century house, it was built by Sir Edward Lovett Pearce and inspired by Italy's Palladian villas. One of the its most famous owners, Charles Coote, Earl of Belamont, was known as "the Hibernian seducer" because of his extra-marital activities. He was eventually shot in the groin by Lord Townshend. A portrait by Sir Joshua Reynolds hangs in the National Gallery of Ireland. The house is privately owned but is occasionally open to the public.

South-east 13 miles (21km) on the R192 to **Shercock**, is where the playwright Richard Brinsley Sheridan once lived; **Kingscourt**, whose Catholic church has some renowned stained glass; **Bailieborough**, on the R165, which has a fine main street; **Virginia**, 19 miles (33km) south-west on the N3, planned as a garrison town in 1610 and now a handsome, peaceful place with Cuilcagh House, owned by playwright Tom McIntyre (private), where Dean Swift began *Gulliver's Travels*, 3 miles (5km) east; and **Ballyjamesduff**, where the Cavan County Museum in Virginia Road (tel: 049-854 4070; Tue–Sat all year, Sun pm June–Sept) houses a collection of pre-Christian and medieval artefacts including the 1,000-year-old Lough Errol dug-out boat and Lavey Sheela-na-gigs. Virginia is also home to the excellent **Ramor Theatre** (www.ramortheatre.com), housed in the former parish church.

BELOW: Cloughoughter Castle, on an island in Lough Oughter.

The Cavan Way

The Cavan Way provides a pleasant hill and valley walking connection between the Leitrim Way at Dowra and the Ulster Way at Blacklion village. The walk follows quiet valley and river-sided landscapes to the enclosed uplands of the river's source at the mystical Shannon "Pot" (from the Irish *Lag na Sionna*, meaning "hollow of the Shannon").

Walkers enjoy the upland section between the "Pot" and Blacklion, which includes the forested Burren area and its cemetery of ancient tombs, stone megaliths and monuments (Cavan

Tourism has more details; tel: 049-433 1942; www.cavantourism.com; *see also margin note opposite*).

Mild Monaghan

To the northeast, in Monaghan, is the small agricultural town of **Clones** ⓳ (pronounced *Clone-ess*), whose most famous son is Barry McGuigan, the "Clones cyclone" who became world featherweight boxing champion in 1985. The town's commercial centre is Fermanagh Street, signalling the town's former significance for the farmers of south Fermanagh.

But, just as partition destroyed its role as an important railway hub, so the Troubles initially hit trade as northerners became reluctant to cross the border. However, the two tills on most shop counters hint that the two different currencies – the British pound in Northern Ireland and the euro in the South – have encouraged a great deal of cross-border price comparing, especially on fuel for vehicles.

The writer Patrick McCabe was born in Clones. His popular novels include *The Butcher Boy* and *Breakfast on Pluto*, both filmed by Neil Jordan.

Clones has an ancient lineage. The remains of a 12th-century Augustinian abbey (known as **"the Wee Abbey"**) can be seen in Abbey Street. An ancient cross in the marketplace shows scenes from the Bible, such as the Fall of Adam and Eve and the Adoration of the Magi. The cemetery has a 9th-century **round tower**, 75ft (23 metres) high and rather dilapidated, and an early Christian carved **sarcophagus**, thought to be the grave of the founder, St Tiarnoch, the key to which can be obtained from nearby Patton's pub.

Several Georgian houses are a reminder of the town's 18th-century prosperity. Another sign of the vanished "Ascendancy" era are the "big houses", once the homes of the well-to-do Anglo-Irish, many of which have fallen into disrepair.

Monaghan is a quiet, trim county of snug farmhouses and tranquil market towns, and lakes and rivers that draw fishermen. Its administrative centre, **Monaghan** ⓴, 12 miles (19km) northeast of Clones, has a **Market House** dating from 1792, an imposing 19th-century Gothic Revival cathedral (**St Macartan's**) and a good **County Museum** (tel: 047-82928; Mon–Sat; free) highlighting prehistoric relics and local arts and crafts. The **Garage Theatre** (tel: 047-81597; www.garagetheatre.com), located in a disused ward of a psychiatric hospital, mounts excellent touring productions.

Rossmore Forest Park, 2 miles (3km) southwest of Monaghan town on the R189 to Newbliss, has several forest walks, a nature trail, a yew walk and good viewing points. The ruins of the 16th-century **Rossmore Castle** provide a viewing point to the surrounding countryside. The park contains examples of a wedge tomb and a court tomb dating to 3,000–1,800 BC. The landscape has many drumlins, laid down during the Ice Age over 10,000 years ago when boulder clay was deposited as small hillocks by moving ice.

Monaghan's mix of monotonous low hills and poor small farms was well captured by the novelist and poet Patrick Kavanagh (1904–67), who grew up here on a farm at Inishkeen. A man whose acerbic wit spared little, including his native county, Kavanagh described Monaghan's natives as being "locked in a stable with pigs and cows forever." His 1948 book Tarry Flynn, *later dramatised, achingly explores the repressed emotions of a young farmer in this area.*

BELOW: traditional thatched cottage, Clones.

Castle Leslie, where Paul McCartney got hitched to Heather Mills.

Castle Leslie

To the north, 5 miles (8km) on the R185, by Glaslough, is the reputedly haunted **Castle Leslie** (tel: 047-88100; www.castleleslie.com), home of the literary Leslie family and now a hotel. Set on an estate of 1,000 acres (400 hectares), Castle Leslie is rich in Victorian splendour, both in its furniture and family portraits. Winston Churchill, a first cousin of the family, stayed here, and Paul McCartney married Heather Mills here in 2002.

To the south, east of **Newbliss**, 10 miles (16km) on the R188, at **Annamakerrig House** is the **Tyrone Guthrie Centre** (tel: 047-54003; www.tyroneguthrie.ie), an international haven for professional artists in all art forms. Six miles (10km) east is **Rockcorry**, where John Gregg invented Gregg's Shorthand, America's favourite.

Continuing along the R183 to **Castleblayney**, a town so steeped in the tradition of country music it has been called the Nashville of Ireland. It's a good centre for walking, fishing and golf, and is situated by the attractive Lough Muckno. Hope Castle (tel: 042-974 9450), built on the site of Blayney Castle in the 18th century, is now a leisure park.

Poet and novelist Patrick Kavanagh grew up 10 miles (16km) east of attractive **Carrickmacross**, at tiny Inishkeen, where a riverside museum, the **Patrick Kavanagh Centre** (tel: 042-937 8560; www.patrickkavanaghcountry.com; Tue–Fri all year plus Sat–Sun in June–Sept), celebrates his work. While he spent most of his life in Dublin, the harsh isolation of his native county informed much of his work during his life. Mocked by the Dublin literary community of the time, Kavanagh claimed he was hated for his gift and described the situation as "the enmity of the Poet". When the *Irish Times* surveyed "the nation's favourite poems", 10 of Kavanagh's poems were in the first 50. *(See margin note on page 277.)*

Traditional local lace is sold in Carrickmacross (www.carrickmacrosslace.ie). Nearby **Ballybay** is unremarkable except for its proximity to **Lough Major** and **Lough Muckno**, both filled with a variety of coarse fish and surrounded by nature trails and picnic sites. ❑

BELOW: the 18th-century Hope Castle, set in Lough Muckno Leisure Park, was once a convent and is now a hotel.

RESTAURANTS AND PUBS

Restaurants

Prices for a three-course dinner per person without wine:
€ = under €25
€€ = €25–40
€€€ = €40–55
€€€€ = over €55

Athlone

Left Bank Bistro
Fry Place, Athlone, Co. Westmeath
Tel: 090-649 4446
Tue–Sat L noon–5pm; Early Bird Mon–Fri all evening, Sat 5.30–7.30pm; D 5.30–9.30pm. L **€**, Early Bird **€€**, D **€€–€€€**
Keenly priced, informal wide-ranging international lunch menu. Dinner based on more costly ingredients, all cooked with skill and flair.

Wineport Lodge
Glasson, Athlone, Co. Westmeath (restaurant with rooms)
Tel: 090-643 9010
Mon–Sat 6–10pm, Sun 3–9pm. L **€€** (set Sun lunch), D **€€€**, Gourmet **€€€€**
Beautiful lakeside location. Seasonal menus make wide use of artisan and speciality Irish foods. Great wine list.

Blacklion

Macnean House and Bistro
Main Street, Blacklion, Co. Cavan (restaurant with rooms)
Tel: 071-985 3022
L Sun only 12.30 and 3.30pm (2 sittings), D Wed–Sat 6.30–9.30pm, Sun 7–8.30pm. L **€€**, D **€€€**, Prestige dinner menu **€€€€**
Owner/celebrity chef Neven Maguire cooks up a storm. Contemporary Irish cooking and a range of menus including set dinner and 9-course Prestige Menu. It is considered one of the best restaurants in Ireland.

Cloverhill

The Olde Post Inn
Cloverhill, Co. Cavan (restaurant with rooms)
Tel: 047-55555
L Sun only 12.30–3pm, D Tue–Sun 5.30–9.30pm, Sun until 8.30pm. L **€€**, Early Bird **€€**, D **€€–€€€**, D set 5 course **€€€**. Gourmet menu **€€€€**
A traditional feel to this comfortable restaurant where traditional themes are given an individual spin. Variety of game in season and separate vegetarian menu.

Carrickmacross

Nuremore Restaurant, Hotel and Country Club
Carrickmacross, Co. Monaghan
Tel: 042-966 1438
Daily, L Sun–Fri 12.30–2.30pm, D 6.30–9.30pm. L **€€**, D **€€–€€€**, Prestige menu **€€€€**,
Children's menu **€**
Talented chef Raymond McArdle has earned a national reputation for this hotel restaurant. Innovative, elegant, classic French meets modern Irish fine dining.

Cavan

Opus One
Cavan Crystal Hotel, Dublin Road, Cavan, Co. Cavan
Tel: 049-436 0600
Daily, L 12.30–3.30pm, D 6–10pm. L **€€**, D **€€–€€€**
Located in the Cavan Crystal Hotel, Opus One serves up a menu to appeal to traditionalists *and* those seeking innovative overtones. Freshness and flavour are the key.

Mullingar

The Belfrey Restaurant
Ballynegal, Mullingar, Co. Westmeath
Tel: 044-934 2488
L Sun 12.30–5.30pm, D Wed–Sat 6–9.30pm. L **€€**, Early Bird set meal (Wed and Thur 6–7pm) **€€**, D **€€**
Combines a converted Gothic-style Church of Ireland chapel with luxury and skilled cooking, and a menu that mixes classic and traditional.

Multyfarnham

Weirs Bar & Restaurant
Multyfarnham, Mullingar, Co. Westmeath
Tel: 044-937 1111
L Mon–Tue noon–3pm, Sun 1–3.30pm, à la carte menu until 7pm, D Wed–Sat 1–9pm, day menu until 7pm, à la carte 6–9pm. L served until 6pm **€–€€**, Early Bird 5–7pm Wed–Sat **€–€€**, D **€€**, children's menu **€**
This stone pub and restaurant is a lovely place to stop while touring the countryside. Popular with locals, the quality of the meat is notable.

Nenagh

Country Choice Café and Delicatessen
25 Kenyon Street, Nenagh, Co. Tipperary
Tel: 067-32596
Mon–Sat 9am–6pm, L menu 12.30–3pm, All day menu **€**
Peter Ward and his wife run this legendary place where you can experience the best of Irish artisan and speciality foods.

The Peppermill
26 Kenyon Street Nenagh, Co. Tipperary
Tel: 067-34598
Tue–Sun D 5–10pm, Sun 4–10pm **€€**
Smart town-centre restaurant. Balanced menu, with traditional meat dishes, but fish options turn up delicious surprises.

Shannonbridge

The Old Fort
Shannonbridge, Co. Roscommon
Tel: 090-967 4973
Wed–Sat, D 4–8pm, Sun L noon–4pm. L **€€**, Early Bird **€€**, D **€€–€€€**
Authentically restored fort, deeply comfortable. Various menus offer good, simple, classic food.

Pubs

A riverside pub worth visiting is **JJ Hough's** in Banagher (Main Street, Banagher). Family-run pub popular with locals. No food. Nightly traditional music.

Sean's Bar, 13 Main Street, Athlone, Co. Westmeath. Certified by the National Museum as the oldest pub in Britain and Ireland, it is hard to resist a visit to a pub that has all the owners listed since the year 900. Landlubbers enter beside Athlone Castle; direct access from river cruisers is through the beer garden and back bar. Memorabilia, antiques, a great pint and traditional music most nights. Quiet by day and lively by night.

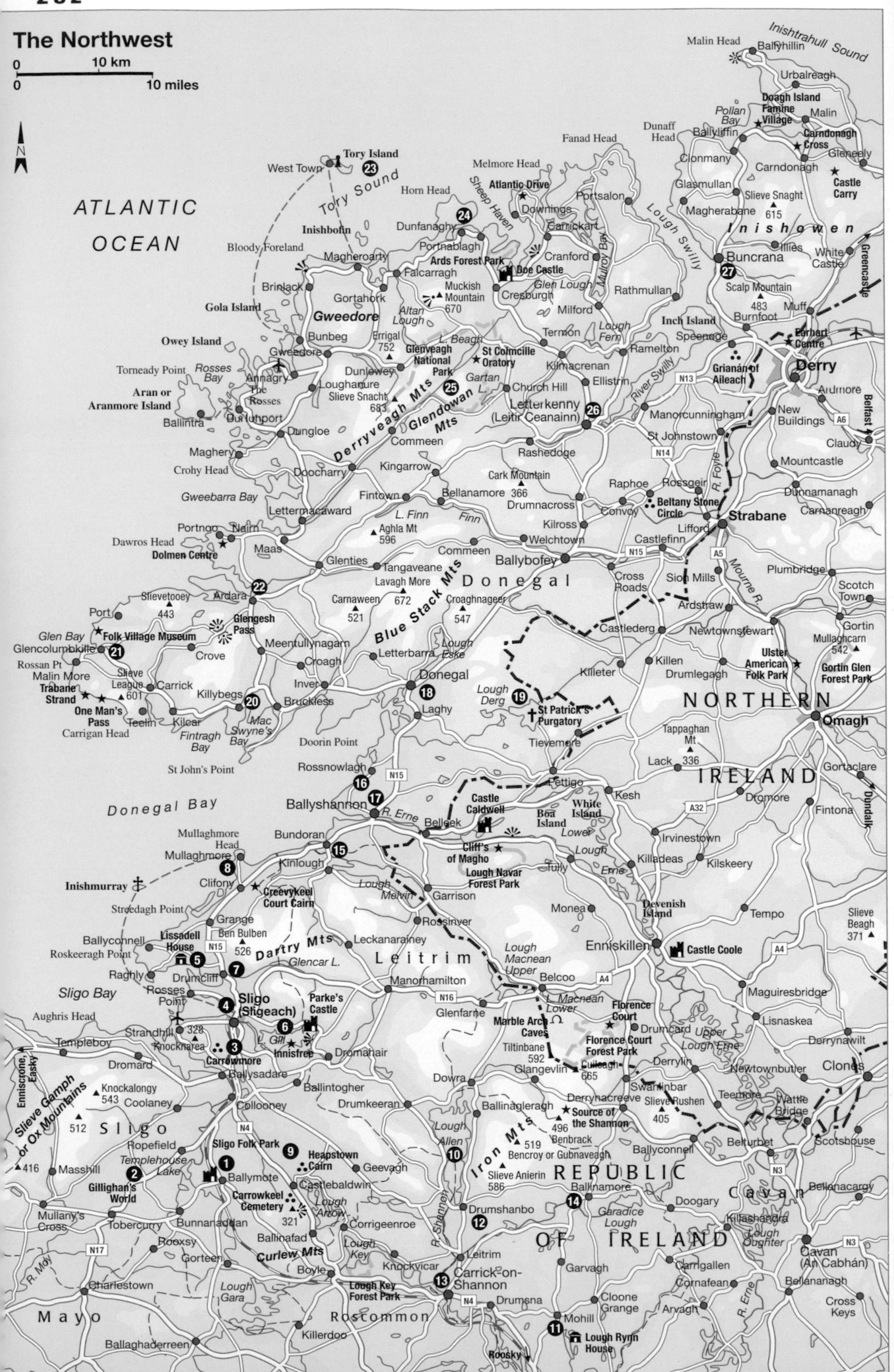
The Northwest
0
10 km
0
10 miles
N
ATLANTIC
OCEAN
Tory Island
West Town
23
Tory Sound
Inishbofin
Bloody Foreland
Gola Island
Owey Island
Torneady Point
Rosses Bay
Aran or Aranmore Island
Ballintra
Annagry
The Rosses
Burtonport
Maghery
Crohy Head
Gweebarra Bay
Portnoo
Narin
Dawros Head
Dolmen Centre
Maas
Melmore Head
Horn Head
Sheep Haven
Atlantic Drive
Downings
24
Dunfanaghy
Portnablagh
Ards Forest Park
Doe Castle
Magheroarty
Falcarragh
Brinlack
Gortahork
Gweedore
Bunbeg
Gweedore
Muckish Mountain
670
Altan Lough
Errigal
752
L. Beagh
Glenveagh National Park
Dunlewey
Loughanure
Slieve Snacht
683
Derryveagh Mts
25
Glendowan Mts
Dungloe
Commeen
Doocharry
Kingarrow
Fintown
Lettermacaward
L. Finn
Finn
Aghla Mt
596
Bellanamore
Cark Mountain
366
Drumnacross
Cresburgh
Glen Lough
Milford
Termon
St Colmcille Oratory
Gartan L.
Church Hill
Kilmacrenan
Letterkenny
(Leitir Ceanainn)
26
Rashedoge
Fanad Head
Portsalon
Carrickart
Cranford
Mulroy Bay
Rathmullan
Lough Fern
Ramelton
Ellistrin
River Swilly
Lough Swilly
Dunaff Head
Malin Head
Ballyhillin
Inishtrahull Sound
Urbalreagh
Doagh Island Famine Village
Malin
Pollan Bay
Ballyliffin
Carndonagh Cross
Gleneely
Clonmany
Carndonagh
Castle Carry
Glasmullan
Slieve Snaght
615
Magherabane
Inishowen
Illies
White Castle
Greencastle
Buncrana
27
Scalp Mountain
483
Muff
Burnfoot
Inch Island
Speenoge
Eglinton
Grianán of Aileach
Derry
N13
Ardmore
Belfast
New Buildings
A6
Claudy
Manorcunningham
St Johnstown
N14
R. Foyle
Mountcastle
Raphoe
Rossgeir
Beltany Stone Circle
Convoy
Dunnamanagh
Carnanreagh
Strabane
Lifford
Kilross
Welchtown
Castlefinn
N15
A5
Glenties
Tangaveane
Commeen
Ballybofey
Donegal
Lavagh More
672
Cross Roads
Sion Mills
Mourne R.
Plumbridge
Scotch Town
22
Slievetooey
443
Ardara
Port
Glengesh Pass
Glen Bay
Folk Village Museum
Glencolumbkille
21
Rossan Pt
Malin More
Trabane Strand
One Man's Pass
Carrigan Head
Teelin
Slieve League
601
Carrick
Kilcar
Killybegs
20
Crove
Meentullynagarn
Croagh
Inver
Bruckless
Fintragh Bay
Mac Swyne's Bay
Carnaween
521
Blue Stack Mts
Croaghnageer
547
Letterbarra
Lough Eske
Donegal
18
Laghy
Lough Derg
19
St Patrick's Purgatory
Doorin Point
St John's Point
Rossnowlagh
16
17
Ballyshannon
N15
R. Erne
Donegal Bay
Castlederg
Newtownstewart
Gortin
Mullaghcarn
542
Ulster American Folk Park
Gortin Glen Forest Park
Killen
Killeter
Drumlegagh
NORTHERN
IRELAND
Omagh
Tappaghan Mt
336
Lack
Tievemore
Pettigo
Kesh
Dromore
Gortaclare
Fintona
Dundalk
A32
Castle Caldwell
Belleek
Boa Island
White Island
Lower
Lough Erne
Irvinestown
Killadeas
Kilskeery
Cliff's of Magho
Lough Navar Forest Park
Tully
Mullaghmore Head
Mullaghmore
8
Bundoran
15
Kinlough
Lough Melvin
Garrison
Inishmurray
Cliffony
Creevykeel Court Cairn
Streedagh Point
Grange
Ben Bulben
526
Rossinver
Monea
Devenish Island
Tempo
Slieve Beagh
371
Ballyconnell
Lissadell House
N15
Roskeeragh Point
5
Dartry Mts
Leckanarainey
Leitrim
Lough Macnean Upper
Enniskillen
Castle Coole
A4
Raghly
Drumcliff
7
Glencar L.
Manorhamilton
Belcoo
A4
Sligo Bay
Rosses Point
4
Sligo
(Sligeach)
Parke's Castle
N16
L. Macnean Lower
Florence Court
Maguiresbridge
Aughris Head
Strandhill
328
6
Glenfarne
Marble Arch Caves
Drumcard
Upper
Lough Erne
Lisnaskea
Templeboy
Knocknarea
3
Carrowmore
L. Gill
Innisfree
Dromahair
Tiltinbane
592
Florence Court Forest Park
Cuilcagh
665
Glangevlin
Derrylin
Derrynawilt
Enniscrone, Easky
Dromard
Ballysadare
Dowra
Swanlinbar
Newtownbutler
Clones
Slieve Gamph or Ox Mountains
Knockalongy
543
Coolaney
Ballintogher
Collooney
Drumkeeran
Derrynacreeve
Slieve Rushen
405
Teemore
Wattle Bridge
512
Sligo
N4
Ballinaglera
Iron Mts
Source of the Shannon
496
Benbrack
Ballyconnell
Belturbet
Scotshouse
Lough Allen
10
519
Bencroy or Gubnaveagh
Sligo Folk Park
9
Heapstown Cairn
Ropefield
Templehouse Lake
1
416
Masshill
2
Ballymote
Gillighan's World
Geevagh
Castlebaldwin
Slieve Anierin
586
REPUBLIC
N3
Carrowkeel Cemetery
Lough Arrow
321
Ballinamore
14
Cavan
Bellanacargy
Doogary
Mullany's Cross
Tobercurry
Bunnanaddan
Corrigeenroe
R. Shannon
Drumshanbo
12
Garadice Lough
Killashandra
Lough Oughter
Rooxsy
N17
Gorteen
Ballinafad
Curlew Mts
Lough Key
OF
IRELAND
Cavan
(An Cabhán)
N3
R. Moy
Boyle
Knockvicar
Leitrim
Carrigallen
Charlestown
Lough Key Forest Park
13
Carrick-on-Shannon
Garvagh
Cornafean
Bellananagh
Lough Gara
R. Erne
Mayo
Roscommon
N4
Drumsna
Cloone Grange
Arvagh
Cross Keys
Killerdoo
Mohill
11
Lough Rynn House
Ballaghaderreen
Roosky

THE NORTHWEST

The counties of Sligo, Leitrim and Donegal combine Stone Age burial sites, a craggy coastline, quiet fishing villages and echoes of William Butler Yeats

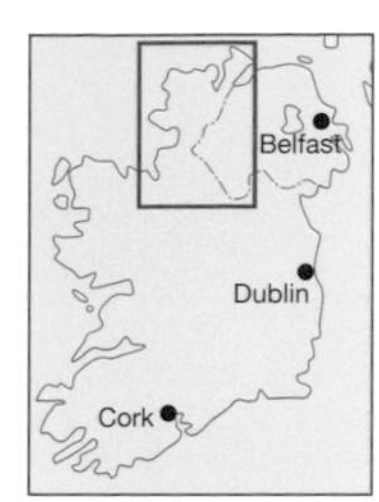

Main attractions
BALLYMOTE
SLIGO
LAKE ISLE OF INNISFREE
DRUMCLIFF
LOUGH ALLEN
ERNE–SHANNON WATERWAY
CARRICK-ON-SHANNON
BUNDORAN
BALLYSHANNON
DONEGAL
LOUGH DERG
GLENCOLMBKILLE
TORY ISLAND
DUNFANAGHY
GLENVEAGH NATIONAL PARK
LETTERKENNY
INISHOWEN PENINSULA

Southwestern Sligo, a land of bright lakes and dramatically carved valleys left behind when the last ice age retreated 10,000 years ago, wears its history on its sleeve. Huts from 2,000 BC cluster on a plateau high in the Bricklieve Mountains west of Lough Arrow.

To their west lie the passage tombs of Carrowkeel Cemetery where Stone Age farmers buried their dead. Cairn K catches the rising sun on the year's longest day, yet the main road to Dublin, the N4, is just a mile west. Across it and across Lough Arrow, south of Riverstown, is the 200ft (70-metre) unexcavated Heapstown Cairn. Almost every hilltop has a passage grave, every lake a defensive artificial island, a crannog, every river confluence a castle, a friary, a priory.

Ancient castles

Along the R295, and 5 miles (8km) northwest from Carrowkeel, Richard de Burgo, the Red Earl of Ulster, has left us the 10ft (3-metre) walls and six towers of his castle, built in 1300, in **Ballymote ❶**. The ruins beside it are of a Franciscan friary where, in 1391, priests wrote the *Book of Ballymote 1*, which enabled scholars to interpret Ireland's ancient Ogham (pronounced *oh-am*) script. At **Collooney**, north again 5 miles (8km) stands a castle, site of a great battle when the English fought off French troops supporting the 1798 rising.

Like bookends, the county begins and ends with seaside resorts. **Enniscrone** (or Innishcrone to some purists), on the shores of Killala Bay, is at the western end, and at the other is Bundoran, which is not in Sligo but a few miles across the county border in Donegal. An eclectic diversion is to visit the seaweed baths at Enniscrone (Kilcullen's Bath House; tel: 096-36238; www.kilcullenseaweedbaths.com; June–Sept daily

PRECEEDING PAGES: the Sligo landscape.
RIGHT: golfers at Enniscrone.

The dolmen at Carrowmore.

10am–8pm, Oct–May Mon–Fri noon–8pm, Sat–Sun 10am–8pm; charge).

From Enniscrone, follow the surfers' coast through **Easky** with its 15th-century Rosalee Castle and two Martello towers built to repel Napoleon in the early 19th century. Another diversion is to take the road south from Easky, past the sparkling waters of Easky Lough deep into the Ox Mountains before joining the N17 at Tobercurry. Young children may wish to stop off at Lavagh, near Tobercurry, to visit **Gillighan's World** ❷ (tel: 071-913 0286; May–Sept Mon–Fri noon–6pm, Sat–Sun 2–7pm; charge), an open-air park and pet zoo where you can explore the kingdom of the fairies with its miniature villages set in an enchanted glade.

Carrowmore

At **Carrowmore** ❸, 5 miles (8km) southwest of Sligo town, the 6,000-year-old Bronze Age graves of Ireland's largest Megalithic cemetery (Visitor Centre; tel: 071-916 1534; www.heritageireland.ie; May–mid-Oct daily 10am–6pm; charge) are easily approached, scattered across the tussocky fields. Above them, on the western horizon, on top of 1,078ft (328-metre) Knocknarea, is the vast cairn, 200ft long by 35ft high (70 by 11 metres), consisting of 40,000 boulders. It is named Mebh's (pronounced Maeve's) Cairn, supposedly for the 1st-century AD Mebh of Connaught whose lust for glitz, baubles and fine clothes would put many a modern royal princess in the shade. The advised approach is from the south.

BELOW: the Garavogue River in Sligo town.

Sligo town

Sligo town ❹ (pop 25,000), best known for its associations with the poet, playwright and Abbey Theatre co-founder William Butler Yeats, is the county's tourist magnet. To the west lie miles of stretches of open beaches, and to the north mountains rise like jutting tablelands dominating the skyline.

Founded by the Normans in the 13th century, Sligo flourished into a prosperous town and has Catholic and Anglican Cathedrals. **Sligo Abbey** was built for the Dominicans in 1252 and was burned in a fire in 1414. It was rebuilt and damaged by fire during the 1641 rebellion and is the only surviving medieval building.

Today the town, with its diverting narrow streets and traditional shop fronts, is the business hub of the northwest of Ireland and with contemporary hotels such as the Glasshouse it is an ideal base for exploring the region. Like so many Irish towns, the waterfront has been developed and along Rockwood Parade cafés, bars and restaurants offer alfresco dining, allowing you to watch swans struggling against the strong current of the River Garavogue.

W. B. Yeats (1865–1948), who spent most of his childhood holidays here, is the main attraction and his legacy is to be found all around. The **Yeats Memorial Building**, Hyde Bridge, (Yeats Society; tel: 071-914 2693; www.yeats-sligo.com; Mon–Fri 10am–5.30pm; charge) is the venue for the Yeats International Summer School in August. A permanent Yeats photographic exhibition is on display and the River Café offers refreshment. A bronze statue portraying the poet stands across the bridge. Upstairs in the Yeats Memorial Building, **Sligo Art Gallery** (tel: 071-914 5847; www.sligoartgallery.com; Mon–Sat 10am–5.30pm) houses exhibitions of contemporary works. The **Sligo County Museum**, housed in a former presbytery on Stephen Street (tel: 071-911 1679; Tue–Sat 9.30am–5pm; free) contains Yeats's letters, a complete collection of his poems, photographs of his funeral, and his Nobel Prize citation.

The arts and theatre thrive in Sligo. The **Model, home of the Niland Collection** (The Mall; tel: 071-914 1405; www.themodel.ie) reopened in May 2010 following extensive redevelopment. It houses one of Ireland's most unique cultural spaces featuring a nationally significant art collection with works by Jack Yeats and Paul Henry.

The town supports two active theatre companies. **Hawk's Well Theatre** (tel: 071-916 1526; www.hawkswell.com) shares a building with the tourist information office (Temple Street; tel: 071-916 1201; www.discoverireland.ie/northwest) while the **Blue Raincoat Theatre Company** is based at the Factory Performance Space on Lower Quay Street (tel: 071-917 0431; www.blueraincoat.com).

Lissadell House

Seasoned travellers, after asking for directions to the offices of the local solicitors Argue and Phibbs, will head out of town and branch west, 4 miles (6km) along the northern shore of Drumcliff Bay where they will come to the extensively restored **Lissadell House** ❺, Ballinful (www.lissadellhouse.com; currently closed to the public).

Designed in the neoclassical Greek Revival style, it was built of local cut grey limestone for the Gore Booths in 1833. By the end of the 20th century it had fallen into a dilapidated state, but even if the house were to crumble, Yeats has immortalised it: *The light of evening, Lissadell, / Great windows open to the south, / Two girls in silk kimonos, both / Beautiful, one a gazelle*. The girls were poet Eva and her sister Constance, later to become Countess Markievicz, a

The Yeats Room at the Sligo County Museum.

BELOW: Lissadell House.

TIP

Lough Gill fish

The lough is noted for brown trout and salmon. February, March and May are good months for salmon, while mid-May to mid-June is the best time for brown trout. There is public access to the lough from a pier on the south side of the mouth of the Garavogue River, at Innisfree pier and from the pier at Sriff Bay in the east.

friend of the Irish President Eamon de Valera who read her funeral oration. Constance, although sentenced to death for her heroic part in the 1916 Easter Rising, was the first woman to be elected to the British House of Commons. She never took the seat, preferring Ireland's equivalent, the Daíl. The neglect of the house was reversed in 2003 when the new custodians – Edward S. Walsh, a barrister from Dublin, and his wife, Constance Cassidy – bought the house for €4.55 million after the Government declined to buy it on behalf of the Irish State.

Unfortunately the property is currently at the centre of a legal battle over rights of way, which will determine the future of Lissadell and whether this spectacular building is ever opened up to the public again.

Lake Isle of Innisfree

South-east of Sligo town, the R286 follows the north side of beautiful **Lough Gill** ❻ swinging south, just into Co. Leitrim, at the elegant 17th-century lakeside **Parke's Castle**, Fivemile Bourne (tel: 071-916 4149; Apr–Sept daily 10am–6pm; charge) and then joins the R288 to **Dromahair** and the 15th-century Creevylea Abbey ruins.

The final stage of the journey, a visit to Yeats's Lake Isle of Innisfree, or a tour of Lough Gill can be taken with local boat companies. Innisfree is a tiny island, just a mile square, and poor weather can make if difficult to replicate Yeats's vision.

The Yeats brothers spent their holidays at windswept **Rosses Point**, 4 miles (6km) north-west on the R291. The view across to Knocknarea is inspiring; mid-channel is a seafarer's marker, the Metal Man – according to Yeats "the only Rosses Point man who never told a lie."

North of Sligo, 5½ miles (9km) on the N15 is tiny **Drumcliff** ❼ at the foot of the majestic cliffs of Ben Bulben. Although he died in France, Yeats by his own request was re-interred here in the dour little Protestant Church of Ireland's graveyard, citing the spot in his poem which begins: *Under Ben Bulben's head* and finishes with the celebrated words inscribed on his tomb: *Cast a cold eye/ On life, on*

BELOW: Drumcliff's Church of Ireland cemetery, resting place of W.B. Yeats.

William Butler Yeats

The son and brother of painters, Yeats (1865–1939) studied art in Dublin and London but became interested in mysticism, the supernatural and Irish nationalism. With Lady Gregory, an Anglo-Irish aristocrat, he founded the Abbey Theatre in Dublin at the same time as his unrequited passion for Maud Gonne, an English-born revolutionary and actress, inspired his early poetry. At 52, he married the 25-year-old Georgie Hyde-Lees, who was deeply into mysticism.

The drama of the 1916 Easter Rising encouraged his interest in politics and he became a senator in the Irish Free State's government from 1922 to 1928, serving as chairman of a commission on coinage. He was awarded the Nobel Prize for Literature in 1923. His status as a major English-language poet is assured.

death, / Horseman, pass by! The church has been restored.

The adjoining round tower is evidence of St Columba's AD 575 monastery, whilst on the 10th-century high cross it is just possible to make out the bible stories of Cain and Abel, Adam and Eve. Glencar Lough, east on the N16 and half in county Leitrim, has a dramatic setting. Earlier literary diversions may be contemplated at Cooldrumman, half-way between Drumcliff and Lissadell. Here, in the Battle of the Books, AD 561, 2,000 monks of various factions, and their supporters, died in an argument as to whether St Finian was right in citing Derry's St Columba for breach of copyright.

Further north off the N15, turn west at Grange for superb **Streedagh Strand** with *Carriag na Spáinneach*, Spaniard's Rock, where three ships of the Spanish Armada foundered in 1588. Most of the shipwrecked, cold and starving were put to the sword. Some re-grouped, joined the *Gerona*, only to suffer similar fates at Port na Spániagh, Dunluce, Co. Antrim. The little road east from Grange leads up Ben Bulben.

Mullaghmore ❽ is a harbour village, a picture-postcard from some perfect childhood holiday. The Blue Flag (EU approved for quality) beach is golden, bright boats rock by the pier and waves splash on Mullaghmore Head.

Offshore is the low-lying uninhabited **Innishmurray Island**, 4 miles (6km) away with one of the most complete and visually exciting early Christian monastic settlements in Europe: the stunning remains of St Molaise's 6th-century monastery, and 3 churches within a 12ft (4-metre) high dry-stone wall – just about the only survivors of Viking raids in the 9th century. If the crossing from Mullaghmore, or Rosses Point, was rough enough, travellers might seek out the island's other curiosity, its cursing stones. Boats to Innishmurray can be hired for day trips (www.sligoheritage.com).

Sligo Folk Park ❾, Millview House, Riverstown, (tel: 071-916 5001; www.sligofolkpark.com; Jun, Jul, Aug Mon–Sat 10–5.30, Sun 12–6; Sep–May Mon–Fri 10–5; charge) is worth a visit

Yeats' statue in Sligo.

LEFT: Mullaghmore. **BELOW:** looking towards Ben Bulben from Drumcliff churchyard.

TIP

Lough Allen is a mixed fishery: pike fishing is particularly popular. There is a good stock of trout and the best trout fishing is in April, August and September. The area from Gobcormongan to the mouth of the Stoney river, on the east shore, is noted for trout and is often referred to as "Murder Mile" by anglers trolling for pike because of the number of trout that come to the baits.

to see traditional craft demonstrations that include thatching, creel-making, butter-making and wood-turning, as well as a working forge. A museum is devoted to rural history with displays of farm implements.

At the end of July into August, Riverstown hosts the **James Morrison Traditional Music Festival** (www.morrison.ie). Morrison (1893–1947), known as "The Professor", was a celebrated fiddle player born nearby in Drumfin.

Leitrim: Rescued by water

North of Mullaghmore, Leitrim is allowed to just dip its toes into 2½ miles (4km) of the Atlantic, before the shore line reaches the **Drowse**, one of the best of salmon rivers and the boundary with Donegal. Ten miles (16km) inland and Leitrim's border is with Fermanagh in Northern Ireland.

Another 20 miles (32km) east and its northern border is with Monaghan. At **Lough Allen** ⑩ – its biggest lake that divides the county into two topographical areas – there are scarcely 5 miles (8km) of Leitrim soil between north Monaghan and south Roscommon.

Thus it has been too easy to dismiss this tiny county of lakes and rushes, meandering rivers, bumpy roads, crumbling farmhouses, drumlins (low rounded hills) and neglected fields, as "Ireland's Cinderella". Sligo even takes credit – via Yeats – for Lough Gill and for Glencar with its waterfall immortalised in Yeats's poem *The Stolen Child*, though the two counties share them. Fermanagh is more associated with salmon-rich Lough Melvin than Leitrim on its southern shore, and the same can be said for the magic of Lough Macnean Upper, which is similarly divided.

The great famine of 1845–46 hit the county hard, and emigration has continued ever since. The unflinching novels of John McGahern (1934–2006) who lived and farmed at Feenagh near **Mohill** ⑪, catch the air of rural desperation that pervaded.

McGahern was one of the most important Irish writers since Samuel Beckett. With his sparse and incisive lyrical style, he was the master of precise language. His stories, set deep in the poor Leitrim soil, tap into the social

BELOW: the beach at Mullaghmore.

Daniel O'Donnell

County Donegal's famous son Daniel O'Donnell is world renowned for his unique blend of country and Irish folk music. Born in Dungloe in 1961, and brought up in Kincasslagh, O'Donnell's success has been attributed to his close and friendly relationship with his enormous fan base and his stage presence.

An initial career founded on a business studies degree was perhaps not the normal grounding for a music legend, but a portfolio of 20 UK Top 40 albums and 15 Top 40 singles unsurprisingly led to him receiving the award of an honorary MBE for services to the music industry in 2002. He has sold over 10 million records.

Today Daniel O'Donnell has returned to his homeland to live and will forever be held an icon in Irish culture.

and economic realities of Irish life in the 1930s and '40s. "There is nothing dramatic about the Leitrim landscape," he once wrote, "but it is never dull." His last published book, the painfully recollected *Memoir* (2005), illuminated much of the fiction that preceded it. The writer and commentator Fintan O'Toole summed up John McGahern's legacy: "He changed Ireland, not by arguing about it, but by describing it."

Erne-Shannon Waterway

That quiet countryside and unspoilt environment so powerfully described in his books is now attracting visitors. Leitrim has much going in its favour. A glance at the map shows a necklace of lakes linking the rivers Shannon and Erne via the Ballinamore–Ballyconnell Canal – more prosaically marketed as the **Erne–Shannon Waterway**. From spring to winter, the banks of the lakes and rivers – where cows drink hock high amongst the flag irises – are dotted with the big green umbrellas of visiting fishermen after bream, eel, perch, pike, roach and rudd.

Hired cruisers flying Austrian, British, Dutch, French and German ensigns ply the canal, their crews clinking their gin 'n' tonic glasses, their skippers nautical in caps, binoculars at the ready. Heron poise in the reed mace, great crested grebe dive before the bow wave. Amid the uncut watermeadows, amateur botanists count sedges, birdwatchers tick off another species of warbler and cup their ear for the cry of corncrake and cuckoo.

Apart from the fishing, boating and birdwatching, tourists come for hill walking, horse-riding, cycling and traditional music. The new money has brought music back to the pubs, turned old market houses into heritage centres and tourist offices, and refurbished town piers and lake fishing stands. The Organic Centre in **Rossinver** offers courses in subjects ranging from "plant to plate" and "growing in polytunnels" (tel: 071-985 4338; www.theorganiccentre.ie).

At the southern tip of Lough Allen, **Drumshanbo** ⓬ dances to the beat of the bodhrán and banjo as well as the piper and fiddler. Music seeps from the pubs at all times of the year but two highlights are An Tóstal (www.antostalfestival.ie), held at the end of May, and in mid-July a week-long annual festival of song and dance, the Joe Mooney Summer School (www.joemooneysummerschool.com).

Slieve Anierin (*Sliabh an Iarainn*, "Mountain of Iron") lies northeast of Drumshanbo and the mountain takes its name from the fact that iron and coal were smelted from it. The mining on the nearby Arigna Mountains ended in 1990 but the memories are retained in the Arigna Mining Experience (tel: 071-964 6466; www.arignaminingexperience.ie; Mon–Sun 10am–5pm; charge), which explains the social and mining traditions of the area. A 45-minute underground tour, led by ex-miners, shows what it was like to work in some of the narrowest coal seams in the western world. An exhibition area traces 400 years of mining history in the area and a

TIP

No licence is needed for fishing on the Shannon for pike, brown trout or coarse fish, but a licence must be held for the Erne. Conservation has become an important issue in Irish angling circles. Local fishery bye-laws are strict. Details of regulations governing coarse angling and game angling can be obtained from Shannon Fisheries (www.shannon-fishery-board.ie).

BELOW: a necklace of lakes link the rivers Shannon and Erne.

Anthony Trollope's first novel, The McDermotts of Ballycloran, *is highly melodramatic, involving illegal distillers, a ruthless attorney, a wronged woman and a murder. Trollope himself said of it: "As to the plot itself, I do not know that I ever made one so good, – or, at any rate, one so susceptible of pathos." He thought it painted an accurate picture of what Irish life was like before the devastating 1846 potato famine.*

DVD gives an insight into the mining process. A visit to the coffee shop is rewarded with stunning views of the natural surroundings.

Carrick-on-Shannon

The county town, **Carrick-on-Shannon** ⓭, (pop 4,500) is a buzz of activity, much of it centred on the riverside and bustling marina with its opulent cruising boats, quality restaurants and luxury hotels. A walk around town with its attractive shop fronts is rewarding. Carrick boasts some striking architecture including the remarkable **Costello Memorial Church**, a tiny Catholic chapel on Bridge Street which is the smallest in Ireland and reputedly the second smallest in the world. The tourist office is based in the Old Barrel Store, at the Marina (tel: 071-962 0170; www.leitrimtourism.com).

Drumsna, just southeast, where Anthony Trollope wrote his first novel, *(see margin note)*, and Roosky 9 miles (14km) south again, have also found prosperity. **Lough Rynn House** (tel: 071-963 2700), once home to the Earl of Leitrim, has now been converted to a luxury hotel where non-guests are welcome for afternoon tea and a stroll in the splendid gardens. It is 10 miles (16km) east of Carrick-on-Shannon. Lough Rynn Caravan Park (tel: 071-963 1022) is adjacent to the house.

Ten miles (16km) to the northeast, **Carrigallen** has a flourishing theatre, the Corn Mill (tel: 049-433 9612; www.cornmilltheatre.com).

The Leitrim Genealogy Centre at Main Street in **Ballinamore** ⓮ (tel: 071-964 4012; www.leitrimroots.com) will help those interested in delving into their Irish past. The staff will compile a family history report.

For another take on the past then the **Glenview Folk Museum**, Aghoo, Ballinamore, (tel: 071-964 4157; www.glenview-house.com; Apr–Oct daily; free) houses a private collection of 3,000 agricultural items from the 19th and 20th centuries. Nearby, fragments of the old Sligo Leitrim and Northern Counties Railway, whose initials were interpreted locally as the Slow Late and Never Completely Reliable, can be traced.

BELOW: fishing at Carrick-on-Shannon.

Donegal

The Atlantic storms into Donegal's rocky coves, rumbling round white boulders up in banks beside the sheep cropped grass. Rusty winches, skeletal memories of long-lost fishing enterprises, paint red the stone of crumbling piers. Dreamers and poets, and stressed-out business executives from Continental Europe, put thatch back on the roofs of old stone cottages, whilst locals, seemingly with no planning constraints erect new bungalows higgledy-piggledy, despoiling (for the tourist) the silent landscape of empty valleys, purple mountains, rushing streams and towering sea-cliffs.

Donegal's people, like Leitrim's, will argue that they are hard done by. In Donegal, tenuously linked to the rest of the Republic by a slender isthmus, they say Dublin forgets them. Certainly much of the county harks back to another age: tiny fields bound by dry-stone walls, the hay cut by scythe then tossed in cocks; a scattering of sheep, woolly dots on a distant, bare, impossibly steep, mountainside.

Bundoran

County Donegal contains seven Blue Flag beaches recognised for their safety as well as the quality and cleanliness of water and recycling facilities. The beaches start at **Bundoran** ⓯, which 30 years ago, was described in an architectural guide as "a squalid place with little of interest." In the intervening years the town has worked hard to clean up its act capitalising on its seaside location, marine wildlife and magnificent **Tullan Strand.** It is a popular centre for surfing and in 2001 hosted the World Master Championship with many taking up the challenge offered by "The Peak", a classic left-hander that runs to about 100 metres and a body-boarding wave known as 3D. Regular sea angling and sightseeing trips with whale, seal, porpoise and dolphin-watch cruises are available in the summer.

Amongst the family attractions are the **Waterworld and Seaweed Baths**, Sea Front (tel: 071-984 1172; www.waterworldbundoran.com; June–Aug daily 10am–7pm, Apr–May, Sept Sat–Sun only; charge), with its wave pools, water slides and sauna and steam rooms.

Rossnowlagh ⓰, its smaller quieter cousin round the coast to the north, is a base for surfers. The extensive Blue Flag beach is very popular with families and there are lifeguards on duty during the summer months.

In the one-time garrison town of **Ballyshannon** ⓱, where the waters of the Erne are tamed to produce hydroelectricity, pretty Georgian houses survive and literary folk commemorate the town's most famous son, poet William Allingham (1824–89) remembered for his verse *Up the airy mountain,/ Down the rushy glen,/ We daren't go a-hunting / For fear of little men.*

The more recent memory of another son of Ballyshannon, the rock musician Rory Gallagher (1948–95), is honoured in an annual musical tribute during the June Bank Holiday weekend attracting up to 5,000 visitors to the town. Gallagher, who blazed a trail for rock bands, enjoyed a successful solo career

TIP

Surfers' delight

Bundoran has been called Ireland's surfing capital, not least because the variety of beach breaks suits all levels of ability, from beginners to advanced surfers. Bundoran Surf School offers lessons that cover various options (tel: 071-984 1968; www.bundoransurfco.com).

BELOW: good surfing at Bundoran.

TIP

More about monks
Visitors interested in the influence of the Cistercian monks in Ireland can trace their history in the Abbey Water Wheels Visitor Centre at Assaroe, Rossnowlagh (tel: 071-985 1580; Easter week, June–Sept Mon–Sun 11am–7pm, Oct–May Sun only 2.30–7pm; free).

BELOW: St Patrick's Purgatory, Lough Derg.

selling millions of albums worldwide. His concerts have gone into the pantheon of rock history and his music is enjoying a resurgence of interest. **Rory Gallagher International Tribute Festival:** www.goingtomyhometown.com.

Inis Saimer, the little island situated in the Erne Estuary is said to be the spot where the first inhabitants of Ireland landed, led by a chieftain from Scythia (near modern Macedonia) around 2,700 BC.

The county town

Donegal ⓲, the lively county town, has a busy triangular "Diamond" market square, congested with tourist traffic all summer. The town's history has a familiar ring. It has a notable castle (tel: 074-972 2405; Mar–Oct Mon–Sun 10am–6pm, Oct–Mar Thur–Mon 9.30am–4.30pm; charge). Once an O'Donnell stronghold, it was redesigned, as was the town itself, by the Brookes, planters who took over the land after the O'Donnells were deported in the so-called "Flight of the Earls" at the turn of the 17th century. In the now ruined O'Donnell-financed Franciscan abbey, south on the estuary of the Eske, monks compiled, in the 1630s, *The Annals of the Four Masters*, tracing Ireland's history back to the time of Noah's granny.

Complementary to tourism, the weaving and making up of tweeds is the main industry, and Magee's, the town's largest shop, is the industry's principal outlet. A mile south, **Donegal Craft Village** (tel: 074-972 2225; www.donegalcraftvillage.com; some workshops closed out of season) established in 1985, demonstrates weaving and other craftworks.

Three miles (5km) south of Donegal town, at **Laghy**, the R232 runs south-east for Pettigo from where the R233 bears north 3 miles (5km) across desolate bogland to **Lough Derg** ⓳, with its tiny Station Island, focal point for a major act of pilgrimage, St Patrick's Purgatory. The island, now covered with buildings, looks from a distance like a Canaletto painting and the pilgrims commemorate the 40 days Ireland's saint spent on it, praying, fasting and expelling evil spirits. There can be few Irish Catholics over the age of 40 who have not spent the required three days of ritual there, walking barefoot, repeating prayers and consuming nothing but black tea and dry toast.

Pilgrims are increasingly coming for "time": time to pray, time to reflect, time for themselves and time away from their hectic everyday world. An increasing number of men are visiting the island, marking a change from the popular belief that the women came to the island to pray for the men. Recent figures show that 20,000 pilgrims a year come to Lough Derg – not only from Ireland but from 35 countries around the world.

Craggy coastline

The road west from Donegal town runs past Bruckless, where there are live oysters and mussels for sale, then through the fishing port of **Killybegs** ⓴ where hefty trawlermen, drinking amongst the Victorian villas, give the town a raffish, frontier air. The Maritime & Heritage Centre in the carpet factory building combines the traditions of hand-knotting carpets and the history of fishing in Ireland's premier port (tel: 074-974 1944; www.visitkillybegs.com; Mon–Fri 10am–6pm, July–Aug also Sat–Sun 1–5pm; charge). The centre has installed Ireland's only interactive Navigation Wheelhouse Simulator where one can step into the boots of a seafarer to steer a boat into the harbour.

Kilcar, 7 miles (11km) on along the craggy, beautiful coastline, is another vacation, traditional music and tweed centre somewhat overshadowed by **Ardara** 20 miles (33km) to the northeast. It is rewarding to continue further west over the steep Glengesh Pass through quiet **Carrick**, then turning south for the precipitous drive past Teelin to Carrigan Head at the eastern end of 2,000ft (650-metre) **Slieve League** whose sheer cliffs – the highest marine cliffs in Europe – drop a scary 765ft (235 metres) into the indigo sea beyond. An alternative is to leave transport at Teelin, walking the signposted One Man's Pass in the same direction. The views from *Amharc Mór* are, when not shrouded in mists, spectacular – and vertiginous.

For those in need of a calming cup of coffee afterwards the **Slieve League Cultural Centre** houses a tea shop and craft gallery, as well as archaeological, geological and tourist information (tel: 074-973 9077; www.sliabhleague.com).

Glencolmbkille

Glencolumbkille ㉑, further west in the lowlands at the head of Glen Bay, represents a landmark in the development of a particular kind of Irish tourism. The idea was devised here that the draughty, cold traditional thatched white-washed cottage could be up-graded, given central heating, pine furniture, shower, television and fridge and clustered into a marketable group. Purists dismiss it, while its protagonists argue that it sustains life and employment in distressed rural communities. Four cottages in the **Folk Village Museum** (tel: 074-973 0017; www.glenfolkvillage.com; Easter–Sept Mon–Sat 10am–6pm, Sun noon–6pm;

TIP

St Patrick's Purgatory

The season begins in May with one-day retreats; the traditional three-day pilgrimage season starts on 1 June and runs until 15 August. Remember to bring warm and waterproof clothing. Address: St Patrick's Purgatory, Lough Derg, Pettigo, tel: 071-986 1518. Pilgrimage fee includes boat fare and accommodation; www.loughderg.ie.

BELOW: Killybegs harbour.

Saturday night music session at a pub in Ardara.

charge) present traditional life over the centuries; one cottage, the Shebeen, sells seaweed and fuchsia wine.

Tiny **Port**, hard to reach in the next valley north, demonstrates what happens when a village dies, but most travellers continue north-east the 16 miles (26km) to **Ardara** ㉒, where the Heritage Centre (tel: 074-953 7905; Easter–Sept Mon–Sat 10am–6pm, Sun 2–6pm; charge) has a tourist information point, then Glenties, both awash in season with Northern Ireland's holidaymakers buying Guinness, tweeds, Aran sweaters, salmon flies for the Owena and Owentocker rivers, and tapping their toes to fiddlers.

Drive north of Ardara to the gloriously soft sandy beach at **Nairn** (known as Tramore strand) where sanderlings frequently perform like clockwork toys, and en route you will pass the wind turbine at the Dolmen Centre, Kilclooney, Portnoo, the first eco-tourism centre in Ireland which uses the latest in green energy (tel: 074-954 5010; www.dolmencentre.com; Mon–Fri 10am–4pm, 7–10pm).

North, the N56 continues to **Dungloe**, capital of the Rosses, a raggedly charming peninsula of islands, trout lakes and inlets. From **Burtonport**, 4 miles (6km) northwest, a 25-minute ferry service (tel: 074-952 0532; www.arranmoreferry.com) runs to Aranmore island, 3 miles (5km) offshore, with its 900 souls, dry-stone walls, holiday cottages and an abundance of wildlife. There are a number of activities to enjoy on the island including excellent lake and shore fishing. A brisk walk can be combined with a stop at one of the island's six traditional Irish pubs renowned for their charming atmosphere. The west of the island has many marine caves and stacks carved from solid rock resulting in a spectacular cliff coastline, and there are great views of the mainland from Glen Head.

Ferries for bare and windswept **Tory Island** ㉓ (tel: 074-953 1320; www.toryislandferry.com), a popular tourist destination, run the 15-mile (24km) sea journey regularly from Bunbeg almost 15 miles (24km) by the coast road north and from Magheroarty round the Bloody Foreland near Gortahork. Home once to Balor, the one-eyed God of Darkness, Tory gave its name (meaning outlaw) to Britain's right-wing political party when it opposed James II in 1680. The island's main village, West Town, has a 51ft (15-metre) round tower and the ruins of two churches. This area, like Gweedore to the north, is traditionally Irish speaking.

The dramatic conical quartz mountain north of Dunlewy is **Errigal**, Donegal's highest at 2,466ft (752 metres). The peak south is Slieve Snaght, 200ft (70 metres) less. At the Dunlewy Visitor Centre (tel: 074-953 1699; www.dunleweycentre.com;

BELOW: Tory Island.

mid-Mar–Nov Mon–Fri 10.30am–6pm, Sun 11am–6.30pm) the traveller can regress to the mid-20th century within the cottage of Manus Ferry, a renowned Donegal weaver. Boat cruises are available on the lake and visitors are entertained with tall tales of the "ghost" of the Green Lady.

Dunfanaghy

Twenty-one miles (37km) north on the N56, **Dunfanaghy** ㉔ is a popular resort, especially with golfers, but also offers opportunity for walking, cycling and horse-riding. The Workhouse, where people fled from the distress of the famine, was the scene of horrific suffering. Today part of the building has been turned into an interpretative centre and exhibition gallery (tel: 074-913 6540; www.dunfanaglyworkhouse.ie; Mon–Sat 10am–4pm, extended hours July–Aug; free).

Right next door, the long-established **Art Gallery** (tel: 074-913 6224) has been attracting visitors for many years, its walls decorated with some of the most evocative and moody images of Donegal captured by contemporary Irish painters.

Round the coast, the **Falcarragh Visitor Centre**, *An tSean Bheairic*, fuses culture, heritage, history and tourist information (tel: 074-918 0888; www.falcarraghvisitorcentre.com; Mon–Fri 9am–5pm, Sat 11–5pm; free) in a former police station.

From Falcarragh, travel southeast 8 miles (13km) along the R255 to walk through the 10,000 acres (400 hectares) of **Glenveagh National Park** ㉕ (tel: 074-913 7090; www.glenveaghnational park.ie; charge for castle). The park was given to the nation by Henry McIlhenny who made his fortune from Tabasco Sauce.

With its castle and its formal French and Italian gardens mixing with the wild mountains, the park has a further surprise in the Regency-style **Glebe House Gallery** (tel: 074-913 7071; daily 11am–6.30pm, closed Fri June–Sept; charge), which displays paintings by Degas, Renoir, Picasso and the primitive painters of Tory Island. Much photographed is **Gartan Lough**, 3 miles (5km) south via a narrow bog road.

Letterkenny ㉖, the prosperous county town on the River Swilly 10 miles (16km) to the southwest, is useful as a base. Its most prominent landmark is the Cathedral, built in modern Gothic style by local masons using Donegal stone. **Colmcille Heritage Centre**, Churchill, (tel: 074-913 7306; Easter–Sept Mon–Sat 10.30am–6.30pm, Sun 2–6pm; free) tells the story of the saint through an audio-visual display.

A choice of routes

The traveller could turn southeast from Letterkenny and head through little-known east Donegal. If the mood takes you, a tour of the 18th-century courthouse and jail in **Lifford** will fill you in on the severe punishment meted out and the grim conditions endured by the inmates (tel: 074-914 1733; www.liffordoldcourthouse.com; Mon–Fri 9am–5 .30pm, Sun 12.30–4.30pm; charge).

At **Raphoe**, a well-signposted 20-minute drive from Letterkenny off

TIP

Going to the dogs
Fans from both sides of the border flock to **Lifford Greyhound Stadium** on Saturdays (7.40pm) and Sundays (6pm). The stadium has been modernised and there are a variety of restaurants and bars (tel: 074-914 1083; www.lifford greyhounds.com).

BELOW: Dunfanaghy Workhouse.

WHERE

Tourism in the Inishowen area has been boosted by the Foyle Ferry between Greencastle and Magilligan Point in Co. Derry. A year-round shuttle service operates on the route (www.loughfoyleferry.com; 074-938 1901). In the summer months a regular ferry service also operates across Lough Swilly from Buncrana on the west side of Inishowen across to Rathmullan on the Fanad peninsula. Both options avoid the long drive around the lough shores.

the N13, those interested in archaeology will want to inspect the impressive 64-stone **Beltany Stone Circle**, a Celtic ritual site (tel: 074-912 1160). Back on the N13 travelling south, the road transverses the rugged Barnesmore Gap, a scenic mountain pass that cuts through the Blue Stack Mountains. For centuries the gap has been a strategic gateway between northern and southern parts of County Donegal, hence, up to about 1800, it was the notorious haunt of brigands and highwaymen.

To the north of Letterkenny a choice of routes presents itself. One option is to follow the N56 southeast from Dunfanaghy, then take the R245 north chasing the Atlantic Drive past the golfer's haven of Rosapenna around Mulroy Bay with its farmed mussel rafts and salmon cages. Continue around windswept Fanad Head, then south again to Rathmullan, from whence, in 1607, the leading clan chiefs took flight by ship for Spain. Their story is recalled in the **Flight of the Earls Heritage Centre** (tel: 074-915 8131; June–Sept Mon–Sat 10am–6pm, Sun 12.30–6pm; charge).

Beyond, 7 miles (11km) southwest, is charmingly preserved, riverside **Ramelton**, in whose Heritage Centre you can find your local roots – should you have any – in Donegal Ancestry (tel: 074-915 1266; www.donegalancestry.com; June–Sept Mon–Fri 9.30am–5pm, July–mid-Sept also Sat; free): thence to Letterkenny again. From here it's a tempting run northwest, for 16 miles (26km), to the 4,000-year-old **Grianán of Aileach**, a spectacular circular stone enclosure atop an 800ft (240-metre) mound. Its name is translated, controversially, as "sun-palace".

BELOW: at Malin Head.

Buncrana

Even more tempting now is the drive 40 miles (64km) north to Ireland's most northerly point, **Malin Head** on the **Inishowen peninsula.** On the way there are a number of attractions to entice the visitor. Along the shores of Lough Swilly, military historians will want to see the Fort Dunree Military Museum near **Buncrana** ㉗ (tel: 074-936 1817; www.dunree.pro.ie; charge) which has a heritage centre with an underground bunker and an extensive collection of military artefacts and memorabilia.

Further along near Ballyliffin, stop off at the **Doagh Island Famine Village** where the charge includes a guided tour with tea and coffee, soda bread and biscuits (tel: 074-937 8078; www.doaghfaminevillage.com; Easter–Sept Mon–Sun 10am–5pm; charge) for a thought-provoking look at the past.

On the other side of the peninsula, and for some deeper contemplation and reflection, call in to the **Iosas Centre** in Muff to visit the Celtic prayer garden (www.columbacommunity.com). The **Inishowen Maritime Museum and Planetarium** (tel: 074-938 1363; www.inishowenmaritime.com; daily 9.30am–5.30pm; charge,) is drawing in visitors to Greencastle. As well as the emphasis on astronomy, dazzling laser light shows are performed live here every weekend in summer, accompanied by recorded traditional and modern Irish music.

Most of Buncrana's many pubs have live music at weekends. ❑

RESTAURANTS AND PUBS

Restaurants

Prices for a three-course dinner per person without wine:
€ = under €25
€€ = €25–40
€€€ = €40–55
€€€€ = over €55

County Donegal

Annagry

Danny Minnie's Restaurant
The Rosses, Annagry, Co. Donegal (close to airport)
Tel: 074-954 8201
D June–Sept Mon–Sat 6–10pm, Oct–May Thur–Sat 6–10pm **€€€**
Delightful decor, relaxed atmosphere, excellent and imaginative cooking. Set dinner and a wide-ranging à la carte menu.

Ballyshannon

Herons Cove
Rossnowlagh Road, Ballyshannon, Co. Donegal
Tel: 071-982 2070
Easter–May Fri–Sat 1–10pm, June–Sept Thur–Sun 1–10pm. L **€**, D **€€**
Close to a lovely beach and the picturesque harbour at Creevy Pier, this family-run restaurant is a haven of the best Irish cuisine and hospitality. The tasteful dining room provides a relaxing setting to enjoy some of the finest steaks and fresh seafood in Donegal.

Buncrana

The Beach House Bar & Restaurant
The Pier Swilly Road, Buncrana, Co. Donegal
Tel: 074-936 1050
Daily, L noon–4pm, winter Fri–Sun, D 5–10pm, winter Wed–Sun, closed last 3 weeks in Jan. L **€€**, D **€€**
In a gorgeous spot right on the pier with great views across Lough Swilly, the head chef Niall Gorham cooks exciting dishes and sources as much local and organic produce as possible; the fish is as fresh as it comes.

Donegal

Aroma
The Craft Village, Donegal, Co. Donegal
Tel: 074-972 3222
Mon–Sat 9.30am–5.30pm **€**
All-day café and bakery that offers more than tea and cakes. The seasonally driven blackboard menu leans towards modern Mediterranean-style.

Dunfanaghy

The Mill Restaurant
Figart, Dunfanaghy, Co. Donegal
Tel: 074-913 6985
D Tue–Sun 7–9pm, check opening days off-season. D **€€€**
A place of character with family art, antiques, comfort and views. Accomplished, creative cooking.

Rathmullan

Weeping Elm Restaurant
Rathmullan House, Co. Donegal
Tel: 074-915 8188
Restaurant: daily 7am–8.45pm, later Fri–Sat **€€€**; Batts Bar and Café: 1pm–2.30am **€€**: Cellar Bar: July–Aug daily 12.30–7pm **€€**
A lovely 19th-century house set in a stunning location on the shores of Lough Swilly. Exceptional food based on natural ingredients. Children's menu.

County Leitrim

Carrick-on-Shannon

Boarwalk Café
Landmark Hotel, Dublin Road, Carrick-on-Shannon, Co. Leitrim
Tel: 071-962 2222
Daily, L noon–4pm, D 5–9pm. L **€€**, D **€€€**
Choose from a wide-ranging innovative menu of well-cooked, unpretentious dishes. The dining space blends neon lighting with wood floors and cobblestone walkways.

Oarsman Café/bar
Bridge Street, Carrick-on-Shannon, Co. Leitrim
Tel: 071-962 1733
L Tue–Sat noon–3pm, D Thur–Sat 5–9. L **€**, D **€€**
Riverside location, full of character, family run, combining traditional pub with comfortable informal dining areas. Great desserts.

Victorian Hall
Quay Road, Carrick-on-Shannon, Co. Leitrim
Tel: 071-962 0320
Daily, L 12.30–5pm, D 5–10pm. L **€**, D **€€**
Stylishly converted Victorian hall near the waterfront. Well-executed Thai and Irish dishes – a feature is the boxty wrap, a potato pancake associated with Irish cooking.

County Sligo

Castlebaldwin

Clevery Mill
Castlebaldwin, Co. Sligo
Tel: 071-912 7424
L Sun 12.30–4pm, D Fri–Sat 6.30–9.30pm. L **€€**, D **€€€**
Deep in the heart of the countryside, the lantern-lit dining room has intimate alcoves and views of an 18th-century waterwheel. The kitchen tempts with a mix of modern Irish dishes using local ingredients.

Moira's Restaurant
Cromleach Lodge, Castlebaldwin, Co. Sligo
Tel: 071-916 5155
Daily, informal food: 11.30am–6pm, L noon–4pm, D 6–9pm. L **€€**, D **€€€**
With great views over Lough Arrow this elegant restaurant offers enticing choices of carefully sourced Irish food.

Sligo

Montmartre
1 Market Yard, Sligo, Co. Sligo
Tel: 071-916 9901
D Tue–Sun 5–11pm **€€**; Early Bird 5–7pm **€**
Owner/chef is French and this leading restaurant pleases locals and homesick French visitors. Children welcome.

Pubs

Sheermore Inn at Kilclare, Co. Leitrim, gives a glimpse of the past, combining a bar, grocery and hardware shop on the banks of the Shannon-Erne waterway.

Nancy's Bar in Ardara (the Donegal tweed village). Run by the same family for seven generations it's a haven of warmth and impromptu live music on many evenings during peak season. Wholesome bar food. **€**.

Austie's, Rosses Point, Co. Sligo. Packed with nautical memorabilia this 200-year-old pub is a quiet daytime place. Traditional music on Sunday evenings.

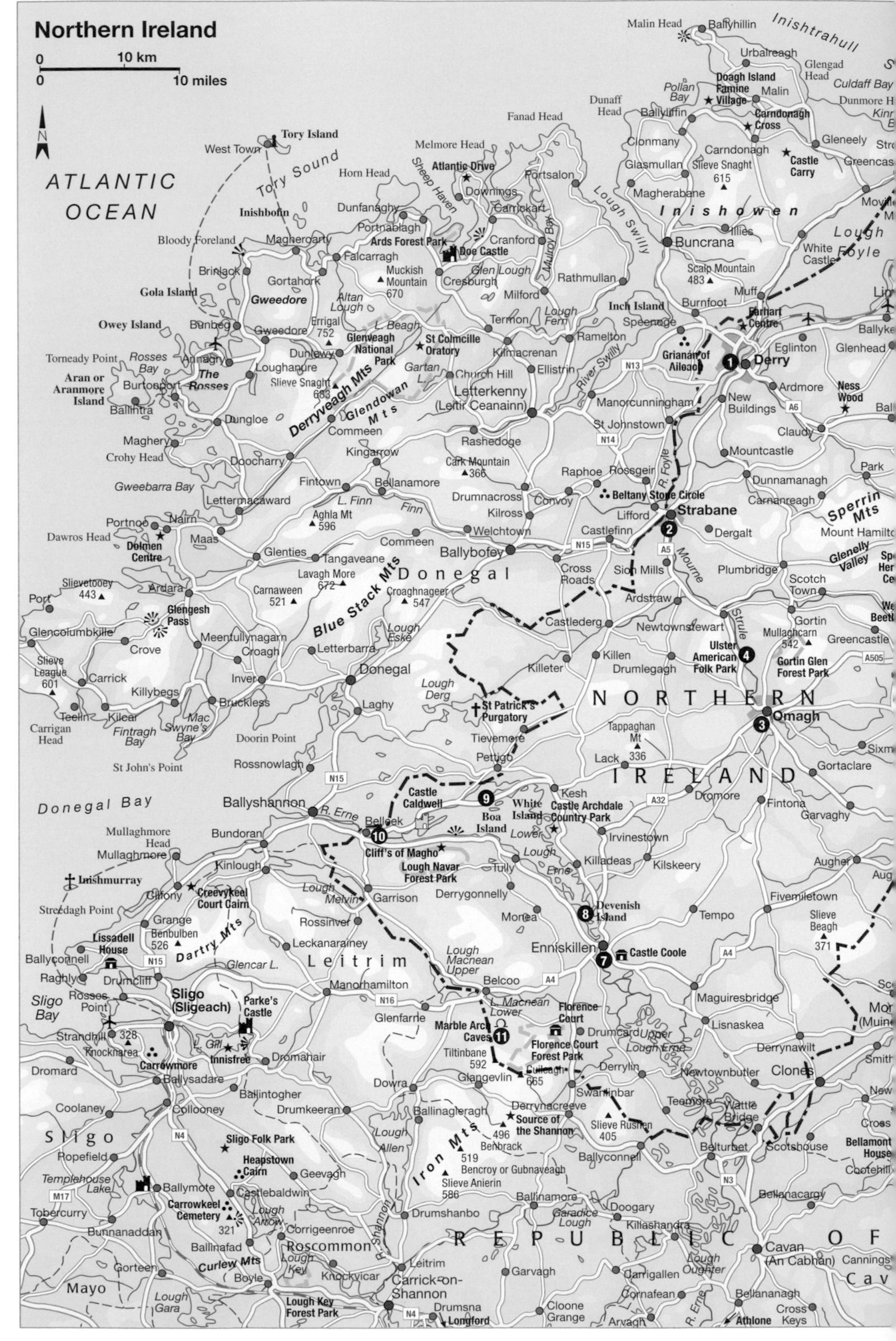
Northern Ireland
0 10 km
0 10 miles
N
ATLANTIC OCEAN
Tory Island
West Town
Tory Sound
Inishbofin
Bloody Foreland
Horn Head
Dunfanaghy
Magheroarty
Portnablagh
Ards Forest Park
Doe Castle
Falcarragh
Brinlack
Gortahork
Gola Island
Gweedore
Muckish Mountain 670
Altan Lough
Errigal 752
Owey Island
Bunbeg
Gweedore
L. Beagh
Glenveagh National Park
St Colmcille Oratory
Torneady Point
Rosses Bay
Annagry
The Rosses
Aran or Aranmore Island
Burtonport
Ballintra
Dunlewy
Loughanure
Slieve Snaght 683
Derryveagh Mts
Glendowan Mts
Gartan L.
Church Hill
Letterkenny (Leitir Ceanainn)
Dungloe
Maghery
Crohy Head
Commeen
Kingarrow
Doocharry
Gweebarra Bay
Lettermacaward
Fintown
Bellanamore
L. Finn
Finn
Aghla Mt 596
Portnoo
Nairn
Dawros Head
Dolmen Centre
Maas
Glenties
Tangaveane
Commeen
Slievetooey 443
Ardara
Port
Carnaween 521
Lavagh More 672
Blue Stack Mts
Croaghnageer 547
Glengesh Pass
Glencolumbkille
Crove
Meenfullynagarn
Croagh
Lough Eske
Letterbarra
Slieve League 601
Carrick
Killybegs
Inver
Donegal
Bruckless
Teelin
Kilcar
Carrigan Head
Fintragh Bay
Mac Swyne's Bay
Doorin Point
St John's Point
Rossnowlagh
Laghy
Lough Derg
Donegal Bay
Ballyshannon
R. Erne
Belleek
Mullaghmore Head
Mullaghmore
Bundoran
Kinlough
Inishmurray
Cliffs of Magho
Lough Navar Forest Park
Castle Caldwell
Boa Island
White Island
Lower Lough Erne
Castle Archdale Country Park
Gilfony
Creevykeel Court Cairn
Streedagh Point
Grange
Benbulben 526
Dartry Mts
Lissadell House
Ballyconnell
Raghly
Drumcliff
Glencar L.
Lough Melvin
Garrison
Rossinver
Leckanarainey
Leitrim
Derrygonnelly
Tully
Monea
Devenish Island
Enniskillen
Castle Coole
Lough Macnean Upper
Sligo Bay
Rosses Point
Sligo (Sligeach)
Parke's Castle
Manorhamilton
Belcoo
L. Macnean Lower
Florence Court
Marble Arch Caves
Florence Court Forest Park
Strandhill 328
Knocknarea
Carrowmore
L. Gill
Innisfree
Dromahair
Glenfarne
Tiltinbane 592
Cuilcagh 665
Glangevlin
Dromard
Ballysadare
Ballintogher
Coolaney
Collooney
Drumkeeran
Dowra
Ballinagleragh
Derrynacreeve
Source of the Shannon
Swanlinbar
Slieve Rushen 405
Sligo
Ropefield
Sligo Folk Park
Lough Allen
Iron Mts
496 Benbrack
519 Bencroy or Gubnaveagh
Slieve Anierin 586
Heapstown Cairn
Geevagh
Templehouse Lake
Ballymote
Castlebaldwin
Carrowkeel Cemetery 321
Lough Arrow
Tobercurry
Bunnanaddan
Corrigeenroe
Ballinafad
Curlew Mts
Roscommon
Lough Key
Knockvicar
Boyle
Gorteen
Mayo
Lough Gara
Lough Key Forest Park
Leitrim
Carrick-on-Shannon
R. Shannon
Drumshanbo
Drumsna
Longford
Ballinamore
Garadice Lough
Garvagh
Cloone Grange
Arvagh
Ballyconnell
Doogary
Killashandra
REPUBLIC OF
Carrigallen
Cornafean
Lough Oughter
R. Erne
Cavan (An Cabhan)
Bellananagh
Cross Keys
Athlone
Cannings
Cav
Malin Head
Ballyhillin
Inishtrahull
Urbalreagh
Glengad Head
Culdaff Bay
Dunmore H
Pollan Bay
Doagh Island Famine Village
Malin
Carndonagh Cross
Dunaff Head
Ballyliffin
Fanad Head
Melmore Head
Atlantic Drive
Sheep Haven
Downings
Carrickart
Portsalon
Lough Swilly
Clonmany
Carndonagh
Castle Carry
Gleneely
Glasmullan
Slieve Snaght 615
Greencas
Magherabane
Inishowen
Buncrana
Illies
Lough Foyle
White Castle
Cranford
Mulroy Bay
Glen Lough
Cresburgh
Rathmullan
Scalp Mountain 483
Milford
Lough Fern
Muff
Burnfoot
Inch Island
Speenoge
Farhart Centre
Termon
Ramelton
Kilmacrenan
Grianan of Aileach
Derry
Eglinton
Glenhead
Ellistrin
River Swilly
Ardmore
Ness Wood
New Buildings
Manorcunningham
St Johnstown
Claudy
Rashedoge
Mountcastle
Cark Mountain 366
R. Foyle
Raphoe
Rossgeir
Park
Dunnamanagh
Drumnacross
Convoy
Beltany Stone Circle
Kilross
Lifford
Strabane
Carnanreagh
Sperrin Mts
Welchtown
Castlefinn
Dergalt
Mount Hamilto
Commeen
Ballybofey
Donegal
Cross Roads
Sion Mills
Mourne
Plumbridge
Glenelly Valley
Scotch Town
Ardstraw
Castlederg
Newtownstewart
Strule
Gortin
Mullaghcarn 542
Greencastle
Ulster American Folk Park
Gortin Glen Forest Park
Killen
Drumlegagh
Killeter
NORTHERN IRELAND
Omagh
St Patrick's Purgatory
Tappaghan Mt 336
Tievemore
Pettigo
Lack
Gortaclare
Kesh
Dromore
Fintona
Garvaghy
Irvinestown
Killadeas
Kilskeery
Augher
Fivemiletown
Tempo
Slieve Beagh 371
Maguiresbridge
Lisnaskea
Drumcard
Upper Lough Erne
Derrynawilt
Derrylin
Newtownbutler
Clones
Teemore
Wattle Bridge
Belturbet
Scotshouse
Bellamont House
Cootehill
Bellanacargy
N13
N14
N15
A5
A6
A32
A505
A4
N15
N16
N4
M17
N3
N4
A4

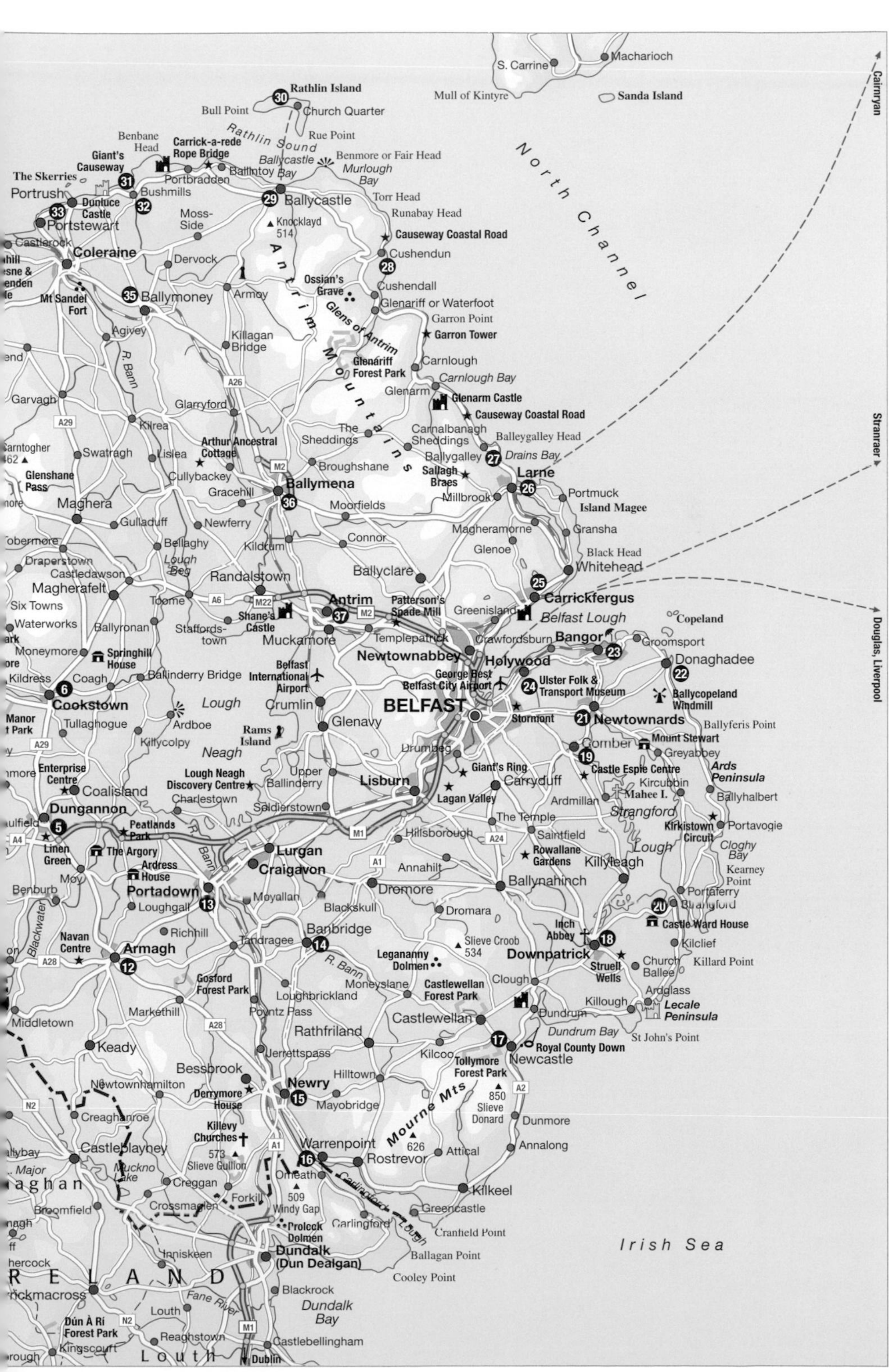
S. Carrine
Macharioch
Mull of Kintyre
Sanda Island
Cairnryan
Rathlin Island
Bull Point
Church Quarter
Rue Point
Rathlin Sound
Benbane Head
Carrick-a-rede Rope Bridge
Giant's Causeway
Ballycastle Bay
Benmore or Fair Head
Murlough Bay
The Skerries
Ballintoy
Portbradden
Portrush
Bushmills
Dunluce Castle
Ballycastle
Torr Head
Runabay Head
Moss-Side
Knocklayd 514
Portstewart
Castlerock
Causeway Coastal Road
Cushendun
Coleraine
Dervock
Antrim Mountains
North Channel
Ossian's Grave
Cushendall
Glenariff or Waterfoot
Mt Sandel Fort
Ballymoney
Armoy
Garron Point
Garron Tower
Glens of Antrim
Agivey
Killagan Bridge
R. Bann
Glenariff Forest Park
Carnlough
Carnlough Bay
A26
Garvagh
Glenarm
Glenarm Castle
Glarryford
A29
Kilrea
Causeway Coastal Road
The Sheddings
Carnalbanagh Sheddings
Balleygalley Head
Swatragh
Lislea
Arthur Ancestral Cottage
Ballygalley
Drains Bay
Stranraer
Glenshane Pass
Cullybackey
M2
Broughshane
Sallagh Braes
Larne
Ballymena
Gracehill
Millbrook
Portmuck
Island Magee
Maghera
Moorfields
Gulladuff
Newferry
Magheramorne
Gransha
Tobermore
Bellaghy
Kildrum
Connor
Glenoe
Black Head
Draperstown
Lough Beg
Whitehead
Castledawson
Randalstown
Ballyclare
Magherafelt
Carrickfergus
Six Towns
Toome
A6
M22
Antrim
Patterson's Spade Mill
Greenisland
Belfast Lough
Copeland
Waterworks
Ballyronan
Shane's Castle
M2
Douglas, Liverpool
Staffords-town
Muckamore
Templepatrick
Crawfordsburn
Bangor
Groomsport
Moneymore
Springhill House
Newtownabbey
Holywood
Donaghadee
Belfast International Airport
George Best Belfast City Airport
Kildress
Coagh
Ballinderry Bridge
Ulster Folk & Transport Museum
Ballycopeland Windmill
Cookstown
Lough
Crumlin
BELFAST
Stormont
Newtownards
Ballyferis Point
Tullaghogue
Ardboe
Glenavy
Rams Island
Killycolpy
Drumbeg
Comber
Mount Stewart
A29
Neagh
Greyabbey
Giant's Ring
Castle Espie Centre
Ards Peninsula
Enterprise Centre
Upper Ballinderry
Lough Neagh Discovery Centre
Lisburn
Carryduff
Kircubbin
Coalisland
Charlestown
Lagan Valley
Ardmillan
Mahee I.
Ballyhalbert
Dungannon
Soldierstown
Strangford
The Temple
A4
Peatlands Park
M1
Hillsborough
Kirkistown Circuit
Portavogie
Linen Green
The Argory
Lurgan
A24
Saintfield
Lough
Cloghy Bay
Ardress House
A1
Annahilt
Rowallane Gardens
Killyleagh
Kearney Point
Benburb
Moy
Craigavon
Portadown
Dromore
Ballynahinch
Portaferry
Moyallan
Blackskull
Loughgall
Dromara
Castle Ward House
Inch Abbey
Blackwater
Richhill
Banbridge
Slieve Croob 534
Navan Centre
Armagh
Tandragee
Kilclief
A28
R. Bann
Leganany Dolmen
Downpatrick
Church Ballee
Killard Point
Struell Wells
Gosford Forest Park
Moneyslane
Castlewellan Forest Park
Clough
Loughbrickland
Ardglass
Markethill
Poyntz Pass
Killough
Lecale Peninsula
Middletown
A28
Dundrum
Castlewellan
Rathfriland
Dundrum Bay
St John's Point
Keady
Jerrettspass
Kilcoo
Royal County Down
Newcastle
Bessbrook
Tollymore Forest Park
Hilltown
Newtownhamilton
Newry
A2
Derrymore House
Mourne Mts
850 Slieve Donard
Mayobridge
N2
Creaghanroe
Dunmore
Killevy Churches
626
Warrenpoint
Annalong
Castleblayney
A1
Rostrevor
Attical
573 Slieve Gullion
Muckno Lake
Omeath
Creggan
509
Kilkeel
Forkill
Carlingford Lough
Windy Gap
Crossmaglen
Greencastle
Broomfield
Proleek Dolmen
Carlingford
Cranfield Point
Irish Sea
Inniskeen
Dundalk (Dun Dealgan)
Ballagan Point
Cooley Point
Blackrock
Fane River
Dundalk Bay
Louth
Dún Á Rí Forest Park
N2
M1
Reaghstown
Kingscourt
Castlebellingham
Louth
Dublin

NORTHERN IRELAND

The visual evidence of Northern Ireland's civil strife is increasingly hard to find. But the traditional attractions are as alluring as ever: the gorgeous lakes and glens, the stunning coastline and a wealth of golf courses

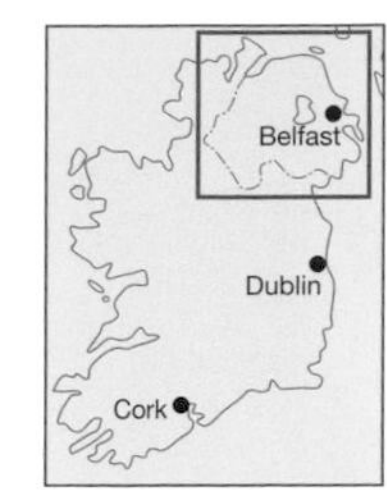

To the surprise of visitors, passports were never required to travel between the Republic and Northern Ireland and they are certainly not needed today as both territories are part of the EU, and the peace process has bought more stability. Indeed, it can be hard to tell when you've crossed the border. Perhaps you'll notice that post boxes and phone booths are no longer green but red, and prices change from euros to pounds. But that's about it.

The troublesome border

One reason it is so difficult to be sure of the border's exact location is that it snakes its way along 18th-century county boundaries through farming land that is sometimes bleak, more often beautiful. It takes little account of natural boundaries, such as rivers, or of the cultural differences that separate Republican-minded Roman Catholics and British-oriented Protestants. A priest may find part of his parish on one side of the border, the rest on the other. Houses straddle it so that, as the joke has it, a man may sleep with his head in the United Kingdom and his heart in the Republic of Ireland.

Political expediency accounts for the absurdities. It had been intended to redraw the border rationally after partition in 1920, and a Boundary Commission was set up to advise. But in the end the British and Irish governments, hoping to avoid further trouble, suppressed the commission's report and left things as they were. Had they decided differently, much of the subsequent conflict might have been averted.

Much confusion was created. Whereas the ancient Irish province of Ulster consisted of nine counties, the new state of Northern Ireland, popularly known as Ulster, consisted of only six: **Antrim**, **Down**, **Armagh**, **Derry**, **Fermanagh** and **Tyrone**. Yet the three counties that went to the Republic –

Main attractions

- DERRY CITY
- STRABANE
- ULSTER-AMERICAN FOLK PARK
- PEATLANDS PARK
- ENNISKILLEN CASTLE
- DEVENISH ISLAND
- BELLEEK
- MARBLE ARCH CAVES
- ARMAGH
- BRONTË INTERPRETIVE CENTRE
- MOURNE MOUNTAINS
- DOWNPATRICK
- STRANGFORD LOUGH
- MOUNT STEWART
- ULSTER FOLK AND TRANSPORT MUSEUM
- CAUSEWAY COASTAL ROAD
- GIANT'S CAUSEWAY

LEFT: the Giant's Causeway. **RIGHT:** dual signage in Armagh.

Derry's symblic Hands Across the Divide *sculpture by Maurice Harron.*

Donegal, **Cavan** and **Monaghan** – are still bound to the other six by firm family and trading ties. To many locals, therefore, the border is an abstraction. And indeed it's hard to take it seriously when the states it divides can't even agree about its length, the Republic claiming it is 280 miles (448km) and Northern Ireland authorities adamant that it is 303 miles (485km).

Following on from the preceding coverage of Donegal, this chapter begins in Derry and proceeds counter-clockwise round the province. Belfast is given a chapter of its own.

Old Derry's walls

Across the border from Donegal, is the county of Londonderry and its famously friendly chief city, Northern Ireland's second, whose very name has long been a bone of contention for its main two communities. Catholics refer to Derry, for both county and city, while Protestants stick to Londonderry, with officialdom increasingly resorting to the clumsy **Derry/Londonderry ❶** in a nervous effort to maintain neutrality, resulting in local broadcaster Gerry Anderson to nickname it "Stroke City". The 19th-century Scottish historian Thomas Carlyle called it "the prettiest looking town I have seen in Ireland" and, though it was scarred by the Troubles, there has been increasing redevelopment since the peace process kicked in during the 1990s. Today the changing skyline attracts more international visitors than ever to Londonderry, a centre of culture and creativity famous for its confident outlook.

But the city, rising each side of the River Foyle, doesn't set out to be a calendar girl; it prefers to provide exhilarating company, and it succeeds. There has

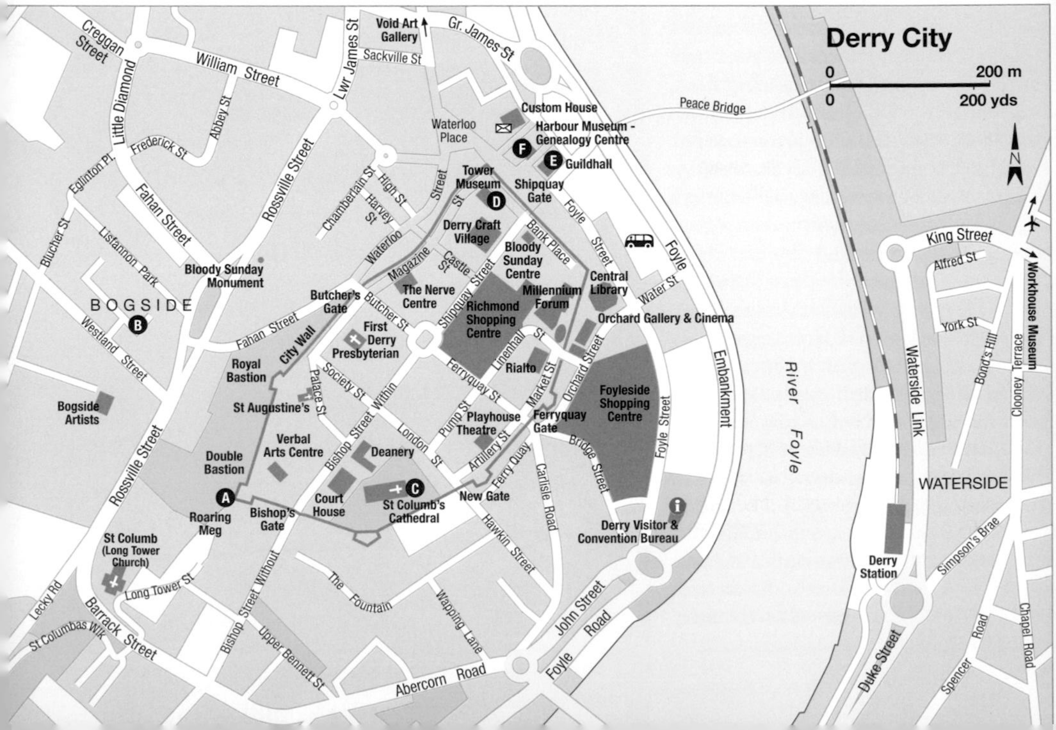

Derry City

0 200 m
0 200 yds

been a renaissance in community activity, especially in the arts, and, in recent years, it has made great efforts to oblige the visitor with new attractions and major festivals such as the Halloween Carnival and the City of Derry Jazz and Big Band Festival in April/May.

The city's growth was financed by London guilds, which in 1613 began creating the last walled city in Europe. Its purpose was mercantile success and you can still see traces of its former economic confidence in the ornamental facades of the old shirt-making factories, which provided the city with its livelihood for generations.

The walls, 20ft (6 metres) thick and complete with watch-towers and cannon such as the 18-pounder **Roaring Meg** **A** (dating from 1642), are marvellously intact (Tours tel: 028-7134 7176; charge, otherwise free access).

The Bogside

Two 17th-century sieges failed to breach the walls, earning the sobriquet "maiden city". Some say the city still has a siege mentality, a theory reinforced by the IRA's daubed slogan "You are now entering Free Derry." This was the name given to the **Bogside** **B**, a densely populated Roman Catholic housing estate, when its inhabitants barricaded it against the police in 1969. Their grievances were old ones. After Ireland's partition in 1920, the city's governing Unionists had fixed constituency boundaries to ensure a "permanent" majority for themselves in what was a mainly nationalist area – an artificial majority that wasn't overturned until the mid-1970s. Feeling isolated from the prosperous eastern counties, Derry's citizens built up both a wonderful community spirit and a resentment that finally boiled over. A good way to experience the political history of the Bogside is to visit the **Bogside Artists** (46 Derry Street; tel: 028-7137 3842; www.bogsideartists.com), whose studio is in the centre of the area. Guided tours of all 12 murals are available. For more on the people's story of the civil rights movement visit the Museum of Free Derry (55 Glenfada

Derry's Guildhall.

BELOW: Celtic, a Scottish football team, has a historic connection with the people of Ireland.

City of Culture

Derry/Londonderry is buzzing with excitement and pride after winning their bid for 2013 City of Culture, a date which will also commemorate 400 years of the founding of the city walls. The city was shortlisted alongside Birmingham, Norwich and Sheffield and citizens waited until July 2010 for the winner to be announced.

Derry's regeneration plans, still under way, put arts and culture at the heart of its redevelopment, with a focus on harnessing the creative energy that now pulses through the modern city. Scooping the prestigious title is considered an important opportunity to share the diversity of the area and its extraordinary history with the rest of the world; as well as demonstrate that the city, emerging from the shadow of its past, now deserves to shine.

The Planter's Gothic-style St Columb's Cathedral.

Park, Bogside; tel: 028-7136 0880; www.museumoffreederry.org; Mon–Fri 9.30am–4.30pm, Apr–Sept Sat 1–4pm, also July–Sept Sun 1–4pm; charge).

The most famous siege – which is still commemorated by Protestant marches today – took place in 1689, when the Catholic forces of James II blockaded the Protestant supporters of William of Orange for 15 weeks, almost forcing them into submission. About 7,000 of the 30,000 people packed within the city's walls died of disease or starvation. One member of the besieged garrison chillingly recorded the selling prices of horse-flesh, dogs' heads, cats and rats "fattened by eating the bodies of the slain Irish."

The city's eventual relief is depicted on the siege memorial window of **St Columb's Cathedral** **C** (London Street; tel: 028-7126 7313; donation) a graceful 17th-century Anglican church built in "Planter's Gothic" style. The chapter house contains siege relics. Outside the walls, off Bishop Street Without, St Columba's Long Tower Church (tel: 028-7126 2301; free), built 1784, and known just as Long Tower Church, has a lavish interior.

The award-winning **Tower Museum** **D** (Union Hall Place; tel: 028-7137 2411; www.derrycity.gov.uk/museums; Tue–Sat 10am–5pm, with exceptions July–Aug; charge) skilfully uses audio-visuals and photography to tell its story from both sides of the sectarian divide. There's also an exhibition on the recovery of a ship from the 1588 Spanish Armada, wrecked off Donegal's coast.

BELOW: Apprentice Boys prepare to parade to celebrate the ending of the siege of Londonderry in 1689.

The Guildhall

Streets from the city's original four gates (Shipquay, Ferryquay, Bishop's and Butcher's) converge on The Diamond, a perversely square-shaped market place at the top of Shipquay Street, the steepest main thoroughfare in Ireland. At the bottom of the street, the **Guildhall** **E** (Guildhall Square; tel: 028-7137 7335; Mon–Fri 9am–5pm; free), one of those Tudor-Gothic structures popular in Northern Ireland, clearly shows the influence of the London merchants.

Behind the Guildhall is Derry Quay, celebrated in song by hundreds of thousands of emigrants who sailed down the Foyle from here, bound for a new life in America. The city's maritime past is covered in the **Harbour Museum** **F** (Harbour Square; tel: 028-7137 7331; www.derrycity.gov.uk/museums; Mon–Fri 10am–1pm, 2–4.30pm; charge); see a replica of a 30ft (9-metre) curragh in which St Columba sailed to Iona in AD 563.

Across the river, the **Workhouse Museum** at 23 Glendermott Road (tel: 028-7131 8328; www.derrycity.gov.uk/museums; Mon–Thur and Sat 10am–5pm; free) has exhibitions on the Famine, Victorian poverty and a memorial exhibition on the role of the city in the Battle of the Atlantic and World War II.

There are now various tours to guide you around the city and its environs. The best place to enquire about these and all other tourist information is the **Derry Visitor and Convention Bureau**

(44 Foyle Street; tel: 028-7126 7284; www.derryvisitor.com), who also run their own walking tours of the city. Free Derry Tours (Gasyard Centre, Lecky Road, Brandywell; tel: 028-7126 2812) takes you through the history of the Bogside and Fountainwell areas, pivotal locations during the Troubles. Tours begin at 10am and 2pm daily. Open-top bus tours are a big draw on rainless days (Top Tours Ireland, 6 Pinetrees; tel: 077-9116 4431), leaving from the Guildhall seven days a week from 10am to 4pm. You can also now take yourself on a digital "Walled City to Wireless City" tour with a handset that delivers a multimedia background to the historic walls (available from Tourist Information).

VOID (Patrick Street; tel: 028-7130 8080; www.derryvoid.com) showcases both established Irish and international artists in some eight exhibitions a year in its two galleries and six studios, while the **Verbal Arts Centre** (Stable Lane and Mall Wall; tel: 028-7126 6946; www.verbalartscentre.co.uk) is the only centre in Ireland dedicated to all kinds of literature. Many in the city's resurgent arts community have links to the **Nerve Centre** (7–8 Magazine Street; tel: 028-7126 0562; www.nerve-centre.org.uk), which also stages live music and film festivals, and arts activities. A dynamic programme of events from drama and dance to comedy and musicals is hosted at the **Millennium Forum** (Newmarket Street; tel: 028-7126 4455) and the renovated **Playhouse** (5–7 Artillery Street; tel: 028-7126 8027; www.derryplayhouse.co.uk). The latter, which houses the Context Art Gallery and various theatre and dance companies, hosts Northern Ireland's biggest comedy festival, "The Big Tickle", each September.

Craft Village

Shoppers will find plenty of modern centres to keep them occupied but perhaps the most engaging destination is the **Craft Village** at the bottom of Shipquay Street, a historic recreation of the city between the 16th and 19th centuries with various workshops and shops relating to traditional crafts.

About 8 miles (13km) from the city centre, the City of Derry Airport has scheduled flights to London, Glasgow, Liverpool, East Midlands and Dublin.

TIP

Tracing your roots

At the Harbour Museum is the Derry Genealogy Centre (tel: 028-7137 7331), which will, for a fee, assist those tracing their roots in Co. Derry and the Inishowen Peninsula of Donegal.

BELOW: celebrating Hallowe'en in downtown Derry.

TIP

Tracing ancestors
Irish-Americans can often find their ancestor date and port of arrival in the New World by consulting the US National Archives. They can also contact the Public Record Office of Northern Ireland, 66 Balmoral Avenue, Belfast BT9 6NY (tel: +44-28 9025 5905; www.proni.gov.uk). There will be no access to the Public Record Office between September 2010 and May 2011 while the records are moved to new premises located in the Titanic Quarter.

As with many border towns and cities in Northern Ireland, you'll find a general acceptance of euros if you're travelling from the Republic.

Small-town Tyrone

Thirteen miles (21km) southwest of Derry city, in county Tyrone on the A5 is **Strabane** ❷, a border town paired with Lifford on the Donegal side. John Dunlap, printer of America's Declaration of Independence, trained in **Gray's Printing Press** (49 Main Street; tel: 028-8674 8210; restricted opening days, call for details; charge). In Dergalt, 2 miles (3km) to the southeast, signposted off the B47, is a whitewashed cottage, the ancestral home of US president Woodrow Wilson (tel: 028-7138 4444; July–Aug Tue–Sun 2–5pm; free).

Sion Mills, 3 miles (5km) south of Strabane, is a village whose name betrays its origins. The linen-workers' old cottages are charming. The Parish Church of the Good Shepherd is a striking Italian-style edifice, contrasting with the modern architecture of St Teresa's Catholic Church, whose façade displays an image on slate of the Last Supper.

As you drive into **Omagh** ❸, the county town of Tyrone, 16 miles (25km) along the A5, the religious fragmentation of Northern Ireland is immediately apparent. On the right is the Presbyterian Church (Trinity); on the left, the Methodist Church; next, St Columba's Church of Ireland; then the Gothic spires of the Roman Catholic Church of the Sacred Heart, a poor man's Chartres Cathedral. There are many more. The joining of the Rivers Camowen and Drumragh to form the Strule make the location pleasant enough, but Omagh is more a town for living (and praying) in than for visiting. Locals still recall the Saturday afternoon in August 1998 when a maroon Vauxhall Astra exploded in the town, killing 29 people. In its shops, alongside the usual linen souvenirs, are plaques and statuettes made of turf (peat). This is cut from the **Black Bog** between Omagh and Cookstown, 27 miles (43km) to the east.

American connections

During tough times in the 1800s, the area's strong Scots-Presbyterian work ethic spurred many to seek their fortune

BELOW: Ulster-American Folk Park.

in America. The results were remarkable and Northern Ireland claims that 11 US presidents have had roots in the province: Andrew Jackson, James Knox Polk, Andrew Johnson, James Buchanan, Ulysses S. Grant, Chester Alan Arthur, Grover Cleveland, Benjamin Harrison, William McKinley, Theodore Roosevelt and Woodrow Wilson. Many Americans visit to seek out ancestral homes.

The Mellon banking family of Pittsburgh, having traced their roots to 4 miles (6km) north of Omagh, off the A5, endowed the **Ulster-American Folk Park** ❹ on the site at Camphill (tel: 028-8224 3292; www.nmni.com; Mar–Sept Tue–Sun 10am–5pm, Oct–Feb Tue–Fri 10am–6pm; charge) as part of Northern Ireland's contribution to the bicentenary of America. To illuminate the transition made by the 18th-century emigrants, craftsmen's cottages, a schoolhouse, a blacksmith's forge and a Presbyterian meeting-house from the Old World have been rebuilt on a peat bog alongside log cabins, a Pennsylvania farmstead and a covered wagon from the New World. Peat is kept burning in the cottages, and there are demonstrations of candle-making, fish-salting and horse-shoeing as well as periodic "living history" recreations of battles between redcoats and native Americans. An indoor exhibit recreates the main street of an Ulster town 100 years ago, its hardware shop displaying foot warmers and lamp wicks. A replica of an emigrant ship links the continents. There's not a whiff of Disney, due to the attention to detail, though the American "half" looks more prosperous than the original settlers found it. The award-winning park has a number of annual celebrations, including Fourth of July and an Appalachian and bluegrass festival.

A Centre for Migration Studies on the site has a reference library open to the public for research and staff will help with enquiries about migration history.

Relics of old industries

There's nothing Northern Ireland likes better than history, and almost every village in Tyrone – Castlederg, Donaghmore, Fivemiletown, Newtownstewart

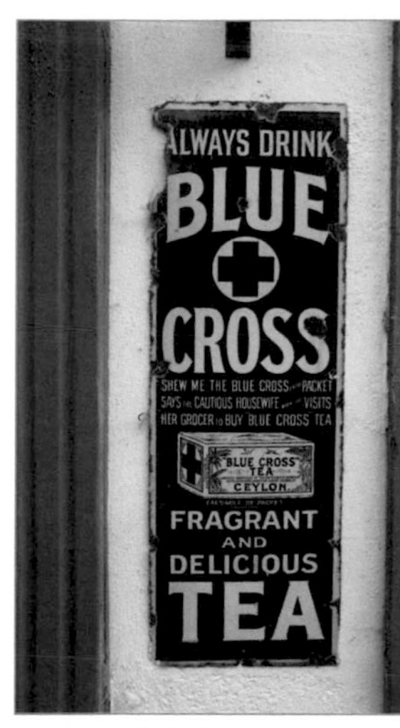

Old advertisement at the Ulster-American Folk Park.

BELOW: television presenter Chris Tarrant and champion fisherman Bob Nudd display their catch.

Peatlands Park
The park is rich in insects, particularly butterflies, moths, dragonflies and damselflies. Many woodland and wetland birds and several species of waterfowl nest here. Grey squirrels, badgers and hares are also here, while lizards and newts can be found in the open bog areas.

– has its heritage centre. One of the more interesting is along the A505 from Omagh. The An Creagan Visitor Centre in **Creggan** (tel: 028-8076 1112; www.an-creagan.com), at the foothills of the blue-tinged Sperrin Mountains, hosts an interpretative exhibition of the area, craft shop, bar/restaurant, self-catering cottages and regular cultural events.

Dungannon

In and around **Dungannon** ❺, 13 miles (21km) south of Cookstown and once the seat of the great O'Neill clan, there are several attractions. One of the more atmospheric places to shop here is the Linen Green (1 The Linen Green; tel: 028-8775 3761; Mon–Sat 10am–5pm) in Moygashel, on the fringes of the town. Based in an old linen mill, it includes a factory outlet of local hero, Paul Costelloe, one of the few leading fashion designers from Northern Ireland. Less than 2 miles (3km) from Dungannon is the village of **Castlecaulfield**, created in the 17th century by Sir Toby Caulfield as part of the Ulster Plantation. It contains the remains of his mansion, where Oliver Plunkett is said to have preached.

BELOW: Tyrone's lush countryside.

Signposted from the M1 motorway, exit 13, 7 miles (11km) east of Dungannon, is **Peatlands Park** (Peatlands Park Centre and Railway; tel: 028-3885 1102; park: Easter–Sept daily 9am–9pm, Oct–Easter 9am–5pm, visitor centre: closed Oct–Easter, miniature railway: Easter–Sept Sat–Sun noon–5pm, June–Aug daily; charge for railway), a unique preservation of the flora and fauna of an Irish bog viewed on foot or from the train *(see margin note)*.

Take the A45 from Dungannon and on the outskirts of Coalisland you will find its **Enterprise Centre**, with its celebration of the Irish bog, the Island Turf Crafts Gift Shop And Visitor Centre (Coalisland Enterprise Centre, 51 Dungannon Road, Coalisland; tel: 028-8774 9041; www.islandturfcrafts.com). There's an indoor bog, a museum exploring Ireland before and after the Ice Age and a shop selling turf crafts. Also at the Enterprise Centre is the **Irish World** genealogy centre (tel: 028-8774 6065; www.irish-world.com), which offers a range of services to people tracing ancestors in Tryone and Fermanagh, and the **Craic Theatre Company** (tel: 028-8774 1100; www.craicartscentre.com). Perhaps Northern Ireland's only (non-council-owned) community theatre, Craic stages everything from Shakespeare to musicals, plus visiting productions from the likes of Dubbeljoint at its 200-seat theatre.

Twenty-five miles (40km) east of Omagh, **Cookstown** ❻, the exact middle of Northern Ireland, is renowned for its main street, 2 miles (3km) long and 160ft (50 metres) wide, and can be located from miles away by the 200ft (61-metre) spire of the Gothic-style Catholic church. The town has a strong tradition of nationalism, often refined in its many old-fashioned pubs. Local livestock sales give a good insight into the rough amiability of the rural Ulster character. Four miles (7km) west, the water-powered **Wellbrook Beetling Mill** (20 Wellbrook Road, Corkhill; tel: 028-8675 1735; July–Aug Sat–Thur 2–6pm, mid-Mar–June and Sept Sat–Sun only; charge) has demonstrations of linen processing by costumed guides. Three miles north of Cookstown, at Moneymore, is a rare treat for lovers of historic costumes. A National Trust property, the 17th century **Springhill House** (tel: 028-8674 8210; July–Aug daily 1–6pm, mid-Mar–June and Sept Sat–Sun 1–6pm; charge) has acquired an award-winning collection of costumes dating from 1690 to the 1930s. The impressive grounds, which house a children's adventure centre, are open daily all year. Look out for the allegedly friendly ghost, Olivia Lenox-Conyngham, a one-time inhabitant of the house.

Just east of Cookstown an 18-hole golf course (200 Killymoon Road; tel: 028-8676 3762) occupies the grounds of **Killymoon Castle**, designed in 1803 by John Nash, architect of London's Regent Street. Some years ago, a farmer bought the castle, then derelict, for £100.

Many Neolithic graves and stone circles are sprinkled around both towns. The best are at **Beaghmore**, (free access) 10 miles (16km) west of Cookstown, off the A505. Villages such as **Clogher** and **Coagh**, **Moneymore** and **Pomeroy** are noted for fine traditional musicians and a variety of ecclesiastical architecture. There's a run-down air about some, the result of chronic unemployment. But it's as well to remember writer John Broderick's advice in *The Pilgrimage*: "The city dweller who passes through a country town and imagines it sleepy and apathetic is very far from the truth: it is watchful as the jungle."

The poet Seamus Heaney is celebrated near his native village at the 17th-century fortified house Bellaghy Bawn (Bellaghy; tel: 028-7938 6812; Easter–Sept Wed–Sun 10am–5pm, Oct–Easter Wed 10am–4pm, Sun noon–4pm; charge). Much of Heaney's poetry derives its imagery and colloquial language from his rural upbringing in this part of Northern Ireland.

Ulster's lakeland

To the southwest, **Fermanagh**, adjacent to Monaghan and Cavan, has many things in common with them, particularly its tempo. Politically it is part of Northern Ireland and is the province's lakeland playground: a third of it is under water. But political divisions are less of a barrier these days: the restoration of the

TIP

Seamus Heaney

The best introduction to Heaney's rich and allusive poetry is through his early collections *Death of a Naturalist* (1966) and *North* (1979). In 1999 he published an acclaimed translation of the Old English heroic poem *Beowolf*.

BELOW: uncrowded cruising on Fermanagh's lakes.

Devenish Island.

Ballinamore–Ballyconnell cross-border canal means that you can now travel all the way here from Limerick by inland waterway.

Enniskillen

The county town, **Enniskillen** ❼, a Protestant stronghold since Tudor times, is built on an island between two channels of the River Erne as it flows from **Upper** to **Lower Lough Erne**. In summer, pleasure boats (MV *Kestrel*, Round O Quay; tel: 028-6632 2882; www.ernetoursltd.com; June–Aug daily 2.15 and 4.15pm, May, Sept, Oct Tue, Sat, Sun; with exceptions) ply the lakes, and visitors cruise them in hired craft (Manor House Marine, Killadeas; tel: 028-6862 8100; www.manormarine.com).

The town's strategic importance is shown by **Enniskillen Castle** (Castle Barracks; tel: 028-6632 5000; July–Aug daily 2–5pm, May, June and Sept Mon–Sat, Oct–Apr Mon–Fri; charge). The earliest parts date from the 15th century and the imposing water gate from the late 16th century. The castle houses two museums, one specialising in prehistory, the other in military relics.

Enniskillen is rich in small bakeries and butcher's shops, and there's a gossipy atmosphere as farmers mix with townsfolk in Blakes of the Hollow, one of the North's finest pubs. A secret is soon shared in such a place. Adjoining are now two excellent restaurants, Café Merlot and Restaurant 6. Confusingly, the main street, best viewed from the head of the 108 stairs of **Cole's Monument** (Forthill Park; tel: 028-6632 3110; mid-Apr–Sept 1.30–3pm; charge) changes its name six times between the bridges at either end. One of the best-preserved towns in Northern Ireland, Enniskillen has several appealing areas, not least the Buttermarket (Mon–Sat 10am–5pm) in the centre, a restored 19th-century courtyard specialising in crafts and art galleries.

A true taste of the region's flavour can be gained by circling Lower Lough Erne by road or by boat. **Devenish Island** ❽ is reached by ferry (accessible Easter–mid-Sept daily; boat fare and charge) from Trory Point, signposted 3 miles (5km) north of the town at the A32/B82 junction. It is the best known of the lough's 97 islands because of its elabo-

BELOW: fishing by Enniskillen Castle.

rate, well-preserved round tower, which you can climb by internal ladders. Close by are the decorative ruins of the 12th-century Augustinian Abbey of St Mary.

Ten miles (16km) northwest of Enniskillen, **Castle Archdale Country Park** (Countryside Centre; tel: 028-6862 1588; Easter–Sept daily 10am–6pm, Oct–Easter Sun noon–4pm, park: daily 9am–dusk) has pony trekking, boating and 230 acres (90 hectares) of lovely parkland with walks and cycle rides. The Archdale Centre is in the last remaining part of Archdale Manor House, the courtyard buildings. A ferry departs from Castle Archdale Park Marina (tel: 028-6862 1892; Easter–Sept Sat–Sun 11am–6pm, July–Aug daily; charge for ferry) for **White Island** with its 12th-century church along one wall of which are lined up eight mysterious pagan statues, discovered only in the 20th century. Their origins fox experts; some speculate that seven may represent the deadly sins.

A few miles on, past the village of **Kesh** is the strangest of all local stone figures: the two-faced Janus on **Boa Island** ❾, which is joined to the mainland by a bridge at each end *(see box below)*.

Following the lough's shoreline, you reach **Pettigo**, an old plantation town once the railhead for pilgrims visiting the holy sites at **Lough Derg**, across the border in Co. Donegal. The River Termon, running through Pettigo, marks the border and is said to be stuffed full of bilingual trout. It is also said that when a man had his skull fatally cracked during a fist fight in the middle of the bridge a surveyor had to be called to determine whether he had died within the jurisdiction of the Northern police or the Republic's gardai. An oak tree on one side of the bridge was planted in 1853 to mark the British victory at Sebastopol. A statue on the other side commemorates four IRA men who died fighting the British in 1922.

Castle Caldwell

Castle Caldwell, on the A47 4 miles (6km) east of Belleek, a ruined 17th-century castle by the loughside nearby, has become the centrepiece of a working forest (tel: 028-6634 3165; daily dawn–dusk; free access), popular with picnickers and bird watchers. It's one of a number of areas where modern growth

Enniskillen facts

- *One of Ulster's worst terrorist outrages took place in Enniskillen when a bomb exploded during a Remembrance Day service at the war memorial in 1987, killing 11 people.*
- *On the outskirts of the town, to the northwest, is Portora Royal School, founded in 1608. Its most famous pupils were playwrights Oscar Wilde and Samuel Beckett.*

BELOW: the two-faced Janus carving on Boa Island.

Ancient monuments

In most countries, a find such as the ancient Janus statue on Boa Island would have been turned into a major tourist attraction. Here, you have to watch for an easily missable road sign pointing to "Caldragh Cemetery" (free access), then tramp through cowpats down a farm lane until you come across a field full of overgrown, moss-covered gravestones, in the middle of which lurks the inscrutable Celtic figure. The lack of refurbishment makes the place feel splendidly eerie; you notice the figure's sexual arousal and the hollow in its head and wonder whether that hollow once held sacrificial blood.

A second Janus figure was discovered on the little island of Lustybeg, near the small village of Kesh. There are holiday chalets for hire on this island.

The intricate detail on a bowl at Belleek Pottery.

is being cut back and ancient woodland regenerated. A fiddler who, the worse for drink, fell off a barge and drowned is remembered on a fiddle-shaped monument with a cautionary verse that ends: *On firm land only exercise your skill. There you may play and safely drink your fill.*

The border touches the River Erne again at **Belleek** ⑩, where anglers assure you that you can hook a salmon in the Republic and land it in Northern Ireland. It was after inheriting nearby Castle Caldwell estate in 1849 that John Caldwell Bloomfield discovered all the requisite ingredients to make pottery. He located his new company in Belleek in 1857 (it celebrated 150 years in 2007), and with many changes of ownership since, **Belleek Pottery** is still thriving. Today, the Visitor Centre (tel: 028-6865 9300; www.belleek.ie; July–Aug Mon–Sat 9am–6pm, Sun noon–6pm, Nov–Dec and Mar–June Mon–Sat 10am–5.30pm, Jan–Feb Mon–Fri 10am–5.30pm; tours every half-an-hour 9.30am–4pm; free) at the distinctive 1893 factory building is one of Ireland's most popular attractions with a museum, showroom, tearoom and audio visual display.

You can take the scenic drive back to Enniskillen along the south side of the lough, stopping 5 miles (8km) north-west of Derrygonnelly on the A46 at **Lough Navar Forest Park** (tel: 028-6634 3165; daily 10am–dusk; free access), where a lookout point offers a panorama of five counties. Peregrine falcons and merlins are among various birds flying overhead, while plentiful deer herds graze. Two monuments here commemorate the crew of two American seaplanes that crashed locally during World War Two. At **Tully**, off the A46, 3 miles (5km) north of the village, is one well-preserved 17th-century castle (Easter–mid-Sept daily 10am–6pm, Oct–Easter Sun noon–4pm; free) whilst at **Monea**, 7 miles (11km) north-west of Enniskillen on the B81, is another with free access at all times.

Marble Arch Caves

"Over 300 million years of history" – impressive even by Irish standards – is the slogan used to promote **Marble Arch Caves** ⑪ (Marlbank, Florencecourt; tel: 028-6634 8855; www.marblearchcaves.net; Mar–June and Sept daily 10am–4.30pm,

BELOW: Marble Arch Caves.

July–Aug until 5pm, Oct Mon–Fri 11–3, weather permitting; charge), a network of limestone chambers containing remarkable stalactites. A 75-minute tour includes an underground boat journey. The "Moses Walk" is so called because the dammed walkway has been created through a lake, with more than a metre of water on either side.

Twelve miles (20km) south-west of Enniskillen, the caves are reached by following the A4 southwest for 3 miles (5km), then following signposts after branching off on the A32 towards Swanlinbar. The complex includes car parking, souvenir shop and restaurant and you can get information on the nearby **Cuilcagh Mountain Park**, designated alongside Marble Arch Caves as a Unesco Global Geopark.

Florence Court

Florence Court (National Trust; tel: 028-6634 8249; house: May–Sept daily 11am–5pm, Mar–Apr and Oct Sat–Sun only, with exceptions, grounds: daily 10am–dusk; charge) is a beautiful 18th-century mansion 4 miles (6km) back. Contents include fine rococo plasterwork and 18th-century furniture. The grounds include an ice house, a water-powered sawmill, a walled garden, extensive park and woodland and a yew tree reputed to be the parent of all Irish yew trees. You can sample homemade delights served in the Stable restaurant.

Two miles (3km) southeast of Enniskillen on the A4 is Ireland's finest classical mansion, **Castle Coole** (National Trust; tel: 028-6632 2690; June–Aug daily 11am–5pm, mid-Mar–May and Sept Sat–Sun only, with exceptions, grounds: daily 10am–dusk; charge). Completed in 1798, it is a perfect example of late 18th-century Hellenism and has furniture dating from before 1830. A state bedroom is presented as it was for George IV. The park lake's graylag geese were established here 300 years ago.

County Armagh

To the east is County Armagh, known as the Apple Orchard of Ireland, and during the 1980s and '90s, its southern acres, thanks to terrorist activity near its border with the Republic, by the less inviting sobriquet of Bandit Country.

Its county town of **Armagh** ⓬ (always called a city despite a population of just over 15,000) symbolises many of Northern Ireland's problems. Its two striking cathedrals – one Protestant, one Catholic, both called **St Patrick's** – sit on opposite hills like, someone once said, the horns of a dilemma. The two communities live mostly in separate parts of the city, with little interaction.

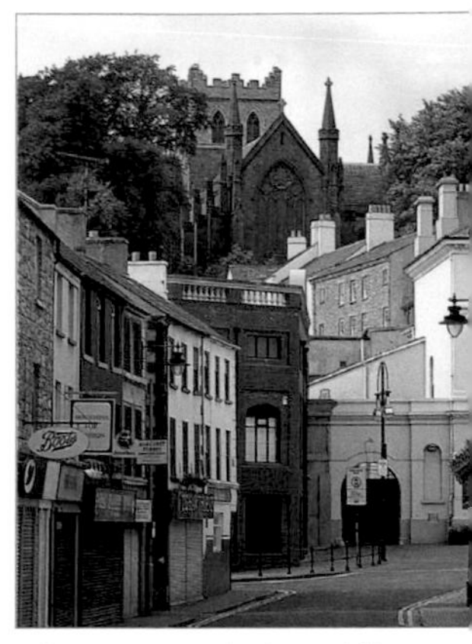

Armagh's St Patrick's Protestant Cathedral.

Armagh is known for its dignified Georgian architecture. At one end of an oval **Mall** – where cricket is played in summer – is a classical courthouse, at the other a jailhouse. The Ionic-pillared **County Museum** (The Mall; tel: 028-3752 3070; www.nmni.com; Mon–Fri 10am–5pm, Sat 10am–1pm, 2–5pm; free) contains many local artifacts, as well as records of Ireland's worst railway disaster, which happened in 1889 just outside Armagh; 80 Sunday School

BELOW: St Patrick's Roman Catholic Cathedral, Armagh.

WHERE

Armagh's location makes it a good base from which to explore the southern part of Northern Ireland. It is 37 miles (60km) from Belfast, 81 miles (130km) from Dublin, and a 45-minute drive from Belfast International Airport.

excursionists died when 10 uncoupled carriages ran down a steep incline into the path of a following train.

The Planetarium

Access is free into the gardens of the 1790 Observatory that accommodates Ireland's main **Planetarium** (College Hill; tel: 028-3752 3689; www.armaghplanet.com; Mon–Fri 1–5pm, Sat 11.30am–5pm, pre-booking essential for shows; charge). Astronomical shows have been enhanced by a major refurbishment to the Digital Theatre, including the world's most advanced digital projection system. There are also interactive exhibitions and an outdoor Astropark with scale models of the planets. It also hosts regular activities.

Somehow the contemporary design of the **Market Place Theatre** (Market Street; tel: 028-3752 1821; www.marketplacearmagh.com) sits comfortably within Armagh's historic centre. It is one of Northern Ireland's most important venues for drama, music and comedy and also has a popular bar and restaurant.

The Palace Demense covers 70 acres of beautiful parkland, where the original palace building and stables, designed by Thomas Cooley in 1768, take centre stage. Today, it is a public park in the town centre that hosts many events.

In the city centre is **St Patrick's Trian** (English Street; tel: 028-3752 1801; www.stpatrickstrian.com; Sept–June Mon–Sat 10.30am–5.30pm, July–Aug until 8.30pm, Sun 2–8.30pm; charge). This explains St Patrick's connections with the city, including the 9th-century *Book of Armagh* *(see margin note, right)*, and cashes in on Dean Swift's habit of holidaying nearby with a "Land of Lilliput" presentation aimed at children.

Two miles (3km) west of the city, off the A28, is the high-tech **Navan Centre** (tel: 028-3752 1801; Apr–Sept daily 10am–7pm, Oct–Mar until 4pm; charge), celebrating Emain Macha, Ulster's Camelot around 600BC. Until restored, it was a neglected hilltop; now it comes complete with hands-on computers and audio-visual interpretation facilities. Access to the hilltop is free.

Armagh's villages

The city is surrounded by neat villages, reached through a network of pleasant

BELOW: Saturday afternoon cricket on Armagh's Mall.

lanes, some of which host the local sport of road bowling, culminating in the Ulster Finals *(see page 90)*. In May, the countryside around **Loughgall** is radiant with apple blossom. In the village the **Dan Winter Ancestral Home** (9 The Diamond, Derryloughan Road; tel: 028-3885 1344; www.orangenet.org/winter; May–Sept Mon–Sat 10.30am–8.30pm, Sun 2–8.30pm, Oct–Apr 10.30am–5.30pm, Sun 2–5.30pm; free) recounts the founding of the Orange Order. Lovers of art should investigate the quaint **Dispensary House Gallery** (88 Main Street; tel: 028-3889 2010; www.dispensaryhousegallery.com; Mon, Wed–Sat 2–5pm).

Near **Markethill**, in **Gosford Forest Park** (tel: 028-3755 1277; 10am–dusk; charge), Gosford Castle is a large turreted mock-Norman edifice built of local granite. **Bessbrook** is a model linen-making town.

Crossmaglen, a village at the heart of this fiercely republican area – known as Bandit Country during the Troubles – has a large market square, containing a striking bronze monument to the IRA; this village was in the front line of many battles between the IRA and the security forces in the 1970s and '80s. Remarkably, after enduring many sectarian murders, Crossmaglen has begun promoting tourism with some degree of success.

But it's the beauty of the Ring of Gullion, and the mystical **Slieve Gullion**, source of myths like Deirdre of the Sorrows, which is the focus of modern tourism. There are fine walks, and cycle rides, around **Slieve Gullion Forest Park** (tel: 028-3755 1277; Easter–Sept 10am–dusk), where a forest drive winds up to two mountain-top Stone Age cairns. In the vicinity are three trails, also for walking or cycling, around Mullaghbane, Forkhill and Creggan, which trace the history of local 18th-century Ulster poets. Traditional music can be enjoyed at pubs, such as the Welcome Inn in **Forkhill**, on Tuesdays from 9pm.

Portadown and Lurgan

Between Armagh and Belfast is a chain of towns built on commerce. **Portadown** ⓭, 10 miles (16km) to the northeast, has found its role scaled down from that of a major railway junction to a prosperous market town noted for rose growing and coarse fishing. Linen manufacturing has diminished, as it has in **Lurgan**, 6 miles (10km) further along the A3. In the 1960s it was decided to link the two towns to form the "lineal city" of **Craigavon**, thereby reducing congestion in Belfast; but the new city's population didn't arrive in the expected numbers and civic pride has kept the separate identities of Portadown and Lurgan very much alive despite the mushrooming between them of housing estates, schools and traffic circles.

Lough Neagh's wildlife is well explained in the **Lough Neagh Discovery Centre** (Oxford Island; tel: 028-3832 2205; daily 9am–5pm, with exceptions; free). The best way to explore the Lough is on board *The Maid*, which departs from various points from April until October (tel: 028-2582 2159).

Seven miles (11km) west of Portadown, off the B28 are two National Trust mansions. 17th-century **Ardress House** (64 Ardress Road, Annaghmore; tel:

The Book of Armagh

The Book, written in 807 by the scribe Ferdomnach, is a precious historic record because of the information it provides about the elusive Saint Patrick. Touch screens in St Patrick's Trian exhibition allow visitors to question three people who were connected with the Book and discover how to make medieval inks and a quill pen.

BELOW:
Co. Armagh's lush countryside.

Men Who March

Parades and bunting, bands and bibles... it's hard to escape these provocative rituals during July and August. What lies behind them?

Northern Ireland is unique in its flourishing popular culture: there are bands in every village and every housing estate, and nowhere else in the UK do normally discreet citizens sing and dance in the streets. There are many processions throughout the year, and some quiet church parades, but the prolonged marching season in July and August can heighten sectarian tensions.

The main Orange procession, which celebrates the 1690 Battle of the Boyne in which William III (William of Orange) cemented the Protestant heritage, takes place on 12 July. On 13 July, the Black Men (the Orange Order's elite) dress up in period costume to re-enact King Billy's routing of the Catholic King James II in the "Sham Fight" at Scarva, County Down. On 12 August the Apprentice Boys march through Derry City in memory of 13 apprentices who closed the city's gates against the forces of James II.

The Green Orangemen

Lady's Day, in honour of the Madonna, Mary Mother of God, is held on 15 August by the Ancient Order of Hibernians, sometimes known as the Green Orangemen. (Green symbolises Catholic Ireland, orange Protestant Ulster.) Like their Orange counterparts, the Hibernians mix prayer with pageantry.

Now that the Troubles have ceased, such pageantry is slowly becoming less political and more of a tourist attraction. Traditionally it appeared to Catholics a sign of "triumphalism" and to Protestants as another nationalist provocation.

A big investment

Flautist James Galway started his career in a Belfast band, and there can be few parts of Europe where such a high percentage of the population plays an instrument. In late spring and early summer, motorists driving through the leafy lanes of Ulster must be prepared to round a corner to find the road blocked by columns of men in bowler hats solemnly drumming and tootling their way to a local band contest. Scottish and Gaelic pipers compete with ecumenical harmony, at their own expense and "for the glory of it", in villages and towns throughout summer. With a set of pipes costing £1,500 or so, there may be £2.5 million worth of pipes keening at a typical contest. ❑

LEFT: the very loud Lambeg drum.

028-8778 4753; mid-Mar–June and Sept Sat–Sun 1–5pm, July–Aug Thur–Sun 1–5pm, with exceptions; charge) has a fine collection of 18th-century furniture. The 19th-century **Argory** (144 Derrycaw Road, Moy; tel: 028-8778 4753; house: July–Aug daily 11am–5pm, mid-Mar–June, Sept–Oct Thur–Mon, grounds: daily 10am–5pm, until 6pm summer; charge) has delightful grounds and a tea-room featuring great local baking. The house has been well refurbished.

Echoes of the Brontës

Banbridge ⓮, 10 miles (16km) south of Lurgan, has a peculiar main street, bisected by an underpass taking through traffic, with sections of road on either side serving a collection of small shops. Just outside the town, off the dual carriageway, the Outlet shopping centre is among the biggest in Northern Ireland.

To its southeast, off the B10, is "**Brontë Homeland**", promoted from the **Brontë Interpretive Centre** (Church Hill Road, Rathfriland; tel: 028-4062 3322; mid-Mar–Sept Fri–Sun noon–4.30pm, other times by appointment; charge), a confusingly signposted trail invented by the tourist authorities to capitalise on the fact that Patrick Brontë (or Brunty or Prunty), father of the novelists Charlotte, Emily and Ann, was born in a cottage at Emdale, 3 miles (5km) southeast of Loughbrickland. The family's fame was cemented in Yorkshire, not in Emdale, and there's nothing here to conjure up the claustrophobia of *Wuthering Heights* or *Jane Eyre*. But the drive through country lanes so narrow that the hedges almost meet is worth taking and, if you lose track of Patrick Brontë's trail on Ballynaskeagh Road, or Ballynafern or Lisnacroppin, it doesn't much matter.

The river valleys are peppered with the tall chimneys of disused linen mills so for access to the history and impact of what was the province's major industry go northwest along the Lagan valley to the impressive **Irish Linen Centre and Lisburn Museum** (Market Square, **Lisburn**; tel: 028-9266 3377; Mon–Sat 9.30am–5pm; free) with its hand-loom weaving workshop. A range of damask table linen is sold in the museum shop

The Legananny Dolmen is near Banbridge. It can be found off the B7, 7 miles (11km) south of Dromara, signposted from Dromara and Castlewellan. Entrance is free.

BELOW: view of Lough Neagh.

TIP

Cycling vacations
The minor roads and lanes that criss-cross the Mournes included many marked cycle trails. For a list of suggested itineraries, such as the Beetler's Trail and the Poet's Trail, visit www.newryand mourne.gov.uk.

with a flax flower pattern designed by the museum staff.

With its key location equidistant between Dublin and Belfast the newly appointed city of **Newry** ⓯, 19 miles (10km) to the southwest of Banbridge, was bound to prosper once the peace process began. The process began in 2007 when the motorway was extended north and south. Newry's two huge shopping centres, the Quays and Buttercrane, are the hubs of a city not overwhelmed with visitor attractions.

Since 2007, Newry and Mourne Museum and the tourist information centre have been relocated in the restored 16th-century **Bagenal's Castle** (Castle Street; tel: 028-3031 3182; Mon–Sat 10am–4pm, Sun 1–4.30pm; free) and its adjoining warehouse. Exhibitions explore the history of the area and building, and there is a café and shop too.

From Newry you can drive 12 miles (19km) north on the A27, or walk or cycle along towpaths, to the **Scarva Visitor Centre** (Main Street; tel: 028-3883 2163; Apr–Sept Tue–Sun 9am–5pm; free). Four miles (6km) west of Newry, on the A25, the thatched 18th-century **Derrymore House** (National Trust; tel: 028-8778 4753; May–Sept daily 10am–6pm, Dec–Apr 10am–4pm; charge) recalls a more sheltered world.

BELOW: the Mourne Mountains meet the sea at Newcastle.

Seaside relaxations

From Newry it's 5 miles (8km) southeast to the pretty seaside resort of **Warrenpoint** ⓰, overlooking Carlingford Lough. Its Maidens of Mourne festival each August is a poor copy of the "Rose of Tralee" but it has become celebrated in recent times for "Blues in the Bay" each May, one of the best blues festivals in the UK, when places like the Whistledown Hotel host acts from across the world. A few minutes around the coast **Rostrevor**, sheltered by hills, is smaller but prettier with more of a Victorian atmosphere.

A steep half-mile walk up the slopes of **Slievemartin** (1,595ft/486 metres) brings you to **Cloghmore**, a "Big Stone" supposedly hurled by the Irish giant Fionn MacCool at a rival Scot. The geological explanation for this misplaced piece of granite is more mundane, having to do with glacial drift.

Skirting round the **Mourne Mountains**, past 14th-century **Greencastle**, takes you to the active fishing village of **Kilkeel**, capital of the so-called "Kingdom of Mourne." Despite its idyllic location between mountain and sea, there is little to recommend the charmless Kilkeel to the visitor, except perhaps the restored Hanna's Close holiday cottages (tel: 028-4176 5999) on the outskirts of town, an ideal base from which to explore the Mournes.

There's a choice here: you can proceed along the coast via **Annalong**, a smaller fishing village with old cottages and a **cornmill** (Marine Park; tel: 028-4175 2256; opening times by arrangement; charge) with waterwheel, or you can turn inland into the Mournes.

Meandering in the Mournes

The Mournes are "young" mountains (like the Alps) and their chameleon qualities attract walkers. One moment the granite is grey, the next pink. You walk by an isolated farmhouse, and

 Map on pages 298–9

within moments are in the middle of a wilderness. One minute, the Mournes justify all the songs written about them; the next, they become plain scrubland and unexceptional hills. The weather has a lot to do with it.

Off the B27 the remote **Silent Valley Mountain Park** (Head Road; daily 10am–dusk; charge) cradles a large dam, which supplies Belfast and Co. Down with water. In the heart of the Mournes, this beautiful and tranquil spot is ideal for picnics and hiking, and there is an innovative exhibition in the modern information centre.

Slieve Donard, the highest peak at 2,796ft (850 metres), has exhilarating panoramic views.

As you reach the foothills of the Mournes, turn right just before Hilltown towards **Newcastle** ⓱. This is east Down's main resort, with a fine, sandy beach, an inordinate number of cake shops and the celebrated Royal County Down Golf Club, one of the world's top 10 links courses. Home to the famous Slieve Donard Hotel and adjacent to the tranquil Murlough nature reserve, Newcastle has undergone a serious makeover, including a smart new promenade, but even that can't quite remove its old-fashioned seaside resort atmosphere.

Several forest parks – **Donard, Tollymore, Castlewellan** (charges) – are good for riding (by pony or bicycle). This is an area that invites you to unwind, that doesn't understand people in a hurry.

Five miles (8km) inland from Newcastle, **Castlewellan** is a picturesque village with a wide main street. Nine miles (14km) to the west, **Rathfriland** is a steep-streeted plantation town with livestock sales and views of the Mournes.

As an alternative to heading into the Mournes from Newcastle, one can

Pony trekking at low tide, Newcastle.

BELOW: Castlewellan Park.

St Patrick
At 16, St Patrick was captured in Britain by raiders and taken to Ireland as a slave. Six years later, he escaped back to Britain, became a bishop, and returned to Ireland as a successful missionary. He probably died around AD493. The legend that he banished snakes from the island disregards the fact that snakes hadn't existed in post-glacial Ireland.

continue round the coast, via, at **Dundrum,** Ireland's finest Anglo-Norman castle to **Ardglass,** where several smaller, ruined castles hint at its strategic importance in the Middle Ages to unwelcome kings visiting from Britain. A source of wonderful local seafood, Dundrum has two excellent restaurants to enjoy it, the Buck's Head and Mourne Seafood Bar.

Downpatrick

Seven miles (11km) inland to the northwest is **Downpatrick** ⓲, which has a Georgian air and a cathedral supposedly built on the site of St Patrick's first stone church. The saint himself is said by some to be buried here. You can follow Patrick's story in a high-tech interactive exhibition with audio-visual film at the **St Patrick Centre** (Lower Market Street; tel: 028-4461 9000; www.saintpatrickcenre.com; June–Aug daily 9.30am–6pm, Apr–May and Sept Mon–Sat 9.30am–5.30pm, Sun 1–5.30pm, Oct–Mar Mon–Sat 10am–5pm; charge), itself the hub of Downpatrick's famous week of celebrations around St Patrick's Day, 17 March. A hundred yards or so away the atmospheric **Downpatrick and County Down Steam Railway** (tel: 028-4461 5779; www.downrail.co.uk) runs weekends between June and September and special holidays.

Down County Museum (The Mall; tel: 028-4461 5218; www.downcountymuseum.com; Mon–Fri 10am–5pm, Sun 1–5pm; free) housed in an old gaol, explores the local heritage. The Christian theme continues, off the A7 a mile northwest at riverside Cistercian **Inch Abbey** (charge). The **Struell Wells** (free access), off the B1, 1½ miles (2.5km) east of the town, are evidence of pagan worshippers long before Christianity.

North of the town there begins a prosperous commuter belt, populated by well-spoken professionals who put their money into making their homes ever more comfortable. The source of their prosperity and the commercial magnet to which they are drawn each working day lies to the north: Belfast.

BELOW: St Patrick's grave in Down Cathedral – though the saint's last resting place is a matter of dispute.

Comber

Comber ⓳, 17 miles (27km) to the north at the head of Strangford Lough, was a linen town and still has a working mill. The town centre retains its old character, despite the developers, with cottage shops and a square. **Castle Espie** (Wildfowl and Wetlands Trust; tel: 028-9187 4146; daily 10.30am–dusk; charge), on the shores of Strangford Lough, is base for Ireland's largest collection of ducks, geese and swans.

The conservation area of **Strangford Lough** is noted for its myriad islands, most of which are sunken drumlins, the smooth glacial hillocks that characterise Co. Downs landscape. There are rocky shores on this side of the lough at places like **Whiterock Bay**. **Mahee Island**, accessible by bridge, has a golf course and the remains of **Nendrum Abbey** (Visitor Centre: tel: 028-9181 1491; Easter–Sept daily 10am–6pm, Oct–Easter noon–4pm; free), an early monastery.

The Ards Peninsula

You can reach the **Ards Peninsula**, a 23-mile (37km) long finger dotted with villages and beaches, by means of a regular car ferry which chugs a slanted course from **Strangford** ⓴, 8 miles (13km) from Downpatrick, across to Portaferry. The Vikings are said to have had a trading post at Strangford in the 9th century. Nearby is **Castle Ward House** (tel: 028-4488 1204; www.ntni.org.uk; house: mid-Mar–Oct daily 11am–5pm, grounds: daily 10am–4pm, Apr–Sept until 8pm; charge), an 18th-century Georgian mansion, once the home of the Lord of Bangor. Overlooking the lough, the house has two "fronts" in differing styles (classical and Gothic) because the Lord and his Lady had diverging tastes. There are wildfowl in the 700-acre (280-hectare) grounds and the **Strangford Lough Wildlife Centre** (tel: 028-4488 1411) is located at the water's edge. There's also a Victorian laundry, two small 15th-century castles and an adventure playground for children.

The ferry across the mouth of the lough deposits you where the sunsets are as fine a sight as anywhere in the world and where the local lobster and the **Exploris** (Castle Street; tel: 028-4272 8062; www.exploris.org.uk; Mon–Sat 10am–5pm, Sun noon–5pm, with exceptions; charge), Northern Ireland's only sea aquarium, are not to be missed.

The Exploris aquarium charts the marine life of Strangford Lough and has a seal rehabilitation centre.

Nine miles (14km) north of Portaferry along the A20 is the one-street town of **Kircubbin**, a boating centre with a small pier jutting into Strangford Lough. Two miles (3km) inland takes you to the **Kirkistown Circuit**, a wartime airport and the home of car racing in Northern Ireland. Motor sport has a keen following in Northern Ireland; motorcycle racing and rallying can take place on public roads closed by Act of Parliament for the events.

Four miles (6km) further north on the A20 in the pretty village of **Grey-**

BELOW: Strangford Lough.

Mount Stewart.

abbey is the site, with "physick garden", of a Cistercian abbey dated 1193, and one of the most complete of its type in Ireland (tel: 028-9181 1491; Easter–Sept daily 10am–6pm, Oct–Easter Sun only noon–4pm; free).

Two miles (3km) north of the village is another National Trust treasure, **Mount Stewart** (tel: 028-4278 8387; www.ntni.org.uk; gardens: daily 10am–6pm, house: mid-Mar–Oct Thur–Tue 11am–6pm; charge). It is an 18th-century house, which has several fine gardens and a mild microclimate that fosters delicate plants untypical of the area. The rhododendrons are particularly fine, and the gardens contain a variety of statues of griffins, satyrs, lions and the like. The **Temple of the Winds**, an 18th-century folly in the grounds, was built by James Stewart, a rival of Robert Adam, and is modelled on another in Athens. It offers a splendid view of the lough.

BELOW: Donaghadee.

Newtownards

Newtownards ㉑, a sprawling commuter town at the head of Strangford Lough, belies its name; it's an old town, dating back to the 17th century. It was an old market town and still is a bustling shopping centre with a blend of traditional shops and a covered shopping centre. There is a fine sandstone town hall and other buildings of historical interest include **Movilla Abbey** on the site of a 6th-century monastery about 1 mile to the east of the town.

The **Somme Heritage Centre** (Bangor Road; tel: 028-9182 3202; July–Aug Mon–Fri 10am–5pm, Sat–Sun noon–5pm, Sept–June Mon–Thur 10am–4pm, with exceptions; charge), on Bangor Road, reconstructs elements of the 1916 battle in which many Ulstermen died.

Overlooking the town is **Scrabo Tower** (Scrabo Country Park; tel: 028-9181 1491), a 19th-century memorial to the third Marquess of Londonderry, offering vistas of the lough and the soft-hilled countryside and good walks in the nearby **Killynether Wood**.

Donaghadee ㉒, 8 miles (13km) to the east, is notable for its much-painted harbour and lighthouse, and summer boat trips (Nelson's Boats; tel: 028-9188 3403) up Belfast Lough and to **Copeland Island** (a bird sanctuary), just offshore. The twisting road passes 18th century **Ballycopeland Windmill** (Millisle; tel: 028-9181 1491; visitor centre: July–Aug daily 10am–5pm; free) and quieter beaches at **Ballywalter** and **Ballyhalbert**, and the fishing port of **Portavogie**, which has occasional evening quayside fish auctions.

Popular resort

Bangor ㉓ was originally a small seaside resort, noted for its abbey. The expensively rejuvenated seafront still has to gentrify some of its fast-food bars and souvenir shops to do justice to the new marina packed with yachts and cruisers. Rowing around the bay in hired punts and fishing trips from the pier are evergreen attractions. The town has a leisure centre with heated swimming and diving pools. For some reason, perhaps the bracing sea air, Bangor is favoured by evangelists who trawl for souls along the sea wall by the little harbour.

The **North Down Heritage Centre** (Town Hall, Castle Park Avenue; tel: 028-9127 1200; Tue–Sat 10am–4.30pm, Sun 2–4.30pm, also Mon July–Aug; free) could provide a refuge.

The old Bangor has been overgrown by acres of new housing developments and shopping centres, many of them inhabited by people who work in Belfast. It is a busy town with a weekly open-air market, plenty of pubs and eating places, and parkland. The best beach is nearby **Ballyholme Bay**, a sandy arc which can becomes very crowded.

If you leave Bangor by the A2, a detour to the right will take in the beaches of **Helen's Bay**, the nearby wooded **Crawfordsburn Country Park** (tel: 028-9185 3621; free) and the picturesque village of **Crawfordsburn** with its charming **Old Inn**. Such havens are unusual so close to a city the size of Belfast.

Seaside fun at Bangor's Pickie Pool.

The "Gold Coast"

The A2 from Bangor to Belfast runs through what locals enviously describe as the **"Gold Coast"**. This is stockbroker country, where lush lawns meet mature woodland. Hillside sites, overlooking the shipping lanes, have traditionally lured the well-heeled. **Cultra**, 6 miles (10km) from Bangor, has leafy lanes and the resplendent **Culloden Hotel**. They go in for yachting, golf and horse riding around here.

Holywood, an ancient religious settlement a mile further on, enjoys a quiet prosperity since it was bypassed. Nothing much happens here, apart from summer jazz and rumours of the odd dance around the Maypole, but it has pleasant craft shops and art galleries, and good pubs and restaurants.

Nearby, at Cultra Manor is the award-winning **Ulster Folk and Transport Museum** ㉔ (tel: 028-9042 8428; www.

BELOW: Ulster Folk and Transport Museum.

WHERE

The **Ulster Folk and Transport Museum** is situated 7 miles (11km) east of Belfast, near Holywood, on the main Belfast to Bangor Road (A2), just 15 minutes outside Belfast City Centre and close to Belfast City Airport. The nearest rail station is Cultra Halt. Buses stop outside the museum entrance. There is plenty of parking.

nmni.com; Mar–Sept Tue–Sun 10am–5pm, Oct–Feb Tue–Fri 10am–4pm, Sat–Sun 11am–4pm; charge), which brings social history to life. Farmhouses, cottages, churches and mills have been painstakingly reconstructed – often brick by brick from their original locations. Freshly made soda bread, a local speciality, is sometimes baked over a traditional peat fire. On another part of the site the Transport Museum has its own fascination; exhibits range from horse-drawn chariots right up to a prototype of the ill-fated Belfast-built De Lorean sports car. There is a *Titanic* exhibition and the state-of-the-art X2 Flight Exhibition, where you can simulate flying.

From here it's a straight run into Belfast (*see next chapter*).

North of Belfast

If you aren't in the mood for city life, however, a good ring-road system will take you through the city to the north shore of Belfast Lough and the suburbs of **Whiteabbey** and **Greenisland**, with some opulent housing.

Carrickfergus ㉕, 12 miles (19km) north from Belfast along the A2, is yet another market and dormitory town. Its big synthetic-fibre plants are empty now – a contemporary monument to its industrial past. The imposing 12th-century Norman **Castle** (The Marine Highway; tel: 028-9335 1273; Easter–Sept daily 10am–6pm, Oct–Easter until 4pm; charge) beside the harbour, scene of gun-running exploits early in the 20th century, still attracts attention for its authenticity. It is a real castle in every sense, with a portcullis, ramparts, chilling dungeons, cannons and a regimental museum in the keep. Looking to the new age of leisure, the town's **marina** has 300 berths. The parish church of St Nicholas (with stained-glass windows to Santa Claus) is 12th-century.

In Antrim Street, **Carrickfergus Museum** (tel: 028-9335 8049; Apr–Sept Mon–Sat 10am–6pm, Oct–Mar until 5pm; free) provides general historical information about the town. **Flame**, the Gasworks Museum, (Irish Quarter West; tel: 028-9336 9575; May–Aug daily 2–5pm, Sept Mon–Fri 2–5pm; charge) is Ireland's last surviving gasworks.

A mile to the east at Boneybefore, the **Andrew Jackson Cottage** (tel: 028-9335 8049; by appointment only) is a reconstruction of the thatched cottage home of Andrew Jackson, the seventh President of the United States.

The countryside north of Carrickfergus becomes rich meadowland, with the sleepy seaside town of **Whitehead,** base for the Railway Preservation Society of Ireland on Castleview Road, from where occasional steam excursions run. The town nestles at the mouth of the lough, with a seashore walk to the Black Head lighthouse.

Beyond this begins the peninsula of **Island Magee**, with unspoilt beaches and caves, which wraps around Larne Lough. From here, the road runs into unlovely **Larne** ㉖, a port with frequent ferries to and from Stranraer in Scotland (70 minutes away). The **Larne Museum and Arts Centre** at 2 Victoria Road (tel: 028-2827 9482; Mon–Sat 10am–4.30pm; free) has modern displays reflecting the history and heritage of the area.

BELOW: Carrickfergus Castle.

The Causeway Coastal Road

The rewards of continuing along the coast are spectacular views of brown moorlands, white limestone, black basalt, red sandstone and blue sea along the **Causeway Coastal Road.** A notable engineering achievement, it is explained in the Larne Interpretive Centre based in the Tourist Information Centre (Narrow Gauge Road; tel: 028-2826 0088; Mon–Fri 9am–5pm, Sat 10am–6pm, closed Sat Oct–Easter; free). The road, designed in 1834 by Sir Charles Lanyon as a work of famine relief, opened up an area whose inhabitants had previously found it easier to travel by sea to Scotland than overland to the rest of Ireland.

At various points, you can turn into one or other of Antrim's celebrated nine glens – **Glenarm**, **Glencloy**, **Glenariff**, **Glenballyeamon**, **Glenaan**, **Glencorp**, **Glendun**, **Glenshesk** and **Glentaisie** – and into another world. It's a world of weather-beaten farmers in tweeds; a world of sheep sales conducted by auctioneers who talk like machine guns; a world with a baffling dialect that turns an ewe into a *yow* and "six" into *sex*; a world where poteen, the "mountain dew", is distilled in lonely places. It's not hard to track down this illicit (and potentially lethal) alcohol. "It's floating about," they'll tell you. "In fact it's practically running down the streets."

Ballygalley ㉗, at the start of the famous scenic drive, has a 1625 fortified manor house (now a hotel) and, inland from the coast road, a well-preserved old mill and pottery. **White Bay** is a picnic area around which small fossils can be found. **Glenarm** has a beautiful park adjoining a fussy castle, home of the Earls of Antrim. **Carnlough** has a fine harbour and, running over its main street, a white bridge built in 1854 to carry limestone from the quarries to waiting boats. The Londonderry Arms hotel (also 1854) retains the charms of an old coaching inn. An eponymous literary summer school at **Garron Tower**, 5 miles (8km) north, celebrates John Hewitt, an acerbic dissenter poet.

The village of **Waterfoot** is the entrance to **Glenariff Glen**, a deep wooded gorge dubbed by Thackeray "Switzerland in miniature". Wild flowers carpet the upper glen in spring and early summer, and rustic footbridges

It was in Larne's harbour that Ulster Unionists, opposed to a Roman Catholic-dominated united Ireland,unloaded a large consignment of German-made rifles in 1914. It was probably only the intervention of World War I that postponed bitter conflict in the province of Ulster.

BELOW: Cushendun.

The Causeway Coastal Road was built by the engineer William Bald between 1832 and 1842 to replace the dangerous Old Irish Highway. Originally called the Grand Military Way, it was intended to make not only accessibility to the Glens and coastal areas possible but also to create a quick access route for troops in the event of a rebellion.

carry walkers over the Glenariff River, past postcard-pretty waterfalls.

About 1½ miles (2km) to the north, **Cushendall**, "capital of the glens", was created largely by a wealthy 19th-century landowner, Francis Turnly. His most striking structure was the four-storey red sandstone **Curfew Tower**, built as "a place of confinement for idlers and rioters". The village has a good beach and is a popular sailing centre. Just to the north is **Layde Old Church**, dating back to the 13th century and containing some ancient vaults. Six miles (10km) further on, **Cushendun** ㉘ is a village of Cornish-style white cottages, graceful old houses and friendly pubs, has been captured on countless canvases and is protected by the National Trust.

The northern coast

Crossing the towering **Glendun Viaduct** (1839), just before arriving at Ballycastle, one passes the ruins of **Bonamargy Friary**, founded around 1500. A vault contains the massive coffins of several MacDonnell chieftains who stood out successfully against the forces of England's Queen Elizabeth I.

The best time to visit **Ballycastle** ㉙ is during the **Auld Lammas Fair**, held on the last Monday and Tuesday of August. Then this unspoiled town turns into one throbbing market place as farmers with impenetrable accents bring their livestock in from the glens and hundreds of stalls sell souvenirs, bric-a-brac, dulse (dried, edible seaweed) and yellowman (a sweet confectionery).

The big attraction is the *craic* – pronounced "crack" (a Scots-Irish word for talk, enlivened by a glass or two of Bushmills). It's great fun – an authentic folk event that owes nothing to the manipulations of tourist boards.

The **Ballycastle Museum** (59 Castle Street; tel: 028-2076 2942; July–Aug daily noon–6pm; free) concentrates on the folk social history of the Glens.

Rathlin Island

A sea-front memorial marks the spot where, in 1898, Guglielmo Marconi first seriously tested wireless telegraphy. He made his historic transmission between here and **Rathlin Island** ㉚, 8 miles (13km) off the coast towards Scotland's Mull of Kintyre. The boomerang-shaped

BELOW: the Auld Lammas Fair.
RIGHT: Carrick-a-Rede Rope Bridge.

Map on pages 298–9

island, whose population has slumped from 2,000 to 80 since 1850, makes its living from farming and fishing and attracts geologists, botanists and birdwatchers; there is a reserve (tel: 028-2076 3948) managed by the Royal Society for the Protection of Birds, an estimated 250,000 birds of 175 species.

A ferry (tel: 028-2076 9299; daily year round; reservations advised) makes the journey from Ballycastle in 45 minutes. There is one pub, a hotel, guesthouse and youth hostel – but no policeman, and no need for one.

Five miles (8km) west, off the A2, is the **Carrick a Rede Rope Bridge** (tel: 028-2076 9839; Mar–Oct daily 10am–6pm, Nov–Feb 10.30am–3.30pm; charge), 65ft (20 metres) wide swinging over a 80ft (24-metre) chasm to an island salmon fishery. Past Whitepark Bay is **Dunseverick Castle**, the slight remains of a 6th-century fortress perched on a high crag overlooking a fishing harbour.

The Giant's Causeway

The castle is at the eastern end of the **Giant's Causeway** ㉛, an astonishing assembly of more than 40,000 basalt columns, mostly perfect hexagonals formed by the cooling of molten lava. Dr Samuel Johnson, when asked by his biographer James Boswell whether this wonder of the world was worth seeing, gave the immortal reply: "Worth seeing? yes; but not worth going to see." It was a shrewd judgment in the 1770s when roads in the region were primitive enough to turn a journey into an expedition; indeed, the existence of the Causeway hadn't been known at all to the outside world until a gadabout Bishop of Derry stumbled upon them in 1692. Today this geological curiosity is accessible to the most monstrous tourist coaches, but it can still disappoint some visitors, who expect the columns to be bigger (the tallest, in the **Giant's Organ**, are about

Atlantic views from Whitepark Bay, 7 miles (11km) west of Ballycastle.

BELOW: the Giant's Causeway.

Carrick-a-Rede Rope Bridge

The Carrick-a-Rede-Rope Bridge provides a novel way to get an alternative view of the coastline. Spare a thought for the salmon fishermen who traversed this chasm, braving a bridge of widely spaced wooden slats and a single rope handrail. Today you get two handrails and a more substantial suspension bridge.

Fortunately no accident ever occurred on the bridge and old photographs even show people performing stunts, such as riding a bicycle across and doing handstands on a chair.

Once across on Carrick Island the view is fantastic and complemented by an array of diverse seabirds. Of course the only way back is to cross the bridge again – although a few visitors have been known to need a boat.

Rock climbing at Fair Head, on the north coast.

BELOW: Dunluce Castle.
RIGHT: Bushmills Distillery.

39 ft (12 metres) or who find their regularity diminishes their magnificence. It remains worth seeing, though. The formal approach is via the Causeway Visitor Centre (44 Causeway Road; tel: 028-2073 1855; www.giantscausewaycentre.com; car park charge) 2 miles (3km) north of Bushmills on the B146.

One of the most pleasant ways to reach the Giant's Causeway from Bushmills is on the Giant's Causeway and Bushmills Railway **steam train**, which operates daily July, August and Easter (Sat–Sun Mar–Oct).

The world's oldest distillery

The distillery at **Bushmills** ㉜ (Distillery Road; tel: 028-2073 3218; www.bushmills.com; guided tours: Mar–Oct Mon–Sat 9.15am–5pm, Sun noon–5pm, Nov–Feb Mon–Fri 9.30am–3.30pm, Sat–Sun 12.30–3.30pm; charge), a couple of miles away, boasts the world's oldest whiskey-making licence (1608). Old Bushmills, Black Bush and Bushmills Malt, made from local barley and the water that flows by in St Columb's Rill, can be tasted after a tour. Connoisseurs tend to prefer the classic Black Bush to the more touted (and expensive) malt. The main difference between Scotch whisky and Irish whiskey, apart from the spelling, is that Scotch is distilled twice and Irish three times.

About 2 miles (3km) along the coast road are the romantic remains of **Dunluce Castle** (tel: 028-2073 1938; Apr–Sept daily 10am–6pm, Oct–Mar 10am–4pm; charge). Poised on a rocky headland besides sheer cliffs, the 14th-century stronghold is huge and dramatic. It was abandoned in 1641, two years after part of the kitchen collapsed into the sea during a storm, carrying many servants to their death. In the graveyard of the adjacent ruined church are buried sailors from the Spanish Armada galleass *Girona*, which was wrecked on nearby rocks in 1588 with 1,300 men on board and was located on the seabed in 1967. Many of the *Girona*'s treasures are in Belfast's Ulster Museum.

Portrush and Portstewart

Next along the coast are two seaside resorts. **Portrush** ㉝ is the brasher, tackier, offering amusement arcades, burger bars, karaoke pubs, souvenir shops,

guest-houses, a children's adventure play park, boats trips for sea fishing and viewing the Causeway and two championship golf courses. The **Dunluce Centre** (tel: 028-7082 4444; Easter, July and Aug daily 11am–6pm, Apr–June and Sept–Oct Sat–Sun noon–5pm; charge), offers a virtual-reality "Treasure Fortress". **Portrush Countryside Centre** (Bath Road; tel: 028-7082 3600; Easter–Sept daily 10am–6pm, Oct–Easter Sun only noon–4pm; free) has rock pool animals in a touch tank.

Portstewart is the quieter, a tidy Victorian town with a huge strand, popular with anglers for its fine beach casting.

Nearby **Coleraine** is a busy market town whose traffic schemes make little of its setting on the wide River Bann or of the fact that the earliest human settlement in Ireland was found at the 200ft (60-metre) **Mount Sandel** in its southern suburbs. However, its university's **Riverside Theatre** (Colmore Road; tel: 028-7032 3232) imports interesting productions during term.

A choice of routes

Here, you can either continue westwards towards Derry City or south towards the international airport and Belfast.

Along the first choice, the A2 towards Derry City, on a windswept headland is **Downhill Demesne** ㉞ (Mussenden Road, Castlerock; tel: 028-2073 1582; grounds: dawn–dusk, house: Easter–Sept daily 10am–5pm; charge), concealing the ruins of Downhill Castle and Hezlett House, and Mussenden Temple, perched precariously on a cliff, which housed an eccentric bishop's library and possibly his mistress; it was inspired by the temples of Vesta at Tivoli and Rome. Downhill Forest has lovely walks, a fish pond and waterfalls.

Beyond is **Benone Beach**, part of Magilligan Strand, one of Ireland's best with golf, tennis, heated pools and children's play areas at its excellent adjoining Tourist Complex (tel: 028-7775 0555). At the beginning of the strand is a famous **Martello Tower**, built during the Napoleonic wars.

The alternative route is southwards through the relatively prosperous farming country "east of the **Bann**". This long, under-used river, which flows from the southeast of the province through Lough Neagh and into the Atlantic near Portstewart, is a rough and ready political dividing line between the western counties of Londonderry and Tyrone, with their preponderance of nationalists and Roman Catholics, and the eastern counties of Antrim and Down, with their Unionist/Protestant majority.

In a thriving market town like **Ballymoney** ㉟, 17 miles (27km) southwest of Ballycastle, archaic words that would have been familiar to Shakespeare crop up in conversation – a legacy of the Scots Presbyterians who settled in the 1800s.

As elsewhere in Ulster, churches loom large. There's one on each of the four roads leading into a small village like **Dervock**, for instance, 4 miles (6km) north of Ballymoney and ancestral home of America's President William McKinley (assassinated in 1901). Legend says that this strategic siting of churches keeps the Devil out. Locals suggest it probably keeps him in. Off the B96,

WHERE

Long-distance walkers can pick up the North Antrim Coast Path at Portstewart Strand. It forms part of the Ulster Way and extends eastwards for 40 miles (64km) to Murlough Bay.

BELOW: the Mussenden Temple.

Within the Antrim Castle Gardens is ***Clotworthy Arts Centre*** *(currently closed for restoration until 2011), a restored coach house and stables, which has art galleries and a theatre for music and drama as well as its very own ghost, a servant girl who perished in the fire that destroyed Antrim Castle, to which the coach house and stables belonged, in 1922.*

20 miles (33km) south, the restored **Arthur Ancestral Cottage** (Dreen, Cullybackey; tel: 028-2563 5900; Apr–Sept Thur–Sat 10.30am–4pm; charge) commemorates Chester Alan Arthur, US president from 1881 to 1885, whose father emigrated from it in 1815.

Ballymena ㊱, 19 miles (30km) southeast of Ballymoney, is the staunchly Protestant business centre of Antrim and, though not over-blessed with things to do, has the Ecos Millennium Environmental Centre (Kernohan's Lane, Broughshane Road; tel: 028-2566 4400; Mon–Fri 10am–5pm, also Easter, July–Aug Sat–Sun noon–5pm; free), raising children's awareness of the environment with fun activities inside and around its extensive grounds.

Antrim ㊲, the county town, 11 miles (18km) to the southeast, offers a little more to see. At **Pogue's Entry** (Church Street; tel: 028-9448 1338; June–mid-Sept Thur–Fri 2–5pm, Sat 10am–1pm, 2–5pm) is the 18th-century cottage, preserved in its original state, which was the birthplace of Alexander Irvine who became a missionary on New York's Bowery. There's an almost perfectly preserved round tower, more than 1,000 years old, in **Steeple Park**.

The **Antrim Castle Gardens,** (Randalstown Road; tel: 028-9448 1338; free) are laid out like a miniature Versailles and run down to the shore of Lough Neagh *(see margin note)*. The gardens are currently under restoration until June 2011 so there could be some access restrictions in place.

BELOW: Lough Neagh.

Lough Neagh

Lough Neagh (pronounced *Nay*), 17 miles long and 11 miles broad (27 by 18km) is the largest inland sheet of water in the British Isles. Legend has it that the warrior giant Finn McCool created the lake by scooping up a mighty handful of earth to fling at a rival Scottish giant (he missed, and the rock and clay fell into the Irish Sea to create the Isle of Man). Due to the lough's marshy edges, it has few access points – a reason, perhaps, why it is still one of western Europe's most important bird habitats.

The **Lough Neagh Discovery Centre** on Oxford Island *(for opening times, see page 315)* runs audio-visual shows about the wildlife and has a gift shop and café. There is sailing and water-skiing, with marinas at **Oxford Island** (south shore) and **Ballyronan** (west shore).

A large eel fishing industry is based at **Toome**. Until it became a fishermen's cooperative, gun battles used to take place on Lough Neagh between the police's patrol boats and the vessels of organised poachers.

The atmospheric, **Patterson's Spade Mill** (751 Antrim Road, Templepatrick; tel: 028-9443 3619; June–Aug Wed–Mon 2–6pm, mid-Mar–May and Sept Sat–Sun 2–6pm; charge) is Ireland's last working water-powered spade mill. And you can buy a spade, always remembering the Ulster saying about people who "dig with the other foot" – a reference from the days when the shapes of spades were very localised and a stranger's home and therefore, by inference, his religion could be told from the cut of his spade. Some obsessions in Ulster don't change much in centuries. ❑

RESTAURANTS AND BARS

Restaurants

Prices for a three-course dinner per person without wine:
£ = under £16
££ = £16–25
£££ = £25–40
££££ = over £40

Armagh

Manor Park Restaurant
2 College Hill, The Mall, Armagh, Co. Armagh
Tel: 028-3751 5353
Daily, L 11am–2.30pm, D 5.30–10pm, Early Bird 5–6.30pm. L **£**, Early Bird **££**, D **£££**
Lovely old-world character, French through and through (staff, menus, cuisine) albeit with a pride in local Irish ingredients, which are treated with care and cooked with skill by chef James Nelly who worked with Paul Rankin for 10 years.

Ballycastle

The Cellar Restaurant
11b The Diamond, Ballycastle, Co. Antrim
Tel: 028-2076 3057
Daily, L noon–3.30pm, D 3.30–10pm, winter D only. L **££**, D **£££**
Barrel-vaulted ceiling and cosy snugs. Menus, including daily specials, favour seafood with good steaks and vegetarian options. Children welcome up to 7pm.

Ballygally

Lyndon Heights Restaurant
97 Drumnagreagh Road, Ballygally, Co. Antrim
Tel: 028-2858 3560
D Fri–Sun 5–9pm, L Sun only 12.30–3pm. L **££**, D **££**
Located on the Antrim coastal drive. There are great views from this conservatory restaurant. Seafood and game in season are a strength on the menus. Carefully sourced ingredients, reliable cooking, generous portions and efficient service.

Bangor

The Boathouse
1A Seacliff Road, Bangor, Co. Down
Tel: 028-9146 9253
Wed–Sun, L noon–2.30pm, D 5–9.30pm. L **££**, D **£££**
Located in the old Harbour Masters Office beside the Marina. Original features have been retained to provide an enchanting setting in which to savour superior locally sourced food from an ever-changing menu.

Belleek

The Thatch
Belleek, Co. Fermanagh
Tel: 028-6865 8181
Food served: Mon–Sat 9am–5pm, from 10 in winter **£**
An essential stop on the main street through Belleek. The 18th-century coffee shop is the only thatched building remaining in the county, and its old-world charm and tradition of serving home-made food since the early 1900s is very much preserved; sandwiches and cakes to tempt the taste buds.

Bushmills

Bushmills Inn
9 Dunluce Road, Bushmills, Co. Antrim
Tel: 028-2073 3000
Daily noon–6pm, D 6–9.30pm, Sun L noon–3pm. L **££**, D **£££**
Delightful and comfortable 19th-century coaching inn where they take pride in offering traditional Ulster menus with a modern twist that respect local specialities. Roast carvery served Sunday lunch.

Tartine
The Distillers Arms, 40 Main Street, Bushmills, Co. Antrim
Tel: 028-2073 1044
L Sat–Sun 12.30–2.30pm, D daily 5–9pm, Fri–Sat until 9.30, closed Mon, Tue Oct–Mar. L **££**, D **£££**
Under new management since April 2009, the restaurant at the Distillers Arms has a new image and a new name. The refined dining room has low lighting and paintings by local artists on the walls. Simple but flavoursome modern dishes.

Dundrum

The Bucks Head Inn
77 Main Street, Dundrum, Co. Down
Tel: 028-4375 1868
Daily, closed Mon Oct–Apr, L noon–2.30pm, High tea 5–6pm, D 7–9pm, Sun until 8.30pm. Set L **£**, HT **££**, set D **£££**
Comfortable, welcoming bar and restaurant. Well planned menu reflecting seasonal availability of local seafood and local produce and traditions. Fine food in a relaxed atmosphere. Children welcome. Bar food, home baking, available all day.

RIGHT: fresh seafood is a local speciality.

Prices for a three-course dinner per person without wine:
£ = under £16
££ = £16–25
£££ = £25–40
££££ = over £40

Enniskillen

Café Merlot
6 Church Street, Enniskillen, Co. Fermanagh
Tel: 028-6632 0918
Daily, L noon–3pm, D 5–9pm, Fri–Sat until 9.30pm. L **£**, Early Bird 5.30–7.30pm **£**, D **££**
Informal bistro offering prompt service and reliable cooking in a downstairs, cosy dining space with vaulted ceilings.

Hillsborough

The Plough Inn
3 The Square. Hillsborough, Co. Down
Tel: 028-9268 2985
Daily pub hours; food served 10am–9.30pm. L **£**, D **£££**
Known for its friendly welcome and well-honed hospitality. With three food operations majoring on seafood you can eat at any time of day in this old coaching inn established in 1752. Choose from simple bar food or from a wider menu in the Plough restaurant (part of the original pub and also open most of the day). The Baretto Café and Bistro offer international dishes. Children are welcome in the café.

Holywood

Fontana Restaurant
61A High Street, Holywood, Co. Down
Tel: 028-9080 9908
Tue–Fri, L noon–2.30pm, Sun brunch 11am–3pm, D 5–9.30pm, Sat 6–10pm. L **£**, D **££**
Modern European cuisine served in sleek surroundings. Casual food style and menus. Imaginative use of locally sourced foods. Good seafood and vegetarian options.

Mitre Restaurant
Culloden Estate and Spa, Bangor Road, Co. Down
Tel: 028-9042 1066
L Sun only 12.30–2.30pm, D daily 7–9.30pm. L **£££**, D **£££**
Fine dining in luxury room overlooking the lough. Beautifully appointed and comfortable. Classic cuisine, impeccable cooking. Children welcome.

Killinchy

Baloo House
1 Comber Road, Killinchey, Co. Down
Tel: 028-9754 1210
Food served daily noon–9pm, Sun–Mon until 8.30pm. L **£**, D **££**
Choose to eat in either the downstairs Bistro or the upstairs restaurant. Top-class ingredients.

Kircubbin

Paul Arthur's Restaurant
66 Main Street, Kircubbin, Newtownards, Co. Down
Tel: 028-4273 8192
Daily, L noon–2.30pm, D Tue–Sun 5–9pm. L **£££**, D **£££**
Apart from a menu advertising the dishes on offer that night, the exterior gives little sign of the delights that await within. Simply, but comfortably furnished. The cooking is excellent, the menu is enticing and carefully constructed: seafood, local game in season, beef from their own farm and vegetarian options.

Limavady

Lime Tree
60 Catherine Street, Limivady, Co. Londonderry
Tel: 028-7776 4300
Tue–Sat, D 6–9pm, Sat until 9.30pm **££**; Early Bird 6–7pm **£**
Warm hospitality, carefully sourced local food and good cooking in the classic mode with occasional modern twists. Menus are concise but do change even though old favourites remain. Good value for money.

Londonderry

Browns Restaurant, Bar and Brasserie
1–2 Bond's Hill, Londonderry
Tel: 028-7134 5180
L Tue–Fri noon–2.30pm, Sun 10.30am–3pm. D Tue–Sat 5.30pm–late. L **£**, Early Bird Tue–Fri 5.30–6.45pm **£**. D **££**
Despite new ownership in 2009, the city's leading restaurant continues to offer consistently good creative cooking in the modern style.

Fitzroys
2–4 Bridge Street, Londonderry
Tel: 028-7126 6211
Daily noon–9.30pm, food served all day. L **£**, D **££**
Welcoming city-centre bistro with strong Mediterranean influences.

Mange 2
110–115 Strand Road, Londonderry
Tel: 028-7136 1222

L Tue–Fri 12.30–2.30pm, Sun noon–3.30pm, D daily 5–9.30pm. L **£**, D **£££**
Top quality French-inspired cuisine in the heart of Derry's historic walls with views of the river. The changing menu features unpretentious signature dishes that make the most of the fine fresh and local produce available, cooked to perfection.

Newcastle

Hugh McCanns
119–121 Central Promenade, Newcastle, Co. Down
Tel: 028-4372 2487
Daily 10am–9.30pm. L **£**, D **££**
In a great location with both mountain and sea views. The family-owned café-bar cum deli is ideal for a light lunch or something more substantial; renowned for its steaks and mouth-watering desserts.

Portaferry

Portaferry Hotel and Restaurant
The Strand, Portaferry, Co. Down
Tel: 028-427 28231
Daily, L noon–2.30pm, D 5.30–9pm, Sun until 8.30pm. L **££**, Early Bird **££**, D **£££**
A place of great character and comfort. A deserved reputation for good traditional and unpretentious local food, especially seafood, lamb and game in season. Children's menu.

Strabane

Oysters Restaurant
37 Patrick Street, Strabane, Co. Tyrone
Tel: 028-7138 2690
Daily, L noon–3pm, Sat–Sun until 4pm, D 5–9.30pm, Sat until 10pm. L **££**, D **££**
An innovative chef and speciality dishes have made Oysters worthy of its fine-dining reputation. Irish favourites fused with a modern twist, using locally sourced ingredients, are served by attentive staff who have an extensive knowledge of the menu.

Warrenpoint

Copper Restaurant
4 Duke Street, Warrenpoint, Co. Down
Tel: 028-4175 3047
L Wed–Sun noon–3pm, D Tue–Sun 5.30–9.30pm, Sun until 8.30pm. L **££**, D **££–£££**
Comfortable, welcoming room offers concise but imaginative set menu, a tasting menu and extensive à la carte. Talented chef cooks great soups, seafood and meat casseroles. Service good, prices fair.

Restaurant 23
23 Church Street, Warrenpoint, Co. Down
Tel: 028-4175 3222
Wed–Sun, L 12.30–3pm, D 6.30–9pm, Fri–Sat until 10pm. L **£**, D **££–£££**
Elegant, comfortable room. A great team led by talented head chef Trevor Cunningham are in charge of this wonderful addition to Warrenpoint. Enticing mid-week set menu and à la carte with highest quality foods; eclectic mix of traditional and cutting edge modern, presented with style and top-class cooking.

Bars

The House of McDonnell in Ballycastle has been run by the same family since it first opened in April 1766, who have retained and maintained its classic style. Traditional music sessions on Friday nights.

Distillers Arms, Bushmills. A contemporary style bar set in renovated 19th-century building. Food on offer in restaurant (lunch and dinner) features signature dish of salmon cured in Bushmills whiskey.

Grace O' Neill's, Donaghadee. A good stop on the Ards Peninsula, this inn dates back to 1611 and claims to be one of the oldest in all Ireland. The old has been left unspoilt; behind, a stylish contemporary restaurant has been built serving good value traditional dishes with an imaginative spin. Traditional Irish music.

Sweeney's public house and wine bar, Portballintrae, Co. Antrim. Close to the Giant's Causeway and Portrush golf club is an attractive stone building with open fires in the bar, a choice of places to drink, including the wine bar/bistro where food is on offer. Live folk and country music can be found here during peak times and over some weekends.

Coyle's Bar, Bangor. A very pleasant, modernised bar and bistro in Bangor where well cooked and presented modern food is on offer both day and evening.

Denvirs in Downpatrick is bang in the centre of the town. This wonderful old pub has genuine old-world original features (some uncovered during renovations). Bar and restaurant food available.

The Cuan, Strangford, has a well-kept, cosy lounge and homely bar, close to the ferry. Bar and restaurant food available.

The Bank in Newry is a fine old former banking hall near the main bridge. It has now become an upmarket contemporary bar that serves food all day.

LEFT: whiskey casks at Bushmills.
RIGHT: the Ulster Fry, a classic local breakfast.

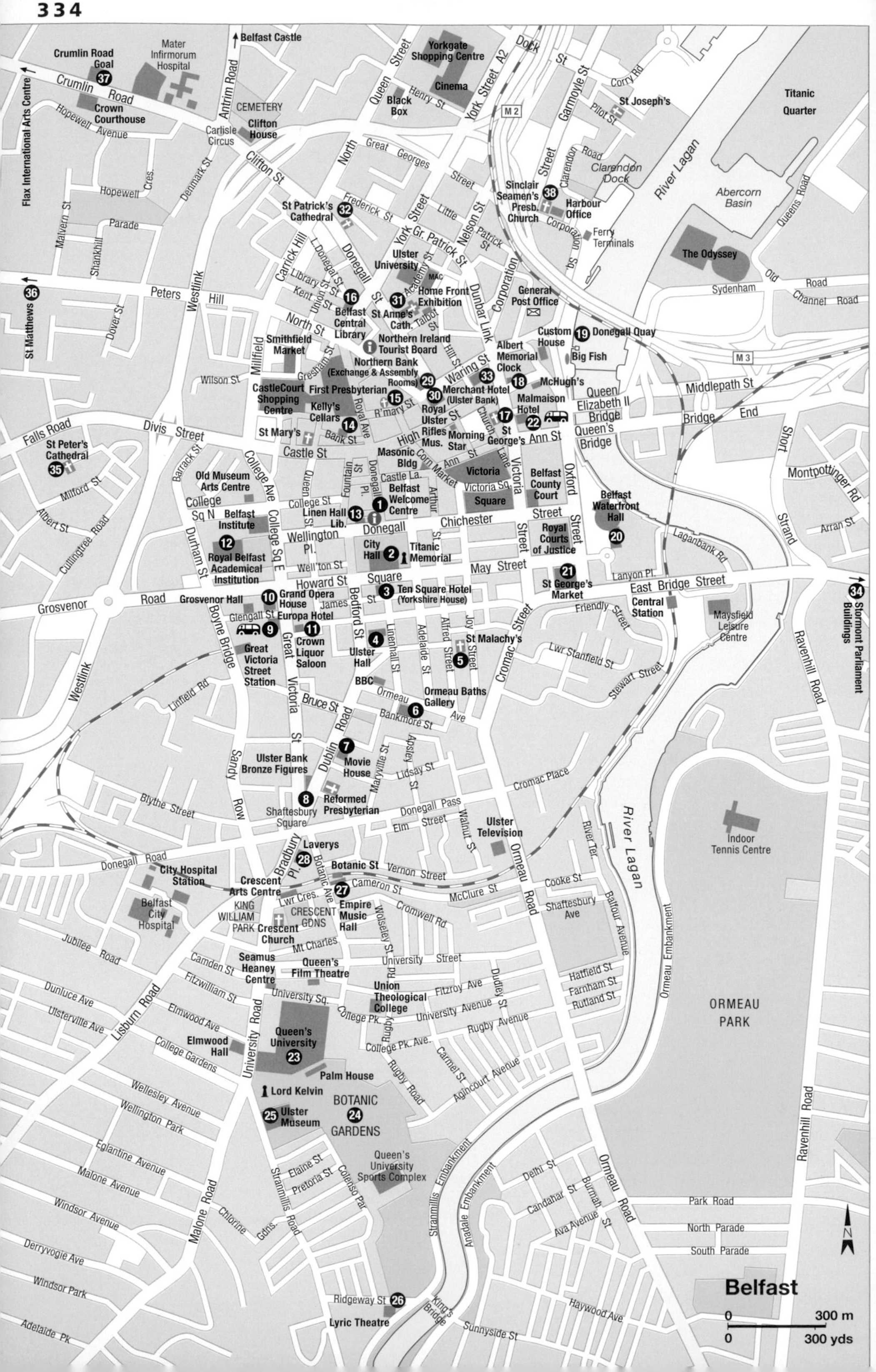
Belfast
0 300 m
0 300 yds
N
Belfast Castle
Crumlin Road Goal
Mater Infirmorum Hospital
Yorkgate Shopping Centre
Cinema
Black Box
Crown Courthouse
CEMETERY
Clifton House
Carlisle Circus
Flax International Arts Centre
St Joseph's
Titanic Quarter
Clarendon Dock
River Lagan
Abercorn Basin
The Odyssey
St Patrick's Cathedral
Sinclair Seamen's Presb. Church
Harbour Office
Ferry Terminals
Ulster University
MAC
Home Front Exhibition
General Post Office
Belfast Central Library
St Anne's Cath.
Northern Ireland Tourist Board
Smithfield Market
Custom House
Donegall Quay
Big Fish
Albert Memorial Clock
Northern Bank (Exchange & Assembly Rooms)
First Presbyterian
CastleCourt Shopping Centre
Merchant Hotel (Ulster Bank)
McHugh's
Malmaison Hotel
Kelly's Cellars
Royal Ulster Rifles Mus.
St George's
Morning Star
St Mary's
St Peter's Cathedral
Masonic Bldg
Victoria Square
Belfast County Court
Old Museum Arts Centre
Belfast Welcome Centre
Belfast Waterfront Hall
Linen Hall Lib.
Belfast Institute
City Hall
Titanic Memorial
Royal Courts of Justice
Royal Belfast Academical Institution
St George's Market
Ten Square Hotel (Yorkshire House)
Grosvenor Hall
Grand Opera House
Europa Hotel
Central Station
Maysfield Leisure Centre
Stormont Parliament Buildings
Crown Liquor Saloon
Great Victoria Street Station
Ulster Hall
St Malachy's
BBC
Ormeau Baths Gallery
Ulster Bank Bronze Figures
Movie House
Reformed Presbyterian
Shaftesbury Square
Ulster Television
Laverys
Botanic St
City Hospital Station
Crescent Arts Centre
Empire Music Hall
Belfast City Hospital
KING WILLIAM PARK
CRESCENT GDNS
Crescent Church
Indoor Tennis Centre
Seamus Heaney Centre
Queen's Film Theatre
Union Theological College
Queen's University
Elmwood Hall
ORMEAU PARK
Palm House
Lord Kelvin
BOTANIC GARDENS
Ulster Museum
Queen's University Sports Complex
Lyric Theatre
Crumlin Road
Antrim Road
Clifton St
Peters Hill
Westlink
Falls Road
Divis Street
Grosvenor Road
Donegall Road
Lisburn Road
Malone Road
University Road
Ormeau Road
Ravenhill Road
East Bridge Street
Queen Elizabeth II Bridge
Queen's Bridge
Middlepath St
Sydenham Road
Channel Road
Bridge End
Short Strand
Montpottinger Rd
Oxford Street
May Street
Chichester Street
Donegall Square
Donegall Place
Royal Ave
High St
Ann St
Victoria Street
Cromac Street
Dublin Road
Great Victoria St
Bedford St
Sandy Row
Botanic Ave
Stranmillis Road
Stranmillis Embankment
Ormeau Embankment
M2
M3
A2
St Matthews

BELFAST

Forget the television coverage. This is a city of unexpected charms, mixing splendid Victorian architecture with a genuine hospitality

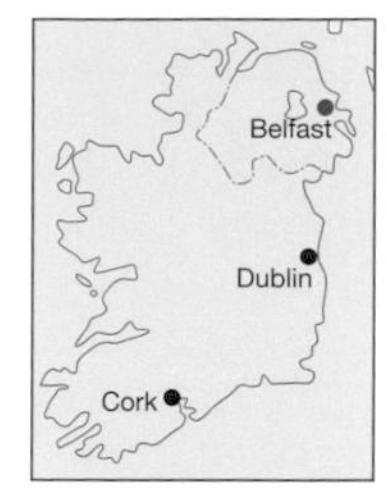

Main attractions
CITY HALL
ULSTER HALL
GRAND OPERA HOUSE
CROWN LIQUOR SALOON
LINEN HALL LIBRARY
ALBERT MEMORIAL CLOCK
BELFAST WATERFRONT HALL
QUEEN'S UNIVERSITY
ROYAL BOTANIC GARDENS
ULSTER MUSEUM
PARLIAMENT BUILDINGS
BELFAST ZOO

Belfast's dominant Victorian and Edwardian architecture resembles more a northern English city, such as Leeds or Liverpool, than the softer Georgian elegance of Dublin, just a hundred miles south. But Northern Ireland's capital has other attributes. A low-rise, open city, framed between lofty green Cave Hill and the great blue bowl of Belfast Lough, it is dotted with lovely parks and open spaces and, for a major city, is surprisingly easy to get around and out of, into the beginning of Northern Ireland's beautiful rural hinterland.

Above all, it's the people of Belfast who remain its great attraction. Despite preconceptions to the contrary, Belfast people remain among the friendliest you will meet, with an easy and down-to-earth sense of humour. And, ironically, it is precisely that synthesis of Ulster Scots and native Irish, so long a source of division, that gives the people of Belfast their distinct personality.

Belfast sells itself today as the birthplace of the legendary *Titanic*, whose luxurious embellishment symbolised the apex of Belfast's Edwardian heyday as one of the world's greatest ports, and whose watery fate barely predated Belfast's own long industrial and manufacturing decline. Now the city, rejuvenated with the help of huge investment from the UK government, has been enjoying a renaissance as a short-break destination. Visitors will find a dynamic, forward-thinking city with an infectious vitality. There are ongoing projects both sides of River Lagan including the development of the Cathedral Quarter, and the city's Quays are core to the revitalisation of the riverfront.

The city centre

Belfast Welcome Centre ❶ (47 Donegall Place; tel: 028-9024 6609) is a good place to pick up informative brochures. It has a multilingual staff who can advise on everything from attractions and events to restaurants and bars and book

RIGHT: the view from City Hall.

EAT

Belfast has a collection of fine places to eat under the auspices of Belfast's Michelin-starred chef Michael Deane. He started his career in London and moved back to Northern Ireland in 1993, gaining his star in 1997 for the flagship Restaurant Michael Deane in Howard Street, now renamed Deanes *(see page 350)*. Along from the Ulster Hall are the New York-style Deane's Deli and Parisian flavoured Café Vin, and Deanes at Queens completes the set.

accommodation, not just for Belfast but Northern Ireland as a whole.

Around the corner is the **City Hall** ❷ (Donegall Square; tel: 028-9027 0456; tours: Mon–Fri 11am, 2pm, 3pm, Sat 2pm, 3pm; free). Dubbed a "Wren-aissance" building due to its shameless borrowing from St Paul's Cathedral in London, it is at the heart of Belfast. Famed for its marbled halls, its plush Council Chamber has resounded to some of the liveliest debate in the history of public affairs. The portraits of the lord mayors in the corridors tell their own story of Belfast's divided history, a long line of formally dressed unionists eventually reaching the first Catholic (SDLP) lord mayor in 1997. Not until 2002, with Sinn Féin's informally attired Alex Maskey, do you find a republican.

City Hall reopened in October 2009 following major refurbishment, which resulted in a new coffee shop and an exhibition area focusing on Belfast industries from the 17th century to the present day. The surrounding gardens are a favourite summer lunchtime spot. Its many monuments include Thomas Brock's frumpy statue of **Queen Victoria** while his marble figure of **Thane,** erected to mark the sinking of *Titanic* in 1912, is a place of commemoration during the "Titanic – Made in Belfast" festival, which takes place every April. City Hall's gardens are also the venue for many annual events.

On the south side of City Hall remain several buildings from Belfast's linen era, including Yorkshire House, an old warehouse, now a chic hotel, **Ten Square** ❸ (10 Donegall Square South; tel: 028-9024 1001) whose Linenhall Street facade has some interesting carvings.

Ulster Hall

Also in Linenhall Street, the style of this part of the Linen Conservation Area is typified by the work of the celebrated architect Charles Lanyon *(see box on opposite page)* at number **35–37.** Running parallel on the west side is Bedford Street, home to the distinguished **Ulster Hall** ❹ (No. 30; tel: 028-9033 4400). Built in 1862 as a music hall, it now hosts rock and classical concerts, and cultural events. After being restored to its Victorian splendour in 2009, it has become home of the Ulster Orchestra.

BELOW: Ulster Hall. **RIGHT:** Linen Hall Library.

Around the corner at 24 **Alfred Street** is the Catholic **St Malachy's Church** ❺, noted for its Tudor-style exterior and delightful fan-vaulted ceiling, famously described as an upside down wedding cake. The church was reopened after an extensive restoration in March 2009.

Around the corner at 18a Ormeau Avenue, one of Belfast's leading art galleries has been established at a beautifully converted Victorian bathhouse. The **Ormeau Baths Gallery** ❻ (tel: 028-9032 1402; Tue–Sat 10am–5.30pm) has regular exhibitions of leading contemporary Irish and international artists.

Touring the BBC

Across the road you can now take a behind-the-screen tours of **BBC Northern Ireland's** headquarters (tel: 0370 901 1227; tours: Mon and Tue at noon; free). This is one of many "hard hat" tours of unusual buildings (pick up a brochure at the Belfast Welcome Centre).

Once an integral part of what was known as Belfast's "Golden Mile" when the city's tourism offering was constricted by the Troubles, the Dublin Road remains a collection of fast food outlets, short-lived Asian restaurants and cheerful, noisy pubs and clubs. The street's best and most enduring restaurant is the glass-fronted **Square** (tel: 028-9023 9933), at No. 89. On the other side of the road, **Auntie Annie's Porterhouse** (tel: 028-9050 1660), at No. 44, typifies Belfast's growing reputation for unpretentious fun and is known for promoting good local rock bands. You can check out the latest blockbusters at the **Movie House** complex ❼ at No. 14 Dublin Road (tel: 028-9024 5700).

Though Belfast's antique scene is disappearing fast, the best of what remains can be found in **Donegall Pass,** which also has two good Chinese restaurants, the Water Margin (Nos 159–161) in a converted church at the bottom of the road, and the atmospheric and authentic Sun Kee (Nos 42–47). **Shaftesbury Square** ❽ contains Belfast's celebrity chef Paul Rankin's acclaimed Cayenne, elegantly refurbished and still amongst the best in the city. On the Portland stone façade of the Ulster Bank opposite are two bronze figures by Elizabeth Frink, nicknamed "draft" and "overdraft" by locals.

Though some political opponents elected to the Northern Ireland Assembly found it hard to sit at the same table, the same wasn't true of those elected to Belfast City Council. Once dominated by Unionists, the council's membership now reflects the city's divisions, yet business gets done. Sinn Féin holds 14 of the 51 seats, closely followed by the Democratic Unionist Party with 13. Other Unionist and nationalist parties are more or less matched.

BELOW: City Hall and Donegall Square.

Lanyon's legacy

Charles Lanyon (1813–89), an English architect, carpet-bagger and engineer, conferred on the city's new bank buildings the majestic solidity of the palazzi of northern Italian merchant princes. He understood the essence of the architectural faddishness. He caught the spirit of early Victorian righteousness.

His Piranesian Crumlin Road County Gaol promises unbridled retribution. Queen's University's spoof Elisabethanry unashamedly appropriates Oxford's Magdalen. His Doric façade of the Union Theological College promises dour Presbyterianism. His Palladian Custom House intimidates. He was responsible for 14 churches. Although a philanderer who openly bought election votes, Lanyon was knighted, became the city's mayor and also one of its Conservative MPs.

Belfast's Heady History

The history of Ireland's only industrial city is brief by European standards, but it is a turbulent one of power struggles in factories and politics

Belfast could barely said to have existed before the arrival of Arthur Chichester at the very end of the 16th century. Tasked with the anglicisation of the fiercely Irish province of Ulster, Chichester defeated the rebellious Hugh O'Neill, last of the great Irish Chieftains, and cleared the land of its original owners. By introducing English and Scottish settlers, he changed the nature of Ulster forever.

Chichester built a striking timber castle in 1611 (which later burnt down) and developed a small "towne of good forme" around it. For almost two centuries, Belfast grew slowly, handicapped by a corrupt and incompetent corporation. Despite a growing importance as a trading port, the town did not register its first major shipbuilder until the arrival of William Ritchie (whose first dry dock, dating from 1796, can be seen near Clarendon Dock).

It was not until the 19th-century industrial revolution, when Belfast added world-leading roles in shipbuilding, engineering and various kinds of manufacturing to its existing pre-eminence in the linen industry, that the now populous town hit its stride. It was now that the buildings that dominate Belfast today began to take shape as the great industrialists and entrepreneurs turned to architects such as Sir Charles Lanyon to reflect the town's increasing prestige in a more permanent way. Lanyon himself was responsible for many of Belfast's most iconic buildings *(see panel, page 337)*.

Despite a growing Catholic population, however, God's blessing seemed still to have a strong Protestant bias in the city. While many thousands of Catholics had flocked to the linen mills of west Belfast during the 19th century, power remained in the hands of Belfast's unionist ascendancy (a power base locked in by the partition of Ireland in 1920).

By the 1870s, a young William Pirrie had added his insatiable ambition and extraordinary abilities as a salesman to the firm of Edward Harland and Gustav Wolff, who were on their way to becoming the world's greatest shipbuilders from their fast expanding base at Queen's Island.

Following Queen's Victoria's conferring of city status on Belfast in 1888, Belfast Corporation invited designs for a new city hall be built on the site of the old White Linen Hall. The competition was won by Brumwell Thomas, an Englishman who happily admitted his debt to Christopher Wren and London's St Paul's Cathedral. Similarly clad in finest Portland stone, City Hall was adorned with marble from the same quarry that supplied classical Rome and no expense was spared to impress. When the building opened in 1906 critics of its budget busting extravagance were silenced and the ambition of the new city, now with a population of 450,000, appeared to have no limit. In fact, Belfast was already nearing the apex of its prestige.

Today, tourism chiefs have divided Belfast into a series of quarters, and though boundaries tend to be vague, each has a distinct personality. ❑

ABOVE: Belfast's High Street in around 1910.
LEFT: Belfast in 1911, with *Titanic* in the background.

Despite damage from bombs and planners, **Great Victoria Street**, which runs north off Shaftesbury Square, contains several of Belfast's best-known tourist honey-pots. It also contains the much-bombed four-star Hastings **Europa** ❾, a base for hundreds of journalists during the Troubles and almost a tourist attraction in itself.

Grand Opera House

The street's highlights are at the northern end, on opposite sides of the road. Extensively refurbished and extended in 2006, the twin-domed **Grand Opera House** ❿ (tel: 028-9024 1919; www.goh.co.uk), with its plush brass and velvet, gilded elephant heads supporting the boxes, and excellent acoustics, was designed by theatre architect Frank Matcham. Thanks to its now extended wing space, the venue, where Luciano Pavarotti made his UK debut and Sarah Bernhardt, Orson Welles and Laurel and Hardy all appeared, can now house the grandest West End productions.

Diagonally opposite the Opera House, you can't help but notice the rusticated sandstone Tudor Gothic bulk of the **Presbyterian Assembly Rooms** now given over to an elegant shopping centre, the Spires Mall. Also on this side of the road, it's worth taking time to enjoy Guinness and oysters at one of the world's most beautiful Victorian pubs, the **Crown Liquor Saloon** ⓫, (tel: 028-9024 3187; www.crownbar.com), which was elegantly restored by the National Trust on the advice of John Betjeman. Its tiling and stained-glass windows were the work of some of Italy's finest craftsmen, in Belfast to work on Catholic churches and the White Star liners, in the 1880s.

As Great Victoria Street continues, **College Square East** reveals one of the city's finest buildings, Sir John Soane's dignified red brick **Royal Belfast Academical Institution** ⓬. The baroque Portland stone building to the north, now part of **Belfast Metropolitan College**, has one of the last working steam-engine-powered ventilating and heating systems.

Around the corner the **Old Museum Arts Centre** (7 College Square North; tel: 028-9023 3332; www.oldmuseumartscentre.org) specialises in groundbreaking theatre, comedy and arts. Its relocation

DRINK

Two doors north of the historic Crown Liquor Saloon is **Robinson's Bar** (www.robinsonsbar.co.uk), entirely new but rebuilt to its original 1846 design. It is now home to five bars, including the Irish-themed Fibber Magees, which hosts traditional Irish music sessions, the Bistro and Roxy, a New York loft-style club.

BELOW: the Crown Liquor Saloon, preserved by the National Trust.

Linen Hall Library.

to the new Metropolitan Arts Centre, or MAC *(see page 345)*, in the Cathedral Quarter is due to take place early 2012.

Linen Hall Library

East along **Wellington Place**, the **Linen Hall Library** ⓭ (17 Donegall Square North; tel: 028-9032 1707; www.linenhall.com; Mon–Fri 9.30am–5.30pm, Sat 9.30am–4pm), is Ireland's last public subscription library. As well as the definitive Troubles, Northern Ireland theatrical, C.S. Lewis and Irish Studies collections, it also has a pleasant café and literary-themed shop. Each Monday at 5pm (not in winter) enthralling literary tours of Belfast leave from here (call the Belfast Welcome Centre on 028-9024 6609 to book).

To the north is Donegall Place, with its streetscape of British chain stores. Off it, past Castle Junction, west down Bank Street, is **Kelly's Cellars** ⓮ (Nos 30-32; tel: 028-9024 6058), dating from 1780. Though considerably refurbished, the bars retain much of the charm, which appealed to Henry Joy McCracken and other Protestant leaders of the United Irishmen as they plotted here in 1798. It is also known for excellent Irish traditional music sessions held Monday to Thursday evenings.

Across High Street, you can take two routes. The first, north, brings you to **Rosemary Street** where, at **No. 33, William Drennan**, founder of the United Irishmen was born and where, at No. 41, in the 1783 **First Presbyterian (Non-Subscribing) Church** ⓯, the oldest place of worship within the city, its congregation once included *Titanic* designer Thomas Andrews, no doubt attracted by its charming boat-like interior. One of Belfast's oldest thoroughfares, Rosemary Street also hosts that shrine to freemasonry, the **Provincial Masonic Hall.** A plaque on the wall commemorates radical Belfast Presbytarian Henry Joy McCracken who worshipped in the church that once stood here.

Further up Royal Avenue the red sandstone **Belfast Central Library** ⓰ (tel: 028-9050 9150; Mon–Thur 9am–8pm, Fri–Sat 9am–4.30pm) is a good place to

BELOW: boat tours explore Belfast's port.

Aristocrat owners

The industrial revolution was facilitated by a change in land ownership. Until the mid-19th century, Belfast was the only Irish town to be run as a private fiefdom by a single family, lying as it did within the Donegall estate in Co. Antrim, owned by the descendants of British administrator Sir Arthur Chichester.

The first Marquis of Donegall, though he lived in England, was enlightened enough to fund fine public buildings and insist on decent architectural standards. His spendthrift son, who succeeded to the estates in 1799, continued this policy but ran up such huge debts that he was forced to start selling off leases. By 1855 virtually the whole town had been sold to tenants or rich speculators.

The family's legacy lies in the number of Belfast streets named after them.

start for those wishing to research Belfast or Northern Irish history and culture, with extensive collections and a wide range of periodicals and news-papers going back to the 19th century.

High Street

The other route takes you up High Street. Off High Street is the narrow alleyway Wineceller Entry and the charming and, by Belfast standards, ancient **White's Tavern** (No. 2; tel: 028-9024 3080), where Irish traditional music is played on Fridays and Sundays. Further along High Street is the excellent Wicker Man gift shop (Nos 44–46; tel: 028-9024 3550).

The striking portico of the magnificent **St George's Church** ⓱ (1816) was transported by canal from the house of the eccentric Earl Bishop of Derry (tel: 028-9023 1275 for visiting hours). At Queen's Square, across Victoria Street, the **Albert Memorial Clock** ⓲ was, until its recent restoration, threatening to rival the Leaning Tower of Pisa, while the renovated **McHugh's bar** claims to be housed in Belfast's oldest building.

Around the corner, Lanyon's glorious **Custom House**, where Anthony Trollope once worked, looks over what is now Belfast's premier public space. Since its transformation in 2005, Custom House Square has become a premier outdoor venue, used for all kinds of events from carnivals to live music.

Donegall Quay

Donegall Quay ⓳ is the place to catch the Lagan Boat Company's fine tours *(see margin tip)* and see local sculptor John Kindness's now famous **Big Fish**, a 32ft (9.8-metre) salmon whose ceramic "skin" tells the history of Belfast.

Across the River Lagan, at what is the developing Titanic Quarter, the **Odyssey Pavillion** (Queen's Quay; tel: 028-9045 1055; www.odysseypavillion.com) is home to the Belfast Giants ice hockey team and is a venue for sporting events and pop concerts. The Pavilion hosts the interactive discovery centre, **W5** (tel: 028-9046 7700; www.w5online.co.uk; during school term Mon–Thur 10am–5pm, Fri–Sat 10am–6pm, Sun noon–6pm; charge), with nearly 200 interactive exhibits; a 20-lane tenpin bowling alley; Ireland's only 2D and 3D Imax Cinema

WHERE

Titanic tours

On the Lagan Boat Company's *Titanic* tours, you can see the drawing rooms where the ill-fated ship was designed, its dry dock and the slipway from which it was launched in 1912. The company also runs boat trips down the river. www.laganboatcompany.com.

LEFT: festival time at the Albert Memorial Clock. **BELOW:** the Big Fish, celebrating the return of salmon to the once polluted Lagan.

Waterfront Hall.

(tel: 028-9046 7000); the 12-screen Storm Cinema Complex (tel: 028-9073 9134) and a number of cafés, bars, restaurants and nightclubs.

Waterfront Hall

South along the Lagan is the copper-domed **Belfast Waterfront Hall** ⓴ (2 Lanyon Place; tel: 028-9033 4455; www.waterfront.co.uk), a forerunner of Belfast's renaissance when built in 1997 and a venue for top international performers.

Beside the Waterfront Hall is the Hilton, across the road the neoclassical **Royal Courts of Justice**, fashioned from Portland Stone.

At the corner of Oxford Street and May Street, **St George's Market** ㉑, Ireland's oldest covered market, has been elegantly refurbished and now has many stalls selling superb locally produced food, including cheeses, organic meats, fish and seafood, and plants at the Saturday **Food and Garden Market** (9am–3pm). The Friday **Variety Market** (6am–2pm) has many of those food stalls plus books, antiques and more.

Head down May Street and turn right into Victoria Street, where you will see the spectacular glass dome of Belfast's biggest and most impressive shopping centre, the £230 million **Victoria Square**, opened in 2008.

On the other side of Victoria Square is the triangular **Bittles** bar, with its literary paintings and, nearby, the **Kitchen Bar**, one of Belfast's most famous traditional pubs, still picking up awards despite its recent move from its original location to make way for Victoria Square. Further along Victoria Street is the excellent **Malmaison Hotel** ㉒ (Nos 34–38; tel: 028-9022 0200), with its dramatic Goth meets Lewis Carroll decor, housed in two Victorian warehouses famous for their exterior carvings.

Queen's Quarter

Based around Sir Charles Lanyon's distinguished Queen's University, Queen's Quarter is a curious mixture of student haunts, elegant academia and Belfast's designer-label heartland, the Lisburn Road. **Queen's University** ㉓, its blue-tinged red brick at its best near dusk, is one of Lanyon's delights, appropriating the Tudor of Oxford's Magdalen Col-

BELOW: graduation, Queen's University.

lege. There are over 100 listed buildings around the campus and surrounding area and it's worth picking up the "Walkabout Queen's" leaflet from the **Queen's Welcome Centre** (tel: 028-9097 5252; Mon–Fri 9.30am–4.30pm, Sat–Sun 10am–1pm) to help you on a signposted tour. In particular, search out the Great Hall, which Lanyon based on the medieval great halls of the Oxbridge universities. Also check out the **Naughton Gallery** (tel: 028-9097 3580; www.naughtongallery.org) in the Lanyon Building, which houses the university's own collection and often hosts interesting touring exhibitions.

You can find the best of world cinema at the **Queen's Film Theatre** near Queen's University (20 University Square; tel: 028-9097 1097; www.queensfilmtheatre.com), which now has two screens and a comfortable bar/lounge. Opposite the University's lawns stands its modernised **Student's Union**.

Nearby is the delightful Italianate deconsecrated wedding cake, **Elmwood Hall,** which hosts concerts. Towards the end of October Queen's is the hub of the annual Belfast Festival at Queens (tel: 028-9097 1345).

Northwards down University Road from Queen's is a selection of atmospheric cafés and restaurants. Leading novelist Glen Patterson teaches creative writing across the road at the **Seamus Heaney Centre** (tel: 028-9097 1070), which organises literary events such as poetry readings, book launches and talks around Queen's.

Royal Botanic Gardens

South of the University, the **Royal Botanic Gardens** ㉔ (tel: 028-9031 4762; 7.30am–dusk; free) contain another Lanyon gem, his restored curvilinear **Palm House** (Apr–Sept Mon–Fri 10am–noon, 1–5pm, Sat–Sun 1–5pm, Oct–Mar until 3.45pm; free). In the **Tropical Ravine** (same details as Palm House), water drips from banana leaves in a miniature sunken rainforest.

On the park's Stranmillis Road boundary, the **Ulster Museum** ㉕ (Botanic Gardens; tel: 0845-608 0000; www.nmni.com; Tue–Sun 10am–5pm; free), which reopened in 2009 following an exciting transformation, now features a 75ft (23 metre) high atrium that leads into fascinating history, art and science galleries. The museum also has a new enclosed rooftop gallery to house its glass, jewellery and Belleek collections.

Further south takes you to the pleasant villagey atmosphere of Stranmillis and the site of the **Lyric Theatre** ㉖ at 55 Ridgeway Street, (tel: 028-9038 1081), where Ulster-born actor Liam Neeson first trod the boards. Currently, a new theatre is being built by the River Lagan, due to open in spring 2011.

Evening entertainment

North from Queen's again is the heavily student-influenced Botanic Avenue, home to excellent cafés such as Café Renoir (No. 95; tel: 028-9031 1300) and AM:PM (No. 67–69; tel: 028-9023 9443), some of Belfast's best-value food at outlets like Maggie May and The Other Place, the excellent crime bookshop No Alibis (No. 83; tel: 028-9031 9607), known for book launches and a regular

The University

Queen's University's campus is modest in size and so, as the university expanded to around 24,000 students and 1,600 teaching and research staff, it began buying up every vacant building in the area. Currently it owns more than 250 buildings. A large proportion of students come from Northern Ireland and, as many of those with families outside Belfast travel home at weekends, social activities at weekends are less extensive than one might expect.

BELOW: Botanic Gardens.

TIP

Finding a taxi
Taxis operate from "taxi ranks" and do not stop when hailed. One of the main taxi ranks in Belfast city centre is in front of City Hall and there are further ranks at the airports and main stations. There are two types of taxi: London-style hackneys and saloon car "radio cab" companies such as Value Cabs (tel: 028-9080 9080), fonaCAB (tel: 028-9033 3333) or Citi Cabs (tel: 028-9066 5566).

haunt of Belfast writer Colin Bateman), and retro clothes shops like Rusty Zip at No. 28 (tel: 028-9024 9700). The focus of the street is the all-purpose Madisons (No. 59–63; tel: 028-9050 9800), a lively hotel/bar/restaurant/nightclub with an up-front decor worthy of Barcelona.

The **Empire Music Hall** ㉗ (42 Botanic Avenue; tel: 028-9024 9276), a deconsecrated church, features comedy, live music and entertainment most nights (in university term time). Around the corner in Lower Crescent Avenue is the 19th-century **Crescent Townhouse** hotel at No. 13 (tel: 028-9032 3349), with its stylish Metro brasserie and Bar Twelve, and Taphouse (5–6 Lower Crescent Street; tel: 028-9050 9750), a student hotspot where a heady mix of sport and music are the focus of attention.

At the meeting point of Lower Crescent Street and University Road is the **Crescent Arts Centre** (2–4 University Road; tel: 028-9024 2338), a 19th-century building of Scrabo stone, which also houses the excellent Fenderesky art gallery, which majors in contemporary Irish art. The centre reopened in April 2010 following major refurbishment.

BELOW: a Belfast blues band play the Kitchen Bar.

Left up University Road are two of Belfast's most enduring restaurants, Italian cuisine Belfast-style at **Villa Italia** (No. 37–41; tel: 028-9032 8356) and **Beatrice Kennedy** (No. 44; tel: 028-9020 2290).

Around the corner in Bradbury Place is one of the city's liveliest nightspots, **Laverys** ㉘ (Nos 12–16; tel: 028-9087 1106), with live music and sounds at its five bars over three levels. Over the road at No. 31; the **M-Club** (tel: 028-9023 3131) packs them in for party nights of music, not least for its gloriously tacky 1970s tribute night, Groovy Train.

Lisburn Road

You're now at the start of the **Lisburn Road,** a long tree-lined avenue studded with fine restaurants like Shu (No. 253; tel: 028-9038 1655), chic bar/restaurants such as the Chelsea Wine Bar (No. 346; tel: 028-9068 7177), café/delis like the Yellow Door at No. 427 (tel: 028-9038 1961) and a range of boutiques, such as **Bison** (No. 713a; tel: 028-9066 9988) and **Hugo Thomas** (No. 669; tel: 028-9066 2060), displaying the latest designer names. It's also home to many of Belfast's finest private art galleries, including the **Eakin Gallery** at No. 237 (tel: 028-9066 8522), the **Tom Caldwell Gallery** at No. 429 (tel: 028-9066 1890) and **Gormley's** at No. 251 (tel: 028-9066 3313).

Cathedral Quarter

Gradually the transformation of Belfast's historic Cathedral Quarter to a cultural and entertainment district to rival Dublin's Temple Bar is acquiring some credibility. Beginning where Bridge Street meets Waring Street is the Soviet-themed **Northern Whig** with its chunky sofas and fine range of vodkas.

Opposite, the historic 1769 **Exchange and Assembly Rooms** ㉙ (converted to the Northern Bank by Sir Charles Lanyon), hosted a famous harp festival attended by rebels Wolfe Tone (who disapproved) and fellow United Irishman Henry Joy McCracken.

Across Donegall Street, the lovely façade of the Four Corners building has been preserved as a Premier Inn. Worth visiting on Waring Street is the **Royal Ulster Rifles Museum** ㉚ (No. 5; tel: 028-9023 2086; Mon–Fri 10am–12.30pm, 2–4pm, Fri until 2.30pm; charge).

Take a left down Donegall Street, passing two fine pubs, the traditional **Duke of York** (Nos. 7–11 Commercial Court; tel: 028-9024 1062) and the **John Hewitt** at No. 51 Donegall Street (tel: 028-9023 3768), a superb community-run pub which features live music and is a key venue in the area's excellent Cathedral Quarter Arts Festival each April.

Also on Donegall Street, **Belfast Exposed** at Exchange Place (tel: 028-9023 0965) hosts contemporary photo exhibitions and allows access to its digital archive of 250,000 images of Belfast.

St Anne's Cathedral

Further along the neo-Romanesque **St Anne's (Belfast) Cathedral** ㉛, dates from the beginning of the 19th century but wasn't completed until 2007 when its striking stainless steel "Spire of Hope" was added. Check out the mosaic roof over the baptistery, composed of 150,000 pieces of glass. The famed unionist leader Edward Carson is interred here. Opposite, Writers' Square contains sculptural pieces by John Kindness and Brian Connolly, and during the festival hosts musical and comedy events. On the cathedral's east side in Talbot Street is the **Home Front Exhibition**, which gives an in-depth account of wartime Northern Ireland. To the rear, St Anne's Square is a rejuvenation project that will eventually be home to the MAC, Belfast's multi-million pound arts centre.

Donegall Street continues past the junction with Royal Avenue and on to **St Patrick's Cathedral** ㉜, where society painter Sir John Lavery used his beautiful wife Hazel (rumoured to have had an affair with Irish rebel leader Michael Collins) as the face of Madonna in his famous triptych of St Patrick.

The **Front Page** (Nos 106–110; tel: 028-9032 4269), renowned for live bands (and a fine collection of photos of old Belfast) is city's last family-run pub.

Two forerunners of Belfast's burgeoning gay scene are here too. The elegant gay-friendly **Union Street Bar and Restaurant** (8–14 Union Street; tel: 028-9031 6060) off Donegall Street has good gastro food and relaxing surround-

Funding St Patrick's

In the early 19th century Roman Catholics accounted for around one-sixth of Belfast's population and their numbers were growing. A new church was needed, and a plot of ground was leased in 1809 from the Marquis of Donegall. Of the £4,100 raised to finance St Patrick's construction, £1,300 was subscribed by Protestants – an indication that the two communities were not always at each others' throats.

BELOW: St Anne's Cathedral.

The Merchant Hotel with its elaborate cast iron balustrade and Thomas Fitzpatrick's carvings.

BELOW: Parliament Buildings at Stormont, designed to look like Buckingham Palace, only grander.

ings in the day but comes alive in the evenings with music, karaoke and more. The adjoining **Kremlin** nightclub (96 Donegall Road; tel: 028-9031 6060) is more outrageous. The Cathedral Quarter is also home to the annual Belfast Pride festival in July/August.

Returning east from Donegall Street, along the atmospheric cobbled Hill Street, is one of Belfast's finest restaurants, **Nick's Warehouse** (No. 35; tel: 028-9043 9690), while the **Black Box** (Nos 18–22; tel: 028-9024 4400; www.blackboxbelfast.com), a dedicated performance space for new theatre, music and comedy, is another key venue for the Cathedral Quarter Arts Festival, the Belfast Film Festival and many others.

At the junction across the road at the corner of Waring Street and Skipper Street (named for being the lodging place for captains of ships tied up in nearby High Street when the River Farset ran through), is the **Spaniard** bar and restaurant (tel: 028-9023 2448).

Just along Waring Street is the area's new social hub, the **Merchant Hotel** 33 (No. 35–39; tel: 028-9023 4888), converted from one of Belfast's finest buildings, the 1860s Ulster Bank. The five-star hotel, Belfast's finest, radiates luxury from the Great Room restaurant where Ireland's largest chandelier hangs beneath a glass cupola to its 26 lavish rooms and five suites. The adjoining New York-style Cloth Ear pub and opulent Ollie's nightclub in the basement also belong to the hotel. An expansion, adding 38 rooms and a rooftop garden, is due for completion summer 2010.

Opposite the Merchant is **Cotton Court**, the home of **Craft NI**. In the same building you can visit the ground-floor gallery of the **Belfast Print Workshop** (tel: 028-9023 1323), which has free exhibitions of leading print artists.

East Belfast

Not yet designated a quarter but the largest district of the city, it was here that three of Belfast's most famous sons were born: singer Van Morrison, footballer George Best (after whom Belfast City Airport is now named) and C.S. Lewis. "Jack" Lewis, author of the *Chronicles of Narnia*, who was baptised at **St Mark's Church** on the Holywood Road by his formidable grandfather, the Rev

Thomas Hamilton, is now celebrated with his own festival in December. Ken Harper of **Harper Taxi Tours** (tel: 028-9074 2711, mobile 07711-757 178) will guide you on tours exploring locations relevant to each of the three or all.

Stormont

East Belfast's most famous building is the grand **Parliament Buildings** ❸❹, Stormont, off the Upper Newtownards Road, now again the home of the rejuvenated Northern Ireland Assembly. Visitors don't have access to the building but can walk the 300 acres (120 hectares) of grounds (daily 7.30am–dusk), including the impressive one-mile driveway.

Though not exactly dominating the tourist map, east Belfast has some much-visited attractions to offer. Watching sweets and chocolates made in the traditional way will tempt children to **Aunt Sandra's Candy Factory** (60 Castlereagh Road; tel: 028-9073 2868; www.irishcandyfactory.com; Mon–Fri 9.30am–4.30pm, Sat until 5pm; tour charge).

On the outskirts of Belfast, **Dundonald Ice Bowl** (111 Old Dundonald Road; tel: 028-9080 9100; www.theicebowl.com) has Ireland's only Olympic-sized ice rink, one of the biggest indoor play worlds in Ireland and 30 state-of-the-art bowling lanes. Adjoining is the American-style mini-golf centre the **Pirates Adventure Golf Course** (111a Old Dundonald Road; tel: 028-9048 0220; www.piratesadventuregolf.com; Mon–Fri 11am–9pm, Sat–Sun 10am–9pm; charge), while a short walk away is **Streamvale Open Farm** (38 Ballyhanwood Road; tel: 028-9048 3244; www.streamvale.com; Easter, July–Aug daily 10.30am–5pm, Apr–June, Sept–Oct 11am–5pm; charge) offering lots of domestic animals for children to meet.

A street parade during the West Belfast Festival.

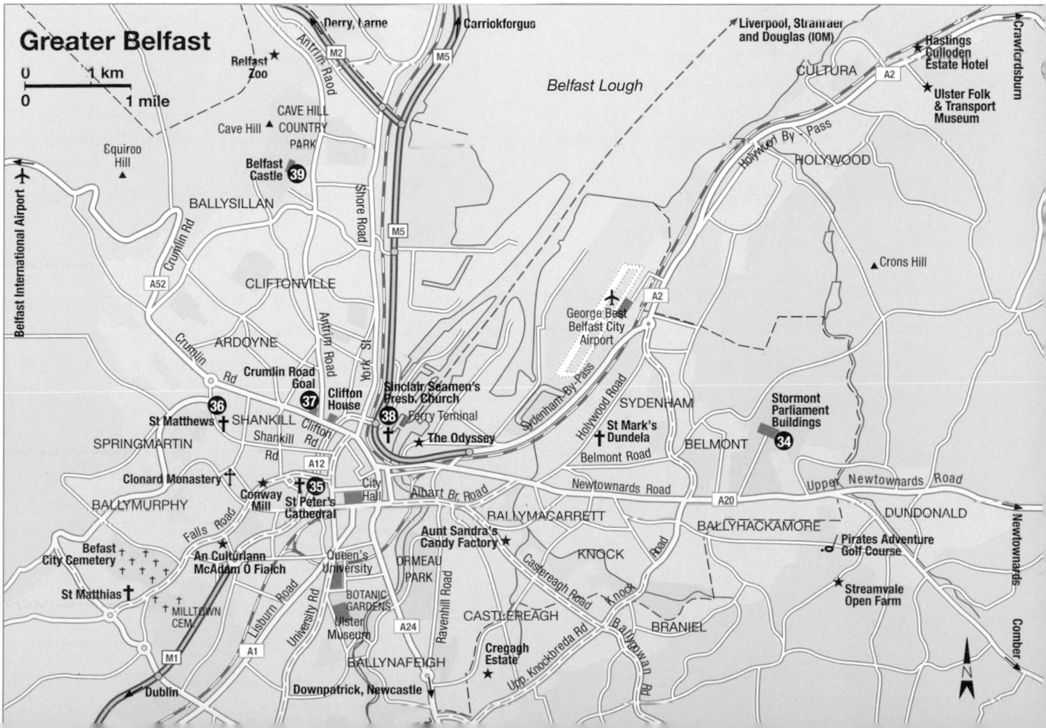

Greater Belfast

Falls and Shankill
Though lack of resources still affects both communities, this seems more evident in the Shankill, a heartland of loyalism. Compared to the more cohesive and vibrant republican community on the Falls, there is a listlessness and lack of bustle. This is typified by the two summer festivals, with the nationalist West Belfast Festival (Féile an Phobail), claiming to be Europe's biggest community festival, dwarfing the more modest Shankill version.

Gaeltacht Quarter

This is essentially the nationalist part of west Belfast (omitting the Protestant Shankill area) and is focused on the **Falls Road**. A good introduction to the people and area is to take one of the cheap, shared black cabs that drive along the Falls Road from their HQ at Castle Junction (TaxiTrax; tel: 028-9031 5777).

In ascending order up the Falls Road, you should begin your tour at the 1866 **St Peter's Cathedral** ㉟ (Peter's Square; tel: 028-9032 7573), whose two great towers with rising spires were used as sightlines by German bombers in the war. The first flax spinning mill in west Belfast, **Conway Mill** (5–7 Conway Street; tel: 028-9032 9646) is now a centre of local community arts with an interesting gallery (closed for major building work until the end of 2010). The lovely French-Gothic style **Clonard Church** (1 Clonard Gardens; tel: 028-9044 5950) is notable for its remarkable Rose Window, organ and mosaics.

The Irish language arts centre **An Cultúrlann McAdam Ó Fiaich** (216 Falls Road; tel: 028-9096 4180; www.culurlann.ie), with an Irish language book and gift shop, hosts Irish music and theatre and art exhibitions. It has a good-value restaurant, too.

One of the best ways to understand Belfast's history is to investigate **Belfast City Cemetery**, just off the Falls Road. Here are buried the powerful unionists who made modern Belfast. Over the road, in the Milltown Cemetery is the famous "Republican Plot" where hunger striker Bobby Sands is buried.

BELOW: Belfast Castle.

Shankill and North Belfast

The rundown Shankill area lacks the vitality of nationalist west Belfast but Shankill Road itself is worth visiting for the famous political murals and the "shamrock church", **St Matthews** ㊱. A shared cab service run by the North Belfast Mutual Association (400 Shankill Road; tel: 028-9032 8775), will take you cheaply up and down the road.

Parallel to the Shankill Road is the **Crumlin Road**, highlighted by Lanyon's imposing **Crumlin Road Gaol** ㊲, which was restored in 2007. An underground tunnel connects it with Lanyon's **Courthouse** across the road.

Further towards the city centre is the most elegant Georgian building **Clifton House** (2 North Queen Street; tel: 028-9089 7534 for group tours), opened in the 1770s as the Belfast Poor House.

Down in the docks area of north Belfast is another Lanyon building the nautically themed **Sinclair Seamen's Church** ㊳ (Corporation Square; tel: 028-9071 5997). Its pulpit is shaped like a ship's prow and its bell is from the ill-fated HMS *Hood*, sunk by the *Bismarck* in 1941 with the loss of more than 1,400 lives. Further north is the Italianate Harbour Office, which leads into attractive tree-lined riverside plazas at the newly developed Clarendon Dock.

Outside Belfast

Seven miles (11km) east of Belfast on the main A2 towards Holywood is the excellent **Ulster Folk and Transport Museum** at Cultra *(see page 324)*.

To the north of the city centre, a 30-minute bus ride away, is the Scottish

Baronial-style sandstone **Belfast Castle** 39 (tel: 028-9077 6925; www.belfastcastle.co.uk; Mon–Sat 9am–10pm, Sun until 6pm; free), built in 1870 as an aristocratic residence with fine views of the city, and **Cave Hill Country Park. Belfast Zoo** (off Antrim Road; tel: 028-9077 6277; www.belfastzoo.co.uk; Oct–Mar daily 10am–4pm; charge) built into Cave Hill, is known for its conservation policies.

Tours worth taking

Much of Belfast's history is contained in the fairly small city centre, which forms the basis of Belfast's **Historical Walking Tours.** Using trained Blue Badge guides, these 90-minute tours take place from May to October and, like most of the other tours, can be booked at the Belfast Welcome Centre, 47 Donegall Place (tel: 028-9024 6609) as can the rewarding **Historical Pub Tours.** The many different Black Taxi guides do not need the Blue Badge accreditation and the commentary is entirely subjective, and no less enjoyable for that.

Belfast by Bike (available at the Belfast Welcome Centre) informs you of the National Cycle Network lanes around the city. You can hire a bike at **McConvey's Cycles** (183 Ormeau Road; tel: 028-9033 0322), just yards away from one of these routes, and spend a day cycling up the Lagan towpath and back.

The lure of *Titanic* proves a bigger draw each year. The **Lagan Boat Company** has regular boat trips to the Harland and Wolff shipyards where the ship was built *(see page 341)*.

You can tour the city on an open-topped bus with **Belfast City Sightseeing** (tel: 028-9045 9035). The tour includes the Botanic Gardens, the Harland and Wolff shipyards and the famous wall murals of the Falls and Shankill.

Mini-Coach (tel: 028-9031 5333) also include the Titanic Quarter as part of a Belfast City Tour.

Belfast Safaris (Spectrum Centre, 331–333 Shankill Road; tel: 028-9022 2925) take you in the footsteps of George Best, the United Irishmen and bring you in for a cup of tea with the locals, while **Coiste** (10 Beechmount Avenue; tel: 028-9020 0770), offer political tours of west Belfast with former republican prisoners and can arrange similar loyalist tours of the Shankill area. ❑

City bus preserved at the Ulster Folk and Transport Museum.

BELOW: murals are a reminder of Belfast's recent history as a bus passes Sinn Féin's headquarters on the Falls Road.

RESTAURANTS AND BARS

Restaurants

Prices for a three-course dinner per person without wine:
£ = under £16
££ = £16–25
£££ = £25–40
££££ = over £40

Alden's Restaurant
229 Upper Newtownards Road, Belfast
Tel: 028-9065 0079
Mon–Fri L noon–2.30pm, D Mon–Thur 6–10pm, Fri–Sat until 11pm. L and D **££**
Chic modern restaurant with food to match. International menu, consistently good cooking and service.

Beatrice Kennedy
44 University Road, Belfast
Tel: 028-9020 2290
L Sun only 12.30–2.15pm, D Tue–Sun 5–10.30pm. L **££**, D **££**
Located in the university area inside a Victorian terrace that has retained its original character. Soft jazz, fresh flowers and candles create an intimate setting for a fusion menu; the homemade food speaks for itself.

Cayenne
7 Ascot House, Shaftesbury Square, Belfast
Tel: 028-9033 1532
L Tue–Fri noon–2.15pm, D daily 5–10.30pm. L **£**, D **£££**
Main restaurant of celebrity chefs Paul and Jeannie Rankin. Adventurous, creative food with Asian twists. Children welcome.

Cargoes Café and Deli
613 Lisburn Road, Belfast
Tel: 028-9066 5451
L Mon–Sat 9am–4.30pm, Sun 10am–3pm, D Thur–Fri 6–9pm. L **£**, D **££**
Modern European; Thai with Indian influences makes this an exciting place to eat; the food quality is top-class and the cooking sound. Children welcome.

Coco
7–11 Linenhall Street, Belfast
Tel: 028-9031 1150
L Mon–Fri noon–3pm, Sun noon–4pm, D Mon–Sat 6–9.30pm. L **££**, D **£££**
Only opened in April 2009, Coco has gained a reputation as one of the best and coolest restaurants in the city. Owned by a new talented chef from Northern Ireland, Jason More, the eclectic interior is complemented by a no-nonsense menu.

Deanes Restaurant
36–40 Howard Street, Belfast
Tel: 028-9033 1134
Tue–Sat, L noon–2.30pm, D 6–9.30pm. L **££**, D **£££–££££**
Michael Deane's Michelin Star, flagship restaurant may have undergone a minimalist makeover but the diverse menu still delivers his extraordinary skill in combining sophistication with modernism.

The Edge
The Edge, May's Meadows, Belfast
Tel: 028-9032 2000
L Mon–Fri noon–2.30pm, D Tue–Sat 5.30–9.30pm. L **£**, D **££**
Overlooking the Waterfront with balconies for soaking up the view. Fine chef with cosmopolitan ideas, using local produce (especially seafood); good service and value.

James Street South
21 James Street South, Belfast
Tel: 028-9043 4310
L Mon–Sat noon–2.45pm, D daily 5.45–10.45pm, Sun 5.30–9pm. L **£**, Early Bird **££**, D **£££**
An exceptional place. Exciting, innovative, top class cooking with service to match. Classic/European/Mediterranean menu. Fair prices with lunch and pre-theatre menu (Mon–Thur) offering exceptional value. Children welcome.

Menu by Kevin Thornton
The Fitzwilliam Hotel, 1–3 Great Victoria Street, Belfast
Tel: 028-9044 2080
L daily 12.30–2.30pm, D Sun–Thur 5.30–10pm, Fri–Sat until 11pm. L and D **£££**
With a menu overseen by Michelin-star restaurateur Kevin Thornton, this is one of Belfast's newest and smartest hotel restaurants. Wonderfully uncomplicated cooking served in a modernistic and sumptuous setting.

Mourne Seafood Bar
34–36 Bank Street, Belfast
Tel: 028-9024 8544
Mon noon–5pm, Tue–Thur noon–9.30, Fri–Sat noon–10.30pm, Sun 1–6pm. L **£**, D **££**
Informal – a new concept for Belfast. Creature comforts are few. However, with their own shellfish beds on Carlingford Lough and a philosophy

that food is what matters, there is a wide choice of locally caught of fish and seafood, skillfully cooked. Children welcome.

Nick's Warehouse
35–39 Hill Street, Belfast
Tel: 028-9043 9690
Tue–Sat, L noon–3pm, D 6–10pm. L **£**, D **££**
An informal, love it or loathe it place in the heart of the Cathedral district. Top class interesting ingredients offering rare breed pigs and game in season.

No27
27 Talbot Street, Belfast
Tel: 028-9031 2884
L Mon–Fri noon–3pm, D Tue–Sat 6–10pm. L **££**, D **£££**
You can't fail to be impressed with No27's contemporary brasserie-style interior, superior service and accomplished, innovative Irish cooking from a bold, yet unpretentious menu.

Shu
253 Lisburn Road, Belfast
Tel: 028-9038 1655
Mon–Sat, L noon–2.30pm, D 6–10pm. L **££**, D **£££**
Very much an "in" place and always busy. Ultra-modern with courteous service, well chosen ingredients, classic/brasserie style menus, consistently good cooking and value for money. Vegetarian menu. Children welcome.

Tedfords
5 Donegall Quay, Belfast
Tel: 028-9043 4000
L Wed–Fri noon–2.30pm, D Tue–Sat 5–9.30pm. L **£**, Early Bird 5–6.30pm **££**, D **£££**
Once a ship's chandlers, it retains the nautical theme and the menu favours seafood. Informal (the formal upstairs only open at weekends). Creative food and value for money wine list.

Ten Square
10 Donegal Square South, Belfast
Tel: 028-9024 1001
Mon–Fri 7am–10pm, Sat–Sun from 8am, food available all day. L **£**, D **££**
The hugely popular Grill Room at this ultra-modern hotel is informal and offers a wide ranging menu including steaks and fish with traditional accompaniments.

The Water Margin
159–161 Donegal Pass, Belfast
Tel: 028-9032 6888
Mon–Thur noon–2.30pm, Fri–Sat noon–11pm, Sun 2–8pm. L and D **££**, Early Bird **£**
In a converted church at the bottom of the Ormeau Road, this is the largest Chinese restaurant in Ireland, seating 200. The menu has nearly as many options, ranging though dim sum to authentic dishes like fish heads and steamed tripe. Western favourites, too.

Zen
55–59 Adelaide Street, Belfast
Tel: 028-9023 2244
L Mon–Fri noon–2.30pm, D daily 5–10.30pm. L and D **££**
Zen leads the way for either authentic or cutting-edge Japanese cuisine. Choose to eat upstairs in spectacularly chic surroundings with booth-style seating, or downstairs in a more traditional Japanese setting where you can choose from the sushi bar.

LEFT: homegrown coffee shop on Royal Avenue.
RIGHT: Belfast's dining has been rapidly improving.

Bars

Belfast has some great pubs and many of their landlords take pride in maintaining the original decor. The best known of these is the **Crown Liquor Saloon**, one of the Victorian gin palaces that flourished in industrial cities. Settle in one of the famous "snugs" for a pint to wash down a plate of oysters, or Irish stew.

The **John Hewitt Bar and Restaurant**, 51 Donegall Street. Once a newspaper office and originally set up by the poet and socialist John Hewitt. People love the combination of traditional pub interior, good bar food and music three nights a week. Closed Sunday.

McHugh's Bar, 29–31 Queen's Square, Belfast. Built in 1711. Belfast's oldest listed building. A collection of memorabilia relating to Belfast make it worth a visit alone (bar food available).

The **Kitchen Bar** (36–40 Victoria Square) was for many the most genuine of Belfast's traditional pubs. Forced to move to an old Victorian seed warehouse around the corner, the atmosphere has changed from quirky intimacy to spacious elegance. All the same, it's still friendly, still serves, unusually for Belfast, a good choice of beers, and offers live traditional Irish music and jazz.

The Northern Whig, 2 Bridge Street, Belfast. Yet another pub located in the former offices of a news paper of the same name. Trendy and popular with the business community. Bar food available.

The Duke of York (7 Commercial Court) is a former journalists' pub (though most famous for former barman Gerry Adams), hence the printing artefacts. It retains an old-fashioned intimacy. A pretty good mix of live music and disco as well.

INSIGHT GUIDES TRAVEL TIPS IRELAND

Transport

Accommodation

Activities

Shopping

A – Z

Further Reading

Transport

Getting There and Getting Around

Getting There

By Air

Irish Republic

There are three major international airports in the Republic of Ireland, at Dublin, Cork and Shannon.

There is a regular bus service from **Dublin Airport** (tel: 01-814 1111; for general transport information, www.dublinairport.com) to the city centre and the main bus station, taking about 30 minutes. Aircoach (www.aircoach.ie) departs every 10–20 minutes for various city locations. The bus from **Cork Airport** (tel: 021-431 3131; www.corkairpot.com) to the city takes about 10 minutes. From **Shannon Airport** (tel: 061-712 000; www.shannonaiarport.com) there is a regular bus service to Limerick city operating between 7am and midnight. It takes about 30 minutes.

Frequent flights from UK airports also arrive at regional airports such as Kerry, Galway, Waterford and Knock. There are connections from Dublin and/or Shannon to many destinations in Britain and Europe. Low-cost airlines cover many destinations in eastern and southern Europe. Carriers serving Ireland from North America are **Aer Lingus** (www.aerlingus.com), **Air Canada** (www.aircanada.com), **American Airlines** (www.aa.com), **Continental** (www.continental.com), **Delta** (www.delta.com) and **US Airways** (www.usairways.com).

For flights to the United States from Dublin and Shannon, passengers clear US immigration before boarding the plane, enabling them to proceed straight to the baggage carousel and Customs at their destination.

Ryanair (www.ryanair.com) flies to Dublin and Shannon. Irish airports have a low-cost rival in **Aer Arann** (www.aerarann.com), which flies to London Luton, Edinburgh, Isle of Man and Bristol. Other key airlines include **Aer Lingus**, **British Airways** (www.ba.com), **bmibaby** (www.bmibaby.com) and **BMI** (www.flybmi.com).

Northern Ireland

Northern Ireland has two major airports, **Belfast International** (a 30-minute bus ride from town, 6am–11pm) and **George Best Belfast City Airport**, a short bus or taxi ride from the town centre.

Belfast International (tel: 028-9448 4848; www.belfastairport.com) has services to New York with **Continental**, and to many UK cities and European capitals with **BMI** and **Easyjet**. George Best Belfast City (tel: 028-9093 9093; www.belfastcityairport.com) serves the UK via **BMI**, **Aer Arann** and **flybe** airlines.

By Sea

Main ferry routes include Dublin/Dun Laoghaire to Holyhead (Wales) or Liverpool (England); Rosslare to Pembroke or Fishguard (Wales), Roscoff and Cherbourg (France); Larne to Fleetwood, Cairnryan or Troon (Scotland); Belfast to Stranraer (Scotland) and Cork to Swansea (Wales). Many routes vary by season; seas are rough in winter.

Irish Ferries (www.irishferries.com; tel: 08717-300 400) *Services*: Holyhead–Dublin North Wall (3 hours 15 minutes) two crossings daily; Holyhead–Dublin fast service (1 hour 49 minutes) four crossings daily; Pembroke–Rosslare (3 hours 45 minutes). Also offers sailings every second day between Rosslare and Roscoff and Cherbourg.

Stena Line, www.stenaline.co.uk, tel: 01-204 7700 in Dublin, 08705 707 070 in the UK. *Services*: Holyhead–Dublin (3 hours 15 minutes); Holyhead–Dun Laoghaire (1 hour 39 minutes); Fishguard–Rosslare (3 hours 30 minutes or 1 hour 50 minutes); Stranraer–Belfast (1 hour 45 minutes); Larne–Fleetwood (8 hours).

Fastnet Ferries, www.fastnetline.com, tel: 021-437 8892 in Cork, 0844-544 3323 in the UK. *Services*: Swansea–Cork (10 hours).

P & O Irish Sea Ferries, www.poirishsea.com, tel: 0871-664 4999 in the UK. *Services*: Cairnryan–Larne (1 hour 45 minutes); Troon–Larne (1 hour 49 minutes, mid-Mar–mid-Oct); Liverpool–Dublin (8 hours).

By Bus

Bus companies run through services from various points in England and Wales via the ferries. The ride to Galway from London, for example, takes around 17 hours by **National Express/Bus Eireann**, tel: 01-836 6111 in Dublin or 08705-808 080, www.nationalexpress.com

Getting Around

Public Transport

In the Republic, there are two national service providers: Bus Éireann Expressway (serving provincial areas nationwide) and Iarnród Éireann (operating inter-city trains as well as the DART, the Dublin Area Rapid Transit system).

Express bus timetables are sold in newsagents. Once off the main routes, small towns and villages may only be served by a couple of buses a week. For information on Expressway services, tel: 01-836 6111 (Bus Eireann, www.buseireann.ie). For information on bus travel within Dublin tel: 01-873 4222 (Dublin Bus, www.dublinbus.ie). The city's bus service can be maddeningly unpredictable. The LUAS tram system (tel: 1-800-300 604; www.luas.ie) offers a handy connection between Connolly and Heuston train stations.

Citylink.ie (www.citylink.ie, no phone, online service only) is a private bus company linking Cork to Galway and Clifden via Shannon Airport. **Aircoach.ie** (tel: 01-844 7118; www.aircoach.ie) has daily services from Dublin Airport via the city centre and six stops en route to Cork.

Trains radiate from Dublin on different lines. A new line links Limerick and Galway via Ennis, and there are commuter lines from Cork to Cobh and Midleton, and from Dublin along the coast. Booking online with Irish Rail can lead to great savings if you can travel on off-peak trains. Dublin-Cork, for example, is €10 each way off-peak, compared to the regular fare of €65 return. For information on rail travel, tel: 01-836 6222 (Iarnród Éireann, www.irishrail.ie).

Eurailpasses are valid for bus and train travel in the Republic, excluding city services. Reduced-rate Rambler passes provide unlimited travel on buses and/or trains, excluding city services, for either 8 or 15 days. Tickets can be bought from any bus or train station in the Republic, or through a travel agent abroad.

Golden Trekker is a scheme offering free rail travel within the Republic of Ireland for visitors aged 66 or over, introduced in 2010, and set to continue, subject to demand. Details at Failte Ireland's website www.discoverireland.com. Register your date of birth and passport number with Failte Ireland (85 Amiens Street, Dublin 1, tel: 01-884 7700), online or at any Tourist Information Office in Ireland, to arrange for a "Golden Trekker Reservation", then tickets can be purchased in blocks of four days for unlimited free travel on mainline and commuter trains.

In Northern Ireland, trains run from Belfast northwest to Derry via Ballymena and Coleraine; east to Bangor; and south to Dublin via Newry. For bus/rail information, call Translink in Belfast, tel: 028-9066 6630.

Private Transport

Driving

Outside the cities the roads are still amongst the least congested in Europe, although it's hard to believe this when stuck in a traffic jam in Dublin's ever-expanding suburbs or on the ring roads of Galway, Cork or Killarney. Drive on the left is the rule on both sides of the border, although there is a predilection in some rural areas for the middle of the road. Drivers and front-seat passengers must wear seat belts as must back seat passengers when belts are fitted.

In the Republic, the speed limit is 45kmh, 60kmh or 80kmh (28mph, 37mph or 50mph) in urban areas, and 80kmh or 100kmh (50mph or 62mph) on National routes (green signposts), with 120kmh (75mph) permitted on motorways. On-the-spot fines can be issued for speeding offences. Drink driving laws are strict. It is an offence to drive with a concentration of alcohol exceeding 80 mg per 100ml of blood.

In Northern Ireland, the limit for country roads is 60mph (96kmh), and 70mph (113kmh) is allowed on motorways and dual-carriageway trunk roads.

Car Rentals

Irish Republic

At the height of summer, hire cars can be hard to find, so book in advance. If you're heading west, the smaller the car, the better – the most alluring lanes are the narrowest. Shop around – rental prices are lower outside the Dublin area. You must be over 23 with two years' full licence and under 76 to hire a car in the Irish Republic. To compare prices go to www.irelandcarhire.ie.

Alamo/National Car Rental, Arrivals hall, Dublin Airport, tel: 1800-301 401 in Ireland, 01-260 3771 in Dublin. www.alamo.com.
Avis, 1-890-405 060 in Ireland, Dublin Airport, tel: 01-605 7500; Shannon Airport, tel: 061-715 600; Cork Airport, tel: 021-432 7460; Killarney (Kerry Airport), tel: 064-36655; Galway, tel: 091-786 440. www.avis.ie.
Hertz Rent-a-Car, Dublin Airport, tel: 01-844 5466; Shannon Airport, tel: 061-471 369; Cork Airport, tel: 021-496 5849. www.hertz.ie.

Northern Ireland

Avis Rent-a-Car, Great Victoria Street, Belfast, tel: 028-9024 0404; Belfast International Airport, tel: 028-9442 2333; Belfast City Airport, tel: 028-9045 2017; City of Derry Airport, tel: 028-7181 1708; Larne, tel: 028-2826 0799. www.avis.co.uk.
Budget Rentacar, Belfast, tel: 028-90230 700; Belfast City Airport, tel: 028-9045 1111; Belfast International Airport, tel: 028-9442 3332. www.budget-uk.com.
Europcar, Belfast City Airport, tel: 028-90450 904; Belfast International Airport, tel: 028-9442 3444.www.europcar.co.uk.
Hertz Rent-a-Car, Belfast International Airport, tel: 028-9442 2533; Belfast City Airport, tel: 028-9073 2451. www.hertz.co.uk.

Cycling

Throughout the Republic, Rent-a-Bike dealers hire out sturdy Raleigh Tourer bicycles, which can sometimes be delivered to airports. Expect to pay upwards of €70 a week for rental. For a list of Raleigh Rent-a-Bike dealers, see www.raleigh.ie. In Dublin, you can hire a bicycle from **Cycleways**, 185–186 Parnell Street, Dublin, tel: 01-873 4748; www.cycleways.com. See also cycling tip on page 120.

BELOW: Dublin's trams offer a quick way of getting to outlying areas.

Accommodation

Hotels, Youth Hostels, Bed and Breakfast

The Choice

It is possible to pay as much as €350 or more for a room in a top-rated hotel, or as little as €30 each for "bed and breakfast" in a family home which takes visitors. Dearer is not necessarily better, of course, but generally speaking the more you pay, the more facilities are on offer.

Nowadays most B&Bs now have rooms with "en-suite" shower or bath, and in the cities TV and phone. Some – especially farmhouses – offer first-class food. B&Bs are not necessarily budget options: large rooms decorated with antiques in stately homes like Ballymaloe House may cost the same as a good hotel, but the experience will be much more memorable.

Both the Irish Republic and Northern Ireland classify hotels on broadly the same grading system, as follows:

★★★★★ Top-grade hotels, some in former castles; all rooms have private bathrooms and suites are available. High-quality restaurant.

★★★★ Hotels, ranging from modern, purpose-built premises to converted period houses, offering a high standard of comfort and service. With few exceptions all rooms have private bathrooms.

★★★ Medium-priced hotels, ranging from small, family-run places to larger, more commercial operations. Most of the rooms have private bathrooms.

★★ Mostly family-run hotels, with a limited but satisfactory range of food and comfort. Some rooms have private bathrooms.

★ Simple but acceptable accommodation and services.

Guesthouses

This is a category for B&Bs with over five rooms. Some but not all guesthouses have restaurant facilities, and those public facilities that you would expect in a hotel, such as residents' lounge, may be limited or non-existent. Guesthouses are not licensed to sell beer and spirits (unless the guesthouse is also a pub), but some have wine licences.

Bed and Breakfast

B&B accommodation is offered both in towns and in the countryside. Irish B&Bs have increased greatly in professionalism – at the price, in some places, of a friendly welcome. The newer B&Bs have often been designed for that purpose, with ensuite bathrooms. If there is no restaurant nearby, evening meals can often be provided if notice is given before noon.

Hostels

The Irish Youth Hostel Association (An Oige) 61 Mountjoy Street, Dublin 7, tel: 01-830 4555; fax: 01-830 5808; www.irelandyha.org, has 23 hostels in the Republic, with fees varying from €18 to €25 per person per night, with a €2 discount per night for members. Hostels in Northern Ireland are run by Hostelling International Northern Ireland (www.hini.org.uk). Members of the International Youth Hostel Federation can use any of these.

Independent Holiday Hostels of Ireland is an umbrella organisation for about 125 privately-owned hostels. Like An Oige, these are relaxed places, with no curfews. Bedlinen is supplied, but towel hire is usually extra. As well as traditional dormitory accommodation, many also have private double and family rooms, and offer cooked breakfast as an optional extra, as well as kitchen facilities. For a brochure, contact the IHH Office, 57 Lower Gardiner Street, Dublin 1, tel: 01-836 4700; fax: 836 4710; www.hostels-ireland.com.

All independent hostels are privately owned, and can vary from scenic organic farms to a tiny townhouse stacked with bunk beds. The one drawback is a tendency to overcrowding in July and August and at festival times. Some hostels prefer not to belong to any organisation, and may not have been inspected for compliance with fire regulations.

Budget Accommodation

The Irish student and youth travel company USIT (www.kinlayhouse.ie) runs Kinlay House year-round centres in Dublin (tel: 01-679 6644), Galway (tel: 091-565 244) and Cork (tel: 021-450 8966). Prices start at around €16. During the long vacation from mid-June to mid-September, they also offer self-catering apartments in UCD Village, Belfield Campus, Dublin 4 (tel: 01-269 7111). Brookfield Holiday Village, also offer apartments at College Road, Cork (tel: 021-434 4032) with prices starting at €25.

Self-catering Accommodation

This is available in houses, cottages (some thatched), apartments, caravans and even a few castles. If you are looking for a "traditional Irish cottage" be warned that many are newly built in artificial "clusters", and used solely for holiday rentals. Be sure you are getting what you want when you book. If touring the Republic, you can ask one of the local tourist offices to book ahead for you; a small charge is made for telephone costs.

ACCOMMODATION LISTINGS

DUBLIN

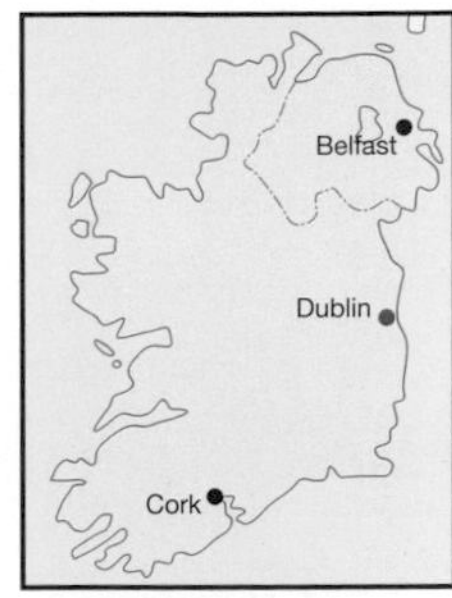

These categories are based on standard prices, but rates shoot up at all Dublin hotels when international sporting events and big festivals take place. Since the recession hit, Dublin room prices are often reduced, so check the internet for special deals.

Aberdeen Lodge
53 Park Avenue, Dublin 4
Tel: 01-283 8155
www.aberdeen-lodge.com
Well-equipped guesthouse in pair of Edwardian houses on an elegant road in Ballsbridge. **€€**

Abraham House
82–3 Lower Gardiner Street, Dublin 1
Tel: 01-855 0600
www.abraham-house.ie
Inexpensive hostel in two large Georgian houses, offering double rooms, dormitories and parking. **€**

Aishling House
19–20 St Lawrence Road, Clontarf, Dublin 3
Tel: 01-833 9097
www.aishlinghouse.com
Escape the stress of the city centre in this substantial villa in a seaside suburb only 2 miles (3km), a 10-minute bus journey away. **€**

Avalon House
55 Aungier Street, Dublin 2
Tel: 01-475 0001
www.avalon-house.ie
Well-located cheap hostel near Grafton Street and Temple Bar. Single rooms, double rooms, family rooms and dorms. **€**

Bewley's Hotel Ballsbridge
Merrion Road, Ballsbridge, Dublin 4
Tel: 01-668 1111
www.bewleyshotels.com
A substantial Victorian building next door to the RDS, a short bus ride from the centre, offers great value and good comfort with an excellent restaurant and a lively basement lounge bar. **€€**

Blooms Hotel
6 Anglesea Street, Temple Bar, Dublin 2
Tel: 01-671 5622
www.blooms.ie
Don't expect a quiet time if you stay at Blooms. It's perfect for partygoers and offers good facilities and modern rooms. **€**

Buswell's Hotel
23–7 Molesworth Street, Dublin 2
Tel: 01-614 6500
www.buswells.ie
Former Georgian townhouses used as a hotel since the 1920s, which oozes period charm. A haunt of politicians because of its proximity to Leinster House. **€€**

Central Hotel
1–5 Exchequer Street, Dublin 2
Tel: 01–679 7302
www.centralhotel.ie
Has more character than some of the bigger, pricier places, with interesting paintings on the walls. Close to Grafton Street. **€€**

The Clarence
6–8 Wellington Quay, Dublin 2
Tel: 01-407 0800
www.theclarence.ie
City-centre, riverside location, backing onto Temple Bar. Refurbished and redesigned, but still retaining its keynote art deco panelling with stylish restraint, this place delights the eye as well as the stomach (the restaurant is first-class). Owners include members of the U2 rock group and the clientele is self-consciously hip. **€€€**

Conrad Dublin
Earlsfort Terrace, Dublin 2
Tel: 01-602 8900
www.conradhotels1.hilton.com
American-style, gleaming five-star hotel across the street from the National Concert Hall and just a few metres from St Stephen's Green. Ask for a room near the top. Telephones even in the bathrooms. **€€€**

The Dylan Hotel
Eastmoreland Place, Dublin 2
Tel: 01-660 3000
www.dylan.ie
A redbrick Victorian hotel midway between the centre and leafy Ballsbridge, has been given the ultimate boutique make-over, from candle and champagne extravaganzas in lobby and bar, to bedside speakers for your iPod. **€€€€**

Four Seasons
Simmonscourt Road, Dublin 4
Tel: 01-665 4000
www.fourseasons.com/dublin
Vast and very swanky hotel near the RDS horse show grounds. Stylish and spacious, with two bars – traditional or ultra modern – and a classic restaurant, Seasons. **€€€€**

Gresham Hotel
23 Upper O'Connell Street, Dublin 1
Tel: 01-874 6881
www.gresham-hotels.com
Combining tradition with luxurious modern facilities is key at this landmark hotel that has undergone a thorough refurbishment. **€€€**

Harcourt Hotel
60 Harcourt Street, Dublin 2
Tel: 01-478 3677
www.harcourthotel.ie
Georgian house just off Stephen's Green. Rooms are small and can be noisy due to hotel's nightclub, but great location and ambience. **€**

Hotel Isaacs
Store Street, Dublin 1
Tel: 01-813 4700
www.isaacs.ie
Small, efficient, friendly place handily situated close to Connolly Station (rail) and Busaras (central bus station). **€**

Hotel St George
7 Parnell Square, Dublin 1
Tel: 01-874 5611
www.hotel-st-george.ie
Comfortable hotel in two converted Georgian houses. Close to the Hugh Lane Art Gallery, Gate Theatre and O'Connell Street. **€€**

King Sitric
East Pier, Howth
Tel: 01-832 5235
www.kingsitric.ie
This is one of Howth's finest fish restaurants but it also has 8 seaside rooms. The gourmet breakfast is just as impressive as the evening meals. **€€€**

Kinlay House
2–12 Lower Edward Street, Dublin 2
Tel: 01-679 6644
www.kinlayhouse.ie
Close to Christ Church Cathedral, backing onto Temple Bar. Singles, doubles, 4–6 bedded rooms, dorms. Cheap. **€**

The Merrion
Upper Merrion Street, Dublin 2
Tel: 01-603 0600
www.merrioinhotel.com
Four Georgian town houses have been converted into a top-class hotel that combines luxury with quiet good taste – and priceless original art. So discreet it even lacks a hotel sign, using instead the traditional Georgian small brass plaque. **€€€€**

Merrion Hall
54 Merrion Road, Ballsbridge, Dublin 4
Tel: 01-283 8155
www.merrionhall.com
Peaceful manor house-style

PRICE CATEGORIES

Price categories are for a double room without breakfast:
€ = under €90
€€ = €90–140
€€€ = €140–220
€€€€ = more than €220

hotel near the Royal Dublin Society grounds, which offers good breakfasts. €€

The Morrisson
Lower Ormond Quay, Dublin 1
Tel: 01-887 2400
www.morrisonhotel.ie
Vies with the Clarence *(see above)* for title of most media-hip hotel in town. Contemporary design, organic fare in Halo restaurant and the new look Morrison Bar, the perfect place for a cocktail overlooking the River Liffey. Good value. €€

Mount Herbert Hotel
Herbert Road, Lansdowne Road, Sandymount, Dublin 4
Tel: 01-614 2000
www.mountherberthotel.ie
Family-run guesthouse in an extended Victorian house near Lansdowne Road stadium. There's also a children's playground. €€

Number 31
31 Leeson Close, Dublin 2
Tel: 01-676 5011
www.number31.ie
Friendly guesthouse based in two houses, one modern, one Georgian. Just off Leeson Street. Delicious breakfasts. €€€

O'Callaghan Davenport Hotel
Merrion Square, Dublin 2
Tel: 01-661 5663
www.ocallaghanhotels.com
A profusion of polished wood and marble in a impressive 1860s building, with benefit of modern facilities. €€€

O'Callaghan Mont Clare Hotel
Clare Street, Merrion Square, Dublin 2
Tel: 01-607 3800
www.ocallaghanhotels.ie
Excellent location on the corner of Merrion Square, near the National Gallery and southside shops. €€€

O'Callaghan Stephen's Green Hotel
83 St Stephen's Green North, Dublin 2
Tel: 01-612 9200
www.ocallaghanhotels.com
A surprise is in store beneath the glass atrium of this boutique hotel. Skillfully incorporated are two Georgian houses with a Georgian library within. €€€

The Oliver St John Gogarty
58–9 Fleet Street, Temple Bar, Dublin 2
Tel: 01-671 1822
www.gogartys.ie
Popular budget hostel above a busy pub of the same name in the heart of Temple Bar. Hostel accommodation is cheap but the penthouse self-catering apartments cost up to €300 at weekends (up to 6 people). €

Othello House
74 Lower Gardiner Street, Dublin 1
Tel: 01-874 0225
www.othellodublin.com
Handy, inner north-city location near rail and bus stations. Well equipped. €

St Aiden's Guesthouse
32 Brighton Road, Rathgar, Dublin 6
Tel: 01-490 6168
www.staidens.com
Redbrick Victorian guest-house in a pleasant south-side suburb of Rathgar. €

Shelbourne Hotel
27 St Stephen's Green, Dublin 2
Tel: 01-663 4500
www.marriot.co.uk
Dublin's most prestigious hotel, with plenty of old-world atmosphere, it had a major refurbishment in 2007. The lounge is a great place for afternoon tea, the Horseshoe Bar is popular with some of the city's "heavy hitters". €€€€

Temple Bar Hotel
Fleet Street, Dublin 2
Tel: 01-612 9200
www.templebarhotel.com
Sited in trendy Temple Bar. Great location if you're not a light sleeper. €€

Westbury Hotel
Balfe Street, off Grafton Street, Dublin 2
Tel: 01-679 1122
www.doylecollection.com
Modern, luxury hotel right in the city centre, popular with jet-setters, with a shopping mall next door. First-class food. €€€

The Westin
Westmoreland Street, Dublin 2
Tel: 01-645 1234
www.thewestindublin.com
Formerly a bank, this fine hotel has luxurious rooms, a gym and a fine restaurant. The Atrium Bar is a lovely venue for an afternoon tea or glass of bubbly. €€€

BELOW: the Oliver St John Gogarty.

SOUTHEAST REGION

Cahir, Co. Tipperary

Kilcoran Lodge
Cahir
Tel: 052-744 1288
www.kilcoranlodgehotel.com
Charmingly old-fashioned former hunting lodge in its own grounds on the main N8 with views over the Knockmealdown Mountains, pool and self-catering lodges available. €€

Cashel, Co. Tipperary

Cashel Palace Hotel
Main Street, Cashel
Tel: 062-62707
www.cashel-palace.ie
Queen Anne-style Bishop's palace sumptuously converted into fine hotel. View of the Rock of Cashel from back rooms. €€€

Glen of Aherlow, Co. Tipperary

Aherlow House Hotel and Lodges
Tel: 062-56153
www.aherlowhouse.ie
Simple hunting lodge surrounded by pine forest and overlooking the Galtee mountains. Good base for walking/climbing. €€

Gorey, Co. Wexford

Courtown Hotel
Courtown Harbour, near Gorey
Tel: 055-942 5210
www.courtownhotel.ie
Small hotel run by owner-manager, with indoor heated pool in family-oriented seaside resort. €€

Marlfield House
Gorey
Tel: 055-21124
www.marlfieldhouse.com
Grand Regency country house with first-class restaurant in large conservatory. €€€€

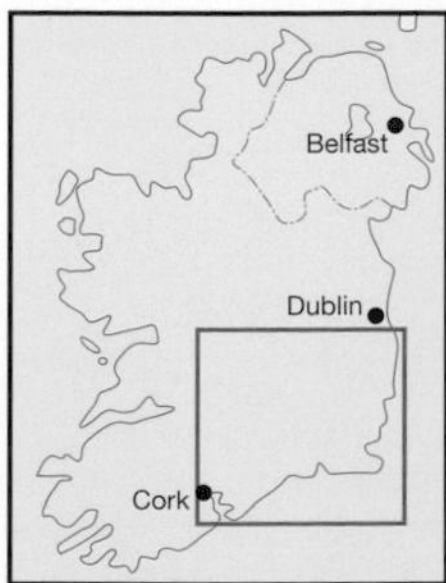

Hook Peninsula, Co. Wexford

Dunbrody Country House Hotel

Arthurstown
Tel: 051-389 600
www.dunbrodyhouse.com
Stylish Georgian manor in 20 acres (8 hectares) of parkland now an informal hotel and restaurant run by the award-winning owner-chef and his wife. €€€€

Kilkenny, Co. Kilkenny

Hotel Kilkenny
College Road, Kilkenny
Tel: 056-776 2000
www.hotelkilkenny.ie
Modern hotel and leisure complex built around Georgian house. Pool, jacuzzi, conservatory. €€€

Zuni Townhouse
26 Patrick Street
Tel: 056-772 3999
www.zuni.ie
Town-centre boutique hotel with minimalist decor, parking and a popular Asian-themed restaurant. €

Rosslare, Co. Wexford

Hotel Rosslare
Rosslare Harbour
Tel: 053-913 3110
www.hotelrosslare.ie
Modern cliff-top hotel overlooking Rosslare Bay and ferryport. €€

Kelly's Resort Hotel
Rosslare Village, Co. Wexford
Tel: 053-913 2114
www.kellys.ie
Beachfront resort hotel established 1895, and run by the Kelly family ever since. Outstanding sports facilities and fine food. €€€

Thomastown, Co. Kilkenny

Mount Juliet Conrad
Thomastown
Tel: 056-777 3000
www.mountjuliet.ie
Elegant 18th-century house on its own estate which includes a Jack Nicklaus golf course, equestrian centre and tennis centre. €€€€. Informal, budget accommodation in Hunter's Yard Clubhouse rooms.€€.

Waterford, Co. Waterford

Arlington Lodge Town House and Restaurant
John's Hill
Tel:051-878 584
www.arlingtonlodge.com
Charming former bishop's palace, eight minutes' walk from centre. €€

Dooley's Hotel
The Quay
Tel: 051-873 531
www.dooleys-hotel.ie
Family-run hotel with good food and lively bar in centre of town on the River Suir. €€

Wexford, Co. Wexford

Ferrycarrig Hotel
Ferrycarrig Bridge, near Wexford
Tel: 053 912 0999
www.ferrycarrighotel.ie
Stylish modern hotel in nice setting by Slaney River 3 miles (5km) outside town on Enniscorthy road. €€€

Riverbank House Hotel
The Bridge
Tel: 053-912 3611
www.riverbankhousehotel.com
Small waterside hotel looking across harbour to the old town, close to sandy beaches. €

Bed & Breakfast

Graiguenamanagh, Co. Kilkenny

Waterside
The Quay
Tel: 059-972 4246
www.watersideguesthouse.com
These simple, comfortable rooms above a popular restaurant are in a converted stone-built corn mill overlooking the River Barrow, and are popular with outdoor types. The quiet village has some old-fashioned pubs. €€

Kilkenny Town, Co. Kilkenny

Butler House
Patrick Street
Tel: 056-776 5707
www.butler.ie
Once the Dower House of Kilkenny Castle, this town-centre Georgian house has large gardens. Combines period elegance with contemporary design. €€

Lacken House
Dublin Road, Kilkenny
Tel: 056-776 1085
www.lackenhouse.ie
Award-winning restaurant with owner-chef offers comfortable, well-equipped rooms in small Georgian house. Restaurant is closed Sunday and Monday. €

Nire Valley, Co. Waterford

Hanorah's Cottage
Ballymacarbry
Tel: 052-613 6134
www.hanorascottage.com
Hikers in Waterford's Comeragh mountains appreciate the comfort of this award-winning riverside retreat, and its imaginative home cooking. €€

Waterford, Co. Waterford

Foxmount Farm and Country House
Passage East Road
Tel: 051-874 308
www.foxmountcountryhouse.com
This working dairy farm, only 15 minutes from Waterford city centre, has a 17th-century house, which offers simple, relaxing rooms and home-baked breakfast. €€

Wexford Town, Co. Wexford

Faythe Guest House
Swan View, Wexford
Tel: 053-912 2249
www.faytheguesthouse.com
Simple town house with views over Wexford Harbour. €

St George Guest House
Georges Street
Tel: 053-914 3473
www.stgeorgeguesthouse.com
Pleasant traditional-style guest house three minutes' walk from town centre. €

Southwest Region

Ballylickey, Co. Cork

Seaview House Hotel
Ballylickey, Bantry
Tel: 027-50073
www.seaviewhousehotel.com
Elegant but relaxed country house hotel set in wooded grounds on the edge of Bantry Bay.
€€

Price Categories

Price categories are for a double room without breakfast:
€ = under €90
€€ = €90–140
€€€ = €140–220
€€€€ = more than €220

Blarney, Co. Cork

Blarney Castle Hotel
Tel: 021-438 5116
www.blarneycastlehotel.com
Small traditional family-run hotel overlooking the village green with popular bar and restaurant. €€

Clonakilty, Co. Cork

The Lodge & Spa at Inchydoney Island
Inchydoney Island
Tel: 023-883 3143
www.inchydoneyisland.com
A relaxing modern hotel

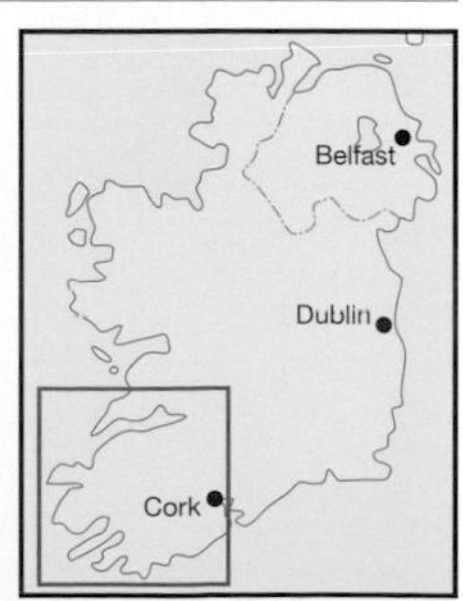

with great views across two vast beaches to the open sea. The main attraction is the thalassotherapy (seawater) spa offering a wide range of treatments. **€€€€**

Cork City

Ambassador Hotel
Military Hill, St Lukes
Tel: 021-453 9000
www.ambassadorhotelcork.ie
An imposing Victorian building has been converted into a stylish, hill-top hotel with great views of the city and harbour. **€€**

Clarion Hotel
Lapp's Quay
Tel: 021-422 4900
www.clarionhotelcorkcity.com
Pioneer landmark building of city's proposed docklands development. Large six-storey modern building with central atrium and chic boutique hotel-style bedrooms. Asian cuisine in bar. **€€**

Hayfield Manor Hotel
Perrott Avenue, College Road
Tel: 021-484 5900
www.hayfieldmanor.ie
This modern luxury hotel is built in the country house-style on carefully landscaped grounds near University College. A haven of tranquillity only five minutes' drive from the centre. **€€€**

Hotel Isaac's
48 MacCurtain Street
Tel: 021-450 0011
www.isaacs.ie
Charming Victorian hotel with contemporary interior tucked away under an archway off a busy road. Handy for both bus and train stations.
€€

Dingle, Co. Kerry

Dingle Skellig
Co. Kerry
Tel: 066-915 0200
www.dingleskellig.com
Well designed modern hotel on the water's edge. Sea view on request. Indoor pool.
€€€

Killarney, Co. Kerry

Cahernane Hotel
Muckross Road
Tel: 064 663 1895
www.cahernane.com
Once the shooting lodge of the Earl of Pembroke, this elegant old house has a lakeside location ½ mile (1km) outside town. Most bedrooms are in a modern wing. **€€€**

Loch Lein Country House Hotel
Killarney
Tel: 064-663 1260
www.lochlein.com
Small, quiet hotel, newly built in a traditional style in secluded location 2½ miles (4km) from town centre with soothing lake views.
€€

Kinsale, Co. Cork

Trident Hotel
Kinsale
Tel: 021-477 2301
www.tridenthotel.com
Modern waterfront hotel adjacent to main town pier, with sea views from all rooms. Lively bar. **€€**

Mallow, Co. Cork

Longueville House
Co. Cork
Tel: 022-47156
www.longuevillehouse.ie
Relaxed family-run country house in a magnificent classical-style 18th-century house overlooking the Blackwater River midway between Cork and Killarney. The restaurant is renowned. **€€€€**

Ring of Kerry, Co. Kerry

Ard-na-Sidhe
Caragh Lake, Killorglin
Tel: 066-976 9105
www.killarneyhotels.ie
Luxurious lakeside Victorian mansion with antiques, open fires and extensive gardens. **€€€**

Butler Arms Hotel
Waterville
Tel: 066-947 4144
www.butlerarms.com
Well-established, informal family-run hotel overlooking the sea. Golf, tennis, fishing. **€€**

Derrynane Hotel
Derrynane
Tel: 066-947 5163
www.derrynane.com
Striking modern hotel situated on rocky shoreline near sandy beaches. Friendly service, children welcome. Good walking base, horse riding nearby. **€€**

Park Hotel
Kenmare
Tel: 064-664 1200
www.parkkenmare.com
Luxurious, impeccably decorated hotel in grand 1897 greystone building with 11 acres (4.5 hectares) of gardens. Excellent food. **€€€€**

Sheen Falls Lodge
Kenmare
Tel: 064-664 1600
www.sheenfallslodge.ie
Kenmare's famous luxury hotel is in a rambling lodge on a 300-acre (120-hectare) waterside estate. Award-winning restaurant.
€€€€

Bed & Breakfast

Cork City

Garnish House
Western Road
Tel: 021-427 5111
www.garnish.ie
Sample real Irish hospitality at this comfortable Victorian house near the university, a short walk from the city centre. **€**

Lancaster Lodge
Lancaster Quay, Western Road
Tel: 021-425 1125
www.lancasterlodge.com
This four-storey modern building near the city centre was designed as a guesthouse, and offers free parking, hotel-standard bedrooms, lifts to all floors and an extensive breakfast menu. **€**

Dingle, Co. Kerry

Emlagh House
Tel: 066-915 2345
At the entrance to town, near the Dingle Skellig Hotel, this elegant, Georgian-style house offers high standards of comfort, great sea views and plentiful local knowledge.
€€€

Heaton's Guesthouse
The Wood
Tel: 066-915 2288
Luxurious family-run guesthouse on water's edge, five minutes' walk west of the town. Splendid breakfasts. **€**

Killarney, Co. Kerry

Killarney Lodge
Countess Road, Killarney
Tel: 064-663 6499
www.killarneylodge.net
Bright, modern guesthouse built in traditional farmhouse-style with welcoming open fires, set in private gardens a short walk from town centre. **€**

Earls Court House
Woodlawn Junction, Muckross Road
Tel: 064-663 4009
www.killarney-earlscourt.ie
A purpose-built modern guesthouse near the town centre, with spacious bedrooms, antique furniture and an open fire in the foyer, where tea and cake are served on arrival.
€

Kinsale, Co. Cork

Friar's Lodge
Friar Street
Tel: 021-477 3445
www.friars-lodge.com
Sumptuously converted Georgian townhouse with large rooms offering excellent value bed and breakfast. **€€**

Old Presbytery
43 Cork Street
Tel: 021-477 2027
www.oldpres.com
Characterful old town house furnished with an attractive medley of antiques offering high standard of comfort. Quiet town centre location.
€€

Pier House
Pier Road
Tel: 021-477 4169

www.pierhousekinsale.com
A small enclosed garden overlooking the harbour and an outdoor balcony with hot tub add to the pleasure of this family-run guesthouse. Children welcome. €

Midleton, Co. Cork

Ballymaloe House
Shangarry, Midleton
Tel: 021-465 2531
www.ballymaloe.ie
One of Ireland's leading guest houses, virtually indistinguishable from a luxury hotel, Ballymaloe is a large, impeccably run and stylishly decorated Georgian house, still surrounded by the family farm. The establishment is renowned for its kitchen, which pioneered the imaginative use of fresh local produce. Children welcome.
€€€€

Ring of Kerry

Carrig Country House
Caragh Lake, near Glenbeigh
Tel: 066-976 9100
www.carrighouse.com
Charming Victorian manor in lovely lakeside gardens with renowned restaurant. Boating, fishing. **€€**

Sallyport House
Glengarriff Road, Kenmare
Tel: 064-664 2066
www.sallyporthouse.com
Exceptionally comfortable family home on the edge of town overlooking Kenmare harbour. Interesting antique furniture. **€€**

Tahilla Cove Country House
near Sneem
Tel: 064-664 5204
www.tahillacove.com
Secluded waterside retreat with 14-acre (5.6-hectare) estate, run by the friendly Waterhouse family. Fully licensed. Home-cooked dinner. **€€**

LIMERICK AND SHANNON REGION

Adare, Co. Limerick

Dunraven Arms Hotel
Adare
Tel: 061-605 900
www.dunravenhotel.com
Beautifully refurbished historic inn in picture-book pretty village. Equestrian and golf holidays a speciality. **€€€**

Fitzgeralds Woodlands House Hotel
Knockanes, Adare
Tel: 061-605 100
www.woodlands-hotel.ie
This is a friendly, family-run modern hotel with a lively bar and a busy local trade. A good base for touring.
€€

Ballyvaughan, Co. Clare

Gregan's Castle
Ballyvaughan
Tel: 065-707 7005
www.gregans.ie
Renowned and relaxed country house hotel in extensive gardens at the base of the Burren's famous Corkscrew Hill with breathtaking views over Galway Bay. The best restaurant for miles around.
€€€

Hyland's Burren Hotel
Ballyvaughan
Tel: 065-707 7037
www.hylandsburren.com
Rambling, much-extended, family-run hotel in village centre with a lively bar and busy restaurant.
€€

Doolin, Co. Clare

Ballinalacken Castle
Doolin
Tel: 065-707 4025
www.ballinalackencastle.com
A converted shooting lodge with a modern bedroom wing, located beside the ruined castle for which it is named, on the coast road outside town. Superb views of the Atlantic and the Aran islands. **€€€**

Hotel Doolin
Doolin
Tel: 065-707 4111
www.hoteldoolin.ie
Small contemporary hotel bringing urban chic to a small fishing village-turned tourist mecca. Comfortable touring base. **€€**

Ennis, Co. Clare

Old Ground Hotel
Ennis
Tel: 065-682 8127
www.flynnhotels.com
Venerable, ivy-clad hotel partly 17th-century, with a quiet but central location 30 minutes from Shannon Airport. Lots of golfers. **€€**

Ennistymon, Co. Clare

Falls Hotel & Spa
Ennistymon
Tel: 065-707 1004
www.fallshotel.ie
Family-owned and managed large spa hotel near waterfalls on River Inagh on the edge of a quietly attractive old world village. Retains charm and atmosphere in spite of its relatively large size (130 rooms).
€€

Kinvarra, Co. Galway

Merriman Inn
Main Street Kinvarra
Tel: 091-638 222
www.merrimanhotel.com
A large thatched building dating from 1997 in the centre of this attractive little fishing village, blends modern and traditional design. **€€**

Limerick City

Radisson Blu
Ennis Road
Tel: 061-456 200
www.limerick.radissonblu.ie/hotel-limerick
Pleasantly located in extensive gardens 5 minutes from city centre and 15 minutes from Shannon Airport. There are some lively bars and a good restaurant.
€€€

Clarion Hotel
Steamboat Quay
Tel: 061-444 100
www.clarionhotellimerick.com
This 17-storey city-centre hotel on the banks of the Shannon, Limerick's only landmark modern building, has panoramic views, uncluttered design and good leisure facilities.
€€

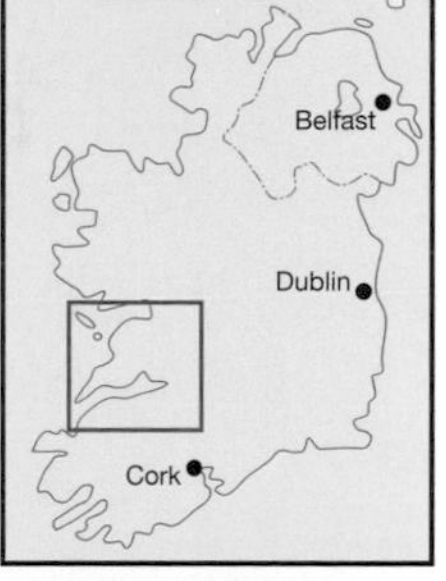

Lisdoonvarna, Co. Clare

Sheedy's Country House Hotel
Lisdoonvarna
Tel: 065-707 4026
Small, much-loved family-run hotel with turf fires. The main attraction is owner-chef John Sheedy's exceptional food, using herbs and vegetables from the garden. **€€**

Newmarket on Fergus, Co. Clare

Dromoland Castle Hotel
Newmarket on Fergus
Tel: 061-368 144
www.dromoland.ie
One of the great Irish castle

PRICE CATEGORIES

Price categories are for a double room without breakfast:
€ = under €90
€€ = €90–140
€€€ = €140–220
€€€€ = more than €220

hotels, former seat of the O'Briens, direct descendants of the High King of Ireland, Brian Ború, in its own park with large lake. Private golf course, clay shooting, golf academy, and horse riding on the estate. Interior decor is atmospheric and stylish. **€€€€**

BED & BREAKFAST

Ballyvaughan, Co. Clare

Cappabhaile House
Ballyvaughan
Tel: 065-707 7260
www.cappabhaile.com
Large, unpretentious stone-faced bungalow on the edge of the Burren purpose-built for the B&B business. Walking distance to lively village pubs. **€**

Lahinch, Co. Clare

Vaughan Lodge
Ennistymon Road
Tel: 065-708 1111
www.vaughanlodge.ie
New hotel built in a sumptuous country house style with large, well-equipped bedrooms, knowledgable local hosts and a super seafood restaurant. **€€€**

Moy House
Milltown Malbay Road
Tel: 065-708 2800
www.moyhouse.com
This is the ultimate romantic retreat, an 18th-century country house with 15 acres (6 hectares) of grounds, on a cliff-top overlooking the wild Atlantic. It's a three-minute drive from the busy surfing-and-golfing village, but a world apart, with an atmosphere more like a private country house than a guesthouse. **€€€€**

Newmarket-on-Fergus, Co. Clare

Carrygerry Country House
Tel: 061-360 500
www.carrygerryhouse.com
Rural seclusion within 10 minutes' drive of Shannon Airport, the comfortable, unpretentious Victorian house overlooks calm pastures and is run by the owner-chef and his wife: the conservatory restaurant is outstanding. **€€**

Note: Many hotels in small towns dispense with a street name in their letterhead and websites, as we have here. This means the community is small enough for the hotel to be prominent, and it will usually be well signed.

MIDLANDS REGION

Arvagh, Co. Cavan

Breffni Park Hotel
Tel: 049-433 5127
www.breffniarms.com
Small hotel in village centre, newly-built in traditional style. Indoor pool and leisure centre. Simple comfort, good touring location, bar and restaurant. **€–€€**

Athlone, Co. Westmeath

Hodson Bay Hotel
Athlone
Tel: 090 644 2000
www.hodsonbayhotel.com
Large, nicely modernised hotel with a superb location on the water's edge at Lough Ree just west of Athlone on the N61 Roscommon road. **€€€**

Sheraton
Gleeson Street, Athlone
Tel: 090-645 1000
www.sheratonathlonehotel.com
Athlone's newest hotel shines high over the town, a 12-storey tower of glass providing spectacular views. Excellent pool and spa facilities and a contemporary restaurant opening on to a pleasant roof garden. **€€**

Ballyconnell, Co. Cavan

Slieve Russell Hotel and Country Club
Tel: 049-952 6444
www.slieverussell.ie
A phenomenon. One of the first of a tidal wave of new hotels, with luxury interior contrasting with Disney-like exterior suggesting Palladio on steroids. Pool, jacuzzi. Fine food. **€€**

Birr, Co. Offaly

County Arms Hotel
Railway Road, Birr
Tel: 057-912 0791
www.countyarmshotel.com
Small, owner-managed hotel in converted Georgian mansion on 9-acre (3.6-hectare) estate. Leisure club with pool, spa. **€€**

Clones, Co. Monaghan

Hilton Park
Tel: 047-56007
www.hiltonpark.ie
In the Madden family since Samuel, a friend of Dr Samuel Johnson, bought it in 1734. An interesting stay guaranteed at one of the best country houses open to guests: a magnificent house and warm welcome **€€€**

Glaslough, Co. Monaghan

Castle Leslie
Tel: 047-88100
www.castleleslie.com
The ancestral home of the Leslie family is expensive, but many find it worth it for the genuine historic house, the luxury accommodation, the great restaurant and the choice of on-site activities including cooking school, equestrian centre and angling. Self-catering packages can reduce the cost. Check the website for special deals. **€€€**

Longford, Co. Longford

Viewmount House
Dublin Road, Longford
Tel: 043-334 1919
www.viewmounthouse.com
This lovely Georgian house, once owned by Lord Longford, is set in beautiful gardens. Elegant rooms, vaulted dining room and first-class restaurant in the converted stables. **€€**

Mullingar, Co. Westmeath

Bloomfield House Hotel
Belvedere, Tulla more Road, Mullingar

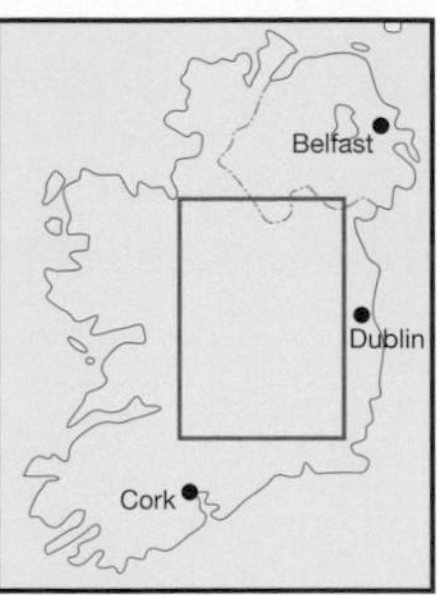

Tel: 044-934 0894
www.bloomfieldhouse.ie
Friendly hotel in old, castellated house on the shores of Lough Ennell. **€€**

Nuremore, Co. Monaghan

Nuremore Hotel and Country Club
Tel: 042-966 1438
www.nuremore.com
Lakeside hotel with golf course and indoor pool in tranquil countryside, with excellent cuisine. Popular weekend retreat for

PRICE CATEGORIES

Price categories are for a double room without breakfast:
€ = under €90
€€ = €90–140
€€€ = €140–220
€€€€ = more than €220

ABOVE: Slieve Russell Hotel and Country Club.

Dubliners, only one hour's drive from the city. €€€

Roscommon, Co. Roscommon

Abbey Hotel
Galway Road
Tel: 090-662 6240
www.abbeyhotel.ie
Modern hotel in venerable castellated shell, parts of which date from the 18th century. Peaceful location surrounded by lawns. €€

BED & BREAKFAST

Athlone, Co. Westmeath

Wineport Lodge
Glasson
Tel: 090-643 9010
www.wineport.ie
Restaurant in striking contemporary design, with very comfortable rooms in a peaceful lakeside setting. Luxury spa with a range of treatments and cedar hot tub, boat jetty, adjacent golf club. €€€

Banaher-on-the-Shannon, Co. Offally

The Harbour Masters House
Shannon Harbour, Banagher-on-the-Shannon
Tel: 057-915 1532
Lovely waterside setting for this pretty characterful house only minutes from a pub serving good food. Charming rooms and antique furnishings. The perfect spot for anglers and boat lovers. €

Birr, Co. Offaly

The Maltings
Castle Street
Tel: 057-912 1345
www.themaltingsbirr.com
Converted stone malthouse in picturesque riverside setting beside Birr Castle in town centre is now a guesthouse with full bar and restaurant. Children welcome. €

Cootehill, Co. Monaghan

Riverside House
Tel: 049-555 2150
www.riverside.irlguide.com
Farmhouse B&B (and self-catering accommodation) on a working dairy farm, favoured by anglers and those seeking peace and tranquility. Dinner by arrangement, restaurants in nearby town. €

Nenagh, Co. Tipperary

Ashley Park House
Ardcroney
Tel: 067-38223
www.ashleypark.com
Charming family home in venerable lakeside Georgian house. Woodland walks and a rowing boat on the lake, evening meal and wine licence. €

Tullamore, Co. Offaly

Eskermóre House
Daingean, Tullamore
Tel: 086-824 9574
www.eskermore.com
A sympathetically restored early Georgian farmhouse in the heart of the picturesque Bog of Allen, rural peace one hour from Dublin. Proprietor Ann Mooney can arrange activity holidays and provide evening meals.
€

Terryglass, Co. Tipperary

Tír na Fiúise (Land of Fuchsia)
Borrisokane
Tel: 067-22041
www.countrycottages.ie
Quiet farmhouse well off the beaten track – this is genuine rural solitude. Good walking country near scenic Lough Derg. Offers self-catering accommodation in restored old-style farm cottages. Price per week ranges from €250–500 during high season.
€

FAR WEST REGION

Achill, Co. Mayo

Gray's Guest House
Dugort
Tel: 098-45245
Run by the legendary Vi McDowell until her death, aged 100, in 2009, this occupies a row of small houses on dramatically scenic island connected to the mainland by a causeway. Children's play area, and drawing room with open fire in case of bad weather. €

Aran Islands, Co. Galway

Ostan Inis Oirr
Lurgan Village, Inisheer
Tel: 099-75020
Whether you fly or take the ferry, this simple modern hotel makes a comfortable base for exploring the smallest of the Aran Islands. Traditional music nightly in the bar. €

Cashel Bay, Co. Galway

Cashel House Hotel
Cashel Bay
Tel: 095-31001
www.cashel-house-hotel.com
Elegant, antique-filled country hideaway in lovely gardens overlooking bay and backed by the hills of Connemara. €€€

Clifden, Co. Galway

Abbeyglen Castle
Sky Road
Tel: 095-22832
www.abbeyglen.ie
Beautifully sited turreted mock castle on outskirts of Connemara's "capital". Friendly staff, free afternoon tea, loyal Irish clientele. €€

Ardagh Hotel
Ballyconneely Road
Tel: 095-21384
www.ardaghhotel.com
Quiet family-run hotel 2km from Clifden on Ardbear Bay.

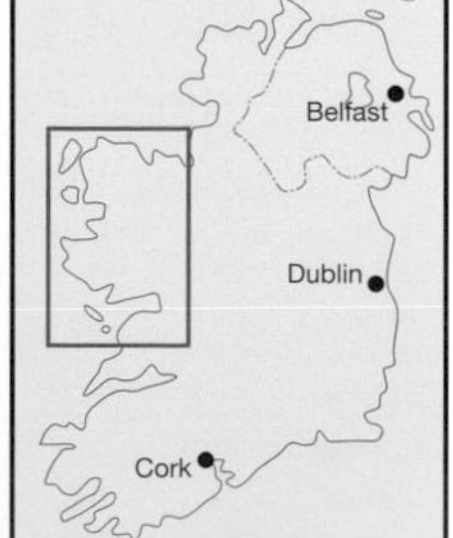

Excellent restaurant specialising in seafood. €€

Cong, Co. Mayo

Ashford Castle

Cong
Tel: 094-954 6003
www.ashford.ie
A castellated fairy-tale castle, standing on the isthmus between Lough Corrib and Lough Mask. American-owned with very high standards of comfort and decor. Private golf course, tennis, fishing, boating, horse riding and shooting are part of the "total resort" experience. Ronald and Nancy Reagan stayed here during their presidential visit to Ireland in 1984. **€€€€**

Furbo, Co. Galway

Connemara Coast Hotel
Furbo
Tel: 091-592 108
www.connemaracoasthotel.com
Well-run, imaginatively designed modern hotel. Swimming, tennis. **€€**

Galway City

"G" (The)
Wellpark
Tel: 091-865 200
www.theg.ie
Contemporary design with an extravagant sense of fun, including a "vertigo rug" and live seahorses. Designed by hat-maker extrordinaire Phlilip Treacy, indulging his wildest fantasies. Stylish luxury. Edge-of-town location avoids Galway's traffic grid-lock. **€€€€**

Glenlo Abbey Hotel
Bushy Park
Tel: 091-526 666
www.glenlo.com
Luxuriously converted monastery on the banks of Lough Corrib, 4km west of city centre, surrounded by its own golf course. Orient Express restaurant car. **€€€€**

Grand Hotel Meyrick
Eyre Square
Tel: 091-564 041
www.greatsouthernhotels.com
Grand old railway hotel on city's main square, formerly the Galway Great Southern, still a major landmark and social centre. **€€€**

Park House Hotel
Forster Street, off Eyre Square
Tel: 091-564 924
www.parkhousehotel.ie
The bar and lobby of this centrally located hotel are popular with Galway natives, while the rooms in the cleverly disguised warehouse conversion are triple-glazed against noise from night revellers. **€€**

Radisson SAS
Lough Atalia Road
Tel: 091-538 300
www.radissonhotelgalway.com
Sparkling glass-and-steel modern hotel in city centre, with large windows and terrace backing on to watery views, and four floors of luxuriously appointed rooms. Its Atrium Bar is the busiest and the coolest place in town, especially during Race Week. **€€€**

Leenane, Co. Galway

Delphi Mountain Resort
Tel: 095-42208
www.delphimountainresort.com
New spa and hotel aimed at those who enjoy a touch of luxury while enjoying their wilderness experience. Bold modern design using glass and stone. Organic kitchen, no televisions and no mobile phone reception. **€€€**

Letterfrack, Co. Galway

Rosleague Manor Hotel
Letterfrack, Connemara
Tel: 095-41101
www.rosleague.com
Beautifully situated Georgian house in scenic Connemara with grounds running down to the sea. Relaxed country house hotel atmosphere, memorable location. **€€€**

Oughterard, Co. Galway

Sweeney's Oughterard House
Oughterard
Tel: 091-552 207
www.sweeneys-hotel.com
In spite of its main road location, this 200-year-old country house hotel retains an attractive, slightly faded, old-world charm. Tea can be taken in the pretty gardens while a beautiful stretch of the Owenriff River runs in front of the hotel. **€€**

Recess, Co. Galway

Ballynahinch Castle Hotel
Ballynahinch
Tel: 095-31006
www.ballynahinch-castle.com
Historic house full of character, splendidly sited in the wilds of Connemara at the foot of one of the "Twelve Bens", overlooking the Owenmore River. Private salmon fishing. **€€€**

Westport, Co. Mayo

Hotel Westport
The Demense, Newport Road, Westport
Tel: 098-25122
www.hotelwestport.ie
Comfortable, modern two-storey hotel with spacious rooms near the town centre. Surrounded by gardens with pleasant rural views. Good sports facilities. **€€€**

Westport Plaza and Castlecourt Hotel
Castlebar Street, Westport
Tel: 098-55088
www.westporthotelsresort.ie
Neighbouring hotels in town centre share pool and spa. Castlecourt is a comfortable traditional hotel, while the Plaza is a more snazzy (and expensive) boutique-style hotel with pleasantly luxurious bedrooms. **€€–€€€**

BED & BREAKFAST

Aran Islands, Co. Galway

Kilmurvey House
Inis Mór
Tel: 099-61218
www.kilmurveyhouse.com
B&Bs abound on all three Aran Islands, and you can book a room when booking your ferry or flight. Kilmurvey House is an 18th-century stone-built house, situated at the foot of Dun Aengus prehistoric fort midway between the island's two villages, and serves dinner nightly (wine licence). **€**

Clifden, Co. Galway

Dun Rí Guesthouse
Hulk Street
Tel: 095-21625
www.dunri.ie
A short step away from the busy town centre, rooms in this traditional town house are well-equipped, and there is a friendly guest lounge with tea, coffee. **€**

The Quay House
Beach Road
Tel: 095-21369
www.thequayhouse.com
Beautifully located on a tranquil quay below the busy town, the large harbourmaster's house (1829) has been converted into a stylish and characterful guest house, with a wing of new self-catering apartments. **€€**

Galway City

Adare Guest House
9 Father Griffin Place
Tel: 091-582 638
www.adarebedandbreakfast.com
Well-located, unpretentious accommodation with private parking three minutes' walk from city centre. **€**

Leenane, Co. Galway

Delphi Lodge
Leenane
Tel: 095-42222
www.delphilodge.ie
Romantic Georgian country house in remote Connemara valley. Lovely lakeside setting, private fly fishing, elegant but informal atmosphere. Freshly prepared gourmet dinner daily at 8pm. **€€**

PRICE CATEGORIES

Price categories are for a double room without breakfast:
€ = under €90
€€ = €90–140
€€€ = €140–220
€€€€ = more than €220

NORTHWEST REGION

Ardara, Co. Donegal

Nesbitt Arms Hotel
Tel: 074-954 1103
www.nesbittarms.com
Historic town centre pub, patronised by the area's famous tweed weavers down the years. A warm welcome and live music. **€€**

Woodhill House
Tel: 074-954 1112
www.woodhillhouse.com
Scenically located historic house overlooking the Donegal Highlands. Great base for outdoor pursuits. Restaurant with French menu that highlights seafood, bar and occasional music. **€€**

Ballyshannon, Co. Donegal

Heron's Cove
Creevy Pier, Rossnowlagh Road, Creevy
Tel: 071-982 2070
www.heronscove.ie
Small, friendly modern inn with traditional stone-facing has a waterside location and makes an excellent touring base. Close to big beach at Rossnowlagh just north of Ballyshannon on the coast road. **€€**

Carrick-on-Shannon, Co. Leitrim

Bush Hotel
Carrick-on-Shannon
Tel: 071-967 1000
www.bushhotel.com
One of Ireland's oldest provincial hotels, in the centre of a bustling riverside town.
€€

Coolooney, Co. Sligo

Markree Castle
Tel: 071-916 7800
www.markreecastle.ie
Massive castellated mansion on an extensive estate of gardens and parkland. One of the more affordable castle hotels. Dog friendly.
€€€

Donegal Town, Co. Donegal

Harvey's Point Country Hotel
Lough Eske
Tel: 074-972 2208
www.harveyspoint.com
Modern luxurious lakeside complex with sports facilities. A recommended restaurant with rooms.
€€€–€€€€

Dunfanaghy, Co. Donegal

Arnolds Hotel
Dunfanaghy
Tel: 074-913 6208
www.arnoldshotel.com
One of the great seaside family hotels, on the water's edge and close to miles of sandy beaches. Excellent traditional cooking. Painting tuition, photography weekends, creative writing, horseback riding. **€€**

Inishowen, Co. Donegal

McGrorys of Culdaff
Culdaff
Tel: 074-937 9104
www.mcgrorys.ie
Traditional pub on the Inishowen peninsula, famed for its hospitality, and also for its great music sessions. Also a fine restaurant. **€**

Killybegs, Co. Donegal

Bayview Hotel
Main Street, Killybegs
Tel: 074-973 1950
www.bayviewhotel.ie
Lively modern hotel overlooking busy harbour of small fishing port. Pool and leisure centre. **€€**

Letterkenny, Co. Donegal

Mount Errigal Hotel
Ballyraine, Letterkenny
Tel: 074-912 2700
www.mounterrigal.com
Modern facilities include sauna and leisure centre.
€€

Malin, Co. Donegal

Malin Hotel
Malin, Inishowen
Tel: 074-937 0606
www.malinhotel.ie
Situated in a small town at the tip of the Inishowen Peninsula, a great base for walking in scenery. **€€**

Rathmullan, Letterkenny, Co. Donegal

Fort Royal Hotel
Rathmullan
Tel: 074-915 8100
www.fortroyalhotel.com
Small country hotel in own grounds on edge of Lough Swilly. Sandy beach, tennis and friendly welcome. **€€€**

Rathmullan House
Lough Swilly
Tel: 074-915 8188
www.rathmullanhouse.com
Large country house on shores of Lough Swilly. Beautiful gardens. Period-style rooms. Indoor pool, all-weather tennis courts and excellent restaurant. **€€€€**

Rossnowlagh, Co. Donegal

Sand House Hotel Rossnowlagh
Tel: 071-985 1777
www.sandhouse-hotel.ie
Right on the beach, and run the way seaside hotels used to be. **€€€**

Sligo Town, Co. Sligo

Sligo Park Hotel
Pearse Road, Sligo
Tel: 071-919 0400
www.sligoparkhotel.com
Scenic location a mile south of town with own gardens and leisure facilities. **€€**

BED & BREAKFAST

Ardara, Co. Donegal

The Green Gate
Ardvally
Tel: 074-954 1546
www.thegreengate.eu

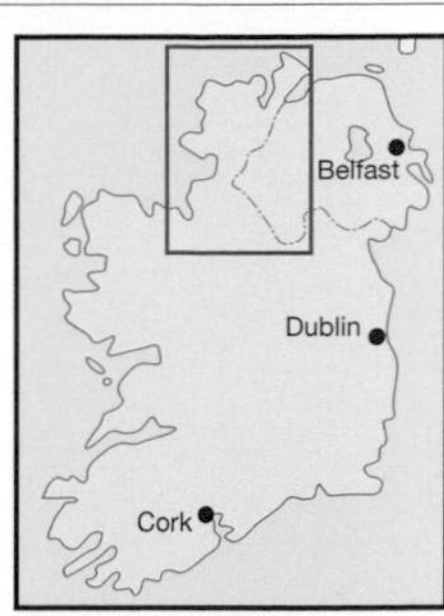

Traditional cottage with ocean views. **€–€€**

Ballymote, Co. Sligo

Temple House
Ballymote
Tel: 071-918 3329
www.templehouse.ie
Lakeside Georgian mansion overlooking 13th-century Templar castle. Excellent touring base. **€€€**

Donegal Town

Atlantic Guest House
Main Street, Donegal
Tel: 074-972 1187.
www.atlanticguesthouse.ie
Family-run, very central. **€**

Rhu-Gorse
Lough Eske, Donegal
Tel: 074 972 1685
www.lougheske.com
Expect a warm welcome at this modern B&B. Pets welcome. **€**

Mohill, Co. Leitrim

Glebe House
Ballinamore Road, Mohill
Tel: 071-963 1086
www.glebehouse.com
In 50 acres (20 hectares) of farmland and mature trees, this former Georgian rectory is a tranquil haven. **€–€€**

Riverstown, Co. Sligo

Coopershill House
Tel: 071-916 5108
www.coopershill.com
Georgian country house in own grounds, luxurious rooms, croquet lawn. Children welcome. Dinner by arrangement. **€€€**

Northern Ireland

County Antrim

Bayview Hotel
2 Bayhead Road, Portballintrae
Tel: 028-2073 4100
www.leighinmohrhotel.com
Come here for fine views and modern comfort. **££–£££**

Bushmills Inn
9 Dunluce Road, Bushmills
Tel: 028-2073 3000
www.bushmillsinn.com
Conveniently near the world's oldest whiskey distillery. **£££**

Dunadry Hotel and Country Club
2 Islandreagh Drive, Dunadry
Tel: 028-9443 4343
www.mooneyhotelgroup.com
Attractive old building, conveniently close to the airport. **££**

Fullerton Arms
22 Main Street, Ballintoy
Tel: 028-2076 9613
www.fullertonarms.co.uk.
Modernised coaching inn. B&B. **£**

Galgorm Resort & Spa
136 Fenaghy Road, Ballymena
Tel: 02825-881 001
www.galgorm.com
Set within 163 acres, this former gentleman's residence has an exceptional spa. **££–£££**

Glens Hotel
6 Coast Road, Cushendall
Tel: 02821-771 223
www.theglenshotel.com
Comfortable hotel in the "capital of the glens". **££**

Londonderry Arms Hotel
Harbour Road, Carnlough
Tel: 028-2888 5255
www.glensofantrim.com
Charming old coaching inn that once belonged to Sir Winston Churchill. Some of the rooms have a sea view, so check in advance for availability. The Arkle Bar has memorabilia devoted to the famous racehorse, **££**

Magherabuoy House
41 Magherabuoy Road, Portrush
Tel: 028-70-82 3507
www.magherabuoy.co.uk
A Best Western hotel near resorts with fine beaches. **££**

Marine Hotel
1–3 North Street, Ballycastle
Tel: 028-2076 2222
www.marinehotel.net
Lacking in personality, but excellent views, this hotel is popular for weddings. **££**

Rosspark Hotel
Kells
Tel: 028-2589 1663
www.rosspark.com
City standards in heart of country. **££**

Templeton Hotel
882 Antrim Road, Templepatrick, Ballyclare
Tel: 028-9443 2984
www.templetonhotel.com
A lodge-style hotel with old-fashioned charm, en route to airport. **££**

County Armagh

Armagh City Hotel
2 Friary Road, Armagh
Tel: 028-3751 8888
www.armaghcityhotel.co.uk
Somewhat characterless but handy location and panoramic views. **££**

Charlemont Arms Hotel
57–65 English Street, Armagh
Tel: 028-3752 2028
www.charlemontarmshotel.com
An old building with character but there is some traffic noise. **££**

Seagoe Hotel
Upper Church Lane, Portadown
Tel: 028-3833 3076
www.seagoe.com
Refurbished hotel that serves good food. **££**

County Derry

Ardtara Country House
8 Gortead Road, Upperlands, Maghera
Tel: 028-7964 4490
www.ardtara.com
Deep in Seamus Heaney country, this elegant manor house features distinctive cuisine and live music. **££**

Beech Hill Country House Hotel
32 Ardmore Road, Derry
Tel: 028-7134 9279
www.beech-hill.com
Offers elegant grounds and a fine kitchen. **££**

Camus House
27 Curragh Road, Coleraine
Tel: 028-7034 2982
B&B that will appeal to salmon fishers, **£**

City of Derry Travelodge
22 Strand Road, Derry
Tel: 028-7127 1271
www.travelodge.co.uk
One of three city-centre business hotels. **£**

Radisson Blu Roe Park Hotel and Golf Resort
Roe Park, Limavady
Tel: 028-7772 2222
www.radissonroepark.com
Charles Lanyon-designed mansion conversion. **££**

County Down

Burrendale Hotel and Country Club
51 Castlewellan Road, Newcastle
Tel: 028-4372 2599
www.burrendale.com
Closed to fantastic countryside and serves a decent menu. **££**

Glassdrumman Lodge
85 Mill Road, Annalong
Tel: 028-4376 8451
www.glassdrummanlodge.com
Exquisite small hotel on edge of the Mourne mountains. **££**

La Mon House
41 Gransha Road, Castlereagh, Belfast
Tel: 028-9044 8631
www.lamon.co.uk
Country hotel with pool, quite close to Belfast. **££**

Marine Court Hotel
The Marina Bangor
Tel: 028-9145 1100
www.marinecourthotel.net
Overlooking the new marina, and with a health and fitness club too. **££**

Old Inn
15 Main Street, Crawfordsburn

Price Categories

Price categories in Northern Ireland are for a double room without breakfast:
£ = under £80
££ = £80–150
£££ = £150–200
££££ = more than £200

Below: breathtaking interiors at Belfast's Merchant Hotel.

Tel: 028-9185 3255
www.theoldinn.com
A pleasant, friendly hotel, with the benefit of being renowned for its food. **££**

Portaferry Hotel
10 The Strand
Tel: 028-4272 8231
www.portaferryhotel.com
Overlooking Strangford narrows, the kitchen here serves good seafood. **££**

Slieve Donard Hotel
Downs Road, Newcastle
Tel: 028-4372 1066
www.hastingshotels.com
Mansion on beach with pool and superb view of Mourne Mountains. **£££**

Strangford Arms
92 Church Street, Newtownards
Tel: 028-9181 4141
www.strangfordhotel.com
Country town hotel, recently renovated. **£–££**

County Fermanagh

Arch House
59 Marble Arch Road, Florencecourt, Enniskillen
Tel: 028-6634 8452
www.archhouse.com
A warm welcome and good home cooking. **£**

Belle Isle Castle
Lisbellaw, Enniskillen
Tel: 028-6638 7231
www.belleislecastle.com
Set in glorious countryside and full of period grandeur. **£££**

Killyhevlin Hotel
Dublin Road, Enniskillen
Tel: 028-6632 3481
www.killyhevlin.com
With an idyllic lakeland setting, popular for its spa and good food. **£££**

Mahon's Hotel
Enniskillen Rd, Irvinestown
Tel: 028-6862 1656
www.mahonshotel.co.uk
Well located for exploring, plus a good menu. **££**

County Tyrone

Blessingbourne
Fivemiletown
Tel: 028-8952 1188
www.blessingbourne.com
Self-catering apartments and courtyard adjacent to Elizabethan lakeside manor, with carriage museum. Minimum two night stay. **£**

Grange Lodge
7 Grange Road, Dungannon
Tel: 028-8778 4212
www.grangelodgecountryhouse.com
A charming guesthouse famed for its food. **££**

BELFAST

Belfast Central Travelodge
15 Brunswick Street
Tel: 0871-984 6188
www.travelodge.co.uk
Bright, inexpensive hotel, right in the centre of it all. **£**

Benedicts Hotel
7–21 Bradbury Place
Tel: 028-9059 1999
www.benedictshotel.co.uk
Good value boutique-style hotel with an excellent restaurant, which uses local produce. **££**

The Crescent Town House
13 Lower Crescent
Tel: 028-9032 3349
www.crescenttownhouse.com
Inexpensive, busy hotel within easy walking distance of restaurants and nightlife. **££**

Culloden Estate & Spa
142 Bangor Road, Holywood
Tel: 028-9042 1066
www.hastingshotels.com
Plush hide-away for top people in baronial-style mansion with wooded grounds outside the city on Belfast Lough shore. **£££**

Duke's at Queens
65–67 University Street
Tel: 028-9023 6666
www.dukesatqueens.com
A make-over and a new name makes this sophisticated hotel a good choice. In the university area, 10-minute walk to city centre. **££**

Europa Hotel
Great Victoria Street
Tel: 028-9027 1066
www.hastingshotels.com
Large hotel with conference suites in heart of city. Once a popular target for bombers, now a watering hole for expense-account executives. **££–£££**

Fitzwilliam Hotel
1–3 Great Victoria Street
Tel: 028-9044 2080
www.fitzwilliamhotelbelfast.com
Unassuming from the outside, the inside is contemporary and sleek. Kitchen is overseen by Michelin-starred chef Kevin Thornton. **££–£££**

Holiday Inn Express
106A University Street
Tel: 028-9031 1909
www.oxhi belfast.com
At the lower end of the Holiday Inn range. Impersonal, but fills a gap in the university area. **£**

Madison's
59–63 Botanic Avenue
Tel: 028-9050 9800
www.madisonshotel.com
A stylish café-restaurant and bright rooms are the attractions of this venture in an off-campus milieu. **££**

Malmaison Belfast
34–38 Victoria Street
Tel: 028-9022 0200
www.malmaisonhotel.com
This imaginative conversion from two beautiful Victorian seed warehouses in the Cathedral Quarter, known for its artistic and gay scene, has a dramatic decor, plus popular brasserie and art deco bar. **£££–££££**

Malone Lodge Hotel
60 Eglantine Avenue
Tel: 028-9038 8060
www.malonelodgehotelbelfast.com
There are fine reviews for this attractive Victorian townhouse hotel in the leafy Queen's Quarter. **££**

Merchant Hotel
35–39 Waring St
Tel: 028-9023 4888.
www.themerchanthotel.com
Formerly a richly ornamented Italianate bank headquarters, this opulent hotel aims to be ranked for luxury and service alongside Claridge's in London. **£££–££££**

Stormont Hotel
587 Upper Newtownards Road
Tel: 028-9065 1066
www.hastingshotels.com
Smart hotel beside former Parliament buildings and government offices. **££–£££**

Ten Square
10 Donegall Square South
Tel: 028-9024 1001
www.tensquare.co.uk
A listed Victorian linen warehouse transformed into an ultra-luxury hotel with an oriental flavour. Faces City Hall. **££–££££**

Wellington Park Hotel
21 Malone Road
Tel: 028-9038 1111
www.wellingtonparkhotel.com
Smart suburban Best Western, close to university. Live music in the popular Wellie Bar. **££**

GUESTHOUSES

Avenue Guesthouse
25 Eglatine Avenue
Tel: 028-9066 5904
www.avenueguesthouse.com
Lovingly restored Victorian townhouse 10 minutes' walk from the city centre. **£**

An Old Rectory
148 Malone Road
Tel: 028-9066 7882
www.anoldrectory.co.uk
Charming former rectory, this guesthouse serves a particularly fine breakfast. **£**

Windermere House
60 Wellington Park
Tel: 028-9066 2693
www.windermereguesthouse.co.uk
A friendly guesthouse a short walk from the university area. **£**

ACTIVITIES

CALENDAR OF EVENTS, THE ARTS, NIGHTLIFE, SPORT AND TOURS

CALENDAR OF EVENTS

The number of events and festivals, big and small, seems to increase every year. There are folk festivals, music festivals, oyster festivals, walking festivals, regattas, angling competitions, drama festivals, chess congresses, sporting competitions of all kinds, beauty contests, song contests, parades, car rallies, boat rallies, literary festivals, jazz festivals, exhibitions, agricultural shows, horse shows, dog shows, cat shows, commemorations, celebrations, hunt meetings, marathons, summer schools, community festivals, *ceílís*... the list seems endless. The biggest growth area is arts festivals – theatre and film in winter, and multi-disciplinary summer events, including the Cork Midsummer Festival (June), Galway Arts Festival (July) and Kilkenny Arts Festival (August).

In many cases, dates and venues are variable and some festivals – particularly the smaller, local ones – may appear and disappear from year to year according to the availability of funds, enthusiasm or organisers.

Here is a small selection, listed in calendar order. Exact dates often vary, and local tourist boards can provide precise dates and details.

January Races, Leopardstown, Dublin: top-class National Hunt (jumping) meeting. Opening of Point-to-Point season: races run at different venues every Sunday over unfenced courses.

Temple Bar Traditional Irish Music & Cultural Festival, Dublin. January.

Walking Wild Ireland, Leitrim. January.

Holiday World Show, King's Hall, Belfast. Mid-January.

Six Nations Rugby Championship (Ireland versus England, Wales, Scotland, France, Italy). Home matches at Lansdowne Road, Dublin. February/March.

Powers Whiskey Ulster National, Downpatrick: steeplechase. Late February/early March.

Irish Dancing Championships. February/March.

Dublin Film Festival. **Belfast Film Festival**. March/April. Irish premieres of a selection of Irish and international cinema.

St Patrick's Day (17 March): Festival of Ireland's national saint. Celebrated throughout Ireland and much of the world, notably in New York City.

World Irish Dancing Championships: venue variable. March/April (Easter).

The Cathedral Quarter Arts Festival lively celebration of the arts in Belfast's vibrant "left bank" district.

Irish Grand National (steeplechase), Fairyhouse. Easter Monday.

Circuit of Ireland Car Rally. Easter weekend.

Dublin Grand Opera Society Spring Season, Gaiety Theatre. Late March/April.

Belfast Civic Festival and Lord Mayor's Show. May.

Belfast City Marathon road race. Mass masochism. May.

Northwest 200: fastest motorcycle road race in Britain or Ireland. Along the Portrush–Causeway Coast, County Antrim. May.

Feile na Bealtaine/Dingle Peninsula Arts and Political Festival, Dingle Peninsula, Co. Kerry. Bilingual festival of culture and debate.

Kinsale Sevens by the Sea, Kinsale, Co. Cork. Europe's largest rugby 7s festival takes place on the May Bank Holiday weekend.

Irish 2,000 Guineas (for 3-year-old colts) and **1,000 Guineas** (for fillies), both run over one mile. First classics of the flat-racing season, staged on consecutive Saturdays at the Curragh in May.

Ulster Classic Fishing Festival, Fermanagh Lakeland. Anglers' cornucopia. May.

Balmoral Show of the Royal Ulster Agricultural Society, Belfast. May.

Writers' Week, Listowel, Co. Clare. Late May/June

Castle Ward Opera, Strangford, Co. Down. Country house opera with supper in marquee. Opera Fringe Festival based at Down Arts Centre.

Smithwick's Cat Laughs Comedy Festival, Kilkenny. International festival of stand-up comedy, with over 50 comedians hoping to bring a smile to the medieval city of Kilkenny.

Music in Great Irish Houses Festival: held in various mansions near Dublin. Early June.

Bloomsday Literary Festival, 16 June, Dublin. Held on the date on which Joyce's *Ulysses* takes place. Principally for Joyce buffs, but there is no shortage of those.

Walk the Glens, Glens of Antrim. Walking festival in an area known for breathtaking scenery.

World Oceans Festival, Tramore, Co. Waterford. A celebration of wildlife and surfing in seaside resort famed for its long sandy beach.

Ballybunion International Bachelor Festival, Ballybunion, Co. Kerry. Irish manhood's answer to the Miss World contest. Seeing is believing. Late June.

Irish Derby (1½-mile flat-race for 3-year-old colts). Most glamorous day in the Irish racing calendar. Held at the Curragh. Late June.
Westport Sea Angling Festival, Westport, Co. Mayo. Late June.
Irish Oaks, the Curragh. Equivalent of the Derby for fillies. Early July.
Willie Clancy Summer School, Miltown Malbay, Co. Clare (uillean piping, set dancing). July.
Ulster Harp Derby, Downpatrick, Co. Down. July.
Orangeman's Day, all over Northern Ireland. 12 July.
International Rose Trials, Sir Thomas and Lady Dixon Park, Belfast. July–September.
Oxegen Festival, Punchestown Racecourse, Naas, Co. Kildare. Ireland's biggest open-air rock festival. July.
Galway Arts Festival. Massive celebration of international and Irish theatre, film, art, literature and music precedes the races *(see below)* to create a mighty buzz. Mid-July.
Galway Races – heady, often hilarious, holiday horse-racing. Late July/August.
Ulster Steam Traction Rally, The Showgrounds, Ballymena, Co. Antrim. July, huffing and puffing.
Stradbally Steam Rally, Stradbally, Co. Laois. Early August, more huffing and puffing.
Yeats International Summer School. Sligo. Academics, writers and poetry enthusiasts from all over the world assemble to listen and learn. The biggest and oldest of many summer schools taking place in August.
Dublin Horse Show, RDS, Ballsbridge. Greatest event in the show-jumping calendar. August.
Puck Fair, Killorglin, Co. Kerry. Ancient pagan festival at which a goat is crowned. August.
Féile an Phobail, West Belfast's massive community festival with concerts, debates, tours, exhibitions and street theatre. July–August.
The Auld Lammas Fair, Ballycastle, Co. Antrim. The North of Ireland's most popular old fair, at which you traditionally "treat your Mary Ann to some dulse and Yellow Man." For elucidation, go to Ballycastle. Last Monday and Tuesday in August.
Festival of World Cultures, Dun Laoghaire, Co. Dublin. Artistes from over 50 countries take part in Ireland's multi-cultural artsfest. July.
Ulster Grand Prix (motorcycling), Dundrod, near Belfast. August.
Merriman Summer School, Ennis, Co. Clare. A week in August of intense intellectual debate about the nation's culture, liberally laced with drinking and partying.
Rose of Tralee International Festival, Tralee, Co. Kerry. Late Aug.
Fleadh Ceoil na Eireann (All-Ireland festival of Irish music, with competitions therein). Venue variable. August.
Match-making Festival of Ireland, Lisdoonvarna, Co. Clare. More fun than computer dating. August–September.
Hurling and Gaelic Football: All-Ireland finals, Croke Park, Dublin. September.
Galway Oyster Festival, Galway city. Late September.
National Ploughing Championships. Venue variable. Late September. One of Europe's biggest agricultural shows with 60-acre tented city.
Dublin Theatre Festival. Late September/October.
Banks of the Foyle Halloween Carnival, Derry City, Co. Londonderry. Halloween events for all the family; carnival parade. October.
Cork Jazz Festival, Cork City. October.
Dublin City Marathon, More self-inflicted punishment. Late October.
Belfast Festival, Queen's University, Belfast. Ambitious, event-packed two weeks of music, drama, folksong, cinema, with many international participants. November.
Dublin Grand Opera Society Winter Season, Gaiety Theatre, Dublin. December.

BELOW: banging the drum at the Rose of Tralee International Festival.

THE ARTS

Theatre

Dublin

Abbey Theatre, Lower Abbey Street, Dublin, tel: 01-878 7222, www.abbeytheatre.ie. Ireland's national theatre. Founded in the early years of the 20th century by Yeats, Lady Gregory and their collaborators, it quickly won a world reputation with some outstanding plays and a unique style of acting. Many Irish classics feature in its programme. The Abbey's sister theatre, the **Peacock**, is used to try out new, experimental work.
Gaiety Theatre, South King Street, tel: 01-677 1717, www.gaietytheatre.com. A fine Victorian building restored in 2007. The programme includes opera, ballet, pantomime, variety concerts and serious drama.
Gate Theatre, 1 Cavendish Row, Parnell Square, tel: 01-874 4045, www.gate-theatre.ie. Founded by the noted actor Micheál MacLiammóir (1899–1978). The programme includes opera, ballet, pantomime, variety concerts and serious drama.
Grand Canal Theatre, Grand Canal Square, Docklands Dublin 2, tel: 01-677 7999, www.grandcanaltheatre.com. A spanking new design set in the brand new Docklands development on the Grand Canal. Drama, musicals, concerts, ballet, opera and more.
Lambert Puppet Theatre, Clifton Lane, Monkstown, Co. Dublin, tel: 01-280 0974, www.lambertpuppettheatre.com. Where the country's only permanent professional puppet theatre company performs.
Olympia Theatre, 72 Dame Street, tel: 01-679 3323, www.olympia.ie. Similar shows to the Gaiety. Once a Victorian music hall.
Project Arts Centre, 39 Essex Street East, Temple Bar, tel: 01-881 9313, www.projectartscentre.ie. Dublin's original "alternative" performance space.
Samuel Beckett Theatre, Trinity College, tel: 01-896 1334, www.tcd.ie/drama. Based in the university that produced such dramatists as Goldsmith, Synge and Beckett, and run in association with the university's Samuel Beckett Centre.

Other Theatres

Armagh: The Market Place, Market Street, tel: 028 3752 1821, www.marketplacearmagh.com. Adventurously-designed arts centre.
Belfast: Grand Opera House, Great Victoria Street, tel: 028-9024 1919,

www.goh.co.uk. Lyric Theatre, Ridgeway Street, tel: 028-90381 081, www.lyrictheatre.co.uk.
Clare: Glór Irish Music Centre, Causeway Link, tel: 065 684 3103, www.glor.ie. Modern building with two auditoria. Irish music shows in summer, theatre rest of the year.
Cork: Opera House, Emmet Place, tel: 021-427 0022, www.corkoperahouse.ie. Everyman Palace, 15 MacCurtain Street, tel: 021-450 1673, www.everymanpalace.com. Both mix touring productions, popular entertainment and local productions.
Derry: Riverside Theatre, University of Ulster, Coleraine, Co. Derry, tel: 028 7032 3232. New auditorium.
Fermanagh: Ardhowen Theatre, Dublin Road, Enniskillen, Co. Fermanagh, tel: 028-6632 5440, www.ardhowentheatre.com.
Galway: Druid Theatre Company, Druid Lane Theatre, Chapel Lane, off Quay Street, tel: 091-568 660, www.druidtheatre.com. One of Ireland's most successful repertory theatre companies, presenting a mix of new work and revivals. Galway's other professional companies, Punchbag and Macnas, share the Town Hall Theatre with the Druid.
Limerick: Belltable Arts Centre, 69 O'Connell Street, tel: 061-319 866, www.belltable.ie. Small auditorium.
Sligo: Hawk's Well Theatre, Temple Street, tel: 071-916 1526/1518, www.hawkswell.com. Modern theatre hosting touring and local shows.
Tralee: Siamsa Tíre: National Folk Theatre of Ireland, tel: 066-712 3055, www.siamsatire.com. Evokes Irish rural tradition in song, dance and mime.
Tyrone: Burnavon Arts & Cultural Centre, Burn Road, Cookstown, tel: 028 8676 9949, www.burnavon.com. Mid-Ulster's main venue for theatre, dance, comedy and live music.

Music

Ireland has some of the most vital traditional music in the world. You can hear it in pubs almost everywhere in the country, but visitors who want to be sure of hearing some good stuff are best advised to attend an organised session, such as one of those presented in summer, Mondays to Thursdays at 9pm at Culturlann na hEireann, the headquarters of Comhaltas Ceoltoiri Eireann (the traditional music association). The address is 32 Belgrave Square, Monkstown, Co. Dublin, tel: 280 0295 www.comhaltas.ie. Buses No. 7 and 8 from Dublin city centre stop nearby and the Seapoint DART rail station is only a short walk away. For pub sessions try the Auld Dublin in Temple Bar, tel: 01-677 0527 or check out *The Ticket*, the entertainment supplement of Friday's *Irish Times for other venues*. See also the website www.entertainment.ie.

ABOVE: the pub's the place for Irish music.

The biggest change in Irish popular music over the past few years, particularly among the younger people, is how "club" music has become the new and dominant means of musical expression. In European terms, Dublin is seen as a "clubbing capital" and venues like The TriPod (still referred to as POD for Place of Dance) and D Two are two of the best places in the city in which to experience the modern musical sound of youthful Ireland. Local DJs are bringing out their own records on their own labels and dabbling in the contemporary genres of music such as Garage, Drum 'n' Bass and Trance.

The Ticket also carries details of jazz, rock and classical music events. The top venue for the latter is the National Concert Hall in Earlsfort Terrace, off St Stephen's Green, Dublin. There are also three auditoria used for jazz and classical music, theatre and dance at The Helix, Dublin City University, Collins Avenue, Glasnevin, Dublin 9, tel: 01-700 7000 www.thehelix.ie. A variety of musical genres can be found at the 0_2 arena (formerly the Point), tel: 01-819 8888, www.the02.ie.

Art Galleries

Dublin Area

Those interested in the visual arts should visit the National Gallery, the Dublin City Art Gallery, The Hugh Lane, the Irish Museum of Modern Art and the Chester Beatty Library. There are also many smaller exhibition centres and commercial galleries which often contain interesting work. Details in *The Ticket* (see above) or at www.recirca.com
Chester Beatty Library, tel: 01-407 0750, www.cbl.ie. Oct–Apr Tue–Fri 10am–5pm; May–Sept Mon–Fri 10am–5pm; Sat 11am–5pm; Sun 1–5pm. This superb collection of oriental art and manuscripts is housed in the Clocktower Building at Dublin Castle.
Combridge Fine Arts, 17 South William Street, tel: 01-677 4652, www.cfa.ie. Mon–Sat 9.30am–5.30pm. Conventional landscapes in oil and watercolour.
Douglas Hyde Gallery, Trinity College, tel: 01-608 1116, www.douglashydegallery.com. Mon–Fri 11am–6pm (7pm on Thur), Sat 11am–4.45pm. Contemporary Irish and international painting, sculpture and photography.
Dublin City Gallery, The Hugh Lane, Charlemont House, Parnell Square North, tel: 01-222 5550, www.hughlane.ie. Tue–Thur 10am–6pm, Fri–Sat 10am–5pm, Sun 11am–5pm. Sumptuously restored Palladian villa with a major collection of Impressionists and 20th-century Irish art. Also Francis Bacon's rebuilt studio.
Gallery of Photography, Meeting House Square, Dublin 2, tel: 01-671 4654, www.galleryofphotography.com. Tue–Sat 11am–6pm, Sun 1–6pm. Irish and international exhibitions; postcards, prints and posters.
Green on Red Gallery, 26–28 Lombard Street East, Dublin 2, tel: 01-671 3414, www.greenonredgallery.com. Tue–Fri 10am–6pm, Sat 1–4pm. Cutting-edge contemporary art.
Irish Museum of Modern Art, Royal Hospital, Kilmainham, tel: 01-612 9900, www.imma.ie. Tue–Sat 10am–5.30pm, Sun noon–5.30pm. Irish and international art of the 20th century.
Kerlin Gallery, Ann's Lane, South Ann Street, Dublin 2, tel: 01-670 9093, www.kerlin.ie. Mon–Fri 10am–5.45pm, Sat 11am–4.30pm. Contemporary European, Irish artists.
Malahide Castle, Malahide, Co. Dublin, tel: 01-846 2516. Mon–Sat 10am–5pm, Sun and bank holidays 11am–5pm, closed for lunch (Apr–Oct); weekends and bank holidays 2–5pm (Nov–Mar). Houses a selection of Irish portraits from the National Gallery.
National Gallery of Ireland, Merrion Square West, tel: 01-661 5133, www.

nationalgallery.ie. Mon–Sat 9.30am–5.30pm (8.30pm on Thur), Sun noon–5.30pm. Old Masters, Irish and international art from the 16th to the 19th centuries. Permanent Yeats exhibition, mainly dedicated to the work of Jack B. Yeats.

Oriel Gallery, 17 Clare Street, Dublin 2, tel: 01-676 3410, www.theoriel.com. Mon–Fri 10am–5.30pm, Sat 10am–1pm. Has 19th- and 20th-century Irish paintings, mostly landscapes. Established names such as Paul Henry, Jack B. Yeats, "AE".

RHA Gallagher Gallery, 15 Ely Place, Dublin 2, tel: 01-661 2558, www.royalhibernianacademy.ie. Wed–Sat 11am–7pm (Mon and Tue until 5pm), Sun 2–5pm. Exhibitions by Irish and international artists in large modern gallery.

Rubicon Gallery, 10 St Stephen's Green, Dublin 2, tel: 01-670 8055, www.rubicongallery.ie. Tue–Sat noon–6pm and by appointment. Contemporary Irish and international art.

Taylor Galleries, 16 Kildare Street, Dublin 2, tel: 01-676 6055, www.taylorgalleries.ie. Mon–Fri 10am–5.30pm, Sat 11am–3pm. Represent some of Ireland's leading contemporary artists.

Temple Bar Gallery and Studios, 5–9 Temple Bar, Dublin 2, tel: 01-671 0073, www.templebargallery.com. Tue–Sat 11am–6pm, Thur until 7pm. Avant-garde contemporary Irish and international art.

Southeast

Butler Gallery, Kilkenny Castle, Kilkenny, tel: 056-776 1106, www.butlergallery.com. Daily 10am–7pm. Late 19th-century and 20th-century Irish art.

Garter Lane Arts Centre, O'Connell Street, Waterford, tel: 051-877 153. Daily 10am–6pm. Exhibitions by lively young artists.

Wexford Arts Centre, Cornmarket, Wexford, tel: 053-23764, www.wexfordartscentre.ie. Mon–Sat 10am–6pm. General-purpose arts centre in 18th-century market house which hosts touring exhibitions.

Southwest

Catherine Hammond Gallery, Main Street, Glengarriff, tel: 027-62812, www.hammondgallery.com. Thur–Sun, 11am–5pm or by appointment. Contemporary Irish and American painting.

Crawford Municipal Art Gallery, Emmet Place, Cork, tel: 021-427 3377, www.crawfordartgallery.com. Mon–Sat, 10am–4.45pm. Irish and European paintings, sculpture, silver, glass. Excellent café.

Frank Lewis, 6 Bridewell Lane, Killarney, tel: 064-31108, www.franklewis.com. Commercial gallery hosting regular shows by artists living or temporarily working in the southwest.

Green Lane Gallery, Holy Ground, Dingle, Co. Kerry, tel: 066-915 2047, www.greenlanegallery.com. Seascapes and other work by distinguished local artists.

Keane on Ceramics, Pier Road, Kinsale, tel: 021-477 4553. Open daily. Represents a number of major Irish ceramic artists.

Lavit Gallery, Father Matthew Street, Cork, tel: 021-427 7749. Mon–Sat 10am–6pm. Fortnightly exhibitions by Irish artists.

Lewis Glucksman Gallery, University College, Cork, tel: 021 490 1844, www.glucksman.org. Architecturally distinguished building with mainly contemporary shows.

The Private Collector, Main Street, Innishannon, Co. Cork, tel: 021-477 6777. Large space with big names in Irish art alongside new up-and-coming talent.

Triskel Arts Centre, Tobin Street, Cork, tel: 021-427 2022, www.triskelart.com. Mon–Sat 10am–5.30pm. Exhibitions, plays, poetry readings and music.

Siamsa Tíre, Town Park, Tralee, tel: 066 712 3055, www.siamstire.com. Kerry's main public-sector-funded contemporary arts centre.

Siopa Cill Rialaig, Dun Geagan, Ballinskelligs, Co. Kerry, tel: 066-947 9277. The gallery linked to remote artists' retreat near Waterville in a circular thatched building. Exhibitions by visiting artists, café and workshops.

West Cork Arts Centre, Old Bank House, North Street, Skibbereen, Co. Cork, tel: 028-22090, www.westcorkartscentre.com. Mon–Sat 10am–6pm. Community arts centre with exhibitions of contemporary paintings, sculpture, ceramics. Directory of local artist and craft makers on request. Interesting shop.

The Shannon Region

Belltable Arts Centre, 69 O'Connell Street, Limerick, tel: 061-319 866, www.belltable.ie. Mon–Sat 10am–9pm. Community arts centre hosting travelling exhibitions and shows by local artists.

Ennis Art Gallery, 2 Francis Street Ennis, Co. Clare, www.ennisartgallery.com. Contemporary Irish art.

Limerick City Gallery of Art, Pery Square, Limerick, tel: 061-310 633. http://gallery.limerick.ie. Mon–Fri 10am–1pm, 2.30–8pm, Sat 10am–1pm. Collection of 18th- to 20th-century oils and watercolours. Local and touring exhibitions.

Far West

Ballinglen Arts Foundation, Main Street, Ballycastle, Co. Mayo, tel: 096-43366, www.ballinglenartsfoundation.org. Gallery open June to September showing work by international artists who have had residencies on the North Mayo coast.

Bold Art Gallery, Merchants Road, Galway, tel: 091-539 900, www.boldartgallery.com. Friendly city centre gallery with a mix of contemporary and traditional work.

Galway Arts Centre, 47 Dominick Street, Galway, tel: 091-565 886, www.galwayartscentre.ie. Mon–Sat 10am–

BELOW: Dublin's National Gallery of Ireland is an inspiring setting for amateur artists.

6pm. Regular exhibitions by younger artists. Information centre for the lively Galway arts scene.
Linenhall Arts Centre, Linenhall Street, Castlebar, tel: 094-902 3733, www.thelinenhall.com. Mon–Fri 10am–5.30pm, Sat 11am–5pm. Community centre for all kinds of artistic activity including shows of local work.
Norman Villa Gallery, 86 Lower Salthill, Galway, tel: 091-521 131, www.normanvillagallery.com. Tue–Sat 11–6. Contemporary painting and sculpture in a Victorian townhouse.

Northwest Region

The Cat and the Moon Art Gallery, 4 Castle Street, Sligo www.thecatandthe moon.com. Selection of paintings, sculptures and prints by artists resident in Ireland.
Glebe Gallery, Churchill, Co. Donegal, tel: 074-913 7071. Tours June–Sept daily 11am–6.30pm, (closes Fri June and Sept). Derek Hill collection; English-born artist associated particularly with paintings of Tory Island.
The Model, The Mall, Sligo, tel: 071-914 1405, www.themodel.ie. Major provincial gallery housed in a recently renovated model school dating back to 1862 and enlarged for 2010. Visiting shows, and important collection of Jack B. Yeats.
Sligo County Museum, Stephen Street, Sligo, tel: 071-911 1679. Open all year Tue–Sat (am only Oct–May). Local archaeological artefacts and geological samples, plus the Yeats Collection including photographs, prints, letters, portraits and his Nobel medal. Also memorabilia of Countess Markievicz and the Gore-Booth family.

Northern Ireland

Island Arts Centre, Lagan Valley Island, Lisburn, tel: 028-9250 9509, www.islandartscentre.com. Purpose-built contemporary arts venue for Lisburn City with a lively programme of exhibitions.
The Market Place Theatre and Arts Centre, Market Street, Armagh City, tel: 028-3752 1820, www.themarketplace armagh.com. Purpose-built multi-purpose arts venue with striking modern design.
Strule Arts Centre, Townhall Square, Omagh, Co. Tyrone, tel: 028-8224 7831, www.struleartscentre.co.uk. A complete arts venue including an art workshop with ceramics facility, print workshop and exhibition space.

Belfast

Belfast Exposed, The Exchange Place, 23 Donegall Street, Belfast, tel: 028-9023 0965, www.belfastexposed.org. Tue–Sat 11am–5pm. Based in a 19th-century warehouse, the gallery shows work from both local and international photographers.
Bradbury Gallery, 1 Lyndon Court, College Street, Belfast, tel: 028-9023 8450, www.bradburygallery.co.uk. Irish and international artists.
Catalyst Arts Gallery, 5 College Court, Belfast, tel: 028-9031 3303, www.catlystarts.org. Contemporary art in converted industrial space.
Eakin Gallery, 237 Lisburn Road, Belfast, tel: 028-9066 8522, www.eakingallery.co.uk. Traditional and modern Irish paintings.
Fenderesky Gallery, Crescent Arts Centre, 2–4 University Road, Belfast, tel: 028-9023 5245. Tue–Sat 11.30am–5pm. Contemporary and avant-garde Irish painting.
Golden Thread Gallery, The Switch Room, 84-94 Great Patrick Street, Belfast, tel: 028-9033 0920, www.gtgallery.co.uk. Contemporary visual art in converted industrial warehouse space.
Gormley's Fine Art Gallery, 251 Lisburn Road, Belfast, tel: 028-9066 3313, www.gormleys.ie. On three floors of a charming terrace, featuring well-known Irish artists such as William Conor and Rita Duffy but also the less well-known.
Naughton Gallery, Lanyon Building, Queen's University, Belfast, tel: 028 9097 3580, www.naughtongallery.org. Work from the university's own collection and touring shows of contemporary art.
Nicholas Gallery, 571 Lisburn Road, Belfast, tel: 028-9068 7767, www.nicholasgallery.co.uk. Paintings and sculptures by leading British and Irish artists including Sean Scully, Howard Hodgkin and Bridget Riley.
Old Museum Arts Centre, 7 College Square North, Belfast, tel: 028 9023 3332, www.oldmuseumartscentre.org. Fine classical building now used as a centre for contemporary arts (moving to new Cathedral Quarter premises in 2012).
Ormeau Baths Gallery, 18a Ormeau Road, Belfast, tel: 028-9032 1402, www.ormeaubaths.co.uk. Tue–Sat 10am–5.30pm. Free public gallery in converted public baths. Contemporary shows, often of conceptual art.
Tom Caldwell Gallery, 429 Lisburn Road, Belfast, tel: 028-9066 1890, www.tomcaldwellgallery.com. Large commercial gallery with paintings and scupture by contemporary Irish artists, and Italian designer furniture.

Outside Belfast

Flowerfield Arts Centre, 185 Coleraine Road, Portstewart, Co. Derry. Tel; 028-7083 1400, www.flowerfield.org. Georgian house extended to incorporate multi-purpose arts centre with craft retail area.
Void Art Centre, Old City Factory, Patrick Street, Derry, tel: 028 7130 8080, www.derryvoid.com. With two large galleries and six artists studios, Void showcases adventurous contemporary art by local and international artists.

BELOW: viewing the latest exhibition at Belfast's Ormeau Baths Gallery.

NIGHTLIFE

Dublin

Late Spots

If you're under 30 and believe in having a good time, the chances are you've heard of Dublin's club scene. Much has been written internationally about how the city has begun to rival fashionable European cities for exciting clubs. The reality behind the hype is improving all the time.

You don't have to dance till dawn. Those more sophisticated in years can enjoy late-night bars, cabarets or smart nightclubs where tables positioned away from the dance floor allow for meaningful conversations.

A word about smoking: it doesn't matter where you go or how late you stay out – if you're indoors, all Irish pubs and clubs are smoke-free and smokers spend much of their time keeping bouncers from getting lonely.

Nightclubs

Club M, Blooms Hotel, 6 Anglesea Street, Dublin 2, tel: 01-671 5274, www.clubm.ie. If you don't feel like posing and just want to bop the night away. City centre disco playing chart, dance and R'n'B. Smart dress preferred.
Gaiety Theatre, South King Street, tel: 01-677 1717. At night the theatre opens its doors to the after-hours crowd. The atmosphere is relaxed and spacious as the punters are spread out over three floors – one with a DJ, one with a live act and one left with only the sound of conversation.
The George, 89 South Great Georges Street, Dublin 2, tel: 01-478 2983. Probably the city's most popular gay club. The George pub from which the club gets it name is a favourite meeting place among gay men. Stylish dress.
La Cave, 28 South Anne Street, Dublin 2, tel: 01-679 4409. Cosy and compelling late-night venue which falls somewhere between a restaurant, wine bar and nightclub, although there's no dance floor as such. The soothing Latino sounds and intimate atmosphere mean this is a winner with thirty-somethings wanting to kick back. Smart dress.
Lillie's Bordello, Adam Court, Grafton Street, Dublin 2, tel: 01-679 9204, www.lilliesbordello.ie. One of the most exclusive clubs in town, and one which prides itself on its VIP lounge where high-profile party animals rub shoulders with fellow celebrities. Non-members are not guaranteed entry, but looking like a celeb can work wonders on the bouncers. Stylish clothes essential.
Ri-Ra, Dame Court, Exchequer Street, Dublin 2, tel: 01-671 1220, www.rira.ie. Groovy club for babes with attitude and cool dudes. Funk, hip-hop and audio-visual shows. As for clothes, the hipper the better.
Sugar Club, 8 Lower Leeson Street, Dublin 2, tel: 678 7188, www.thesugarclub.com. Live bands most nights are followed by DJ dancing. The bar has one of the city's most extensive cocktail menus.
The TRIPOD, Harcourt Street, Dublin 2, tel: 01-476 3374, www.pod.ie. Still referred to as the POD, but now three-clubs in one: ultra-hip venue where everyone who's anyone in rock music, the media and modelling congregate. The dance floor is home to the young and beautiful. You probably already know to wear hip clothes.
The Vaults, Harbourmaster Place, IFSC, Dublin 1, tel: 01-605 4700, www.thevaults.ie. Lots of atmosphere in this converted venue with its cave-like setting. The VI Nite Club at the Vaults is one Dublin's hottest night spots with top Irish and international DJs spinning the decks.
The Viper Room, 5 Aston Quay, Dublin 2, tel: 01-672 5566. This late-night lounge bar, with its decadent purple and red decor, doesn't really get going until after 10pm but it then pulsates to the disco beat downstairs or live music upstairs until the early hours.

Late Bars

Late-night bars continue to be popular in Dublin thanks to revised – though still not exactly liberal – licensing laws. The following pubs are open on various nights, mainly weekends, until the crazy hour of 1.30am.
Bleeding Horse, 24 Upper Camden Street, Dublin 2, tel: 01-475 2705.
Czech Inn, Essex Gate, Temple Bar, Dublin 2, tel: 01-671 1535.
Fitzsimons, East Essex Street, Dublin 2, tel: 01-677 9315.
Foggy Dew, 1 Upper Fowne's Street, Dublin 2, tel: 01-677 9328.
The Globe, Georges Street, Dublin 2, tel: 01-671 1220.
Hogans, 35 Great South Georges Street, Dublin 2, tel: 01-677 5904.
Market Bar, Fade Street, Dublin 2, tel: 01-613 9094.
Mercantile Bar, Dame Street, Dublin 2, tel: 01-670 7100.
Sinnotts, South King Street, Dublin 2, tel: 01-478 4698.
Turk's Head Chop House, 27–30 Parliament Street, Temple Bar, Dublin 2, tel: 01-679 2606.
Whelans, 25 Wexford Street, Dublin 2, tel: 01-478 0766.

Cabaret

Celtic Rising, Burlington Hotel, Upper Leeson Street, Dublin 4, tel: 01-660 5222. Cabaret that brings a fresh and contemporary slant on Irish heritage and culture. See some of Ireland's top dancers, musicians and singers perform in a vibrant new show, choreographed by international Irish dance master Ronan McCormack.
The Sugar Club, 8 Lower Leeson Street, Dublin 2, tel: 01-678 7188, www.thesugarclub.com. A new multimedia theatre geared towards the over-25s with a vast range of entertainment from classic and cult cinema screening to international live music, comedy, live theatre, cabaret, burlesque, etc. Check the programme before you go. Open 7 nights a week with a bar licensed until 2.30am.

Comedy

Battle of the Axe, Ha'penny Bridge Inn, 42 Wellington Quay, Dublin 2, tel: 086-815 6987, www.battleofaxe.com. Every Tuesday night new and experienced acts from around the world battle it out for the No. 1 spot.
International Bar, Wicklow Street, Dublin 2, tel: 01-677 9250. Home to various comedy acts upstairs.
Laughter Lounge, Basement 4, 8 Eden Quay, Dublin 1, tel: 01-878 3003, www.laughterlounge.ie. Ireland's premier purpose-built comedy venue has top Irish and international acts on stage every Thursday, Friday and Saturday nights. There's a bar and food, too and the After Lounge to dance the night away after the show.
Vicar Street, 58–59 Thomas Street, Dublin 8, tel: 01-775 5800. Primarily a hugely successful music venue, Vicar Street also stages top comedians. Call or check press for details of performances.

Dance

Culturlann na hEireann *(see page 370)* is the best place to find out about traditional Irish dance. May sees the Dublin Dance Festival featuring all manner of dance performance.

Cork

Nightclubs

Cubins, Hanover Street; tel: 021-427 9250, http://cubins.ie. Late night DJs with wide mix of music Thursday to Sunday from 11pm.
Havana Browns, Hanover Street, tel: 021-427 1969, www.havana-browns.com. Open from 11pm, seven nights.
Mangan's, Careys Lane, tel: 021-427 5530. Well-established venue for the over-25s, open Thursday to Sunday from 11pm.
Savoy Music Venue, Patrick Street, Cork, tel: 021-425 4281 www.savoycork.com. Two venue club with live bands in foyer. Indie-Alternative, or Retro classics on Friday, Local DJ's mix on Saturdays.

ABOVE: some pubs have become trendy bars.

Galway

Cuba, Eyre Square, tel: 091-565 991 www.cuba.ie. Mainly Latin, DJs and live bands.
GPO, Eglinton Street, tel: 091-563 073, www.gpo.ie. Popular dance club. Free admission with student ID.
Roisin Dubh, Dominick Street, tel: 091-586 540. Big pub venue for emerging rock and traditional Irish bands.
Sally Longs, Upper Abbeygate Street, tel: 091-565 756. Heavy metal in famous bikers' pub.

Limerick

Dolan's Pub, 3–4 Dock Road, tel: 061-314 483. Live music venue with big-name acts.
Nancy Blake's Pub, 19 Denmark Street, tel: 061-416 443. The Outback at this lively pub is a great venue for live bands, chiefly rock.

Belfast

Clubs

Belfast has earned a surprising reputation for a new generation of stylish bars and nightclubs. Perhaps hedging its bets, the **Robinson's** (38–40 Great Victoria Street, tel: 028-9024 7447) complex, next to the Crown, includes the now rather dated-looking but still popular Irish-themed pub, Fibber Magee's, but also the quirkily upmarket BT1 and even newer Roxy, home to dance nights and live music.

Another big draw is the eastern-influenced **Bar Bacca** (43 Franklin Street, tel: 028-9023 0200), with a large and inventive range of cocktails and regular DJs. Upstairs is sister nightclub **La Lea**.

Another cocktail menu worth investigating is at the kitsch US-style 1950s interior of the popular **Irene and Nan's** (12 Brunswick Street, tel: 028-9023 9123).

Another of the original style bars that Belfast took to its heart is the **Northern Whig** (2 Bridge Street, tel: 028-9050 9888), housed in what was once an old Belfast newspaper office. Now Soviet-themed (big chunky furniture, several vodka-based cocktails, statues of Lenin etc), its bar, restaurant and nightclub are usually heaving on weekends.

Rain attracts large queues to the unpromising Tomb Street (tel: 028-9032 7308) since opening in 2009. The state-of-the-art nightclub oozes opulence and features various themed nights.

In the Queen's Quarter, the **M-Club** (23 Bradbury Place, tel: 028-9023 3131) and **Club Capri** (701 Lisburn Road, tel: 028-9066 4442), one of Belfast's newest venues, are renowned as major hot spots for a good night out.

Traditional Music

The John Hewitt, 51 Donegall Street, tel: 028-9023 3768. Sessions on Tue and Wed.
Kelly's Cellars, 30 Bank Street, tel: 028-9032 4835. Wed, Fri, Sat and Sun. Less purist.
Kitchen Bar, 16 Victoria Square, tel: 028-9024 5268. Music most nights.
McHugh's. 29–31 Queen Street, tel: 028-9050 9999. Music Wed–Sat.

SPORT

Spectator

Gaelic Football and Hurling

You can carry the ball, which is round, and slightly smaller than a soccer ball, but you must bounce or kick it every three steps. Hurling is one of the world's oldest and fastest ball games, played by teams of 15 players with a curved wooden stick made from ash and a leather-wrapped ball, or *sliotar*. Most matches at Croke Park are between county teams, and a great part of the fun lies in observing the passionate zeal of the supporters, who wear their team's colours and roar themselves hoarse. Matches are held most weekend afternoons between May and August. Tickets can be bought at the stadium (from €20–55), except for championship matches. To attend a match elsewhere in the country at County and local level, ask about fixtures at the Tourist Information Office, Cumann Luthchleas Gael, Croke Park, Dublin 3, tel: 836 3222, www.gaa.ie. This houses a museum devoted to the history of this uniquely Irish sport. Further details, tel: 819 2323, fax: 819 2324.

Rugby

Irish Rugby Football Union, 62 Landsdowne Road, Ballsbridge, Dublin 4, tel: 647 3800, www.irishrugby.ie.

For local fixtures, ask at the Tourist Information Office.

Soccer

Soccer Football Assocation of Ireland, 80 Merrion Square, Dublin 2, tel: 703 7500, www.fai.ie.

Landsdowne Road Stadium has been closed for rebuilding and reopened in 2010 as the Aviva Stadium with a 50,000 capacity. During rebuilding, both rugby and football internationals were played at Croke Park (in north Dublin). To buy tickets for internationals you have to join the Irish Rugby Supporters' Club – see website.

Participant

Golf

Visitors are welcome to play at over 400 golf courses in Ireland. Green fees range from about €50 to €250. Most clubs offer discounts to groups and societies. Some courses have sets of clubs for hire, but it's wise to book in advance. Caddies are also available by prior booking at 11 high-profile clubs. Most clubs hire out pullcarts, and some have a few motorised buggies, though some clubs, particularly the links, with severely undulating terrain, do not have this service. Visitors should bring only light golf-bags, as they may have to carry their own. Bear in mind that it is possible to play golf from 7am up to 8pm in May, and August to mid-September, while in late June and July there is sufficient daylight to play golf up to 10pm.

Golfing in Ireland is a new publication available from tourist information offices in Ireland and overseas, or tel: 0800 039 7000. It includes details of golf accommodation offers, tour operators, golf clubs, access travel and golfing fixtures in both the Republic and Northern Ireland. See also www.discoverireland.com/golfing. There is also a useful website, www.golfireland.ie which represents an affiliation of companies offering customised golfing holidays in Ireland including transport, accommodation and tee times. Packages range from short breaks to 10 days with eight rounds of golf. Companies such as Golfbreaks.com offer three days' golf breaks with 2 nights B&B (tel: 0800 279 7988; www.golfbreaks.com).

A Northern Ireland Tourist Board brochure (tel: 028-9024 6609) lists the province's 80 golf courses. For a Gold Pass for Northern Ireland giving three rounds of golf for €70 at a choice of seven top courses, see www.discovernorthernireland.com/golfing.

Sea Angling

Shore fishing (from rocks, piers, beaches and promontories), inshore fishing (in bays and inlets) and deep sea fishing are popular in Ireland all the year round. No permits are required. There are over 250 competitions organised throughout the country February–November.

Boats can be hired from more than 700 operators around the country. Expect to pay between €20 and €40 per angler per day, or between €225 and €400 for a daily charter. Full details of events and of boats for hire are contained in the free Tourism Ireland publication, *Angling in Ireland*, which covers both coarse and sea angling or go to their designated website www.discoverireland.com/angling.

Coarse Angling

The species of freshwater fish in this category are pike, arch, bream, rudd, tench, dace and various hybrids. The main area for coarse fishing is the Midlands, stretching from the River Erne system in the North southwards through the Shannon basin, the Monaghan and Westmeath lakes, the Grand and Royal Canals, to the Barrow River and Canal and the Munster Blackwater. There is no legal closed season, but a conservation order on pike was introduced in 1990. No licence is required in the Irish Republic.

In Northern Ireland, anglers require an annual general coarse fishing permit and a coarse fishing rod licence (for 15 days or a season).

Tackle can be bought but seldom hired in Ireland. Boat hire works out at around €30 per head per day based on six sharing. Pre-packed bait, such as pure breadcrumbs, white maggots and worms can be bought from a number of stockists, but it is best to pre-order from Irish Bait and Tackle, Ballyconnell, Co. Cavan, tel: 049-952 6258. If you are bringing your own bait into Ireland, do not pack it in soil or vegetable material, the importation of which is illegal.

Game Angling

The species are salmon, sea trout and brown trout. The season for salmon fishing is from 1 January to 30 September, depending on district. A licence is essential, and usually a fishery permit also – though some loughs, for example Corrib and Conn, are free of permit charge. (Permits are not the same as licences and are paid to individual fishery owners.)

An annual licence costs €62, a 21-day licence €23, a district licence €29 and juvenile and one-day licences €10 and €16 respectively.

A salmon licence and permit also covers fishing for sea trout, which is in season from June to 30 September (12 October in some areas). For brown trout, a licence is required in Northern Ireland only and much of the fishing is free. Full details are in Tourism Ireland's brochure *Game Angling in Ireland*.

Angling Information

Tourism Ireland (tel: 0800 039 7000 www.discoverireland.com) publishes free visitors' guides on Game Angling, Coarse Angling, Pike Angling and Sea Angling in Ireland. Tourist offices in main cities and towns throughout country will provide up-to-date information on every aspect of angling.
Department of Communications, Marine and Natural Resources, Inland Fisheries Administration, Leeson Lane, Dublin 2, tel: 01-678 2000, www.dcmnr.gov.ie.
Central Fishing Board, Balnagowan House, Glasnevin, Dublin 9, tel: 01-884 2600, www.cfb.ie.
Eastern Regional Fisheries Board Blackrock, Dublin, tel: 01-278 7022, www.fishingireland.net.
Southern Regional Fisheries Board, Anglesea Street, Clonmel, Co. Tipperary, tel: 052-80055, www.srfb.ie.
Southwestern Regional Fisheries Board, Neville Terrace, Massey Town, Macroom, Co. Cork, tel: 026-41221, www.cfb.ie.
Shannon Regional Fisheries Board, Ashbourne Business Park, Dock Road, Limerick, tel: 061-300 238, www.shannon-fishery-board.ie.
Western Regional Fisheries Board, Weir Lodge, Earls Island, Galway, tel: 091-563 110, www.wrfb.ie.
Northwestern Regional Fisheries Board, Abbey Street, Ballina, Co. Mayo, tel: 096-22623, www.northwestfisheries.ie.
Northern Regional Fisheries Board, Station Road, Ballyshannon, Co. Donegal, tel: 071-985 1435 www.nrfb.ie.

Adventure Sports

Canoeing, boardsailing, caving, hang-gliding, mountaineering, orienteering, parachuting, scuba diving, sailing and water-skiing are among the main activities provided for in a growing number of Outdoor Education Centres located in suitably stunning locations from Cork to Galway to Donegal to Wexford and beyond. Courses range from day or half-day introductions to a sport, to full-time courses for aspiring instructors, and everything in between. Full details of the nine centres are affiliated to the Outdoor Education Ireland are on the website, www.oec.ie. Alternately, contact: Victor Fusco, Kinsale Outdoor Education Centre, St John's Hill, Kinsale, Co. Cork, tel: 021-477 2896.

Surfing

Surfing is one of Ireland's fastest-growing sports. Notable venues with Atlantic swells, stimulating breezes and foaming surf are at Strandhill and Easkey, Co. Sligo, and Lahinch, Kilkee, Doolin Point, along the coast of Co. Clare. Coaching, including surf-board and wet-suit, costs about €35 per hour. There are over 30 approved surfing schools listed on the website of the Irish Surfing Association, www.isasurf.ie.

Alternately, contact Zoe Lally, Development Officer, The Irish Surfing Association, Easkey Surf and Information Centre, Easkey, Co. Sligo, tel: 096-49428, www.isasurf.ie.

Bird-watching

There are more than 55 recognised birdwatching sites in Ireland. For details of these, and of the various species to be seen at different times of year, contact Birdwatch Ireland, Rockingham House, Newcastle, Co. Wicklow, tel: 01-281 9878, www.birdwatchireland.ie. There are two bird observatories at which visitors can stay. These are Cape Clear Bird

ABOVE: a stroll through the Sperrin Mountains in Co. Tyrone.

Observatory (bookings via Mr Steve Wing , Cape Clear Bird Observatory, Cape Clear, West Cork or book through the Birdwatch Ireland website above); and Copeland Bird Observatory, Co. Down (bookings Secretary is Mr N. McKee, 67 Temple Rise, Templepatrick, Co. Antrim, tel: 028-9443 3068, www.cbo.org.uk).

Cycling

Walking Cycling Ireland is an association of approved tour operators offering guided and self-guided holidays for walking and cycling enthusiasts, www.walkingcycling ireland.com.

Irish Cycling Safaris offer a choice of routes in scenic areas including the Ring of Kerry, Connemara and the Burren. Choose a self-led tour with pre-booked accommodation, bike hire, luggage transfer and route details, or opt to join a group tour with a set departure date, organised lunch and dinner stops, and a local guide driving the support van (tel: 01-260 0749, www.irishcyclingsfaris.com).

For other options, contact Tourism Ireland for their free brochure, Cycling in Ireland, tel: 0800 039 7000, www.discoverireland.com.

Hill-Walking, Rambling and Climbing

There is surely no need for further propaganda about the unspoilt beauty of Ireland's hills and mountains. Few of them rise above 3,000ft (1,000 metres), but they have great character and variety, from the soft, bog-covered domes of Wicklow to the jagged peaks of Connemara, the ridges of Cork and Kerry, the strange, basalt outcrops of the Antrim plateau or the sweeping Mountains of Mourne. Most of Ireland's mountains command marvellous views of the sea. A network of way-marked footpaths covers the whole island, combining off-road walking with short stretches on less frequented backroads.

The best-known long-distance walking path in the Republic is the Wicklow Way,which extends for about 79 miles (126km) southwards from Marlay Park, Co. Dublin to Clonegal, Co. Carlow. The route switchbacks along the eastern flanks of the Dublin and Wicklow mountains, the largest unbroken area of high ground in Ireland, very sparsely inhabited. Another spectacular, lesser-known footpath is the Central Sperrins Way in County Tyrone which winds for 25 miles (40km) along the heather-covered slopes of a large upland area of outstanding natural beauty.

Other marked long-distance walking routes include the Cavan Way, the Tain Trail around the Cooley mountains and Carlingford in the northeast, the Ulster Way, the Slieve Bloom Way, the Aran Island Way , the Kerry Way, Munster Way, Dingle Way and many more. One of Europe's great long-distance paths, the Ulster Way, virtually encircles Northern Ireland, stretching for 500 miles (800km). Many people choose to walk only short sections of the path, and there are an increasing number of shorter circular routes of about 3–10 miles (5–16km) being introduced. To locate a way-marked path in the area you wish to visit see www.walkingireland.ie or www.discovernorthernireland.com or ask at the local tourist information office. In addition to a map of the way-marked trail, long-distance walkers will also need an Ordnance Survey map.

There are about 10 companies offering organised walking holidays, which can range from self-guided walking tours for any number from two people upwards, with luggage transfer and pre-booked accommodation, to hotel-based groups, walking a different route each day with an expert local guide. Details of organised walking holidays can be found at www.irelandwalkingcycling.com and on www.discoverireland.com/walking or contact Tourism Ireland for their free brochure, *Walking in Ireland*, tel: 0800 039 7000 (from UK), www.discoverireland.com.

Another popular option is the walking festival, often held in an off-peak season in spring or autumn, which consists of a weekend of guided walks (some catering for special interests such as archaeology or wildlife), offered for varying degrees of fitness, on which like-minded people can get to know each other, and socialise in the evening, when there is a programme of music sessions, set dancing and talks. Participants organise their own accommodation and meals. Kenmare, County Kerry, Glengarriff, County Cork, Clifden in Connemara, the Slieve Bloom Trail in County Tipperary and the Bluestacks in Donegal all have walking festivals. See www.walkingireland.ie.

Horse-drawn Caravan Holidays

Horses and caravans are available for hire in Counties Cork, Kerry and Wicklow. Expect to cover only about 10 miles (16km) a day – but going slowly is just the point, giving you time to appreciate the countryside, meet and talk to passers-by and let your inner rhythms settle down to a more sensible pace. Feeding, grooming and harnessing the horse is time-consuming too, and can prove quite hard work.

The caravans, which have gas cookers, are mostly for four people, with berths that convert into seating for daytime. Utensils, crockery, etc are provided. Fastidious people should note that caravans do not have toilets (well, didn't you want the real thing?). However, there are showers and toilets at the farms where you make overnight stops. In high season, expect to pay from €930 a week, in May, June and September, €720; allow €15–20 a night for overnight parking.

Operators include **Clissman's Horse-Drawn Caravans** in Co. Wicklow (tel: 0404-46290), **Mayo Horse-Drawn Caravan Holidays** in Co. Mayo (tel: 094-903 2054), and **Into the West** in Co. Galway (tel: 090-974 5211, fax: 974 5987). For full details visit www.irishhorsedrawncaravans.com.

Horse Riding

Equestrian Holidays Ireland has details of residential and non-residential riding holidays around the country. Choose between post-to-post trail riding, staying in a different guesthouse every evening, or equestrian centres with on-site accommodation and indoor and outdoor riding facilities. The Galway-Clare-Burren Trail is a six-day holiday on horseback through the forests, national parks and bogs of rural Ireland, ending at the Cliffs of Moher, staying each night in friendly guesthouses. Alternatively, you can base yourself in a guest room at the equestrian centre, and have a relaxed horse-riding holiday in the quiet lanes and paths of the Slieve Aughty Mountains. Contact Equestrian and Leisure Ireland, Derryoran East, Whitegate, County Clare (tel: 061 927 411). The Bel Air Hotel and Equestrian Centre on a 200-acre farm specialises in cross-country ride-outs. Ashford, Co. Wicklow (tel: 0404 401 090.

See www.ehi.ie for further options, or contact Tourism Ireland for their free brochure, *Horse Riding in Ireland* (tel: 0800 039 7000, www.discoverireland.com).

Cruising on Inland Waterways

The three main waterways for cruising are the River Shannon, navigable for 150 miles (240km) downstream from Lough Key, Co. Roscommon; the Grand Canal, which runs westward from Dublin across the central plain to the Shannon, and is joined in Co. Kildare by a branch line running south to the River Barrow; and the River Erne, navigable for 50 miles (80km) from Belturbet, Co. Cavan through Upper and Lower Lough Erne to Belleek, near Enniskillen, Co. Fermanagh. All three waterways are marvellous for fishing, birdwatching, rowing, photography or just pottering peacefully along.

In the Republic, several companies offer cabin cruisers for hire on the River Shannon and the Grand Canal. In Northern Ireland, several companies approved by the Erne Charter Boat Association operate on Lough Erne and on the Lower Bann, a canalised river, navigable from Lough Neagh to the sea near Portstewart; ask for the *Holidays Afloat* brochure from the Northern Ireland Tourist Board. For details of cruiser hire in both the Republic and Northern Ireland contact Waterways Ireland, 5–7 Belmore Street, Enniskillen, County Fermanagh BT74 6AA, tel: 028-6632 3004 www.waterwaysireland.org.

Cruisers range in size from two berths to eight; all have refrigerators and gas cookers; most have heating, hot water and showers, dinghies, charts and safety equipment. Experience in handling a boat is an advantage, but instruction or guided cruises are provided for novices.

Artistic Activity Holidays

There is a growing niche market for holidays that focus on artistic activities, and give you time out to indulge creative impulses.

The **Burren College of Art** is beautifully located near the waterside village of Ballyvaughan. A fully-accredited art school, in the summer it offers five-day courses in various aspects of painting (botanical, landscape, watercolour, abstract) or digital photography from €315. Accommodation can be provided at the school for an extra €105, or booked locally. Burren College of Art, Newtown Castle, Ballyvaughan, County Clare, tel: 065 707 7200, www.burrencollege.ie

Anam Cara Writer's and Artist's Retreat offers a quiet environment on the beautiful Beara Peninsula for those who would like to spend time on that unfinished book, or concentrate on their art. Hosted by editor Sue Booth Forbes in her comfortable home, guests work on their own projects from 9.30am to 5.30pm, helping themselves to lunch, and then have the option of sharing an evening meal. A minimum of one week's stay is recommended. There is also a summer programme of week-long workshops for aspiring writers and artists, between June and September led by experienced writers and artists, suitable for all levels. Anam Cara, Eyeries, Beara, County Cork, tel: 027-74441, www.anamcararetreat.com.

BELOW: cruising on the River Shannon.

Ceramic artist Adrian Wistreich of **Kinsale Pottery** offers a range of courses in ceramic art year-round for adults and children, from an intensive one-week introduction to weekend workshops. Adrian can also organise packages for people wishing to study with local craftmakers in their workshops. Choose from pottery, wood carving, greenwood chair making, bookbinding, photography, stained glass, bronze casting or drawing and painting. Accommodation can be arranged locally in hotels or in bed and breakfasts. Olcote, Kinsale, County Cork, tel: 021-477 7758 www.kinsaleceramics.com.

Islands

Most of Ireland's inhabited offshore islands are accessible by scheduled ferry services, and can be visited on a day trip. Many also have overnight accommodation. To find out more about visiting 26 of Ireland's islands, ask for the free map and a guide, *Explore Ireland's Islands*, tel: 0800 039 7000 www.irelandsislands.com.

TOURS

Sightseeing Tours

Dublin

Bus Eireann sightseeing tours from Dublin offer tours of Glendalough and Wicklow, Newgrange and the Boyne Valley, Kilkenny and the Nire Valley, the Mountains of Mourne and Waterford Crystal with a River Barrow Cruise. Prices start from €30 per adult for a day trip. Tickets can be booked online or at Dublin Tourism's office on Suffolk Street, at the office of Dublin Bus, O'Connell Street or at the Central Bus Station, Store Street, tel: 01-8366 6111, www.buseireann.ie.

Dublin Bus offers a city tour lasting one hour and 15 minutes, with a 24-hour hop-on hop-off ticket, making it an ideal city orientation. There are 20 stops, and buses run every 10 minutes. €15 for adults. They also offer half-day trips to the south coast and Powerscourt Gardens, and the north coast and Malahide Castle. Their evening Ghost Tour covers a thousand years of Dublin's history in a theatrical experience with real actors. Dublin Bus, 59 Upper O'Connell Street, tel: 01-873 4222, www.dublinsightseeing.ie.

Coach Tours of Ireland offer a full day tour of Wicklow (Glendalough, Avoca/Ballykissangel and the Meeting of the Waters) in a midi-bus, combining the comfort of a large coach and the agility of a mini-bus, plus Fáilte Ireland approved guides for €26, (tel: 087 996 6660, www.coachtoursofireland.com).

Southwest

Bus Eireann offers day and half-day guided tours from June to September, operating out of the bus stations at Cork, Limerick and Tralee. A full-day tour costs €30, half-day about €18. Options include the Ring of Kerry, Bunratty and the Cliffs of Moher and an open-top bus tour of Cork City, tel: Cork 021-450 8188, Limerick 061-313 333, Tralee 066-712 3566, www.buseireann.ie.

Dero's Tours and organise day and half-day trips by coach or mini-bus around Killarney and the Ring of Kerry. Dero's Tours, 22 Main Street, Killarney, Tel: 064-31251 www.derostours.com. For other options, call at the Killarney Tourist Information Office.

Shannon

Keatings Coaches offer day trips and half-day tours of the Shannon Region from Limerick City, tel: 069-68201, www.limericktours.com.

West

The only guided bus tours in this region start from Galway. From early June to mid-October, **Bus Eireann** offers two full-day tours, Connemara or the Burren. These can be booked at the Tourist Information Office, which is also the departure point, tel: 091-562 000, www.buseireann.ie.

Healy Tours provides historical sightseeing tours with professional guides, inclyding Kylemore Abbey and Connemara, or the Burren and the Cliffs of Moher. Book at the Galway Tourist Information Office, tel: 091-770 066 www.healytours.ie.

Northwest

Discover Sligo offers day tours of Sligo, Donegal and Leitrim in luxury air-conditioned coaches, which must be booked in advance. Special interest tours, including one of places associated with the poet W. B. Yeats, can be arranged in advance, tel: 087-244 8643, www.discoversligo.com.

Lovers of the poetry of W. B. Yeats are catered for by scheduled daily mini-bus tours of Sligo and Leitrim from **Yeats Country Tours**, whose commentary combines myths, legends and poetry, tel: 086-050 7393, www.yeatscountrytours.com.

Northern Ireland

Belfast City Sightseeing Tours take in city-centre sights from an open-top bus and tours before 2pm include Stormont's parliament buildings, www.belfastcitysightseeing.com.

Translink Tours run a wide variety of day tours on Ulsterbus coaches around the province and into the Republic, tel: 028-9033 7004, www.translink.co.uk.

Water-based Tours

Most water-based tours are seasonal, and run from March to October (inland) or mid-May to mid-September (sea-based).

Dublin Area

The Liffey Voyage is an hour-long cruise of Dublin's River Liffey in an all-weather air-conditioned boat, with commentary on the river's history, tel: 01-473 4082 www.liffeyvoyage.ie.

Sea Safari takes you out on to Dublin Bay in a fast-moving inflatable boat. Enjoy a wide variety of sea birds, and regular sightings of seals, porpoises and dolphins. One-hour trip for €30 per person, tel: 01-855 7600, www.seasafari.ie.

Viking Splash Tours gives you a fresh angle on Dublin's tourist attractions using an amphibious military vehicle with an exuberant, shouting crew wearing horned Viking helmets. Great for kids, tel: 01-707 6000, www.vikingsplashtours.com.

Southwest

Dingle Marine and Leisure operate a ferry service from Dingle Town to the Blasket Islands or Dunquin Pier, and also offer Eco Tours, tel: 066-915 1344, www.dinglebaycharters.com.

Kinsale Harbour Cruise offers an hour-long cruise of the harbour with historical commentary daily from May to October for €12, tel: 012-477 8946, www.kinsaleharbourcruises.com.

Seafari runs a 2-hour, 10-mile eco-cruise from Kenmare Pier around the sheltered waters of the Kenmare River (a sea estuary). Seals are regularly spotted, and there is a commentary on other wildlife, tel: 064-42059, www.seafariirelad.com.

Whale of a Time uses top-of-the-range Rigid Inflatable Boats (RIBS) fully-licensed by the Department of the Marine to offer exciting sightseeing trips ("a gripping experience") in search of whale or dolphin off the Old Head of Kinsale, tel: 087-120 3463, www.whaleofatime.ie.

Shannon Region

Dolphinwatch, Carrigaholt, Co. Clare, Tel: 065-905 8156. Offers boat trips on the Shannon Estuary with a chance of spotting bottle-nosed dolphins, www.dolphinwatch.ie.

The Spirit of Killaloe, Killaloe, Co. Clare, Tel: 0509-51112 offers half-day cruises on Lough Derg, www.killaloe.ie/thespiritofkillaloe.

West

Corrib Cruises operate regular services and also offer tours of Lough Corrib, the Republic of Ireland's largest lake. One and two-hour cruises depart from Oughterard in County Galway, and Ashford Castle, Cong, County Mayo, tel: 092-46029, www.corribcruises.com.

Corrib Tours run scenic cruises from Wood Quay, the centre of Galway City, travel up the Corrib River towards Lough Corrib on the all-weather *Corrib Princess*, and run daily at 2.30 and 4.30pm, also at 12.30pm July and

BELOW: breathing in Dublin's atmosphere on an open-top bus.

August, tel: 091-592 447, www.corribprincess.ie.
Killary Cruises guarantees no seasickness aboard their catamaran which cruises on Killary Lough in Connemara, Ireland's only fjord. Daily from April to October. Leenane, Co. Galway, tel: 1800-415 151.

Northwest

The Rose of Innisfree departs daily (Easter to October, weather permitting) from Parke's Castle for a leisurely cruise on Lough Gill in the heart of Yeats Country, with live commentary and poetry readings, tea, coffee and home-baking (tel: 071-916 4266, www.roseofinnisfree.com).

Literary and Historical Walking Tours

Dublin

Historical walking tours of Dublin are conducted by history graduates of Trinity College (tel: 01-688 9412), and cost €12. Meeting point Trinity College front gate, www.historicalinsights.ie.

Pat Liddy's Walking Tours of Historic Dublin take you into some unusual corners of the city. Choose from four themes including Georgian Dublin and Viking and Medieval Dublin. Start daily at Bachelor's Walk, O'Connell Bridge at 10.15am, and cost €10 for adults. Tel: 01-448 7711, www.walkingtours.ie.

A general **Literary Pub Crawl** starts at the Duke Pub nightly during the summer and Thurs–Sun during the winter. Tel: 01-670 5602, www.dublinpubcrawl.com. Tickets available The Duke Pub, 9 Duke Street from 7pm (tours begin at 7.30pm) or from Dublin Tourism on Suffolk Street.

Cork

The Titanic Trail is a 90-minute guided walking tour of Cobh, County Cork, last port of call of the *Titanic*, and covers Cork Harbour's fascinating maritime history. Trips start from outside the Commodore Hotel at 11am (tel: 021-481 5211, www.titanic-trail.com).

Killarney

An expert on the legends and history of Killarney, Richard Clancy, offers a two-hour guided walk in Killarney National Park daily at 11am (and at other times by arrangement). Departure point is the Shell petrol station on Lower New Street (tel: 064-33471, www.killarneyguidedwalks.com).

The Hidden Ireland Tours with Con Moriarty specialises in walks around the wilder parts of Killarney – the Gap of Dunloe and Carruantoohil areas (tel: 064-22844, www.hiddenirelandtours.com).

ABOVE: a guided tour of historic Dublin.

Limerick

St Mary's Action Centre organises the **Angela's Ashes Walking Tour** of locations highlighted in Frank McCourt's 1996 memoir of the same name. Twice daily, subject to demand. Tel: 061-318 106, www.iol.ie/~smidp, or ask at Limerick City's Tourist Information Office.

Galway

The **Galway City Walking Tour** departs daily from the Galway Tourist Information Office in Forster Place. It takes one-and-a-half hours, and gives a cultural and historical experience of the city (tel: 091-845 400 or 091-537 700, www.irelandwest.ie).

Belfast

Belfast City Walking Tours runs both general tours and tailored walks to appeal to church groups and doctors, www.belfast-city-walking-tours.co.uk.

Package Tours

CIE Tours International offers a selection escorted bus tours, with all travel and accommodation within Ireland included in the price. The Irish Odyssey is a 11-day bus tour, starting with two nights in Dublin, and including Blarney, Killarney, Bunratty Castle and Folk Park, Galway City, Connemara, the Giant's Causeway and the Ulster American Folk Park, staying in top hotels for €1,100. 35 Lower Abbey Street, Dublin 1, tel: 01-703 1829, www.cietours.ie.

Myguideireland is a young company offering customised self-drive itineraries as well as escorted bus tours, using local guides. Self-guided holidays consist of an itinerary agreed after consultation, and include car rental, prepaid accommodation vouchers, and activities such as golf, cycling or hiking can be added on. A seven-day tour for two people works out at about €300 per person, which represents good value compared to independent travel. Escorted tours have an all-inclusive price that includes airport transfers, hotels, breakfast, most dinners, admission to attractions and the services of a tour director. The Irish Heritage Tour at €675 is a good introduction for a first-time visitor. The company will also help with buying cut-price air tickets to and from Ireland, which are not included in the package prices. Myguideireland, Skibbereen, County Cork, tel: 0800-912 8728 (from UK) 1800-927 313 (within Ireland); or 021-465 5500, www.myguideireland.com.

Railtours Ireland utilises the Irish railway network for long-distance transfers, and local coaches for sightseeing at the destination, thus avoiding long stretches of coach travel. The five-day tour starts with a train ride from Dublin to Cork (2 hours 45 minutes) including breakfast, and continues with a bus tour to Blarney, train to Killarney, bus tour of the Ring of Kerry, and also visits Galway, the Cliffs of Moher and Connemara, starting at about €420 per person sharing accommodation in B&Bs and modest hotels. Railtours House, 16 Amiens Street, Dublin 1, tel: 01-856 0045, www.railtoursireland.com.

For a full list of UK tour operators with inclusive packages, see Tourism Ireland's brochure *Your Very Own Ireland Holiday Planner* (tel: 0800-039 7000 for a free copy or visit www.discoverireland.com).

Adams and Butler specialises in customised tours for the upper end of the market. Most tours are for small groups in chauffeur-driven cars or stretch limos. Helicopters are used to avoid traffic congestion, or create special itineraries. An eight-day garden tour, for example, includes private tours from owners of heritage gardens, and talks by horticultural experts, with accommodation in the best country house hotels and castles. Start thinking at $5,500 (£2,700), including admissions, meals, guided tours and talks. Similar packages cover interior design and antiques, literary Ireland, VIP horse racing and even a ghost tour. Adams & Butler, tel: 01-660 7975 (Dublin); www.privateluxurytravel.com.

SHOPPING

WHAT TO BUY AND WHERE

WHAT TO BUY

Ireland is famous for the high quality of its traditional crafts, from Donegal tweed to fine Irish linen sheets, hand-knitted Aran sweaters or Waterford cut crystal. Such traditional crafts can be expensive, but they last a lifetime. There is a wide range of other Irish-made home wares, tailoring, high fashion and contemporary giftware.

Large retailers like Avoca Handweavers, the Kilkenny Shop and Blarney Woollen Mills cater as much for the domestic market as they do for visitors. Waterford Crystal rang the changes by commissioning designer John Rocha to add a contemporary line to its traditional cut crystal range, and Tyrone and Galway Crystal have followed suit.

Irish designers pride themselves on using Irish linen, wools and tweeds, as seen in such high fashion lines as Lainey Keogh's exquisite knitwear, Louise Kennedy's softly feminine designs in luxurious fabrics (available at her showrooms in Merrion Square and Mayfair) and Helen MacAlinden's reworking of Irish linen for classic day and evening wear (available at her own boutiques in Cork and Dublin).

There's a big price difference between hand-knitted (expensive) and hand-loomed sweaters. The latter are made by machine but, provided the wool is virgin wool (and it nearly always is) they will be good quality – just not quite as special. Outside the designer boutiques, you can find finely-woven linen or tweed scarves and stoles, at surprisingly affordable prices, and an good range of knitwear. Linen and lace remain remarkably delicate. Some designers are working in felt and fleece, and experimenting with natural plant dyes with very attractive results.

Rainwear and outdoor wear is a practical buy, with several lines of locally-designed waxed jackets, duck-down-filled waistcoats and full-length or short rain-proof jackets.

Ceramic art and pottery are widely available in a range of designs, from ultra-modern to traditional. It is worth seeking out some of the potters with their own retail outlets, notably Louis Mulcahy on the Dingle Peninsula and Nicholas Mosse at Bennettsbridge, Co. Kildare. There are craft trails in west Cork, County Kilkenny and Donegal, incorporating a number of workers who open their studios to the public and sell directly.

Irish-made jewellery in modern designs (often based on traditional motifs) is widely available, while traditional shapes like Galway's Claddagh ring, are equally sought-after. Basket-weaving has gone through a revival, and provides such souvenirs as table mats and St Brigid crosses, as well as attractive hand-made baskets, large and small. Hand-made candles, traditional music CDs and walking sticks made of blackthorn are good choices at the lower end of the price scale.

Artisan food – hand-made farmhouse cheeses, wild smoked salmon, hand-made chocolates, mustards, jams and traditional chutneys – also make popular gifts. Not forgetting the famous Irish whiskeys – Bushmills, Jameson, Paddy – and Irish coffee liqueurs, the original being Bailey's.

In Dublin and Cork, look out for antiques, books new and second-hand, and galleries selling original art at affordable prices. Many small towns also have at least one independent bookshop, always worth investigating. Dublin's Temple Bar is crammed with off-beat fashion and design shops, while Cork's equivalent is the Paul Street area. Galway has several art galleries, and funky young fashion boutiques and vintage clothing outlets. Kilkenny is known for the high quality of its crafts.

There is tweed-making country in Connemara and Donegal, and yes, they still make hand-knitted Aran sweaters on the Aran Islands. The label will even tell you the name of the person who knitted it.

Shopping Hours

Most shops are open from 9am to 5.30pm. Shopping centres stay open until 9pm on Thur and Fri. Many small grocery stores are open until late at night and there are a few 24-hour shops in Dublin.

Outside the large cities, there is often an all-day or early-closing (1pm) day once a week. This is usually on Wed or Thur.

WHERE TO BUY

Dublin

The two main areas for shopping in Dublin are Grafton Street and its tributaries; and Henry Street area, off O'Connell Street north of the river. Most shops open 9am–6pm, Mon–Sat, and many city centre shops stay open until 8pm on Thursday. Some of the bigger city centre shops open on Sundays, from noon to 6/7pm.

Generally speaking, shops north of the river are less fashionable but better value than those in the Grafton Street area. Recent years have seen a major invasion of the city by British-owned multiples such as Marks and Spencer, Boots and Debenhams, and Dublin now retains only three indigenous department stores: Brown Thomas, on Grafton Street, the most upmarket; Arnott's on Henry Street; and Clery's on O'Connell Street. The stylish Chq shopping mall is a welcome addition north of the river in Custom House Square.

Henry Street runs westward from O'Connell Street, past the famous Moore Street Market where colourful local characters sell flowers, fruit, vegetables and other bargains with an inimitable sales patter featuring razor-sharp Dublin wit. Smaller shops sell footwear, CDs and clothing. Moore Street is also home to several ethnic shops from Asian and African to Polish and Lithuanian. Mary Street, Henry Street's continuation has, Penneys, the city's biggest Primark outlet, the Ilac Centre, Dublin's first large shopping mall, and the bigger, newer Jervis Street Shopping Centre.

Grafton Street is pedestrianised. It runs north from St Stephen's Green, and starts beside the massive, glass-roofed, greenhouse-like St Stephen's Green Shopping Centre, which contains over 100 small shops, mainly selling clothes and gifts. At the rear of this is a large branch of Dunnes Stores, the Irish version of Marks & Spencer.

Don't miss the Powerscourt Townhouse Centre, signposted off Grafton Street on the left as you walk up it (north), a large square 18th-century mansion and courtyard. The courtyard has been roofed over, and converted into a stylish shopping complex with crafts, fashion and antiques shops and restaurants. The Westbury Mall nearby has expensive high fashion and jewellery. The Royal Hibernian Way on the opposite side of Grafton Street is a plush arcade with about 20 exclusive boutiques.

Suffolk Street at the top left of Grafton Street (leading to the Dublin Tourism Centre) is home to a large branch of Avoca Handweavers, one of the most successful chains selling Irish-designed fashion and gifts. The Kilkenny Shop on Nassau Street, on the opposite side of Grafton Street, is a more upmarket showcase for Irish-made crafts and clothes. On the same street, the Celtic Note specialises in Irish music, and Blarney Woollen Mills and Kevin and Howlin stock classic Irish knitwear and tweeds. The Celtic Whiskey Shop on Dawson Street has a huge range.

Dawson Street and Nassau Street are great places for bookshops – due to the proximity of Trinity College, whose side entrance is on Nassau Street. Waterstones at No. 7 Dawson Street, and Hodges Figgis at 56–58, face each other across the road. Dublin Bookshop, 24 Grafton Street, is a pleasant general interest bookshop. Across from the main entrance to Trinity College, Books Upstairs, 36 College Green, is Dublin's major alternative bookshop. Cathac Books, at 10 Duke Street, specialises in collectable Irish books and has many first editions. The Winding Stair, across the Liffey at 40 Ormond Quay, is an excellent second-hand bookshop with café. The Temple Bar Book Market takes place every Saturday and Sunday in Temple Bar Square.

Francis Street (near Christchurch Cathedral) is in the Liberties, the traditional area for antique dealers, with many specialist shops and a couple of contemporary art galleries. The doyen of Dublin antique dealers is O'Sullivan Antiques at 43–44 Francis Street, which specialises in 18th- and 19th-century furniture.

BELOW: Dublin's upscale Grafton Street.

Temple Bar has a small but compelling selection of ultra-trendy shops selling everything from vintage clothes to comic books to outrageous clubbing outfits. Cow's Lane Design Mart, held on Saturday on the western edge of Temple Bar is the place to catch one-off pieces from up and coming fashion designers. Claddagh Records at 2 Cecilia Street stocks an extensive range of Irish music and spoken word recordings.

There's an excellent range of Irish cheeses at Sheridan's on St Anne Street; hard cheeses travel best. The Kilkenny Shop in Nassau Street has a selection of Irish-made jams, chutneys, cakes, biscuits and confectionery. Butler's Irish Chocolates in Grafton Street and Nassau Street offers many delights for the sweet-toothed. Meeting House Square Market in Temple Bar is a good place to buy artisan food on Saturdays.

Dublin Day Trips

Avoca Handweavers, Avoca, Co. Wicklow (tel: 0402-35105; www.avoca.ie) is the oldest hand-weaving mill in Ireland still in operation, and has a shop selling a wide selection of its fabrics, and woven and knitted items. The same company has its flagship shop at suburban Kilmacanogue, Bray, Co. Wicklow. Both have excellent self-service restaurants.

Kildare Village is a fancy name for a discount retail outlet built in the form of a pastiche village, at which a range of international brands offer last season's collections for home and wardrobe at up to 60 percent off in more than 50 boutiques (Nurney Road, Kildare Town, tel: 045-520 501, www.kildarevillage.com).

The Southeast

Kilkenny is the centre of the Irish hand-made crafts trade. The town's leading outlet, The Kilkenny Design Centre in the stableyard of Kilkenny Castle (tel: 056-772 2118), is a retail outlet showcasing the best of Irish-made ceramics, jewellery, knitwear, and weaving. The Jerpoint Glass Studio at Stoneyford, Co. Kilkenny (tel: 056-772 4350) produces an attractive heavy, modern uncut glass, which is blown on site. Nicholas Mosse Pottery, **Bennettsbridge**, Co. Kilkenny (tel: 056-772 7505) makes rustic stoneware decorated with spongeware designs of flowers and animals. His Irish Country Shop offers a big selection of crafts, a riverside café and the chance to decorate your own pot. Stoneware Jackson pottery, Bennettsbridge (tel: 056-772 7175) makes distinctive hand-thrown tableware and lamps. Rudolf Heltzel, 10 Patrick Street, Kilkenny (tel: 056-772 1497) is a gold and silversmith known for striking modern designs.

Wexford has a compact centre with most of its shops on one street running parallel to the shore one street inland. Westgate Design, 22 North Main Street (tel: 053-23787) has a good selection of Irish crafts. The Wool Shop 39–42 Main Street (tel: 053-22247) stocks souvenirs, knitting yarns and Aran sweaters.

The Waterford Crystal Experience (The Mall, tel: 051-351 936) has a retail area with the biggest selection of Waterford Crystal around, and also Wedgwood china (made by the same group). Joseph Knox, 3 Barronstrand Street (tel: 051-875 307) is a city centre craft shop with a good selection of Waterford Crystal.

Cork and Surroundings

Cork city centre has two new shopping malls, but Patrick Street itself continues to ply a busy trade. Brown Thomas at 18 Patrick Street is the most expensive department store, while Debenham's, also on Patrick Street, has the nicest building, lit by a central glass dome. Penneys at 27 Patrick Street is a branch of Primark, and other high street multiples line the street. The younger hipper boutiques will be found in the pedestrianised Paul Street area (also known as the Huguenot Quarter) to the west of Patrick Street. Upgrade your outdoor clothing at the Great Outdoors, 23 Paul Street. For a good selection of mainly upmarket fashion boutiques try Oliver Plunkett Street, parallel to Patrick Street near the GPO.

For antiques, head north of the river to MacCurtain Street where there is a cluster of shops selling antiques, oriental carpets and up-market bric-a-brac for the home.

The English Market (entrances on Grand Parade and Princes Street, Monday to Saturday midday) is a large covered market with numerous artisan food producers selling local farmhouse cheeses, charcuterie, smoked salmon, handmade bread and other delicacies.

Blarney Castle is one of the busiest visitor attractions outside Dublin, and the village also has one of the biggest craft shops, The Blarney Woollen Mills. Beyond the usual tourist tat, there are some tempting ranges of top-quality outdoor clothing

ABOVE: insane bargains in Cork City.

and Irish-made fashion for men and women: locals keep an eagle eye on the annual sale.

The Southwest

The *County Cork Craft Guide* lists details of over 60 craft makers in the area with a map showing their location. It is available locally from Tourist Information Offices. The cream of west Cork's craftmakers are members of the West Cork Craft and Design Guild, and put on several shows a year (tel: 028-21890; www.westcorkcraft.org).

Kinsale has a good range of craft and designer home ware shops. Cronin's, Pearse Street is the biggest craft shop, while Boland's, across the road, has a good range of designer rain gear, sweaters, hats and jewellery. Keane on Ceramics, Pier Road, shows work by some of Ireland's best ceramic artists. Granny's Bottom Drawer, 53 Main Street, sells fine linen and lace.

Kenmare, Co. Kerry, is another small town packed with craft shops. Cleo's, 2 Shelbourne Street, is famous for strikingly designed clothes in Irish-made wool and linens. Black Abbey Crafts, 28 Main Street, specialises in hand-made Irish crafts. At PFK, 18 Henry Street, designer Paul Kelly makes modern jewellery in gold and silver.

Avoca Handweavers at **Molls Gap** on the N71 road to Killarney is the first of many craft shops in this town, and as it happens, one of the best. Another good **Killarney** shop is Bricín Craft Shop, 26 High Street. House of Names is a shop for those with Irish roots, selling name-lore and heraldic crests on key rings, coasters, sweaters and T-shirts.

An Daingean/Dingle has succumbed to a rash of the worst kind of leprechaun and T-shirt Irish souvenir shops down near the pier. Walk up Green Street from the pier to find Brian de Staic's jewellery shop, which uses motifs from ancient Irish artefacts in well-designed modern pieces, and the Weaver's Shop where Lisbeth Mulcahy sells outstanding hand-woven, vegetable dyed woollen goods. Her husband Louis Mulcahy's pottery studio at Clogher Strand, **Ballyferriter**, is also worth a visit, both for his tableware and his huge decorative bowls and lamps.

The Shannon Region

Limerick has a compact city centre, with most of the main department stores on O'Connell Street. Cruises Street, off O'Connell Street, has the liveliest boutiques. Things are more lively at the Crescent Shopping Centre, **Dooradoyle**, Co. Limerick, a snazzily-designed, vast indoor shopping mall, signposted off the N20 just south of Limerick City, or a short bus ride from O'Connell Street.

Adare Heritage Centre, Main Street, **Adare**, has a selection of craft shops, including a heraldry specialist.

The Antique Loft, **Clarecastle**, Co. Clare (tel: 065-684 1969), is a good place for pine and mahogany antiques.

Ennis's town centre is largely reconstructed on a user-friendly scale in traditional small-shop style, with plenty of pedestrianised areas. The Belleek Shop, 36 Abbey Street, carries Waterford Crystal, Belleek china, Donegal Parian, as well as Lladró, Hummel, Wedgwood and other collectible s. The Rock Shop, 2 O'Connell Street, sells polished gemstones, fossils and other rocks, as well as jewellery. Clare Craft and Design, 20 Parnell Street, sells art, pottery and crafts by local makers.

You can buy direct from a co-op of local craft makers at Ballyvaughan village hall in the Burren, Saturdays from May to October, www.burrencrafts.net.

The Midlands

The **Rathdowney** Designer Outlet, Co. Laois (www.rathdowneyoutlet.ie) is a huge indoor mall bizarrely situated on the outskirts of a quiet country town, selling a mix of designer labels at attractive prices. Side attractions include a children's play centre and sometimes even circus shows.

The Far West

Galway's town centre is great fun to shop in – as long as you are on foot. Most shops are on or just off the one long street that runs down from Eyre Square to the Spanish Arch, starting with a pocket-sized branch of the deparment store, Brown Thomas. Treasure Chest, William Street has china, crystal and classic clothing behind its Wedgwood-like facade. O'Máille's, at 16 High Street, has Aran sweaters, hand-woven tweed and classic tailoring. Twice as Nice, 5 Quay Street, has new and vintage clothing, linens and lace. Design Concourse Ireland, Kirwan's Lane, showcases the work of potter Judy Greene and other hand-crafted design. Cobwebs, 7 Quay Street, has antiques and jewellery. Thomas Dillon's, 1 Quay Street, is a jeweller who specialises in the local Claddagh ring. P. Powell and Sons, The Four Corners, William Street, is the best place for Irish music CDs and instruments. Sheridan's Cheese-mongers, 16 Churchyard Street, has the best range of farmhouse cheeses.

An Spidéal, Co. Galway

Ceardlann – Spiddal Craft and Design Studios (tel: 091-553 376) is a collection of 10 workshops, making and selling pottery, weaving and jewellery on site. Café, open all year.

Aran Islands

Inis Meáin Knitting (tel: 099-73009) produces high-quality fashion knitwear, and sells great bargains from its factory showroom, a five-minute walk from the pier.

Roundstone

Malachy Kearns is a master-maker of the hand-held drum, the bodhrán, near this attractive seaside village. The craft is demonstrated in his workshop in an old monastery, and other craft workers have congregated on site, in addition to a fine record shop and a café (tel: 095 35088; www.bodhran.com). There are also craft shops in the village, including the Dalkey Design Shop which sells linen clothes and kitchenware.

Clifden

Millar's Connemara Tweeds, Main Street, has traditional tweeds and knits. The Station House Courtyard, Old Railway Station, Bridge Street, is a cobbled courtyard surrounded by craft studios and designer-wear outlets.

Westport

O'Reilly/Turpin, Bridge Street, sells the best of contemporary Irish design in knitwear, ceramic and small decorative items. Treasure Trove, Bridge Street (tel: 098-25118), has a good stock of antiques and curios including linen. Who could resist a shop called Interesting Books (James Street, tel: 098-56944)? It's just nearby, and sell military memorabilia as well as secondhand and antique books. O'Reilly/Turpin Bridge Street, (tel: 098-28151) sells the best of Irish contemporary design in knitwear and decorative items for the home. Thomas Moran's at the top of Bridge Street (tel: 098-25562) is a wonderfully old fashioned souvenir shop: get your blackthorn stick here.

The Northwest

Sligo

Carraig Donn, 41 O'Connell Street has a wide selection of knitwear including Aran sweaters for children. The Cat and the Moon, 4 Castle Street, is an interesting craft shop.

Donegal Town

Magee's, The Diamond, is a long-established purveyor of hand-woven tweeds, stocking jackets, hats, scarves and suits for both men and women. Donegal Craft Village, **Ballyshannon**, a mile south of town, is a complex of workshops selling hand-woven goods, jewellery, knitwear and ceramics (tel: 074-972 2225; www.donegal.net).

Ard an Ratha (Ardara)

This is Donegal's chief hand-woven tweed producing area, and is also a good place to buy a hand-knitted Aran sweater. Campbells Tweed Shop, Front Street, has ready-to-wear tweeds including sports jackets. E. Doherty (Ardara) Ltd, Front Street, sells hand-woven tweeds, glassware and linen. John Molloy, Main Street, is a factory shop offering high-quality hand-woven tweed and hand-knitted Aran sweaters.

Belfast

All the big names from the British High Street can be found around the city centre and large shopping centres like Castle Court, on Royal Avenue (82 stores, including Debenhams) and the spectacular Victoria Square retail site.

The success of its linen industry made a huge contribution to the development of Belfast. Today, you can still find locally-made linen products, including tableware, at Smyth's Irish Linens (tel: 028-9024 2232) at 65–67 Royal Avenue. Beautiful hand-finished Irish linen shirts are among the main attractions at the very upmarket Smyth and Gibson (tel: 028-9023 0388) at Bedford House, Bedford Street.

In the same location is Steensons (tel: 028-9024 8269), where Bill and Christina Steenson's Irish jewellery has proved a long-standing success. Queen's Arcade, off Donegall Place, is also a centre for jewellery shops.

Best of the Irish crafts shops is the Wicker Man at 44–46 High Street (tel: 028-9024 3550) with a large range of Irish knitwear, Celtic jewellery, pottery and more. Utopia in the Fountains Centre, College Street (tel: 028-9024 1342), has distinctive gifts from around the world like stylish Italian chess sets. Chinacraft (tel: 028-9023 0766), at 24 Queens Arcade, has locally produced crafts and gifts, including Belleek Pottery and Tyrone Crystal.

Smithfield Market, at the junction of Winetavern and West Streets, has some interesting shops to explore, from collectable models to comics.

BELOW: window-shopping in Belfast, which has all the big British retailers.

A Handy Summary of Practical Information, Arranged Alphabetically

Accidents and Emergencies

For **emergency services**, such as police, ambulance, fire service, lifeboat and coastal rescue, tel: 999 in Northern Ireland and either 999 or 112 in the Republic. The **Samaritans**, who help lonely, depressed and suicidal people, can be contacted on 1850-609 090 and in Northern Ireland on 028-9066 4422. See www.samaritans.org for your local branch.

Other Useful Numbers

Aids Helpline Dublin, tel: 1800-459 459 and Belfast, tel: 0800-137 437.
Alcoholics Anonymous, Dublin, tel: 01-842 0700; Belfast, tel: 028-9043 4848.
Drug Advisory Treatment Centre, tel: 01-648 8600.
Poisons Information Service, Dublin, tel: 01-809 2566.
Rape Crisis Centre, Dublin, tel: 01-661 4911 and Belfast, tel: 028-9032 9002.

Budgeting For Your Trip

Ireland is in the Eurozone, and has relatively high levels of VAT at 21 and 13.5 percent (17.5 percent in Northern Ireland). Restaurant meals, pub prices, wine, sweets and even newspapers all come under the 21 per cent band, making everyday life more expensive than in many other European countries. Two people should budget using the guidelines below (though variables in meals and hotels can cause prices to rise considerably). Prices in Dublin will be higher than in rural areas. Most hotels and some B&Bs outside Dublin raise their rates in July and August. Major sporting fixtures, bank holidays and other big events also mean rises.
Double room per night in a three-star hotel: €90–140
Simple lunch for two: €16–24
Two-course dinner for two: €40–55
Car hire per week: €190
Charges: about €20 per day
Miscellaneous (drinks, tips etc): €30 per day (for two).

Business Etiquette

The Irish are highly social and are great networkers, and it is important to recognise this and make the most of opportunities yourself, as you will be judged on your ability to get along with others. Business entertaining plays a big role in everyday life, whether it's playing golf, eating in a smart restaurant, or simply enjoying a pint of Guinness in the pub.

Ideal characteristics for someone planning to manage a team in Ireland include being a good social mixer, being technically competent, a strong decision maker, a sensitive leader and having a degree of flexibility. Good communication skills are important, whether it's delivering an eloquent and convincing presentation, or being persuasive around the meeting table. It is important to realise that the Irish have a desire to please and tend to put a positive spin on things. Giving negative feedback may be avoided, or dressed up as less serious than it is, or hidden behind humour. The Irish tend to be indirect communicators, so visitors must learn to read between the lines and interpret body language, before reacting to a situation.

The Essentials (10 Key Tips)

1 It is important to remember that while people from the north and the south share certain common characteristics, culture and history, the two areas are separate political entities.

2 Building a relationship is important before getting down to business. Socialising plays a big part in Irish business life. Family life is highly valued. When building trust with you, the Irish will want to know about you , "the whole person".

3 Networking is also important. Your Irish counterparts will assist you in networking at first and you are expected to make use of these new relationships.

4 The business community is small and close-knit, so be careful what you say and to whom.

5 The Irish like a combination of hard facts and technical knowledge as well as eloquent presentations.

6 The Irish find arguments and opinionated conversation entertaining so don't hesitate to express your views as long as they are sincere and well-informed.

7 Even though most Irish business people will admit that locally there is a relaxed attitude to time in many situations, it is still advisable to be punctual. But manage your expectations accordingly and do not get frustrated at "minor" delays.

8 The Irish are tough negotiators; do not be fooled by their apparent relaxed attitude and friendly nature.

9 Cynicism is an important part of the national character. The Irish hold a great respect for the "underdog" so it is best to stay modest about your personal achievements until a relationship has been established.

10 The Irish are quick to criticize themselves but are not always open to criticism from others. If there is a conflict in the workplace, it is advisable to discuss it one-to-one.

• *The above information is provided by Transnational Management Associates as part of its Country Navigator series of information packs (visittmaworld.com).*

Children

Irish people love children, and give them a warm welcome. Baby supplies are easily obtained from supermarkets and smaller stores. Children are usually welcome at hotels and B&Bs, and most can supply special cots or babysitting services. Many hotels allow children under a certain age to stay in their parents' room at no extra charge, but the age limit varies. Most middle-range restaurants can supply high-chairs, and there is usually a children's menu. The bigger restaurants and pubs should have nappy-changing facilities. Some of the grander establishments will only accept children over a certain age, usually about 12. Children are usually welcome in pubs frequented by visitors, but children are expected to be under the control of an adult at all times. Some landlords like children to be off the scene by early evening, and the law prohibits under-18 on any premises that serve alcohol after 9pm. Young people cannot drink alcohol until they are 18, and photo ID should be carried. During holiday periods, there are plenty of child-oriented activities designed by museums, local festivals and outdoor centres – Tourist Information Centres *(see page 389)* will have full details. Look out for family tickets, offering good value deals.

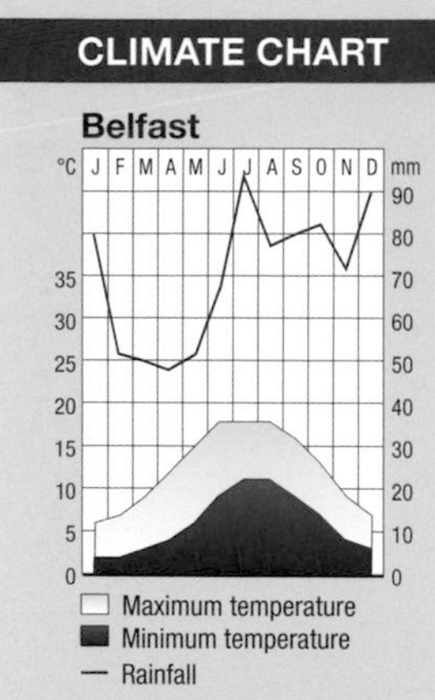

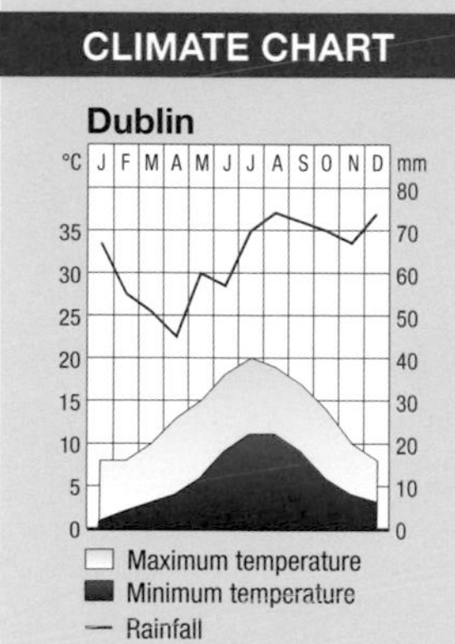

Climate

Although Ireland lies at roughly the same northerly latitude as Newfoundland, it has a mild, moist climate, because of the prevailing southwesterly winds and the influence of the warm Gulf Stream along its western coast. As no part of the island is more than 70 miles (110km) from the sea, temperatures are fairly uniform over the whole country.

Average air temperatures in the coldest months, January and February, are mainly between 4°C and 7°C (39–45°F). The warmest months, July and August, have average temperatures between 14°C and 16°C (57–61°F), but occasionally reaching as high as 25°C (77°F). The sunniest months are May and June, with an average of between 5½ and 6½ hours a day over most of the country. The sunniest region is the extreme southeast.

Parts of the west of the country, with annual rainfall averaging 59 inches (1,500 mm), are twice as wet as the east because of the prevailing Atlantic winds.

Clothing

Casual clothing is acceptable almost everywhere in Ireland, including smart hotels and restaurants. Because of the unpredictability of the weather, pack an umbrella, some rainproof clothing and a warm sweater, even in summer. But bring the suntan cream as well: when the summer sun shines, the ozone-laden winds from the Atlantic can intensify the burning effect of its rays.

Crime and Safety

While rural Ireland is generally a low-risk area for crime, visitors are often considered easy pickings. Hired cars are easy targets for criminals, and thefts from cars are commonplace in Dublin, other major towns and cities, and also in the car parks of visitor attractions. Never leave anything in sight in your car. Pickpockets operate in small gangs in central Dublin.

If you should have a bad experience in Dublin, **Victim Support** (29 Dame Street, Dublin, tel: 01-679 8673) provides invaluable help.

Disabled Travellers

Ireland is still introducing facilities such as ramps and accessible toilets for people with disabilities. Public transport also lags behind, especially outside Dublin. However, visitors with disabilities often find that peoples' helpfulness makes up for the lack of amenities. The key organisation to contact for practical information, including wheelchair sales and rental, parking permits and holidays is the

Irish Wheelchair Association, Ara Cuchulainn, Blackheath Drive, Clontarf, Dublin, tel: 01-818 6400, www.iwa.ie.

The official government body responsible for the rights of people with disabilities is **National Disability Authority**, 25 Clyde Rd, Ballsbridge, Dublin 4, tel: 01-608-0400 (www.nda.ie). They will have up to date information on disability issues. The Head Office of **Fáilte Ireland** can advise on attractions and accommodation suitable for disabled visitors. 88–95, Amiens Street Dublin 1, tel: 01-884 7700, www.discoverireland.ie.

In Northern Ireland the campaigning body **Disability Action** also offer practical advice. 2 Annadale Ave, Belfast, tel: 028-9029 7880 www.disabilityaction.org.

Electricity

220 volts AC (50 cycles) is standard. Hotels usually have dual 220/110 voltage sockets for electric razors only. To use their own small appliances, visitors may need a plug adaptor (best purchased in their home country) to fit Ireland's 3-pin flat or 2-pin round wall sockets.

Embassies and Consulates

Dublin

Australia: Fitzwilton House, Wilton Terrace, Dublin 2; tel: 01-664 5300, www.ireland.embassy.gov.au.
Britain: 29 Merrion Rd, Dublin 4; tel: 01-205 3700, www.britishembassyinireland.fco.gov.uk.
Canada: 7–8 Wilton Terrace, Dublin 2; tel: 01-231 4000, www.canada.ie.
US: 42 Elgin Rd, Dublin 4; tel: 01-668 8777, www.usembassy.ie.

Belfast

American Consulate General, 223 Stranmillis Road, Belfast, tel: 028-9038 6100, http://london.usembassy.gov/nireland.

Gay and Lesbian Travellers

There should be no major problems for gay and lesbian travellers in Ireland. Be as safety-conscious as you would in any foreign city or country. But Ireland has only become an inclusive, non-discriminatory society relatively recently, and the best advice is "don't flaunt it." The development of the Irish gay scene is recent, and most openly gay Irish are young. Discrimination does still exist, and you are more likely to encounter it the further you get from Dublin, Galway and Cork cities. Gay men looking for a double room may find that all rooms in the B&B have suddenly been booked. Openly gay couples may attract unwanted attention in small-town pubs.

The following Lesbian and Gay Resource Centres offer advice and contacts:
Dublin: Outhouse, 51 Capel Street, Dublin 1, tel: 01–873 4933, www.outhouse.ie.
Cork: The Other Place, 85 South Main Street, tel: 021-427 8470, www.theotherplaceclub.ie.
Belfast: Queer Space, Cathedral Buildings, 68 Donegall Street, www.queerspace.org.uk.
Gay Switchboard, Dublin, tel: 01-872 1055, offers information and advice.

Information on bars, clubs accommodation and friendly contacts can be found on http://gayinireland.com.

www.gcn.ie is a lively gay magazine based in Dublin's Temple Bar area.

Gays, lesbians and bisexuals west of the Shannon network through www.outwestireland.ie, PO Box 58, Castlebar, Co. Mayo, tel: 087-972 5586.

Health and Medical Care

Medical Services

Medical insurance is highly advisable for all visitors. However, visitors from EU countries are entitled to medical treatment in Ireland, North and South, under a reciprocal arrangement.

With the exception of UK citizens, visitors from EU states should obtain form E111 from their own national social security office. These forms entitle the holders to free treatment by a doctor and free medicines on prescription. If hospital treatment is necessary, this will be given free in a public ward. UK visitors need only go to a doctor (or, in an emergency, a hospital), present some proof of identity (eg driving licence) and request treatment under EU health agreement.

Liquor Laws

The legal drinking age is 18, but some pubs will only serve patrons over 21 carrying photo identity. Pubs in the Republic of Ireland are open seven days a week, from 10.30am. Opening time is at the discretion of the landlord, and can vary from 12.30pm to 4pm or 6pm depending on local trade. Closing time, in contrast, is defined by law, but can vary depending on what sort of licence the pub has. Normal closing time is 11.30pm, but this can extend to 3 am

ABOVE: all bars are now smoke-free.

on Fridays and Saturdays and during festivals. Sunday opening hours are 12.30pm to 11pm. You are allowed half an hour "drinking up time" after the official closing time, before you have to leave the premises. All bars in the Republic of Ireland are smoke-free, but heated outdoor "smoking decks" are often provided. All pubs close on Good Friday and Christmas Day, but hotel bars are open for guests. Persons under the age of 18 are not allowed in the bar areas of licensed premises after 9pm (10pm May to September). Persons aged 18 to 21 can be required to produce evidence of age in order to remain in the bar area after those hours.

Opening hours in Northern Ireland are, generally, 11.30am to 11pm Monday to Saturday and 12.30pm to 11pm Sunday. Many pubs have extended opening hours at weekends.

Maps

If you intend to do the sort of driving that takes you off the main routes, it is worth buying the Complete Road Atlas of Ireland (Ordnance Survey Ireland and Ordnance Survery of Northern Ireland) which sells for about €9.99. Cyclists and walkers may want smaller scale maps: these can be bought locally from Tourist Information Centres, newsagents and bookshops. Insight Fleximaps to Ireland and Dublin are laminated for ease of use and durability.

Media

Magazines

Hot Press is a lively local pop culture paper. The *Dubliner Magazine* is a monthly covering all aspects of entertainment, media and dining in the capital. The *Irish Arts Review* is a quality glossy magazine published four times a year covering all aspects of fine and decorative arts in Ireland. The *Irish Theatre Magazine* is a quarterly giving in-depth coverage of theatre nationwide.

Newspapers

The Irish devour newspapers, and have no fewer than five morning newspapers to serve the island's population of 5 million. The *Irish Times* and the *Irish Independent* are published in Dublin. The *Irish Examiner* is published in Cork.

The *Irish Times*, the most serious and comprehensive, is best for foreign news, arts and business, and has a great letters page. The *Independent* broadly supports the Fine Gael party and aims for a hard-hitting style. The *Examiner* is the staple diet of business and farming people in the southwest. Two morning papers are published in Belfast: the Unionist/ Protestant *Newsletter* and the nationalist/Catholic *Irish News*; it can be fascinating and instructive to compare their treatments of a controversial story.

There are three evening papers: the *Evening Herald* (from the Independent stable in Dublin), the *Echo* (Cork) and the *Belfast Telegraph*, which also publishes a tabloid Saturday morning edition. All contain lots of sport and showbiz.

The *Independent* has a Sunday version; also published from Dublin are the *Sunday Tribune*, which aims to be a serious paper of political analysis, arts review, etc., the *Sunday World*, a lurid tabloid (pin-ups, shocks, scares, scandals, etc) and the *Sunday Business Post*, which concentrates on business and politics. The London *Sunday Times* Irish edition is published in Cork and distributed nationally. From Belfast, there is *Sunday Life* from the Telegraph stable.

Since all the British dailies and Sundays are readily obtainable on both sides of the border, even the most news-hungry visitor should be satisfied. UK readers can expect an "Irish edition" of their usual paper, with a focus on Irish topics.

There are nearly 100 local papers, which may be entertaining and informative if you are interested in a particular region, or interested in newspapers themselves.

Radio

RTÉ1 is the main station for news, current affairs and drama; RTÉ2 has a staple output of pop music and the recently launched Lyric FM is for lovers of classical music. There are also a number of independent local radio stations.In Northern Ireland the commercials-free BBC Radio Ulster has full local coverage, as do the advertising-funded Downtown Radio (MW) and Cool FM.

Television

The national broadcasting service, Radio Telefis Éireann (RTÉ) has three TV channels (one of them, TG4, broadcasting exclusively In the Irish language). Ireland's first independent television network TV3, was launched in 1998 to provide an alternative to RTÉ – "a middle-of-the-road service aimed at Middle Ireland".

In addition, the British TV channels (both BBC and commercial channels) can be received over much of the country – which accounts for the unsightly height of TV aerials. Several satellite channels, including Sky and Screensport, are widely available via cable.

In Northern Ireland, BBC1 includes local coverage, as does its commercial counterpart, Ulster Television.

Money

In 2002 Ireland became one of the first 12 countries to adopt the euro (€). It is divided into 100 cents. The coins used are 1¢, 2¢, 5¢, 10¢, 20¢, 50¢,€1, €2. The notes are €5, €10, €20, €50 and €100.

In Northern Ireland, the British pound (£) is used. Exchange rates vary but many shops in border areas will accept either currency.

In the Irish Republic, banks are open 10am–4pm, Mon–Fri , and to 5pm once a week. Branches in small towns may close from 12.30pm to 1.30pm. Most Dublin banks are open until 5pm on Thursday. In Northern Ireland, bank opening hours are 9.30–4.30, Mon–Fri.

British visitors to Northern Ireland can cash personal cheques with a bank card. Travellers cheques are accepted at all banks, money-change kiosks and many hotels.

MasterCard and Visa are the most commonly acceptable credit cards, followed by American Express and Diners Club. But many small guesthouses and bed-and-breakfast places will expect payment to be made in cash.

Opening Hours

Shops and department stores usually open at 9.30am and close at 5.30 or 6pm, Mon–Sat. In smaller towns, some shops close for lunch between 1pm and 2pm. **Supermarkets** and convenience stores generally open until 9pm, seven days a week. **Post Offices** open 9am–5.30pm, Mon–Fri, and 9–1 Sat; some of the smaller ones close for lunch. **Government offices** are open to the public Mon–Fri, 9am–5pm.

Museums and other tourist sights are often closed on Monday, and outside Dublin and Belfast most have restricted opening hours between Nov and Easter or late May.

In hotels and B&Bs **breakfast** is generally served from 8–10am, and in restaurants and pubs until noon. **Restaurants and pubs** generally serve a lunch menu between 12.30 and 2.30pm, and dinner from 6 to 9.30pm.

Postal Services

At the time of writing, letters, postcards and airmail weighing less than 50 grammes (approximately the weight of an envelope containing up to three regular A4 sheets of paper) cost €0.55 within Ireland, €0.82 to the UK, all European Union countries, and the rest of the world.

In Northern Ireland, British postal rates apply.

Most newsagents and postcard outlets also sell stamps.

Philatelists may obtain information on Irish stamps from the Controller, Philatelic Section, GPO, Dublin 1.

Public Holidays

1 January, 17 March (St Patrick's Day), Good Friday (Northern Ireland only),

Below: Tourist Information Centres are a good source of free local maps.

ABOVE: St Patrick's Cathedral, Dublin.

Easter Monday, First Monday in May, Spring Holiday (last Monday in May in Northern Ireland, first Monday in June in Republic), 12 July (Northern Ireland only), Summer Holiday (first Monday in August in Republic, last Monday in August in Northern Ireland) last Monday in October (Republic only), Christmas Day and 26 December.

Religious Services

All hotels and B&Bs will have details of nearby Roman Catholic and Church of Ireland services.

Roman Catholic

Dublin's principal Catholic cathedral is the place to hear the Palestrina Choir which showcases the best Irish male voices. Latin Mass is sung here every Sunday morning at 11am. Pro-Cathedral, Marlborough Street, off O'Connell Street.

Church of Ireland

At 6pm on Wednesday and Thursday you can enjoy a choral evensong in Dublin's oldest church. Christchurch Cathedral, Christ Church Place.

Muslim

The Islamic Cultural Centre at the Dublin Mosque provides services and information for Ireland's rapidly growing Muslim population, now the third largest congregation after the Church of Ireland. Dublin Mosque, 163 South Circular Road, Dublin 8, tel: 01-453 3242, www.islamireland.ie.

Presbyterian

The Presbyterian Church of Ireland serves the whole island, north and south, and has a membership of about 300,000 in over 560 congregations, 527 of which are in Northern Ireland. The Information Office, Presbyterian Church in Ireland, Church House, Belfast BT1 6DW, Northern Ireland, tel: 028-9032 2284, www.presbyterianireland.org.

Methodist

There are about 250 Methodist congregations in Ireland. See www.irishmethodist.org for contact details and meeting times. Secreatary of Conference, 1 Fountainville Avenue, Belfast, BT9 6AN, tel: +44 (0)28 9032 4554, www.irishmethodist.org.

Other churches

Unitarian

A lively congregation meets on Sundays at 11am in this handsome 19th-century church in the centre of Georgian Dublin to share a bond of religious sympathy rather than a creed-bound faith. There are also lunchtime talks series. Contact Rev. Bill Darlison, Minister, Unitarian Church, 112 St Stephen's Green West, Dublin 2, tel: 01-478 0638, www.unitarianchurchdublin.org.

Quaker

There are meetings every Sunday at 11am at the Quaker Meeting House, Frederick Street, Off York Street, Belfast. In Dublin meetings are held at 11am on Sundays and 6.15 on Thursdays at the Quaker Meeeting House, 4–5 Eustace Street, Temple Bar, Dublin 1. There are about 30 other meeting houses in Ireland. For details tel: 01-668 3864, or see www.quakers-in-ireland.org.

Jewish

The Terenure Hebrew Congregation welcomes visitors to join them for daily, Shabat (8.30am) or Yom Tov services conducted according to the Ashkenazi tradition. Rathfarnham Road, Dublin 6. Or contact The Jewish Community Office, Herzog House, 1 Zion Road, Rathgar, Dublin 6, tel: 01492 3751.

Smoking

Since 2004 smoking has been banned in all enclosed places of work in Ireland, including public transport, airport terminals, cinemas, banks, offices, shops, pubs, restaurants and cafés. Exceptions include hotel and B&B bedrooms and private rented accommodation. Hotels and B&Bs may choose to allow smoking in some bedrooms, or may opt to have smoke-free bedrooms. Ask about their policy when booking. Most pubs and some restaurants have adapted existing beer gardens or patios to cater for smokers.

Telephones

The international dialling code for the Republic of Ireland is **353**. Northern Ireland's code is **44**. If you are calling the North from the Republic, just substitue the code 028 with 048, rather than using the international dialling code.

There are several telecommunications companies operating in Ireland – the largest one being Eircom (www.eircom.ie). A local call from a public telephone costs 40¢. Public telephones mainly use phone cards which are widely available from post offices, newsagents and supermarkets, Phonecards cost from €5 up. Telephone boxes are gradually disappearing, as the mobile (cell) gains dominance.

International calls can be dialled direct from private phones, or dial 114 for the international operator. To contact the local operator, dial 10. The long-distance services of AT&T, Sprint and MCI are also available.

Telephone services in Northern Ireland are operated by British Telecom; dial 100 for the operator.

Mobile (Cell) Phones

Only mobile phones with GSM will work in Ireland. If your phone is non-GSM, consult with your provider before travelling. It may be cheaper to buy a local SIM card and top up with prepaid calls. Local providers include 3, Meteor, O_2, Tescomobile and Vodafone.

If you are coming from the UK, your mobile should work in Northern Ireland, but you will need international roaming in the Republic.

Time Zones

Ireland follows Greenwich Mean Time. In spring, the clock is moved one hour ahead for Summer Time to give extra daylight in the evening; in autumn it is moved back again to GMT. At noon according to GMT, it is: 4am in Los Angeles; 7am in New York; 1pm in western Europe; 8pm in Singapore; 10pm in Sydney; midnight in New Zealand.

Tourist Information

Irish Tourist Board (Fáilte Ireland)

General enquiries: Fáilte Ireland, 88-95, Amiens Street Dublin 1, tel: 01-884 7700; (0808-234 2009 in UK) www.discoverireland.com. Within the Republic see www.discoverireland.ie

Dublin City: Dublin Tourism, Suffolk Street, (near Grafton Street) Dublin 2, tel: 01-605 7700 (0800-039 7000 in UK); www.visitdublin.com.

For tourist information within Ireland tel: 1850-230 330; for accommodation reservations in Dublin, tel: 1800 363 626.

Regional offices

Local tourist offices can be found throughout Ireland. A number are mentioned in the Places chapters. For details see www.discoverireland.ie.

Northern Ireland Tourist Board

www.discovernorthernireland.com.

Belfast: 59 North Street, Belfast BT1 1NB; tel: 028-9023 1221, fax: 028-9024 0960.

Dublin: 16 Nassau Street, Dublin 2; tel: 01-679 1977, fax: 01-679 1863.

Tourism Ireland Offices Abroad

For information on the whole island.

Australia: Sydney: 5th level, 36 Carrington Street, Sydney 2000, NSW, tel: 02-9299 6177, fax: 9299 6323; www.tourismireland.com.au.

Britain: Nations House, 103 Wigmore Street, London W1U 1QS; tel: 020-7518 0800, fax: 020-7493 9065, www.tourismireland.com.

Canada: 2 Bloor Street West, Suite 3403, Toronto, ON M4W; tel: 800 223 6470/416-925 6368, fax: 925 6033; www.tourismireland.com.

New Zealand: Level 6, 18 Shortland Street, Private Bag 92136, Auckland 1; tel: +649-977 2255, fax: +649-977 2256; www.tourismireland.com.au.

US: 345 Park Avenue, New York, NY 10154; tel: +1 800 2223 6470/212-418 0800, fax: 212-371 9052; www.tourismireland.com.

Websites

General

(For regional tourist information, see list above.)

www.discoverireland.com. The official website of Tourism Ireland, it covers both the Republic of Ireland and Northern Ireland, from accommodation to activities.

www.discovernorthernireland.com Detailed information on Northern Ireland

www.irishabroad.com celebrates all things Irish, and has some quirky stories.

www.ireland-information.com is a free information service covering everything from genealogy to Irish jokes.

www.irelandofthewelcomes.com carries extracts from Tourism Ireland's excellent magazine, *Ireland of the Welcomes*.

www.overheardindublin.com. Genuine vox pops. Prepare for the capital by familiarising yourself with its famous wit. Not for the prudish.

Accommodation

www.gulliver.ie is the electronic information and reservation network of Fàilte Ireland.

www.goireland.ie You can reserve accommodation online anywhere in Ireland, north and south, and also book ferries, flights and car hire.

www.irelandhotels.com. Book a hotel online at the website of the Irish Hotels Federation.

www.nihf.co.uk. The Northern Ireland Hotels Federation.

www.irelandbluebook.com contains Ireland's most upmarket country house hotels and restaurants.

www.hostels-ireland.com. Book a Tourist Board-approved holiday hostel online.

Eating Out/Food

www.slowfoodireland.com. News and events for serious foodies.

www.bordbia.ie to locate the nearest farmers' market.

Genealogy

www.nli.ie. The Genealogy Office of the National Library in the best starting place.

www.proni.gov.uk. In Northern Ireland begin at The Public Record Office.

Below: the website www.dublinbus.ie will help you find your way around.

Heritage

www.heritageireland.ie gives details of the National Monuments, historic houses, parks and gardens in State care.

www.heritageisland.com introduces over 80 places to visit, with a map to download and a discount scheme to join.

www.castlesireland.com has details of all the major historical houses, castles and gardens that can be visited in both the Republic and Northern Ireland

www.nationaltrust.org.uk for historic houses to visit in Northern Ireland.

Leisure and Sport

www.hri.ie for details of all horse racing fixtures.

www.irishgolf.ie. All that golfers need to know.

www.isasurf.ie. Surfing updates

www.mountaineering.ie for serious climbers, also good advice for walkers.

www.waterbased.ireland.ie For information on all watersports in the Republic.

www.sportni.net. Website of the Sports Council of Northern Ireland for both participants and spectators.

www.gaa.ie. To track down a game of hurling or Irish football.

www.discoverireland.com/activities has a wealth of information on walking, cycling, angling, golf, horse riding and cruising the Shannon and the canals.

Transport

www.aaireland.ie. Driving advice, time and distance between cities etc.

www.irishrail.ie. Get timetables and book tickets on Ireland's railways.

www.buseireann.ie for local and intercity bus services outside Dublin.

www.dublinbus.ie for bus services within Dublin

www.translink.co.uk for Northern Ireland Railways Ulsterbus and Belfast's bus service.

www.dublinairport.com live flight information and links to all airlines.

www.shannonairport.com

www.corkairport.com

Weather

www.met.ie for the latest forecast.

What's On

www.entertainment.ie will tell you what's on in theatres, cinemas, clubs and at festivals.

www.comhaltas.com. For news of the Irish traditional music scene.

Visas and Passports

Passports are required by everyone visiting the Republic except British citizens. Visas are not required by citizens of EU countries, Australia, Canada or the USA.

FURTHER READING

Irish Classics

Easons, the Dublin book retailer and wholesaler, compiled a list of the top Irish classics of all time. It serves as a useful introduction to the key figures from the past:

Gulliver's Travels by Jonathan Swift (1667–1745). The Dean of Dublin's St Patrick's Cathedral was also great satirist, the original book is a savage indictment of mankind's folly, far removed from the many children's adaptations.

The Vicar of Wakefield by Oliver Goldsmith (1728–74). A graduate of Trinity College, Dublin, like many others he headed for London where his comic novel about a hapless vicar, and his hilarious play *She Stoops to Conquer* gave him enduring fame.

Castle Rackrent by Maria Edgeworth. Published in 1800, Edgeworth's novel uses pointed humour to question Anglo-Irish identity and absentee landlords.

The Complete Works of Oscar Wilde (1854–1900). Besides his sparkling drawing room comedies, Wilde also wrote, poetry, essays, charming children's stories and a novel.

The Complete Works of W. B. Yeats (1865–1939). Winner of the 1923 Nobel Prize for Literature, beside his achievements as poet and dramatist, he played a key role in the struggle for Irish independence, was a founder of the National Theatre and a Senator.

Dracula by Bram Stoker (1847–1912). The only novel of Dublin-born Stoker's large output still read.

The Playboy of the Western World by J. M. Synge (1871–1909). The masterpiece of a multi-faceted writer who invented a new language using the poetry inherent in the Irish vernacular. Its earthy realism caused riots at its Abbey premiere.

Portrait of the Artist as a Young Man; Dubliners; Ulysses by James Joyce (1882–1941). His coming-of-age novel and the collection of Dublin stories will help you decide whether to tackles his magnum opus, *Ulysses*.

Shadow of a Gunman; Juno and the Paycock; The Plough and the Stars by Sean O'Casey (1880–1964). His trilogy of tragicomedies are set in the Dublin tenements, and deal with the problems of ordinary families caught up in historic events.

Essential Contemporary Fiction and Poetry

Fiction

More Pricks than Kicks by Samuel Beckett (John Calder). People are often surprised at how funny the Nobel Laureate's first story collection is, with its cast of outrageous Dublin characters.

BELOW: bookshop at the Dublin Writers Museum.

Murphy by Samuel Beckett (John Calder). Aspiring authors may be encouraged to know that this comic first novel was rejected by 41 publishers.

The Third Policeman by Flann O'Brien (Picador). Straight-faced novel of absurdist humour.

An Old Woman's Reflections by Peig Sayers. Memoir written in Irish by a natural storyteller about life on the Great Blasket Island.

The Islandman by Tomás O Crohan (OUP). Vivid memoir of a Great Blasket Island farmer-fisherman, written originally in Irish.

The Ginger Man by J.P Donleavy (Penguin). Exuberant, often hilarious, account of post-war Dublin, as seen by a hard-living American.

Langrishe, Go Down by Aidan Higgins (New Island). The last great Irish "big house" novel, chronicling its decline, championed by Samuel Beckett and Harold Pinter.

The Country Girls; **A Fanatic Heart: Selected Stories** by Edna O'Brien (Weidenfeld/Penguin). While Ireland's leading female author's first novel is a witty picture of Dublin in the 1950s, the stories are darker and deeper.

Troubles by J.G. Farrell (Penguin). Wry, atmospheric account of sitting out the Civil War in a crumbling hotel.

The Book of Evidence and **The Sea** by John Banville (Picador). A leading intellectual as well as a novelist, his 1989 novel is the disturbing story of a sleazy Dublin murderer, while his 2005 Booker Prize-winner is a tender account of lost love.

The South by Colm Toibín (Picador). Now an internationally-known novelist and travel writer, his first novel about an Irishwoman's love affair with Spain remains one of his best.

Collected Short Stories; The Last September by Elizabeth Bowen (Penguin). One of the last writers in the Anglo-Irish tradition, her compelling novel is set in the Troubles.

Collected Short Stories by William Trevor (Penguin). Set in both England and Ireland, among the plain people. Trevor is a master of the quiet epiphany.

Creatures of the Earth: New and Selected Stories by John McGahern

(Faber). One of the most understated and highly-rated chroniclers of rural Ireland.
There are Little Kingdoms by Kevin Barry (The Stinging Fly Press). Short stories that use anarchic comedy to skewer the absurdities of post-Celtic Tiger rural Ireland. A name to watch.
All Names Have Been Changed by Claire Kilroy. A wry look at 1980s Ireland and its literary culture by an up-and-coming young novelist, set at Trinity College Dublin in a tight-knit group of creative writing students.

Poetry

Penguin Book of Contemporary Irish Poetry edited by Peter Fallon and Derek Mahon (Penguin). Well-balanced selection of today's poets.
Collected Poems by Louis MacNeice (Faber). A major 20th-century poet, born in Ulster and educated in England, where he lived.
Collected Poems and **Finders Keepers** by Seamus Heaney (Faber). Superbly crafted lyric poems by Ireland's latest winner of the Nobel Prize for Literature, and a collection of his incisive literary essays and lectures.
Collected Poems by Derek Mahon (Penguin). A major 20th-century poet in the metaphysical mode, his more sophisticated œuvre is considered by many to be superior to Heaney's.
Collected Poems by Michael Longley. At his best, his perceptive lyrics, often nature-inspired, can stand beside fellow Ulster poets, Heaney and Mahon.
A Snail in My Prime by Paul Durcan (Harvill). Popular, readable poet, known for his quirky humour and often agonising honesty.

ABOVE: browsing at The Hugh Lane's bookshop.

Further Reading

History

Luck and the Irish: A Brief History of Change, 1970–2000 by Roy Foster (Allen Lane History). An enjoyable analysis of how the Celtic Tiger came to growl and how everyday life was transformed.
Modern Ireland 1600–1972 by R.F. Foster (OUP). Readable academic history with many new insights.
The Course of Irish History edited by T.W. Moody and F. X. Martin (Mercier). General narrative history, by established experts in each period, revised and updated.
Ireland – A History by Robert Kee (Weidenfeld). Readable illustrated history, good on disentangling the Troubles; recently updated.
How the Irish Saved Civilization by Thomas Cahill (Doubleday). A humorous look at Irish achievements down the years, with a serious core.
The Great Hunger: Ireland 1845–1849 by Cecil Woodham Smith (Penguin). The classic account of the Famine is a harrowing but compelling narrative.
That Neutral Island by Clair Wills (Faber & Faber). Anecdotal cultural and social history of life in neutral Ireland during World War II.
Twilight of the Ascendancy by Mark Bence Jones (Constable). Well-informed social history documenting the demise of the "big house". Wonderful old photos.

Biography

James Joyce by Richard Ellman (Hamish Hamilton). One of the finest literary biographies.
W.B Yeats, a Life by R. F. Foster (OUP). Definitive two-volume life of the poet by leading historian.
Damned to Fame: A Life of Samuel Beckett by James Knowlson (Bloomsbury). The official biography.
Michael Collins by Tim Pat Coogan (Arrow). The life of the pro-Treaty politician on which Neil Jordan's 1996 film was based.

Memoirs and Journalism

Angela's Ashes by Frank McCourt (Harper). Best-selling account of a miserable childhood in Limerick, subsequently filmed in 1999.
Are You Somebody by Nuala O'Faolain (New Island). The 200-page introduction to her collected journalism is admirably candid about her problems with alcohol and sex.
To School Through the Fields by Alice Taylor (Brandon). A quiet account of a rural childhood in the 1940s, which became an international best-seller.
McCarthy's Bar by Pete McCarthy (Sceptre). Humorous account of an Englishman's discovery of his Irish roots. Excellent on pubs.

Current Affairs

A Place Apart by Dervla Murphy (John Murray). Her 1978 account of Northern Ireland is still first-rate.
After the Ball by Fintan O'Toole (New Island). One of Ireland's sharpest cultural commentators on the legacy of the Celtic Tiger.
The Pope's Children by David McWilliams (Pan Books). A sardonic profile of Ireland's new elite.
Ship of Fools – How Stupidity and Corruption Sank the Celtic Tiger by Fintan O'Toole (Faber & Faber). All you need to know about Ireland's economic catastrophe presented as a tightly argued polemic.

Genealogy

Surnames of Ireland by Edward McLysaght (Irish Academic Press). There are numerous pocket books, but this is the standard work.

Architecture

The Architecture of Ireland by Maurice Craig (Batsford). An early account of the uniqueness of Irish architecture and still one of the best.
Georgian Dublin by Desmond Guinness (Batsford). Enduring illustrated study of Dublin's 18th-century architecture.
The Irish Round Tower by Brian Lalor (The Collins Press). Scholarship at its most readable.

Art and Decorative Arts

A Concise History of Irish Art by Bruce Arnold (Thames and Hudson). The definitive account, updated to include more on Irish modernism.
Modern Art in Ireland by Dorothy Walker (The Lilliput Press). Irish visual art in the mid-to-late 20th-century.

Irish Country Furniture by Claudia Kinmonth (Thames & Hudson). Interesting insights into Ireland's underestimated decorative arts.
Irish Gardens by Olda FitzGerald. Lavishly illustrated guide to the best gardens in the land.

Cookery

Irish Traditional Cooking by Darina Allen (O'Brien). Authentic recipes.
Best of Irish Potato Recipes by Biddy White Lennon (O'Brien). Over 50 recipes for the Irish spud.

Drama

The Complete Dramatic Works by Samuel Beckett (Faber). Includes the famous *Waiting for Godot*.
Plays: One and **Plays Two** by Brian Friel. Includes *Dancing at Lughnasa* and *Translations*.
McPherson: Four Plays by Conor McPherson. Eerie dramas, including *The Weir*, set in the west of Ireland.

Folklore

In Ireland Long Ago by Kevin Danaher (Mercier Press). A highly readable account of the fast-disappearing old ways.
Irish Folk Ways by Estyn Evans (Routledge). Pioneering ethnographical study.
Irish Trees – Myths, Legends and Folklore by Niall MacCoitir (The Collins Press). From the Celts onwards, trees have had a special place in Irish folklore.

Music

Irish Traditional Music by Ciaran Carson (Appletree Press). Complete guide to playing techniques, singing and instruments, including pub etiquette.
Bringing It All Back Home by Nuala O'Connor. Updated account of the history of Irish traditional music at home and abroad.
Irish Rock by Tony Clayton-Lea and Richard Taylor. The growth of the Irish rock scene, strong on punk and new wave, including U2.

Travel

Belfast: A Pocket History by Jonathan Bardon and David Burnett (Blackstaff Press). Best-selling account of 13 centuries.
Dublin edited by Peter Somerville Large (Hamish Hamilton). History of the city, rich in anecdote.
In Search of Ireland by H.V Morton (Metheun). Wallow in nostalgia as an Englishman gets to grips with 1938 Ireland.
The Aran Islands by J.M. Synge (Penguin). Published in 1907, it is the best book to read on a first visit.
A Place Near Heaven by Damien Enright (Gill & Macmillan). A calendar year in west Cork as observed by an amiable nature lover.
The Height of Nonsense by Paul Clements (The Collins Press). Light-hearted account of climbing the highest peak in each of Ireland's counties.
Connemara: Listening to the Wind and **Connemara: The Last Pool of Darkness** by Tim Robinson. Magisterial and mesmerising two-volume exploration of Ireland's great wilderness landscape, from polymath mathematician and artist turned map-maker and author.
Eating Scenery: West Cork, the People and the Place by Alannah Hopkin (The Collins Press). A close look at a scenic corner of rural Ireland, concentrating on the huge social changes of the past 30 years.

Landscape and Topography

The Shell Guide to Reading the Irish Landscape by Frank Mitchell and Michael Ryan (Town and Country). Explaining the natural, historical and geological factors that have shaped the Irish landscape.
Atlas of the Rural Irish Landscape Edited by F.H.A. Allen, Kevin Whelan, Matthew Stout (Cork University Press). Case studies of the effects on the landscape of changes in land use from prehistoric times to the present day.
Farming and the Burren by Brendan Dunford (Teagasc). Analyses the impact man's activities have had on this strange limestone landscape from Neolithic times to the present.
Handbook of the Irish Seashore by Matt Murphy (Sherkin Island Marine Station). What lurks in the rock pool.
The Blasket Islands – Next Parish America by Joan and Ray Stagles (O'Brien Press). The moving story of the hardy inhabitants of a small island off the coast of Dingle who persisted in the old way of life until 1953.

Other Insight Guides

More than 180 **Insight Guides** and **Insight City Guides** cover every continent, providing information on culture and all the top sights, as well as superb photography and detailed maps. In addition, a companion series of **Insight Guides Great Breaks** provides a selection of clearly timed walks and tours within UK locations; while **Insight Smart Guides** present comprehensive listings in a snappy, easy-to-find way, held together by an A–Z theme and with a street atlas showing major attractions, hotels and public transport.
Titles which highlight destinations in this region include:
Great Breaks: Belfast
Smart Guide: Dublin
Insight Guide: Great Britain

Send Us Your Thoughts

We do our best to ensure the information in our books is as accurate and up-to-date as possible. The books are updated on a regular basis using local contacts, who painstakingly add, amend and correct as required. However, some details (such as telephone numbers and opening times) are liable to change, and we are ultimately reliant on our readers to put us in the picture.

We welcome your feedback, especially your experience of using the book "on the road". Maybe we recommended a hotel that you liked (or another that you didn't), or you came across a great bar or new attraction we missed.

We will acknowledge all contributions, and we'll offer an Insight Guide to the best letters received.

Please write to us at:
Insight Guides
PO Box 7910
London SE1 1WE
Or email us at:
insight@apaguide.co.uk

Art and Photo Credits

4 Corners 69,
Alamy 7TL, 72, 73R,
Amanda Anderson 238
Amerune 175T
Aonghus Flynn 287L
Athean 169T
Belfast Visitor and Convention Bureau 340/T, 341L/R, 345, 346T, 347, 368, 369, 386, 387
Julie Berlin 311T
John Brennan 259R
Julian Carnott 164
Collections 98, 99
Corbis 6R, 7BR, 10B, 11T, 22, 25, 30T, 31B/M, 51, 65, 68L, 70, 73L, 83, 90B, 91, 96, 153B/T, 155/T, 157, 179/T, 194/195, 200, 202, 203, 205, 210, 215, 229, 233T, 234T, 237, 253T, 256, 258, 260, 269, 270/T, 274/T, 276, 277, 278, 283, 290, 291, 292, 293, 304/T, 305, 315, 337, 349
APA Kevin Cummins 5T, 6B, 9T, 16/17, 21, 30B, 56, 64, 80T, 84, 86, 95, 104/105, 207, 300, 301,302, 303, 306, 307T, 313, 316T, 317/T, 318, 320, 321, 322/T, 323, 328R, 330, 332, 335, 336L/R, 342T, 343, 345, 350
Richard Cummins 12/13, 106/107, 286
Chris Dlugosz 335L
courtesy Dunbrody Hotel 181
Shaun Dunphy 235R
Cyril Dousin 170T
Kyle Eertmoed 239
Mary Evans Picture Library 66, 328T
Fáilte Ireland 71
Beay Fendi 253
Eoin Gardinier 252R
Alain le Garsmeur 313T325
Getty Images 43, 61, 68R, 90T, 92, 172, 201
Gunnar Grimes 246
APA Glyn Genin 4T, 6T, 7BR/MR/TR, 8B, 9B, 11B, 19B/T, 20B, 34, 35, 109/T, 116T, 117T, 118B/M/T, 119B/T, 12/T, 121T, 124, 125/T, 126, 127BL/BR/T, 128/T, 129T, 130/T, 131T, 132/T, 133/T, 134T, 135, 136/T, 138/t, 139/T, 140, 142, 143, 145, 148, 149, 150, 151/T, 160/161, 162, 163, 165, 166/T, 167, 168T, 170, 172, 175, 176/T, 177, 178, 182, 183, 184, 185BL/BR/T, 186/T, 187, 188/T, 189/T, 190/T, 191BL/BR/T, 192, 193/T, 196, 197, 198, 199/T, 211, 212/T, 213/T, 214/T, 215T, 217, 219, 222, 225, 230, 231, 248T, 255/T, 257, 259T, 261/T, 265, 266, 267/T, 268/T, 269T, 272/T, 289. 352, 354, 355, 356, 357, 370, 371, 372, 378, 379, 381, 382, 384, 388, 389
Phil Guest 5B
Jimmy Harris 129
Christopher Hill 314, 339, 342
Emmett Hume 208
Irish Museum of Modern Art 76, 77, 78, 79
Marty Johnson 7ML, 97
Kashmera 262T
Thomas Kelly 1, 271, 275, 284T
Courtesy Kilkenny Design Centre 174
Lebrecht 10
Michael Kirwan 280/281
Tony McGrath 55
Kevin McManus 363
John Mernard 262
William Murphy 227
Jeremy Nichol 316
Northern Ireland Tourist Board 303T, 307, 308, 309, 310, 311, 319/T, 321T, 323T, 324, 351331, 326L/R, 327T, 328L/T, 329, 333, 376, 377, 380, 383
PA Photos 2, 8T, 57, 60, 88, 89, 236
Courtesy Le Petit Poulailler 313T
Photolibrary 122T, 272
Photoshot 327
Pictures Colour Library 7M
Rona Proudfoot 251
Dainee Ranaweera 366
G.P Reichelt 52
Ciaran Roarty 294
M Ryan 259L
Sde Santi 239T
Seth Sawyers 204T
Shadowgate 312
Grace Smith 296
Jacob Sutton 53
Geray Sweeney 117B, 154, 205T, 249T
Michael Taylor/Image Ireland 348
Tim Thompson 94, 204, 185, 294T
Topfoto 31T, 58
Tourism Ireland 93
B B Tucker 228
Courtesy Warterford Crystal 169
Andrew Wilkinson 137
Willowherb 295
APA Corrie Wingate 3B, 4B, 9M, 14/15, 18, 20T, 23L/R, 24, 62/63, 67, 80, 81, 82, 85, 87, 102/103, 108, 114, 115, 121L/R, 122B , 123, 131, 144, 171T, 206, 209, 220/221, 223, 224T, 226, 228T, 232, 233, 234, 242, 244/245, 247, 249L/R, 250, 252L, 256T, 272T, 284, 285T, 287R/T, 288, 390, 391
Marcus Wilson Smith 173

Photo Features

26/27: Roanld Grant 26/27, 26BL, Kobal 26BR/M, 27M, Pictorial Press 27BL, Getty 27BR

38/39: Corbis 138/139, 139TR, Robert Harding 138M, APA Glyn Genin 138BL, 139BL/BR/ML Alamy 139BR/MR

48/49: Mary Evans Picture Library 48TL,48BR, 49BR/M, AKG London 48/49, Topfoto 48BL, 49TR

74/75: St Patrick's Festival 74/75, Baboro International Children's Arts Festival 75T, Darragh MacSweeney74M, Devo 75M, John Allen74BL, Rang Puhar 75BR

100/101: Alain Le Garsmeur/ Image Ireland 100B, Thomas Kelly 101TR, The Slide File 100BL/M/TL, 100/101, 101BL/BR

146/147: Alamy 146/147, 147BR, Corbis 147TR, 146BL/BR, Rex Features 147BL/ML, PA Photos 147MR

158–159: Corbis 158/159, APA Glyn Genin 158BR, 159MR/TR, Getty Images 159ML, Glyn Genin, Glyn Genin, Glyn Genin, Photolibrary.com 159BL, Axiom 159BR

242–243: All Pictures Marty Johnson except Alain le Garsmeur 242BL/BR

Map production: original cartography Berndston & Berndtson, updated by Phoenix Mapping and Apa Cartography Department

Production: Linton Donaldson and Rebeka Ellam

INDEX

D

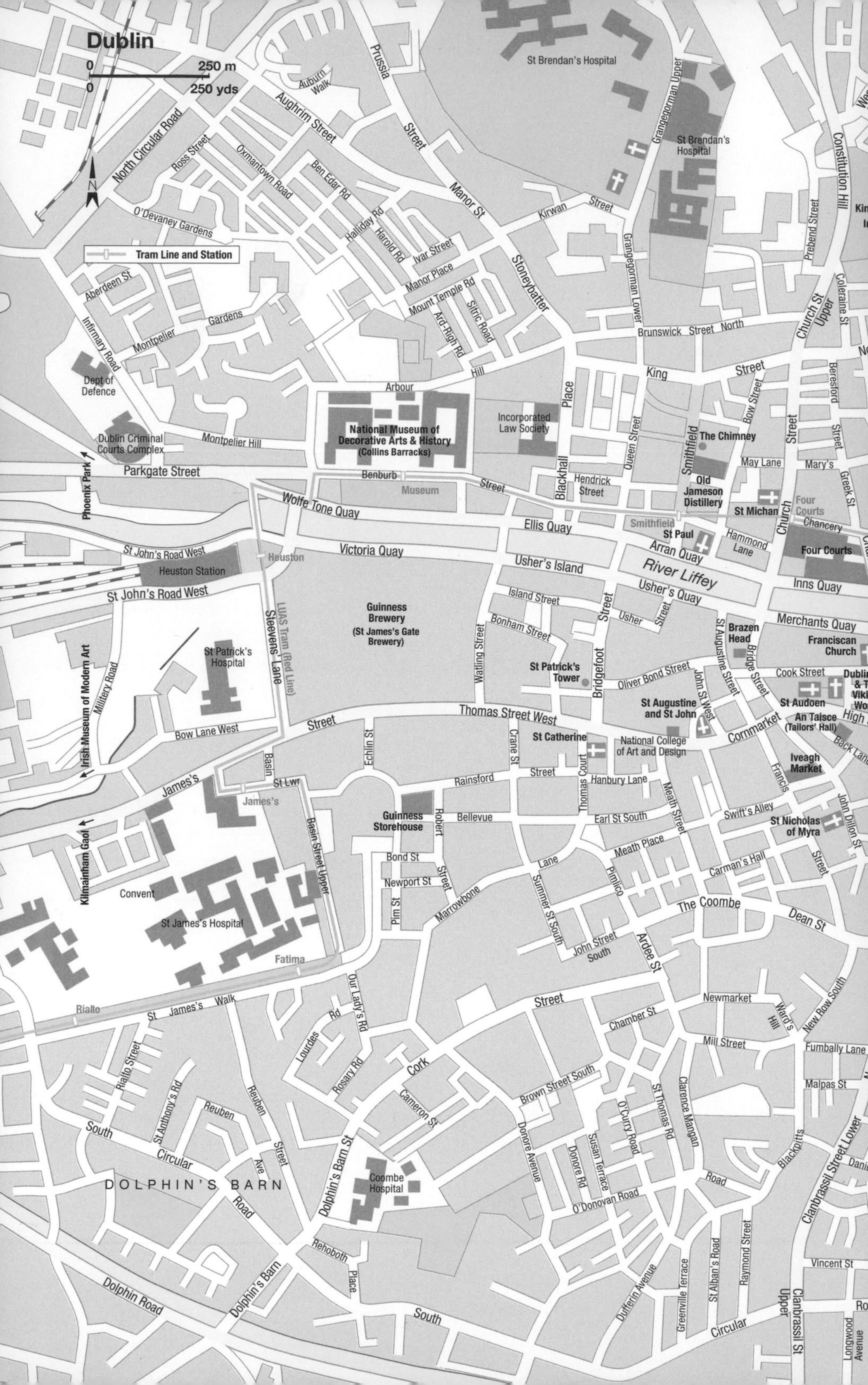
Dublin
0
250 m
0
250 yds
N
Tram Line and Station
St Brendan's Hospital
Prussia
Street
Auburn Walk
Aughrim Street
North Circular Road
Ross Street
Oxmantown Road
Ben Edar Rd
Manor St
Grangegorman Upper
St Brendan's Hospital
Constitution Hill
O'Devaney Gardens
Halliday Rd
Harold Rd
Ivar Street
Kirwan
Street
Prebend Street
Aberdeen St
Manor Place
Mount Temple Rd
Sitric Road
Ard-Righ Rd
Stoneybatter
Grangegorman Lower
Coleraine St
Church St Upper
Infirmary Road
Montpelier
Gardens
Brunswick
Street North
Dept of Defence
Hill
Arbour
King
Street
Beresford
Bow Street
Place
Incorporated Law Society
National Museum of Decorative Arts & History
(Collins Barracks)
Queen Street
Smithfield
The Chimney
Street
Street
Dublin Criminal Courts Complex
Montpelier Hill
Phoenix Park
Parkgate Street
Benburb
Museum
Street
Blackhall
Hendrick Street
May Lane
Mary's
Old Jameson Distillery
Greek St
Wolfe Tone Quay
Ellis Quay
Smithfield
St Michan
Four Courts
Church
Chancery
St Paul
Hammond Lane
Arran Quay
Four Courts
Victoria Quay
St John's Road West
Heuston
Heuston Station
Usher's Island
River Liffey
Inns Quay
St John's Road West
Guinness Brewery
(St James's Gate Brewery)
Island Street
Usher's Quay
Usher
Street
Street
Merchants Quay
LUAS Tram (Red Line)
Steevens' Lane
Bonham Street
St Augustine Street
Brazen Head
Bridge Street
Franciscan Church
St Patrick's Hospital
Watling Street
St Patrick's Tower
Bridgefoot
Oliver Bond Street
John St West
Cook Street
Military Road
Irish Museum of Modern Art
Thomas Street West
St Augustine and St John
St Audoen
An Taisce (Tailors' Hall)
High St
Street
Cornmarket
Bow Lane West
Echlin St
Crane St
St Catherine
National College of Art and Design
Back Lane
Iveagh Market
James's
Basin
St Lwr
Street
Thomas Court
Rainsford
Hanbury Lane
Francis
James's
Kilmainham Gaol
Guinness Storehouse
Robert
Bellevue
Earl St South
Meath Street
Swift's Alley
St Nicholas of Myra
John Dillon St
Basin Street Upper
Bond St
Street
Lane
Meath Place
Pimlico
Carman's Hall
Street
Newport St
Convent
Pim St
Marrowbone
Summer St South
The Coombe
Dean St
St James's Hospital
John Street South
Ardee St
Fatima
Rialto
St
James's
Walk
Our Lady's Rd
Street
Newmarket
Ward's Hill
New Row South
Rd
Chamber St
Mill Street
Fumbally Lane
Rialto Street
Lourdes
Cork
Rosary Rd
Malpas St
Brown Street South
St Anthony's Rd
Reuben
Reuben
Cameron St
O'Curry Road
St Thomas Rd
Clarence Mangan
South
Street
Donore Avenue
Blackpitts
Circular
Ave
Dolphin's Barn St
Coombe Hospital
Donore Rd
Susan Terrace
Road
Clanbrassil Street Lower
DOLPHIN'S BARN
Road
O'Donovan Road
Rehoboth
Place
Raymond Street
St Alban's Road
Vincent St
Dolphin Road
Dolphin's Barn
Dufferin Avenue
Greenville Terrace
Upper
Clanbrassil St
South
Circular
Donore Avenue